Environmental Science, E

Psychological Approaches to Sustainability: Current Trends in Theory, Research and Applications

ENVIRONMENTAL SCIENCE, ENGINEERING AND TECHNOLOGY SERIES

Nitrous Oxide Emissions Research Progress
Adam I. Sheldon and Edward P. Barnhart (Editors)
2009. ISBN: 978-1-60692-267-5

Fundamentals and Applications of Biosorption Isotherms, Kinetics and Thermodynamics
Yu Liu and Jianlong Wang (Editors)
2009. ISBN: 978-1-60741-169-7

Environmental Effects of Off-Highway Vehicles
Douglas S. Ouren, Christopher Haas, Cynthia P. Melcher, Susan C. Stewart, Phadrea D. Ponds, Natalie R. Sexton Lucy Burris, Tammy Fancher and Zachary H. Bowen
2009. ISBN: 978-1-60692-936-0

Agricultural Runoff, Coastal Engineering and Flooding
Christopher A. Hudspeth and Timothy E. Reeve (Editors)
2009. ISBN: 978-1-60741-097-3

Agricultural Runoff, Coastal Engineering and Flooding
Christopher A. Hudspeth and Timothy E. Reeve (Editors)
2009. ISBN: 978-1-60876-608-6
(Online book)

Conservation of Natural Resources
Nikolas J. Kudrow (Editor)
2009. ISBN: 978-1-60741-178-9

Conservation of Natural Resources
Nikolas J. Kudrow (Editor)
2009. ISBN: 978-1-60876-642-6
(Online book)

Directory of Conservation Funding Sources for Developing Countries: Conservation Biology, Education and Training, Fellowships and Scholarships
Alfred O. Owino and Joseph O. Oyugi
2009. ISBN: 978-1-60741-367-7

Forest Canopies: Forest Production, Ecosystem Health and Climate Conditions
Jason D. Creighton and Paul J. Roney(Editors)
2009. ISBN: 978-1-60741-457-5

Soil Fertility
Derek P. Lucero and Joseph E. Boggs (Editors)
2009. ISBN: 978-1-60741-466-7

The Amazon Gold Rush and Environmental Mercury Contamination
Daniel Marcos Bonotto and Ene Glória da Silveira
2009. ISBN: 978-1-60741-609-8

Process Engineering in Plant-Based Products
Hongzhang Chen
2009. ISBN: 978-1-60741-962-4

Buildings and the Environment
Jonas Nemecek and Patrik Schulz (Editors)
2009. ISBN: 978-1-60876-128-9

Tree Growth: Influences, Layers and Types
Wesley P. Karam (Editor)
2009. ISBN: 978-1-60741-784-2

Potential of Activated Sludge Utilization
Xiaoyi Yang
2010. ISBN: 978-1-60876-019-0

Psychological Approaches to Sustainability: Current Trends in Theory, Research and Applications
Victor Corral-Verdugo, Cirilo H. Garcia-Cadena and Martha Frias-Armenta (Editors)
2010. ISBN: 978-1-60876-356-6

ENVIRONMENTAL SCIENCE, ENGINEERING AND TECHNOLOGY SERIES

PSYCHOLOGICAL APPROACHES TO SUSTAINABILITY: CURRENT TRENDS IN THEORY, RESEARCH AND APPLICATIONS

VICTOR CORRAL-VERDUGO
CIRILO H. GARCIA-CADENA
AND
MARTHA FRIAS-ARMENTA
EDITORS

Nova Science Publishers, Inc.
New York

Copyright © 2010 by Nova Science Publishers, Inc.

All rights reserved. No part of this book may be reproduced, stored in a retrieval system or transmitted in any form or by any means: electronic, electrostatic, magnetic, tape, mechanical photocopying, recording or otherwise without the written permission of the Publisher.

For permission to use material from this book please contact us:
Telephone 631-231-7269; Fax 631-231-8175
Web Site: http://www.novapublishers.com

NOTICE TO THE READER

The Publisher has taken reasonable care in the preparation of this book, but makes no expressed or implied warranty of any kind and assumes no responsibility for any errors or omissions. No liability is assumed for incidental or consequential damages in connection with or arising out of information contained in this book. The Publisher shall not be liable for any special, consequential, or exemplary damages resulting, in whole or in part, from the readers' use of, or reliance upon, this material. Any parts of this book based on government reports are so indicated and copyright is claimed for those parts to the extent applicable to compilations of such works.

Independent verification should be sought for any data, advice or recommendations contained in this book. In addition, no responsibility is assumed by the publisher for any injury and/or damage to persons or property arising from any methods, products, instructions, ideas or otherwise contained in this publication.

This publication is designed to provide accurate and authoritative information with regard to the subject matter covered herein. It is sold with the clear understanding that the Publisher is not engaged in rendering legal or any other professional services. If legal or any other expert assistance is required, the services of a competent person should be sought. FROM A DECLARATION OF PARTICIPANTS JOINTLY ADOPTED BY A COMMITTEE OF THE AMERICAN BAR ASSOCIATION AND A COMMITTEE OF PUBLISHERS.

LIBRARY OF CONGRESS CATALOGING-IN-PUBLICATION DATA

Psychological approaches to sustainability : current trends in theory, research and applications / editors, Victor Corral-Verdugo, Cirilo H. Garcia-Cadena, Martha Frias-Armenta.
     p. cm.
  Includes index.
  ISBN 978-1-60876-356-6 (hardcover)
 1. Environmental psychology. 2. Environmentalism--Psychological aspects. 3. Human ecology.
I. Corral Verdugo, Víctor. II. García Cadena, Cirilo Humberto. III. Frías Armenta, Martha.
  BF353.P7735 2009
  155.9--dc22
                                2009038998

Published by Nova Science Publishers, Inc. ✢ New York

Contents

Preface		xi
Part I.	**The Psychology of Environmental Problems and Solutions**	
Chapter 1	Introduction to the Psychological Dimensions of Sustainability *Victor Corral-Verdugo, Martha Frías-Armenta and Cirilo H. García-Cadena*	3
Chapter 2	Global Warming, Climate Change And Human Psychology *Taciano L. Milfont*	19
Chapter 3	Social-Psychological and Contextual Predictors of Sustainable Water Consumption *Giuseppe Carrus, Mirilia Bonnes, Victor Corral-Verdugo, Gabriel Moser and Jai Sinha*	43
Chapter 4	How to Promote Energy Savings among Households: Theoretical and Practical Approaches *Linda Steg and Wokje Abrahamse*	61
Part II.	**Antecedent Psychological Dimensions of Sustainability**	81
Chapter 5	Ecological Worldviews *Bernardo Hernández, Ernesto Suárez, Stephany Hess and Victor Corral-Verdugo*	83
Chapter 6	Leverage for Sustainable Change: Motivational Sources behind Ecological Behavior *Nina Roczen, Florian G. Kaiser and Franz X. Bogner*	109
Chapter 7	The Socio-psychological Affinity towards Diversity: From Biodiversity to Socio-ecological Sustainability *Mirilia Bonnes, Giuseppe Carrus, Victor Corral-Verdugo and Paola Passafaro*	125

Chapter 8	Promoting Pro-environmental Intentions. Theoretical Background and Practical Applications of Travel Feedback Programs for Car Use Reduction *Satoshi Fujii and Ayako Taniguchi*	141
Chapter 9	Altruism and Beyond: The Motivational Bases of Pro-environmental Behavior *Verónica Sevillano, Juan I. Aragonés and P. Wesley Schultz*	161
Chapter 10	Equity and Sustainable Lifestyles *Victor Corral-Verdugo, Cirilo H. García-Cadena, Laura Castro, Iván Viramontes and Rafael Limones*	185
Chapter 11	Time Perspective and Sustainable Behavior *Jose Q. Pinheiro and Victor Corral Verdugo*	205
Chapter 12	Promoting Pro-environmental Competency *Blanca Fraijo-Sing, Victor Corral-Verdugo, César Tapia-Fonllem and Daniel González-Lomelí*	225
Chapter 13	Emotions and Pro-environmental Behavior *César Tapia-Fonllem, Victor Corral-Verdugo, Claudia Gutiérrez-Sida, José Mireles-Acosta and Hugo Tirado-Medina*	247
Part III:	**Contextual Determinants of Sustainable Behavior**	267
Chapter 14	Contextual Influences on Sustainable Behavior *Dawn Hill, Aurelio José Figueredo and W. Jake Jacobs*	269
Chapter 15	Why do People Fail to Act? Situational Barriers and constraints on Pro-ecological Behavior *Rui Gaspar de Carvalho, José Manuel Palma-Oliveira and Victor Corral-Verdugo*	295
Chapter 16	Community Sustainability: Orientations and Implications from Environmental Community Psychology *Esther Wiesenfeld and Euclides Sánchez*	317
Chapter 17	Place Atachment and the Social Acceptance Of Renewable Energy Technologies *Patrick Devine-Wright*	337
Chapter 18	Cultural Background and Environmental Context of Water Perception and Use *Gabriel Moser, Oscar Navarro, Eugenia Ratiu and Karine Weiss*	361
Chapter 19	Influence of Social and Legal Norms on Anti-Ecological Behaviors *Martha Frías-Armenta and Ana M. Martín*	385

Part IV:	**The Positive Psychological Impacts of Sustainable Behavior**	**409**
Chapter 20	Urban Sustainability, Psychological Restoration and Soundscapes *Sarah R. Payne*	411
Chapter 21	Happiness and Sustainable Behavior *Robert B. Bechtel and Victor Corral-Verdugo*	433
Index		**451**

PREFACE

An international team of leading scholars and young researchers in environmental psychology offers a relatively new perspective on the origin and solutions of the current environmental crisis. They explain how human nature has played a prominent role in the emergence of ecological problems such as global warming, threats to biodiversity, resources scarcity and pollution. But also, they demonstrate that such problems are interlinked with social problems such as poverty, famine, social and economical inequities and violence. According to this book's authors, psychological theories and empirical evidence show that the solutions for those socio-ecological problems are to be found in human nature and its psychological predispositions. These include personal motives, world-visions, future perspective, environmental emotions, altruistic tendencies and behavioral capacities among other psychological predispositions that could allow the adoption of sustainable lifestyles. Meeting the ideals of sustainability requires the participation of the natural and social sciences, including psychology, in order to guarantee the fulfillment of its purposes. Behavioral sciences study the psychological characteristics and the contextual factors that lead people to adopt more sustainable lifestyles. In addition, these sciences investigate how sustainable behaviors promote happiness, psychological well being and restoration, which are considered among the aims of sustainable development by governments throughout the world. The authors, who are recognized experts in these areas, offer a state-of-the-art review and data on what it is known regarding the psychological dimensions of the environmental crisis, its behavioral solutions and the repercussions of sustainable behavior on human well being.

PART I.
THE PSYCHOLOGY OF ENVIRONMENTAL PROBLEMS AND SOLUTIONS

In: Psychological Approaches to Sustainability
Editors: V. Corral-Verdugo et al.

ISBN 978-1-60876-356-6
© 2010 Nova Science Publishers, Inc.

Chapter 1

INTRODUCTION TO THE PSYCHOLOGICAL DIMENSIONS OF SUSTAINABILITY

Victor Corral-Verdugo, Martha Frías-Armenta
Universidad de Sonora, Mexico
and Cirilo H. García-Cadena
Universidad Autónoma de Nuevo León, Mexico

ABSTRACT

Environmental problems represent a serious threat to life on Earth. In present days, those problems manifest as global climatic change, degradation and depredation of natural resources, species extinction, violence, socio-economic crises, and an infinitude of social and ecological disturbances. Since most of the current environmental crisis has been caused by human behavior, knowledge regarding what predisposes people to behave sustainably is required. Sustainable behavior is the set of actions resulting in the conservation of natural and social resources, and psychology and other behavioral sciences are committed to study what incites people to engage in conservationist actions. The elucidation of the psychological dimensions of sustainability is a primordial step in designing interventional strategies aimed at encouraging people to behave in accordance with sustainability principles. These principles establish that human lifestyles have to be re-directed to meeting the needs of present generations without compromising the future; in doing this, the integrity of natural resources should be guaranteed. Environmental psychology (EP) is the branch of science dealing with the study of environment-behavior interactions, including those aimed at conserving the natural and social resources of our planet. In this sense, EP studies the psychological dimensions of sustainability. Those dimensions involve *psychological tendencies and capacities* (pro-environmental attitudes, motives, beliefs, norms, skills, etc.) influencing *sustainable behavior* (pro-ecological, altruistic, frugal, and equitable actions). EP is also interested in the physical and social *contexts* that induce the adoption of more sustainable lifestyles. Sustainable behavior has a special purpose: achieving people's *wellbeing* in diverse spheres of human existence. These spheres include enjoying a healthy and meaningful life, as well as experiencing happiness. Thus, the psychology of sustainability addresses the personal and contextual determinants of sustainable behavior, the lifestyles that constitute such behavior, and its positive consequences on people's wellbeing. This book is aimed at describing and discussing what is known regarding all these factors. Its chapters deal with sustainable behaviors, their antecedents and consequences, trying to provide a coherent and integral view of the psychology of sustainability. An overview of the composition and content of this text is presented, by integrating its chapters' topics in terms of the specified characterization of psychological dimensions of sustainability.

INTRODUCTION

Not so long ago, the mention of environmental problems sounded more like a pessimistic premonition than a crude reality. But reality has already arrived: It is not nice, and is universal. The recent annual reports on the state of the world (Starke, 2008; Mastny, 2009, for instance) indicate that. The three levels of the biosphere (atmosphere, water and soil) present such a grave degradation that, if continued, will significantly affect life on Earth as we know it.

Flavin and Engelman (2009, p. 5) clearly synthesize the current state of our planet's atmosphere: "For several decades now, Earth's heat balance has been severely out of equilibrium. Earth is absorbing more heat than it is emitting, and across the planet ecological systems are responding." As a consequence, the Arctic Sea ice has declined to its lowest level since satellite assessments began (leaving, for the first time the Northwest Passage open for navigation). Warm summers have caused Greenland's most extreme ice melting in fifty years. Nearly 50 million people in coastal cities are likely at risk from flooding; this risk will increase by more than three-fold by the 2070's (Flavin & Engelman, 2009; Mastny, 2009).

Southeast Asia's oceans are rapidly running out of fish, threatening the livelihoods of some 100 million people. Irregular rain seasons make it difficult to figure out the best time for cultivation in areas where irrigation depends on rain water (Dodman, Ayers & Huq, 2009). The number of "dead zones" in marine ecosystems due to the low content of oxygen has increased from 149 to 200 (Starke, 2008). Starke also reports that the hole in the ozone layer has grown to a record of 28 million squared kilometers, that the two largest rain forests (Amazonas and Congo) could disappear in less than fifty years, and that carbon emissions have doubled since 1990.

In Asia, the forecast for a water crisis is seen as "unprecedented." This crisis is caused by climate change, population growth and mismanagement of water (Mastny, 2009). Natural ecosystems are progressively degraded and animal and vegetal species are disappearing due to their habitats' destruction, as the World Wildlife Foundation (WWWF, 2008) reports. According to this organization, birds are at risk to become extinct because of global warming. Earth's ecosystem has worsened faster during the last fifty years than in the rest of the historical record (Millennium Ecosystem Assessment, 2005).

On a more human level, the Chinese government reported that birth defects have soared around 40 percent since 2001 due to pollution and worsening environmental degradation. Twenty-four percent of men and twenty-seven percent of women worldwide are obese, which indicates poor nutritional habits and wasteful consumption of food (Mastny, 2009). Air pollution in urban areas causes two million premature deaths yearly, especially in underdeveloped countries (World Health Organization, 2008). Although no global conflicts have occurred in almost sixty years, regional wars are abundant, especially in poorer zones of the planet (Renner, 2005); epidemics like AIDS and diverse variants of influenza (flu) expand; an international financial crisis affects entire nations (Flavin & Engelman, 2009); inequity to the access to natural resources, as well as gender, age, class and racial discrimination still prevail in broad sectors throughout the world (Talbert, 2008); and the phantom of terrorism threatens communities in developed and underdeveloped countries (Mastny & Cincotta, 2005). According to Renner (2005) terrorist acts and the reaction they provoke are exclamations produced in a toxic broth of profound socio-economic, environmental and political pressures. Among these pressures, Renner mentions endemic poverty and convulsive economic transitions causing inequity and unemployment, international crime, large-scale migrations, ecosystems disruption, new and resurgent transmissible diseases, and a growing competition for land, water, oil, and other natural resources. In this scheme, the results are clear that the integrities of biological and human ecosystems are linked.

Humankind faces a predicament: On the one hand, people's needs expand as population grows and their desires for achieving a decent life, equitable access to water, food, lodging, job, and other basic resource satisfying those needs, also grow. On the other hand, there are limits to the use of natural resources that satisfy those needs; such resources are progressively scarcer, they are monopolized by a reduced sector of the population, and many of them have become polluted due to irresponsible use. The dilemma is that if we continue exploiting nature's assets in the (irrational, inequitable, unsustainable) way we have been doing it, soon there will be nothing to use for our benefit. This *environmental dilemma* -as it is called- emerges as a conflict between human desires for obtaining and consuming more resources, and the need for conserving those resources (Tanimoto, 2004).

How can we successfully cope with that predicament? There is not an easy answer for this question, but yet, a number of possible solutions have been expressed. For instance, the *preservationist* solution establishes that the option of protecting natural resources should prevail over the option of meeting human needs, especially when those resources' integrity is threatened (Siurua, 2006). This means that, in facing the danger of ecological deterioration, the restoration of environmental conditions should be priority and, after that, human needs could be considered. Alternatively, there are positions assuming that meeting human needs should be achieved coincidently with the solution of environmental problems. These positions –called *conservationists*- acknowledge natural resources conservation as a key element in solving the environmental dilemma; yet, they establish that human beings have rights to use those resources in order to survive and meet decent life standards (Bonnes & Bonaituo, 2002). *Sustainable development* (SD) is one of those positions opposing the preservationist claim, by considering that the environmental dilemma can be perfectly manageable if human needs are made compatible with ecosystems needs.

SUSTAINABLE DEVELOPMENT

Defined as "a development that meets the need of the present generations without compromising the future" (WCED, 1987), the SD principles establish that natural resources can and should be used to satisfy human requirements; yet, SD recognizes that environmental integrity is a fundamental pre-condition to meet human needs.

The sustainable development paradigm calls for replacing the preservationist static perspective with a more dynamic vision of human-environment relations. The radical preservationist view is more concerned with the physical and biological aspects of today's environment; according to this perspective, change has to be avoided since it leads to the disturbance of current environmental conditions (Siurua, 2006). Therefore, this view emphasizes ecosystems preservation, limits to economic growth, the avoidance of human intervention in natural areas, etc., which often result in neglecting people's needs in long-term scenarios due to their dependence on the use of natural resources (Pearce & Warford, 1993). Alternatively, for the SD approach, the human aspect is as relevant as the bio-ecological component of nature, and the future is as important as the present. Thus, from the sustainable development perspective, ecological conservation is as crucial as social conservation, which does not imply a static vision of the world: ecosystems and human cultures have to change in their adapting to the evolving conditions of our planet. However, these changes should not necessarily have to conduce to either environmental degradation or humankind extinction (or both).

Another issue differentiating the sustainability concept from the preservationist perspective is the SD's view of an active and strategic role assigned to humans in balancing their needs with the needs of natural ecosystems (Corral-Verdugo, Bonnes, Tapia, Fraijo, Frías & Carrus, 2009). The SD concept stresses the idea that human beings are responsible for the use of natural resources by actively promoting their renewal and recovery. In this way, the resilience of ecosystems is considered by guaranteeing their existence and sustainable use over time (Pradhan, 2006). This implies that people, in meeting their needs, can and should produce changes in environmental conditions; yet, such changes should not compromise the integrity of natural resources. Therefore, the sustainability notion appears more comprehensive and open to continuous environmental and social change, as compared to the preservationist perspective, which focuses mainly on the integrity of the present physical environment (Bonnes & Bonaiuto, 2002).

SD also looks for coherence with ecological principles, so that the basic rules of ecosystems' functioning have to be respected in promoting both human development and sustainable behaviors. Those rules include the principles of interdependence, diversity, cyclicity, flexibility, association and sustainability, which are applicable both to natural and human ecosystems.

The *interdependence* principle establishes that all the elements of an ecosystem depend on each other, so that losing a component compromises others' integrity (Capra & Pauli, 1995). That is why preventing species from massive extinction is so important since its occurrence could result in a global ecosystem unbalance, as observed throughout the planet. Therefore, the ideas of equilibrium and reciprocal dependence among the components of a system are enhanced. *Diversity* is another basic ecological principle. Ecosystem integrity depends on the variety of its components so that one missing can be compensated by the remaining elements. An ecosystem of higher diversity is more resilient than a less diversified ecosystem (Pradhan, 2006). *Flexibility* is a rule manifested as versatility or the potential for change after the occurrence of environmental modifications. Ecological systems maintain a state characterized by fluctuations in their variables, allowing adaptations in order to face environmental changes. *Ciclicity*, in turn, means that the interdependence among the elements of an ecosystem involves energy and resource interchanges within continued cycles, as in life-death and water cycles, for instance. *Association* is the principle encompassing competition and cooperation played by ecosystems' elements with each other; ultimately, this rule establishes that all the elements are interrelated. Finally, *sustainability* is conceived as a particular rule emerging from the remaining principles governing the functioning of all ecosystems. In this context, sustainability implies that the long-term survival of every species depends on a limited stock of resources (Capra & Pauli, 1995).

Intriguingly, evidence seems to show that all these ecological principles have a corresponding psychological dimension, which can (and should) be considered when looking for people's sustainable responses to environmental dilemmas. For instance, the interdependence principle seems to be incorporated in people's world-visions (i.e., environmental beliefs); according to Corral-Verdugo, Carrus, Bonnes, Moser, & Sinha (2008) individuals recognize the mutual human-nature dependence, which leads individuals to conservationist practices. Also, the perception of bio and socio-diversity generates a preference for variety in physical and social settings, and –most interestingly- such preference incites environmental conservation, as Corral-Verdugo *et al* (2009) suggest. Moreover, flexibility is a component of pro-environmental competency, a versatile set of skills used to solve environmental problems (Geller, 2002). Association includes cooperation, which is an important element of altruism, a sustainable lifestyle (Schultz, 2001). These examples suggest that looking for the psychological dimensions of sustainability, as associated to general ecological principles, is a pertinent task in the development of sustainable-oriented actions.

SUSTAINABILITY AND PSYCHOLOGY

Every scientific field contributes to implementing the ideals of sustainable development. Psychology plays a particularly important role, since the origins of environmental problems are to be found in human behavior, and psychology is the scientific field for the study of behavior. Several decades ago, psychologists established that environmental problems should be –at least partially- solved by using "behavioral solutions" (Cone & Hayes, 1980), implying that these solutions correspond with the nature of the causes (i.e., human environmentally-destructive behaviors). The ultimate behavioral solution implies the instauration of a sustainable lifestyle, i.e., a set of persistent and deliberate actions intended to conserve the physical and social resources of the planet (Centre for Sustainable Development, 2004).

Environmental psychology (EP) is a particular area or sub-field of psychology, especially involved in delimiting the causes and solutions of environmental problems (Oskamp & Schultz, 2006). This area deals with the study of interactions between human behavior and the socio-physical components of the environment (Aragonés & Amérigo, 2000). Gifford (2007) indicates that several environmental psychologists acknowledge and accept the broader concept of sustainability as outlined in the Brundtland Report (WCED, 1987), and this is manifested in a growing interest in studying sustainability issues from a psycho-environmental perspective. As a part of such interest, EP is aimed at studying the psychological dimensions involved in sustainable actions; we call these components the "psychological dimensions of sustainability."

Those dimensions include psychological tendencies, capacities and behaviors covarying with sustainable actions. In playing its research role, EP tries to determine what personal characteristics and aptitudes predispose individuals towards more sustainable lifestyles. Those characteristics and aptitudes include perceptions, attitudes, motives, beliefs, norms, values, knowledge and skills leading people to behave pro-socially and pro-ecologically (Bamberg & Möser, 2007; Carrus, Pasafaro & Bonnes, 2008; Geller, 2002; Hernández, Suárez, Martínez-Torvisco, & Hess, 2000; Schultz, 2001). This set of pro-environmental *dispositional variables* (i.e., personal tendencies and capacities biasing individuals to act sustainably) constitutes an important component of the psychological dimensions of sustainability.

A second set of psychological variables encompasses *sustainable behaviors*, actions aimed at conserving the integrity of the socio-physical resources of this planet. In order to be sustainably-oriented, people have to be pro-ecological (Kaiser & Wilson, 2000) and non-consumerist (Fujii, 2006) so that the physical environment is conserved; but individuals should also practice altruistic (Schultz, 2001) and equitable behaviors (Winter, 2002) for protecting their social environment. Therefore, sustainable actions include pro-ecological, altruistic, frugal, and equitable conducts, which –when systematically practiced- constitute *sustainable lifestyles* (Centre for Sustainable Development, 2004; Corral-Verdugo, Tapia, Fraijo, Mireles & Márquez, 2008). Pro-environment dispositional variables are assumed to exert a positive influence on these behaviors; so that the former could be considered as dispositional antecedents of sustainable actions.

Human behavior always occurs in a setting or situation; therefore, environmental psychology studies the ways diverse *contextual factors* influence sustainable behaviors. Contexts could be physical or social; the former include aspects such as temperature, technological tools, distance to resources, and the presence or absence of natural resources; while the latter consider social norms, laws, collective values, religion and costumes. Both, social and physical contexts can also be inductors of sustainable behaviors (Barr, 2007; Wiesenfeld, 1996; Fujii, 2006). Since perceptual factors are key elements in mediating the effect of contexts on pro-environmental behavior (i.e., a context only affects behavior after some or all of its components are perceived by the individual), the psychological dimensions of sustainability also act at the level of situational influences on behavior (Gardner & Stern, 2002).

Moreover, the psychological dimensions of sustainability include *consequent variables*; that is: positive repercussions resulting from practicing pro-environmental actions. So far, two of these consequences have been investigated: happiness and psychological restoration (Brown & Kasser, 2005; Fuller, Irvine, Devine-Wright, Warren, & Gaston, 2007). The classical categorization of "impact levels" considers ecological, economic, social and institutional positive repercussions of sustainability (Gouveia, 2002). Recent findings add psychological positive impacts, as the above mentioned (happiness, restoration), to this list. Thus, SD psychological dimensions cover the entire range (antecedents-actions-consequences) of sustainable practices, and environmental psychologists are committed to study them, as the authors of this book demonstrate.

By considering the general framework above exposed, the main aim of this book is to illustrate how environmental psychology addresses the conservationist approach of sustainability in studying sustainable behavior, its determinants and its positive consequences. The authors are recognized scholars, joined by a select group of young researchers specialized in conservation psychology issues. In following the book's general plan, Part 1 (chapters 1-4) addresses the psychology of environmental problems and solutions, while Part 2 (chapters 5-13) is about the antecedent psychological dimensions of sustainability. In turn, Part 3 (chapters 14-19) deals with the contextual influences on sustainable behavior, and, finally, Part 4 (chapters 20-21) addresses the positive psychological impacts of sustainable behavior. A brief overview of the chapters' content follows.

OVERVIEW OF CHAPTERS

Part one constitutes an introduction to the human dimension of environmental problems. By analyzing how people's tendencies, capacities and behaviors have led us to endanger Earth's environmental balance, the authors stress the need of considering the psychological dimension of environmental problems in searching for their integral solution.

Chapter 1, as readers have so far noticed, declares the conservationist goal of environmental psychology, which addresses the study of sustainable behavior, its psychological antecedents and also its psychological consequences. The following chapters are devoted to discussing psychological approaches and solutions to three major environmental problems: global warming, water scarcity and energy conservation. Without minimizing the importance of additional ecological problems (solid waste control, overpopulation, etc.), these three main instances of environmental problems deserve an urgent and special attention, as authors of this part of the book declare.

In Chapter 2, Milfont introduces the topic of the psychological causes and human reactions linked to global warming. His writing also reviews the scientific evidence of the consequences of climate change, and some of the issues in environmental psychology that attend to its investigation. The main section of this chapter reviews the characteristics of global warming and climate change that function as psychological barriers for the awareness of their existence and for willingness to act. Milfont presents five psychologically inadvertent barriers (psychophysiological, temporal, judgemental, socio-geographical, and social-dilemma) that help to understand why most people are not acting to solve issues related to global warming. The author also discusses positive actions for tackling climate change.

In turn, Carrus, Bonnes, Corral-Verdugo, Moser, and Sinha, in chapter 3, discuss the psychological dimensions involved in the water-scarcity problem that most countries of the world face, offering an overview of water problems that challenge a sustainable development for people. They also present a multi-national study showing that water conservation is inhibited by water accessibility, the country's developmental level, individuals' socio-economic status, and people's indifference regarding water problems. Sustainable water consumption is promoted by human-interdependence beliefs, according to these authors. The level of economic affluence, indicated by the HDI, SES and water accessibility also instigates negative dispositional tendencies towards water conservation, such as indifference regarding water problems and the perception of water externalities.

Chapter 4, written by Steg and Abrahamse reviews the contribution of social and environmental psychology to understand and promote household energy conservation. Since households are responsible for a large part of total energy requirements and world's CO_2 emissions (which lead to global warming), conceptual approaches are required to explain what makes people to conserve energy. A general framework is proposed by these authors, comprising the identification and measurement of behaviors to be changed, examination of the main factors underlying these behaviors, design and implementation of interventions to change behavior to reduce household energy use, and evaluation of the effects of interventions.

Part two of this book is devoted to analyze antecedent psychological dimensions of sustainability as well as those actions that constitute sustainable behaviors. Human behavior is importantly determined by dispositional psychological factors -studied as tendencies, propensities and capacities- and also by psychological states -such as emotions. In this part of the book, the authors try to determine the most important psychological inductors of sustainability, conceiving them as "potentials" of human mind that lead people's behavior towards adaptive pro-environmental behavior. In addition, these authors show that sustainable behavior presents at least four facets: the pro-ecological, frugal, equitable, and altruistic manifestations of a sustainable lifestyle.

In Chapter 5, Hernández, Suárez, Hess, & Corral-Verdugo address the relationship between ecological worldviews and sustainable behavior. Worldviews provide a framework for the way a person or a whole community makes sense of life and the world in its most significant aspects and dimensions. Thus, an influence of worldviews is expected on people's behavior and predisposition towards their socio-physical environment. The authors discuss the way ecocentric and anthropocentric ecological visions affect daily interactions with the environment, and develop the notion of *interdependence worldviews* in the form of an integrative paradigm combining eco and anthropocentric environmental beliefs, which should affect sustainable behavior. Data from an empirical study seems to confirm the authors' presumptions.

Chapter 6, written by Roczen, Kaiser, and Bogner discuss three *motives* that psycho-environmental authors regard the top reasons behind people's environmental conservation: environmental attitude, prosocial/moral considerations, and appreciation for nature. The authors argue that environmental attitude represents the extent to which people realize their personal conservation goals. Yet this attitude should not be seen as a motive behind pro-environmental behavior, but as the disposition itself to act ecologically. Moral considerations, a person's moral norms and values, and his/her social value orientation are also considered important motives for environmental conservation. Nevertheless, the most promising motivation for large-scale behavior change seems to be a person's appreciation for nature, which, according to the authors, is corroborated in its significance for people's ecological performance.

In turn, in chapter 7, Bonnes, Carrus, Corral-Verdugo, and Passafaro address a recent topic of interest for conservation psychology: the affinity towards diversity (ATD) that seems to be intrinsic among humans. ATD manifests as a liking for variety in physical and social scenarios and as a significant determinant of sustainable actions. Results of an empirical study conducted by the authors showed that ATD, altruism, future orientation, attitudes towards integration of urban green areas, and feelings of indignation were significantly interrelated, constituting a higher-order factor that they called Pro-Sustainability Orientation (PSO). PSO, in turn, influenced the self-report of pro-environmental behaviors. Their model's results also confirmed that people more attracted to bio and socio-diversity are also more tolerant individuals.

Deliberation is an important component of sustainable behavior, which is manifested in people's intentions to engage in pro-environmental actions. Fujii and Taniguchi in chapter 8 describe a model to develop intentions for various types of pro-environmental behaviors, based upon pro-environmental goals, perceived ease and perceived efficiency of behavior. They argue that providing information regarding actual effectiveness in CO_2 reduction and information about how to reduce car use are indispensable for promoting car-use-reduction behavior. Based on these findings, the authors suggest that travel feedback programs providing such information could be successful in reducing car use. Two application studies from their interventional programs are described to illustrate their model and results.

In chapter 9, Sevillano, Aragonés & Schultz elaborate on altruistic behavior, one paramount component of sustainable actions. Most psycho-environmental scholars agree in considering sustainable actions as altruistically-motivated; altruistic motivation has also been related to the attribution of personal responsibility and to experiencing feelings of sympathy and empathy with nature, as this chapter's authors establish. They conclude that collectivistic motivation is linked to accepting social norms and to people's pro-social value orientation, while also discussing how *principalism* -the motivation concerned with upholding a moral principle- might lead to sustainable behavior. Finally, the authors review the Value-Belief-Norm Theory and the Empathy Model, as explanatory frameworks of altruistically-motivated behaviour.

Chapter 10, written by Corral-Verdugo, García-Cadena, Castro, Miramontes, and Limones, approaches the topic of equitable behavior, conceived as a sustainable lifestyle. Defined as a tendency to fairly distribute resources, power and benefits among people, avoiding bias or favoritism, equitable actions imply dealing with and treating fairly and equally all concerned, regardless of social, economic and demographic differences. A literature review conducted by the authors reveals significant links between equitable actions and sustainable behavior, which is reinforced by the empirical study they conducted. Their findings show that equitable behavior saliently and significantly correlates with austere, pro-ecological, and altruistic actions, suggesting that equity is an important component of sustainable lifestyles.

In chapter 11, Pinheiro and Corral-Verdugo stress the importance of the psychological temporal component of sustainability. Since sustainable development implies a concern for the integrity of forthcoming generations, a future time perspective is expected to predominate in sustainable-oriented people. By using the Zimbardo's Time Perspective Inventory, they contrast the effect of present (both hedonistic and fatalistic), past (both negative and positive) and future orientations on pro-environmental behavior as indicated by a responsible water consumption. Their results confirmed that hedonistically and fatalistically present-oriented individuals tend to waste water; past orientation –either positive or negative- did not affect water consumption (at least, directly), and future-oriented individuals exhibited a pro-environmental use of water.

Effectiveness, a psychological dimensions referring humans' capacity to successfully deal with everyday problems is the topic of chapter 12, written by Fraijo-Sing, Corral-Verdugo and Tapia-Fonllem. Environmental knowledge, efficiency, the ability to perceive affordances, and environmental skills are instances of people's effective responses. Sustainability requires effective actions to deal with ecological problems but, as the authors discuss, people have also to face pro-environmental requirements (i.e., challenges and opportunities) to act in a sustainable way. By combining pro-environmental requirements with their corresponding effective (knowledgeable, skilled) responses, individuals develop *pro-environmental competency*, as these authors demonstrate in a study with Mexican children. In this study, such a competency was a powerful determinant of sustainable behavior.

The last chapter (13) of this section is presented by Tapia-Fonllem, Corral-Verdugo, Gutiérrez-Sida, Mireles-Acosta and Tirado-Medina. These authors, as others in the field, regret that the study of psychological predictors of pro-environmental behavior had neglected the role that emotions play in inducing sustainable actions. Their study illustrates the way emotions influence pro-environmental behaviors by assessing pro-environmental intentions, pro-ecological behavior, emotional interest in nature, feelings of indignation due to environmental deterioration, and affinity towards biodiversity. The three latter factors constituted a second-order latent variable, which they labeled "environmental emotions." The influence of emotions on pro-ecological behavior was higher than the one promoted by intentions. The combined effect of emotions and intentions explained more than half of the pro-environmental behavior variance

Part three of this text is devoted to discussing the role that *contexts* play in the emergence and sustenance of pro-environmental behaviors. As authors of this section demonstrate, physical settings and social situations contribute substantially to the display of sustainable actions and lifestyles. Moreover, contextual factors are psychologically processed by humans so that their effect on behavior is mediated by perceptual and emotional mechanisms. This means that even external environmental situations should be subject to psychological analysis in determining contextual effects on sustainable behavior.

Hill, Figueredo & Jacobs, in chapter 14, criticize the person-centered approach assuming that the primary determinants of behavior are a person's attributes. They assure that the causal role played by context (setting/situation) should be considered in studying the determinants of pro-environmental behavior. Their research focused on various contexts presenting adaptive problems which displayed affordances, cues, and stimuli guiding adaptive (pro-environmental) behavior. Contexts accounted for by a significant proportion of variance in both pro- and anti-environmental behavior. They also found that a person-centered theory did not predict context-specific behavior; however, components of the theory did predict behavior in the aggregate.

In turn, in chapter 15, Gaspar de Carvalho, Palma, and Corral-Verdugo address the "negative" approach to the relationship between contexts and sustainable behaviors, showing that people's sustainable behavior is inhibited by a number of situations, even if individuals have the "right" pro-environmental attitudes, intentions and goals. This approach stresses the importance of contextual and psychological factors working as barriers and constraints to ecological behavior change and to the promotion of pro-ecological behavioral goals. The authors introduce a model aimed at representing a process-view regarding how a conflict between pro-ecological and anti-ecological behavioral goals can be produced, given the presence of two types of barriers and constraints: a) *perceived* barriers and constraints, and b) *unconscious* barriers and constraints.

Wiesenfeld and Sánchez, in chapter 16, propose a model based on environmental community psychology (ECP), which is intended to promote sustainability at the community level. According to these authors, community members are fundamental in conserving social and natural resources, as interpreters of their daily living conditions, and as managers of the transformations that are required to improve such conditions. Yet, most sustainable-development programs are planned and implemented in a vertical way, privileging the opinion of experts, without consideration of the involved citizens. These authors illustrate their point with a case study conducted in Venezuela and offer a series of ECP principles guiding the study of community sustainable practices.

Devine-Wright, in chapter 17 shows that public responses to large-scale non-contaminant technologies for energy generation could be negative if people perceive that their place of residence could be altered. In his study, the project for installing wind farms in a touristic resort was experienced as a threat to identity for those residents with strong attachment to that place, leading to negative attitudes to the project and oppositional behavior. Thus, both place identity and attachment could serve as pro-environmental instigators but –as this author demonstrates- also as inhibitors of sustainable interventions. The conclusion is that situational aspects in interaction with psychological processes should be considered in designing large-scale sustainable projects. Yet, the author recognizes that it should not be presumed that place attachment inevitably leads to resistance to place change. Rather, future studies should be aware of the diverse positions that local residents can adopt in response to sustainable development proposals.

The significant influence of culture and social context on sustainable use of natural resources is addressed by Moser, Navarro, Ratiu & Weiss in chapter 18. These authors show that environmental concern, attitudes, perceptions, social representations and sustainable use of water widely differ from one country to another. They review research results from their studies conducted in Europe, Latin America, the Far East, and Africa, concluding that economic affluence and the country's cultural context predispose people to differentially perceive and use water in either a responsible or wasteful way. In elaborating a model of people's relations to water, they distinguish four consecutive levels of interrelated factors: contextual characteristics and value systems, social representations of water, awareness of water-related issues and elaboration of a diagnosis, and enacted behaviors.

Chapter 19 was written by Frías-Armenta and Martín. They analyze the role that social and legal contexts play in the induction of personal norms and investigate how these norms affect people's commission of illegal anti-ecological conducts. After reviewing theories and factors related to the inhibition of anti-ecological behaviors they present results from an empirical study on the determinants of such behaviors. Their conclusion is that personal norm and antisocial behavior had a direct effect on illegal anti-ecological behavior; social norm produced an indirect effect on that behavior through personal norm. Deterrence (i.e., the threat of sanctions established to obtain compliance with the law) also exerted its effect through social norm. Legitimacy correlated with social norm and deterrence, and emotional volatility affected personal norm. Clearly, situational social aspects interacted with psychological processes in inhibiting anti-environmental behavior.

Part four is about the psychological positive repercussions of sustainability and pro-environmental behaviors. This is a very recent area of research in environmental psychology, which explains the limited knowledge we have regarding the psychological consequences of being sustainable. So far, two of those consequences have been subject to scientific scrutiny: psychological restoration and subjective well-being (or happiness). As the authors in this section show, these two consequences should be enough to motivate the promotion of sustainable behaviors.

Payne, who wrote chapter 20, discusses how sustainable environments are able to provide restorative experiences to people. After reviewing how visual components of green spaces allow recovery from exhausted psychological functions, she presents a study on *soundscapes* (i.e., the mixture of sounds from the natural elements and built elements of a due space) of two urban parks. The author concludes that park users perceived five different types of soundscapes, and these significantly related to the level of restoration participants achieved. The soundscape predominated by natural sounds, along with happy people sounds and object sounds due to people, was perceived by park users who recovered the most while in the park, and had a restorative experience. As with viewing natural elements, natural sounds tend to be restorative.

Finally, in chapter 21, Bechtel and Corral-Verdugo show and discuss evidence of a significant link between sustainable behavior and happiness. According to such evidence, people who engage in altruistic, equitable, frugal and pro-ecological behaviors tend to be happier than individuals who are not prone to practicing those sustainable activities. The authors illustrate their point with a study conducted with Mexican and American undergraduate students. Results of this study showed a significant relationship between the self-report of pro-environmental behaviors and students' levels of happiness. Based upon the reviewed antecedents and their data, Bechtel and Corral-Verdugo conclude that engaging in sustainable behaviors should be added to the list of actions-to-practice in order to obtain happiness.

Conclusion

In summary, this book intends to present an overview of what is known about the psychological causes and benefits of being sustainable. Human psychology is intimately linked to environmental problems and their solutions have to consider what makes us to act pro or anti-environmentally, how we can develop sustainable lifestyles, and what the consequences that might emerge from acting sustainably are.

In trying to address those situations, a question arises regarding whether or not humans are attuned with the principles ruling the functioning of ecological systems, or, if -as the anthropocentric ideas establish- we are an exceptional species, exempted from attending to those natural mechanisms. Recent findings, as the ones reported in this book, suggest that the first option (human psychological attunement with ecological rules) is a pertinent answer to such a question.

The principles ruling ecosystems functioning seem to be incorporated in human psychological structure, providing hope -and clues- to professionals interested in developing interventions for pro-environmental behavioral change. As authors of this book show, the rules of interdependence and diversity are not only perceived but also appreciated –in varying degrees- by people. Even more interestingly, such appreciation conduces individuals to sustainable practices. Hernández et al.'s review in this book demonstrates that adhering to *interdependence* principles makes people prone to pro-environmental actions, and Bonnes et al.'s chapter concludes that appreciating bio and socio-*diversity* shapes an important component of pro-sustainability orientation. These are not the only ecological principles grasped and used by the human mind. Fraijo et al.'s chapter suggests that the *flexibility* principle corresponds with a basic mechanism of pro-environmental competency: such a capacity is characterized by versatile (i.e., flexible) effective responses facing environmental problems and challenges. Moreover, Sevillano et al., in their chapter, demonstrated that cooperation, in the form of altruistic responses, implies the ability of perceiving *association* (one more ecological rule) as a plausible strategy in conserving socio-environmental resources. Since these psychological tendencies and capabilities are not uniform across individuals, increasing their level is an interesting and promising challenge.

Sustainability, as applied to human issues, requires a temporal component allowing the anticipation of behavioral consequences. Pinheiro and Corral-Verdugo in their chapter confirm previous findings establishing that future orientation predisposes people towards the conservation of the environment. Although no ecosystem rule has been established in the form of a time perspective, the interdependence principle contains a temporal component (present-future interdependence) as suggested by these and other authors. Unfortunately, this time perspective is not always on our side: As Milfont's chapter shows, humans are not very good in associating distant-future environmental troubles with present conservationist practices and concerns.

Apparently, the correspondence between ecological principles and human psychology resulted from evolved adaptive mechanisms, which permit people to both perceive environmental opportunities and get adapted to constantly changing ecological conditions, as Hill et al.'s chapter indicates. This situation closely resembles Gibson's (1979) *affordances* notion, the human capability to perceive environmental opportunities in the daily interactions with our surroundings.

Emotions are also evolved mechanisms allowing the survival of our species. Tapia-Fonllem et al.'s chapter questions whether or not emotions will serve the purpose of long-term humans' endurance (i.e., avoidance of extinction from environmental degradation), as much as they have facilitated short-term individual survival. Their response seems to be positive. In addition, Frías-Armenta and Martín, in their writing, show the importance of emotional control in integrating norms that lead to pro-ecological behavior, and Roczen et al.'s chapter establishes that a particular emotion (appreciation for nature) is a most promising leverage for large-scale behavior change. Thus, emotions should be incorporated in every strategy intended to establish sustainable lifestyles among people.

Of course, humans are rational agents, as well as emotionally-motivated subjects. Rationality, as manifested in beliefs, norms, values, and intentions, lead people's behavior towards pro-social and pro-ecological activities, since these are consciously anticipated to produce positive outcomes in oneself and other individuals, as Fujii and Taniguchi illustrate in their chapter. Yet, not all psychological drivers are conscious: an important component of human behavior is automatic, as Gaspar de Carvalho et al.'s writing in this book establishes. Studying both conscious and automatic processes that lead to sustainability will be more fruitful than solely investigating conscious pro-environmental dispositions.

Contexts (i.e., social situations and physical settings) are fundamental inductors of sustainable behavior. People living in a pro-environmental society and having the physical means to behave pro-ecologically will act in a responsible way. But, as the chapters by Devine-Wright, Frias-Armenta & Martín's, Wiesenfeld & Sánchez, Moser & Navarro, and Gaspar de Carvalho et al. demonstrate, psychological processes (i.e., perceptions, emotions) interacting with contexts should be considered in trying to understand how situations and settings affect people's reactions. This is especially important in designing large-scale sustainable projects. This also reinforces the idea that the psychological dimensions of sustainability permeate every human-environment transaction.

Milfont's, Carrus et al.'s and Steg and Abrahamson's chapters remind us of the behavioral causes of environmental degradation, as manifested in global warming, water scarcity, and depletion of energy sources. Moreover, these writings also offer clues for behavioral solutions. Sevillano et al., and Corral-Verdugo et al., in their chapters, specifically study those behavioral facets required to cope with environmental problems: pro-ecological, altruistic, equitable and frugal actions that are the kind of behaviors constituting the sustainable lifestyles aimed at conserving the socio-physical environment.

The expected consequences of practicing these sustainable lifestyles are not trivial: psychological restoration of exhausted psychological capacities is one, as Payne discusses in her chapter; happiness or psychological wellbeing is another, as Bechtel and Corral-Verdugo demonstrate in their writing. But, overall, the most important of those consequences is guaranteeing the long-term endurance of humankind, along with the survival of our sister animal and vegetal species that join us in the marvelous journey of life on Earth.

REFERENCES

Aragonés, J.I. & Amérigo, M. (Eds.), (2000). *Psicología Ambiental* [Environmental Psychology], 2d. Edition. Madrid: Pirámide.

Bamberg, S. & Möser, G. (2007). Twenty years after Hines, Hungerford, and Tomera: A new meta-analysis of psycho-social determinants of pro-environmental behavior. *Journal of Environmental Psychology, 27*, 14-25.

Barr, S. (2007). Factors influencing environmental attitudes and behaviors. *Environment & Behavior, 39*, 435-473.

Bonnes, M., & Bonaiuto, M. (2002). Environmental psychology: from spatial-physical environment to sustainable development. In R.B. Bechtel & A. Churchman (Eds.), *Handbook of Environmental Psychology* (pp. 28-54). New York: Wiley.

Brown, K.W. & Kasser, T. (2005). Are Psychological and Ecological Well-being Compatible? The Role of Values, Mindfulness, and Lifestyle." *Social Indicators Research, 3*, 49–68.

Carrus, G., Pasafaro, P. & Bonnes, M. (2008). Emotions, habits and rational choices in ecological behaviours: The case of recycling and use of public transportation. *Journal of Environmental Psychology, 28*, 51-62.

Capra, F & Pauli, P. (1995). *Steering business toward sustainability*. Nueva York: The United Nations University.

Centre for Sustainable Development. (CSD, 2004). *"Every little bit helps..." Overcoming the challenges to researching, promoting and implementing sustainable lifestyles*. CSD. University of Westminster, U.K.

Cone, J.D. y Hayes, S.C. (1980). *Environmental problems. Behavioral solutions*. Monterey, CA: Brooks Cole.

Corral-Verdugo, V., Bonnes, M., Tapia, C., Fraijo, B., Frías, M., & Carrus, G. (2009). Correlates of pro-sustainability orientation: the Affinity Towards Diversity. *Journal of Environmental Psychology, 29*, 34-43.

Corral-Verdugo, V., Carrus, G., Bonnes, M., Moser, G. & Sinha, J. (2008). Environmental beliefs and endorsement of Sustainable Development principles in water conservation: towards a *New Human Interdependence Paradigm* scale. *Environment & Behavior, 40*, 703-725.

Corral-Verdugo, V., Tapia, C., Fraijo, B., Mireles, J. & Márquez, P. (2008). Determinantes psicológicos de los estilos de vida sustentables [Psychological determinants of sustainable lifestyles]. *Revista Mexicana de Psicología, 25*, 313-327.

Dodman, D., Ayers, J., & Huq, S. (2009). Building resilience. In World Watch Institute (Ed.), 2009 *State of the World. Into a warming world*. Washington, DC: World Watch Institute.

Flavin, C., & Engelman, R. (2009). The perfect storm. In World Watch Institute (Ed.), 2009 *State of the World. Into a warming world*. Washington, DC: World Watch Institute.

Fujii, S. (2006). Environmental concern and ease of behavior as determinants of pro-environmental behavior intentions. *Journal of Environmental Psychology, 26*, 262-268.

Fuller, R., Irvine, K., Devine-Wright, P., Warren, P. & Gaston, K. (2007). Psychological benefits of greenspace increase with biodiversity. *Biology Letters, 3*, 390-394.

Gardner, G.T. & Stern, P.C. (2002). *Environmental problems and human. behavior* (2nd ed.). Boston, MA: Pearson Custom Publishing.

Geller, E.S. (2002). The challenge of increasing pro-environment behavior. In R.B. Bechtel & A. Churchman (Eds.), *Handbook of Environmental Psychology*. New York: Wiley.

Gifford, R. (2007). Environmental psychology and sustainable development: expansion, maturation, and challenges. *Journal of Social Issues, 63*, 199-212.

Gouveia, V. (2002). Self, culture and sustainable development. In P. Schmuck y P.W. Schultz (Eds.), *Psychology of Sustainable Development*. Norwell, Massachusetts: Kluwer.

Hernández, B., Suárez, E., Martínez-Torvisco, J. & Hess, S. (2000). The study of environmental beliefs by facet analysis. Research in the Canary Islands, Spain. *Environment & Behavior, 32*, 612-636.

Kaiser, F., & Wilson, M. (2000). Assessing people´s general ecological behavior: A crosscultural measure. *Journal of Applied Social Psychology, 30*, 952-978.

Mastny, L. (2009). State of the world: a year in review. In World Watch Institute (Ed.), *2009 State of the World. Into a warming world*. Washington, DC: World Watch Institute.

Mastny, L. & Cincotta, P. (2005). Examining the connections between population and security. In Brown, L. (Ed.), *State of the World 2005: Global Security*. Washington, DC: World Watch Institute.

Millennium Ecosystem Assessment (2005). *Ecosystems and Human Well-being: Synthesis*. Washington, DC: Island Press.

Oskamp, S. y Schultz, P.W. (2006). Using psychological science to achieve ecological sustainability. In S. Donaldson, D. Berger & K. Pezdek (Eds.), *Applied Psychology. New Frontiers and Rewarding Careers*. New York: Routledge.

Pearce, D., & Warford, M. (1993). *World without end: Economics, environment, and sustainable development*. New York: Oxford University Press.

Pradhan, S.K. (2006). Building resilience in local institutions for natural resources management. *Proceedings of the XI Biennal Conference of the International Association for the Study of Common Property (IASCP)*. Bali, Indonesia: IASCP.

Renner, M. (2005). Security redefined. In Brown, L. (Ed.), *State of the World 2005: Global Security*. Washington, DC: World Watch Institute.

Schultz, P.W. (2001). The structure of environmental concern. Concern for self, other people, and the biosphere. *Journal of Environmental Psychology, 21*, 327-339.

Siurua, H. (2006). Nature above people. Rolston and "fortress" conservation in the south. *Ethics and the Environment, 11*, 71-96.

Starke, L. (Ed.) (2008). *State of the World*. New York, W. W. Norton & Company.

Talbert, J. (2008). Redefining progress. In Starke, L. (Ed.), *State of the World*. New York, W. W. Norton & Company.

Tanimoto, J. (2004). Environmental dilemma game to establish a sustainable society dealing with an emergent value system. *Physica D: Nonlinear Phenomena, 200*, 1-24.

WCED: World Commission on Environment & Development (1987). *Our Common Future*. Oxford, U.K.: Oxford University Press.

Wiesenfeld, E. (1996). The concept of "we": A community social psychology myth? *Journal of Community Psychology, 24*, 337-346.

Winter, D. (2002). (En)Gendering sustainable development. En P. Schmuck & P.W. Schultz (Eds.), *Psychology of Sustainable Development*. Norwell, Massachusetts: Kluwer.

World Health Organization. (2008). Retrieved March 31, 2008 from http://www.who.int/research/en/.

WWF (World Wide Fund). (2008) Retrived April, 2008 from http://www.wwf.org.mx/wwfmex/wwfmundo.php.

In: Psychological Approaches to Sustainability
Editors: V. Corral-Verdugo et al.

ISBN 978-1-60876-356-6
© 2010 Nova Science Publishers, Inc.

Chapter 2

GLOBAL WARMING, CLIMATE CHANGE AND HUMAN PSYCHOLOGY

*Taciano L. Milfont**
Centre for Applied Cross-Cultural Research and
Victoria University of Wellington, New Zealand

ABSTRACT

This chapter considers psychological aspects of global warming and climate change. It begins with a brief consideration of the public and political recognition of global warming and climate change as significant environmental issues. The chapter then turns to a review of the scientific evidence of the causes and consequences of climate change, and some of the issues in psychology that attend its investigation. The main section of the chapter reviews of characteristics of global warming and climate change that function as psychological barriers for the awareness of their existence and for willingness to act. Using Construal Level Theory, a new integrative approach is then outlined that links climate change barriers with psychological distance, and implications of the high-level construals of climate change are discussed. Thereafter some research agendas for further psychological research addressing global warming and climate change is proposed and delineated. This is followed by a section highlighting that the rate and consequences of global warming and climate change can be downgraded by global and local reductions of greenhouse gas emissions. The chapter finishes with some concluding remarks.

Keywords: global warming, climate change, psychology, barriers, climate change construals

---

* Correspondence: Taciano L. Milfont. E-mail: www.milfont.com.

INTRODUCTION

Discussion of issues related to global warming and climate change are increasingly frequent in public discourse. The last few years have seen the release of several movies dealing with the topic, including *An Inconvenient Truth, The 11th Hour, The Great Global Warming Swindle, The Day After Tomorrow* and *The Age of Stupid*. Media coverage has also appeared in popular magazines, including a special report on *Time* magazine (April 3, 2006) under the banner "*Global warming: Be worried. Be very worried.*" An increasing number of scientific publications have also been dealing with the topic. The large and increasing number of scientific studies have been routinely assessed, and the main conclusions are summarised, in the reports by the Intergovernmental Panel on Climate Change (IPCC; discussed below). There is also an increasing number of psychological studies dealing with the topic (e.g., Gifford, 2008a; Heath & Gifford, 2006; Nilsson, von Borgstede, & Biel, 2004; Pawlik, 1991; Sundblad, Biel, & Gärling, 2009). The majority of lay people also seem to be aware of the problem. The results of a Gallup survey in the early 90s with representative samples from six nations (Brazil, Canada, Mexico, Portugal, Russia and USA) shows that the majority of lay persons in four of the six nations rated "global warming or the 'greenhouse' effect" as a very serious problem (Dunlap, 1998). Similarly, a more recent public opinion survey from Yale University also showed that 71% of the American public is convinced that global warming is happening (Leiserowitz, 2007).

Concern about climate change and the emission level of greenhouse gases is also evident in political discourse. For example, in a 2007 speech UN Secretary General Ban Ki-moon has warned that climate change poses as much of a danger to the world as war, and in a 2004 speech the former Prime Minister Tony Blair called climate change the world's greatest environmental challenge in a foreword to a book published in 2005 ("*Avoiding Dangerous Climate Change*").[1] As a result, global warming and climate change are a concern in many nations (see also Brouwer, Akter, Brander, & Haque, 2007; Harré & Atkinson, 2007), and they are seen as one of the most significant environmental issues in recent years (Heath & Gifford, 2006), or even the greatest challenge to our civilization (Triandis, 2008). However, despite the increasing certainty about the evidence for anthropogenic climate change (i.e., climate change caused by human activities), public opinion and political changes have been very slow (or even non existent). This raises the question of "why"? Why do we not seem to be worried? This chapter tackles this question by specifically focusing on characteristics of global warming and climate change that function as psychological barriers for the awareness of their existence and for willingness to act.

In the first section, I will provide a brief overview of the evidence for global warming and climate change. It will be argued that global warming and climate change are happening, that they are anthropogenic issues, and that their effects pose real threats for human living conditions and ecosystems. In the second section, I will discuss the psychological barriers that allow us to understand human failure to become aware of global environmental changes and to act properly to address these changes. These barriers will be illustrated with data from my ongoing programme of research as well as from other published data. The third section briefly

---

[1] Political discourse is an unfortunate measure of what people feel because politicians would not address global warming and climate change if they did not think they would have the support of a sufficiently large fraction of their voters.

outlines a new integrative approach for understanding the climate change barriers based on Construal Level Theory (Trope & Liberman, 2003). This approach holds that climate change is a psychologically distant event, and for that reason people mentally construe climate change in terms of high-level, abstract, and stable characteristics. In the fourth section, I discuss research agendas through which the psychological barriers can be reduced, eliminated or overcome. Four interrelated psychological research areas that deserve special attention in dealing with global warming and climate change are discussed. In the forth section, I will highlight the challenges of change. This section briefly outlines the importance of both individual and community actions for tackling global warming and climate change. Some conclusions are presented in the fifth and last section of the chapter.

Table 1. Brief summary of important historical events and initiatives related to climate change and global warming

Year	Event/Initiative
1859	John Tyndall, a UK scientist, discovers that greenhouse gases keep the Earth warmer than it would be otherwise
1896	Svante Arrhenius, a Swedish chemist, was the first to postulate that increasing carbon dioxide concentrations in the atmosphere could raise global temperatures
1979	First World Climate Conference organized by the World Meteorological Organization
1985	The Vienna Convention for the Protection of the Ozone Layer was signed
1987	The Montreal Protocol on Substances that Deplete the Ozone Layer was signed
1987	The International Geosphere-Biosphere Programme was established
1988	The establishment of the Intergovernmental Panel on Climate Change (IPCC)
1988	James Hansen, an American scientist, alerted a U.S. Senate Committee that rise in temperature was a result of the greenhouse effect
1990	The IPCC First Assessment Report was released
1992	The United Nations Framework Convention on Climate Change (UNFCCC) was signed by 154 nations during the Earth Summit in Rio de Janeiro.
1995	The IPCC Second Assessment Report was released
1996	The International Human Dimension Programme on Global Environmental Change was established
1997	The Kyoto Protocol was agreed under the UNFCCC
2001	The IPCC Third Assessment Report was released
2005	The Kyoto Protocol came into effect
2007	The IPCC Fourth Assessment Report was released
2008	Kyoto Protocol First Commitment Period started (from 1/1/2008 to 31/12/2009)
2009	University of Copenhagen Congress on Climate Change
2009	Discussions for further climate change actions are being negotiated under the UNFCCC and Kyoto Protocol

FACTS ABOUT GLOBAL WARMING AND CLIMATE CHANGE: IT IS A HAPPENING THING!

The notion of global warming and climate change can be briefly summarised as follows. Some gases present in the Earth's atmosphere act like the covering of a greenhouse, allowing the sun's energy to enter but then keeping the heat from escaping back into space, thus helping to make our planet a warm and habitable place. Although greenhouses gases (e.g., carbon dioxide, methane and nitrous oxide) are emitted naturally from trees and animals, they are also emitted from human activities like burning coal, driving cars, farming and deforestation. An increase in such human activities leads to higher emissions of the greenhouse gases into the atmosphere and increases their concentrations. Rising concentrations of greenhouse gases in the atmosphere means that even more heat is being trapped from the sun, causing the planet to warm up and our natural weather patterns to change. *Global warming* refers to this process. However, it is preferable to think of *climate change* because the changes currently observed and predicted are not limited to temperature alone but also embrace changes in climate patterns and related events (sea rise, floods, cyclones, droughts and landslips) (Ministry for the Environment, 2007).

Although global warming and climate change are currently a *hot topic* (double meaning intended), a historical overview clearly shows that these are not new issues (see Table 1). It is true that evidence has increased since the late 1980s (Flavin & Engelman, 2009), but scientists have long indicated that human activities could cause large-scale changes in climate. Nowadays most of the widely disseminated scientific evidence relating to global warming and climate change comes from the assessment reports produced by the IPCC. The IPCC was established in 1988 by the World Meteorological Organization and the United Nations Environment Programme, and is open to 192 countries that are members of these organizations. The IPCC regularly assesses the scientific, technical and socio-economic information important to comprehending the science of climate and climate change, potential impacts of climate change and options for adaptation and mitigation. This assessment is provided via Assessment Reports, Special Reports, Methodology Reports and Technical Papers, and is used to inform the work of the United Nations Framework Convention on Climate Change (UNFCCC). The UNFCCC is the political multi-lateral process by which countries agree on measures to counteract the negative consequences of climate change through placing limits on greenhouse gas emissions, and through adapting to the unavoidable consequences of a changing climate.

The UNFCCC definition of climate only encompasses climate change attributed to human activities. In contrast, the IPCC defines climate change as any "change in the state of the climate that can be identified (e.g. using statistical tests) by changes in the mean and/or the variability of its properties, and that persists for an extended period, typically decades or longer. It refers to any change in climate over time, whether due to natural variability or as a result of human activity" (IPCC, 2007a, p. 30). In other words, in IPCC usage there is no pre-judgement whether a given change in climate was caused by human activities or may be a natural phenomenon. Rather, scientific research must be used to answer such questions. This chapter uses the broader climate change definition of IPCC, but focuses on anthropogenic climate change.

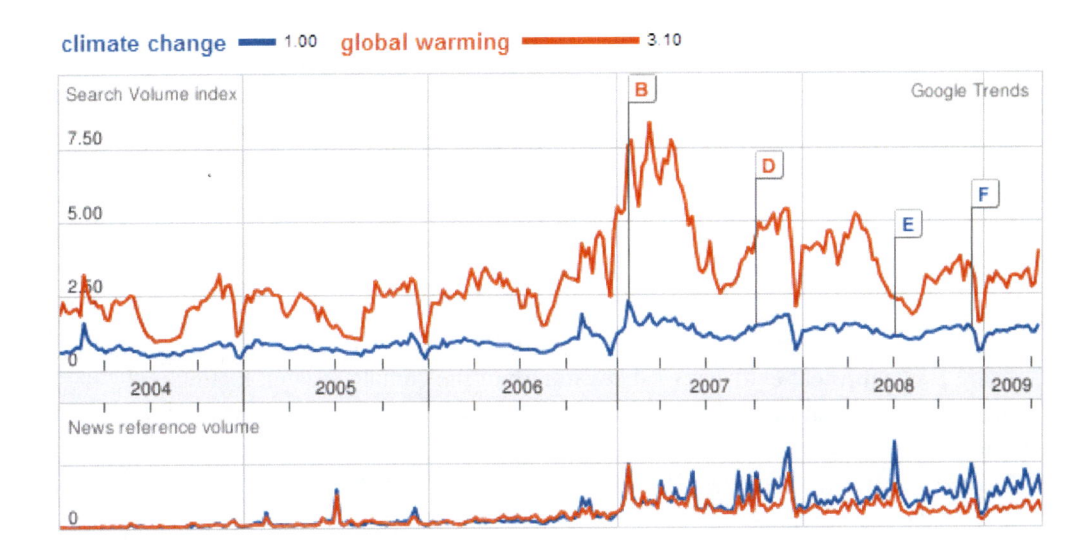

Figure 1. Worldwide web search volume for climate change vs. global warming.

The IPCC has established three working groups that prepare reports on specific thematic areas. The IPCC Working Group I assesses available scientific information on the climate system and climate change. The IPCC Working Group II assesses the impacts of climate change and the vulnerability of natural and socio-economic systems to climate change, and options and ability to adapt to such changes. The IPCC Working Group III assesses the technical and economic feasibility of strategies to reduce greenhouse gas emissions and hence reducing the rate and magnitude of future changes in climate. Reductions in greenhouse gas emissions are usually referred to as "mitigation", while efforts to adapt to changes in climate are referred to as "adaptation". Each working group is co-chaired by one scientist from a developing country and another from a developed country. IPCC reports are prepared by teams of scientific authors, and undergo a two-stage peer-reviewed process (first by experts and then by both experts and governments). This peer-review process is followed by an adoption and approval process in which a plenary with IPCC members accept the final reports and agree on the wording of the report's executive summary (know as "Summary for Policymakers"). None of the authors who prepare the assessments are paid by the IPCC for their work, and authors are drawn from the current global and active scientific community (IPCC, 2004). These features of the IPCC work provide robust support for the scientific integrity, transparency and reliability of its assessments. Figure 1 shows the worldwide web search volume for "climate change vs. global warming" on Google Trends, and serves as a crude indicator of the impact of IPCC work on people's awareness of these issues. As can be seen, the spikes in the graph in 2007 coincide with the release of the IPCC reports and the announcement of the Nobel Peace Prize award for the IPCC and Al Gore for their efforts to build up and disseminate greater knowledge about anthropogenic climate change.

Note. This Google Trends data is scaled based on the average search traffic of the terms from January 2004 to April 2009. The label letters in the graph refer to automatically selected Google News stories (not shown) written about the search terms. The numbers next to the search terms correspond to their total average traffic in the time frame. The first term has a fixed value of 1.0; the number for the second term (3.10) means that global warming has about 3 times more traffic in the time frame than climate change. There is an interesting preference trend in the use of the search terms by the top 10 regions. Although the list of regions is similar, we can see the prevalence of commonwealth/English-speaking regions using the more neutrally-charged term "climate change" (i.e., Australia, New Zealand, South Africa, United Kingdom, Canada, Ireland, Singapore, India, United States, Switzerland), whereas the more emotionally-charged term "global warming" tend to be the preferred term in Asian regions (i.e., Indonesia, Philippines, India, South Africa, Australia, New Zealand, Singapore, United States, Canada, United Kingdom).

The IPCC (IPCC, 2007a; 2007b) has provided international peer-reviewed scientific evidence for (amongst other findings) the following:[2]

There is unequivocal evidence of the warming of the climate system, including increases in global average air and ocean temperatures, pervasive melting of snow and ice, and rising global average sea level

Global mean temperature has risen approximately 0.76° Celsius since 1850 and continues to rise from decade to decade

- Changes in arctic temperatures and sea ice, widespread changes in precipitation amounts, ocean salinity and wind patterns are long-term changes already observed due to climate change; recent warming has already affected many natural systems on every continent and most oceans
- Concentrations of greenhouse gases (carbon dioxide, methane and nitrous oxide) have increased strikingly since 1750 as a result of human activities (i.e., from deforestation, land use change, burning fossil fuels)
- Human activities that increase the concentration of greenhouse gases in the atmosphere are largely responsible for the observed increase in temperature over the past 50 years
- Increasing emissions will further enhance the greenhouse effect and result in an additional warming of the Earth's surface over the 21st century that will very likely be greater than the warming observed over the 20th century
- Climate models predict a increase of the global mean temperature between 1.1 to 6.4°C over the next 100 years, depending on future greenhouse gas emissions
- Extreme weather events including droughts, heavy precipitation, heat waves and the intensity of tropical cyclones have also been observed and in many places are expected to become more frequent and/or intense as the climate warms
- Sea level is projected to rise by about 0.5m by 2100, and would continue to rise inexorably for many centuries in a warmer world (more recent studies suggest that this rise could occur even faster)

---

[2] Interestingly enough, some commentators argue that because not all scientists agree or fully endorse these evidences they should be ignored. Would they give the same advice for say a cancer patient who is testing a new treatment for her/his disease? Should the patient wait until a full scientific consensus is reached about the new treatment before undertaking it? Likewise, should we wait for a similar consensus before acting to solve the environmental problems we face? As the reader will soon see, the scientific evidence for climate change is more compiling and consensual than the evidences for most of the medical treatments we readily accept and employ.

- The projected changes in climate will result in many negative impacts on ecological systems and socio-economic sectors, including e.g. food supply, water resources, and human health
- The impacts of climate change will be felt in all countries, but developing countries and some key ecosystems are generally most vulnerable

This evidence is very serious. It shows that the planet is warming up, that our natural weather patterns are changing, that human activities are largely responsible for these changes, and that projected future changes are likely to have significant impacts on the most vulnerable people. Scientists are now very confident that the observed changes in climate are not just a natural weather cycle (Collins, Colman, Haywood, Manning, & Mote, 2007). Indeed, IPCC revised its conclusion that most of the warming observed since the mid-20th century is attributable to humans from *likely* (more than 66 percent probable) in the 2001 report to *very likely* (more than 90 percent probable) in the 2007 report (Collins et al., 2007). More worrying still is the fact that although very accurate, the 2007 IPCC report has been seen as too cautious as new scientific data are reported on unexpectedly rapid changes, such as the dramatic further reduction in Artic sea ice during 2007 and 2008 (Kintisch, 2009).

Evidence thus supports the claim that global warming and climate change are anthropogenic. Ecological systems in many regions of the world are now more controlled by anthropogenic rather than by natural forces. The Italian geologist Stoppani created the term "anthropozoic era" in 1873 to refer to humans as a new factor (a new geological force) in nature (as cited in Clark, 1988, Footnote 1). More recently, Crutzen and Stoermer (2000) coined the term "anthropocene" to refer to this same idea of humans as a major geological force, and to characterise the current geological epoch of a global-level impact of human activities on geology and ecology.

Given the key role of human behaviour in the current environmental issues, psychology and in particular environmental psychology can boldly lead initiatives that address these issues, as several publications in the area have already made clear (see, e.g., Gifford, 2008a; Oskamp, 2000; Schmuck & Schultz, 2002; Schmuck & Vlek, 2003; Vlek & Steg, 2007). In the next section, I will explore the psychological barriers or constraints that affect the ability of people to think and act about global warming and climate change.

ENVIRONMENTAL NUMBNESS AND PSYCHOLOGICAL CHARACTERISTICS OF CLIMATE CHANGE

Gifford (2008a) has recently expanded his concept of "environmental numbness." He argues that "most people, most of the time, simply are not thinking at all about climate change. Instead, they are (understandably) thinking about their work, their friends and family, or the big game." (p. 277). Environmental numbness thus implies that people can be intentionally thinking about climate change but choose not too. However, there are also unintentional psychological mechanisms that work as barriers or constraints preventing people from becoming aware of climate change and from acting on this awareness. These psychological characteristics were addressed in one of the first psychological papers dealing with global environmental changes published by Pawlik (1991). In a concise but important work, Pawlik proposed five "psychologically inadvertent characteristics" related to climate change. These characteristics influence people's evaluations of climate change, and can help us to understand the human failure to become aware of global environmental changes. These inadvertent characteristics of climate change are reviewed and expanded next.

1. Psychophysiological Barriers

The first psychologically inadvertent characteristic of climate change is humans' psychophysiological barrier to perceiving the physical signs of these climate changes. Pawlik (1991) referred to this as the 'low signal-to-noise ratio of global change'. As presented above, evidence shows that the global mean temperature has risen approximately 0.76°C and is going to increase between 1.1 to 6.4°C over the next 100 years. However, the variation in temperatures that humans normally experience from summer to winter, or even variations in temperatures during a single day, are typically higher than the evident warming due to climate change. The physical 'signals' of changes in temperature due to climate change are thus weak in value if compared to the strong 'noise' of changes in temperature due to daily, seasonal and regional variations (Pawlik, 1991). Because of the weak physical signals of climate change, sensory and memory mechanisms are unable to discern them as they are below the common thresholds of discernability. Its weak physical signals make climate change harder to notice than other environmental problems. It is easier to notice deforestation, air and water pollution than small variations in temperature.

Pawlik does not assume that global changes in temperature are not important, just that people tend not to notice them. Indeed, it would be incorrect to assume that because the magnitude of climate change appears small compared with day-to-day variability, it is irrelevant. Global annual average temperatures normally only vary by a few tenths of a degree from one year to the next. Hence an increase in several degrees in global average temperature is a significant change on geological proportions. In addition, small changes in average temperature can lead to a disproportionate increase in extremes, for example heat waves. Apart from temperature, changes in average rainfall of several tens of percent are projected in many already dry regions of the globe, with attendant increase in drought risk. Combining all these changes, the physical signals will therefore soon become very noticeable as the consequences of changes in the climate increase in ecosystems and for human activities such as agriculture, coastal storms and public health. If we were to wait for rapid and catastrophic changes before taking global action the situation would get worse than already is now.

2. Temporal Barriers

Another psychologically inadvertent characteristic refers to temporal barriers related to awareness of climate change. There is a great time lapse between human actions and their influence on environmental change. As pointed by Reisinger (2003) for the example of ozone depletion, "there is a lag of about 30 years from the first discovery of a global environmental risk to the period of maximum environmental damage, and a lag of more than 60 years from the beginning of concerted international action until the environmental perturbation will have been reduced to levels prior to anthropogenic interference" (p. 111). This means that in the case of ozone depletion there is a time lapse of about one hundred years from discovery of the potential environmental problem to its eventual resolution.

This temporal barrier was referred to by Pawlik (1991) as the 'extreme masking and delay of cause-effect gradients'. The great temporal delay between human actions and their perceptible influence on environmental systems (i.e., cause-effect gradient) means that the consequences of human actions go beyond a single generation. The environmental problems we are facing now are a result of maladaptive human behaviour of previous generations, and our current maladaptive behaviours will have consequences for our generation as well as for several generations to come. Indeed, climate scientists agree that the consequences of climate change will be felt by plants, animals and humans for at least the next thousand years (Collins et al., 2007). Our current actions will thus influence how the world will develop over centuries to come. Conversely, it means that actions to reduce risks from climate change will present costs to the current generation but the main benefits of such actions would be accrued only by future generations.

This second characteristic of climate change can be expanded to include another temporal barrier that is more related to individuals' temporal orientations rather than to the phenomenon of climate change *per se*. This second temporal barrier of climate change is related to people's capacity and interest in thinking long-term. Research has shown that environmental issues entail not only a social conflict (discussed below) but also a temporal conflict (a conflict between short- and long-term interests) (Joireman, Van Lange, & Van Vugt, 2004). More specifically, research has shown that future-oriented individuals (those who are aware of and concerned about the future consequences of their actions) tend to care and act more to address environmental issues than present-oriented individuals (for a review, see Pinheiro & Corral-Verdugo, this volume). This means that individuals who care about environmental issues focus more on public and long-term interests, rather than on their immediate needs and concerns (Milfont & Gouveia, 2006).

Extending this line of research on the impact of individuals' time orientation on environmental awareness, we recently showed that attitudes toward climate change responsibility predict differential support for political parties *only* for people who have children (Milfont, Harré, Sibley, & Duckitt, 2008). Attitudes toward climate change responsibility predicted increased support for a center-left party in New Zealand (The Labour Party) and decreased support for a center-right party (The Labour Party) but only for people with children. For people without children, such attitudes did not predict support for either of these political parties. We proposed an 'environmental generativity' account to theoretically ground this finding, based upon Erickson's (1950) theory of life-span psychological development. Erickson sees generativity as the challenge underlying the seventh stage of human development, and is manifest as a desire to leave a social legacy and provide positive guidance for others. Following this idea, we argued that parenting may help prompt an 'environmental generativity' so that parents (compared to non-parents) feel more inclined to preserve the environment for their children. This indicates that the desire to leave a social legacy and the future orientation underlying generativity tendencies are characteristics related to climate change. This seems self-evident given that parents have a clear stake in the welfare of future generations and thus have an obvious motivation to care about the future of the planet. As a result, political parties perceived as more pro-environmentally oriented may be more likely to attract the votes of people who are concerned about climate change when they have a vested interest in preserving the environment for future generations, and particularly one's children.

There is therefore robust evidence for the role of temporal barriers as psychologically inadvertent characteristic of climate change. This is expressed in respect of the delay between current actions and their future consequences on environmental systems, as well as the impact of people's time orientation on their awareness of such issues. It has even been argued that it is difficult for humans to adopt a future-centered conceptualization of problem-solving, which is needed for addressing environmental issues, because of evolutionary characteristics of human personality (Shackelford, 2006).

3. Judgemental Barriers

The third psychologically inadvertent characteristic of climate change refers to human tendency to underestimate the occurrence of low-frequency events. Pawlik refers to this as the 'psychophysics of low-probability events'. People tend to underestimate the increasing frequency of natural disasters produced by global warming and climate change, such as hurricanes and major flooding, because of their low absolute rate of occurrence (Pawlik, 1991). This tendency to minimize events with a small probability of occurrence is a cognitive bias that originates from judgmental heuristics (mental strategies or cognitive short-cuts). When making judgements under uncertainty we tend to use such heuristics for reaching subjective probabilities (Tversky & Kahneman, 1974). Judgement by availability is one of the heuristic postulated by Tversky and Kahneman (1974), and is used when "people assess the frequency of a class or the probability of an event by the ease with which instances or occurrences can be brought to mind" (p. 1127). Because instances or occurrences of global warming and climate change (or natural disasters produced by those) cannot be easily brought to mind, its probability of occurrence is underestimated due to a cognitive bias. Uncertainty related to environmental problems not only influences risk perception but also behaviour. For example, research has shown that increasing the level of certainty (or probability of occurrence) that negative effects of resource depletion would occur increases participants' willingness to limit resource consumption (Kortenkamp & Moore, 2006).

Another related cognitive bias that functions as a psychologically inadvertent characteristic of climate change refers to more specific analyses of risk perception. Research has shown that we tend to evaluate hazards as more threatening when such hazards are perceived as unknown (Slovic, 1987). Slovic (1987) reports a study that asked participants to rate 81 hazards (e.g., DNA technology, pesticides, pollution from coal burning) on 18 risk characteristics (e.g., common, immediate, fatal, controllable). Using a factor-analytic approach to provide a spatial representation of the relationships among the hazards and the risk characteristics, two risk factors were identified: a Dread Risk factor and an Unknown Risk factor. These two risk factors have been confirmed in several other cross-cultural studies (Boholm, 1998). The Dread Risk factor (uncontrollable, global catastrophic, consequences fatal, not easily reduced) included hazards such as nuclear technology and radioactive waste. The Unknown Risk factor (not observable, unknown to those exposed and to science, effect delayed) included chemical technology hazards. While people were more afraid of hazards that are both dreaded and unknown, people wanted to reduce the current risks and wanted stricter regulation especially for hazards scoring high on the Dread Risk factor.

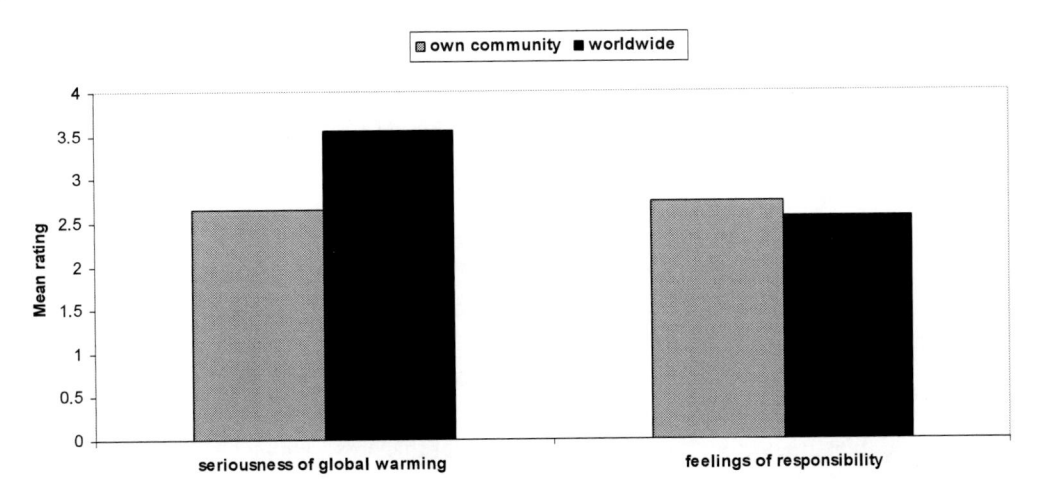

Figure 2. Environmental hyperopia in a cross-cultural sample (source Milfont, Sibley & Duckitt, in press).

These two cognitive biases are related to climate change. Natural disasters caused by changes in global climate are underestimated because of their low frequency of occurrence as well as because of their familiarity. Risks from climate change (e.g., floods, sea rise) are by and large known and thus underestimated (Weber, 2006). Hence, risks from say nuclear reactor accidents (low-frequency event but unknown) are perceived as more threatening than increasing hurricanes due to climate change (low-frequency event but known).

4. Geographical and Social Barriers

Another psychologically inadvertent characteristic of climate change signed by Pawlik (1991) refers to the 'social distance between actors and victims of global change.' As discussed above, the environmental consequences of global warming and climate change have impacts across temporal social distances, so that future generations will have to deal with the environmental problems caused by the behaviour of our generation. But these consequences not only operate across temporal social distances; environmental impacts due to global warming and climate change are also carried across spatial social distances. Our maladaptive behaviours will have negative consequences for generations living away apart in both place and time.

Research looking at the way people evaluate environmental problems in distinct geographical places helps us to understand the social distance underlying climate change. Uzzel (2000) observed people's tendency to perceive environmental problems as more worrying when they take place at greater distances, which he calls 'environmental hyperopia.' As a result of environmental hyperopia, people are typically more concerned about environmental problems at the global and international level than they are at the local and regional level. Several empirical studies have supported this phenomenon (see, e.g., Freury-Bahi, 2008; García-Mira, Real, & Romay, 2005). As an illustration, I re-analysed cross-cultural data of 468 participants from 59 countries (Milfont, Sibley, & Duckitt, in press). As can be seen in Figure 2, while showing significantly higher ($p < .001$, $d = .21$) feelings of responsibility for environmental problems in their community than for environmental problems worldwide, participants rated the seriousness of global warming worldwide as significantly higher ($p < .001$, $d = 1.04$) than the seriousness of global warming in their community. This supports the environmental hyperopia and shows that we tend to perceive global warming and climate change as more threatening to others than to ourselves.

A similar phenomenon that has been related to environmental issues is optimistic bias (Hatfield & Job, 2001; Pahl, Harris, Todd, & Rutter, 2005; Uzzell, 2000). Weinstein (1980) was the first to demonstrate optimistic bias by showing that people tend to believe their chances of experiencing positive events to be higher than that of other people, and their chances of experiencing negative events to be lower. Some studies have investigated environment-related optimistic bias. Hatfield and Job (2001) investigated optimistic bias regarding environmental hazards. Contrary to their expectations, they found only low levels of optimistic bias regarding general environmental hazards. However, higher levels of optimistic bias were found regarding both the likelihood of hazards affecting the participant's local area, and the participant's perception of their own knowledge of suitable ecological behaviours to reduce environmental problems produced by the hazards. More recently, Pahl et al. (2005) conducted two studies investigating whether optimistic bias exists in relation to environmental risks and also whether this bias can be used to predict self-reported ecological behaviour. Although Pahl et al.'s (2005) findings indicate that optimistic bias is relevant to environmental issues, no direct association was found between optimistic bias for environmental risks and ecological behaviour.

Conceptually integrating environmental hyperopia with optimistic biases, Freury-Bahi (2008) investigated environmental risk perception for four distinct targets (i.e., risk to oneself, inhabitants of the town, inhabitants of the country, and humanity) and three categories of hazards (including climate change). In line with environmental hyperopia and optimistic biases, he observed that participants' perceived risk of climate change increased as both the size of local area and the number of people under consideration also increased. Climate change was thus rated as a greater risk for humanity than for inhabitants of the country, inhabitants of the town, and for oneself (i.e., humanity > country > town > oneself). These findings support the notion of a psychologically inadvertent characteristic of climate change related to the actors-victims social distance: even if people are convinced climate change is a major issue facing the planet, they do not feel climate change will affect them much.

5. Social Dilemma Barriers

The final psychologically inadvertent characteristic of climate change signed by Pawlik (1991) refers to the 'low subjective cost-effectiveness of environment-conserving behaviour.' This characteristic stands for the practical understanding that many (if not most) of one's detrimental acts to the environment are more cost-effective for oneself than acts that are less detrimental. Put in other words, from an individualistic point of view pro-environmental behaviours (e.g., walking, biking or taking public transport to work) are often more costly in terms of personal comfort and convenience than anti-environmental behaviours (e.g., driving to work).

This low subjective cost-effectiveness of pro-environmental behaviours can be understood through the conceptualisation of social dilemmas. When in a social dilemma situation we are caught between two competing alternatives: to act serving our own interests or to act serving the needs of the group we belong to or wider society. Hardin (1968) was the first to describe the notion of social dilemma in his paper *The Tragedy of the Commons* dealing with the risks of overexploitation of natural resources as a result of the conflict between individual interests and the common good. A prototypical example of the tragedy of commons is the situation in which fishermen have little incentive to act alone to preserve the shared fish stocks and as a result suffer collectively from overfishing. Environmental issues are understood as social dilemmas because they represent a conflict between the collective interest of society and the individual interests of its members (Milfont & Gouveia, 2006; Osbaldiston & Sheldon, 2002; Van Vugt, 2001; Van Vugt & Samuelson, 1999). This conflict between private and public interests comprises the social dimension of the dilemmas. But a temporal dimension (see discussion above) has also been acknowledged as another conflict underlying social dilemmas (Joireman, 2005; Joireman et al., 2004; Messick & Brewer, 1983). Hence, environmental issues are social dilemmas with a conflict between short-term individual interests and long-term collective interests (Milfont & Gouveia, 2006).

There is also a distinction in the literature of two types of social dilemmas: The resource dilemma and the public goods dilemma (Van Vugt, 1998). The resource dilemmas are situations that require individuals' cooperation to preserve a valuable resource (e.g., rain forest), while public good dilemmas are situations that require individuals' cooperation to create a valuable good (e.g., creation of a community centre for edible gardening). Although specific environmental issues might encompass mainly a resource dilemma, broader environmental problems such climate change clearly involves both resource dilemmas and public good dilemmas. In fact, Gifford (2008b) have developed a theoretical model that can be applied to both types of social dilemmas. The model integrates influences on and outcomes of social dilemmas with relevance to environmental issues, including climate change (Gifford, 2008a). According to the model, five categories of influence (i.e., geophysical, governance, interpersonal, decision-maker and dilemma-awareness influences) have important consequences for the outcomes of social dilemmas. The influenced outcomes are: outcomes for the decision-maker (e.g., emotional, financial and social satisfaction) and outcomes for the environment (e.g., public good is completed or not; resource depleted or sustained).

Overall, the imbalance between private good and public good comes from the fact that environmental issues are usually the result of a large number of individual destructive acts. Hence, *one* individual choosing not to commit such an act has a very small influence on the overall outcome, but for the specific individual concerned, the choice between committing or not committing such an act can be significant. Individuals will benefit more in a social dilemma if he or she defects, but the group as a whole is worse off if everyone defects than if everyone cooperates. As a result, individualistic orientations tend to produce negative outcomes in social dilemmas. As research has shown, individuals who place higher priorities in individualistic, self-centred value orientations tend to be less concern about environmental issues and to act accordingly (Coelho, Gouveia, & Milfont, 2006; Milfont, Sibley & Duckitt, in press; Schultz, Gouveia, Cameron, Tanka, et al., 2005). For example, we found that self-enhancement values were negative predictors of ecological behaviour (while altruistic values were positive predictors) in samples from Brazil, New Zealand and South Africa (Milfont, Duckitt, & Wagner, in press).

Construal Levels and Psychological Distance: Towards an Integrative Approach to Understand Climate Change as a Psychologically Distant Situation

Climate change is an environmental risk characterized by weak physical signals, high uncertainty, time-delayed consequences, low subjective cost-effectiveness, and great geographical and social distance. These characteristics were outlined in Pawlik (1991) and expanded upon above. These climate change characteristics are implicitly discussed by other scholars (e.g., Dunlap & Jones, 2002; Gattig & Hendrickx, 2007), and there are also other individual and social perceived barriers to engaging with climate change that are not discussed here (Lorenzoni, Nicholson-Cole, & Whitmarsh, 2007). However, no previous attempt has been made to integrate the several barriers related to climate change. I use the Construal Level Theory (Liberman & Trope, 1998; Trope & Liberman, 2003) to briefly outline a novel integrative approach for understanding climate change (and other environmental risks) as a psychologically distant situation.

According to Construal Level Theory (CLT), temporal distance influences people's responses to future events: events in the distant future are viewed in more abstract and superordinate terms (high-level construals), while events in the near future are viewed in more concrete and detailed terms (low-level construals). The theory has later been expanded to include not only temporal distance but also other dimensions of psychological distance (Trope, Liberman, & Wakslak, 2007). An event is more psychologically distant as it takes place farther into the future (temporal distance), as it occurs in more remote locations (spatial distance), as it is less likely to occur (hypotheticality), and as it happens to people less like oneself (social distance). The basic premise of CLT is that the more psychologically distant an event is (i.e., the greater the temporal, spatial, hypothetical, or social distance from an event), the more distant it appears and the more it will be represented at higher levels of abstraction. Therefore, CLT posits that similar mental construal processes underlie psychological distance dimensions, and that these construal processes guide the way people predict, evaluate, and plan psychologically near and distant situations (Liberman & Trope, 2008). Indeed, several studies testing CLT hypotheses have shown that dimensions of psychological distance are (i) interrelated, (ii) affect and are affected by the level of construal (i.e., people think more abstractly about distant than about near situations, and more abstract construals also lead people to think of more distant situations), and (iii) have similar effects on prediction, evaluation, and action (for reviews, see Liberman & Trope, 2008; Trope et al., 2007).

All climate change barriers discussed above involve some form of psychological distance. Climate change has weak physical signals and uncertain outcomes so is perceived to be less likely to occur (hypotheticality), takes place farther into the future (temporal distance), and is perceived to be more likely to occur in more remote locations (spatial distance) and to people less like oneself (social distance). Thus, psychophysiological and judgemental barriers are related to hypotheticality, and temporal, geographical and social dilemma barriers are linked to temporal, spatial and social distances, respectively. The links between barriers and psychological distance indicates that climate change can be regarded as a psychologically distant situation. And because climate change is a psychologically distant situation, CLT would predict that the way people mentally represent it is by abstract representations, or high-level construals. High-level construals consist of general, structured, parsimonious, superordinate, and essential features of a situation (Trope & Liberman, 2003). This means that climate change is likely to be represented in terms of a few abstract features that convey its perceived essence rather than in terms of more concrete and incidental details.

A CLT account of climate change has important implications for understanding the way people evaluate environmental risks in general and also on action plans related to these risks. Take the role of feasibility and desirability considerations of climate change, for example. Whilst desirability refers to the value of an action's end state (superordinate, *why* aspects of an action), feasibility refers to the ease or difficulty of reaching the end state (subordinate, *how* aspects of an action) (Liberman & Trope, 1998). So, desirability concerns the value (why) of overcoming climate change, whereas feasibility concerns the amount of effort we have to invest (how) to tackle climate change. Although climate change involves both desirability (moral principals and ideals) and feasibility (difficulty, cost, and situational pressures) considerations, moral principles are more likely to guide decisions involving high-level construals and psychologically distant situations. Therefore, moral principles and ideals should be key variables guiding people's decisions to tackle climate change. This prediction might explain the known role of values in predicting environmental attitudes and behaviours (see discussion below). Using CLT as a framework for understanding the construal of climate change and other environmental risks seems a fertile endeavour for theoretical and empirical development in the area.

PSYCHOLOGICAL RESEARCH FOR TACKLING CLIMATE CHANGE

As it is clear from the discussion and research examples discussed earlier, psychological research is important for understanding and overcoming barriers related to climate change. This section focuses on research agendas to help this process. Important actions for addressing climate change have been proposed and discussed by other commentators (Crompton, 2008; Gifford, 2008a). Here I will concentrate my analyses on four interrelated areas for further psychological research that deserve special attention. An effort is made to highlight the importance of the integrative approach discussed above in the research agendas.

Risk Perception

Climate change is an example of "hidden hazards," or risks that are unnoticed or unattended until they reach disaster proportions, despite their serious consequences for society (Kasperson & Kasperson, 1991). In line with this, public opinion polls and academic studies examining the relative importance of several environmental problems have shown that global warming and climate change are not salient issues in people's minds (e.g., Bord, Fisher, & O'Connor, 1998; Leiserowitz, 2004). This hidden feature of climate change is further exacerbated by the psychophysiological barriers of climate change discussed above. Future studies should investigate the specific mechanisms by which people perceive climate change as a risk or not. Considering the fact that climate change is a psychologically distant situation, research should focus on the interrelationship of all dimensions of psychological distance in affecting people's perception of climate change as a risk (cf. Gattig & Hendrickx, 2007). An inclusive approach that takes into account all these factors will provide a way to understand how individuals consider the potential climate outcomes of their past and current behaviours for themselves and others (away in place and time), and also the extent to which they are influenced by these potential future outcomes.

Risk Communication

Communication seems the ideal tool for making climate change an "unhidden" risk. Pawlik (1991) argues that communication can address many of the barriers outlined above. Likewise, Gifford (2008a) argues that to challenge environmental numbness we need, among other things, "to get as many people around the world as possible actively thinking about climate change" (p. 277). These positions seem to support the knowledge-deficit model (cf. Kellstedt, Zahran, & Vedlitz, 2008), according to which providing information about global warming and climate change would increase public concern about these issues. Communication is thus expected to create awareness and willingness to act even considering the uncertain, gradual, long-term signals of climate change. However, the effect of communication and information on increased concern is not that simple. For example, some researchers were unable to find a clear effect of perceived information about global warming and climate change on concerns and intention to act (Heath & Gifford, 2006; Kellstedt et al., 2008). Further psychological research is therefore needed to examine whether increased information about climate change can indeed lead to higher concern and proper actions. Three general areas of research could be explored.

1. It has been recently suggested that climate communication should use a combination of top-down (regulatory approaches that forces green behaviour) and bottom-up (fostering voluntary action to reduce emissions) approaches to both facilitate public acceptance of regulations related to climate change and to stimulate grass-roots action (Ockwell, Whitmarsh, & O'Neill, 2009). This combination of approaches for climate communication seems reasonable. It seems that we cannot rely only on individuals to take collective action; we have to make collective action normative and subject to social sanctions through policies and laws. However, the psychological reasons for combining top-down and bottom-up approaches have not been spelled out nor tested.
2. Environmental risks are more likely to be accepted when they are presented as gains rather than as losses (Gattig & Hendrickx, 2007). This suggests that framing climate communications in a way that it is perceived as an increase of an existing risk may prove more effective. Another possibility is to tailor climate change messages to the specific processes underlying behaviour change, and to frame these messages as a function of the intrinsic versus the extrinsic costs or benefits of the behaviour (Pelletier & Sharp, 2008). It is a question for future research whether these tailoring and framing strategies are more effective in climate communication.
3. Besides addressing broad climate communication approaches and framings, future research should also explore specific issues related to communicating uncertainty. A recent study has shown that the way the IPCC reports communicate uncertainty

(using a set of probability terms accompanied by global interpretational guidelines) leads to imprecision and errors in communication related to climate change information (Budescu, Broomell, & Por, 2009). Future studies could address whether changes in the way IPCC reports communicate uncertainty can lead to higher risk awareness and actions.
4. Future research should also explore the implications of the high-level construals of climate change in risk communication. As discussed above, climate change is likely to be represented in terms of a few abstract features that convey its perceived essence. Climate change communication should thus take these features into account.

Intertemporal and Interpersonal Issues

Climate change comprises a conflict between short-term individual interests and long-term collective interests. Current destructive behaviours will have negative consequences for generations living away apart in both place and time. Moreover, while actions to reduce risks from climate change represent costs to the current generation, their resulting benefits would be accrued only by future generations. Climate change therefore encompasses intertemporal and interpersonal issues. Future research should further examined the link between temporal and social distances in the climate change dilemma (cf. Joireman, 2005; Milfont & Gouveia, 2006; Milfont et al., 2008). One possibility would be to link the social dilemma framework with the CLT account of climate change. CLT predicts that more abstract construals should be applied to other people and out-group while more concrete construals should be applied to self and in-group (Liberman & Trope, 2008). In line with this, CLT may be expanded into the social dilemma framework by considering the influence of both temporal and social distance on climate change construals. One might postulated that events in the distant future are viewed in more abstract and selfless terms (i.e., "a tax on gas will reduce fuel consumption and pollution"), while events in the near future are viewed in more concrete and selfish terms (i.e., "a tax on gas will cost me more money when I fill up my gas tank"). Given that climate change is a distant future event, the information and evaluative implications of high-level construals and cooperative orientations, compared to low-level construals and competitive orientations, should have more impact on the way people mentally represent climate issues. Empirical studies could address this possibility. The link between intertemporal and interpersonal issues is also important because social influence can be enhanced by future thinking. Research has shown that reflecting on the future, or thinking about future consequences, increases persuasive attempts by influencing choices in the present (Sherman, Crawford, & McConnell, 2004).

Dominant Values

The areas of research discussed above are important for addressing climate change. Enhancing risk perception and communication could increase awareness, and understanding the link between intertemporal and interpersonal issues can facilitate the promotion of personal and collective actions for overcoming environmental issues. However, these research areas do not question nor address the implicit causes of climate change or other environmental issues. Most (if not all) current environmental problems are a result of the assumption that the ever-increasing economic growth should be the main drive for development. This growth paradigm and its underlying values, such as individualistic, materialistic and consumeristic values, influence the way we relate to nature.[3] Commentators and researchers have argued that these values have to be challenged if we are to successfully address environmental issues (Brown & Cameron, 2000; Crompton, 2008; Flavin & Engelman, 2009). No action will be completely effective if the dominant values that lead to the current environmental problems are not challenged. This is because any agreement or action built on the assumptions of ever-increasing economic growth is doomed to failure (Flavin & Engelman, 2009). A core role of psychological research should thus be to identify ways and means by which the underlying growth paradigm, and its underlying values, can be challenged without leading to an immediate blockage by the people whose growth would be halted. Furthermore, values constitute moral principles and ideals that, according to CLT and the approach described above, are more likely to guide decisions for situations with high psychological distance, like climate change, because they represent desirability concerns (cf. Liberman & Trope, 1998). Values are thus crucial psychological variables for challenging the state of affairs for the way we relate to nature. Indeed, research has shown the predictive power of values in explaining people's environmental attitudes and behaviours (e.g., Milfont, Duckitt et al., in press; Milfont & Gouveia, 2006; Milfont, Sibley et al., in press)

THE CHALLENGE OF CHANGE

The focus of this chapter has so far been on evidence, facts and research agendas. The evidence reviewed is worrying and can be overwhelming. There is the possibility that we might end up in a state of inertia due to what the New Zealand journalist Margie Thompson calls eco-anxiety: feelings of guilt with overtones of fear followed by feelings of being overwhelmed by all the changes you know you should make to your lifestyle. However, it is important to highlight that apart from the mounting scientific evidence about the impact of human behaviour on the global climate, there is also rapidly increasing evidence about options to reduce greenhouse gas emissions and thus reduce the rate and magnitude of climate change (see, e.g., IPCC, 2007a). This means that hope, awareness and action should overcome despair, denial and inertia, and the focus should be on ways we can ameliorate the impact of climate change in our lives.

Although climate change cannot be prevented entirely, its rate and consequences can be downgraded by global and local reductions of greenhouse gas emissions (Hare, 2009). In virtually every sector of human activities (energy, industry, buildings, agriculture, forestry, and waste management) there exists a significant potential to reduce emissions through new technologies, use of existing more efficient technologies, and changes in behaviour. The overall economic costs of such changes are estimated to be small, reducing the global average growth rate of GDP by less than about 0.1 percentage points (Stern & Taylor, 2007), but they would require significant policy changes including placing a cost on the emission of greenhouse gases.

---

[3] Annie Leonard's movie *The Story of Stuff* provides an interesting portrait of these underlying values.

Because climate change is caused by human behaviour, its solution lies in changing human behaviour. Actions to reduce emissions, including use of clean-energy technologies, policy changes, domestic regulations and international treaties, will be a result of community and individual decisions. Individual actions have thus a meaningful impact in addressing climate change. Research supports this by showing that individuals must believe that even small personal actions can make a meaningful difference before they decide to act against climate change (Heath & Gifford, 2006). Governmental and non-governmental agencies have also indicated the need to enhance the power of small individual actions (Crompton, 2008; Ministry for the Environment, 2007). For instance, the Ministry for the Environment (2007) in New Zealand recognises that the difference in addressing climate change will be made by the small steps taken by individuals (supported by the bigger steps of governments and businesses).

However, such changes generate significant debate and opposition from vested interests, since they would inevitably make some activities less profitable and others more so. As a result, community action is also necessary for achieving widespread changes. Communities should be encouraged to share their experiences and learn from each other. For example, the movie *The Power of Community: How Cuba Survived Peak Oil* shows how Cubans developed community initiatives and creative strategies to overcome the collapse of their formal economy. We have much to learn from their experiences and resilience strategies. Specific resilience strategies for climate change have also been discussed (Brouwer et al., 2007; Dodman, Ayers, & Huq, 2009). Therefore, psychological research should also contribute for enhancing community and individual actions.

CONCLUSION

This chapter dealt with the issues of global warming and climate change. The evidence and research summarized in this chapter indicate a number of important conclusions about the role of psychological research aimed to address these major environmental problems we are facing. First, evidence was shown demonstrating that these issues are happening and that they will have negative impacts on our lives. Second, five psychologically inadvertent barriers were presented that can help to understand why most people are not acting to solve these issues. Third, construal level theory was used to provide an integrative approach for understanding climate change as a psychologically distant situation. Fourth, research agendas were outlined to guide future psychological studies aiming to tackle climate change. Finally, considerations of positive actions for tackling climate change were briefly discussed.

Before concluding, I would like to point out that we tend to use broader and (at some degree) contestable concepts, such as 'climate change', 'global warming' and even 'sustainability', that are regrettably often used for political rhetoric rather than for political and social action. However, what is really at stake is environmental degradation. Even if the reader does not agree with such terminologies, remember that the underlying concern encompassing these concepts is the degradation of the environment. And now there is compelling evidence that human behaviour has been producing unprecedented environmental problems (e.g., Millennium Ecosystem Assessment, 2005).

I am grateful for this opportunity to discuss psychological aspects of environmental issues alongside distinguished colleagues in the field. I hope that this chapter, along with the others, will contribute to enhancing psychological theory and research for ameliorating the environmental challenges we face. We need to be aware (and make other people aware) of the negative impacts of our behaviours in the environment. And we need to lead by example. Our actions to reduce the effects of global warming and climate change will certainly encourage others to do the same. I hope the reader can join us in tackling these issues.

ACKNOWLEDGMENTS

I thank Víctor Corral-Verdugo for the invitation to contribute with this volume. I am also grateful to John McClure (Victoria University of Wellington), Andy Reisinger (New Zealand Climate Change Research Institute), Quentin Atkinson (University of Oxford) and Niki Harré (University of Auckland) for their helpful comments and criticisms. Whilst their comments and encouragement is in no small measure responsible for this chapter, this is not meant to imply that they agree with all my views, and I am, of course, solely responsible for any remaining shortcomings.

REFERENCES

Boholm, A. (1998). Comparative studies of risk perception: A review of twenty years of research. *Journal of Risk Research, 1*, 135-163.

Bord, R. J., Fisher, A., & O'Connor, R. E. (1998). Public perceptions of global warming: United States and international perspectives. *Climate Research, 11*, 75-84.

Brouwer, R., Akter, S., Brander, L., & Haque, E. (2007). Socioeconomic vulnerability and adaptation to environmental risk: A case study of climate change and flooding in Bangladesh. *Risk Analysis, 27*, 313-326.

Brown, P. M., & Cameron, L. D. (2000). What can be done to reduce overconsumption? *Ecological Economics, 32*, 27-41.

Budescu, D. V., Broomell, S., & Por, H.-H. (2009). Improving communication of uncertainty in the reports of the Intergovernmental Panel on Climate Change. *Psychological Science, 20*, 299-308.

Clark, W. C. (1988). The human dimensions of global environmental change. In Committee on Global Change (Ed.), *Toward an understanding of global change: Initial priorities for U.S. contributions to the International Geosphere-Bisphere Program*. Washington, DC: National Academy Press.

Coelho, J. A. P. M., Gouveia, V. V., & Milfont, T. L. (2006). Valores humanos como explicadores de atitudes ambientais e intenção de comportamento pró-ambiental [Human values as predictors of environmental attitudes and pro-environmental behavior]. *Psicologia em Estudo, 11*, 199-207.

Collins, W., Colman, R., Haywood, J., Manning, M. R., & Mote, P. (2007). The physical science behind climate change. *Scientific American 297*, 64-71.

Crompton, T. (2008). *Weathercocks & signposts: The environment movement at a crossroads*. London: WWF-UK. Retrieved May 17, 2008, from http://wwf.org.uk/strategiesforchange.

Crutzen, P. J., & Stoermer, E. F. (2000). The "Anthropocene". *Global Change Newsletter, 41*, 12-13.

Dodman, D., Ayers, J., & Huq, S. (2009). Bulding resilience. In T. W. Institute (Ed.), *State of the world 2009: Into a warming world*. Washington, DC: The Worldwatch Institute.

Dunlap, R. E. (1998). Lay perceptions of global risk: Public views of global warming in crossnational context. *International Sociology, 13*, 473-498.

Dunlap, R. E., & Jones, R. E. (2002). Environmental concern: Conceptual and measurement issues. In R. E. Dunlap & W. Michelson (Eds.), *Handbook of environmental sociology* (pp. 482-524). Westport, CT: Greenwood Press.

Erikson, E. H. (1950). *The life cycle completed*. New York: Norton.

Flavin, C., & Engelman, R. (2009). The perfect storm. In The Worldwatch Institute (Ed.), *State of the world 2009: Into a warming world*. Washington, DC: The Worldwatch Institute.

Freury-Bahi, G. (2008). Environmental risk: Perception and target with local versus global evaluations. *Psychological Reports, 102*, 185-193.

García-Mira, R., Real, J. E., & Romay, J. (2005). Temporal and spatial dimensions in the perception of environmental problems: An investigation of the concept of environmental hyperopia. *International Journal of Psychology, 40*, 5-10.

Gattig, A., & Hendrickx, L. (2007). Judgmental discounting and environmental risk perception: Dimensional similarities, domain differences, and implications for sustainability. *Journal of Social Issues, 63*, 21–39.

Gifford, R. (2008a). Psychology's essential role in alleviating the impacts of climate change. *Canadian Psychology, 49*, 273-280.

Gifford, R. (2008b). Toward a comprehensive model of social dilemmas. In A. Biel, D. Eek, T. Gärling & M. Gustaffson (Eds.), *New issues and paradigms in research on social dilemmas* (pp. 265–280). New York: Springer.

Hardin, G. (1968). The tragedy of the commons. *Science, 162*, 1243-1248.

Hare, W. L. (2009). A safe landing for the climate. In T. W. Institute (Ed.), *State of the world 2009: Into a warming world*. Washington, DC: The Worldwatch Institute.

Harré, N., & Atkinson, Q. D. (Eds.). (2007). *Carbon neutral by 2020. How New Zealanders can tackle climate change*. Nelson, New Zealand: Craig Potton.

Hatfield, J., & Job, R. F. S. (2001). Optimism bias about environmental degradation: The role of the range of impact of precautions. *Journal of Environmental Psychology, 21*, 17-30.

Heath, Y., & Gifford, R. (2006). Free-market ideology and environmental degradation: The case of beliefs in global climate change. *Environment and Behavior, 38*, 48-71.

IPCC (Intergovernmental Panel on Climate Change). (2004). *16 years of scientific assessment in support of the climate convention* (Anniversary Brochure). Cambridge: Cambridge University Press. Retrieved February 25, 2009, from http://www.ipcc.ch.

IPCC (Intergovernmental Panel on Climate Change). (2007a). *Climate change 2007: Synthesis report*. Cambridge: Cambridge University Press. Retrieved February 25, 2009, from http://www.ipcc.ch.

IPCC (Intergovernmental Panel on Climate Change). (2007b). *Summary for policy makers. A report of Working Group I of the Intergovernmental Panel on Climate Change*.

Cambridge: Cambridge University Press. Retrieved February 25, 2005, from http://www.ipcc.ch.

Joireman, J. A. (2005). Environmental problems as social dilemmas: The temporal dimension. In A. Strathman & J. A. Joireman (Eds.), *Understanding behavior in the context of time: Theory, research, and apllication* (pp. 289-304). Mahwah, NJ: Lawrence Erlbaum.

Joireman, J. A., Van Lange, P. A. M., & Van Vugt, M. (2004). Who cares about the environmental impact of cars? Those with an eye toward the future. *Environment and Behavior, 36*, 187-206.

Kasperson, R. E., & Kasperson, J. X. (1991). Hidden hazards. In D. G. Mayo & R. D. Hollander (Eds.), *Acceptable evidence: Science and values in risk management* (pp. 9-28). New York: Oxford University Press.

Kellstedt, P. M., Zahran, S., & Vedlitz, A. (2008). Personal efficacy, the information environment, and attitudes toward global warming and climate change in the United States. *Risk Analysis, 28*, 113-126.

Kintisch, E. (2009). Global warming: Projections of climate ghange go from bad to worse, scientists report. *Science, 323*, 1546-1547.

Kortenkamp, K. V., & Moore, C. F. (2006). Time, uncertainty, and individual differences in decisions to cooperate in resource dilemmas. *Personality and Social Psychology Bulletin, 32*, 603-615.

Leiserowitz, A. A. (2004). Surveying the impact of "The Day After Tomorrow". *Environment, 46*, 23-44.

Liberman, N., & Trope, Y. (1998). The role of feasibility and desirability considerations in near and distant future decisions: A test of temporal construal theory. *Journal of Personality and Social Psychology, 75*, 5-18.

Liberman, N., & Trope, Y. (2008). The psychology of transcending the here and now. *Science, 322*, 1201-1205.

Lorenzoni, I., Nicholson-Cole, S., & Whitmarsh, L. (2007). Barriers perceived to engaging with climate change among the UK public and their policy implications. *Global Environmental Change, 17*, 445-459.

Messick, D. M., & Brewer, M. B. (1983). Solving social dilemmas: A review. In L. Wheeler & P. R. Shaver (Eds.), *Review of personality and social psychology* (Vol. 4, pp. 11-44). Beverly Hills, CA: Sage.

Milfont, T. L., Duckitt, J., & Wagner, C. (in press). A cross-cultural test of the value-attitude-behaviour hierarchy *Journal of Applied Social Psychology*.

Milfont, T. L., & Gouveia, V. V. (2006). Time perspective and values: An exploratory study of their relations to environmental attitudes. *Journal of Environmental Psychology, 26*, 72-82.

Milfont, T. L., Harré, N., Sibley, C. G., & Duckitt, J. (2008). *Environmental generativity and the climate change dilemma: Examining the effects of parental status on political party support*. Unpublished manuscript, Centre for Applied Cross-Cultural Research, Victoria University of Wellington, New Zealand.

Milfont, T. L., Sibley, C. G., & Duckitt, J. (in press). Testing the moderating role of the components of norm activation on the relationship between values and environmental behaviour. *Journal of Cross-Cultural Psychology*.

Millennium Ecosystem Assessment. (2005). *Ecosystem and well-being: Synthesis report.* Washington, DC: Island Press.

Ministry for the Environment. (2007). *Understanding climate change. Get a grasp of the facts.* Wellington, New Zealand: Ministry for the Environment. Retrieved February 25, 2009, from www.mfe.govt.nz.

Nilsson, A., von Borgstede, C., & Biel, A. (2004). Willingness to accept climate change strategies: The effect of values and norms. *Journal of Environmental Psychology, 24,* 267–277.

Ockwell, D., Whitmarsh, L., & O'Neill, S. (2009). Reorienting climate change communication for effective mitigation: Forcing people to be green or fostering grass-roots engagement? *Science Communication, 30,* 305-327.

Osbaldiston, R., & Sheldon, K. M. (2002). Social dilemmas and sustainability: Promoting peoples' motivation to "cooperate with the future". In P. Schmuck & P. W. Schultz (Eds.), *Psychology of sustainable development* (pp. 37-58). Boston: Kluwer Academic Publishers.

Oskamp, S. (2000). A sustainable future for humanity? How can psychology help? *American Psychologist, 55,* 496-508.

Pahl, S., Harris, P. R., Todd, H. A., & Rutter, D. R. (2005). Comparative optimism for environmental risks. *Journal of Environmental Psychology, 25,* 1-11.

Pawlik, K. (1991). The psychology of global environmental change: Some basic data and an agenda for cooperative international research. *International Journal of Psychology, 26,* 547-563.

Pelletier, L. G., & Sharp, E. (2008). Persuasive communication and proenvironmental behaviours: How message tailoring and message framing can improve the integration of behaviours through self-determined motivation. *Canadian Psychology, 49,* 210-217.

Reisinger, A. (2003). Science for global environmental problems – lessons learned from Montreal for Kyoto? *New Zealand Science Review, 60,* 111-114.

Schmuck, P., & Schultz, W. P. (2002). Sustainable development as a challenge for psychology. In P. Schmuck & W. P. Schultz (Eds.), *Psychology of sustainable development* (pp. 3-18). Norwell, MA: Kluwer Academic Publishers.

Schmuck, P., & Vlek, C. (2003). Psychologists can do much to support sustainable development. *European Psychologist, 8,* 66-76.

Schultz, P. W., Gouveia, V. V., Cameron, L. D., Tankha, G., Schmuck, P., & Franek, M. (2005). Values and their relationship to environmental concern and conservation behavior. *Journal of Cross-Cultural Psychology, 36,* 457-475.

Shackelford, T. K. (2006). Recycling, evolution and the structure of human personality. *Personality and Individual Differences, 41,* 1551-1556.

Sherman, S. J., Crawford, M. T., & McConnell, A. R. (2004). Looking ahead as a technique to reduce resistance to persuasive attempts. In E. S. Knowles & J. A. Linn (Eds.), *Resistance and persuasion* (pp. 149-174). Mahwah, NJ: Erlbaum.

Slovic, P. (1987). The perception of risk. *Science, 236*(4799), 280-285.

Stern, N., & Taylor, C. (2007). Climate change: risks, ethics and the Stern review. *Science 317,* 203-204.

Sundblad, E.-L., Biel, A., & Gärling, T. (2009). Knowledge and confidence in knowledge about climate change among experts, journalists, politicians, and laypersons. *Environment and Behavior, 41,* 281-302.

Triandis, H. C. (2008). Towards the realistic perception of a culture. *Social and Personality Psychology Compass, 2*, 1812-1823.

Trope, Y., & Liberman, N. (2003). Temporal construal. *Psychological Review, 110*, 403–421.

Trope, Y., Liberman, N., & Wakslak, C. (2007). Construal levels and psychological distance: Effects on representation, prediction, evaluation, and behavior. *Journal of Consumer Psychology, 17*, 83-95.

Tversky, A., & Kahneman, D. (1974). Judgment under uncertainty: Heuristics and biases. *Science, 185*, 1124-1131.

Uzzell, D. (2000). The psycho-spatial dimension of global environmental problems. *Journal of Environmental Psychology, 20*, 307-318.

Van Vugt, M. (1998). The conflicts of modern society. *The Psychologist, 5*, 289-292.

Van Vugt, M. (2001). Community identification moderating the impact of financial incentives in a natural social dilemma: Water conservation. *Personality and Social Psychology Bulletin, 27*, 1440-1449.

Van Vugt, M., & Samuelson, C. D. (1999). The impact of personal metering in the management of a natural resource crisis: A social dilemma analysis. *Personality and Social Psychology Bulletin, 25*, 735-750.

Vlek, C., & Steg, L. (2007). Human behavior and environmental sustainability: Problems, driving forces, and research topics. *Journal of Social Issues, 63*, 1-19.

Weber, E. U. (2006). Experience-based and description-based perceptions of long-term risk: Why global warming does not scare us (yet). *Climatic Change, 77*, 103-120.

Weinstein, N. D. (1980). Unrealistic optimism about future life events. *Journal of Personality and Social Psychology, 39*, 806-820.

Chapter 3

SOCIAL-PSYCHOLOGICAL AND CONTEXTUAL PREDICTORS OF SUSTAINABLE WATER CONSUMPTION

Giuseppe Carrus[*]
Università degli Studi Roma Tre, Italy
Mirilia Bonnes
Università degli Studi di Roma "La Sapienza," Italy
Victor Corral-Verdugo
Universidad de Sonora, Mexico
Gabriel Moser
Université René Descartes-Paris V, France
Jai Sinha
Assert Institute of Management Studies, India

ABSTRACT

Fresh water scarcity represents – along with global warming - the most serious environmental threat humankind currently faces. Environmental psychology, among other branches of science, is committed to investigate and promote more sustainable water consumption throughout the planet, so that every country might be able to respond to the challenge of guaranteeing the supply of fresh water to all individuals. This sustainable consumption would imply not only satisfying human needs but also the consideration of the ecosystems' continuity over time. This chapter offers an overview of water problems that challenge a more sustainable development around the world. It also discusses the way environmental psychology and other social and behavioral scientific

---

[*] Correspondence: Giuseppe Carrus, Ph.D. Università degli Studi Roma Tre, Department of Cultural and Educational Studies Experimental Psychology Laboratory. Via del Castro Pretorio 20 - 00185 Rome, Italy. Tel. +39 06 44703450 - Fax +39 06 44703879. E-mail: carrus@uniroma3.it

fields can contribute to understanding the relationship between human behavior and water related issues. A literature review shows that water consumption – and, specially, water waste - is predicted by individual as well as contextual factors. The findings of a multi-national study are presented, showing complex interrelations between contextual, attitudinal, perceptual and behavioral factors involved in water consumption. Participants from France, Italy, Mexico and India responded to a questionnaire investigating sustainable water behaviors and their psychological determinants. This questionnaire, built up on the basis of four in-depth qualitative studies carried out in each considered country, included items regarding reported water accessibility, perceived lack of contextual water concern (i.e., perceiving that public bodies or private sectors waste or disregard water), perceived temporal uncertainty regarding water supply, indifference towards water problems, pro-environmental worldviews (i.e., endorsement of a New Human Interdependence Paradigm, NHIP), and self-reported water conservation (as the main target variable). These variables were included in a structural model, also considering the respondents' socio-economic status, and the economic affluence of each participating country (i.e., United Nations' Human Development Index, HDI). Results revealed that water conservation is inhibited by high water accessibility, the country's developmental level, participants' socio-economic status and by indifference regarding water problems. More sustainable water consumption was indeed promoted by participants' endorsement of the NHIP. The level of economic affluence, indicated by the HDI, SES and water accessibility also instigated negative dispositional tendencies towards water conservation, such as indifference regarding water problems and contextual water concern. In addition, water accessibility correlated negatively with beliefs in the NHIP. These results might suggest that sustainable water consumption is promoted by interlinked sets of contextual and psychological factors. These should be considered when setting up and implementing public campaigns for the promotion of water conservation.

INTRODUCTION

Human use and perception of fresh water resources represents one of the main priorities in the current environmental agenda, for bio-physical and human-social sciences and for political action. Indeed, the depletion of freshwater resources is, according to experts, one of the most serious changes affecting our global environment. (Brown & Flavin, 1999; Rosegrant, Cai, & Cline, 2003). Freshwater is perhaps the most precious and limited resource currently present in our biosphere. Thus, issues related to the quantity and quality of fresh water resources have increasingly been in the focus of political action, scientific research, and public opinion during the last decades, at a local and global level. Currently about one billion and 400 million of persons in the world do not have free access to fresh water. According to the previsions of intergovernmental bodies, the entire world population in 2025 will be over 8 billions, and 3 billions will be the number of persons without available fresh water (UNESCO-WWAP, 2003).

As a consequence, the importance of promoting sustainable water conservation as a major task for human societies in the new millennium has been clearly remarked at the international level at the latest United Nation Conferences of Rio de Janeiro (1992) and Johannesburg (2002). As time passes by, water is therefore becoming more precious and expensive almost everywhere. This resource is decreasing mainly because of pollution and wastes; it is therefore more and more considered an economic as well as a natural good. As Mastny (2009) establishes, the forecast for an imminent water crisis is seen as "unprecedented," this crisis being caused by climate change, population growth and mismanagement of the resource. Regional and international inequities in the access to water are also a part of the problem. While the levels of domestic water consumption are between 200 and 400 liters per person per day in developed nations, many poorer nations have much lower domestic demands –anywhere between 3 and 100 liters per person per day (Gleick, 1998). According to Thomas and Ford (2005, p. 44), this situation "verifies the hypothesis that increased domestic water demand is a result of economic development and of increased wealth of the community."

Water has been defined as the "blue gold of third millennium" and, according to a report of UNESCO-WWAP (2003), this resource will soon substitute oil in becoming the principal cause of conflicts around the world. The importance of water was also formalized in this decade at the intergovernmental level by the United Nations, who declared the year 2003 as the "UN year of Fresh Water."

Within such a framework, investigating the factors driving human behaviors and perceptions in relation to water resources becomes a relevant issue for applied social psychological research. In fact, since the most significant causes of the water problem arise from human use of this natural resource, the search for determinants of water conservation behavior is one of the main objectives of environmental psychology and other environmental social sciences. Such a search would allow the inclusion of significant predictors of water conservation within interventional programs aimed to promote sustainability (Corral-Verdugo & Pinheiro, 2006).

The aim of this chapter is to offer an overview of psychological dimensions related to water problems that challenge a more sustainable development around the world. In particular, we started from the assumption that the relationship between people and water resources is also affected by a number of diverse factors, from the local environmental context to the ecological phenomena governing water renewal, water quality and water functions as a "common good". It is crucial to stress that a more sustainable consumption of water resources might be strongly hampered or encouraged by specific individual, social, cultural and environmental factors. Thus, co-operation and self restraining behavior in the domain of water-resources use cannot be taken for granted. This typically occurs in the use of any other set of limited common resources (e.g., Hardin, 1968). Moreover, serious disparities in access to fresh water exist between different countries and regions of the world, as well as between different regions and social groups within a single country (Gleick, 1998). Given this frame, specific social psychological factors can play a crucial role in orienting human perception and behavior in this domain. Recent research contributions suggest, for example, the importance of social identity and social representation processes in regulating individuals' and collective's uses of water resources (Bonaiuto, Bilotta, Bonnes, Ceccarelli, Martorella & Carrus, 2008; Moser, 1984; Moser, Ratiu & De Vanssay, 2004; Van Vugt, 2001). However, differences and varieties existing in the domain of water-related perceptions and behaviors (between countries, and between regional or local contexts within the same country) have not yet been addressed in a systematic way by environmental psychological research.

In the remaining of this chapter we will briefly introduce the increasing interest for sustainability issues among environmental psychological research over the last decades. Then we will discuss how environmental psychological research can contribute to understanding human behavior and perceptions in relation to water issues, and how water consumption and water waste might be affected by different socio-psychological and contextual factors. To this end, we will present results of a multi-national study conducted in four countries, differing in geographical and socio-economic conditions: France, Italy, Mexico and India[1].

Psychological Processes, Sustainability and Global Environmental Changes

The concept of Sustainable Development and issues related to sustainability have gained increased relevance within psychological science in the last decades, in particular within Environmental Psychology (e.g., Bechtel & Churchman, 2002; Bonnes & Bonaiuto, 2002; Giuliani & Scopelliti, 2009; Moser, Pol, Bernard, Bonnes, Corraliza & Giuliani, 2002; Moser & Uzzell, 2002; Schmuck & Schultz, 2002; Vlek & Steg, 2007; Winter, 2000). The specific psychological processes and factors related to various environmental global changes occurring in the biosphere have been a focus of this research field (Pawlik, 1991). The relevance of such perspective has led environmental psychology to emphasize the role of the socio-physical environment as a *life-resource* for both human and non-human species. It is also widely acknowledged, among many researchers in this field, that the study of global environmental changes should be addressed taking into account both the global and the local (or place-specific) character of these processes (e.g., Bonnes & Bonaiuto, 2002; Moser et al., 2002). In order to deal with the different social, cultural, economic, and psychological aspects of environmental changes, it is then important to consider these diverse perspectives. It has been suggested, for example, how a deeper connection between bio-physical and human-social science should be pursued to address environmental changes at different local/specific and global/general levels (Bonnes & Bonaiuto, 2002; Uzzell, 2000; Zube, 1991).

Starting from these broad assumptions, a considerable amount of research in environmental psychology has been devoted in the last decades to the investigation of environmentally-relevant behaviors, and to the different psychological factors underlying and regulating such behaviors (Levy-Leboyer, Bonnes, Chase, Ferreira-Marques & Pawlik, 1996; Stern, 2000). To this extent, a primary aim of current research has been to highlight the individual, social-psychological and contextual determinants of environmentally friendly or unfriendly behaviors (many of which often occur even out of people's individual awareness; see Gaspar de Carvalho et al.'s chapter, this volume). Thus, general issues like environmental "awareness", "concern", "responsibility", which were addressed paying particular attention to their globally and locally situated character and implications, occupied an increasing central position in the environmental psychological research agenda over the last 20 years.

Typically, findings from these studies have shown that several personal, environmental, and contextual factors can be related to pro-environmental attitudes and actions. Earlier

---

[1] This research was supported with a 2-years funding by the ICSU (International Council for Science; http://www.icsu.org) Grants Programme 2004, under the Priority Theme on *Science and Technology for Sustainable Development*, with the active support of IUPsyS (International Union of Psychological Science; http://www.am.org/iupsys/). The project was titled "Human Dimension of Global Changes: Human

research contributions focused on more general variables like age, gender, educational level, income, residence, and political orientation (e.g., Dietz, Stern & Guagnano, 1998; Fransson & Garling, 1999). A typical pattern highlighted by such studies is that young, female, well-educated, high-income, urban, liberally oriented subjects express stronger concern for the environment. At the same time, these results clearly show how general pro-environmental values and worldviews, environmental awareness, environmental concern, and pro-environmental attitudes have increasingly become a shared "worldview" for a large portion of the public in modern societies. This shared worldview was defined by Dunlap and Van Liere (1978) as a "New Environmental Paradigm" (NEP) supporting the idea of humankind as a part of nature, which gradually replaced the traditional "Dominant Social Paradigm" supporting the idea of humankind dominating over the rest of nature.

While concern for the environment is, as said, widely shared in present-day societies, more recent research has however highlighted that specific perceptions, attitudes and behaviors regarding the environment still differ from one country to another. Such differences are indeed related to different environmental conditions, state of natural resources, and societal contexts characterizing the respective countries (e.g., national and/or traditional cultures, shared belief systems, values, norms, regulations, infrastructure, media communication, opportunities for action; see Levy-Leboyer et al., 1996; Moser et al., 2004). Earlier research on environmental concern was however often criticized for its insufficient consideration of specific social psychological factors mediating the relationships between social structural variables and pro-environmental actions (Stern, Dietz & Guagnano, 1995). It seems important then to investigate more directly how "global" variables at a personal level (such as value orientations, worldviews, general beliefs and social representations about the environment) may interact with more specific contextual and situational factors promoting or inhibiting individuals specific pro-environmental choices (e.g., Bonaiuto, Carrus, Martorella & Bonnes, 2002; Bonnes & Bonaiuto, 2002; Carrus, Bonaiuto & Bonnes, 2005; Carrus, Passafaro & Bonnes, 2008; Corraliza & Berenguer, 2000; Kaiser, Wolfing & Fuhrer, 1999). As contributions in this field have typically reported, pro-environmental attitudes and behaviors are often only weakly or moderately (usually < .20) correlated (see Fransson & Garling, 1999; Hines, Hungerford & Tomera, 1986); similar findings were also reported in a recent meta-analysis by Bamberg & Moser (2007). It is thus important to strongly emphasize on the possible different subsets of environmentally relevant perceptions, attitudes, behaviors, while at the same time investigating more directly how these behavioral subsets relate to the different kinds of environmental changes and to the related sustainable use of natural resources. Apparently, the best predictors of behaviors towards natural resources are attitudes and values attached to environmental issues, to which it may be added a perceived control, a personal commitment and the fact of having been physically and/or emotionally touched by these aspects (Grob, 1995; see also Roczen et al.'s chapter, this volume). In addition, adhering to ecological ideas which are currently gaining ground (e.g., readiness to become involved in the lasting improvement of environmental quality at local, national, and world level) or to consumerism which is still dominant in western society might also explain human pro-or anti environmental behavior.

Perceptions and Behaviours in Sustainable Water Use. International Psychological Research Project" and coordinated by Mirilia Bonnes and Gabriel Moser.

It should be also taken into account the fact that different kinds of global bio-physical changes can be characterized by different degrees of direct sensorial perceptibility and thus of possible "personal relevance" for individuals' everyday experience and life (Graumann & Kruse, 1990). Different kinds of changes can in fact vary for being:

a) almost unrelated to people's direct sensorial perception and thus to daily activities (e.g. the greenhouse effect, the depletion of the ozone layer);
b) only moderately related to people's perception and daily activities (e.g. the loss of biodiversity, climate changes, over-population);
c) strongly related to people's perception and daily activities (e.g. shortage of fresh water, air and water pollution).

It is therefore appropriate to take such different characteristics of environmental global changes into account, when investigating the psychological factors and human behaviors related to them.

Finally, cultural theory (Douglas & Wildavsky, 1982) clearly put forward these factors. This theory can be used to explain the relation between individuals and environmental problems according to the representation of nature, social relations and preferred behavioral strategies (e.g., Steg & Sievers, 2000). The emphasis in this case is on the way values and beliefs shared in a given culture or society may influence the adoption of cognitive and behavioral strategies at the individual level. According to this approach, systematic individual differences in the perception of environmental problems can represent different "ways of life", connected to particular representations of nature. These representations are in turn linked to support/aversion for different environmental management practices. Although the concept of sustainability is now increasingly acknowledged by large parts of the population (especially in western societies), consequent individual behavior is difficult to promote. Perhaps this happens because people do not find any sense of urgency to protect the environment, which is manifested in "environmental indifference" as Grimsrud and Wandschneider (2003) establish. This happens also because individuals consider their actions as inefficient or insufficient in front of the size of the problem to solve, which might inhibit the quitting of old and/or the adoption of new behaviors (Uzzell, 1997).

ENVIRONMENTAL BELIEFS AND WATER CONSERVATION: A MULTINATIONAL STUDY

Now, about fresh water consumption, it is also worth remarking how societal contexts and ideological factors can make up the framework on which the links between people and freshwater resources are built up and developed. Factors at various levels may affect human relations to water, in both perceptual and behavioral terms. On the one hand, we should mention symbolic dimensions and available information on fresh water (social representations and underlying values, collective memory, information); on the other hand there are aspects related to levels of economic, institutional, and technical development affecting the specific conditions of daily access to fresh water. Indeed, each culture has its own way of perceiving natural elements and common resources, of attaching certain values to them, and of conveying representations of them (e.g., unchanging/changing, renewable/non-renewable, controllable/uncontrollable). The social and individual values assigned to water differ, for example, according to whether fresh water is "natural" or "domestic." These values appear to be the result of a conjunction of environmental, societal, and personal characteristics. Likewise, representations of fresh water could play a role in establishing a standard of comparison, as well as an individual normative framework (Moser et al., 2004). In addition, differentiation may occur between the functional and economic dimensions on the one hand, and aesthetic, affective, ethical, and identity-related dimensions on the other. A functional value may be linked to shortages and to financial difficulties in gaining access to fresh water. This is notably the case amongst the disadvantaged strata of society who are affected by severe disparities in access to good-quality water, notably in many developing countries (Gleick, 1998).

A major aim of the present research was to investigate the impact of individual belief systems on water conservation actions (e.g., Somerville & Briscoe, 2001). In this regard, we were interested in assessing the impact of environmental beliefs and attitudes of indifference towards water issues on water conservation. Environmental beliefs have been previously investigated in their relationship with water conservation. Corral-Verdugo, Bechtel & Fraijo (2003) found that utilitarian water beliefs (believing that water is an unlimited resource without restrictions for human use) promoted water over-consumption while more ecological water beliefs inhibited that behavior. Results of that study showed how the individual endorsement of the New Environmental Paradigm principles indirectly influenced water conservation, through ecological and utilitarian water beliefs. A specific aim of the present study was to further explore this relationship, investigating the influence of a recently proposed "new" set of environmental worldviews and beliefs systems upon water conservation: the New Human Interdependence Paradigm (NHIP, see Corral-Verdugo, Carrus, Bonnes, Moser, & Sinha, 2008; see also Hernández et al., this volume). The NHIP assesses beliefs regarding a spatial human-nature interdependence, as well as a beliefs of temporal interdependence between the human needs of the present and the needs of the future. Our previous study resulted in a significant relationship between adherence to the NHIP and water conservation (Corral-Verdugo et al., 2008).

In addition, in the present study we were interested in assessing the relationship between attitudes of indifference toward water problems. Although environmental indifference (Grimsrud & Wandschneider, 2003) in regard to water problems had not been previously investigated, we hypothesized that such indifference would negatively influence water conservation.

One more aim was to assess the effect of perceptual factors on this conservation behavior. A number of studies suggest that water conservation is predicted by various socio-psychological factors, in which perceptions of environmental issues play a relevant role. Syme, Thomas and Salerian (1983), for example, reported that the individuals' appreciation of the value of their gardens was a positive predictor of water consumption, with higher appreciation corresponding to higher levels of water consumption. In turn, De Oliver (1999) found that the perception of others' engagement in an obligatory campaign of water conservation led people to cooperate with the required conservation effort. In Japan, Hirose and Kitada (1987) found that the perceived efficacy of the government's water management constituted a positive determinant of residential water conservation during a drought. Also, perceiving that other people are wasting water impacts on own water conservation behavior;

Corral-Verdugo, Frías-Armenta, Pérez, Orduño, & Espinoza (2002) found that the more a person perceives that her/his neighbors, the government and other individuals at the city overconsume water, the less his/her motivation for saving this vital resource. In the present study we identified this perception as "contextual concern regarding water usage."

Individual values, motivations and capacities are also linked to water conservation or wasting. A study by Bonaiuto and colleagues (2008) found that social value orientations and community identification are also predictive of water-saving behaviors; the authors reported that pro-social individuals who strongly identify with their local community are the most willing to cooperate in voluntary water conservation actions, while pro-self low identifiers are the least. Conservation skills and competence are also important determinants of water conservation, as various studies indicate (e.g., Corral-Verdugo 2002; Middlestadt, Grieser, Hernández, Tubaishat, Sanchack, Southwell & Schwartz, 2001). People who are skilled or competent in water conservation practices tend to engage in this pro-environmental behavior. By considering the personal motivational system, the more motives a person has for saving water (i.e., conserving for preserving water, for saving money, for avoiding fines, for protecting other people, etc.), the more it is likely he or she will conserve this resource (López, Balboa, Igartúa, and Claramunt, 1994).

This brief review shows the complexity that explanations of water consumption and saving entail. The following sections of this chapter will attempt to provide one of those explanations, by specifying and testing a model of psychological and contextual determinants of water conservation.

METHOD

Participants

A questionnaire assessing perceptual, attitudinal and behavioral dimensions related to a more sustainable use of water resources was set up, on the basis of four preliminary in-depth qualitative studies conducted in each of the four countries considered. The preliminary studies were conducted using semi-structured interviews and focus groups.

The questionnaire was then administered to 759 subjects, recruited in 9 different sites located within the 4 nations involved in the study (Paris and Brest in France; Rome and Cagliari in Italy; Monterrey, Hermosillo and La Victoria in Mexico; New Delhi and Patna in India). Subjects were selected from zones that were representative of high, middle and lower socio-economic classes in the cities considered, and balanced for gender (males = 49%; females = 51%). Age ranged between 18 and 84 years (Mean = 39). The questionnaire was first built in English and then translated into the 4 different languages of each participating country. The distribution of participants across the 9 sites is displayed in Table 1.

Table 1. Distribution of participants a across the four countries and the nine locations

Country	Location	n	f %
France	Paris	126	17
	Brest	70	9
Italy	Rome	127	17
	Cagliari	121	16
India	New Delhi	76	10
	Patna	77	10
Mexico	Monterrey	70	9
	Hermosillo	70	9
	La Victoria	22	3
Total		759	100

Measures

The questionnaire was made of five scales plus a single item, measuring the following variables:

1. *Reported daily water accessibility.* This variable was measured using three items: "I have no constant access to water," "water is scarce during certain months," and "water is not available during certain months." These items responses were reversed to indicate water accessibility.
2. *Perceived contextual lack of water concern.* This variable was measured with three items, indicating respondents' perceptions of insufficient water concern by various environmental actors, such as industries and municipal authorities, in relation to both water supply and water quality, respectively.
3. *Perceived temporal uncertainty regarding access to water.* This variable was measured with three items, concerning perceived uncertainty related to water accessibility in the future, problems with water supply due to climatic change, and the perception that in the past water was more accessible, respectively.
4. *General environmental worldviews.* This variable was measured through five items, assessing respondents' endorsement of what we labeled as a "New Human Interdependence Paradigm" (Corral-Verdugo et al., 2008). These items assessed the belief that human needs are interdependent with nature processes, and that the human-nature balance in the present is interdependent with that balance in the future.
5. *Self-reported water conservation behaviors.* This variable was measured through eleven items, indicating respondents' commitment to save water in everyday life domains. Subjects were asked to indicate what they actually do to conserve water in their everyday life. The items included behaviors such as "reuse water from washing machine and sink," "watering plants at night," and "turning taps off while soaping." For each behavior listed, respondents had to indicate whether they *did* it, they *could do* it, or they did *not want to do* it.

Table 2. The Human Development Index across the four countries involved (Source: United Nations, 2008)

Country	HDI
FRANCE	.955
ITALY	.945
MEXICO	.842
INDIA	.609

A single item, measuring respondents' indifference in regard to local water supply problems was also included: "Water problems are the same everywhere".

In addition, a Human Development Index (HDI) from the United Nations (2008) was used as a proxy of the affluence of each country involved. According to the United Nations, the HDI provides a composite measure of three dimensions of human development: life expectancy, educational opportunities (measured by adult literacy and enrollment at the primary, secondary and tertiary level) and having a decent standard of living (measured by an index of purchasing power parity, and income). The source of this index clarifies that the HDI is not in any sense a comprehensive measure of human development: "It does not, for example, include important indicators such as gender or income inequality and more difficult to measure indicators like respect for human rights and political freedoms. What it does provide is a broadened prism for viewing human progress and the complex relationship between income and well-being." (United Nations, 2008, p. 1). Table 2 displays the HDI for the four countries involved in the study, which ranged from the highest of France (.95) to the lowest of India (.60).

Finally, respondents were asked to provide demographic information, including gender, socio-economic status, age and schooling level.

Procedure

Participants were interviewed at their households, after their informed consent to participate in this study was obtained. It took about 20 minutes to respond to all the questions.

Data Analysis

Univariate statistics and reliability indexes were computed for all the scales. A structural equation model (SEM) was specified and tested. In this model, three exogenous variables were considered: socio economic status (SES), country affluence (HDI), and perceived water accessibility. In turn, contextual concern regarding water usage, temporal uncertainty regarding access to water, indifference towards water problems, and the endorsement of the New Human Interdependence Paradigm (NHIP) constituted the mediating variables, which were influenced by the exogenous variables. Finally, self-reported water conservation was specified as the key criterion variable, and expected to be influenced by water accessibility, the NHIP, indifference, SES, the HDI, and temporal uncertainty. To test the SEM, the items of the water conservation and the NHIP scales were parceled into three indicators for each assessed construct. A *parcel* is the mean of two or more items of a construct, randomly chosen from the total set of items constituting the scale. This procedure simplifies the process of data analysis in the context of structural equation modelling, because a small number of indicators are used in specifying the assessed factors (Little, Cunningham, Shahar & Widaman, 2002). Goodness of fit indicators considered included a classical statistical indicator (*Chi-square*) plus various practical indices, such as the Non-Normed Fit Index (*NNFI*), the Comparative Fit Index (*CFI*) and the Root Mean Square Error of Approximation (*RMSEA*), in line with the literature in this field (Bentler, 2006).

RESULTS

Table 3 shows the univariate statistics and Cronbach's alphas for all the scales: results indicate acceptable reliability levels, with alphas ranging from .60 to .76.

Figure 1 shows the structural relations between the considered predictors and the self-reported water conservation behavior, as well as the interrelations among the exogenous and mediating variables.

All the perceptual, attitudinal and behavioral factors coherently emerged from their indicators (the scale items and parcels), as revealed by salient and significant factor loadings ($p<.05$). The high loadings are indicative of convergent validity for the psychological measures employed. The structural model showed that water conservation is directly and positively affected by personal endorsement of the New Human Interdependence Paradigm, and negatively influenced by reported water accessibility, by socio-economic status, by the affluence of the participants' country, and by indifference regarding water problems. Perceived temporal uncertainty did not correlate with water saving behavior. The whole set of predictors considered is able to account for the 35% of the variance in water conservation.

Results of the SEM also suggest that reported water accessibility negatively influences the endorsement of the NHIP and positively impacts on indifference regarding water problems. Also, believing in the NHIP positively and significantly correlates with temporal uncertainty regarding water access and supply.

The human development index did not affect this perceived temporal uncertainty, but it had a positive impact upon participants' indifference towards water problems, and it negatively affected the perceived contextual lack of concern for water issues (i.e., the perception of water waste from industries and of a scarce interest in efficient water management from public authorities). These contextual perceptions, in turn, correlated positively (although slightly) with perceived temporal water uncertainty. Nonetheless, this uncertainty neither emerge as significantly linked to water conservation behaviors, nor to indifference regarding water problems.

Table 3. Univariate statistics and reliabilities of scales

Scale/Items	Mean	SD	Max	Min	Alpha
Reported water accesibility					.76
I have no constant access to water	1.81	.41	2	1	
Water is scarce during certain months	1.91	.46	2	1	
Water is not available during certain months	1.91	.47	2	1	
Water conservation					.71
Reusing water from washing machine and sink	1.65	.64	3	1	
Using economy shower	2.02	.58	3	1	
Car washing with water in bucket	2.22	.69	3	1	
Tooth brushing using glass instead of running water	2.26	.64	3	1	
Filling sink with water and soak dishes	2.18	.75	3	1	
Using a water-pressure regulator	2.08	.58	3	1	
Turn taps off while soaping	2.55	.61	3	1	
Reducing shower time	2.40	.65	3	1	
Using pressure cooker	2.27	.71	3	1	
Cooking over low heat	2.41	.64	3	1	
Watering plants at night	2.21	.68	3	1	
Perceived contextual lack of water concern					.60
Industries waste water	3.23	.88	4	1	
Municipal services do not care about water supply	2.81	.98	4	1	
Municipal services do not care about water quality	2.61	.99	4	1	
Temporal uncertainty					.65
More water in the past	1.68	.46	2	1	
Less water in future	1.85	.36	2	1	
Less water in future because climatic changes	1.78	.41	2	1	
New human interdependence paradigm					.76
Human progress only by conserving nature	3.72	.57	4	1	
Enjoy nature only if making wisely its resources	3.79	.48	4	1	
Progress achieved only with ecological balance	3.76	.53	4	1	
Preserving nature now ensures the future.	3.79	.55	4	1	
Reduce consumption to ensure present and future	3.70	.59	4	1	

CONCLUSION

Our findings seem to corroborate the arguments put forward in this chapter. As far as the more contextual and structural indicators are concerned, our results highlight an apparent paradox. In fact, these results suggest that conditions indicating economic wealth (such as the individuals' SES and their country's economic affluence as assessed through the HDI), as well as high perceived water accessibility, inhibit water conservation actions, either directly or indirectly (influencing indifference towards water problems and decreasing beliefs about the interdependence between humankind and the natural processes of the ecosystems). Such a paradox stems from the fact that richer individuals are, in general, considered more pro-environmentally oriented than less affluent persons (Dietz et al., 1998; Domina & Koch, 2002). Yet, since water is more accessible in France and Italy, and the HDI is higher in those countries, their inhabitants are less prone to engage in water conservation behaviors, as compared to India and Mexico. Taken together, these apparently paradoxical results replicate previous findings, which indicate that economic affluence is an instigator of over-consumption of water resources. A study by Aitken, McMahon, Wearing and Finlayson (1994), for example, found that richer people, living in big, expensive households, consume significantly more water that poorer individuals. In a similar vein, De Oliver (1999) found that a campaign of voluntary water conservation did not affect consumption among members of higher socioeconomic classes, until this campaign became obligatory. Also, Syme, Thomas, and Salerian (1983), reported that individuals' appreciation of the value of their gardens was a positive predictor of water consumption.

As far as the more individual and personal psychological mediators are concerned, our findings indicate that endorsing a worldview that supports the interdependence between humans and natural resources (the NHIP) can be a relevant driver of positive behaviors in the domain of water conservation. On the contrary, personal indifference to water problems can slightly inhibit these behaviors. The NHIP scale can be therefore considered as a reliable indicator of general environmental concern, encompassing at the same time the concern for the continuity of the environmental processes in the ecosystems and the resources therein, as well as the concern for the wellbeing of human societies. This worldview is in line with the more general principle of Sustainable Development put forward and promoted at various levels since more than two decades by the United Nations (e.g., WCED, 1987). It manifests as a belief in the interdependence between the needs of people and the dynamic balance of the natural resources and processes of the physical environment; therefore, the more the idea of interdependence appears in people, the more their effort for practicing a sustainable use of these natural resources, as our data seem to show (see also Corral-Verdugo et al, 2008, and Hernández et al.'s chapter in this volume). The results concerning the negative influence of indifference towards water problems are also logical: individuals who disregard the importance of local water problems are not interested in water scarcity, perhaps because they are not affected by it. Consequently, their engagement in more sustainable practices of water consumption tends to decrease. Contrary to our expectations, individual perceptions of temporal uncertainty about access to water resources did not emerged as significantly linked to water conservation.

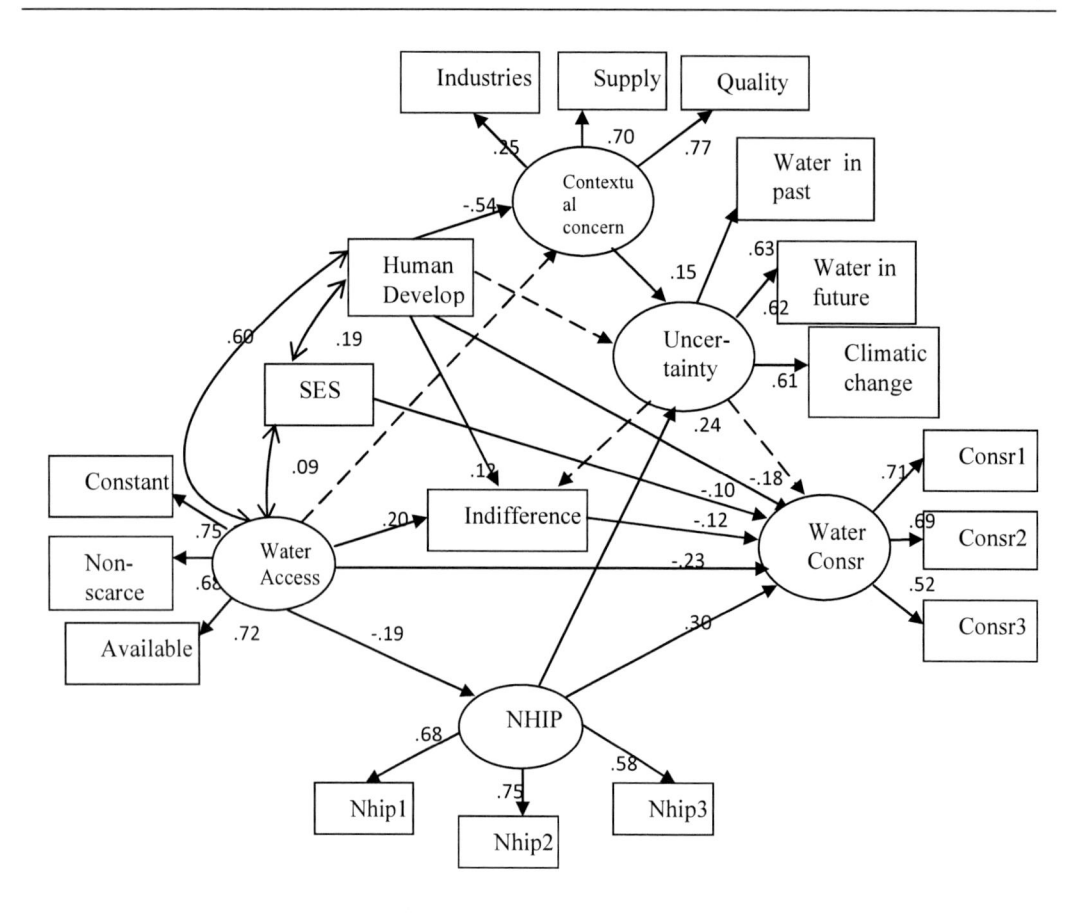

Figure 1. Structural model of water conservation predicted by attitudinal, perceptual and situational factors. All structural coefficients are significant at p<.05, excepting those indicated by dotted arrows. Goodness of fit: X^2= 278.8 (120 df), p <.001; $NNFI$=.92, CFI=.94; $RMSEA$=.04. R^2 for water conservation behavior = .35.

In conclusion, practical implications of these findings for policymaking in the field of water conservation should be outlined. Promoting the idea of an interdependence between human wellbeing and the dynamic processes of the natural and limited resources use and renewal of the ecosystems -well resumed in the basic tenets of the sustainable development principles put forward since more than 20 years within U.N. International Programs- can be a relevant avenue for enhancing the likelihood of concrete domestic water conservation behaviors. As our data suggest, this seems to be the case among the general public in different societies, ranging across a huge variety of geographical, economic and societal contexts. Our findings also suggest that economically affluent people should be a special target in the instrumentation of water-conservation campaigns. In addition, these results emphasize the need of a higher involvement of richer nations and regions in the implementation of water saving measures so that a more equitable distribution of this vital resource can be achieved, benefiting especially the poorer. Last, but not least, environmental education programs have to counteract the noxious influence of environmental indifference on water conservation. Environmental psychology has a preeminent role in suggesting strategies aimed at reversing such a noxious influence.

REFERENCES

Aitken, C., McMahon, T., Wearing, A., & Finlayson, B. (1994). Residential water use: Predicting and reducing consumption. *Journal of Applied Social Psychology, 21,* 611–619.

Bamberg, S. & Moser, G. (2007). Twenty years after Hines, Hungerford, and Tomera: A new meta-analysis of psycho-social determinants of pro-environmental behaviour. *Journal of Environmental Psychology, 27,* 14–25.

Bechtel, R., Churchman, A. (Eds.) (2002). *Handbook of Environmental Psychology.* New York: Wiley, pp. 28-54.

Bonaiuto, M., Bilotta, E. Bonnes, M., Ceccarelli, M., Martorella, H. Carrus, G. (2008). Local Identity and the Role of Individual Differences in the Use of Natural Resources: The Case of Water Consumption. *Journal of Applied Social Psychology, 38,* 947-967.

Bonaiuto, M., Carrus, G., Martorella, H., Bonnes, M. (2002). Local identity processes and environmental attitudes in land use changes: the case of natural protected areas. *Journal of Economic Psychology, 23,* 631-653.

Bonnes, M., Bonaiuto, M. (2002). Environmental Psychology: from spatial-physical environment to sustainable development. In R. Bechtel, A. Churchman, Eds., *Handbook of Environmental Psychology,* New York: Wiley, pp. 28-54.

Brown, L. R., & Flavin, C. (1999). A new economy for a new century. In Linda Starke (Ed.), *State of the World. A Worldwatch Institute Report on Progress Toward a Sustainable Society.* New York: W.W. Norton & Company.

Carrus, G., Bonaiuto, M. & Bonnes, M. (2005). Environmental concern, regional identity and support for protected areas in Italy. *Environment and Behavior, 37,* 237-257.

Carrus, G., Passafaro, P., & Bonnes, M. (2008). Emotions, habits and rational choices in ecological behaviours: the case of recycling and use of public transportation. *Journal of Environmental Psychology, 28,* 51-62.

Corraliza, J.A., Berenguer, J. (2000). Environmental values, beliefs, and actions: A situational approach. *Environment and Behavior, 32,* 832-848.

Corral-Verdugo, V. (2002). A structural model of pro-environmental competency. *Environment & Behavior, 34,* 531-549.

Corral-Verdugo, V., Bechtel, R. & Fraijo, B. (2003). Environmental beliefs and water conservation: an empirical study. *Journal of Environmental Psychology, 23,* 247-257.

Corral-Verdugo, Carrus, G., Bonnes, M., Moser, G. & Sinha, J. (2008). Environmental beliefs and endorsement of Sustainable Development principles in water conservation: towards a *New Human Interdependence Paradigm* scale. *Environment & Behavior, 40,* 703-725.

Corral-Verdugo, V., Frías-Armenta, M., Pérez, F., Orduño, V., & Espinoza, N. (2002). Residential water consumption, motivation for conserving water, and the continuing tragedy of the commons. *Environmental Management.* 30, 527-535.

Corral-Verdugo, V. & Pinheiro, J. (2006). Sustainability, future orientation and water conservation. *European Review of Applied Psychology, 56,* 191-198.

De Oliver, M. (1999). Attitudes and inaction: A case study of the manifest demographics of urban water conservation. *Environment & Behavior, 31,* 372–394.

Dietz, T., Stern, P., Guagnano G.A., (1998). Social structural and social psychological basis of environmental concern. *Environment and Behavior, 30,* 450-471.

Domina, T. & Koch, K. (2002). Convenience and frequency of recycling. Implications for including textiles in curbside recycling programs. *Environment & Behavior, 34*, 216-238.

Douglas, M., & Wildavsky, A. (1982). *Risk and culture: An essay on the selection of technological and environmental dangers*. Berkeley: University of California Press.

Dunlap, R.E., Van Liere, K.D. (1978). The "New Environmental Paradigm". *Journal of Environmental Education*, 9, 10-19.

Fransson, N., Garling, T. (1999). Environmental concern: conceptual definitions, measurement methods, and research findings. *Journal of Environmental Psychology*, 19, 369-382.

Giuliani, M.V. & Scopelliti, M. (2009). Empirical research in environmental psychology: Past, present, and future. *Journal of Environmental Psychology*, in press. doi:10.1016/j.jenvp.2008.11.008.

Gleick, P.H. (1998) Water in crisis: paths to sustainable water use. *Ecological Applications*, 8, 571-579.

Graumann, C.F., & Kruse, L. (1990). The environment: Social construction and psychological problems. In H.T. Himmtelweit, G. Gaskel (Eds.), *Societal Psychology* (pp. 212-229). London: Sage.

Grimsrud, K.M. & Wandschneider, P.R. (2003, July). Empirical Taxonomy of Environmental Ethical Archetypes. *Paper presented at the American Agricultural Economics Association Annual Meeting, Montreal, Canada.*

Grob, A. (1995). A structural model of environmental attitudes and behavior. *Journal of Environmental Psychology*, 15, 209-220.

Hardin, G. (1968). The tragedy of the commons. *Science*, 162, 1243-1248.

Hines, J.M., Hungerford, H.R., Tomera, A.N. (1986). Analysis and synthesis of research on responsible environmental behaviour: a meta-analysis. *Journal of Environmental Education*, 18, 1-8.

Hirose, Y. & Kitada, T. (1987). Determinants of residential consumers' water conservation in urban drought. *Research in Social Psychology*, 2, 21-28.

Kaiser, F.G., Wolfing, S., Fuhrer, U. (1999). Environmental attitude and ecological behaviour. *Journal of Environmental Psychology*, 19, 1-19.

Levy-Leboyer, C., Bonnes, M., Chase, J. Ferreira-Marques, J., Pawlik, K. (1996). Determinants of Pro-Environmental Behaviors: A Five–Countries Comparison. *European Psychologists*, 1, 123-129.

Little, T., Cunningham, W., Shahar, G., & Widaman, K. (2002). To parcel or not parcel: exploring the question, weighing the merits. *Structural Equation Modeling: A Multidisciplinary Journal*, 9, 151-173.

López, E., Balboa, H., Igartúa, A., & Claramunt, R. (1994). Aproximación al estudio de actitudes respecto al ahorro doméstico de agua en Barcelona [Approaches to the study of attitudes regarding residential water conservation]. In B. Hernández, E. Suárez and J. Martínez-Torvisco (Eds.) *Interpretación social y gestión del entorno: Aproximaciones desde la psicología ambiental* (pp. 29-34). Universidad de La Laguna, Tenerife, Spain.

Mastny, L. (2009). State of the world: a year in review. In World Watch Institute (Ed.), *2009 State of the World. Into a warming world*. Washington, DC: World Watch Institute.

Middlestadt, S., Grieser, M., Hernández, O., Tubaishat, K., Sanchack, J., Southwell, J., & Schwartz, R. (2001). Turning minds on and faucets off: Water conservation education in Jordanian schools. *Journal of Environmental Education*, 32, 37-45.

Moser, G. (1984). Water quality perception: a dynamic evaluation. *Journal of Environmental Psychology*, 4, 201-210.

Moser, G., Pol, E., Bernard, Y., Bonnes, M., Corraliza, J.A., Giuliani, V. (Eds.) (2002). *People, Places, and Sustainability*. Gottingen: Hogrefe & Huber.

Moser, G., Ratiu, E., & de Vanssay, B. (2004). Water use and management in the light of sustainable development: Social representations, ideologies and practices in different societal contexts. IHDP Update, 4, 13–15.

Moser, G. & Uzzell, D. (2002). Environmental psychology. In: Millon, T., & Lerner, M.J. (Eds.), *Comprehensive Handbook of Psychology, Volume 5: Personality and Social Psychology*, New York: John Wiley & Sons, 2002, pp 419-445

Pawlik, K. (1991). The psychology of global environmental change: Some basic data and an agenda for cooperative international research. *International Journal of Psychology*, 26, 547-563.

Rosegrant, M.W., Cai, X., & Cline, S. (2003). Will the world run dry? *Environment*, 45, 24-36.

Schmuck, P., & Schultz, W. (2002). *Psychology of sustainable development*. Norwell, MA: Kluwer.

Somerville, C. & Briscoe, J. (2001) Genetic engineering and water. *Science*, 292, 2217.

Steg L. & Sievers, I. (2000). Cultural theory and individual perceptions of environmental risks. *Environment and Behavior*, 32, 250-269.

Stern, P. (2000). Toward a coherent theory of environmentally significant behavior. *Journal of Social Issues*, 56, 407-424.

Stern, P., Dietz, T., Guagnano, G.A. (1995). The new ecological paradigm in social psychological context. *Environment and Behavior*, 27, 723-743.

Syme, G., Thomas, J., & Salerian, S. (1983). Can household attitudes predict water consumption? In *Hidrology and Water Resources Symposium* (pp. 53-56). Canberra: Institution of Australia Engineers.

Thomas, D., & Ford, R. (2005). *The crisis of innovation in water and wastewater*. Northampton, MA: Edward Elgar Publishing.

UNESCO-WWAP (2003). *Water for people – water for life. The United Nations world water development report*. Barcelona, Spain: UNESCO Publishing & Berghahn Books.

United Nations (2008). Statistics of the Human Development Reports. Retrieved on January 2009 from the site: http://hdr.undp.org/en/statistics/

Uzzell, D.L. (1997). Ecological Responsibility and the Action Competent Citizen: Some Methodological Issues. In R. Garcia-Mira, C. Arce and J. M. Sabucedo (eds.), *Responsabilidad Ecológica y Gestión de Los Recursos Ambientales*, A Coruña, Spain: Diputación Provincial de A Coruña, 23-34.

Uzzell, D.L. (2000). The psycho-spatial dimension of global environmental problems. *Journal of Environmental Psychology*, 20, 307-318.

Van Vugt, M., (2001). Community Identification Moderating the Impact of Financial Incentives in a Natural Social dilemma: Water Conservation. *Personality and Social Psychology Bulletin*, 11, 1440-1449.

Vlek, C. & Steg, L. (2007). Human behavior and environmental sustainability: problems, driving forces, and research topics. *Journal of Social Issues*, 63, 1-9.

WCED - World Commission on Environment and Development (1987). *Our common future*. Oxford: Oxford University Press.

Winter, D. (2000). Some big ideas for some big problems. *American Psychologists*, 55, 516-522.

Zube, E. (1991). Environmental Psychology, Global Issues and Local Landscape Research. *Journal of Environmental Psychology*, 11, 321-334.

In: Psychological Approaches to Sustainability
Editors: V. Corral-Verdugo et al.
ISBN 978-1-60876-356-6
© 2010 Nova Science Publishers, Inc.

Chapter 4

HOW TO PROMOTE ENERGY SAVINGS AMONG HOUSEHOLDS: THEORETICAL AND PRACTICAL APPROACHES

Linda Steg[*]
Rijksuniversiteit Groningen, Netherlands
Wokje Abrahamse
University of Surrey, United Kingdom

ABSTRACT

Households are responsible for a large part of total energy requirements and CO_2 emissions. We review the contribution of social and environmental psychology for understanding and promoting household energy conservation. A general framework is proposed, comprising: (1) identification and measurement of the behavior to be changed, (2) examination of the main factors underlying this behavior, (3) design and implementation of interventions to change behavior to reduce household energy use, and (4) evaluation of the effects of interventions. We discuss how psychologists empirically studied these four topics.

INTRODUCTION

Greenhouse gas emissions have steadily increased by about 1% per year during the last decade (e.g., EPA, 2004; RIVM, 2004). CO_2 is the most important greenhouse gas, responsible for about 84% of the total emissions of greenhouse gases (EPA, 2004). Household energy use significantly contributes to greenhouse gas emissions. For example, households are responsible for approximately 15 to 20% of total energy requirements in

---

[*] Correspondence: Linda Steg, Department of Psychology, University of Groningen, Grote Kruisstraat 2/1, 9712 TS Groningen, the Netherlands. E-mail: E.M.Steg@rug.nl.

OECD countries (OECD, 2001) by using electricity, natural gas and fuels; in the Netherlands, this percentage is 23% (Ministerie van EZ, 1999). Many governments aim to reduce household energy use, and consequently, greenhouse gas emissions. However, despite their efforts, household energy consumption is still increasing. In the Netherlands, electricity and fuel use have increased steadily from 1990, due to increases in possession and use of electric appliances, and increases in car use (Steg, 1999). More effective energy policies seem to be warranted to reduce the emission of greenhouse gases by households.

This chapter discusses factors influencing household energy use, and ways to promote household energy savings. Attempts to promote household energy conservation will be more effective when one (1) selects high impact behaviors, that involve relatively large amounts of energy use and CO_2 emissions, and monitors behavior over longer periods of time, (2) examines which factors are related to those behaviors, (3) implements interventions that change these antecedents and the behavior, and (4) systematically evaluates the effects of these interventions in terms of behavior changes, changes in behavioral antecedents, changes in energy use, environmental quality and human quality of life (Geller, 2002; Steg & Vlek, 2008). This chapter provides a brief overview of how psychologists have addressed these issues.

SELECTING AND ASSESSING ENERGY USE BEHAVIORS

If psychologists aim to significantly contribute to the reduction of energy problems, they should study behaviors associated with high energy consumption. Households use energy in a direct and in an indirect way (e.g. Vringer & Blok, 1995). Direct energy use is the use of electricity, natural gas and other fossil fuels, and indirect energy use refers to the energy used in the production, transportation and disposal of goods and services. In European countries, about half of total household energy use is direct energy use, the other half is indirect energy use (Kok, Falkena, Benders, Moll, & Noorman, 2003; Reinders, Vringer, & Blok, 2003). Although a substantial part of total household energy use involves indirect energy use, only few studies examined the indirect use of energy (Abrahamse, Steg, Vlek, & Rothengatter, 2007; Gatersleben, Steg, & Vlek, 2002; Poortinga, Steg, Vlek & Wiersma, 2003).

Household activities vary widely in the amount of energy they use. In 2005, in the UK, about 53% of domestic direct energy use related to space heating, 20% to water heating, 16% to the use of household appliances, 6% to lighting and 5% to cooking (Maslin, Austin, Dickson, Murlis, Owen, & Panizzo, 2007). Environmental scientists have developed various tools for assessing direct and indirect energy use, such as life-cycle analysis, or input-output analysis (e.g., Kok, Benders, & Moll, 2006) that are useful for identifying behaviors associated with relatively high levels of energy use. These data can help practitioners decide which type of conservation behavior would be most worthwhile. Besides impact, psychologists should also consider the feasibility of behaviour changes. Of course, the feasibility can be facilitated via various intervention strategies (see Section Interventions to promote energy conservation).

After a specific energy-related behavior is identified, it needs to be measured properly. That is, valid behavioral measures are needed. Based on this, one can decide which (groups of) individuals should be targeted. Moreover, by monitoring (changes in) environmental behavior over time, one can assess whether interventions have been successful.

Most studies on household energy use rely on self-reported data. Some studies revealed that self-reports are adequate indicators of actual behavior (e.g., Fujii, Hennesy, & Mak, 1985; Warriner, McDougall, & Claxton, 1984), but others reported weak correlations between self-reported and observed behavior (e.g., Corral-Verdugo, 1997). Whenever possible, one should try to measure actual behavior; smart meters and GPS devices could yield useful insights in this respect. When the measurement of people's actual behavior is not feasible, it is important to consider how to collect valid and reliable measures of self-reported behavior (see also Vining & Ebreo, 2002), and to check the accuracy of the employed measures.

Psychologists have studied separate energy conservation behaviors, such as reducing car use, or switching off lights, but they have also tried to assess total household energy use. Meter readings reflect how much electricity, gas, fuel or water has been used by a particular household. However, meter readings do not reveal which specific behaviors contributed most to total energy, fuel or water use. From an educational point of view this is problematic, for people generally do not know which and whose behaviors significantly affect resource use, and people cannot receive specific feedback on the results of their behavioral changes (see also Gatersleben et al., 2002).

Therefore, composite behavioral measures of energy use have been proposed based on a well-defined set of specific behaviors (see Abrahamse et al., 2007; Gatersleben et al., 2002). This approach implies that respondents first indicate which goods they possess (e.g., fridges, cars) and how often they use these. Subsequently, environmental scientists asses the direct as well as indirect 'energy contents' of these behaviors. Next, the energy contents of various behaviors are summed, yielding a measure of total energy use involved in a given household behavior pattern. On the basis of this approach, households can be provided with information on specific ways to reduce their energy use. Also, feedback can be provided about the specific behavior changes that have been most effective in realizing energy savings, and those that have not been effective (see Abrahamse et al., 2007). This is important, as households may gain insight into the relative impact of the various energy-saving options they consider implementing.

FACTORS INFLUENCING HOUSEHOLD ENERGY USE

Behavioral interventions are generally more effective when they target important antecedents of the relevant behavior and remove barriers to change. Therefore, it is important to understand which factors promote or inhibit energy conservation. Various factors influence household energy use and energy savings. Individuals need to be aware of the need for and possible ways to reduce household energy use, they need to be motivated to conserve energy, and they should be able to adopt the relevant behaviors. Each of these factors will be discussed briefly below.

Knowledge

In general, people are well aware of the problems related to household energy use, and are concerned about these problems (Abrahamse, 2007), although there is still confusion about the causal processes involved (e.g. Bord, O'Connor, & Fischer, 2000; Gorsira, Steg, Bolderdijk, & Keizer, in preparation). For example, many people think global warming is caused by the depletion of ozone in the upper atmosphere (which is incorrect), while only a limited number of people think global warming is caused by heating and cooling homes, which is correct (Bord et al., 2000). In 2008, only 21% of a representative sample of the Dutch population knew that global warming does not result in ozone depletion, and only 35% knew that acid rain is not caused by global warming (Gorsira et al., in preparation). Moreover, people know relatively little about the energy use associated with their daily behaviors. For example, when assessing the energy use of household appliances, people tend to rely on a simple heuristic: the size of appliances. The larger the appliance, the more energy it is believed to use (Baird and Brier, 1981; Schuitema and Steg, 2005). Obviously, this heuristic is not always accurate. Moreover, people have a tendency to underestimate the energy use involved in heating water, which suggests that people are not well aware of the fact that energy sources are needed to do this (Schuitema and Steg, 2005). Assessing indirect energy use is even more complicated, as, typically, no information of the 'embedded' energy use of products and services is provided. People know relatively little about the energy use associated with the production, transportation, and disposal of products (Tobler, Visschers, & Siegrist, 2009). For example, people think the term 'organic' means that these products are more environmentally-friendly than non-organic products, while they do not necessarily consider the energy use involved in transporting organic products to the supermarket (e.g., flown in from overseas).

Motivations

Various studies have examined relationships between motivational factors and energy behaviors. Below, we first discuss relationships between motivations and household energy use, and next relationships between motivational factors and specific energy behaviors.

Household Energy Use

Household energy use is most strongly related to socio demographics, in particular income and household size, while motivational factors do not play an important role (Gatersleben et al., 2002). Not surprisingly, wealthier and larger households use more energy. This is true for direct as well as indirect energy use (Abrahamse, 2007), and for energy use in home as well as for transport (Poortinga, Steg, & Vlek, 2004). This implies that households use more energy as soon as they need to (household size) or when they have the opportunity to do so (income). However, larger households use less energy per person than smaller households, because they share appliances, space, cars, etc.

In contrast, intention to reduce household energy use is most strongly related to motivational factors, in particular attitudes towards energy conservation and perceived behavioral control, while socio demographics do not play a significant role. This is true for direct as well as indirect energy use (Abrahamse, 2007). Environmental considerations are less strongly related to intention to reduce household energy use. So, even though concern with environmental and energy problems is generally high in Western countries (Abrahamse, 2007; Poortinga, Steg, & Vlek, 2002; Schultz & Zelezny, 1999), people often do not act in line with their concerns. As well as lacking knowledge of the energy use related to various behaviors (see above), many people attach only a low priority to saving energy. Energy use and energy conservation are not only driven by concerns about environmental and energy problems. Many other factors play a role, such as status, comfort and effort (Stern, 2000). People are less likely to reduce their energy use when saving energy involves high behavioral costs in terms of money, effort or convenience. For example, people are far more likely to carry out pro-environment activities such as recycling, which has a low cost in money and effort, than others such as reducing car use which have higher financial and lifestyle costs (see Lindenberg and Steg, 2007, for a review). This does not imply that environmental and normative concerns do not affect high-cost behavior. Some people do reduce their energy use even at the cost of personal disadvantage. Normative and environmental concerns are important in promoting energy conservation, because they provide the most solid basis for it (Lindenberg and Steg, 2007). If people only conserve energy for hedonic or cost reasons, they will stop doing so as soon as the behavior is no longer attractive or cost-effective. When energy conservation results from normative concerns as well, it is more robust against such changes.

Energy Behaviors

Motivational factors proved to be related to specific energy behaviors. Energy behaviors have been studied from different theoretical perspectives. Below, we elaborate on three types of motivations that are the focus of different theoretical perspectives: perceived cost and benefits, affect, and moral and normative concerns. We also indicate how these different perspectives may be integrated into a coherent framework, and elaborate on the role of habits.

Cost-benefit Considerations

The Theory of Planned Behavior (TPB; Ajzen, 1991) assumes that individuals make reasoned choices and choose alternatives with highest benefits against lowest costs (e.g., in terms of money, effort and/or social approval). The TPB proposes that behavior follows from an individual's intention, which reflects how much effort one is willing to take to engage in a specific behavior. Intentions depend on attitudes towards the behavior (that is, the degree to which engagement in behavior is positively valued), social norms (that is, social pressure from important others to engage in a particular behavior), and perceived behavioral control (that is, beliefs on whether one is capable of performing the behavior). All other factors, such as socio demographics or values, are believed to affect intentions indirectly, via attitudes, social norms and perceived behavioral control. The TPB has proven to be successful in explaining various types of behavior associated with direct or indirect energy use, including travel mode choice (e.g., Bamberg & Schmidt, 2003; Heath & Gifford, 2002), the purchase of energy-saving light bulbs, use of unbleached paper, and meat consumption (Harland, Staats, & Wilke, 1999).

Affect

Various studies demonstrated that affect is related to behavior, in particular energy use related to car use (see Gatersleben, 2007, for a review). Most studies were exploratory and not theory-driven. Dittmar's (1992) theory on the meaning of material possessions provides a promising perspective to study the role of affective and symbolic factors in more detail. This theory proposes that the use of material goods fulfils three functions: instrumental, symbolic, and affective. Interestingly, Steg (2005) showed that commuting car use is most strongly related to symbolic and affective motives, while instrumental motives are less important, indicating that it is important to consider affective and symbolic aspects of energy use.

Moral and Normative Concerns

Many scholars studied the role of moral and normative concerns in relation to energy conservation. This is not surprising, because energy conservation is often costly, e.g., in terms of money, time, or effort. In this case, people probably only conserve energy if they think this helps to benefit the environment, taking the additional behavioral costs for granted. Various theoretical perspectives have been employed to study the role of moral and normative concerns. First, scholars have examined the value-basis of environmental beliefs and behavior (De Groot & Steg, 2007; 2008b; Nordlund & Garvill, 2002; Stern & Dietz, 1994; Stern, Dietz, Kalof, & Guagnano, 1995). These studies revealed that people are more likely to engage in pro-environmental actions such as energy conservation when they endorse values beyond their immediate own interests, that is, self-transcendent, pro-social, altruistic or biospheric values, while egoistic or self-enhancement values are negatively related to pro-environmental behavior.

Second, scholars have studied the role of environmental concern. The most influential perspective here is the New Environmental Paradigm (NEP), which reflects people's beliefs about humanity's ability to upset the balance of nature, the existence of limits to growth for human societies, and humanity's right to rule over the rest of nature (Dunlap & Van Liere, 1978; Dunlap, Van Liere, Mertig, & Jones, 2000). It appeared that a higher environmental concern is associated with acting more pro-environmentally, although these relationships are generally not strong (e.g., Poortinga, Steg, & Vlek, 2004; Schultz & Zelezny, 1998). A recent study revealed that environmental concern is less predictive of behavior-specific beliefs than are values (Steg, De Groot, Dreijerink, Abrahamse, & Siero, in press), probably because values reflect a wider range of motivations than does NEP.

A third line of research is based on the norm-activation model (NAM; Schwartz, 1977; Schwartz & Howard, 1981) and the value-belief-norm theory of environmentalism (VBN theory; Stern, 2000; Stern, Dietz, Abel, Guagnano, & Kalof, 1999). These theories assume that people conserve energy when they feel a moral obligation to do so, which depends on the extent to which people are aware of the problems caused by their behavior, and feel responsible for these problems and their solution. The VBN-theory further proposes that awareness of the problems is rooted in environmental concern (NEP) and values. The NAM and VBN theory appeared to be successful in explaining low-cost environmental behavior and "good intentions" such as willingness to change behavior (e.g., Nordlund & Garvill, 2003; Stern et al., 1999), political behavior (e.g., Gärling, Fujii, Gärling, & Jakobsson, 2003), environmental citizenship (e.g., Stern et al., 1999), or acceptability of energy policies (e.g., De Groot & Steg, 2008a; Steg, Dreijerink, & Abrahamse, 2005), but their explanatory power is generally low in situations characterized by high behavioral costs or strong constraints on behavior, such as reducing car use (e.g., Bamberg & Schmidt, 2003; Hunecke, Blöbaum, Matthies, & Höger, 2001). In such settings, the TPB appears to be more powerful in explaining behavior (Bamberg & Schmidt, 2003), probably because the TPB considers a wider range of factors, notably non-environmental motivations and perceived behavioral control.

A fourth line of research focuses on the influence of social norms on behavior. The theory of normative conduct (Cialdini, Kallgren, & Reno, 1991; Cialdini, Reno, & Kallgren, 1990) distinguishes two types of social norms. Injunctive norms refer to the extent to which behavior is supposed to be commonly approved or disapproved of. Descriptive norms reflect the extent to which behavior is perceived as common. When injunctive and descriptive norms are in conflict, behavior will be most strongly influenced by the norm that is most salient. This theory has been validated in a series of experimental studies about littering in public places and energy use (Cialdini et al., 1990; 1991). It appeared that people are more likely to violate a particular social norm when they see that others violate that specific norm as well. Recent studies revealed that norm violations spread, that is, when people see that a particular norm is being violated, they are more likely to violate other norms as well, suggesting that people are not merely copying the behavior of others, but that perceptions of norm violations reduce the likelihood of normative behavior in general (Keizer, Lindenberg & Steg, 2008).

Multiple Motivations

Various scholars have integrated concepts and variables from different theoretical frameworks, showing that behavior results from multiple motivations (e.g., Harland et al., 1999; Heath & Gifford, 2002; Stern et al., 1995). Goal-framing theory (Lindenberg, 2006) explicitly acknowledges that behavior results from multiple motivations. This theory postulates that goals govern or "frame" the way people process information and act upon it. Three general goals are distinguished: a hedonic goal-frame "to feel better right now", a gain goal-frame "to guard and improve one's resources", and a normative goal-frame "to act appropriately". In a given situation, one of these goals is focal and influences information processing the most (that is, it is the goal-frame), while other goals are in the background and increase or decrease the strength of the focal goal. The hedonic goal-frame is a priori strongest, while in particular the normative goal-frame needs external social and institutional support in order to become focal. The three goal-frames coincide with the three types of motivational factors discussed above (Lindenberg & Steg, 2007). That is, theories and models on affect focus on hedonic goals, the TPB focuses on gain goals, while theories on norms, values and environmental concern (e.g. the NAM, VBN theory) focus on normative goals. As such, goal-framing theory provides an integrative framework for understanding pro-environmental behavior.

Habits

The theoretical frameworks discussed above generally imply that individuals make reasoned choices. However, in many cases, behavior is habitual and guided by automated cognitive processes, rather than being preceded by elaborate reasoning. When people frequently act in the same way in a particular situation, that situation will be mentally associated to the relevant goal-directed behavior. The more frequently this occurs, the stronger and more accessible the association becomes, and the more likely it is that an individual acts accordingly. Thus, habitual behavior is triggered by a cognitive structure that is learned, stored, and retrieved from memory when individuals perceive a particular situation. Various studies revealed that environmental behavior, and more particularly car use, is habitual (e.g., Aarts & Dijksterhuis, 2000; Aarts, Verplanken, & Van Knippenberg, 1998; Klöckner, Matthies, & Hunecke, 2003). Fujii and colleagues found that temporarily forcing car drivers to use alternative travel modes induced long-term reductions in car use (Fujii & Gärling, 2003; Fujii, Gärling, & Kitamura, 2001). The impacts of such temporary changes were particularly strong for habitual car drivers. This suggests that habitual drivers have inaccurate and modifiable perceptions of the pros and cons of different transport modes.

Ability to Engage in Energy Conservation

Obviously, human behavior does not depend on motivations alone. Many contextual factors may facilitate or constrain energy conservation and influence individual motivations (Ölander & Thøgersen, 1995; Stern, 1999; Thøgersen, 2005), such as the availability of energy efficient appliances, the quality of public transport, or pricing regimes (e.g., Santos, 2008; Vining & Ebreo, 1992). In some cases, constraints may even be so strong that motivations make little difference in the environmental outcome (see, e.g., Corraliza & Berenguer, 2000). Only few scholars included contextual factors in their studies (Black, Stern, & Elworth, 1985; Hunecke et al., 2001), and surprisingly, contextual factors are not included in theories to explain energy use. The TPB only considers individuals' perceptions of contextual factors, as expressed in perceived behavioral control. It is highly important to understand how contextual factors influence energy use in order to design intervention strategies that remove important barriers for energy conservation.

INTERVENTIONS TO PROMOTE ENERGY CONSERVATION

The question of how to encourage household energy conservation has been a topic of interest within social and environmental psychological research for a number of decades. Behavioral interventions may be aimed at changing an individual's perceptions, preferences, motivations, and norms via informational strategies. Alternatively, interventions may be aimed at changing the context in which decisions are being made, for instance, through financial rewards, laws, or the provision of energy-efficient equipment. The latter strategy is aimed at changing the pay-off structure, so as to make energy-saving activities relatively more attractive. When energy saving is rather costly or difficult because of external barriers to energy conservation, changes in the circumstances under which behavioral choices are made may be needed so as to increase individual opportunities to conserve energy and to make energy saving behavior choices more attractive (cf. Ölander & Thøgersen, 1995; Stern, 1999; Thøgersen, 2005). The costs and benefits of behavioral alternatives may be changed in various ways. First, the availability and quality of products and services may be altered via changes in physical, technical, and/or organizational systems. Environmentally harmful behavioral options can be made less feasible or even impossible, or new and/or better-quality (energy-saving) behavior options may be provided (e.g., recycling bins, energy efficient technology). Second, legal regulations can be implemented (e.g., prohibiting the use of specific appliances). Legal measures of course require that the relevant laws and regulations are enforced, and that violations are penalized. Third, pricing policies are aimed at decreasing prices of energy saving behavior options and/or increasing prices of less energy-saving alternatives.

Behavioral interventions are typically classified according to the taxonomy for behavior change interventions as proposed by Geller, Berry, Ludwig, Evans, Gilmore and Clark (1990), which distinguishes between antecedent and consequence intervention strategies (see also Lehman & Geller, 2004). Antecedent interventions are assumed to influence one or more determinants *prior* to the performance of energy behaviors. Examples of such interventions are information, commitment, and goal setting. For instance, providing households with information about energy-saving options in the office may result in energy savings, because people have acquired (more) knowledge. Consequence strategies on the other hand are based on the assumption that positive or negative consequences will influence behavioral choices. To illustrate, pro-environmental behavior will become a more attractive alternative when positive consequences are attached to it, e.g., by the provision of a monetary incentive. Feedback, punishments and rewards are well-known examples of this type of interventions. A browse through the social and environmental psychology literature reveals an abundance of intervention studies with an aim to encourage consumers to conserve energy – with varying degrees of success (for reviews see Abrahamse, Steg, Vlek, & Rothengatter, 2005; Dwyer, Leeming, Cobern, & Porter, 1993; Schultz, Oskamp, & Mainieri, 1995).

Antecedent Strategies

Information is a widely used intervention to encourage household energy savings – its success, however, is rather debatable. This may be general information about energy-related problems, or specific information about possible solutions, such as information about various energy-saving measures households can adopt. Providing information serves to increase households' awareness of energy problems and their knowledge about possibilities to reduce these problems. It appears that information provision about energy conservation or environmental issues does indeed generally lead to an increase in knowledge, or awareness, but it does not necessarily translate into behavior changes (Gardner & Stern, 2002; Geller, 1981; Staats, Wit, & Midden, 1996).

The provision of personalized, tailored, information tends to be more effective. An advantage of this approach is that households receive relevant information only, rather than getting an overload of general information, which may not always apply to their specific situation. Examples of such approaches are home energy audits, which have proven to be quite effective in encourage energy savings among households (e.g. Winett, Love, & Kidd, 1982-1983), or personalized information about energy saving options via the Internet, which proved to be effective as well (Abrahamse, Steg, Vlek, & Rothengatter, 2007).

It has been suggested that, the provision of information may be more effective when it makes salient social norms in favor of energy conservation. One particular study found that towels were re-used more frequently by hotel guests when they were provided with information that emphasized descriptive social norms in favor of re-use (e.g. 'did you know 75% of our guests help save the environment by reusing their towels') compared to when they were given environmental information only (e.g. 'help save the environment by re-using your towels') (Goldstein, Cialdini, & Griskevicius, 2008). Alternatively, information provision can also be more effective when it is given in a certain social context. Neighborhood interactions may be important in this respect, as this may lead to the diffusion of information, and it may help people to develop and establish social norms (see Weenig & Midden, 1991).

Commitments are potentially powerful and cost-effective interventions. Commitments essentially entail making a promise to try and engage in a certain pro-environmental behavior (e.g. try driving less often), and in doing so, eliciting a moral obligation to stick to the promise made. In terms of large scale implementation, commitments do not necessarily have to cost a lot of money (in contrast to for instance financial incentives), but they may be difficult to implement when they rely on personal contact. Various studies have found commitment to be effective in encouraging energy conservation (e.g. Pallak & Cummings, 1976) and recycling (e.g. DeLeon & Fuqua, 1995; Wang & Katzev, 1990). Especially in view of the long-term effects found in several studies (Katzev & Johnson, 1983; Pallak & Cummings, 1976), commitment may be a successful strategy for reducing household energy use.

Goal setting entails giving households a reference point, for instance to save 5% or 15% energy. A goal can be set by the experimenters, or by the households themselves. A study by Becker (1978) found that a relatively difficult goal (20%) was more effective when it was combined with feedback, as compared to a relatively easy goal (2%). This indicates that in order for a (difficult) goal to work, households need feedback on how they are performing in relation to the goal. Also, eliciting implementation intentions, in which people are not only asked whether they intend to change their behavior, but also to indicate how they plan to do so (i.e. reach that goal), appeared to be effective (e.g., Bamberg, 2002; Jakobsson, Fujii, & Gärling, 2002).

Consequent Strategies

Feedback is often applied to promote energy conservation. Feedback consists of giving households information about their energy consumption, or energy savings. It can influence behavior, because households can associate certain outcomes (e.g., energy savings) with their behavior. Ideally, feedback is given immediately after the behavior occurs, because households need to understand the relationship between the feedback and their behavior (Geller, 2002). Feedback appears to be an effective strategy for reducing household energy use (e.g., Seligman & Darley, 1977), although some exceptions exist (e.g., Katzev, Cooper, & Fisher, 1980-1981). Results of studies using feedback seem to suggest that the more frequent the feedback is given, the more effective it is. Positive effects have for instance been found for continuous feedback (e.g., McClelland & Cook, 1979-1980). A study by Kantola, Syme and Campbell (1984) showed that high frequency is not necessarily the key to success: by giving feedback one single time, evoking dissonance between people's reported attitudes (i.e. favorable towards energy conservation) and their behavior (i.e. high energy usage), households significantly reduced their energy use.

Feedback about individual performance relative to the performance of others may be helpful in encouraging energy conservation. By providing people with feedback on how they are doing as a group, social norms in favor of a certain pro-environmental behavior may become salient. Similarly, by giving comparative feedback about how a group of individuals is doing relative to other groups may evoke feelings of social comparison, which may be especially effective when important or relevant others are used as a reference group. The results of the use of comparative feedback are mixed, and seem to be dependent on the target group that is studied. In the area of household energy conservation, group feedback is generally no more effective than individual feedback (e.g. Abrahamse et al., 2007; Midden, Meter, Weenig, & Zieverink, 1983). Group feedback has also been implemented to encourage energy conservation in organizational settings, with promising results (e.g. Siero, Bakker, Dekker, & Van den Burg, 1996). Another line of research suggests that the effects of comparative feedback may depend on whether people already behave according to the group norm (see for instance, Schultz, Nolan, Cialdini, Goldstein, & Griskevicius, 2007). In fact, differential effects of feedback have been found for relatively high and low consumers of energy, the latter group (who already behaved in a pro-environmental way) actually increased their energy use as a result of feedback (e.g. Brandon & Lewis, 1999). Apparently, the behavior of others is taken as a reference point to strive for. Interestingly, this boomerang effect was neutralized by adding an injunctive message (in this case a smiley), which probably conveyed social approval (Schultz et al., 2007).

Monetary rewards may serve as an extrinsic motivator to conserve energy. Rewards can either be contingent on the amount of energy saved, or a fixed amount (e.g., when a certain percentage is attained). Overall, rewards seem to have a positive effect on energy savings. Results of several studies (e.g. Slavin, Wodarski, & Blackburn, 1981) do however suggest that the effect of rewards is rather short-lived.

Combining Interventions

Combinations of interventions are generally more effective than single interventions. This makes sense to the extent that different people may have different barriers to change (Gardner & Stern, 2002). A combination of antecedent (e.g., information) and consequence strategies (e.g., feedback) is generally more effective than the individual interventions. Interventions within the realm of social and environmental psychology typically focus on informational strategies, rather than changing contextual factors which may more strongly steer households' behavioral decisions (see Abrahamse et al., 2005; Dwyer et al., 1993; Schultz et al., 1995, for reviews). This is regrettable, because to the extent that contextual factors strongly influence energy use, structural strategies are probably very effective in promoting household energy savings. Moreover, informational and structural strategies could complement one another. For instance, informational strategies may be an important element in the implementation of structural strategies that force individuals to change their behavior (Gärling & Schuitema, 2007). For example, public support for structural strategies may be increased by informing individuals about the need for and the possible consequences of such strategies.

Evaluation of the Effectiveness of Interventions

Studies aimed at evaluating an intervention's effectiveness should follow rigorous experimental research designs that reveal the effectiveness of single as well as combinations of interventions for one or more 'treatment' groups and a comparable control group. In addition, it is important to also study long-term effects as well, as interventions may lose their effectiveness as soon as they are discontinued (e.g. as is often the case with rewards; see Abrahamse et al., 2005). Effect measurements should not only focus on (changes in) energy behaviors. First, it is important to monitor (changes in) determinants of energy use and energy savings as this enhances our understanding of why intervention programs were successful or not. This allows change agents to adapt interventions in order to increase their effectiveness. For instance, failure of group feedback to encourage pro-environmental behaviors may well be attributable to the fact that social norms did not change as a result of the intervention. Second, it is important to monitor (changes in) total energy use and environmental quality, since this is the ultimate goal of behavioral interventions. Here, collaboration with environmental scientists is needed. Based on this, feedback can be provided to the target population so as to inform them about the effectiveness of their efforts to conserve energy and to reduce energy problems. This may strengthen people's commitment to change their behavior, and to maintain the changes already implemented. Third, one would need to know changes in people's quality of life, which is an important component of the more general notion of sustainable development. Studies revealed that people generally expect that environmental policies will not seriously threaten their quality of life (De Groot & Steg, 2006; see also Steg & Gifford, 2005). As yet, most studies (see Steg & Gifford, 2005, for a review) examined expected changes in quality of life, while actual changes resulting from environmental policies or conditions have hardly been monitored over time. Expected changes may differ from actual changes in perceived quality of life, for example, because people do not fully understand or imagine how interventions will affect their life. Also, they may underestimate the positive consequences of energy policies on, for example, environmental quality.

Next to studying actual effects of interventions, psychologists studied the perceived effectiveness and acceptability of environmental policies before policies have been implemented, particularly in the travel domain (e.g., Bamberg and Rölle, 2003; Eriksson, Garvill, & Nordlund, 2006; 2008; Jakobsson, Fujii, & Gärling, 2000; Schade & Schlag, 2003; Schuitema & Steg, 2008; see Steg & Schuitema, 2007, for a review), but also regarding energy use (Nilsson, Von Borgstede & Biel, 2004; Steg et al., 2005). Most studies examined individual factors related to perceived effectiveness or acceptability judgments. These studies revealed, among other things, that policies are more acceptable when they are believed to be more fair, when they are effective in reducing relevant problems, and when they do not seriously affect individual freedom. Moreover, policies are more acceptable to people who have strong environmental values, who are highly aware of the problem, and who feel a strong moral obligation to reduce the problems (De Groot & Steg, 2007; Steg et al., 2005). Thus, normative and environmental concerns are important for the acceptability of policies. Acceptability may increase after policies have been implemented. For example, acceptability of the congestion charge in Stockholm increased after the implementation of the charge, probably because the charge had more positive effects on congestion, environmental problems, and parking problems than expected beforehand, while the additional travel costs for households were lower than expected (Schuitema, Steg, & Forward, 2009).

A few studies examined the extent to which perceived effectiveness and acceptability depends on specific policy features, such as rewards versus penalties, or the type of behaviour being targeted (e.g., Poortinga, Steg, Vlek, & Wiersma, 2003; Steg, Dreijerink, & Abrahamse,

2006). It appeared that policies that increase the attractiveness of pro-environmental behavior (that is, energy savings) are evaluated as more effective and acceptable than policies aimed at decreasing the attractiveness of environmentally harmful behavior (that is, not saving energy; Steg et al., 2006). Moreover, people prefer policies aimed at promoting the adoption of energy-efficient equipment above policies aimed at reducing the use of existing equipment (Poortinga et al., 2003; Steg et al., 2006), and energy savings in home above energy savings in transport (Poortinga et al., 2003). Interestingly, people high in environmental concern evaluate governmental regulations and behavioral strategies as more acceptable, while people with a low environmental concern prefer market-oriented and technological strategies (Poortinga, Steg, & Vlek, 2002).

CONCLUSION

Psychologists have an important role to play in promoting energy conservation via behavioral changes. Behavioral interventions are generally more effective when they are systematically planned, implemented and evaluated. Four key issues to be addressed are: (1) identification of the behavior to be changed, (2) examination of the main factors underlying this behavior, (3) application of interventions to change the relevant behaviors and their determinants, and (4) evaluation of intervention effects on the behavior itself, its main determinants, energy use, environmental quality, and human quality of life. Individuals can contribute significantly to achieving long-term environmental sustainability by reducing household energy use. The challenge for psychologists is to understand the individual and structural factors and processes that threaten environmental sustainability, so that energy saving could be facilitated and emerge worldwide.

Studies on household energy conservation typically have a mono-disciplinary focus. However, multidisciplinary approaches can have clear added value. For instance, sociologists can provide valuable insight into the meanings individuals attach to sustainable practices, with regards to existing institutional and contextual arrangements (e.g. Spaargaren, 2003). Also, as has been mentioned earlier, input from environmental scientists can be of valuable importance to further improve intervention studies. Environmental scientists can help translate energy-related behaviors into energy use and environmental impact, e.g., in terms of CO_2 emissions, and help select high-impact behaviors. It is therefore important to consider energy conservation from an interdisciplinary perspective. Equally well, close collaboration between academia and the policy arena is essential in order to develop and evaluate effective interventions to encourage household energy conservation.

REFERENCES

Aarts, H., & Dijksterhuis, A. P. (2000). The automatic activation of goal-directed behaviour: the case of travel habit. *Journal of Environmental Psychology, 20*, 75-82.

Aarts, H., Verplanken, B., & Van Knippenberg, A. (1998). Predicting behaviour from actions in the past: Repeated decision making or a matter of habit? *Journal of Applied Social Psychology, 28*, 1355-1374.

Abrahamse, W. 2007. Energy conservation through behavioral change: examining the effectiveness of a tailor-made approach. PhD thesis, University of Groningen, The Netherlands.

Abrahamse, W., Steg, L., Vlek, C., Rothengatter, J. A. (2005). A review of intervention studies aimed at household energy conservation. *Journal of Environmental Psychology, 25*, 273-291.

Abrahamse, W., Steg, L., Vlek, C., & Rothengatter, J. A. (2007). The effect of tailored information, goal setting and feedback on household energy use, energy-related behaviors and behavioral determinants. *Journal of Environmental Psychology, 27*, 265-276.

Ajzen, I. (1991). The theory of planned behavior. *Organizational Behavior and Human Decision Processes, 50*, 179-211.

Baird, J.C. & Brier, J.M. (1981). Perceptual awareness of energy requirements of familiar objects. *Journal of Applied Psychology, 66*, 90-96.

Bamberg, S. (2002). Effects of implementation intentions on the actual performance of new environmentally friendly behaviours - Results of two field experiments. *Journal of Environmental Psychology, 22*, 399-411.

Bamberg, S., & Rölle, D. (2003). Determinants of people's acceptability of pricing measures- replication and extension of a causal model. In: J. Schade & B. Schlag (Eds.), *Acceptability of transport pricing strategies* (pp. 235-248). Oxford: Elsevier Science.

Bamberg, S., & Schmidt, S. (2003). Incentives, morality or habit? Predicting students' car use for university routes with the models of Ajzen, Schwartz and Triandis. *Environment and Behavior, 35*, 264-285.

Becker, L.J. (1978). Joint effect of feedback and goal setting on performance: A field study of residential energy conservation. *Journal of Applied Psychology, 63*, 428-433.

Black, J. S., Stern, P. C., & Elworth, J. T. (1985). Personal and contextual influences on household energy adaptations. *Journal of Applied Psychology, 70*, 3-21.

Bord, R.J., O'Connor, R.E., Fischer, A. (2000). In what sense does the public need to understand global climate change? *Public Understanding of Science, 9*, 205–218.

Brandon, G. & Lewis, A. (1999). Reducing household energy consumption: a qualitative and quantitative field study. *Journal of Environmental Psychology, 19*, 75-85.

Cialdini, R. B., Kallgren, C. A., & Reno, R. R. (1991). A focus theory of normative conduct: A theoretical refinement and reevaluation of the role of norms in human behavior. *Advances in Experimental Social Psychology, 24*, 201-234.

Cialdini, R. B, Reno, R. R., & Kallgren, C. A. (1990). A focus theory of normative conduct: Recycling the concept of norms to reduce littering in public places. *Journal of Personality and Social Psychology, 58*, 1015-1026.

Corraliza, J. A., & Berenguer, J. (2000). Environmental values, beliefs and actions. *Environment and Behavior, 32*, 832-848.

Corral-Verdugo, V. (1997). Dual 'realities' of conservation behavior: self-reports vs observations of re-use and recycling behavior. *Journal of Environmental Psychology, 17* (2), 135-145.

De Groot, J., & Steg, L. (2006). Impact of transport pricing on quality of life, acceptability, and intentions to reduce car use: an explorative study in five European countries. *Journal of Transport Geography, 14* (6), 463-470.

De Groot, J. I. M., & Steg, L. (2007). Value orientations and environmental beliefs in five countries: Validity of an instrument to measure egoistic, altruistic and biospheric value orientations. *Journal of Cross-Cultural Psychology, 38*, 318-332.

De Groot, J. I. M. & Steg, L. (2008a). Morality and prosocial behavior: the role of awareness, responsibility and norms in the norm activation model. *Journal of Social Psychology*, in press.

De Groot, J., & Steg, L. (2008b). Value orientations to explain beliefs related to environmental significant behavior: How to measure egoistic, altruistic, and biospheric value orientations. *Environment and Behavior, 40*, 330-354.

DeLeon, I. G., & Fuqua, R. W. (1995). The effects of public commitment and group feedback on curbside recycling. *Environment and Behavior, 27*, 233-250.

Dittmar, H. (1992) *The social psychology of material possessions: To have is to be*. Harvester Wheatsheaf, Hemel Hempstead, UK; St. Martin's Press, New York.

Dunlap, R. E., & Van Liere, K. D. (1978). The 'new environmental paradigm': a proposed measuring instrument and preliminary results. *Journal of Environmental Education, 9*, 10-19.

Dunlap, R. E., Van Liere, K. D., Mertig, A. G., & Jones, R. E. (2000). Measuring endorsement of the New Ecological Paradigm: A revised NEP scale. *Journal of Social Issues, 56* (3), 425-442.

Dwyer, W. O., Leeming, F. C., Cobern, M. K., Porter, B. E., & Jackson, J. M. (1993). Critical review of behavioral interventions to preserve the environment. Research since 1980. *Environment and Behavior, 25*, 275-321.

EPA (2004). *Inventory of U.S. greenhouse gas emissions and sinks, 1990-2002*. Washington, DC: U.S. Environmental Protection Agency (EPA), report nr. EPA 430-R-04-003.

Eriksson, L., Garvill, J., & Nordlund, A.M. (2006). Acceptability of travel demand management measures: The importance of problem awareness, personal norm, freedom, and fairness. *Journal of Environmental Psychology, 26*, 15-26.

Eriksson, L., Garvill, J., & Nordlund, A.M. (2008). Acceptability of single and combined transport policy measures: The importance of environmental and policy specific beliefs. *Transportation Research A, 42*, 1117-1128.

Fujii, S., & Gärling, T. (2003). Development of script-based travel mode choice after forced change. *Transportation Research F, 6*, 117-124.

Fujii, S., Gärling, T., & Kitamura, R. (2001). Changes in drivers' perceptions and use of public transport during a freeway closure: Effects of temporary structural change on cooperation in a real-life social dilemma. *Environment and Behavior, 33*, 796-808.

Fuijii, E. T., Hennesy, M., & Mak, J. (1985). An evaluation of the validity and reliability of survey response data on household electricity conservation. *Evaluation Review, 9*, 93-104.

Gardner, G. T., & Stern, P. C. (2002). *Environmental problems and human behavior* (2nd edition). Boston, MA: Pearson Custom Publishing.

Gärling, T., Fujii, S., Gärling, A., & Jakobsson, C. (2003). Moderating effects of social value orientation on determinants of proenvironmental intention. *Journal of Environmental Psychology, 23*, 1-9.

Gärling, T., & Schuitema, G. (2007). Travel demand management targeting reduced private car use: Effectiveness, public acceptability and political feasibility. *Journal of Social Issues, 63*, 139-153.

Gatersleben, B. (2007). Affective and symbolic aspects of car use. In: T. Gärling & L. Steg (Eds.), *Threats to the quality of urban life from car traffic: problems, causes, and solutions* (pp. 219-233). Amsterdam: Elsevier.

Gatersleben, B., Steg, L., Vlek, C. (2002). Measurement and determinants of environmentally significant consumer behaviour. *Environment and Behavior, 34*, 335-362.

Geller, E.S. (1981). Evaluating energy conservation programs: Is verbal report enough? *Journal of Consumer Research, 8*, 331-335.

Geller, E. S. (2002). The challenge of increasing proenvironmental behavior. In R. B. Bechtel & A. Churchman, *Handbook of environmental psychology* (pp. 525-540). New York: Wiley.

Geller, E. S., Berry, T. D., Ludwig, T. D., Evans, R. E, Gilmore, M. R., & Clarke, S. W. (1990). A conceptual framework for developing and evaluating behavior change interventions for injury control. Health Education Research, 5 (2), 125-137.

Goldstein, N. J., Cialdini, R. B., & Griskevicius, V. (2008). A room with a viewpoint: Using social norms to motivate environmental conservation in hotels. *Journal of Consumer Research, 35*, 472-482.

Gorsira, M., Steg, L., Bolderdijk, J.W., & Keizer, K. (in preparation). Factors influencing energy efficient driving.

Harland, P., & Staats, H., & Wilke, H. (1999). Explaining proenvironmental behavior by personal norms and the theory of planned behavior. *Journal of Applied Social Psychology, 29*, 2505-2528.

Heath, Y., & Gifford, R. (2002). Extending the theory of planned behaviour: Predicting the use of public transportation. *Journal of Applied Social Psychology, 32*, 2154-2185.

Hunecke, M., Blöbaum, A., Matthies, E., & Höger, R. (2001). Responsibility and environment: ecological norm orientation and external factors in the domain of travel mode choice behavior. *Environment and Behavior, 33*, 830-852.

Jakobsson, C., Fujii, S., & Gärling, T. (2000). Determinants of private car users' acceptance of road pricing. *Transport Policy, 7*, 153-158.

Jakobsson, C., Fujii, S., & Gärling, T. (2002). Effects of economic disincentives on private car use. *Transportation, 29*, 349-370.

Kantola, S.J., Syme, G.J., & Campbell, N.A. (1984). Cognitive dissonance and energy conservation. *Journal of Applied Psychology, 69*, 416-421.

Katzev, R., Cooper, L., & Fisher, P. (1980-1981). The effect of feedback and social reinforcement on residential electricity consumption. *Journal of Environmental Systems, 10*, 215-227.

Katzev, R.D., & Johnson, T.R. (1983). A social-psychological analysis of residential electricity consumption: the impact of minimal justification techniques. *Journal of Economic Psychology, 3*, 267-284.

Keizer, K., Lindenberg, S., & Steg, L. (2008). The spreading of disorder. *Science, 322*, 1681-1685.

Klöckner, C. A., Matthies, E., & Hunecke, M. (2003). Problems of operationalising habits and integrating habits in normative decision-making models. *Journal of Applied Social Psychology, 33*, 396-417.

Kok, R., Falkena, H.J., Benders, R., Moll, H.C., Noorman, K.J. (2003). Household metabolism in European countries and cities: comparing and evaluating the results of the cities Fredrikstad (Norway), Groningen (The Netherlands), Guildford (UK), and

Stockholm (Sweden). Integration Report of WP2 (Toolsust Deliverable No. 9), Groningen, The Netherlands: IVEM, University of Groningen. http://www.toolsust.org/documents/D-9%20European%20report.pdf. Accessed at October 10 2007.

Kok, R., Benders, R., & Moll, H. (2006). Measuring the environmental load of household consumption using some methods based on input-output energy analysis: A comparison of methods and a discussion of results. *Energy Policy, 34,* 2744-2761.

Lehman, P. K., & Geller, E. S. (2004). Behavioral analysis and environmental protection: Accomplishments and potential for more. *Behavior and Social Issues, 13* (1), 13-32.

Lindenberg, S. (2006). Prosocial behavior, solidarity and goal-framing processes. In: D. Fetchenhauer, A. Flache, B. Buunk, & S. Lindenberg (Eds.), *Solidarity and prosocial behavior. An integration of sociological and psychological perspectives.* Amsterdam: Kluwer.

Lindenberg, S., & Steg, L. (2007). Normative, gain and hedonic goal-frames guiding environmental behavior. *Journal of Social Issues, 63* (1), 117-137.

Maslin, M., Austin, P., Dickson, A., Murlis, J., Owen, M., Panizzo, V. (2007). *UK Greenhouse Emissions: Are We on Target?* University College London – Environment Institute, London.

McClelland, L., & Cook, S.W. (1979-1980). Energy conservation effects of continuous in-home feedback in all-electric homes. *Journal of Environmental Systems, 9,* 169-173.

Midden, C.J., Meter, J.E., Weenig, M.H., & Zieverink, H.J. (1983). Using feedback, reinforcement and information to reduce energy consumption in households: A field-experiment. *Journal of Economic Psychology, 3,* 65-86.

Ministerie van EZ (1999). *Actieprogramma energiebesparing 1999-2002 [Action Program Energy Conservation 1999-2000].* Den Haag: Ministerie van Economische Zaken (EZ; in Dutch).

Nilsson, A., Von Borgstede, C., & Biel, A. (2004). Willingness to accept climate change strategies: The effect of values and norms. *Journal of Environmental Psychology, 24,* 267-277.

Nordlund, A. M., & Garvill, J. (2002). Value structures behind pro-environmental behavior. *Environment and Behavior, 34,* 740-756.

Nordlund, A. M., & Garvill, J. (2003). Effects of values, problem awareness, and personal norm on willingness to reduce personal car use. *Journal of Environmental Psychology, 23,* 339-347.

OECD 2001. Environmental Outlook. Organisation for Economic Co-operation and Development, Paris.

Ölander, F., & Thøgersen, J. (1995). Understanding of consumer behaviour as a prerequisite for environmental protection. *Journal of Consumer Policy, 18,* 345-385.

Pallak, M.S., & Cummings, N. (1976). Commitment and voluntary energy conservation. *Personality and Social Psychology Bulletin, 2,* 27-31.

Poortinga, W., Steg, L., Vlek, C. (2002). Environmental risk concern and preferences for energy-saving measures. *Environment and Behavior, 34,* 455–478.

Poortinga, W., Steg, L., & Vlek, C. (2004). Values, environmental concern and environmental behavior: A study into household energy use. *Environment and Behavior, 36,* 70-93.

Poortinga, W., Steg, L., Vlek, C., & Wiersma, G. (2003). Household preferences for energy-saving measures. A conjoint analysis. *Journal of Economic Psychology, 24,* 49-64.

Reinders, A.H.M.E., Vringer, K., Blok, K. 2003. The direct and indirect energy requirement of households in the European Union. Energy Policy 31, 139–153.

RIVM (2004). *Greenhouse gas emissions in the Netherlands 1990 – 2002*. Bilthoven: RIVM.

Santos, G. (2008). The London experience. In E. Verhoef, B. Van Wee, L. Steg, & M. Bliemer (Eds., 2007). *Pricing in road transport: a multi-disciplinary perspective* (pp. 273-292). Cheltenham: Edgar Elgar.

Schade, J., & Schlag, B. (2003). Acceptability of urban transport pricing strategies. *Transportation Research F, 6*, 45-61.

Schuitema, G., & Steg, L. (2005). Percepties van energieverbruik van huishoudelijke apparaten (Perception of energy use of domestic appliances). In: A.E. Bronner, P. Dekker, E. de Leeuw, K. de Ruyter, A. Smidts & J.E. Wieringa, *Ontwikkelingen in het marktonderzoek. Jaarboek 2005 MarktOnderzoekAssociatie (Developments in marketing research. Yearbook 2005)*, pp. 165-180. Haarlem (NL): De Vrieseborch.

Schuitema, G., & Steg, L. (2008). The role of revenue use in the acceptability of transport pricing policies. *Transportation Research F: Psychology and Behaviour, 11*, 221-231.

Schuitema, G., Steg, L., & Forward, S. (2009). Explaining differences in acceptability before and acceptance after the implementation of a congestion charge in Stockholm. Manuscript submitted for publication.

Schultz, P. W., Nolan, J., Cialdini, R., Goldstein, N., & Griskevicius, V. (2007). The constructive, destructive, and reconstructive power of social norms. *Psychological Science, 18*, 429-434.

Schultz, P. W., Oskamp, S., & Mainieri, T. (1995). Who recycles and when? A review of personal and situational factors. *Journal of Environmental Psychology, 15*, 105-121.

Schultz, P. W., & Zelezny, L. C. (1998). Values and proenvironmental behaviour. A five-country study. *Journal of Cross-Cultural Psychology, 29*, 540-558.

Schultz, P.W., Zelezny, L.C. 1999. Values as predictors of environmental attitudes: evidence for consistency across 14 countries. Journal of Environmental Psychology 19, 255–265.

Schwartz, S. H. (1977). Normative influences on altruism. In L. Berkowitz (Ed.), *Advances in experimental social psychology, 10* (pp. 221-279). New York: Academic Press.

Schwartz, S. H., & Howard, J. A. (1981). A normative decision-making model of altruism. In: J.P. Rushton, *Altruism and helping behaviour: Social, personality and developmental perspectives* (pp. 189-211). Hillsdale N.J.: Erlbaum.

Seligman, C., & Darley, J.M. (1977). Feedback as a means of decreasing residential Energy consumption. *Journal of Applied Psychology, 62* (4), 363-368.

Siero, F.W., Bakker, A.B., Dekker, G.B., & Van den Burg, M.T.C. (1996). Changing organizational energy consumption behavior through comparative feedback. *Journal of Environmental Psychology, 16*, 235-246.

Slavin, R.E., Wodarski, J.S., & Blackburn, B.L. (1981). A group contingency for electricity conservation in master-metered apartments. *Journal of Applied Behavior Analysis, 14*, 357-363.

Spaargaren, G. (2003). Sustainable consumption: A theoretical and environmental policy perspective. *Society and Natural Resources, 16*, 687 – 701.

Staats, H.J., Wit, A.P., & Midden, C.Y.H. (1996). Communicating the greenhouse effect to the public: evaluation of a mass media campaign from a social dilemma perspective. *Journal of Environmental Management, 45*, 189-203.

Steg, L. (1999). *Verspilde energie? [Wasted energy?]* (SCP Report no. 126). Den Haag, the Netherlands: Social and Cultural Planning Office of the Netherlands.

Steg, L. (2005). Car use: lust and must. Instrumental, symbolic and affective motives for car use. *Transportation Research A, 39*, 147-162.

Steg, L., De Groot, J.I.M., Dreijerink, L., Abrahamse, W., & Siero, F. (in press). General antecedents of personal norms, policy acceptability, and intentions: The role of values, worldviews, and environmental concern. *Society and Natural Resources.*

Steg, L., Dreijerink, L., & Abrahamse, W. (2005). Factors influencing the acceptability of energy policies: testing VBN theory. *Journal of Environmental Psychology, 25*, 415-425.

Steg, L., Dreijerink, L., & Abrahamse, W. (2006). Why are energy policies acceptable and effective? *Environment and Behavior, 38*, 92-111.

Steg, L., & Gifford, R. (2005). Sustainable transport and quality of life. *Journal of Transport Geography, 13*, 59-69.

Steg, L., & Schuitema, G. (2007). Behavioural responses to transport pricing: a theoretical analysis. In: T. Gärling & L. Steg (Eds.), *Threats to the quality of urban life from car traffic: problems, causes, and solutions* (pp. 347-366). Amsterdam: Elsevier.

Steg, L., & Vlek, C. (2008). Encouraging pro-environmental behaviour: An integrative review and research agenda. *Journal of Environmental Psychology*, in press.

Stern, P. C. (1999). Information, incentives, and proenvironmental consumer behavior. *Journal of Consumer Policy, 22*, 461-478.

Stern, P. C. (2000). Toward a coherent theory of environmentally significant behavior. *Journal of Social Issues, 56* (3), 407-424.

Stern, P. C., & Dietz, T. (1994). The value basis of environmental concern. *Journal of Social Issues, 50* (3), 65-84.

Stern, P.C., Dietz, T., Abel, T., Guagnano, G.A., & Kalof, L. (1999). A value-belief-norm theory of support for social movements: the case of environmentalism. *Human Ecology Review, 6*, 81-97.

Stern, P. C., Dietz, T., Kalof, L., & Guagnano, G. A. (1995). Values, beliefs, and proenvironmental action: attitude formation toward emergent attitude objects. *Journal of Applied Social Psychology, 25*, 1611-1636.

Thøgersen, J. (2005). How may consumer policy empower consumers for sustainable lifestyles? *Journal of Consumer Policy, 28*, 143-178.

Tobler, Ch., Visschers, V.H.M. & Siegrist, M. (2009). Environmental food assessment by consumers. *2009 MAPP Workshop: "Food choice and sustainability".* Middlefart (Denmark), May 13-14, 2009.

Vining, J., & Ebreo, A. (1992). Predicting recycling behavior form global and specific environmental attitudes and changes in recycling opportunities. *Journal of Applied Social Psychology, 22* (20), 1580-1607.

Vining, J., & Ebreo, A. (2002). Emerging theoretical and methodological perspectives on conservation behavior. In R. B. Bechtel & A. Churchman, *Handbook of environmental psychology* (pp. 551-558). New York: Wiley.

Vlek, C. (2000). Essential psychology for environmental policy making. *International Journal of Psychology, 35* (2), 153-167.

Vringer, K., & Blok, K. (1995). The direct and indirect energy requirements of households in the Netherlands. *Energy Policy, 23*, 10, 893-910.

Wang, T. H., & Katzev, R. D. (1990). Group commitment and resource conservation: Two field experiments on promoting recycling. *Journal of Applied Social Psychology, 20*, 265-275.

Warriner, G.K., McDougall, G.H., & Claxton, J.D. (1984). Any data or none at all? Living with inaccuracies in self-reports of residential energy consumption. *Environment and Behavior, 16*, 503-526.

Weenig, M. W. H., & Midden, C. J. H. (1991). Communication network influences on information diffusion and persuasion. *Journal of Personality and Social Psychology, 61*, 734-742.

Winett, R.A., Love, S.Q., & Kidd, C. (1982-1983). The effectiveness of an energy specialist and extension agents in promoting summer energy conservation by home visits. *Journal of Environmental Systems, 12*, 61-70.

Part II.
Antecedent Psychological Dimensions of Sustainability

Chapter 5

ECOLOGICAL WORLDVIEWS

Bernardo Hernández[*], *Ernesto Suárez, Stephany Hess*
Universidad de La Laguna, Spain
and Victor Corral-Verdugo
Universidad de Sonora, Mexico

ABSTRACT

Conceptions regarding how the world works and what is humankind's role in its relations with nature are approached as *Ecological Worldviews*. This chapter firstly reviews the Worldview general concept and then discusses the way Environmental Psychology has so far analyzed systems of belief, values, attitudes, ideological principles concerning human being – environment relations, and, especially, how these aspects are integrated within ecological worldviews. Particular attention is paid to a contraposition between the worldview privileging an anthropo-centered and exceptionalist vision of human-environment relations and the alternative bio-centered worldview. This contraposition is reviewed by considering, in the one hand, the New Environmental Paradigm (NEP) and Dominant Social Paradigm (DSP) tenets, and, on the other hand, the anthropocentrism - ecocentrism attitudinal duality that is apparent in ecological worldviews. The chapter also analyzes the Human Interdependence concept at the basis of sustainability and sustainable development notions, by considering this concept as the core of a New Human Interdependence Paradigm, an ecological worldview encompassing and integrating ecocentric and anthropocentric systems of belief. Finally, the chapter presents results from an empirical study aimed at deepening on the conceptualization of this new ecological paradigm.

---

[*] Corresponding author: Prof. Bernardo Hernández, Facultad de Psicología, Campus de Guajara, s/n 38205, La Laguna, Tenerife, Spain. E-mail: bhdezr@ull.es

INTRODUCTION

In the cartography of psychosocial knowledge, beliefs about the person-environment relationship have been repeatedly defined through a dualist approach, according to which it is more or less explicitly assumed that pro-environmental interest and interest in human development are mutually conflicting. The focal point of discussion and debate in this analysis of belief systems about relations between humans and the environment lies in the comparison between the New Environmental Paradigm (NEP) and the Dominant Social Paradigm (DSP) ever since Dunlap and Liere (1978) proposed their assessment through a general, simple and reliable scale. The duality of environmental beliefs represented by the DSP-NEP dichotomy ultimately corresponds to the radical distinction between an anthropocentric and exceptionalist notion of person-environment relations and a biocentric perspective of these relations. This dual approach is endorsed in various fields of psychoenvironmental knowledge. For example, in the field of environmental attitudes it is sustained in terms of anthropocentrism-ecocentrism, as reflected in Thompson and Barton's (1994) scale. Similarly, when analyzing the motives for acting pro-environmentally, a distinction is usually made between attention to the human (selfish or altruistic motives) and attention to the non-human (biospherism and associated reasons) interests (Schultz, 2001; Stern 2000). However, in the face of such approaches, the situation of ecological emergency in which humanity found itself in the latter part of the 20th century compels us to consider an eco-social, holistic and comprehensive view that emerges from the philosophy of sustainability as the only possible option to distance ourselves from the irreversibility of collapse.

Whether considering the entire planet or a specific territory, sustainability depends on the adequate combination of scientific and technological knowledge, economic relations and social habits. This integrated perspective involves at least three basic principles (Fernández-Buey, 2006):

a) Limitation of resources makes the indefinite growth of the Gross Domestic Product inviable, particularly when bearing in mind the unequal distribution of consumption and wealth. That is, environmental sustainability is also social and presupposes the application of the principle of equity, so that human development includes all the inhabitants of the planet.
b) Sustainability implies a far-reaching technological reorientation aimed at achieving ecological efficiency. Nevertheless, eco-efficiency should be considered not only in terms of a responsible consumption of natural resources but also under the assumption that such resource-saving will necessarily generate economic returns. That is, respect for environmental quality should be the origin of economic activity.
c) Sustainable development involves changing both the economic paradigm and the mentality (or social paradigm) that upholds it. In fact, this change of mentality entails revealing, among other aspects, the disparity that exists between the amount of goods produced, and the social and ecological costs associated with production. That is, orientation towards sustainability above all involves transforming ways of interpreting and assessing socio-economic practices, in such a way that they incorporate the environmental dimension as an essentially valuable criterion.

In this sense, analyzing sustainability as the governing principle behind human actions necessarily entails considering the role played by communities' ideological systems, values and beliefs—or any of their strata—in the pursuit of social development, which may be described as sustainable. This chapter reviews how Environmental Psychology has addressed the analysis of such beliefs, values, attitudes, ideological principles and behaviors, and particularly how these aspects are integrated into the worldviews that ultimately configure the relation between people and the environment.

WORLDVIEWS AND THE ENVIRONMENT

The consideration of environmental factors as a dimension central to decision-making about the future of humanity differentiates the social and economic development of the last forty years from the events in previous periods of history. The oil crisis of the 70s made citizens acutely aware of the importance of natural resources and the global dimension of growth models. Nevertheless, if the book *Limits to Growth* (Meadows, Meadows, Randers and Behrens, 1972) emphasized the need to promote -through technological, cultural and institutional change- social innovation to reduce humanity's ecological footprint, the fact is that 30 years later the authors still insist that humanity's footprint continues its unstoppable growth. In fact, in connection with social welfare, they consider that environmental over-exploitation is a much more relevant concept for people's wellbeing in the XXI century than free trade and consumption (Meadows, Randers & Meadows, 2004).

Social diffusion of the awareness of ecological limits has numerous precedents and intellectual roots in scientific fields as wide-ranging as biology, ecology, geology, geography and urban studies. In fact, little doubt remains when stating that the delimitation of the ecological crisis as an object of ethical and social reflection is located within the very core of scientific descriptions and explanations of the world. These explanations were contributed in the late 60s by natural sciences and economics through authors such as Carson (1962), Commoner (1967, 1972), Georgescu-Roegen (1971) and Schumacher (1973), among others.

A return to the practice of including environmental variables into its disciplinary analysis occurred at practically the same time in the field of the social sciences (Lemkow, 2002). Ecological awareness (and its expression and integration in the form of worldviews) presupposes not only the review of relations between humans and their natural surroundings but also tends to expand and equally include relations with the social environment, that is, humans with other humans. In this sense, the most critical and radical perspective is found in works from disciplinary fields, such as social ecology and environmental sociology, which do not hesitate to highlight ecological problems as a fundamental sociological issue. Thus, Bookchin (1982) indicates that the gravity of a joint social and ecological crisis is of such magnitude that it is extremely difficult to expect solutions from the interpretations of reality that have in themselves caused the crises: socially dominant and conservative ways of thinking. The need for a modification in the way person-environment relations are conceived becomes a necessary condition for social change and ecological rehabilitation. Along similar lines, Gorz (1975) points out that the options for overcoming the environmental crisis call for modifying the foundations of the productive economy and instigating a cultural change in notions of wealth, consumption, work and progress.

The epistemological basis of the theoretical approach identified as the "ecological paradigm" must be sought in the usage of the *ecosystem* as a basic unit. This assumption would indeed be particularly significant in disciplinary fields like anthropology or the already mentioned environmental sociology (Liebow, 2002). From this perspective, a holistic, systemic, dynamic and integrated analysis is advocated that also contemplates the human dimension as a major organizing principle of every ecosystem (Bonnes and Bonaiuto, 2002). Moreover, the distinguishing hypothesis of the ecological perspective presupposes contemplating that "community is the essential adaptive mechanism" (Hawley, 1986; Sosa, 1990). Accordingly, this highlights the inevitability of considering individuals as group members who must also be conceived by scrutinizing their complex relations with other groups (or species) and their surroundings.

These new ways of understanding relations between people and the environment constitute what Bechtel (1997, 2000) has called the "Third Revolution in Human Thinking". In this sense, Macy and Brown (1998) identify the current moment as "The Great Turning", characterized by a fundamental shift in worldview and values, associated with actions intended to slow the damage to Earth, and by the identification of its structural causes and the creation of solutions.

Worldviews provide a framework for the way a person or a whole community makes sense of life and the world in its most significant aspects and dimensions (Irzik and Nola, 2009). Moreover, Maxwell (1980) and Morgan and Peters (2006) define a worldview as articulated and enacted answers to such questions as: 1) what kind of world is this? 2) how do we fit into the world and how did we come to be? 3) what is of most value in life and how is it to be achieved? and 4) how can we develop a better world? These questions entail considering ontological, ethico-political and instrumental aspects at the same time. Thus, a worldview implies a broad-ranging and comprehensive set of principles that act as an interpretative framework, in addition to defining the way in which these principles are expressed in social practices.

From this perspective, conceptions about the functioning of the universe and the role of humanity vis-à-vis nature are recognized as ecological worldviews (Devall and Sessions, 1985; Steg, Dreijerink and Abrahamse, 2005), habitually operationalized in psychosocial terms as systems of values, beliefs and environmental attitudes (Dunlap, Van Liere, Mertig and Jones, 2000; Hernández, Suárez, Martínez-Torvisco and Hess, 2000; Stern, Dietz and Guagnano, 1995). There is, in fact, a majority agreement when pinpointing in the analysis of ecological worldviews the distinction between an anthropomorphic tradition and a tradition (or traditions) in which the human dimension is only considered as yet another element in a higher-order system. This view, which does not pivot on the human dimension, tends to be identified as bio- or eco-centered (Bonnes and Bonaiuto, 2002).

ECOLOGICAL WORLDVIEWS:
THE ROLE OF ANTHROPOCENTRISM AND ECOCENTRISM

The value attributed to the environment and the way in which the reasons, motives and explanations of the person-environment link are conceived constitute the basic principles of Ecological Worldviews (EWVs). EWVs are thus looked upon as the interpretative framework on which the collective awareness of ecological crisis is built insofar as a set of phenomena—overexploitation of resources, reduced biodiversity, pollution, climate change, desertification, health threats associated with modernization and industrial production, overdevelopment—resulting from social practices that have disregarded the environmental parameter during their realization.

Taking Cultural Theory as a starting point, Poortinga, Steg and Vlek (2003) identify four Myths of Nature: Benign, Tolerant, Ephemeral and Capricious. Each myth is associated with a corresponding way of life (Individualistic, Hierarchical, Egalitarian and Fatalistic). In addition, each myth successively gives rise to a particular view of nature, a differentiated degree of environmental interest and perception of global warming, and a preference for various environmental management strategies (See Table 1).

Altman and Chemers (1980) develop a similar approach and identify three general conceptions when describing the bond between humans and nature. According to the first orientation, *the human being is subjugated by nature* and lives at the mercy of her powers. These powers are associated with the beneficent or vengeful will of the divinity. This conception has a strong presence in societies and historical periods of limited scientific and technological development. The second orientation proposes a diametrically opposed perspective, according to which *the human being is a different and exceptional being* compared to other living creatures. This superiority confers humans the right to exercise absolute control over nature. Moreover, humans are not ruled by natural laws since they know them and are capable of handling them for their own aims. In the western world, such concerns stemmed from the industrial and scientific revolution that emerged in the Enlightenment. Finally, the third conception defines *the human being as part of nature* and on an equal footing with other creatures. The basic principle of this orientation is the harmonious regulation of the human presence in nature. Traditional eastern cultures (Asian, African) and Native American groups believe that humans exist in a harmonious relationship with nature.

Accordingly, EWVs can be analyzed in the light of anthropological and cultural phenomena or indeed, from the history of civilizations, to the extent that human cultures have attributed a different value to nature. For example, discussions about sustainable alternatives frequently throw up references to concepts such as Traditional Ecological Knowledge, Indigenous Knowledge or, in connection with ways of life, the Indigenous Ways of Living in Nature. This orientation links indigenous tradition to holistic, empirical, intuitive and spiritual knowledge, place-based descriptions and explanations of nature that take the form of a harmonious bond between people and the environment. It is also assumed that such a tradition sustains a series of principles (largely implicit) of a metaphysical, epistemological and normative nature: "that unite most, but not all, Indigenous communities and nations worldwide" (Aikenhead and Ogawa, 2007, p. 556). In turn, these indigenous worldviews appear to confront the Judeo-Christian tradition in which the anthropocentric cultural roots of western thought and technoscience are identified.

Anthropocentrism conceives human beings as dominant entities within nature, insofar as they are considered highly capable of modifying the environment according to their needs and interests, either as specific social groups or as a species. The concept of "natural resource" largely reflects how the environment is regarded as an accessory to human life. Catton and Dunlap (1980) summarize the four basic suppositions of the western world's anthropocentric view: 1) humans are fundamentally different from other living beings, 2) humans have free will and "personal agency", 3) the world provides unlimited opportunities for human growth and 4) the course of human history leads to progress, which must never cease.

From these basic assumptions emerge anthropocentric attitudes, but also those of individualism and industrialism (Corral-Verdugo, Tapia, Fraijo, Mireles, and Márquez, 2008). Furthermore, the anthropocentric presupposition is couched in the value of power and dominion over nature. Environmental quality is defined now and always in relation to humans: the implications for human survival are what make the environment a significant and valuable element (Kortenkamp and Moore, 2001). All in all, the functional and utilitarian trait of the person-environment bond established by anthropocentrism has meant that this orientation is both the origin of practices that have led to the situation of global ecological crisis and the basis of environmental interest.

Hence, White (1967) identified the root of arguments in favour of the indiscriminate exploitation of nature in the predominance of the Judeo-Christian doctrine of the creation of the world and the exceptional role assigned to humans: *"So God created Man in his own image, in the image of God created he them; male and female created he them. And God blessed them, and God said unto them, Be fruitful, and multiply, and replenish the earth, and subdue it; and have dominion over the fish of the sea, and over the fowl of the air, and over every living thing that moveth upon the earth".* (Genesis 1, Verses 27 and 28). According to White, in western societies the Judeo-Christian worldview would have destroyed the biocentric inhibitions that linked preceding cultures. Despite the criticism levelled against these arguments (for a review, see Attfield, 1994 and Schultz, Zelezny and Dalrymple, 2000), the fact is that the exceptionality attributed to humans is historically reinforced by techno-scientific proposals (ever more complex and with increasing environmental impact) incorporated into the lifestyles and patterns of consumption in post-industrial societies (Riechmann, 2006). Ultimately, anthropocentrism suggests the humankind-versus-nature dichotomy.

Moreover, anthropocentrism forms the basis of environmental interest, as knowledge of the effects that the degradation of ecosystems has on human beings acquires more significance (Nordlund and Garvill, 2003). Is it feasible to talk then about radical anthropocentrism vis-à-vis moderate or soft anthropocentrism? In accordance with McCloskey (1983) what surely has occurred is not so much a modification of the basic motivational orientation but a change in beliefs that sustain this perspective. According to this author, anthropocentrism has gradually incorporated beliefs that assume interconnectedness, which have been developed within scientific disciplines.

This moderate interpretation of anthropocentrism in turn implies the identification of a series of normative principles establishing the rational foundation of environmental ethics (Gómez-Heras, 2002): a) the development of intergenerational solidarity and the defense of the rights of future generations, b) the application of deontological criteria of equality and justice to access to environmental resources, c) the identification of basic human needs (nutrition, health, cognitive-affective restoration) directly associated with maintaining a balanced environment and d) the assessment of nature as a result of the value of personal and social identity and in relation to place identity.

Table 1. Myths of Nature and Associated Factors

	View on nature	Environmental Concern	Perceived Global Warming	Management strategy
Benign Nature	Resilient	Low	Low	Free market and Technology
Tolerant Nature	Moderately vulnerable	Average	Average	Government regulation
Ephemeral Nature	Fragile	High	High	Behavioral Change
Capricious Nature	None	Low	Average	No preference

Adapted from Poortinga, Steg and Vlek (2003), p. 281.

Ecocentrism, on the other hand, regards human beings as just another feature of ecological systems. In terms of belief systems, the ecocentric stance on person-environment relations emerged from the inevitable consideration of humans as members of the community of life on earth, or biotic community, as outlined in the seminal work *The Land Ethics* by Leopold (1949). Normative criteria and ideas derived from this central hypothesis include 1) the existence of a complex web (ecosystems) that connects the various components of that community means that the operations (and survival) of some depend on others, 2) actions will be appropriate and "right" if they preserve the integrity and stability of ecosystems and the community, 3) the rejection of the principle of human exceptionality and 4) the development of an attitude of respect for nature and for the diversity of non-human life forms (Attfield, 1994; Sosa, 1990).

The appearance in 1994 of Suzanne Gagnon Thompson and Michelle Barton's scale provided Environmental Psychology with a conceptual and instrumental tool to discern the influence of anthropocentrism and ecocentrism on (pro) environmental interest. These authors contemplated the distinction, in attitudinal terms, between interest in the environment based on an anthropocentric view and interest rooted in an ecocentric conception of person-environment relations. Attitudes rooted in anthropocentrism appraise nature as a source of wellbeing and defend it as a basic feature to maintain quality of life. By way of contrast, attitudes rooted in ecocentrism denote a positive appraisal of the environment and its preservation because of its intrinsic value (Thompson and Barton, 1994).

However, Thompson and Barton discovered in their research that only ecocentrism relates positively to pro-environmental behavior. Anthropocentrism did not correlate with caring for the environment. Therefore, although anthropocentrism, at least the soft version, may form part of the arguments of environmentalism, it has no influence whatsoever on environmentally responsible personal actions. Similar results were found by Nordlund and Garvill (2002). The study was conducted as a mail-back survey of 1414 randomly selected residents between 18 and 65 years of age in Umeå, Sweden. Results showed that only ecocentrism correlated significantly with the general mean calculated from 25 different pro-environmental behaviors. The behaviors represented different domains of everyday actions such as recycling/reuse, environmentally responsible consumption, energy conservation and transportation behavior. Heath and Gifford (2006) analyzed the relation between both factors and the intention to take action to address negative effects of global climate change measured using a simple scale (four items). Once again the results obtained showed only the significance of ecocentric orientation.

In line with these findings, the anthropocentrism-ecocentrism duality, when bearing in mind the behavioral dimension and social practices, only partly helps to distinguish between different EWVs. To discover the extent to which anthropocentric or ecocentric interest shapes the heart of more or less opposing worldviews requires an analysis of the relations of both roots of environmental interest with other psychosocial factors or dimensions, in particular those concerned with value orientations and moral judgements that sustain and justify environmental practices. For example, Karpiak and Baril (2008) indicate that ecocentrism is significantly connected to moral reasoning based on criteria of justice, impartiality, rights and obligations; in other words, the highest level of moral development. However, these authors did not found significant relation between anthropocentrism and this level of moral reasoning.

A consistent line of research promoted by Paul Stern and Wesley Schultz has led to the identification of significant relations between motives and value orientations when explaining interest and environmental behavior. Stern and colleagues (Stern, Dietz and Kalof, 1993; Stern and Dietz, 1994; Stern, 2000) suggested that there are three value bases for environmental concern: self-interest, humanistic altruism and biospheric altruism. The self-interest basis of environmental concern comes from caring about the environment because it influences us and those we care about. The second reason for caring about the environment is altruism toward the social or humanistic environment (from family to a larger community or all of humanity). Obviously, these two approaches are basically anthropocentric and assign instrumental values to the environment. Only the third basis for concern, biospheric altruism, is directed toward other species or the state of ecosystems themselves. In other words, only biospheric altruism acknowledges the intrinsic value of the environment: the ecocentric perspective (Dietz, Fitzgerald and Shwom, 2005).

From a cross-cultural perspective and by comparing the responses of 2160 people in fourteen different countries, Schultz and Zelesny (1999) examined the link between anthropocentrism-ecocentrism and values, among other aspects, using the value structure proposed by Schwartz (1994). Their results show that the relation between ecocentrism and values follows a different pattern than that of anthropocentrism. Accordingly, ecocentrism was predicted by universalism (positively), power (negatively) and tradition (negatively). In contrast, anthropocentric concerns were significantly related to benevolence (negatively), power (positively), tradition (positively) and security (positively). Therefore, while self-transcendent values are positively associated with ecocentrism, the self-enhancement value was negatively related to ecocentrism and positively related to anthropocentrism. This pattern was consistent across different countries.

From these findings, Schultz provides an alternative explanation to that considered by Stern for whom environmental interest responded to an altruistic sense. However, Schultz regards self-transcendence as connected to a broader cognitive representation of self, which would therefore include awareness of the environmental dimension: "self as part of nature" (p.263), while self-enhancement denotes quite the opposite, a narrow definition, centred on egoistic concern. Stemming from this is the different contribution of ecocentrism and anthropocentrism to the dimensional structure of values. Schultz (2001) subsequently found a positive relationship between ratings of the interconnectedness of self and nature and environmental concerns (biospheric and altruistic but not egoistic).

In this sense, there may be evidence to suggest the existence of the mechanics of internalization (and integration in the self) of the reasons that sustain environmental values orientation by differentiating between ecocentrism and anthropocentrism. In research that connected both elements with the reasons behind pro-environmental action, Suárez, Salazar-Laplace, Hernández and Martín (2007) found a significant positive correlation between anthropocentrism and a factor of external motivation (in reference to people's concern to act pro-environmentally to avoid criticism or negative reactions from others), insofar as ecocentrism correlated with internal motivation (pro-environmental action as a result of high personal standards).

A similar conclusion can be drawn from research by Dutcher, Finley, Luloff and Buttolph Johnson (2007) using the concept of connectivity with nature. These authors believe that inclusion with nature is a theoretically sound approach to conceptualizing and measuring environmental values. Connectivity with nature means experiencing nature as a part of a community and not just as the raw material for society. Community and connectivity involve a sense of belonging, and that sense of belonging includes not only each other but also some sense of place, one that exists on a human time scale. The results obtained by these authors show that connectivity accounted for 17% of the variation in environmental concern and 10% of the variation in environmental behavior of a sample of 741 US landowners. From this perspective, both Person and Nature are aspects of a general sense of connectivity ("I see myself as part of a larger whole in which everything is connected by a common essence").

In any case, the environmental interest that defines EWVs must be linked to other dimensions of a cultural kind. Along these lines, Sarigöllü (2009) investigates, among other aspects, the differential role of basic cultural orientations such as factors associated with environmental attitudes, analyzing the influence of four dimensions: a) collectivism-individualism, b) temporal perspectivism (especially orientation to the past and the future), c) materialistic versus post-materialistic values and d) (internal-external) locus of control. Comparing the responses of residents in Istanbul (Turkey) and Montreal (Canada), the results obtained indicate that collectivism, orientation to the past, external locus of control and materialistic values are related to a more positive attitude. The differential effects of cultural factors are also identified when bearing in mind the degree of specificity of attitudes. In accordance with these results, the relative importance of general pro-environmental attitude and specific attitude (attitude towards behavior) varies over populations differing in cultural factors. Thus, in internally controlled cultures (Canada), general attitude accounts for most variance in environmental concern. However, in externally controlled cultures like Turkey, activity attitude accounts for most variance in environmental concern. In line with these conclusions, Hernández, Suárez, Martínez-Torvisco and Hess (1997) identified that anthropocentrism is closer to individualism insofar as ecocentrism is closer to collectivism.

In the final analysis, Dietz (2003) points out that values should not be thought of as having a single value or weight for each individual, but rather that each individual has some variability in the importance (s)he assigns to a value. Individual values exist, but because the importance assigned to them is not fixed, the weight given to a value in making an environmental decision depends on the context (cultural and situational) as defined by the individual.

Therefore, the anthropocentrism versus ecocentrism dimension appears to contribute to shaping a worldview that humans develop particularly with regard to their relationship with the environment. However, several results have indicated that specific value orientations are also present in this cosmoview, in addition to cultural and contextual elements that must be taken into consideration (i.e. Göksen, Adaman and Zenginobuz, 2002). Similarly, the particular conceptions shared by each individual are often the result of a personal synthesis that frequently exceeds dual approaches. However, the anthropocentrism-ecocentrism dichotomy is not the only one that has directed psychoenvironmental research on worldviews and their relation to ecological behavior. On the contrary, from a perspective that transfers the idea of scientific paradigm to social knowledge it has been proposed that the way to understand person-environment relations be explained from the confrontation between social paradigms.

THE NEW ENVIRONMENTAL PARADIGM AS ECOLOGICAL WORLDVIEW

In the field of Environmental Psychology, the most successful approach to the concept of ecological worldviews is undoubtedly the New Environmental Paradigm (NEP), as defined in 1978 by R.E. Dunlap and K.D. Van Liere. In fact, Bechtel (2000) identifies Dunlap and Van Liere's operative contribution, the NEP Scale, as the best way of defining the environmental revolution in thinking as "the realization that humans are not above nature and that there are limits to resources in the environment" (p. 3). The NEP was presented as an opposing worldview to that of the Dominant Social Paradigm (DSP).

The concept of the DSP refers to the prominent worldview through which individuals and society interpret the world. In modern western societies, the DSP supports individualism and laissez-faire government, highlights the belief in material progress, faith in the efficacy of science and technology, and a view of nature as something to be used (Dunlap, 2008). According to the DSP, material progress is the only social value possible and nature only responds to the criterion of satisfying human needs. Likewise, from an environmental perspective, the core belief of the DSP holds that humans are an exception to the laws of nature, and consequently human activity stands apart from ecological principles.

The DSP encompasses political, economic and technological dimensions. The political dimension includes commitment to limited government regulation, support for private property rights, and an emphasis on liberty and economic individualism. Support for free enterprise and belief in the likelihood of unlimited economic growth are characteristic of the dominant economic worldview. The technological dimension of the DSP reflects a faith in the ability of science and technology to solve human problems, including environmental degradation (Shafer, 2006). The antagonism between the DSP and environmental interest was analyzed by Kilbourne Beckmann and Thelen (2002) who found that each of the three DSP dimensions measured (economic, political, and technological) had a significant negative relation with perceived environmental problems, perceived condition of the environment and general environmental concern.

In comparison, the NEP has been defined as a constellation of attitudes that represent adherence to a new view of human relations with nature and the environment (Vining and Ebreo, 1992). According to Dunlap and Van Liere's original proposal, the structure of interest and social evaluation of actions to protect and preserve the environment was organized around four basic elements: 1) the existence of limits to growth, 2) the importance of maintaining the balance of nature, 3) the promotion of a sustainable economy and 4) the need to review the principle of human exceptionality (Dunlap and Van Liere, 1978).

For over three decades, research on the NEP has turned up three parallel lines of work. The first is directed at the operationalization of the NEP through the creation and validation of measuring instruments. The second analyzes the degree of acceptance and sociological distribution of the paradigm. And the third examines the validity of the scale, by relating the NEP to pro-environmental behavior and to other elements of the system of beliefs and social values.

Initially a considerable part of the efforts to analyze the NEP were aimed at creating the scale (Dunlap and Van Liere, 1978; 1984; Van Liere and Dunlap, 1980; 1981). The instrument originally included twelve items: four statements that address concepts connected to the *limits of human growth* (the idea that natural resources are not infinite), four associated with the concept of *ecological balance* (the need to balance the satisfaction of human needs with ecological requirements) and another four referring to the consideration of humans as exceptional (a unique, superior species not limited by the restrictions imposed by how ecosystems function). This scale was administered to 1213 adults living in Washington State, along with another 35 items concerning pollution, population and natural resources. The factorial analysis of the responses to the 12 items on the scale generated a factor on which the eight statements of pro-NEP beliefs saturated, and another factor with four pro-DSP statements (Dunlap and Van Liere, 1978).

However, this structure has not been confirmed in subsequent studies. For example, Albretch, Bultena and Holberg and Nowak (1982) administered this same scale to residents of Iowa (USA) and reported three factors. Some items corresponded to the DSP, but the others that would correspond to the NEP were grouped into two factors named "Balance of Nature" and "Limits to Growth". Moreover, Edgell and Nowell (1989) in Canada, and Kuhn and Jackson (1989) and Noe and Snow (1990a, 1990b) in the USA reported a tri-factorial structure underlying the responses to this scale. Gooch (1995) studied responses from Swedes and residents in the Baltic countries and found a NEP-DSP bi-factorial structure, although both factors did not contain the same statements as in Dunlap and Van Liere (1978). In Mexico, using confirmatory factor analysis, Corral-Verdugo, Bechtel, Armendáriz and Esquer (1997) obtained a tri-factorial structure similar to that of Albretcht et al. (1982). However, the first two factors ("Limits to Growth" and "Balance of Nature") made up a second-order factor that coincided with the NEP.

Nonetheless, although the authors themselves acknowledge that there is little consensus on whether the scale measures a single construct or is multidimensional (Dunlap, Van Liere, Mertig and Jones, 2000), it is assumed in practically all cases that it provides a general positive measure of environmental protection (i.e. Stern, Dietz, Guagnano, 1995). When applying the NEP Scale, Dunlap and Van Liere (1984) and Van Liere and Dunlap (1981) found high percentages of acceptance of their postulates among American participants. These results were replicated in studies carried out in various countries including Sweden and the Baltic States (Gooch, 1995), Turkey (Furman, 1998), Mexico (Corral-Verdugo and Armendáriz, 2000), China (Chung and Poon, 2000), Peru and Japan (Bechtel, Corral-Verdugo, Asai and González-Riesle, 2006), which revealed a high acceptance of ecocentric postulates around the world. The scale was subsequently revised in its items' number -passing from 12 to 15- and formulation of the items, for adaptation to a more systematic view of environmental problems (Dunlap, Van Liere, Merting and Jones, 2000). This instrument, now known as the New Ecological Paradigm Scale (NEPS), has replaced the original NEP almost entirely.

Dunlap and his colleagues justify their review of the NEP because of the appearance of the newly emerging attitude object (p. 427) and the need to redirect the use given to the NEP measure. In fact, it was an attempt to mitigate the ambiguity implied in considering the scale, without distinction, as a measure of approval of a worldview or as a measure of attitudes, beliefs and even environmental values. Indeed, the authors point out that "a consensus that the NEP items measure such beliefs is emerging, and it seems reasonable to regard a coherent set of these beliefs as constituting a paradigm or worldview that influences attitudes and beliefs toward more specific environmental issues" (p. 428).

Having been defined from this perspective as a pro-ecological orientation that gives rise to environmental beliefs in a wide range of issues, the revised scale was constructed around five facets which form a primary dimension: a) limits to growth, b) anti-anthropocentrism, c) fragility of nature's balance, d) rejection of human exemptionalism and e) belief in an eco-crisis (Dunlap et al., 2000). The data gathered indicate that these five facets may be structured into a single factor, though the authors are open to the possibility that the NEPS may be treated as multidimensional in other populations and contexts.

As with the original version of the NEP, the NEPS has been widely used in various cultural and geographical contexts (Berenguer, Corraliza and Martín, 2005; Casey and Scott, 2006; Hunter and Rinnner, 2004; Vozmediano, and San Juán, 2005, among others). In like manner, it has been adapted to specific populations. For example, there is an NEP Scale for use with children aged from 10 to 12 years. This Scale for Children (Manoli, Johnson, and Dunlap, 2007) contains 10 items that measure three interrelated dimensions: Rights of Nature, Eco-Crisis and Human Exemptionalism.

A second line of work, though related to the former, has underscored the degree to which the beliefs that form the NEP are shared by different social groups. The NEP/NEPS was formulated as a unidimensional representation of the environment and its quality in relation to humans, socially well implanted and highly representative of the ideology of politically organized groups concerned about the environmental situation. Thus, no socio-demographic features are found among environmental activists. However, a differentiated socio-demographic profile is observed in individuals from the overall population who share a conception of the environment that fits the characteristics defined by the NEP.

Accordingly, a negative correlation between age and pro-NEP judgements is observed, while the relation is positive vis-à-vis educational level and liberal political orientation (Dunlap and Van Liere, 1978; Dunlap, Van Liere, Merting and Jones, 2000). These results are consistent with those of other studies (Arcury and Christianson, 1990; Scott and Willits, 1994; Zelesny, Chua and Aldricht, 2000). Individuals living in urban areas are also seen to be more pro-NEP (Berenguer, Corraliza and Martín, 2005; Zelesny, Chua and Aldricht, 2000). This same pattern of results was found by Dunlap, Xiao, and McCright (2002), Jones and Dunlap (1992). Results have been less consistent where gender is concerned. Women have been reported to be more environmentally concerned than men (Xiao and Dunlap, 2007; Zelezny, Chua and Aldrich, 2000), but the stability of this relation has also been questioned (Diamantopoulos, Schlegelmilch, Sinkovics and Bohlen, 2003). Neither is it totally clear whether socio-economic status maintains a positive association with environmental concern (Dunlap, 2008).

Johnson, Bowker and Cordell (2004) examined the convergence of ethnic diversity, a reduced version of the NEPS and environmental behaviors of five ethnic groups (African-Americans, US-born Latinos, Latino emigrants, Asian-Americans and European-Americans) in the United States. Their results showed that when holding constant gender, age, education, residence, family size and political leaning, Blacks and Latino emigrants had significantly lower scores on the NEPS than Whites. Blacks and Latino emigrants were least similar to Whites, Asians were most like Whites, and US-born Latinos assumed a middle position between Blacks and Latino emigrants and Asians. Behavioral differences between ethnic groups varied depending on the kind of environmental behavior (environmental reading, recycling, *joining an environmental or conservation group* and nature participation).

Various studies have also been carried out in several countries (in Latin America and Europe) where significant, though not consistent, differences have been found with the United States. Hence, while higher NEP scores have at times been recorded in the US, at others the difference has been the opposite (i.e.: Rauwald and Moore, 2002; Vikan, Camino, Biaggio and Nordvik, 2007). Nevertheless, it is important to point out that in many of these studies, coefficients for internal consistency reported medium to low values. This may be revealing problems with the cultural suitability of the scale.

The third line of work has essentially been occupied with the validity of the concept and scale used. In this sense, as we have already pointed out, liberal orientation has been seen to relate positively to environmental concern (Samdahl and Robertson; 1989). The NEP has also been connected to other psychosocial indicators. Thus, for example, a negative relation has been found with authoritarianism (Schultz and Stone, 1994) or with egoistic and traditional values, while biospheric values relate positively (González and Amérigo, 2008; Stern, Dietz and Guagnano, 1995).

De Groot and Steg (2007) analyzed relationships between values, the NEPS, problem awareness and ascription of responsibility. Their results show that the three value orientations could be clearly distinguished. Value orientations explained around 30% of the variance in the NEPS. The biospheric value orientation was most strongly related to environmental concern; the more respondents ascribe to biospheric values, the more they are concerned with the environment. The egoistic value orientation contributed significantly to the explanation of environmental concern in an opposite direction. Altruistic value orientations were not significantly related to the NEPS. Value orientations contributed strongly to the explanation of environmental concern and were less strongly related to specific environmental beliefs (awareness of consequences, AC and Ascription of Responsibility, AR). In that sense, values affect behavioral specific beliefs (such as AC and AR) indirectly, via general beliefs, such as the NEP. However, not all three value orientations made a unique and significant contribution to the explanation of AC and AR. Only egoistic values contributed significantly to the explanation of AC, whereas only biospheric value orientations contributed significantly to the explained variance of AR.

In the same direction, the NEP has been related to different behavioral measures, though with contradictory results, since correlations are generally low and not significant. On the one hand, Scott and Willis (1994) found significant correlations between these beliefs and pro-environmental conduct, though they were not very high. Corral-Verdugo and Armendáriz (2000) also obtained a significant covariance between the NEP component "Limits of Growth" and a pro-environmental behavior factor, but the "Balance of Nature" dimension presented no significant relation to pro-environmental behavior. In the same vein, Leung and

Rice (2002) found a significant correlation between the NEP and environmental behavior only for females and for Anglo-Australians, but not for males or for Chinese-Australians. Environmental behaviors were positively associated with endorsement of the NEP Scale in research by Casey and Scott (2006). On the other hand, Mainieri, Barnett, Valdero, Unipan, & Oskamp (1997) reported that, in conjunction with other items that measure general pro-environmental beliefs, the NEP does not predict responsible consumption behavior. Likewise, Berenguer, Corraliza and Martín (2005) pinpoint the lack of correlation between the NEPS and pro-environmental behavior, according to their results. Nevertheless, Dunlap (2008, p. 12) indicated that, given that one reason for weak attitude- behavior relations stems from use of broad attitudinal measures to predict specific behaviors, there was never any reason to expect that the NEP Scale would be a strong predictor of behaviors.

The NEP-DSP dichotomy has been questioned by Lester Milbrath in his analysis of environmentalism as a space for political and social action. Milbrath (1986) agrees that these beliefs and values models are divided into two ecological worldviews. Nevertheless, these worldviews also include opposing beliefs about political and social change. From this perspective, he identifies a dimensional space based on two bipolar constructs. In the first construct, the positive assessment of environmental quality (connected with the NEP) is contrasted with the negative assessment of material progress (related to the DSP). The second construct is structured around the disparity between support for and resistance to social change. From this perspective, the environmentalism worldview implies a) a high evaluation of nature, b) empathy with others, future generations and non human species, c) an interest in avoiding risks to people and nature, d) acknowledgement of the existence of limits to growth and e) a desire to promote social, economic and political change (Milbrath, 1986). On the contrary, the development ideology is characterized by a disinterest in nature, low empathy, the acceptance of risk if it will lead to maximum material wealth, an unlimited conception of growth and the acceptance of prevailing political and economic conditions.

Other results question the duality of a view of person-environment relations in confrontational terms. Hence, studies by Bechtel et al. (Bechtel, Corral-Verdugo and Pinheiro, 1999; Bechtel, Corral-Verdugo, Asai and González-Riesle, 2006) and Corral-Verdugo and Armendáriz (2000) revealed that, when examining how people of different nationalities ascribed to the New Environmental Paradigm, ecocentric beliefs did not contradict anthropocentric beliefs, as was expected. By contrasting the responses of samples of different nationalities in the NEP tool, Bechtel et al. noted that the factor structure depended on the group. In other words, NEP dimensions behaved differently in the various national groups studied. In the American groups, a NEP (or ecocentric) factor was formed that was diametrically opposed to or conflicting with the Human Exception Paradigm (anthropocentric). This was the expected result, according to previous reports from different authors. However, in Latin American and Japanese groups, the NEP and the HEP (Human Exception Paradigm) could covariate positively and significantly (Bechtel et al., 1999; 2006; Corral-Verdugo and Armendáriz, 2000).

In Portugal, Castro and Lima (2001) also found that some people had no difficulty in reconciling these apparently incompatible views. Likewise, Hernández, Corral-Verdugo, Hess and Suárez (2001) show that, in Mexican students, the correlation between beliefs in nature (ecocentric) and beliefs in progress (anthropocentric) are not contradictory. Vikan, Camino, Biaggio and Nordvik (2007, p. 225) applied the NEPS to Brazilian and Norwegian samples and concluded that "...Latin culture gives a relatively more significant rating of the interdependence between humans and nature". These findings taken together suggest the likelihood of an alternative worldview capable of combining anthropocentric and ecocentric beliefs with no fear of contradiction and of glimpsing a potential reconciliation and not merely opposition between them. This new framework or paradigm would be based on a conception of interdependent growth, which would involve a dynamic process of integration and inclusion of human needs into the dynamics of environmental balance.

THE NEW HUMAN INTERDEPENDENCE PARADIGM

The concept of interdependence forms the bedrock of notions of sustainability and sustainable development. Some of the early approaches to the psychosocial implications of sustainable development are included in the book *Psychology of Sustainable Psychology* edited by Schmuck and Schultz (2002) and in the *Handbook of Environmental Psychology* (Bechtel and Churchman, 2002), particularly in the chapters on sustainable development (Bonnes and Bonaiuto, 2002) and on the Human Interdependence Paradigm (Gärling, Biel and Gustafsson, 2002). The Interdependence Principle implies that, in a given ecosystem, the survival of one element depends on the integrity of the others. Consequently, if one component is damaged or lost, the entire system is upset and the remaining elements are affected (Capra and Pauli, 1995).

As an epistemological principle, interdependence entails breaking the duality between anthropocentrism and ecocentrism. As a world-view, it combines both environmental beliefs into a vision that favors the idea that the physical environment needs humans in order to be preserved and that people need nature in order to survive. Concern about the degradation of the physical environment and its resources, combined with an interest in satisfying human needs, gives rise to a holistic worldview, in accordance with the postulates of sustainable development. Interdependence involves a new way of understanding person-environment relations that form the core beliefs of an emerging, integrative and non-dichotomic ecological worldview called the New Human Interdependence Paradigm (Gärling, Biel and Gustafsson, 2002). According to Gärling et al. (op cit), a notorious interdependence exists between the social and the physical environments, so that environmental psychologists should assess how people acknowledge the reciprocal dependencies existing between humans and the environment.

An initial approach to the New Human Interdependence Paradigm Scale (NHIP) was outlined by Corral-Verdugo, Carrus, Bonnes, Moser and Sinha (2008) in an intercontinental study. Corral-Verdugo et al. (2008) conducted research whose general objective was to test the validity of the NHIP construct and its influence on pro-environmental behavior. To that end, the NHIP was contrasted against the NEP, in terms of the predictive capacity of both systems of belief on water conservation practices. The authors created a five-item scale to evaluate the NHIP, assessing its reliability and validity. They added a component of temporal interdependence, to the spatial interdependence recognized by Gärling et al. (2002), among all the human and non-human elements of the biosphere because they considered that the integrity of the future depends on the present and that the conservation of the planet's future directs actions that currently seek to preserve its integrity and life therein. Thus, the scale combines three statements incorporating the idea that human welfare depends on the integrity of nature, and another two that underline the importance of preserving today's resources for future generations.

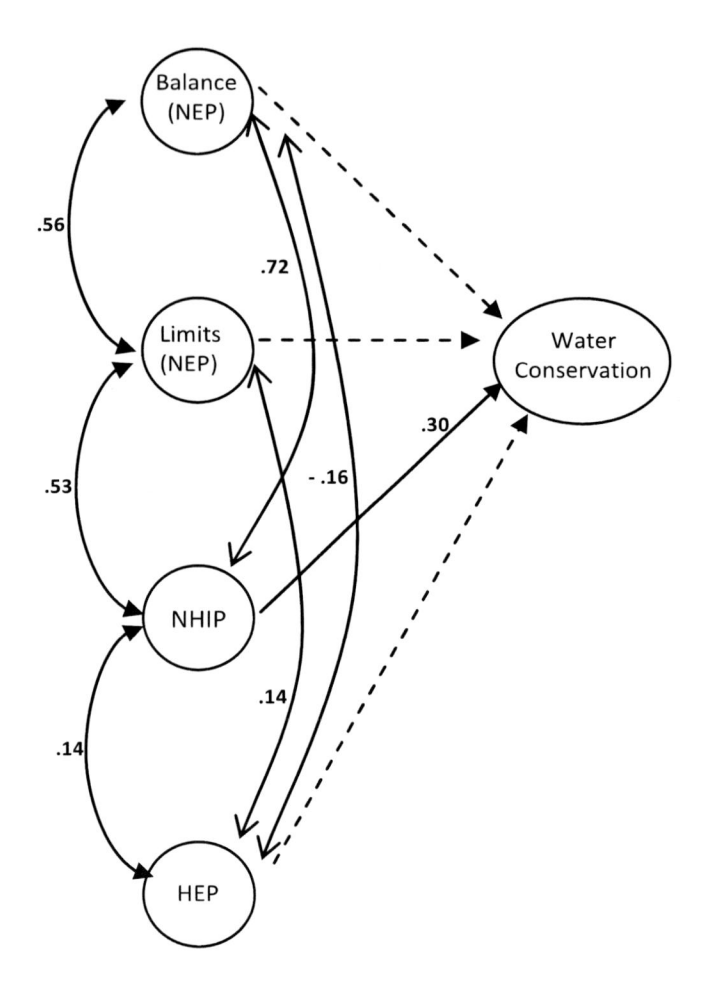

Figure 1. Combined influence of the NEP, HEP and NHIP on Water Conservation practices. Adapted from Corral-Verdugo, Carrus, Bonnes, Moser and Sinha (2008).

The research was conducted using a sample of 759 individuals in France, Italy, Mexico and India. In addition to the NHIP Scale, an eleven-item scale was used to measure water conservation, and the twelve items of Dunlap and Van Liere's NEP Scale (1978). The multi-sample factor analysis confirmed that the NHIP is a uni-factorial construct in the four samples, although the relation between the NHIP and NEP factors varied from country to country. Furthermore, using structural equation model, the results of this study showed that the NHIP was a better predictor of residential water conservation than the NEP (see figure 1).

The significant correlation between the NHIP and the two ecocentric subfactors of the NEP scale (balance and limits) suggest that the NHIP view may have emerged, at least partially, from the NEP. According to these results, the NHIP may constitute a system of beliefs where ecocentric orientation is fundamental, without questioning the importance and centrality of human welfare. Sustainability as a way of life must also include the consideration of socio-cognitive processes involved in the development of expectations, satisfaction of needs and fulfilment of social and individual desires. In other words: elements that are connected with wellbeing and happiness (Schultz, 2001; Winter, 2002).

For the purpose of scrutinizing the conceptualization of the NHIP from its connection to ecocentrism, anthropocentrism and altruism, on the one hand, and of analyzing the predictive power of these variables vis-à-vis pro-environmental behavior, on the other, we conducted an empirical study.

METHOD

The participants were 183 residents of the Tenerife island (Spain). Their age range was 17 to 68 years, with a mean age of 22 years and standard deviation of 5.6. Of the total sample, 84 were women (46.2%) and 98 were men (53.8%).

In addition to the NHIP Scale (Corral-Verdugo et al., 2008), participants completed a smaller version adapted to Spanish (Amérigo, Aragonés, Sevillano and Cortés, 2005) of Thompson and Barton's Anthropocentrism-Ecocentrism Scale (1994), an altruism scale (Corral-Verdugo, Tapia, Frías, Fraijo, and González (2008) and a reduced version of Kaiser's General Ecological Behavior scale (Kaiser, 1998).

RESULTS

Analyzing the responses to individual items of the NHIP, in Table 2 we see that participants show agreement with each item over 90% in all cases, except for item 5, which is 83.6%. The mean obtained for the total scale was 3.49, ranging between 1 (disagreement) and 4 (agreement). The reliability of this scale is indicated by a Cronbach's alpha of 0.70. A principal components analysis showed a single component that explains 46% of the variance with an eigenvalue of 2.3. The saturation of the five items ranged between .58 and .76.

The internal consistency for the Ecocentrism and Anthropocentrism scales was 0.78 and 0.65, respectively. In a range of responses for both scales that varied between 1 and 5, the mean score in Ecocentrism was 4.12, with a standard deviation of 0.63—in other words, very close to the "strongly agree" positions. Conversely, a mean of 2.70 was obtained for Anthropocentrism, with a standard deviation of 0.80—that is, bordering on the central position of "neither agree nor disagree". The Altruism Scale consisted of 10 items; eliminating one of them produced a Cronbach's alpha of 0.69. The *Altruism* variable, created from the mean of the 9 remaining items, has a possible range of 1 to 3. The mean is 1.63, tending towards "nearly always", with a standard deviation of 0.43. On the Ecological Behavior scale, considering a range of possible scores from 0 to 3 (Never-Always), the sample produced a minimum and maximum score of 0.38 and 2.64, respectively. The mean was around 1.66, with a standard deviation of 0.41. The reliability of the scale was indicated by a Cronbach's alpha of 0.72.

The correlations between the analyzed variables show that the NHIP relates significantly to Ecocentrism ($r = 0.38$; $p < 0.05$) and to Ecological Behavior ($r = 0.23$; $p < 0.05$), sharing 5.3% and 14.4% of variance, respectively. In contrast, the correlation of the NHIP with Anthropocentrism and Altruism was not significant. This appears to indicate that we are faced with a system of beliefs in interdependence wherein ecocentric orientation is fundamental and essential without implying the rejection of the objective of satisfying human needs. At least this can be indirectly concluded from the correlation found between Ecocentrism and Altruism ($r = 0.25$; $p < 0.05$).

Table 2. Percentages of agreement for the NHIP items

Item	% Agreed	% Partially Agreed	Total
Humans can progress only by conserving natural resources	61.2	35.5	96.7
Humans can enjoy nature only if we make a wise use of its resources	57.4	37.2	94.5
Human progress can be achieved only by maintaining ecological balance	54.6	36.6	91.3
Preserving nature now means safeguarding the future of humankind	74.3	20.8	95.1
We must reduce our consumption level to ensure wellbeing of the present and future generations	48.6	35.0	83.6

In order to analyze how the inclusion of Ecocentrism, Anthropocentrism and Altruism influences the contribution of the NHIP towards explaining behavior, a hierarchical regression analysis was carried out by first inserting the NHIP into the model, followed by the remaining variables in successives stages. In this way, the contribution of the NHIP was endorsed as significant ($F_{1,114} = 6.382$; $p < 0.05$), although it only explains 5.3% of the variance. Entering Altruism in second place resulted in a significant increase in explained variance, so that both variables explain 12.1% ($F_{1,114} = 7.681$; $p < 0.05$). Anthropocentrism was entered in third place but did not increase the explained variance. By positioning Ecocentrism in fourth place, the NHIP lost the significance of its contribution because it was appropriated by Ecocentrism. Finally, what remained was a predictive model of ecological behavior, based on two predicting variables: Ecocentrism and Altruism. This model explains the 18% variance of ecological behavior ($F_{1,114} = 12.322$; $p < 0.05$), 9.8% is solely explained by Ecocentrism, 3.8% by Altruism and the remaining 4.4% by both variables in a redundant way.

In short, the NHIP is linked to ecocentric and not to anthropocentric orientation in this study, although a significant relation is maintained with altruism. Furthermore, the NHIP is significantly related to general pro-environmental behavior though to a lesser extent than ecocentrism. In fact, the results obtained denote an overlapping of predictive capacity for both elements. The ecocentric view forms the basis of the NHIP. In research conducted by Corral-Verdugo et al. (2008), the NHIP is a more powerful predictor than the ecocentric components of the NEP. A comparison between the NHIP and the ecocentrism factor of Thompson and Barton's scale, however, shows that the latter is a better predictor of behavior. This apparent contradiction is perhaps indicating the existence of a higher communality between the NHIP and the main ecocentric principles included in the Ecocentrism-Anthropocentrism Scale. In this regard, given the complexity and extent of the elements that shapes an EWV, it seems reasonable to extend the measuring scale for use when empirically defining the NHIP.

Addressing interdependence as a fundamental principle of sustainability and in relation to the concept of ecological worldview lends permanent form to the challenge of a comprehensive far-reaching theory of environmental practices. If indeed EWVs comprehensively define both beliefs about the bonds between humans and their surroundings, as well as the patterns that govern their social practices, psychoenvironmental knowledge must advance towards an equally holistic description and explanation of environmental interest and sustainable behavior. In fact, in the same way that there can be no sustainability without referring to pro-environmental lifestyles, neither is it feasible to analyze EWVs without considering socio-cognitive and affective roots and their consolidation as social behavior.

CONCLUSION

A dichotomous view that considers pro-environmental and human development as opposed ends of the same continuum has dominated the analysis of attitudes and beliefs regarding the person-environment relationship. However, the concept of sustainable development is considered a global (holistic) approach to understanding the world and its problems. Therefore, it is plausible to question to what extent sustainability constitutes a new orientation in approaching beliefs, norms and social values, and in which degree this orientation influences behavior and life styles. Results from our research seem to provide an affirmative, although tentative, answer to these questions. These results suggest that sustainability is built on a belief system in which the ecocentric orientation is fundamental without questioning the relevance and centrality of human well-being.

For several decades, Environmental Psychology research has led to the development of partial theoretical models sustained by sufficient empirical evidence to provide a basis for devising comprehensive theoretical models. Hence, the following can be identified: 1) the relations between value orientations, attitudes and behavior, 2) the influence of personal norms and the mediating role of the processes of attributing responsibility and dealing with behavioral consequences, 3) the differential weight of general and specific beliefs in predicting intentional behavior and actions, 4) interrelations with affective factors such as empathy and sense of connection with nature and 6) the importance of place and the associated phenomena of appropriateness and identity as determining factors of environmental behaviors. In turn, it is generally assumed that sustainability will entail a drastic reduction in human impact on ecosystems that will also involve a redistribution of wealth on a worldwide scale. In this sense, the presence of positive attitudes towards behaviors of austerity, equity and solidarity must also be contemplated.

In psychosocial terms, the meaning of this road to integration may entail the internalization (and automation in the form of habits) of arguments of human interdependence shaped according to mechanisms that associate sustainability with personal and social identity. Evidently the development of the concept of the NHIP as an EWV is still far from combining all these dimensions. However, empirical evidence now beginning to emerge reveals the potentiality of the principle that defines the NHIP—interdependence—as a central column around which normative, valuative, attitudinal and belief elements can be inserted to bring behavior closer to sustainability criteria.

The approach to the NHIP that this chapter has presented is circumscribed to its consideration into the individual (non-collective) level. Yet, as Gärling et al (2002) pointed out, this paradigm supposes an understanding of negative environmental impacts as a product of "an aggregate level of choice that individuals and groups make in self-interest" (pag 85). In fact, the elimination of obstacles to sustainability has to be associated with structural changes in the organizational and political levels.

REFERENCES

Aikenhead, G.S. & Ogawa, M. (2007). Indigenous knowledge and science revisited. *Cultural Studies of Science Education, 2,* 39-620.

Albretch, D., Bultena, G., Holberg, E. & Nowak, P. (1982). The New Environmental Paradigm Scale. *Journal of Environmental Education, 13,* 39-43.

Altman, I. & Chemers, M. (1980). *Culture and Environment.* Monterey, CA: Brooks/Cole.

Amérigo, M.; Aragonés, J.I.; Sevillano, V. & Cortés, B. (2005). La estructura de las creencias sobre la problemática ambiental. *Psicothema, 17,* 246-251.

Arcury, T. & Christianson, E. (1990). Environmental worldview in response to environmental problems: Kentucky 1984 and 1988 compared. *Environment and Behavior, 22,* 387-407.

Attfield, R. (1994). *Environmental Philosphy: Principles and prospects.* Avebury. Hampshire, England.

Bechtel, R.B. (1997). *Environment and Behavior. An Introduction.* Thousand Oaks: Sage.

Bechtel, R.B. (2000). The Third Revolution in Thinking and Its Impact on Psychology. *Medio Ambiente y Comportamiento Humano, 1,* 1-7.

Bechtel, R.B. & Churchman, A. (Eds.) (2002). *Handbook of Environmental Psychology.* New York: Wiley.

Bechtel, R.B., Corral-Verdugo, V., Asai, M. y González-Riesle, A. (2006). A crosscultural study of environmental belief structures. USA, Japan, Mexico and Peru. *International Journal of Psychology, 41,* 145-151.

Bechtel, R.B., Corral-Verdugo, V. & Pinheiro, J. (1999). Environmental beliefs U.S., Brazil and Mexico. *Journal of Crosscultural Psychology,* 30, 122-128.

Berenguer, J. Corraliza, J.A. & Martín, R. (2005). Rural-Urban Differences in Environmental Concern, Attitudes, and Actions. *European Journal of Psychological Assessment; 21,* 128-138.

Bonnes, M., & Bonaiuto, M. (2002). Environmental psychology: from spatial-physical environment to sustainable development. In R.B. Bechtel & A. Churchman (Eds.), *Handbook of Environmental Psychology* (pp. 28-54). New York: Wiley.

Bookchin, M. (1982). *Ecology of Freedom: The Emergence and Dissolution of Hierarchy.* Palo Alto, CA: Cheshire Books.

Capra, F & Pauli, P. (1995). *Steering business toward sustainability.* Nueva York: The United Nations University.

Carson, R. (1962). *Silent spring.* Boston: Houghton Mifflin.

Casey, P. & Scott, K. (2006). Environmental concern and behavior in an Australian sample within an ecocentric-anthropocentric framework. *Australian Journal of Psychology, 58,* 57-67.

Castro, P., & Lima, L. (2001). Old and new ideas about the environment and science: An exploratory study. *Environment and Behavior, 33,* 400-423.

Catton, W. & Dunlap, R. (1980). New Ecological Paradigm for Post-Exuberant Society. *American Behavioral Scientist, 24,* 15-48.

Chung, S.S. & Poon, C.S. (2000). A comparison of waste reduction practices and the New Environmental Paradigm in four southern Chinese areas. *Environmental Management, 26,* 195-206.

Commoner, B. (1967). *Science and Survival.* New York: Viking.

Commoner, B. (1972). *The Closing Circle.* New York: Bantam.

Corral-Verdugo, V. & Armendáriz, L.I. (2000). The "New Environmental Paradigm" in a Mexican Community. *Journal of Enviromental Education,* 31, 25-31.

Corral-Verdugo, V., Bechtel, R.B., Armendáriz, L.I. & Esquer, A.B. (1997). La estructura de las creencias ambientales en universitarios mexicanos: El nuevo paradigma ambiental. *Revista Mexicana de Psicología, 14,* 173-181.

Corral-Verdugo, V., Carrus, G., Bonnes, M., Moser, G. & Sinha, J. (2008). Environmental beliefs and endorsement of Sustainable Development principles in water conservation: towards a *New Human Interdependence Paradigm* scale. *Environment and Behavior, 40,* 703-725.

Corral-Verdugo, V., Tapia, C., Fraijo, B., Mireles, J. & Márquez, P. (2008). Determinantes psicológicos de los estilos de vida sustentables. *Revista Mexicana de Psicología, 25,* 313-327.

De Groot, J.I. & Steg, L. (2007). Value Orientations to Explain Beliefs Related to Environmental Significant Behavior: How to Measure Egoistic, Altruistic, and Biospheric Value Orientations. *Environment and Behavior* 2008; 40; 330-354.

Devall, B, & Sessions, G. (1985). *Deep Ecology.* Salt Lake City: Gibbs Smith Publishers.

Diamantopoulos, A., Schlegelmilch, B., Sinkovics, R. & Bohlen, G. (2003). Can sociodemographics still play a role in profiling green consumers? A review of the evidence and an empirical investigation *Journal of Business Research 56,* 465-480

Dietz T. (2003). The Darwinian trope in the drama of the commons: variations on some themes by the Ostroms. *Journal of Economic Behavioral Organization, 57,* 205-25.

Dietz, T., Fitzgerald, A. & Shwom, R. (2005). *Environmental values.* Annu. Rev. Environ. Resour. 30, 335-72.

Dunlap, R.E. (2008). The New Environmental Paradigm Scale: From Marginality to Worldwide Use. *Journal of Environmental Education, 40,* 3-18.

Dunlap, R.E. & Van Liere, K.D. (1984). Commitment to the dominant social paradigm and concern for environmental quality. *Social Science Quarterly, 65,* 1013-1028.

Dunlap, R.E. & Van Liere, K.D. (1978). The "New Environmental Paradigm". *Journal of Environmental Education,* 9, 10-19.

Dunlap, R.E., Van Liere, K., Mertig, A., & Jones, R. (2000). New trends in measuring environmental attitudes: Measuring endorsement of the New Ecological Paradigm: a revised NEP scale. *Journal of Social Issues, 56,* 425-442.

Dunlap, R.E., Xiao, C. & McCright, A. (2002.) Politics and Environment in America: Partisan and Ideological Cleavages in Public Support for Environmentalism. *Environmental Politics 10*, 23-48.

Dutcher, D, Finley, J., Luloff, A. & Buttolph Johnson, J. (2007). Connectivity With Nature as a Measure of Environmental Values. *Environment and Behavior, 39,* 474-493.

Edgell & Nowell (1989) Edgell, M.C. y Nowell, D.E. (1989). The New Environmental Paradigm Scale: Wildlife and environmental beliefs in British Columbia. *Society and Natural Resources, 2,* 285-296.

Fernández-Buey, F. (2006). Filosofía de la sostenibilidad. En J. Riechmann: *Biomímesis.* Madrid: Los libros de la catarata.

Furman, A. (1998). A note on environmental concern in a developing country: Results from an Instanbul survey. *Environment and Behavior, 30,* 504-519.

Gärling, T., Biel, A., & Gustafsson, M. (2002). The new environmental psychology: The human interdependence paradigm. In R. B. Bechtel & A. Churchman (Eds.) (2002), *Handbook of environmental psychology* (pp. 85-94). New York: Wiley.

Georgescu-Roegen, N. (1971). *The Entropy Law and the Economic Process.* Cambridge, Harvard: University Press.

Goksen, F., Adaman, F. & Zenginobus, E. (2002). On environmental concern, willingness to pay and postmaterialistic values. *Environment and Behavior, 34,* 616-633.

Gómez-Heras, J.M.G. (2002). Propuestas de fundamentación de la ética del medio ambiente. En J.M.G Gómez-Heras (Coord): *Ética de la frontera* (pp 13-46). Madrid: Biblioteca Nueva.

González, A. & Amérigo, M. (2008). Relationship among values, beliefs, norms and ecological behaviour. *Psicothema* 20, 623-629.

Gooch, G.F. (1995). Environmental beliefs and attitudes in Sweden and the Baltic states. *Environment and Behavior, 27,* 513-539.

Gorz, A. (1975) *Ecologie et politique.* Paris: Galilée.

Hawley, A. (1986). *Human Ecology. A Theoretical Essay.* Chicago: Chicago University Press.

Heath, Y. & Gifford, R. (2006). Free-market ideology and environmental degradation: The case of belief in global climate change. *Environment and Behavior, 38,* 48-71.

Hernández, B., Corral-Verdugo, V., Hess, S. & Suárez, E. (2001). Sistemas de creencias ambientales: un análisis multi-muestra de estructuras factoriales. *Estudios de Psicología, 22,* 53-73.

Hernández, B., Suárez, E., Martínez-Torvisco, J. & Hess, S. (1997). Actitudes y creencias sobre el medio ambiente. *Papeles del Psicólogo, 67,* 48-54.

Hernández, B., Suárez, E., Martínez-Torvisco, J. & Hess, S. (2000). The study of environmental beliefs by facet analysis. Research in the Canary Islands, Spain. *Environment and Behavior, 32,* 612-636.

Hunter, L. & Rinner, L. (2004). The association between environmental perspective and knowledge and concern with species diversity. *Society and Natural Resources, 17,* 517-532.

Irzik, G. & Nola, R. (2009). Worldviews and their relation to science. *Science and Education. 18,* 729-745.

Johnson, C.; Bowker, B. & Cordell, K. (2004). Ethnic Variation in Environmental Belief and Behavior: An Examination of the New Ecological Paradigm in a Social Psychological Context. *Environment and Behavior,* 36; 157-186.

Jones, R. & Dunlap, R (1992). The social bases of environmental concern: Have they changed over time? *Rural Sociology, 57,* 28-47.

Kaiser, F. (1998). A general measure of ecological behavior. *Journal of Applied Social Psychology, 28,* 395-442.

Karpiak, C. & Baril, G. (2008). Moral reasoning and concern for the environment. *Journal of Environmental Psychology 28,* 203-208.

Kilbourne, W.; Beckmann, S. & Thelen, E. (2002). The role of the dominant social paradigm in environmental attitudes A multinational examination. *Journal of Business Research 55,* 193-204.

Kortenkamp, K. & Moore, C. (2001). Ecocentrism and anthropocentrism: moral reasoning about ecological moral commons dilemmas. *Journal of Environmental Psychology, 21,* 261-272.

Kuhn, R.G. & Jackson, E.L. (1989). Stability of factor structures in the measurement of public environmental attitudes. *Journal of Environmental Education, 21,* 20-26.

Lemkow, L. (2002). *Sociología Ambiental.* Barcelona: Icaria.

Leopold, A. (1949). *A Sand County Almanac.* Oxford: Oxford University Press.

Leung, C. & Rice, J. (2002). Comparison of Chinese-Australian and Anglo-Australian environmental attitudes and behavior. *Social Behavior and Personality, 30,* 251-262.

Liebow, E.B. (2002). Environmental Anthropology. In R.B. Bechtel & A. Churchman (Eds.), *Handbook of Environmental Psychology* (pp. 147-159). New York: Wiley.

Macy, J. & Brown, M.Y. (1998). *Coming Back to Life.* Gabriola Island, BC: New Society.

Mainieri, T., Barnett, E., Valdero, T., Unipan, J. & Oskamp, S. (1997). Green buying: The influence of environmental concern on consumer behavior. *The Journal of Social Psychology, 13,* 189-204.

Manoli, C.; Johnson, B. & Dunlap, R. (2007). Assessing Children's Environmental Worldviews: Modifying and Validating the New Ecological Paradigm Scale for Use with Children. *Journal of Environmental Education, 38,* 3-13.

Maxwell N. (1980). Science, Reason, Knowledge, and Wisdom: A Critique of Specialism. *Inquiry,* 23, 19-81.

McCloskey, H.J. (1983). *Ecological Ethics and Politics.* Totowa, NJ: Rowman & Littlefield.

Meadows, D.H.; Meadows, D.L.; Randers, J. & Behrens, W.W. (1972). *The Limits to Growth.* New York: Universe Books.

Meadows, D.H; Randers, J. & Meadows, D.L: (2004). *The Limits to Growth: The 30-Year Update.* Chlesea, Vermont: Chelsea Green Publications.

Milbrath, L. (1986). Environmental beliefs and values. En M. Hermann (Ed.): political Psychology (pp. 97-138). San Francisco: Jossey-Bass.

Morgan, P.A. & Peters, S.J. (2006). The Foundations of Planetary Agrarianism. Thomas Berry and Liberty Hyde Bailey. *Journal of Agricultural and Environmental Ethics,* 19, 443-468.

Noe, F.P. & Snow, R. (1990a). The New Environmental Paradigm and further scale analysis. *Journal of Environmental Education, 21,* 20-26.

Noe, F.P. & Snow, R. (1990b). Hispanic cultural influence on environmental concern. *Journal of Environmental Education, 22,* 26-32.

Nordlund, A. & Garvill, J. (2002). Value Structures behind Proenvironmental Behavior. *Environment and Behavior,* 34, 740-756.

Nordlund, A. & Garvill, J. (2003). Effects of values, problem awareness, and personal norm in willingness to reduce personal car use. *Journal of Environmental Psychology,* 23, 339-347.

Poortinga, W., Steg, L. & Vlek, C. (2003). Myths of nature and environmental management strategies. A field study on energy reductions in traffic and transport. In G. Moser, E. Pol, Y. Bernard, M. Bonnes, J.A. Corraliza and M.V. Giuliani (Eds.), *People, Place and Sustainability.* (p 280-290). Seattle: Hogrefe & Huber Publishers.

Rauwald, K. & Moore, C.F. (2002). Environmental attitudes as predictors of policy support across three countries. *Environment and Behavior, 34,* 709-739.

Riechmann, J. (2006). *Biomímesis.* Madrid: Los libros de la catarata.

Samdahl, D.M. & Robertson, R. (1989). Social determinants of environmental concern. *Environment and Behavior,* 21, 57-81.

Sarigöllü, E. (2009). A Cross-Country Exploration of Environmental Attitudes. *Environment and Behavior, 41,* 365-386.

Schmuck, P. & Schultz, P. W. (2002). Sustainable development as a challenge for Psychology. In P. Schmuck & P. W. Schultz (Eds.), *Psychology of Sustainable Development.* (pg. 1-17). Norwell, Massachusetts: Kluwer.

Schultz, P.W. (2001). The structure of environmental concern. Concern for self, other people, and the biosphere. *Journal of Environmental Psychology,* 21, 327-339.

Schultz, P.W. & Stone, W.F. (1994). Authoritarianism and attitudes toward the environment. *Environment and Behavior,* 26, 25-37.

Schultz, P.W. & Zelezny, L. (1999). Values as Predictors of Environmental Attitudes: Evidence for Consistency across 14 countries. *Journal of Environmental Psychology, 19,* 255-265.

Schultz, P.W., Zelezny, L. & Dalrympe, N. (2000). A multinational perspective on the relation between Judeo-Christian religious beliefs and attitudes of environmental concern. *Environment and Behavior, 32,* 576-591.

Schumacher, E.F. (1973). *Small is beautiful. A study of economics as if people mattered.* New York: Harper & Row.

Schwartz, S.H. (1994). Are there universal aspects in the structure and contents of human values? *Journal of Social Issues, 50,* 19-45.

Scott, D. & Willits, F.K. (1994). Environmental attitudes and behavior: A Pennsylvania survey. *Environment and Behavior,* 26, 239-260.

Shafer, W.E. (2006). Social paradigms and attitudes toward environmental accountability. *Journal of Business Ethics, 65,* 121-147.

Sosa, N.M. (1990). *Ética ecológica.* Madrid: Libertarias/Prodhufi.

Steg, L., Dreijerink, L. & Abrahamse, W. (2005). Factors influencing the acceptability of energy policies: A test of VBN theory. *Journal of Environmental Psychology, 25,* 415-425.

Stern, P. (2000). Toward a coherent theory of environmentally significant behavior. *Journal of Social Issues,* 56, 407-424.

Stern, P.C., & Dietz, T. (1994). The value basis of environmental concern. *Journal of Social Issues, 50,* 65-84.

Stern, P.C., Dietz, T. & Guagnano, G.A. (1995). The new ecological paradigm in social-psychological context. *Environment and Behavior, 27*, 723-743.

Stern, P.C., Dietz, T. & Kalof, L. (1993). Value orientations, gender, and environmental concern. *Environment and Behavior, 25*, 322-348.

Suárez, E., Salazar-Laplace, M.E., Hernández, B. & Martín, A. (2007) ¿Qué motiva la valoración del medio ambiente? La relación del ecocentrismo y del antropocentrismo con la motivación interna y externa. *Revista de Psicología Social, 22*, 235-244.

Thompson, S.C.G. & Barton, M. (1994). Ecocentric and anthropocentric attitudes toward the environment. *Journal of Environmental Psychology, 14*, 149-157.

Van Liere, K.D. & Dunlap, R.E. (1980). The social bases of environmental concern: A review of hypotheses, explanations, and empirical evidence. *Public Opinion Quarterly, 44*, 181-197.

Van Liere, K.D. & Dunlap, R.E. (1981). Environmental concern: Does it make a difference how it's measured? *Environment and Behavior, 13*, 651-676.

Vikan, A., Camino, C., Biaggio, A. & Nordvik, H. (2007). Endorsement of the New Ecological Paradigm: A comparison of two Brazilian samples and a Norwegian sample. *Environment and Behavior, 39*, 217-228.

Vining, J. & Ebreo, A. (1992). Predicting recycling behavior from global and specific environmental attitudes and changes in recycling opportunities. *Journal of Applied Social Psychology, 22*, 1580-1607.

Vozmediano, L. & San Juan, C. (2005). Escala del Nuevo Paradigma Ecológico: propiedades psicométricas con una muestra española obtenida a través de internet. *Medio Ambiente y Comportamiento Humano, 6*, 37-49.

White, L. (1967). The Historical Roots of our Ecological Crisis. *Science, 155*, 1203-1207.

White, R. V. (1959). Motivation reconsidered: The concept of competence. *Psychological Review, 66*, 297-333.

Winter, D. (2002). Gendering sustainable development. En P. Schmuck & P.W. Schultz (Eds.), *Psychology of Sustainable Development*. (pp. 79-96). Norwell, Massachusetts: Kluwer.

Xiao, C y Dunlap, R.E. (2007). Validating a Comprehensive Model of Environmental Concern Cross-Nationally: A U.S.-Canadian Comparison. *Social Science Quarterly, 88*, 471-493.

Zelezny, L.C., Chua, P. & Aldrich, C. (2000). Elaborating on gender differences in environmentalism. *Journal of Social Issues, 56*, 443-457.

In: Psychological Approaches to Sustainability
Editors: V. Corral-Verdugo et al.
ISBN 978-1-60876-356-6
© 2010 Nova Science Publishers, Inc.

Chapter 6

LEVERAGE FOR SUSTAINABLE CHANGE: MOTIVATIONAL SOURCES BEHIND ECOLOGICAL BEHAVIOR

Nina Roczen[*,1,2,3], *Florian G. Kaiser*[1]
[1]Otto-von-Guericke Universität Magdeburg, Germany
[2]Technische Universiteit Eindhoven, The Netherlands
and Franz X. Bogner[3]
[3]Universität Bayreuth, Germany

ABSTRACT

In this chapter, we focus on three different types of motives behind individual conservation. We reflect upon these motives from a behavior-change perspective. That is, we examine reasons for ecological behavior not only in terms of their behavior relevance but also with respect to how appropriate they are for behavior-change campaigns. First, we discuss environmental attitude as a source of a person's ecological performance. Here, we argue that the apparent gap between individual attitude and behavior represents a chimera fed by a tacit assumption that made us, in conservation psychology, believe in a causal connection between attitude and behavior. Instead, individual attitude and behavior are axiomatically and, thus, formally linked (Greve, 2001). In other words, environmental attitude should not be seen as a motive *behind* ecological behavior but as the disposition itself to act ecologically. Second, we also discuss prosocial and moral considerations as motives for environmental conservation. Different research traditions converge in confirming moral norms and prosocial traits as key forces behind conservation. While their efficacy for behavior is undisputed, their suitability for behavior change nevertheless remains debatable. Third, we discuss a phenomenon that has lately sparked some interest in conservation psychology, which is evidenced in a

---
[*] Correspondence concerning this article should be addressed to Nina Roczen, Otto-von-Guericke University, Department of Psychology I, P.O. Box 4120, D-39016 Magdeburg, Germany; e-mail: nina.roczen@gast.uni-magdeburg.de

rapidly growing body of research. A person's appreciation for nature is a most promising leverage for large-scale behavior change, which is corroborated in its significance for people's ecological performance. At the same time, appreciation for nature might not draw negative consequences when it is promoted sensibly.

INTRODUCTION

Psychology already has a thirty-year tradition of investigating people's motives for environmental conservation. The reason for such a strong interest in these motives is linked with the urgency of initiating changes on a large scale in the near future, to halt progressive environmental deterioration. An exponent of that interest is the desire to effectively promote conservation through behavior change. More precisely, the motives behind ecological behavior are suspected to offer the psychological leverage for change.

With motives, however, it is not only their efficacy that matters, but also their suitability for behavior-change campaigns. Are the identified reasons for action also useful as large-scale behavior-change measures? In this chapter, we want to review the three most popular motives for ecological behavior to date. In doing so, we will not only discuss the different motives' efficacy but also their malleability and how appropriate they are for a large-scale intervention.

Environmental attitude is conventionally seen as the key to ecological behavior, which is also reflected in attitude's prominence in conservation psychological publications (see e.g., Kaiser, Wölfing, & Fuhrer, 1999). Overall, the results are rather disappointing. Repeatedly, the attitude-behavior relationship is found to be moderate at most (e.g., Fransson & Gärling, 1999; Olli, Grendstad, & Wollebaek, 2001). In other words, people seem to say one thing and do another. In this chapter, we argue that, although corroborated by numerous studies, the apparent inconsistency between environmental attitude and ecological behavior derives from a logical misconception and subsequently from inadequate measurement instruments. Fortunately, it can be overcome conceptually (see Kaiser, Byrka, & Hartig, 2009). In fact, we will argue for a formal (not a causal) link between attitude and behavior within which the attitude-behavior inconsistency can be overcome when the costs of behavior in terms of money, time, or social acceptance are considered. Strictly speaking, an environmental attitude is not a motive *behind* behavior but rather the ecological overall performance itself (cf. Greve, 2001).

Moral considerations and prosocial dispositions form a second group of crucial motives for environmental conservation in psychology. Different research traditions converge on the same insights. Research on social value orientation (e.g., Joireman, van Lange, Kuhlman, van Vugt, & Shelley, 1997) as well as the search for motivational sources of behavior in conservation psychology (e.g., Bamberg & Möser, 2007) corroborate people's morality to be an important force behind environmental conservation. Despite its behavior effectiveness, we nevertheless conclude that moral considerations and prosocial dispositions are inappropriate means for large-scale behavior-change campaigns, for three reasons. The first reason refers to the notion that moral exhortation is unfair and draws negative consequences. Specifically speaking, appeals to conscience only reach some and moreover evoke anxiety and stress (Hardin, 1968). The second argument stems from moral philosophy. There are no moral absolutes a campaign could refer to (Mackie, 1977), a fact that will always spark dispute and resistance. The third concerns the presumed rigor of moral convictions and of prosocial traits (see Kaiser & Byrka, 2009). The question is whether moral convictions can be effectively mended: without malleability, no campaign will succeed.

Neither environmental attitude nor people's morality are, as we believe, the leverages that allow us to effectively promote conservation. What psychological motives for ecological behavior should we then focus on? There is one promising phenomenon that has not only been corroborated as a significant motivational force for ecological behavior but that also promises to be suitable for behavior-change campaigns: a person's appreciation for nature. Although theoretically conceptualized differentially, either as "inclusion of nature in self" (Schultz, 2002), "environmental identity" (Clayton, 2003) or as "connectedness to nature" (Mayer & Frantz, 2004), we found evidence that these concepts share substantial amounts of variance, which speaks for a unique psychological phenomenon (see Brügger, Kaiser, & Roczen, 2009).

Different research groups agree on the behavior effectiveness of appreciation for nature (see e.g., Clayton, 2003; Mayer & Frantz, 2004). Concerning nature appreciation's accessibility for behavior-change interventions, the question about origin and development is essential. While the biophilia hypothesis implies an innate need to connect with and, thus, to appreciate nature (Kellert & Wilson, 2003), others suspect nature appreciation to be acquired throughout the course of one's life. A person's appreciation for nature is typically anticipated to stem from joyful and gratifying experiences in nature, probably through conditioning processes (e.g., Kaiser, Roczen, & Bogner, 2008).

ENVIRONMENTAL ATTITUDE

Environmental attitudes are one of the most widely studied constructs in the search for possible motives for ecological behavior. Traditionally, the object of one's environmental attitude is either nature preservation/conservation in general, or certain ecological behaviors in particular (e.g., recycling). An attitude toward a specific behavior normally is conceptualized as one determinant of a person's intention in the planned behavior framework (e.g., Staats, 2003). Attitude toward environmental conservation is commonly based on a multiple-component approach; an approach that can be traced back to Maloney and Ward (1973) and more generally to Rosenberg and Hovland (1960). The former distinguish between affective, intentional, and behavioral indicators of people's environmental attitudes. Others have differentiated between ecocentric, anthropocentric, and egoistic attitude components (Schultz, 2001). Recently, Milfont and Duckitt (2004) suggested the two-component model proposed by Bogner and Wiseman (1999; 2002) as the last word in this line of research. In this model, "Utilization" refers to an anthropocentric, utility-oriented or exploitation-favoring conception. "Preservation," by contrast, reflects an ecocentric perspective that aims at conservation and protection of the natural environment irrespective of any personal profits. Interestingly, only preservation was found to be significantly related to ecological behavior so far (Bogner & Wiseman, 1999; 2002; 2006).

The hopes for attitudes to be the panacea for environmental conservation have genuinely been high. Empirical studies of the relationship between environmental attitude and ecological behavior, however, failed to meet these expectations. Already in early research, doubts emerged concerning a close connection between attitude and behavior (see e.g., Hines, Hungerford, & Tomera, 1986/87; Stern, 1978). These doubts have only been amplified over time (e.g., Bamberg & Möser, 2007; Diekmann & Preissendorfer, 1998; Fransson & Gärling, 1999; Olli et al., 2001) so that, in the meantime, the gap between environmental attitude and behavior has become common knowledge in conservation psychology (e.g., Vining & Ebreo, 2002). And although the gap has been tackled with moderators, such as the differential costs of various ecological behaviors (e.g., Guagnano, Stern, & Dietz, 1995; Schultz & Oskamp, 1996), and technical measures, such as measurement correspondence (e.g., Schultz, Oskamp, & Marinieri, 1995), a dissatisfying lack of convergence between attitude and behavior still persists.

The attitude-behavior inconsistency is, however, an empirical chimera as we learn from Greve (2001) in his insightful reflection on behavior. According to Greve, behavior in psychology has to be conceptualized as a goal-directed or intent-oriented activity (cf. Stern, 2000; Kaiser, 2004). Accordingly, attitudes are not motives *behind* behavior (that can be explored empirically) but rather they are axiomatically linked--in a means-end relation--with behavior. This is equivalent to a person's proficiency in mathematics that is not a factual property, but a latent one that is reflected in the mathematics tasks the person masters. The challenge is to non-trivially link goals/intentions and behavior (cf. Greve, 2001), since such an axiomatic or logical link implies a structural and formal connection between particular behaviors and an actor's intention/goal. Kaiser and colleagues (e.g., Byrka, 2009; Kaiser et al., 2009) developed such model, which describes a formal link between individual attitude and goal-directed behavior (see Kaiser, Oerke, & Bogner, 2007). In reference to the first person, who in principle sketched this very solution to the notorious attitude-behavior gap, Donald T. Campbell (1963), they call their approach Campbell's paradigm (see Kaiser et al., 2009).

According to Campbell's paradigm, verbal evaluative statements (items that are traditionally used to assess personal attitudes) and other behavioral responses toward an attitude object are both expressions of the same underlying disposition or attitude. The apparent inconsistency between verbal evaluations and other behavioral performances can be explained with the disregard of the relative costs or difficulties of the various behavioral responses. For example, verbally admitting the importance of financially supporting a certain environmental organization is probably easier for most people (as it only requires a cross in a questionnaire) than actually donating money to that organization. But still, both the verbal statement and the financial sacrifice are realizations of the same goal (i.e., environmental conservation). In other words, a person's environmental attitude is anticipated to be observable in evaluative statements and ecological behaviors alike. Any discrepancies between declarative and other relevant behaviors are caused by the distinct difficulties of the behavioral responses (see e.g., Byrka, 2009).

If attitudes are directly reflected in a person's behavioral responses, it should also be possible to infer a person's attitude by inspecting what he or she does. Although it is not possible to derive personal attitudes from the engagement or non-engagement in a single specific behavior, a systematic inspection of a set of behavioral responses that are implied by a certain attitude allows for such an inference (Kaiser et al., 2007). If a person holds environmental conservation in high regard, we can expect this person to engage in all sorts of environmental conservation-relevant activities. Such a composite of activities also entails that people can select from various behavioral alternatives to realize their individual level of environmental attitude. Instead of running energy-efficient washing programs, people can abstain from using a dryer or focus more on what washing detergents they use. A person's appreciation for a certain attitude object (e.g., environmental conservation) is most obvious in the face of increasingly demanding hurdles or progressively intolerable sacrifices (Schultz & Oskamp, 1996).

Necessarily, the more obstacles someone overcomes and the more effort a person expends along the way to implement this attitude, the higher the individual's level or extent of that attitude is. When a person, however, admits to be environmentally oriented, but insists on using a car or avoids recycling, he or she probably does not care about environmental conservation that much. Furthermore, any behavior being performed, figuratively speaking, involves costs as it requires personal resources, such as time, money, or effort. If one's attitude level can be expressed by a variety of different acts, we can anticipate a prudent selection of the behavioral means to its manifestation. Naturally, people commonly prefer the more convenient, less socially sanctioned actions over the more complicated, strenuous, or pricey ones. Thus, we can assume that people favor less demanding actions over more demanding ones.

Conceptually, the probability that a certain ecological behavior is performed not only depends on (a) a person's disposition to act, his or her environmental attitude, but also on (b) the composition of all the figurative costs of that particular act. Kaiser and colleagues have repeatedly corroborated that the Rasch model can be used to describe this functional relationship formally (e.g., Kaiser, 1998; Kaiser & Wilson, 2000, 2004; Kaiser et al., 2007).

With an axiomatic, formal (and not an empirical) relationship between environmental attitude and intent-oriented/goal-directed ecological behavior, attitude change necessarily implies behavior change. Therefore, attitudes must not be misunderstood as causes of behavior. Attitudes and behavior are in fact two sides of the same coin. Predictably, an environmental attitude measure is a psychologically suitable criterion for assessing behavior interventions, as long as such a measure represents a goal-directed ecological behavior based on Campbell's paradigm (see e.g., Kaiser, Midden, & Cervinka, 2008). The question remains, however, what shapes people's environmental attitudes; what is the motivational source behind intent-oriented ecological behavior? In the next section, we will review research concerning the most promising of the possible determinants: moral norms and values.

MORAL CONSIDERATIONS

Many of the currently existing environmental problems can structurally be described as social dilemmas (Hardin, 1968). In other words, environmental deterioration stems from self-interest undermining people's environmental conservation in the common interest (Gifford & Hine, 1997). For example, the conservation of natural resources and the preservation of clean air for the benefit of all are compromised by people's personal desires for safe, fast, and comfortable rides. Unsurprisingly, research on social dilemmas is considered essential for environmental conservation. In this line of research, a person's social value orientation--that is the cooperative, individualistic, or competitive orientation of an individual when making decisions that also affect others--is found to be an important determinant for cooperation in social dilemmas generally and specifically concerning environmental conservation (e.g., Joireman et al., 1997; Van Vugt, Meertens, & van Lange, 1995). Similarly, moral considerations, or more precisely, moral norms, have also been recognized as key forces behind ecological behavior within more traditional psychological research (e.g., Bamberg & Möser, 2007; Hunecke, Blöhbaum, Matthies, & Höger, 2001). Next, we will give an overview of these two research traditions that corroborate people's morality to be vital for behavior in the conservation domain, before we take a closer look at some practical problems with moral values and thoughts.

In social dilemmas (i.e., public good or resource dilemmas with open access to the resource; see e.g., Komorita & Parks, 1995), people are confronted with a genuine conflict between their prosocial propensity to cooperate with each other and their inclination to compete for the resource. By and large, people compete rather than cooperate. In other words, the pursuit of self-interest is commonly found to be the dominant strategy. Nevertheless, people differ in their propensity to cooperate with one another in social dilemmas (Kramer, McClintock, & Messick, 1986). Predictably, personality--i.e., one's social value orientation (e.g., Van Lange, 1999)--was one factor that was repeatedly recognized to influence behavior in social dilemmas. Social value orientation refers to three distinct types of persons: prosocials, individualists, and competitors. While prosocials are concerned with maximizing collective benefits and, thus, are more likely to cooperate with others, individualists and competitors, by contrast, prefer to maximize personal outcomes and relative gains (Brucks & van Lange, 2007). Social value orientation was also recognized to be relevant for environmental conservation outside the lab. Joireman and colleagues (1997), for example, confirmed prosocials in contrast to individualists and competitors to prefer public transportation over private cars for their daily commutes if they also hold high levels of trust.

In conservation psychology, the search for motives behind ecological behavior also led to moral considerations, particularly, to a person's moral norms and values (e.g., Bamberg & Möser, 2007; Stern, 2000). In their meta-analysis, Bamberg and Möser (2007) report a mean correlation between moral norms and behavior of about $r = .40$. In their extended version of the planned behavior framework, they estimate moral norms to explain about 10% of people's intention to act ecologically even above and beyond the other determinants of intention (cf. also Harland, Staats, & Wilke, 1999). In Kaiser's research (2006), moral norms not only form the essence of a person's attitude and, thus, a person's intention to act ecologically but also substantially materialize in ecological activities of various sorts (also Kaiser & Scheuthle, 2003). Likewise, Lindenberg and Steg (2007) also speak of a most critical role of normative goals for environmental conservation. Finally, most research in conservation psychology has so far been conducted within some variant of the norm-activation framework by Schwartz (1973, 1977). The original theory holds that ecological behavior occurs when personal moral norms, or a person's feeling of a moral obligation, are activated. The two preconditions for a person to feel morally obliged are (a) the person's belief that a particular environmental condition poses a threat to animals and/or humans (i.e., awareness of adverse consequences) and (b) that one's own actions are regarded as measures to effectively avert these threats (i.e., ascription of responsibility to self). Two typical examples of research inspired by this theory concern public transportation use by Hunecke and colleagues (2001) and recycling by Guagnano and his colleagues (1995).

Further empirical support for the behavior-significance of moral norms in the conservation domain comes from studies employing the value-belief-norm theory by Stern and colleagues (e.g., Stern, 2000; Stern, Dietz, Abel, Guagnano, & Kalof, 1999). This theory integrates a person's ecological worldview and other environment-relevant values (e.g., Stern & Dietz, 1994) into a larger norm-activation-based theoretical frame. It claims moral norms to be the ultimate predictor of ecological behavior. These norms, in turn, are seen as a function of a chain of three beliefs: one's self-ascribed responsibility, one's awareness of the consequences of a behavior, and one's ecological worldview (measured with the New Ecological Paradigm by Dunlap, Van Liere, Mertig, & Jones, 2000), which in turn is determined by environment-relevant values. In other words, in the value-belief-norm model, a person's awareness of the behavioral consequence depends on his or her ecological worldview and, at the same time, determines a person's self-ascribed responsibility to act, which then leads to a person's sense of obligation to act (i.e., his or her moral norm). Stern and colleagues (1999) could confirm their value-belief-norm theory's efficacy in accounting for different types of behavior (i.e., private sphere behavior, policy support action, or environmental citizenship). More precisely, they found their model to cover 19% to 35% of these behaviors' variances, which was considerably more than what an exclusively value-based model was able to address when tested comparatively. The value-belief-norm theory was also tested by Kaiser and his colleagues (Kaiser, Hübner, & Bogner, 2005) using a composite measure of ecological behavior as a dependent variable. They found 64% of their general performance to be accounted for by moral norms.

In summary, we believe these results from different lines of research speak of a person's morality to be a strong, if not the key motivational force behind environmental conservation. Except for some protective reasons (Schultz, 2001), instrumental reasons (i.e., motives based on personal utility) turned out to be comparatively insignificant for the ecological performance of individuals (Kaiser, 2006; Milfont & Duckitt, 2004). Hence, morality's importance for ecological behavior is hard to dispute. Nevertheless and despite morality's impressive behavior efficacy, the following arguments cast some doubt on its suitability for large-scale behavior-change campaigns.

The first argument comes from Garrett Hardin's seminal paper (1968). There, he considers appeals to guilt and other forms of moral exhortation as unfair, because only agreeable, "good" people will voluntarily respond. As an even worse consequence, such appeals would eventually even eliminate the very conscience, or prosocial trait that makes people act morally rather than egotistically. According to Hardin, the most significant ecological sacrifice for an individual would be to refrain from having offspring, which in turn would--eventually--eliminate the prosocial gene that can be held accountable for the self-sacrifice in the first place. If this was not enough, Hardin also expects appeals to guilt and to a person's conscience to be pathogenic as they cause anxiety and stress. The second objection against appeals refers to the content of such moral exhortations. All moral standards are relative from a meta-ethical perspective (Mackie, 1977). Without moral facts (i.e., absolutes) though, advocating certain behaviors based on moral principles will inevitably draw dissent and create conflicts, which in turn renders moral-based campaigns in secular societies more or less impracticable (Wardekker, 2001). The third argument against moral-based behavior-change campaigns concerns the presumed rigor of moral convictions and the very concept of traits. If environmentalism is a virtue and environmentalists are the "better," the more prosocially acting people as some believe, and if environmentalism is a trait rather than a state (e.g., Joireman et al., 1997), we might also lower our expectations against overly high hopes for moral norms in environmental conservation as a viable means to effectively change behavior (Kaiser & Byrka, 2009). The question is whether moral convictions can be effectively mended or not. Without the flexibility for change, campaigning would be a rather futile endeavor.

APPRECIATION FOR NATURE

In our search for the motives behind environmental conservation, it turned out that neither environmental attitudes nor people's morality probably represent the necessary leverage for behavior change to effectively advance conservation efforts of individuals. But what then; what motive or what motives behind ecological behavior should we, as psychologists, address instead? A growing body of research points to an interesting and promising phenomenon: people's appreciation for nature. As we believe, this appreciation might even be suitable for large-scale behavior-change campaigns. Next, we summarize the different theoretical concepts that are to date linked with a person's appreciation for nature. Subsequently, we will provide evidence for its behavior relevance and, finally, we will speculate about nature appreciation's origins and how we believe that it can be systematically promoted. The latter implies that this appreciation for nature represents, as we believe, the wanted leverage for change to a more sustainable performance in individuals.

While some prefer a more cognitive conceptualization, others emphasize the emotional aspects of the nature-appreciation phenomenon more strongly. Schultz (2002), for example, defines, what he calls "inclusion of nature in self," as the extent to which individuals see themselves as part of nature and vice versa, how much they see nature as a constituent of their own self-concepts. Clayton (2003) calls her concept "environmental identity." Similar to Schultz' concept, environmental identity relates to one's belief that the natural environment is important to oneself and to how one sees him- or herself. Mayer and Frantz (2004), by contrast, speak of one's "connectedness to nature." Their concept covers a person's emotional kinship with nature, obvious in one's feelings of a personal connection to the natural world. Nisbet, Zelenski, and Murphy (in press) in turn believe their "nature relatedness" to encompass one's appreciation for nature and one's understanding of the interconnectedness of all living beings on earth. The latter, so to speak, incorporates cognitive and affective elements in parallel.

Although theoretically conceptualized differentially, either as "inclusion of nature in self" (Schultz, 2002), "environmental identity" (Clayton, 2003) or as "connectedness to nature" (Mayer & Frantz, 2004), Brügger and colleagues (2009) found support for their idea that these concepts speak of a unique psychological phenomenon that also is measurable as an attitude, as an attitude toward nature (not to be mistaken for the more common environmental attitude, which refers to nature preservation as attitude object rather than to nature itself; cf. Nisbet et al., in press). Based on data from a large convenience sample of the general population ($N = 1309$), Brügger and colleagues developed a measure that indirectly derived a person's attitude toward nature from inspecting reports of past bonding activities and responses to evaluative statements reflecting appreciation of nature. Their measure closely converged with most of the currently available instruments of concepts, which they thought to represent one and the same psychological phenomenon irrespective of all differences in their theoretical conceptualizations. Fortunately also, different research groups agree on the behavior efficacy of this attitude toward nature as we will see next (see e.g., Clayton, 2003; Mayer & Frantz, 2004).

The suspicion that a person's appreciation for his natural environment might trigger his or her environmentalism already exists for quite some time. Ecologists (Leopold, 1949; Orr, 1994) and ecopsychologists (see e.g., Roszak, Gomes, & Kanner, 1995) alike anticipate one's emotional bond with nature to foster a person's pro-environmental engagement of some sort or another, or, at least, prevent people from further contributing to environmental deterioration (cf. Schultz, Shriver, Tabanico, & Khazian, 2004). For example, to a Sámi reindeer herder, whose subsistence is closely linked to the forest, the idea of felling trees would not even occur. While early approaches remained primarily conceptual, lately, a continuously growing body of research is yielding empirical support for this suspicion. Clayton (2003), for instance, reports a person's environmental identity to substantially covary with ecological behavior ($r = .64$). Convergently, Kals, Schumacher, and Montada (1999), who argue for a better understanding of people's nature connectedness, also found their "emotional affinity for nature" measure to correlate with different pro-environmental performances (coefficients range from $r = .49$ to $r = .60$). Similarly, Davis, Green, and Reed (in press) found what they call a "commitment to the environment" to determine a composite measure of ecological engagement ($r = .60$). With proportions of explained behavior variance between 25% and 40%, there is surprising consensus in the findings of the various research groups.

From the perspective of behavior change, a motive that can be addressed in an intervention not only has to be behavior effective, it also has to be malleable. Theories about the origins and the development of an individual's nature appreciation shed light on its plasticity and, hence, on its suitability as a behavior-change measure. Strictly speaking, the question whether a person's appreciation for nature is genetically determined and, consequently, not susceptible to change or whether it is acquired through learning processes remains to be answered. Two ideas compete here. The first assumes a genetic basis for people's nature appreciation. The second anticipates this appreciation to represent an acquired behavioral disposition.

According to the biophilia hypothesis, humans experience a genetically predetermined bond with nature (Kellert & Wilson, 2003). Kellert and Wilson argue that for millions of years humans lived in (and adapted to) their natural habitat, allowing them to thrive and prosper. Consequently, their genetic make-up has evolved by means of natural selection to prefer this particular (biologically functional) environment (prototypically the East-African Savannah). If a person's appreciation for nature actually stems from such an inborn disposition, shifts in people's preferences and in their appreciation for nature would be connected with the genetic make-up of humans that would be exclusively malleable through natural selection. Correspondingly, we would not see ways to trigger a more intensive appreciation for nature irrespective of the target group by means of psychological interventions.

Others believe a person's appreciation for nature to be an acquired and not a genetically prompted disposition. This view is supported by anecdotal evidence and by notions about possible mechanisms and processes through which individuals *acquire* appreciation for nature. Schultz (2002), for example, stresses the importance of exposure to nature. He suspects technology and with it the advancing separation of humans from their natural environment, to be the main culprit for a continuous loss in people's appreciation for nature.

Spending (more) time in natural environments is his proposed remedy. Clayton (2003), similarly, sees the instrumental value of nature, the psychological and physiological benefits that people derive from experiences in nature, as the essence of a person's appreciation for nature. Typically, this appreciation is anticipated to stem from joyful and gratifying experiences in nature, probably through classical and operant conditioning processes (e.g., Kaiser, Roczen, et al., 2008).

Mundane forms of gratifications in natural environments include an escape from daily demands and the replenishment of mental resources and the recovery from stress (e.g., Hartig, 2007; Kaplan, 1995). The repeated provision of gratifying experiences renders the natural environment into a conditioned stimulus and, at the same time, relief from mental exhaustion negatively reinforces experiences in nature as well. In several studies, Hartig and colleagues established the theoretically anticipated link between a person's propensity to instrumentally use nature to recover from daily demands and the person's ecological engagement (see Byrka, Hartig, & Kaiser, 2009; Hartig, Kaiser, & Bowler, 2001 Hartig, Kaiser, & Strumse, 2007). If a person's appreciation of nature originates from gratifying and joyful learning experiences, then, of course, stimulating this learning process would be the logical measure to widely promote environmental conservation.

Conclusion

Large-scale psychological interventions can be reduced to two primary concerns: one of absolute (and--as cost-effectiveness--of relative) efficacy and one of usability. The first is primarily about the most practically significant motive, the psychological reason that allows us in psychology to reach as many persons and as much amendment in people's performance as possible. For that, we have to know what to address; we need to pinpoint the very motive with the most impact. Second, we have to know whether an intervention will draw possible rebound effects (for a detailed explanation of the concept see e.g., Midden, Kaiser, & McCalley, 2007), such as amplified consumption, or whether it will meet strong opposition and, thus, whether it will eventually be cost effective in the short as well as in the long run. Strictly speaking, usability is the pragmatic side of psychological interventions that aim at knowledge and/or motivation-based behavior amendment. In this chapter, we discussed three motives that we regard the top scholarly reasons behind environmental conservation of individuals in psychology.

With environmental attitude, we argue that it represents the extent to which people realize their personal conservation goals. Here, we claim that the apparent gap between individual attitude and behavior represents an empirical chimera fed by poor measurement instruments. When behavior is defined from a motivational point of view as an intent-oriented, goal-directed performance (e.g., Stern, 2000), i.e., as the behavioral means necessary to realize a specific attitudinal ambition, research did not only confirms that--based on the Rasch model--seemingly diverse types of activities like glass recycling and ownership of private solar panels belong to one class of actions (e.g., Kaiser & Wilson, 2004). Research has also found the attitude-behavior gap to empirically disappear with proportions of explained behavior variance as high as 95% (e.g., Kaiser et al., 2005), indicating that individual goal-directed behavior simultaneously represents a measure of environmental attitude (Kaiser et al., 2007).

As environmental attitude is not the reason behind but rather an individual's ecological overall performance itself (cf. Kaiser et al., 2009), attitude change necessarily implies behavior change. Referring to environmental attitude as the motive behind shifts in people's ecological behavior would accordingly be tautological and, thus, trivial as an explanation for change.

Morality's importance for ecological engagement is hard to dispute as the results from different lines of research speak of a person's morality to be a strong, if not dominant motivational force behind environmental conservation (e.g., Bamberg & Möser, 2007). Despite morality's widely confirmed behavior relevance, its suitability for large-scale behavior change still remains questionable. One question is whether moral convictions can factually be mended (by means of education or by appeals to engage in the "right" behavior) and even if it was malleable the next question would be whether moral exhortation should be used, given all its negative consequences for human health and well-being, and for the make-up of the human gene pool (cf. Hardin, 1968). One more objection against moral exhortation refers to the relative nature of moral standards behind such appeals. Without moral absolutes (i.e., standards that are valid and applicable for everyone under all circumstances), advocating certain behaviors based on moral principles inevitably draws dissent and create conflicts, rendering moral-based campaigns rather impractical.

A person's appreciation for nature is the third phenomenon that we explored as a possible psychological lever to promote behavior change. Irrespective of any conceptual differences, various research groups converge regarding nature appreciation's behavior relevance (e.g., Clayton, 2003; Mayer & Frantz, 2004). Jointly, the significance for people's ecological performance and the absence of apparent negative consequences when actively promoted are appealing when one induces higher levels of attitudes towards nature (not to be mistaken with environmental attitude) as the means to intensify environmental conservation. By endowing people with enjoyable and gratifying experiences in nature and thereby with mental rewards, such as escapes from daily demands, replenishment of cognitive resources, and recovery from stress (e.g., Hartig, 2007), people's appreciation for nature, their personal connection with nature so to speak, is expected to rise through conditioning processes. The repeated parallel provision of spontaneously gratifying experiences renders the natural environment into a conditioned stimulus and, at the same time, rewards, such as relief from mental exhaustion and mundane fun-experiences, will reinforce appreciation for nature (but probably not trigger resistance against the provision of pleasure and fun). If a person's appreciation of nature does indeed originate from gratifying and joyful learning experiences in nature, then, of course, widely and extensively stimulating these learning processes through schools and through health services would be the logical measure to promote environmental conservation on a societal level to turn us all into more sustainable human beings.

ACKNOWLEDGMENTS

This research was financially supported as part of the Priority Research Program 1293, by grant #BO944/5-1 from the German Research Foundation (DFG). The authors thank Steven Ralston for his language support and Caroline Duvier for commenting on an earlier version of this chapter.

REFERENCES

Bamberg, S., & Möser, G. (2007). Twenty years after Hines, Hungerford, and Tomera: A new meta-analysis of determinants of pro-environmental behaviour. *Journal of Environmental Psychology, 27,* 14-25.

Bogner, F. X., & Wiseman, M. (1999). Toward Measuring Adolescent Environmental Perception. *European Psychologist, 4,* 139-151.

Bogner, F. X., & Wiseman, M. (2002). Environmental Perception: Factor Profiles of Extreme Groups. *European Psychologist, 7,* 225-237.

Bogner, F. X., & Wiseman, M. (2006). Adolescents' attitudes towards nature and environment: Quantifying the 2-MEV model. *The Environmentalist, 26,* 247-254.

Brucks, W., & Van Lange, P. A. M. (2007). When prosocials act like proselfs in a commons dilemma. *Personality and Social Psychology Bulletin, 33,* 750-758.

Brügger, A., Kaiser, F. G., & Roczen, N. (2009). *One to bind them all: Connectedness to nature, inclusion of nature, environmental identity, implicit association with nature.* Manuscript submitted for publication.

Byrka, K. (2009). *Campbell's paradigm to reveal attitude-behavior consistency: Environmental and health domains.* Unpublished doctoral dissertation, Eindhoven University of Technology, Eindhoven, The Netherlands.

Byrka, K., Hartig, T., & Kaiser, F. G. (2009). *Environmental attitude as a mediator of the relationship between psychological restoration in nature and ecological behavior.* Manuscript submitted for publication.

Campbell, D. T. (1963). Social attitudes and other acquired behavioral dispositions. In S. Koch (Ed.), *Psychology: A study of a science* (Vol. 6, pp. 94-172). New York: McGraw-Hill.

Clayton, S. (2003). Environmental identity: A conceptual and operational definition. In S. Clayton & S. Opotow (Eds.), *Identity and the natural environment* (pp. 45-65). Cambridge, MA: MIT Press.

Davis, J. L., Green, J. D., & Reed, A. (in press). Interdependence with the environment: Commitment, interconnectedness, and environmental behavior. *Journal of Environmental Psychology.*

Diekmann, A., & Preisendorfer, P. (1998). Environmental behavior-discrepancies between aspirations and reality. *Rationality and Society, 10,* 79-102.

Dunlap, R. E., Van Liere, K. D., Mertig, A. G., & Jones, R. E. (2000). Measuring endorsement of the new ecological paradigm: A revised NEP scale. *Journal of Social Issues, 56,* 425-442.

Fransson, N., & Gärling, T. (1999) Environmental concern: Conceptual definitions, measurement methods, and research findings. *Journal of Evironmental Psychology, 19,* 369-382.

Gifford, R., & Hine, D. W. (1997). Towards cooperation in the commons dilemma. *Canadian Journal of Behavioural Science, 29,* 167-178.

Greve, W. (2001). Traps and gaps in action explanation: Theoretical problems of a psychology of human action. *Psychological Review, 108,* 435-451.

Guagnano, G. A., Stern, P. C., & Dietz, T. (1995). Influences on attitude-behavior relationships: A natural experiment with curbside recycling. *Environment and Behavior, 27*, 699–718.

Hardin, G. (1968). The tragedy of the commons. *Science, 162*, 1243-1248.

Harland, P., Staats, H., & Wilke, H. A. M. (1999). Explaining proenvironmental intention and behavior by personal norms and the theory of planned behavior. *Journal of Applied Social Psychology, 29*, 2505-2528.

Hartig, T. (2007). Three steps to understanding restorative environments as health resources. In C. Ward Thompson & P. Travlou (Eds.), *Open space: People space* (pp. 163-179). London: Taylor & Francis.

Hartig, T., Kaiser, F. G., & Bowler, P. A. (2001). Psychological restoration in nature as a positive motivation for ecological behavior. *Environment and Behavior, 33*, 590-607.

Hartig, T., Kaiser, F. G., & Strumse, E. (2007). Psychological restoration in nature as a source of motivation for ecological behaviour. *Environmental Conservation, 34*, 291-299.

Hines, J. M., Hungerford, H. R., & Tomera, A. N. (1986/87). Analysis and synthesis of research on responsible environmental behavior: A meta-analysis. *Journal of Environmental Education, 18*, 1–8.

Hunecke, M., Blöbaum, A. Matthies, E., & Höger, R. (2001). Responsibility and environment – Ecological norm orientation and external factors in the domain of travel mode choice behavior. *Environment and Behavior, 33*, 845-867.

Joireman, J. A., van Lange, P. A. M., Kuhlman, D. M., van Vugt, M., & Shelley, G. P. (1997). An interdependence analysis of commuting decisions. *European Journal of Social Psychology, 27*, 441-463.

Kaiser, F. G. (1998). A general measure of ecological behavior. *Journal of Applied Social Psychology, 28*, 395-422.

Kaiser, F. G. (2004). Ecological behavior. In Ch. Spielberger (Ed.), *Encyclopedia of applied psychology* (Vol. 1; pp. 473-477). San Diego, CA: Academic Press.

Kaiser, F. G. (2006). A moral extension of the theory of planned behavior: Norms and anticipated feelings of regret in conservationism. *Personality and Individual Differences, 41*, 71-81.

Kaiser, F. G., & Byrka, K. (2009). *Environmentalism as a trait: Gauging people's prosocial personality with environmental engagement.* Manuscript submitted for publication.

Kaiser, F. G., Byrka, K., & Hartig, T. (2009). *Campbell's paradigm: Reviving attitudes as a prolific concept for psychology.* Manuscript under revision.

Kaiser, F. G., Hübner, G., & Bogner, F. X. (2005). Contrasting the theory of planned behavior with the value-belief-norm-model in explaining ecological behavior. *Journal of Applied Social Psychology, 35*, 2150–2170.

Kaiser, F. G., Midden, C., & Cervinka, R. (2008). Evidence for a data-based environmental policy: Induction of a behavior-based decision support system. *Applied Psychology: An International Review, 57*, 151-172.

Kaiser, F. G., Oerke, B., & Bogner, F. X. (2007). Behavior-based environmental attitude: Development of an instrument for adolescents. *Journal of Environmental Psychology, 27*, 242-251.

Kaiser, F. G., Roczen, N., & Bogner, F. X. (2008). Competence formation in environmental education: advancing ecology-specific rather than general abilities. *Umweltpsychologie, 12*, 56-70.

Kaiser, F. G., & Scheuthle, H. (2003). Two challenges to a moral extension of the theory of planned behavior: Moral norms and just world beliefs in conservationism. *Personality and Individual Differences, 35,* 1033-1048.

Kaiser, F. G., & Wilson, M. (2000). Assessing people's general ecological behavior: A cross-cultural measure. *Journal of Applied Social Psychology, 30,* 952-978.

Kaiser, F. G., & Wilson, M. (2004). Goal-directed ecological behavior: The specific composition of a general performance. *Personality and Individual Differences, 36,* 1531-1544.

Kaiser, F. G., Wölfing, S., & Fuhrer, U. (1999). Environmental attitude and ecological behaviour. *Journal of Environmental Psychology, 19,* 1-19.

Kals, E. D., Schumacher, & Montada, L. (1999). Emotional Affinity toward Nature as a Motivational Basis to Protect Nature. *Environment and Behavior, 31,* 178-202.

Kaplan, S. (1995). The restorative benefits of nature: Toward an integrative framework. *Journal of Environmental Psychology, 15,* 169-182.

Kellert, S. R, & Wilson, E. O. (Eds.). (1993). *The Biophilia Hypothesis*. Washington, DC: Island Press.

Komorita, S. S., & Parks, C. D. (1995). Interpersonal relations: Mixed-motive interaction. *Annual Review of Psychology, 46,* 183-207.

Kramer, R. M., McClintock, C. G., & Messick, D. M. (1986). Social values and cooperative response to a simulated resource conservation crisis. *Journal of Personality, 54,* 576-592.

Leopold, A. (1949). *A Sand County Almanac: With essays on conservation from Round River.* New York: Ballantine Books.

Lindenberg, S., & Steg, L. (2007). Normative, gain and hedonic goal frames guiding environmental behavior. *Journal of Social Issues, 63,* 117-137.

Mackie, J. L. (1977). *Ethics: Inventing right and wrong*. New York: Penguin.

Maloney, M. P., & Ward, M. D. (1973). Ecology: Let's hear it from the people. *American Psychologist, 28,* 583–586.

Mayer, F. S., & Frantz, C. M. (2004). The connectedness to nature scale: A measure of individuals' feeling in community with nature. *Journal of Environmental Psychology, 24,* 503-515.

Midden, C. J. H., Kaiser, F. G., & McCalley, L. T. (2007). Technology's four roles in understanding individuals' conservation of natural resources. *Journal of Social Issues, 63,* 155-174.

Milfont, T. L., & Duckitt, J. (2004). The structure of environmental attitudes: A firstand second-order confirmatory factor analysis. *Journal of Environmental Psychology, 24,* 289-303.

Nisbet, E. K. L., Zelenski, J. M., & Murphy, S. A. (in press). The Nature Relatedness Scale: Linking individuals' connection with nature to environmental concern and behavior. *Environment and Behavior.*

Olli, E., Grendstad, G., & Wollebaek, D. (2001). Correlates of environmental behaviors: Bringing back social context. *Environment and Behavior, 33,* 181-208.

Orr, D. W. (1994). *Earth in mind: On education, environment, and the human prospect.* Washington, DC: Island Press.

Rosenberg, M. J., & Hovland, C. I. (1960). Cognitive, affective, and behavioral components of attitudes. In C. I. Hovland & M. J. Rosenberg (Eds.), *Attitude organization and change: An analysis of consistency among attitude components* (pp. 1-14). New Haven, CT: Yale University Press.

Roszak, T., Gomes, M. E., & Kanner, A. D. (Eds.) (1995). *Ecopsychology: Restoring the earth, healing the mind.* San Francisco, CA: Sierra Club Books.

Schultz, P. W. (2001). The structure of environmental concern: Concern for self, other people, and the biosphere. *Journal of Environmental Psychology, 21,* 327-339.

Schultz, P. W. (2002). Inclusion with nature: The psychology of human-nature relations. In P. Schmuck & W. P. Schultz (Eds.), *Psychology of sustainable development* (pp. 61-78). Boston: Kluwer.

Schultz, P. W., & Oskamp, S. (1996). Effort as a moderator of the attitude-behavior relationship: General environmental concern and recycling. *Social Psychology Quarterly, 59,* 375-383.

Schultz, P. W., Oskamp, S., & Marinieri, T. (1995). Who recycles and when? A review of personal and situational factors. *Journal of Environmental Psychology, 15,* 105-121.

Schultz, P. W., Shriver, C., Tabanico, J. J., & Khazian, A. M. (2004). Implicit connections with nature. *Journal of Environmental Psychology, 24,* 31-42.

Schwartz, S. H. (1973). Normative explanations of helping behavior: A critique, proposal, and empirical test. *Journal of Experimental Social Psychology, 9,* 349–364.

Schwartz, S. H. (1977). Normative influences on altruism. In L. Berkowitz (Ed.), *Advances in experimental social psychology* (Vol. 10, pp. 221–279). New York: Academic Press.

Staats, H. (2003). Understanding proenvironmental attitudes and behavior: An analysis and review of research based on the theory of planned behavior. In M. Bonnes, T. Lee, & M. Bonaiuto (Eds.), *Psychological theories for environmental issues* (pp. 171-201). Aldershot, UK: Ashgate.

Stern, P. C. (1978). When do people act to maintain common resources? A reformulated psychological question for our times. *International Journal of Psychology, 13,* 149–158.

Stern, P. C. (2000). Toward a coherent theory of environmentally significant behavior. *Journal of Social Issues, 56,* 407-424.

Stern, P. C., & Dietz, T. (1994). The value basis of environmental concern. *Journal of Social Issues, 50,* 65–84.

Stern, P. C., Dietz, T., Abel, T., Guagnano, G. A., & Kalof, L. (1999). A value-belief-norm theory of support for social movements: The case of environmental concern. *Human Ecology Review, 6,* 81–97.

Van Lange, P. A. M. (1999). The pursuit of joint outcomes and equality in outcomes: An integrative model of social value orientation. *Journal of Personality and Social Psychology, 77,* 337-349.

Van Vugt, M., Meertens, R. M., & van Lange, P. A. M. (1995). Car versus public transportation? The role of social value orientations in a real-life social dilemma. *Journal of Applied Social Psychology, 25,* 258-278.

Vining, J., & Ebreo, A. (2002). Emerging theoretical and methodological perspectives on ecological behavior. In R. Bechtel & A. Churchman (Eds.), *The New Handbook of Environmental Psychology* (pp. 541-558). New York: John Wiley.

Wardekker, W. L. (2001). Schools and moral education: Conformism or autonomy? *Journal of Philosophy of Education, 35,* 101-114.

In: Psychological Approaches to Sustainability
Editors: V. Corral-Verdugo et al.

ISBN 978-1-60876-356-6
© 2010 Nova Science Publishers, Inc.

Chapter 7

THE SOCIO-PSYCHOLOGICAL AFFINITY TOWARDS DIVERSITY: FROM BIODIVERSITY TO SOCIO-ECOLOGICAL SUSTAINABILITY

Mirilia Bonnes[*]
Università degli Studi di Roma "La Sapienza," Italy

Giuseppe Carrus
Università degli Studi Roma Tre, Italy

Victor Corral-Verdugo
Universidad de Sonora, Mexico

Paola Passafaro
Università degli Studi di Roma "La Sapienza," Italy

ABSTRACT

This chapter discusses the concept of Affinity Towards Diversity (ATD), defined as a socio-psychological predisposition to appreciate the dynamic variety of human-nature interactions in everyday life situations. It is posited that ATD goes beyond a mere superficial acceptance for variation in social and physical contexts. Rather, we assume that ATD implies the deep enjoyment and positive evaluation of the diversities existing in the surrounding environment, at both the biological and socio-cultural levels. The topic is addressed in the light of the increasing importance that ecological sciences (biological and social) are assigning to the conservation of biological and cultural diversity within socio-ecological systems, in order to achieve a more sustainable development. The results of an empirical study on the role of ATD, as a socio-psychological driver of a pro-sustainability orientation and pro-environmental friendly behaviors, are presented and discussed. These results show that ATD positively covary with a series of measures of

---

[*] Corresponding author: Prof. Mirilia Bonnes, Sapienza University of Rome, Department of Psychology of Social and Developmental Processes, Via dei Marsi 78 - 00185 Rome, Italy. Tel. +39 06 49917546 - Fax +39 06 49917652. E-mail: mirilia.bonnes@uniroma1.it

altruism, future orientation, feelings of indignation due to environmental degradation, and attitudes towards green areas in the city, which in turn, are interrelated. This interrelation produces a higher-order construct that we called "pro-sustainability orientation" (PSO). Results of a structural equation model show that PSOE positively influences ATD, altruism, future orientation, attitudes towards integration of urban green areas, and feelings of indignation due to environmental degradation, and negatively affects attitudes that oppose integration of urban green areas. PSO also influences the self-report of pro-environmental behaviors. The model results also confirm that people more attracted to bio and socio-diversity are also more tolerant individuals. Thus, ATD seems to be linked to a series of indicators of sustainable practices and predispositions. The practical implications of these results for the promotion of sustainable lifestyles are also discussed.

INTRODUCTION

Diversity has always played a controversial role in the life of human beings. Rejected and beloved at a time, in some cases it appears as the solution to the problem (i.e., environmental or ecological deterioration), while in others it is addressed as the problem itself. Important source of life, renewal and growth, it has nevertheless been continuously menaced in its integrity. Biological diversity (or *biodiversity),* considered under the genetic, functional, and evolutionary points of view, is the key element of all life forms in the biosphere (e.g., Barbault, 1995; di Castri, 1995; Wilson, 1999). According to a definition put forward in 1988 by the IUCN-*International Union of the Conservation of Nature* during its XVIII General Assembly, biodiversity is "the variety and variability of all living organisms." This includes the genetic level of species (intra-species variability), the level of life forms among species (inter-species variability) and the level of ecosystems (variability of complexes of species and related ecological processes). By following the evolutionary paradigm of bio-ecological sciences, diversity is conceived as a mechanism of pre-adaptation of any living system for facing ecological changes, and thus an "opportunity" for the long term continuity of life within any complex system (di Castri & Balayi, 2002; Wilson, 1999).

Biodiversity is thus an inalienable good, although an increasingly threatened resource. Biodiversity loss has been indeed indicated as one of the most dangerous global environmental changes threatening the biosphere in present time (Wilson, 1999). Diversity, however, is not only of biological nature. A number of leading scholars in the field of ecological sciences (both biological and social) have indeed proposed to widen the concept of biodiversity by including the notion of socio-cultural diversity (i.e., *biodiversity* and *sociodiversity*). In this perspective, both aspects can be considered as parts of a broader *diversity* concept (e.g., Alfsen-Norodom & Lane, 2002; Dansereau, 1997; di Castri & Balayi, 2002; Guillitte, 2005). Diversity should then be more generally considered as "the foremost adaptive and evolutionary strategy to face unpredictable changes - and to ensure options for the future – in all biological, cultural and economic systems" (di Castri & Balayi, 2002, p.15).

In sum, diversity is one of the basic principles of ecological sciences. Any socio-ecological system needs a sufficient variety in its constituting elements in order to survive and to develop through time (Pradhan, 2006). This principle applies to both, biological ecology and human ecology (Capra & Pauli, 1995). However, human activities had an increasingly negative impact on biological diversity in the last decades. It is estimated that if this trend remains unchanged, entire species and families of plants and animals will be extinguished in few decades (Starke, 2008). Moreover, economic globalization and increasing urbanization are pushing human societies towards the homologation of cultural systems. Minority languages, traditions and costumes are being threatened by majority cultures, and this leads to a loss of socio-cultural diversity, a fundamental condition for human evolution (Tonn, 2007).

The aim of is chapter is to illustrate the concept of Affinity Towards Diversity (ATD), defined as a socio-psychological predisposition to appreciate the dynamic variety of human-nature interactions in everyday life situations. Specifically, we are aimed to investigate whether the appreciation of both biological and socio-cultural diversity can be a socio-psychological basis leading individuals to care for the quality of their socio-physical environment. The results of a recent empirical study on the role of affinity towards diversity as a socio-psychological driver of pro-sustainability orientation and environmentally friendly behaviors will be presented and discussed.

BIODIVERSITY AND SOCIODIVERSITY

Biodiversity has been defined as the variability existing within species (genetic diversity), among species, and among ecosystems (UNEP, 1992). Ecosystems are in fact composed of a huge number of species, interdependent of each other for obtaining nutrients and other components of the life cycle. If the biological diversity within an ecosystem is seriously damaged, the entire system might collapse because of the negative consequences on the nutrients cycle (Tonn, 2007). The loss of plants and animal species, at a rate that overcomes the birth of new species, is the more tangible manifestation of biodiversity loss (European Communities, 2008). It is important noting that the rate of species extinction caused by humans in the last decades is one thousand times more rapid than the "normal" rate occurred, until now, throughout the history of our planet (Millennium Ecosystem Assessment, 2005). According to some authors, this phenomenon could be even more extreme: The natural extinction rate has ranged between 10 and 100 species lost per year. However, in the second half of the XX century, the extinction of about 27,000 species per year only in the tropical forests has been calculated (Elewa, 2008).

The causes for this phenomenon have been attributed to the same factors that might underlie environmental degradation in human societies. Population growth is a strong factor in this sense: To sustain an increasing number of people in the planet we need to exploit natural resources at an increasingly higher rate, and this might contribute to the loss of biodiversity. The estimates of the United Nations seem also to suggest that this situation could be even worse in the close future: based on predictions regarding population growth, it is estimated that human societies will require 50% more food production compared to current requirements. This increase could be achieved only by substituting current wild lands with land to be used for agriculture and animal farming purposes. Likewise, cereal production will require an increase of 80% by the year 2030, in order to satisfy increasing human demands.

In sum, biological diversity, in its various forms, is currently undergoing serious threats. In regard to plant biodiversity, the IUCN reports that 70% of plant species are at risk from extinction (IUCN, 2008), including important species used for pharmaceutical production (Hawkins, 2008). A similar situation characterizes animal and marine biodiversity, which is increasingly threatened by global environmental changes, such as global warming (Boyle and Grow, 2008; Elewa, 2008), and by direct human activities such as industrial fishing (FAO, 2007).

In parallel to the loss of biological diversity in the biosphere, a decreasing trend seems to also characterize cultural diversity (or socio-diversity) present in human societies (Jimeno, Sotomayor & Valderrama, 1995). Socio-diversity is related to variety in languages, religions, costumes and traditions, as well as to diversity in political, economic, generational and sexual orientations within and between human societies (O'Hara, 1995). The extinction of spoken languages is common as the extinction of species in ecosystems. According to Nettle and Romaine (2000), 90% of languages will be extinguished in the next 100 years. Economic globalization and cultural homologation are also impacting on other forms of socio-diversity, such as food and eating practices, for example (Lacy, 1994). The loss of socio-diversity might also bring serious consequences to human wellbeing. In fact, according to some authors, the evolutionary basis driving human progress requires a sufficient amount of socio-diversity (Tonn, 2007). The same logic applied to bio-diversity as a basis for sustainability can be applied to socio-diversity: the higher the variety of cultural forms, the higher the potential sustainability for human progress. Furthermore, the same kind of factors seems to be responsible for the simultaneous loss of biological and cultural diversity. This might imply that the straightest way to guarantee biodiversity within ecosystems is to maintain socio-diversity among human cultures. Indeed, several authors from ecological sciences have stressed the crucial relation and interdependence between biological and cultural diversity (e.g., Alfsen-Norodom e Lane, 2002; di Castri, 2003; di Castri e Balayi, 2002; Guillitte, 2005).

Taken together, all these considerations suggest the importance of promoting the simultaneous presence of biological and cultural variety existing on the planet. Psychological research can contribute to this task by investigating the existence of socio-psychological factors which might be at the basis of a human tendency to appreciate the diversity characterizing the physical environment, and the consequent individual willingness to engage in pro-environmental behaviors.

The aim of this chapter is to explore a specific socio-psychological dimension which might be at the basis of a more sustainable human behavior: Affinity Towards Diversity (ATD). ATD could be conceptualized as a relevant component of people's pro-environmental and pro-sustainability commitment. According to the assumptions of the ecological sciences mentioned before, we may define ATD as a tendency to prefer diversity and variations in bio-physical and socio-cultural living scenarios. ATD can then be considered as a socio-psychological predisposition to appreciate the dynamic variety of human-nature interactions. ATD should reflect a stable liking for the biophysical and cultural diversity that individuals face in their everyday life: i.e., physical (landscapes, weather), biological (plants, animals) and socio-cultural (ethnicity, religions, sexual orientations, political inclinations) diversity encountered in daily interaction with the social world. As pointed out by Corral-Verdugo, Bonnes, Tapia-Fonllem, Fraijo-Sing, Frias-Armenta & Carrus (2009), this idea can be based upon scientific theories, such as the *Biophilia Hypothesis* (e.g., Kellert, 1997; Kellert & Wilson, 1993; Wilson, 1984; 2001; see also Frumkin, 2001; Penn, 2003) as well as socio-political movements, such as the *deep ecology* movement (Devall & Sessions, 1985; Glasser, 2005); also upon studies modeling environmental preferences (Kaplan, 1992) as we discuss in the following section.

COMPLEXITY, VARIETY, AND ENVIRONMENTAL PREFERENCES

How do human beings perceive diversity? Is there any attraction towards diversity that humans feel? According to a number of psycho-environmental studies, a positive answer to the later question seems plausible. Rachel and Stephen Kaplan (Kaplan, 1992), in their studies on environmental preferences (i.e., the liking a person manifests for a particular setting, and how much people prefer a place instead of another) have found that *complexity* is a significant predictor of this preference. They define complexity as "the richness or number of different objects in the scene" (p. 588). Thus, complexity implies a high degree of elements' variety in a setting, among other aspects. Scenes with few objects are not very attractive since they "do not offer so much to see," according to the Kaplans. We, humans, are information-seeking organisms who look for diversity or complexity since these features offer the promise of potential knowledge, which will be useful in adapting ourselves to a new, or even a familiar, setting (Roberts, 2007). Therefore, the preference towards complexity (or diversity) would be an evolved mental tendency that allows us advantages in perceiving environmental opportunities. This makes complexity a feature of what Gibson (1979) call *affordances*.

Scott (1993) found that complexity is not only manifested in natural settings but also in the built environment, residential interiors for instance. She conducted a study in which complexity was represented by the number and variety of elements in the interior design of a house, the composition of those elements and the spatial geometry of the scene. The correlation between preference and complexity was high and significant. Yet, Kaplan's (1992) studies clarify that, along with complexity, people prefer naturalness; thus, complex stimuli in natural settings would be preferred over those found in built environments. This makes sense because human evolution has transcurred almost completely in contact with nature.

Moreover, Roberts (2007) found a marked preference and aesthetic judgments towards complex visual stimuli (a large number and heterogeneity of objects, that is: higher diversity) which were presented to participants in a series of slides. This seems to imply that humans are born provided with a tendency to prefer diverse stimulant arrangements, which are judged as having a higher gradient of "beauty" in contrast with simpler stimuli.

AFFINITY TOWARDS DIVERSITY AND PRO-SUSTAINABLE ORIENTATION: AN EMPIRICAL STUDY

From the above-revised literature it could be concluded that affinity towards environmental diversity and complexity is inherent to human mind. The question is: Does this affinity lead people towards environmental protection? Diversity is a condition for environmental integrity and humans are attracted to it. Linking ATD to sustainable behavior would be a logical conclusion. Yet, we have to empirically demonstrate that such a link actually exists. In addition, we have to prove the existence of a relation between affinity towards biodiversity and affinity towards sociodiversity.

Some previous studies have indeed showed how people's attitudes towards environmental diversity can be linked to people's attitudes towards socio-cultural diversity. A study by Carrus, Passafaro and Bonnes (2004) revealed for example that attitudes towards urban green areas (conceived as a form of diversity of the urban landscape) are linked to more general attitudes towards human diversity: individuals having less positive attitudes towards nature in the city and urban green spaces are also characterized by higher scores on ethnocentrism and authoritarianism scales. How can we explain these links? It can be hypothesized that ATD is the expression of a general tendency to value the richness of natural and cultural scenarios that characterize all kind of socio-ecological niches where people live in, or interact with. Thus, it might also be part of a more general socio-psychological dimension oriented towards socio-ecological sustainability, which could be defined as a *pro-sustainability orientation.*

Individuals with this tendency to liking and searching for diversity, as a feature of their living environment, should also be more prone to act in defense of such diversity. As a consequence, they should be likely to practice more ecologically friendly and more sustainable behaviors.

The study presented in this chapter aimed at assessing the relations between ATD and a set of potentially related psychological factors, which have been identified by previous research as predictors of pro-environmental attitudes and behaviors. Specifically, these factors refer to altruism and prosocial values (e.g., Bonaiuto, Bilotta, Bonnes, Carrus, Ceccareli, & Martorella, 2008; Cameron, Brown & Chapman, 1998; Ebreo, Hershey & Vinning, 1999; Hooper & Nielsen, 1991; Pol, 2002; Schultz, 2001), future orientation (Corral-Verdugo and Pinheiro; 2006; Joreiman, Lasane, Bennett, Richards & Solaimani, 2001; Pinheiro, 2002), tolerance/intolerance (Corral-Verdugo, Salazar, Contreras, Delgado & Iturralde, 2002), feelings of indignation due to others' anti-environmental actions (Kals, Schumacher, & Montada, 1999; Montada & Kals, 1995; Vining, 2003), positive and negative attitudes towards urban green spaces (Bonnes, Passafaro, & Carrus, 2009; Carrus et al., 2004). All of these factors have been related to sustainably behaviors. Furthermore, a study by Corral-Verdugo et al. (2009) showed that many of these factors, taken together, can constitute a more general socio-psychological dimension that has been defined as a *pro-sustainability orientation* (PSO) This orientation might, in turn, lead individuals to be more willing to ensure the long-term sustainability of human relations to socio-ecological systems, and thus be the more proximal psychological driver of the individual tendency to engage in pro-environmental behaviors.

Essentially, we are aimed at demonstrating that affinity towards diversity is a significant component of pro-sustainability orientation by looking at the interrelations between ATD and the series of pro-environmental attitudes and behaviors that constitute PSO.

METHOD

Participants and Procedure

The study involved 390 participants (196 females, 194 males) living in four different Italian cities, with an average population of about 50,000 inhabitants. The cities are located in central (Latina and Formia) and southern Italy (Salerno and Taranto). The average age of participants was 41 years (S.D.=15,3: range 18-85). Their education level was 4,9% elementary school, 17,9% middle high school, 51% high school and 26,2% university degree.

Participants lived in various areas of the cities considered. They were contacted at home or on the streets, and asked to respond to a university survey on environmental issues.

Measures

A self-reported paper-and-pencil questionnaire assessing the previously mentioned psychological variables together with socio-demographic variables was set up. The variables were measured as follows:

- *Affinity towards diversity* was assessed through 14 items taken from Corral-Verdugo et al. (2009; ATD scale); it encompassed items indicating preference for physical (weather, scenarios) and biological (plants, animals) diversity, as well as human (ethnic, gender, age) and social (religious, social-class, political) diversity. Responses ranged from 0= "Does not apply to me," 1="It almost does not apply to me," 2="It partially applies to me," to 3= "It totally applies to me."
- *Altruism* was measured through 12 items, taken from Corral-Verdugo, Tirado, Mejía, & Lobo (2006). Participants reported the frequency (on a scale ranging from 0= "never" to 3= "always") with which they engage in behaviors such as helping injured people, providing money to homeless people, contributing economically to the Red Cross, etc.
- *Intolerance* was assessed through 13 items, taken from Corral-Verdugo et al. (2002); consisting of statements revealing rejection or criticism against minorities and groups of people including women, young people, homosexuals, HIV-positive individuals, etc. Subjects are asked to express their views on a four-step scale, ranging from 0= "completely disagree", 1 ="slightly disagree", 2 ="slightly agree", to 3="completely agree"
- *Future orientation* was measured through 10 items of the Future Perspective subscale taken from Zimbardo's Time Perspective Inventory (Zimbardo & Boyd, 1998). This subscale assesses differences in the extent to which individuals are influenced by the immediate versus distant consequences of their behavior. Items are assessed on a 4-point Likert scale, according to "how truly" each statement applies to the respondent. Examples of items for this scale are "I believe a person's day should be planned ahead each morning" and "It upsets me to be late for appointments."
- *Feelings of indignation due to others' anti-environmental actions* were measured through 7 items, taken from Corral-Verdugo et al. (2006); this scale includes situations such as "watching jammed and polluted streets" or "watching my neighbors wasting water." Respondents had to rate their reaction before each situation, using the following scale: 0 ="I feel indifference", 1="I feel slightly bad myself"...to 5= "I feel so bad that I'd try to prevent someone from doing it by all means."
- *Positive and negative attitudes towards urban green areas* were measured through 10 items, assessing both a perspective of integration and a perspective of opposition towards green areas in the city. The instrument was taken from Carrus et al. (2004). These items were responded using a 0 (totally disagree) to 3 (totally agree) scale.

- *Pro-environmental behaviors* were measured through 16 items, taken from Kaiser (1998). Participants were asked to report the frequency (on a scale ranging from 0 = "never" to 3 = "always") of their engaging in behaviors such as collecting and recycling used paper, buying products in refillable packages, or turning down the air conditioning when leaving home.

RESULTS

Descriptive statistics and reliability indexes for all the scale used are reported in Table 1. As can be seen from this table, all the measures employed showed an acceptable internal consistency. There were moderate-to-high levels of affinity towards diversity as manifested in responses to the ATD scale's items, and intermediate levels of self-reported altruistic behaviors. The lowest levels of acceptance of the instruments' items were for the intolerance and opposition towards green areas scales.

Structural equation modeling with latent variables (SEM) was used to test our main hypotheses: i.e., affinity towards diversity, together with altruism, future orientation, intolerance, feelings of indignation due to others' anti-environmental actions, positive and negative attitudes towards urban green spaces, should constitute a more general socio-psychological dimension, defined as a Pro-Sustainability Orientation. This, in turn, should predict pro-environmental behaviors. As in our previous study (Corral-Verdugo et al., 2009) intolerance was specified as covariating with ATD; also, in the present analysis we hypothesized a correlation between intolerance and oppositional attitudes towards integration of urban green areas, and one more covariation between intolerance and pro-sustainability orientation. Items of all the scales were parceled into two indicators for each tested construct. Results of the SEM are displayed in figure 1.

As can be seen from figure 1, the salient and significant ($p < .05$) coefficients between the first-order latent factors and their corresponding observed indicators suggest a convergent validity in their assessment. A relation between affinity towards biodiversity and affinity towards sociodiversity was indicated by significant covariations between the items corresponding to those ATD facets. The relations between pro-sustainability orientation and its predictors (the first-order latent variables) were also salient and significant. This indicates that ATD is a part of the more general pro-sustainability orientation. All the factors considered emerged as direct indicators of pro-sustainability orientation. As expected, pro-sustainability orientation showed a strong and significant relation with self-reported pro-environmental behaviors. Intolerance negatively correlated with ATD and positively with oppositional attitudes towards green integration; yet, no significant covariation between intolerance and PSO was found.

Table 1. Univariate statistics and reliability coefficients of scales

Scale/items	N	mean	(sd)	Min	Max	alpha
Affinity towards diversity						.64
Likes the existence of different religions	390	1.85	(0.89)	0	3	
Enjoys getting together with people of diverse ethnicity	389	1.83	(0.96)	0	3	
Sexual diversity is not bad	388	1.30	(1.07)	0	3	
Enjoys being with people of every social classes	390	2.46	(0.73)	0	3	
Only likes the company of people his/her age/generation*	388	2.34	(0.93)	0	3	
Appreciates the existence of diverse political orientations	389	2.25	(0.83)	0	3	
Does not enjoy getting together people not his/her gender*	389	2.33	(0.83)	0	3	
Likes many kinds (species) of animals, not only a few	390	2.34	(0.90)	0	3	
Likes having very few kinds of plants in her/his garden*	390	2.55	(0.80)	0	3	
Likes visiting zoos with many kinds of animals	389	2.03	(1.05)	0	3	
The more the variety of plants exist, better for her/him	388	2.58	(0.67)	0	3	
Only likes a very few domestic animals*	390	1.53	(1.05)	0	3	
Only enjoys one type of weather (cold or hot)*	390	1.83	(1.04)	0	3	
Could gladly live anywhere (forest, beach, desert, etc) (*Reversed)	390	1.21	(1.02)	0	3	
Altruistic behavior						.81
Assists a person in need	390	1.61	(0.84)	0	3	
Contributes financially with the Red Cross	389	0.56	(0.71)	0	3	
Assists senior citizens	389	1.18	(0.89)	0	3	
Gives money to the homeless	390	1.34	(0.77)	0	3	
Participates in fund-collection rallies	390	0.91	(0.87)	0	3	
Cooperates with colleagues	384	1.63	(0.88)	0	3	
Gives clothes to the poor	390	2.09	(0.87)	0	3	
Assists people who fall or get hurt	388	2.26	(0.81)	0	3	
Visits the sick at hospitals	389	1.16	(0.90)	0	3	
Helps a senior citizen crossing the street	389	1.72	(0.93)	0	3	
Guides persons asking for direction	389	2.28	(0.78)	0	3	
Donates blood in response to campaigns	386	0.72	(1.03)	0	3	

Table 1. Continued

Scale/items	N	mean	(sd)	Min	Max	alpha
Intolerance						.78
I frequently see people behaving like losers	388	1.49	(0.94)	0	3	
Gays should not attend young-people parties	387	0.81	(0.99)	0	3	
White people are more likely to be successful	388	0.83	(0.98)	0	3	
My religion is the only one allowing salvation	387	0.78	(1.06)	0	3	
Most gang members are dangerous	389	1.76	(0.97)	0	3	
Women are not equal to men	388	1.47	(1.22)	0	3	
Children should not ask many questions	389	0.36	(0.74)	0	3	
Communists are a danger for world peace	387	0.88	(1.06)	0	3	
Most murderers should receive death penalty	389	1.09	(1.13)	0	3	
AIDS patients should be isolated	389	0.61	(0.87)	0	3	
Homosexuality is a mental disease	388	0.88	(1.05)	0	3	
Thieves should be finger-amputated	389	0.71	(1.03)	0	3	
Mothers should not work out of home	389	1.38	(1.12)	0	3	
Future orientation		.80				
A person's day should be planned ahead	387	1.82	(0.91)	0	3	
Before making a decision, weighs costs/benefits	387	2.35	(0.71)	0	3	
Meets obligations to friends and authorities on time	388	2.32	(0.65)	0	3	
Makes lists of things to do	388	1.70	(1.06)	0	3	
(S)he is able to resist temptations	388	2.12	(0.80)	0	3	
Keeps working at difficult, non interesting tasks	387	2.04	(0.74)	0	3	
It upsets her/him to be late for appointments	387	2.35	(0.87)	0	3	
Sets goals, consider means for reaching those goals	387	2.32	(0.65)	0	3	
Completes projects on time making steady progress	388	2.00	(0.74)	0	3	
Doing necessary work comes before tonight's play	388	2.27	(0.74)	0	3	
Feelings of indignation						.80
Watching someone cutting off a tree	389	1.55	(0.99)	0	5	
Watching someone dropping a cigarette stub	389	1.58	(1.04)	0	5	
Watching someone littering	389	2.37	(0.87)	0	5	
Watching someone hurting somebody else	389	2.69	(0.63)	0	5	
Watching factories dropping wastes	389	2.65	(0.63)	0	5	

Table 1. Continued

Scale/items	N	mean	(sd)	Min	Max	alpha
Watching jammed and smog-polluted streets	389	2.24	(0.84)	0	5	
Watching neighbors wasting water	389	1.83	(1.03)	0	5	
Oppositon to green areas						.81
Maintaining green areas, inacceptable cost	389	0.93	(0.96)	0	3	
Trees in city do not bring advantages but problems	389	0.69	(0.82)	0	3	
Trees on the street obstruct vision from windows	388	0.82	(0.88)	0	3	
Maintenance of green areas, too much on pockets	389	0.88	(0.92)	0	3	
Trees remove too much light to buildings	389	0.67	(0.82)	0	3	
Integration of green areas						.83
In green areas, relations with others improve	389	2.37	(0.70)	0	3	
Watching green areas reliefs tension	388	2.45	(0.73)	0	3	
Less stress by contact with nature in the city	388	2.57	(0.68)	0	3	
Citizens need nature for restoration	389	2.44	(0.67)	0	3	
Presence of green makes feel alive	389	2.50	(0.63)	0	3	
Pro-environmental behavior						.75
Waits until having a full load before doing laundry	383	1.99	(0.96)	0	3	
Drives on freeways at speeds under 100 kph	378	0.95	(0.99)	0	3	
Collects and recycles used paper	390	1.60	(1.12)	0	3	
Brings empty bottles to a recycling bin	390	1.82	(1.16)	0	3	
Has pointed out unecological behavior to someone	389	1.38	(0.88)	0	3	
Buys products in refillable packages	389	1.29	(0.84)	0	3	
Buys seasonal produce	389	2.27	(0.69)	0	3	
Reads about environmental issues	389	1.18	(0.83)	0	3	
Talks with friends about environmental problems	390	1.36	(0.83)	0	3	
Turns down the air conditioning when leaving place	369	2.07	(1.21)	0	3	
Looks for ways to reuse things	390	1.84	(0.86)	0	3	
Encourages friends and family to recycle	390	1.56	(0.98)	0	3	
Conserves gasoline by walking or bicycling	389	1.20	(1.08)	0	3	
Buys convenience foods	390	0.59	(0.75)	0	3	
Uses a clothes dryer	381	0.11	(0.50)	0	3	

Goodness of fit indicators for this model are reported at the bottom of figure 1. Although the resulting Chi-squared value was significant ($p<.01$), the values of other relevant indexes suggest an acceptable fit for the entire model ($NNFI=.92$, $CFI=.93$; $RMSEA=.06$).

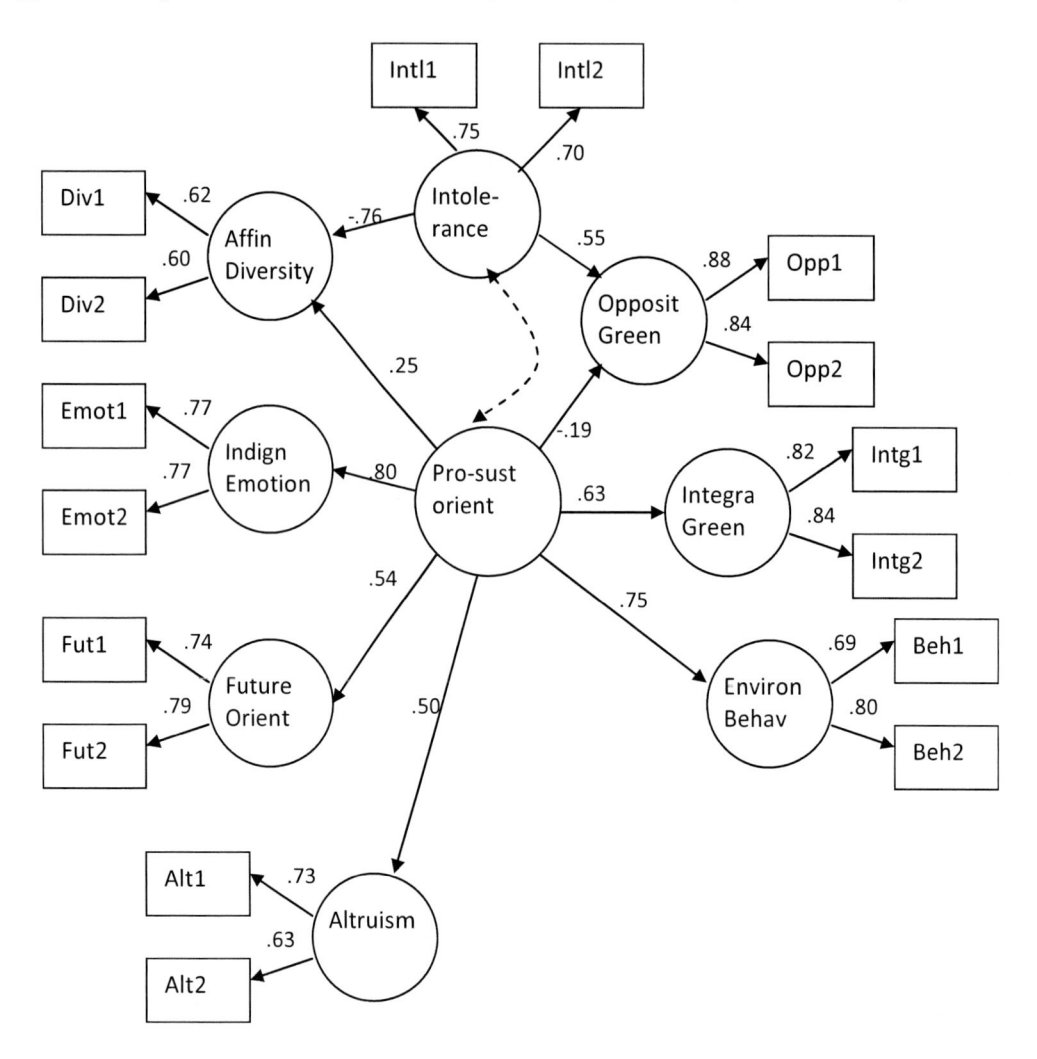

Figure 1. Structural model of relations between Affinity Towards Diversity and other Pro-Sustainability Orientation indicators. The dotted arrow indicates a non significant ($p > .05$) covariance. Goodness of fit: $X^2 = 242.8$ (102 $d.f.$), $p < .001$. $NNFI=.92$, $CFI=.93$; $RMSEA=.06$. Pro-Environmental Behavior's $R^2 = .56$.

Conclusion

The study presented in this chapter confirms that affinity towards diversity (ATD) might support pro-environmental behaviors and could be an important component of what we define as pro-sustainability orientation (PSO). An argument in favor of considering ATD as an important part of pro-sustainability orientation is offered by the salient predictive power of the model that was specified in the present study. The R^2 for pro-environmental behavior was

.56. This means that the combination of ATD plus other psychological factors considered explains 56% of the variance in participants' general ecological behavior. This explanatory power is higher compared to what is usually reported by the literature in this field, as revealed in a recent meta-analysis by Bamberg and Möser (2007).

Our study replicated the previous findings from Corral-Verdugo et al.'s (2009) study showing that ATD opposes a tendency towards intolerance, which is confirmed by the positive correlation between intolerance and the negative attitudes towards green areas in the city. This means that people with favorable attitudes towards bio-diversity and –at the same time- attracted to socio-diversity are tolerant individuals, as expected. However, tolerance was not significantly related to pro-sustainability orientation, the set of behaviors and psychological dispositions that get people closer to a sustainable way of life. This non-significant result might be due to the fact that, sometimes, intolerance is required to fight against anti-environmental attitudes and actions. For instance, Corral-Verdugo et al. (2009) found a significant *and positive* relation between intolerance and pro-environmental behavior. A degree of intolerance is also found in feelings of indignation due to others' anti-environmental action. Both, pro-environmental behaviors and feelings of indignations are a part of PSO. Since some other components of PSO (such as ATD and attitudes towards green areas) correlate in a *negative* way with intolerance, the resulting effect is the non-significant correlation between PSO and intolerance.

From a more practical point of view, the results presented here show a potentially useful approach for studying pro-sustainability orientation: the idea that we, as humans, have a certain degree of affinity for a crucial feature of ecology: diversity. As suggested by the *Biophilia Hypothesis* (e.g., Kellert, 1997) and by studies on the implicit affective evaluation of nature (Korpela, Klemettilä & Hietanen, 2002; Schultz, Shriver, Tabanico & Khazian, 2004), people might be implicitly attracted by diversity in nature and by the variety of non-human life forms.

At the same time, the present results are compatible with the more general idea, put forward by a number of leading scholars in the field of ecological sciences, that the concept of biodiversity should be broadened so to include a social cultural diversity component. Both *biological* and *social-cultural* diversity should then be considered as parts of a broader *diversity* concept, at the basis of the dynamic functioning of any socio-ecological system, as well as at the basis of human progress and evolution (e.g., Alfsen-Norodom & Lane, 2002; Dansereau, 1997; di Castri & Balayi, 2002; Guillitte, 2005).

As our findings seem to suggest, several socio-psychological factors are involved in the human tendency to appreciate diversity in the physical and social environment, and the consequent individual willingness to engage in pro-environmental behaviors. As a practical consequence, if ATD is a relevant component of a more general pro-sustainability orientation, then making ATD more salient among the general public might help to enhance the impact of environmental campaigns and interventions for the promotion of more sustainable behaviors in everyday life contexts.

REFERENCES

Alfsen-Norodom, C. & B. Lane. (2002). Global knowledge networking for site specific strategies: The International Conference on Biodiversity and Society. *Environmental Science & Policy*, 5, 3-8.

Bamberg, S. & Möser, G. (2007). Twenty years after Hines, Hungerford, and Tomera: A new meta-analysis of psycho-social determinants of pro-environmental behaviour. *Journal of Environmental Psychology*, 27, 14-25.

Barbault, R. (1995). Biodiversity: stakes and opportunities. *Nature & Resources*, 31, 18-26.

Bonaiuto, M., Bilotta, E., Bonnes, M., Carrus, G., Ceccarelli, M., & Martorella, H. (2008). Local identity moderating the role of individual differences in natural resource use: the case of water consumption. *Journal of Applied Social Psychology*, 38, 947-967.

Bonnes, M., Passafaro, P., Carrus, G. (2009). The ambivalence of attitudes towards urban green areas: Between pro-environmental worldviews and daily residential experience. *Environment and Behavior*. Manuscript under revision.

Boyle, P. & Grow, S. (2008). The global amphibian crisis. *Endangered Species Bulletin, 33*, 4-6.

Cameron, L.D., Brown, P.M., & Chapman J.G. (1998). Social Value Orientations and decisions to Take Proenvironmental Action. *Journal of Applied Social Psychology*, 28, 675–697.

Capra, F & Pauli, P. (1995). *Steering business toward sustainability*. Nueva York: The United Nations University.

Carrus, G., Passafaro P., & Bonnes, M. (2004). Environmentalism, ethnocentrism and authoritarianism: an attitude toward urban green scale. *Bollettino di Psicologia Applicata*, 242, 3-12.

Corral-Verdugo, V., Bonnes, M., Tapia-Fonllem C., Fraijo-Sing, B., Frias-Armenta, M., & Carrus, G. (2009). Affinity towards diversity as a correlate of sustainable orientation. *Journal of Environmental Psychology,* 29, 34-43.

Corral-Verdugo, V. & Pinheiro, J. (2006). Sustainability, future orientation and water conservation. *European Review of Applied Psychology*, 56, 191-198.

Corral-Verdugo, V., Salazar, M., Contreras, L., Delgado, B. & Iturralde, E. (2002). Creencias en lo mundano y lo divino, rasgos de intolerancia y conductas protectoras del ambiente [Beliefs in worldly and divine dimensions, intolerance and proecological behavior]. In A. Terán & A.M. Landázuri. (Eds.), *Sustentabilidad, Comportamiento y Calidad de Vida* [Sustainability, behavior and quality of life] (pp. 105-114). Mexico City: UNAM.

Corral-Verdugo, V., Tirado, H., Mejía, G. & Lobo, R. (2006). Factores emotivo -emocionales en el deterioro ecológico y sus correlatos [Affective-emotional factors in ecological damage and its correlates]. In AMEPSO (Eds.): *La Psicología Social en México, Vol. XI* [Social Psychology in Mexico] (pp. 691-697). Mexico City: AMEPSO.

Dansereau, P. (1997). Biodiversity, ecodiversity, sociodiversity - Three aspects of diversity: Part 1. *Global Biodiversity*, 6, 2-9.

Devall, B, & Sessions, G. (1985). *Deep Ecology*. Gibbs Smith Publishers. Salt Lake City.

di Castri, F. (1995). The chair of sustainable development. *Nature & Resources*, 31, 2-7.

di Castri, F. (2003). Access to information and e-learning for local empowerment: The requisite for human development and environmental protection. Paper at the European

workshop on "E-learning and grid technologies: a fundamental challenge for Europe". Paris, Ecole Centrale Paris.
di Castri, F., & Balayi, W. (Eds.) (2002). *Tourism, biodiversity and information.* Leiden: Backhuys Publishers.
Ebreo, A., Hershey, J., & Vining, J. (1999). Reducing solid waste: Linking recycling to environmentally responsible consumerism. *Environment & Behavior, 31,* 107-135.
Elewa, A. (2008). *Mass extinction.* Berlin: Springer.
European Communities (2008). *The economics of ecosystems and biodiversity.* Wesseling, Germany: Welsel+Hard.
FAO – Food and Agriculture Organization of the United Nations (2007*).* The State of World Fisheries and Aquaculture 2006. Rome: FAO. Retrieved August 2008 from ftp://ftp.fao.org/docrep/fao/009/a0699e/a0699e.pdf.
Frumkin, H. S. (2001). Beyond toxicity: Human health and the natural environment. *American Journal of Preventive Medicine, 20,* 234-240.
Gibson, J.J. (1979). *The ecological approach to visual perception.* Boston: Houghton Mifflin.
Glasser, H. (2005) (ed), *The Selected Works of Arne Naess,* Volumes 1-10. New York: Springer.
Guillitte, O. (2005). Biodiversity and sociodiversity for a sustainable development. *Liaison Energie Francophonie, 68,* 95-98.
Hawkins, B. (2008) *Plants for Life: Medicinal Plant Conservation and Botanic Gardens.* Richmond, UK: Botanic Gardens Conservation International.
Hooper, J.R. & Nielsen, J.M. (1991). Recycling as altruistic behavior: Normative and behavioral strategies to expand participation in a community recycling program. *Environment & Behavior, 23,* 195-220.
IUCN – International Union for the Conservation of Nature (2008) *2007 IUCN Red List of Threatened Species.* Retrieved August 2008 from: www.iucnredlist.org/.
Jimeno, M., Sotomayor, M. & Valderrama, L. (1995). *Chocó: Diversidad cultural y medio ambiente* [*Chocó: Cultural diversity and environment*]. Bogotá, Colombia: Fondo FEN.
Joreiman, J., Lasane, T., Bennett, J., Richards, D., & Solaimani, S. (2001). Integrating social value orientation and the consideration of future consequences within the extended norm activation model or proenvironmental behaviour. *British Journal of Social Psychology, 40,* 133-155.
Kaiser, F. (1998). A general measure of ecological behavior. *Journal of Applied Social Psychology, 28,* 395-442.
Kals, E., Schumacher, D., & Montada, L. (1999). Emotional affinity toward nature as a motivational basis to protect nature. *Environment & Behavior, 31,* 178-202.
Kaplan, S (1992). Environmental preference in a knowledege-seeking, knowledege-using organism. En J. Barkow, L. Cosmides & J. Tooby (Eds), The Adapted Mind. New York: Oxford University press.
Kellert, S.R. (1997). *Kinship to mastery: Biophilia in human evolution and development.* Washington, DC: Island Press.
Kellert, S.R. & Wilson, E.O. (1993). *The Biophilia Hypothesis.* Washington: Island Press.
Korpela,K., Klemettilä, T. & Hietanen, J.K. (2002). Evidence for rapid affective evaluation of environmental scenes. *Environment and Behavior, 34,* 634-650.
Lacy, W. (1994). Biodiversity, cultural diversity and food equity. *Agriculture and Human Values, 11,* 3-9.

Millennium Ecosystem Assessment (2005) *Ecosystems and Human Well-being: Synthesis.* Washington, DC: Island Press.

Montada, L. & Kals, E. (1995). Perceived justice of ecological policy and proenvironmental commitments. *Social Justice Research, 8*, 305-327.

Nettle, D. & Romaine, S. (2000). *Vanishing voices: the extinction of the world's languages.* New York: Oxford University Press.

O'Hara, S. (1995). Valuing sociodiversity. *International Journal of Social Economics, 22*, 31-49.

Penn, D.J. (2003). The evolutionary roots of our environmental problems: toward a Darwinian ecology. *The Quarterly Review of Biology, 78*, 275-301.

Pinheiro, J. Q. (2002). Comprometimento ambiental: perspectiva temporal e sustentabilidade [Environmental commitment: time perspective and sustainability]. In J. Guevara & S. Mercado (Orgs.), *Temas selectos de Psicologia Ambiental* [Selected themes of environmental psychology] (pp. 463-481). Mexico City: UNAM, GRECO & Fundación Unilibre.

Pol, E. (2002). The theoretical background of the City-Identity-Sustainability Network. *Environment and Behavior, 34*, 8-25.

Pradhan, S.K. (2006). Building resilience in local institutions for natural resources management. *Proceedings of the XI Biennal Conference of the International Association for the Study of Common Property (IASCP)*. Bali, Indonesia: IASCP.

Roberts, M.N. (2007). *Complexity and aesthetic preference for diverse visual stimuli.* Tesis doctoral. Departamento de Psicología, Universitat de les Illes Balears.

Schultz, P.W. (2001). The structure of environmental concern. Concern for self, other people, and the biosphere. *Journal of Environmental Psychology, 21*, 327-339.

Schultz, W., Shriver, C., Tabanico, J.J. & Khazian, A.M. (2004). Implicit connections with nature. *Journal of Environmental Psychology*, 24 31–42.

Scott, S. (1993). Complexity and mystery as predictors of interior preferences. *Journal of Interior Design, 19*, 25-33.

Starke, L. (Ed.) (2008). *State of the World.* New York, W. W. Norton & Company.

Tonn, B. (2007). Futures sustainability. *Futures, 39*, 1097-1116.

UNEP (1992) *Convention on Biological Diversity*. UNEP Environmental Law and institutions Programme Activity Centre. Nairobi: United Nations.

Vining, J. (2003). The connection to other animals and caring for nature. *Research in Human Ecology*, 10, 87-99.

Wilson, E. O. (1984). *Biophilia*. Boston: Harvard University Press.

Wilson, E. O. (1999). *The Diversity of Life*. New York: W.W. Norton.

Wilson, E. O. (2001). Beyond toxicity: Human health and the natural environment. *American Journal of Preventive Medicine*, 20, 241-242.

Zimbardo, P. & Boyd, J. (1999). Putting time in perspective: a valid, reliable individual-differences metric. *Journal of Personality and Social Psychology, 77*, 1271-1288.

In: Psychological Approaches to Sustainability
Editors: V. Corral-Verdugo et al.
ISBN 978-1-60876-356-6
© 2010 Nova Science Publishers, Inc.

Chapter 8

PROMOTING PRO-ENVIRONMENTAL INTENTIONS. THEORETICAL BACKGROUND AND PRACTICAL APPLICATIONS OF TRAVEL FEEDBACK PROGRAMS FOR CAR USE REDUCTION

Satoshi Fujii[*]

Kyoto University, Japan

Ayako Taniguchi

University of Tsukuba, Japan

ABSTRACT

In order to achieve an environmentally sustainable society, pro-ecological policies such as those promoting efficient pro-environmental behaviors that lead to reductions of CO_2 emissions are strongly required. Car-use-reduction behavior is known to be the most pro-environmentally effective for those who drive in daily life. We describe a model to explain behavioral intention of multiple pro-environmental behaviors, and the estimation results of the model reveal that those with higher goals of reducing CO_2 emission more likely will implement diverse types of pro-environmental behavior that they believe are easy and highly effective. Thus, it was implied that providing information regarding actual effectiveness in CO_2 reduction and information about how to reduce car use are indispensable for promoting car-use-reduction behavior. Based on these findings, we suggest that travel feedback programs to provide such information could successfully reduce car use. Two application studies from our interventional programs are described; one is the program for commuting behavior and the other is for new residents (newcomers) at Japanese cities. The field experiments for these two types of program show that these programs could actually promote environmental sustainable travel modes as alternatives to car driving.

---

[*] Correspondence: Dr. Satoshi Fujii, Department of Urban Management, Kyoto University, Japan. E-mail: fujii@trans.kuciv.kyoto-u.ac.jp

INTRODUCTION

For achieving environmentally sustainable society, various types of pro-environmental behavior to reduce CO_2 emission are believed to be called for. These have included adjusting the temperature of air-conditioning, turning off lights and electronic appliances as often as possible, and the reduction of car use. Among various pro-environmental behaviors that people can perform in daily life, car-user-reduction behavior is known to be the most effective option (Fujii & Ohta, 2008). As seen in Table 1, yearly CO_2 reduction by reduction of car use for 10 minutes a day (588 kg;/year) is around 5 times greater than the one resulting from recycling at households everyday (121 kg/year). Also, such a reduction is around 20 times greater than adjusting the thermostat by 1 degree through the year (32 kg/year), and around 300 times greater than the one resulting from turning off a TV (32 kg/year). However, this "fact" is not well known to drivers. Therefore, their pro-environmental behavior would often be *inefficient* in terms of CO_2 reduction even though they were to be highly motivated to reduce such greenhouse gas emissions (Fujii, 2006; Fujii & Ohta, 2006, 2008). Consequently, practical measures to promote people's voluntary behavior change to reduce car use are strongly called for in environmental policy making, and psychologically communicative strategies to make people understand the relative effectiveness of car-user-reduction behavior as compared to other pro-environmental behaviors are especially important.

In order to develop such communicative measures, we need to understand a number of psychological processes; why a certain pro-environmental behavior, such as car-user-reduction behavior, would be selected to be performed from among various types of pro-environmental behavior? In this chapter, we will firstly describe a model of behavioral intention to perform a type of pro-environmental behavior from various options that we previously proposed (Fujii & Ohta, 2006). This will be followed by two sub sections describing practical programs to promote car-user-reduction behavior and the results from tests of their effectiveness.

Table 1. Effect of reducing CO_2 emissions per household per year (Fujii & Ohta, 2004)

Behaviours	Objective effect [kg/yr]
Adjusting the thermostat (1 degree adjustment)	32
Turning off a light (1 hour a day)	2
Turning off a TV (1 hour a day)	13
Refrigerator rearrangement	25
Reducing bathwater reheating (once a day)	80
Reducing showers (2 minutes a day)	44
Shopping with less packaging (every package)	58
Recycling (everything recycled)	121
Reducing automobile use (10 minutes a day)	588
Reducing automobile idling (5 minutes a day)	55

DETERMINANTS OF BEHAVIORAL INTENTIONS FOR PRO-ENVIRONMENTAL BEHAVIOR

With regard to the antecedents of behavioral intentions in multiple types of pro-environmental behavior, we have found that environmental concern, attitudes toward frugality and perceived ease of implementation were all possible determinants (Fujii, 2006). Yet, the significant determinants were found to be different across diverse types of pro-environmental behavior. One study revealed that environmental concern had a positive effect solely for garbage reduction, while attitudes toward frugality had positive effects for gas and electricity reduction. For automobile use reduction, neither environmental concern nor attitude toward frugality produced significant effects (Fujii, 2006). Yet, perceived ease for car-user-reduction behavior was found to be a significant determinant of those intentions. Therefore, educating environmental concern or attitude towards frugality is strongly necessary for promoting almost every type of pro-environmental behavior, but insufficient solely for promoting car-user-reduction behavior. For promoting this reduction, beliefs regarding reduced car use, such as perceived ease, are required. Therefore, it is important to investigate the effects of beliefs or perception regarding multiple types of pro-environmental behavior on behavioral intentions, which are expected to be an important determinant for promoting a specific type of pro-environmental behavior such as reduction of car use behavior.

Having this in mind, the first author of this chapter proposed a model that incorporates determinants of behavioral intentions to perform various pro-environmental behaviors, i.e. perceived ease and perceived effectiveness for each pro-environmental behavior while expanding Fujii's (2006) model by incorporating interactional effects between perceived ease and effectiveness, and a subjective goal to reduce CO_2.

A MODEL OF MULTIPLE PRO-ENVIRONMENTAL BEHAVIORS

Goal Setting Theory (Locke, 1968) suggests that an accepted goal directs attention and actions towards goal-relevant activities. The theory implies that a goal to reduce CO_2 would lead to the intention to perform several types of environmental behaviors, and that the more important the goal, the stronger the behavioral intentions to reach that goal. Studies of socially desirable behaviors, including pro-environmental actions, have revealed that the perceived *effectiveness* of socially desirable behavior is an important behavioral determinant (Chen, Au, & Komorita 1996; Hirose, 1995; Olson, 1965; Strobe & Frey 1982).

When developing behavioral intention, perceived behavioral control also plays an important role. If implementing a specific pro-environmental behavior is believed to be difficult, the behavior may not be attempted even if the motivation to engage in it is present. In other words, the perceived *ease* of pro-environmental behavior has a positive effect on pro-environmental behavior, as implied by Loukopoulos, Jakobsson, Gärling, Schneider, & Fujii (2004).

Although the perceived effectiveness and ease of pro-environmental behaviors positively impact on pro-environmental behavioral intention, they are not sufficient in developing these intentions. Even with a high value of perceived effectiveness and ease, pro-environmental behavioral intention would not develop without a goal to implement that behavior. Thus, perceived effectiveness and ease would have positive effects on pro-environmental behavioral intention only if there is a corresponding goal to implement that pro-environmental behavior. In other words, an effect of goal to implement pro-environmental behavior is assumed to be dependent on various factors.

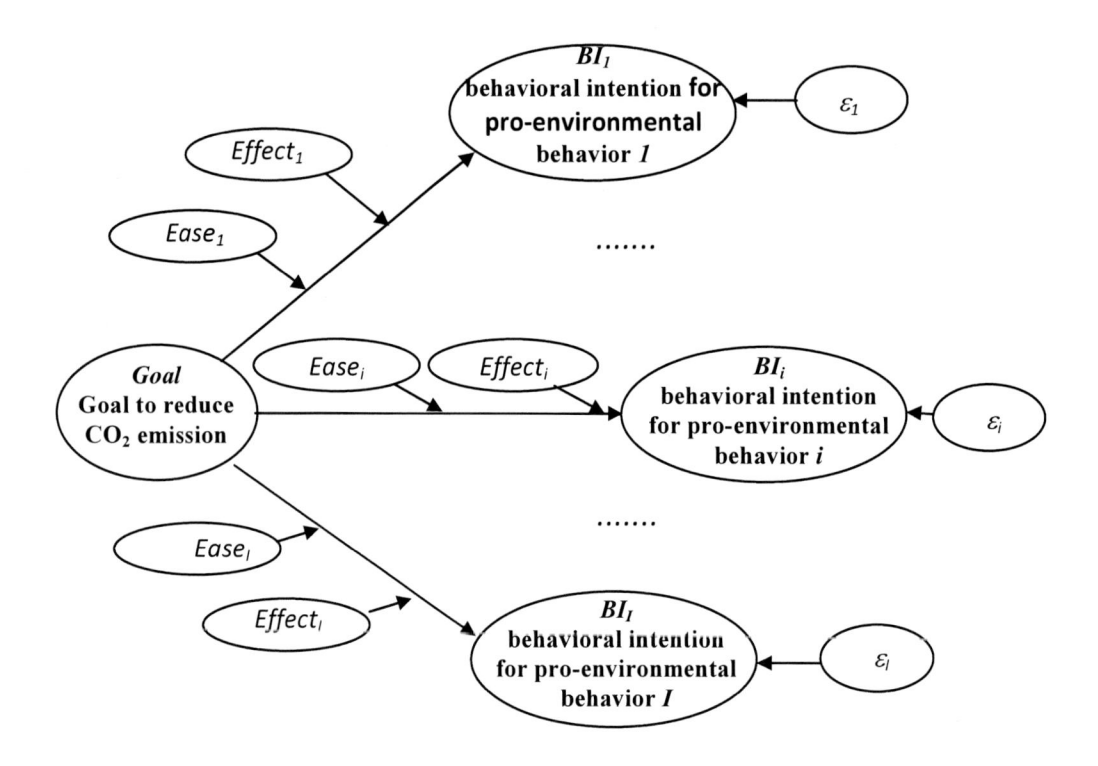

Note: $Effect_i$ = perceived effectiveness of pro-environmental behavior i, $Ease_i$ = perceived ease of pro-environmental behavior i, and ε_i = error term that implies effects of other determinants than $Goal$.

Figure 1. A model of multiple pro-environmental behaviors.

Based on these discussions, we proposed the following model for developing behavioral intention in multiple types of pro-environmental behavior (Fujii & Ohta, 2006). In the model, the relationships between goal, perceived effectiveness, perceived ease, and behavioral intention are represented by the following equation. This model is also represented graphically in Figure 1.

$$BI_i = \alpha_i\, Goal + \varepsilon_i \text{ (for all } i) \tag{1}$$

where, i denotes a type of pro-environmental behavior to reduce CO_2 emissions; $Goal$ is a subjective personal goal to reduce CO_2 emissions; BI_i is a behavioral intention to produce pro-environmental behavior $i,$; ε_i is the error term that denotes effects from factors other than $Goal$ on behavioral intentions to perform pro-environmental behavior i, and α_i denotes the effect size of $Goal$ on a behavioral intention to produce pro-environmental behavior $i,$.

The proposed model assumes, based on the abovementioned discussions, that such variables include perceived effectiveness and ease of pro-environmental behaviors, as follows:

$$\alpha_i = a_i + b_i \, Effect_i + c_i \, Ease_i \text{ (for all } i) \tag{2}$$

where $Effect_i$ denotes the perceived effectiveness of pro-environmental behavior i,; $Ease_i$ indicates the perceived ease of pro-environmental behavior i, and a_i, b_i, and c_i are coefficients to estimate.

Equations (1) and (2) lead to the following equation (3):

$$BI_i = a_i \, Goal + b_i \, Effect_i \, Goal + c_i \, Ease_i \, Goal + \varepsilon_i \text{ (for all } i) \tag{3}$$

This equation indicates that perceived effectiveness and perceived ease have no effect on behavioral intention if there is no goal to reduce CO_2. This is, for example, because $Effect_iGoal$ is 0 when $Goal$ is 0.

This model implies that 1) people are more likely to implement pro-environmental behavior when they have a strong motivation to reduce CO_2 emissions, and that 2) people develop stronger behavioral intentions for pro-environmental behaviors that are associated with higher perceived effectiveness and ease.

FINDINGS FROM THE MODEL ESTIMATION

Equation (3) can be regarded as a linear regression model. The coefficients in the model were empirically estimated using the data obtained in Japan ($n = 341$; see Fujii & Ohta, 2006 for details of the survey). In the survey and model estimation, gas and electricity savings, garbage reduction, and automobile use reduction due to modifying travel behavior were considered as pro-environmental behaviors. An important finding from the empirical analysis in Fujii & Ohta (2006) was that the impact on behavioral intention to perform a type of pro-environmental behavior of goal sensitivity to reduce CO_2 was empirically a function of the perceived effectiveness and ease of the type of pro-environmental behavior, as it was assumed in the model. Thus, it is likely that people with the goal of reducing CO_2 emissions intend to implement types of pro-environmental behavior that they believe are easy and highly effective, as compared to behaviors believed to be difficult and ineffective.

This study's findings implied that pro-environmental behavior could be promoted not only by a campaign that explicitly describes the global environmental problems and seeks to increase people's subjective goal to reduce CO_2, but also by increasing the recognition of effectiveness and ease for various pro-environmental behaviors. Thus, providing information about the objective effectiveness of diverse pro-environmental behaviors and presenting specifically how to behave in favor of the global environment would be effective for global environmental protection.

A Travel Feedback Program Promoting Environmental Sustainable Travel Modes

In our research series, we found that 1) car-user-reduction behavior is objectively the most effective option among various pro-environmental behaviors (Fujii & Ohta, 2008), but 2) environmental concern and attitude toward frugality that were found to be effective in promoting pro-environmental behaviors other than car-user-reduction behavior were not influential determinants for this conservationist behavior (Fujii, 2006), and 3) the informational strategies for strengthen perceived ease and perceived effectiveness would be important in promoting car-user-reduction behavior (Fujii & Ohta, 2006). These three findings imply that practical travel-behavior change programs are highly important for the achievement of a sustainable society, and such programs need to be designed to strengthen the perceived ease and perceived effectiveness of car-user-reduction behavior.

A travel feedback program, as a practical communicative strategy for car-user-reduction behavior that was designed to change perceptions of behavior ease and effectiveness (c.f. Fujii & Taniguchi, 2005, 2006) was proposed. In the following section, we will explain this travel feedback program to promote environmental sustainable travel modes instead of car and the result of the field experiment to investigate the effectiveness of such a program.

The Travel Feedback Program in Workplace Mobility Management

In transportation policy, governments have attempted to change people's travel behavior from car use to sustainable transport modes, such as public transport, bicycles, and walking, to address social issues such as traffic congestion, air pollution and other environmental problems, noise, city center invigoration, and sustained regional mobility. Such measures are usually called *mobility management* (MM; Jones, 2003; Fujii & Taniguchi, 2006).

Mobility management is sometimes categorized into the following three types: workplace, school, and residential (Fujii & Taniguchi, 2006). The important characteristic of communicative workplace mobility management is that it can target commutes between home and the workplace exclusively. Because all commutes to a workplace clearly have an identical destination, *i.e.*, the workplace, we can efficiently provide detailed information on alternative travel modes to car such as public transportation in workplace mobility management. Such information is expected to increase the perceived ease to modal shift from car to public transportation.

We introduced a communicative mobility management measure in the workplace, namely a *travel feedback program* (Fujii and Taniguchi, 2005; 2006), to change employee commuting behavior from car use to alternative travel modes. Similar programs have been implemented in many countries, including the UK, Australia, Germany, Sweden, and Japan (c.f. Brög, 1998; Gärling & Fujii, 2004; Rose & Ampt, 2001; Taniguchi, Hara, Takano, Kagaya, & Fujii, 2003). Recently, a travel feedback program requesting recipients to make a behavior plan about how to change their travel behavior was shown to be more effective than programs that did not, as shown experimentally (Fujii & Taniguchi, 2005) and in a meta-analysis of travel feedback programs (Fujii & Taniguchi, 2006). These results support the abovementioned findings that perceived ease was effective in promoting travel behavior change. In addition, since the typical travel feedback program provides messages about how car-use-reduction behavior is effective in CO_2 reduction and why CO_2 reduction is called for in environmental policy, the results showing effectiveness of these programs in reduction of car use again support the abovementioned model. In this model, the goals to reduce car use and perceived effectiveness in CO_2 reduction, in addition to perceived ease, were all significant determinants of intention for voluntary travel behavioral change.

However, no travel feedback program making such a request has been implemented as workplace mobility management. It may be more difficult to change commutes than discretionary trips, such as shopping or leisure trips, because commuters may feel that changing commutes has a greater subjective cost than changing discretionary trips (c.f. Loukopoulos, et al., 2004). In addition, commuting trip is likely to be more habitual than the other types of trip. A number of results reveal that it is much more difficult to change habitual behavior than non-habitual acting (c.f. Fujii & Gärling, 2007). Therefore, a travel feedback program may not always be effective at changing commutes.

Consequently, an objective of the study we are presenting in this chapter was to test whether a travel feedback program asking participants to make a behavior plan can change commute behavior. To assess the effectiveness of the policy intervention, we administered a panel survey before and after a travel feedback program targeted at employee commutes.

METHOD

The experiment targeted employees of three organizations in the cities of Kobe, Akashi, and Himeji, along the Sanyo railway line, in Japan: Kawasaki Jyuukou and Kikko-man, both industrial plants, and the Akashi city government. The travel feedback program consisted of two steps. First, we distributed a questionnaire to company employees to measure travel behavior before the intervention. A person at each company selected the targets considering the employees' residences. The questionnaire was also used to evaluate commute behavior change. Because only the first step was a communicative intervention involving travel behavior change, this can be called a *"one-shot* travel feedback program."

Respondents who had indicated that they were car commuters were asked to make a behavioral plan about how to change their commuting behavior from car use to another travel mode. This question was included in the questionnaire to give recipients a chance to consider the possibility of using an alternative travel mode (Gollwitzer, 1996; Fujii & Taniguchi, 2005, 2006). To prompt recipients to make a detailed behavioral travel plan, the question on that plan had two components: a request to complete a plan from their office to the nearest railway station, and a request to complete a plan from their home to the nearest railway station from their office (see Figure 2).

Simultaneously, to help recipients complete a plan, they were given information about access trips from the nearest railway station to their office. This information included train and bus timetables, bus lines near the office, the location of bicycle parking, the fee for bicycle parking, taxi fares, and a map showing how to get from the nearest station to the office by walking, cycling, or riding a motorbike. Two months after the first survey, we distributed another questionnaire to the respondents of the first survey to measure the effects of the intervention implemented as workplace mobility management.

Questionnaire for Commuters

This is used for a one-shot intervention to modify commuting behavior.

Q1. Please answer the questions about station XXXX (the station nearest your office):

(1) How often do you use station XXXX?

    1. yearly
    2. monthly
    3. weekly   times

(2) How do you travel between station XXXX and your offices (select all applicable alternatives)?
Note: if the frequency is 0, go to (3).

    1. walk   4. company bus
    2. bicycle   5. taxi
    3. public bus   6. others

(3) **Read the access information about station XXXX.**
Then, answer the questions about how you travel between the station and your office. Read "A Sheet of Access Information to XXX Station"

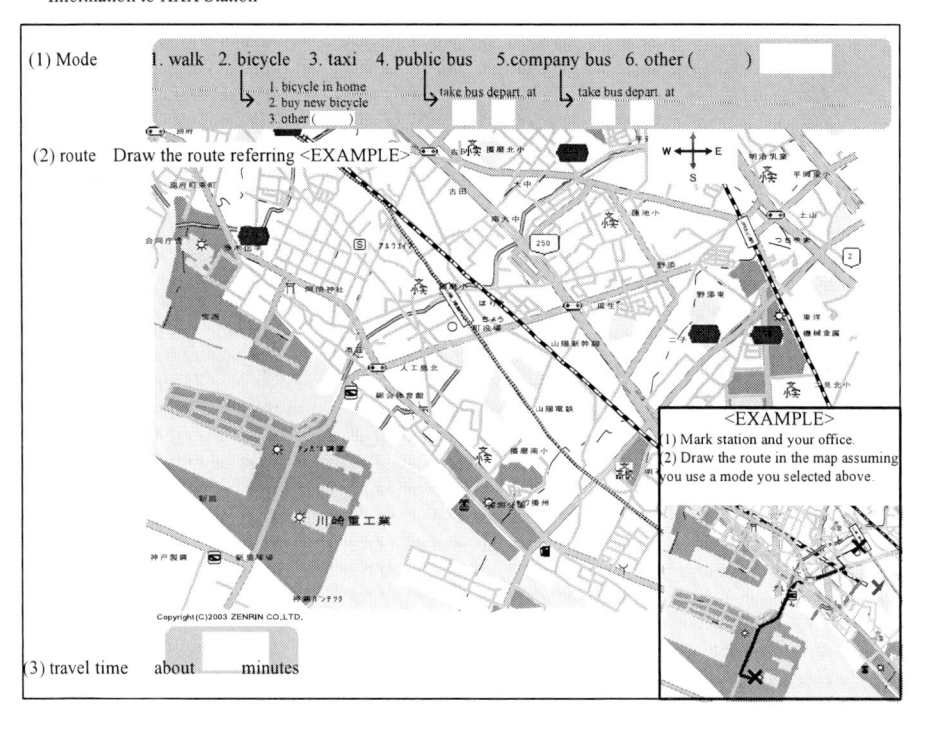

(1) Mode   1. walk   2. bicycle   3. taxi   4. public bus   5. company bus   6. other (   )

    ↓ 1. bicycle in home   ↓ take bus depart. at   ↓ take bus depart. at
        2. buy new bicycle
        3. other (   )

(2) route   Draw the route referring <EXAMPLE>

<EXAMPLE>
1) Mark station and your office.
2) Draw the route in the map assuming you use a mode you selected above.

(3) travel time   about   minutes

Before answering the following questions,
read the pamphlet, "How to use a car wisely."

Q2. Please answer the questions about your daily commute:

(1) How often do you use each travel mode for commuting?

1. car :weekly [ ] days
2. train :weekly [ ] days { 1. Sanyo railway / 2. others }
3. other :weekly [ ] days { 1. walk / 2. bicycle / 3. public bus / 4. company bus / 5. taxi / 6. other ( ) }

(2) If you commute by car,
is it possible to use a travel mode other than a car?

1. definitely impossible → thank you for your cooperation
2. possible, but difficult
3. possible → go to (3)

(3) How do you commute if you do not use a car?

[1] Which travel mode do you use? (select all applicable alternatives)

1. walk   6. company bus
2. bicycle   7. taxi
3. public bus   8. car
4. Sanyo railway 9. other ( )
5. other railway

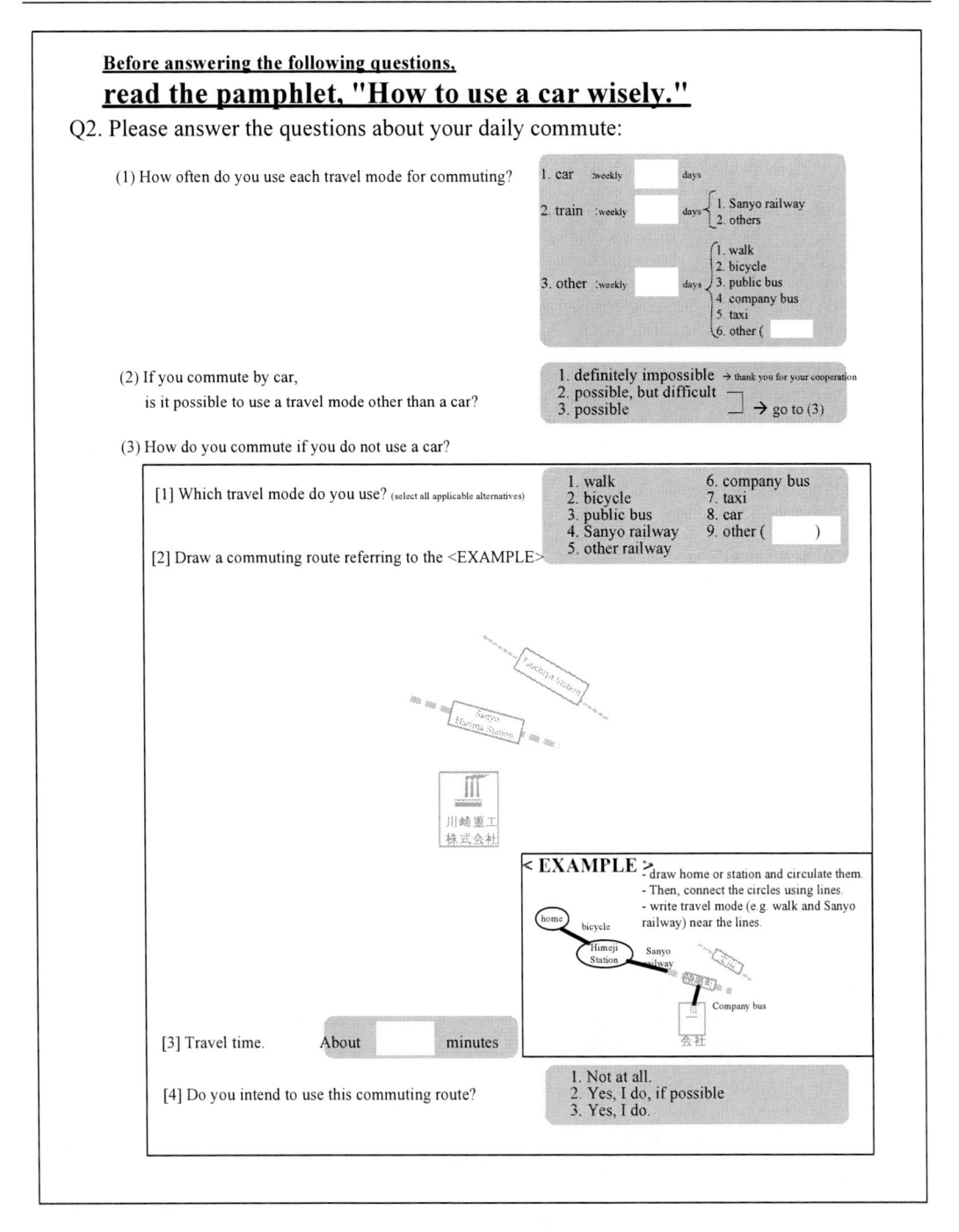

[2] Draw a commuting route referring to the <EXAMPLE>

< EXAMPLE >
- draw home or station and circulate them.
- Then, connect the circles using lines.
- write travel mode (e.g. walk and Sanyo railway) near the lines.

home — bicycle — Himeji Station — Sanyo railway — Company bus

[3] Travel time. About [ ] minutes

[4] Do you intend to use this commuting route?
1. Not at all.
2. Yes, I do, if possible
3. Yes, I do.

Figure 2. An example of both sides of the questionnaire for the behavioral plan.

The questions in the second questionnaire were the same as in the first instrument, but no questions on the travel behavioral plan were included.

RESULTS

In the first step, 300 out of 400 recipients (75%) responded to both questionnaires. Out of the 300 respondents, we selected 99 who commuted by car at the time the first survey was conducted and responded without missing data to analyze the effectiveness of the intervention. The excluded data were for those who did not commute by vehicle at all (200 respondents) and for a respondent for whom commuter trips increased from 1 day a week to 7 days a week during the intervention.

For all 99 samples, the average weekly frequency of commuting by car decreased significantly; by train did not change significantly; and by bicycle and motorbike increased significantly (Table 2). There was no significant change in commute behavior for Kawasaki-Jyuukou. For Kikko-Man and Akashi City, there were significant decreases in car use and significant increases in using a bicycle or motorbike.

In addition, 10 out of 99 (10%) car commuters at the first survey quit commuting by car completely (Table 3): six changed to bicycle, three to train, and one to motorbike.

Table 3 also shows that 19% of the car commuters at Kikko-Man and 12% of the car commuters at Akashi City changed their commuting mode from car to another mode. In contrast, at Kawasaki-Jyuukou, only one (2%) car commuter changed travel mode. All the commute mode changes from car in Akashi City were to railway, while all the changes at Kikko-Man were to bicycle or motorbike.

Table 2. Means (M) and standard deviation (SD) for each travel mode, and t values for one-way analysis of variance (before vs. after the survey)

		n	Car use before M (SD)	Car use after M (SD)	t	Railway use before M (SD)	Railway use after M (SD)	t	Others (bicycle or motorbike) before M (SD)	Others after M (SD)	t
	Total	99	4.68 (1.14)	4.27 (1.84)	2.63 ***	0.27 (1.04)	0.31 (1.11)	-0.56	0.12 (0.61)	0.54 (1.43)	-3.15 ***
Companies	Kikko-man	31	4.87 (0.43)	4.10 (2.07)	1.99 *	0.00 (0.00)	0.00 (0.00)	-	0.03 (0.18)	0.97 (2.01)	-2.56 **
Companies	Kawasaki-jyuukou	43	4.77 (1.13)	4.67 (1.43)	0.66	0.07 (0.46)	0.05 (0.30)	1.00	0.23 (0.90)	0.42 (1.18)	-1.60
Companies	Akashi city	25	4.28 (1.62)	3.80 (2.08)	1.77 *	0.96 (1.84)	1.16 (1.97)	-0.71	0.04 (0.20)	0.20 (0.71)	-1.44

n: number of samples; M: mean; SD: standard deviation; t: t value; *: $p<0.05$; ***: $p<0.01$.

These results imply that the one-shot travel feedback program targeting commutes had a significant effect in reducing car commuters, although the alternative travel modes chosen after intervention differed across companies. This may be due to the difference in the locations of the companies. Kawasaki-Jyuukou is not nearby a railway station or a residential area, making it difficult to use public transport or bicycles for commuting. The Akashi municipal office is close to a railway station and is located in the middle of the city. It takes approximately 10 min to walk through the city center, which may be why all the commuters in Akashi City who changed their commuting trips from car to another mode chose the railway. Finally, from Kikko-Man, while nearby a railway station and residential areas, it takes approximately 15 min to walk to the railway station. In addition, the road from the company to the station may not offer much incentive for pedestrian traffic: there is no sidewalk, and thus people and automobiles share the road, and there are no shops along the road. Therefore, it might not be attractive for commuters to Kikko-Man to change their commute mode from car to train, but it might be feasible to change to bicycle or motorbike.

Table 3. Details on the number of persons who changed travel modes from car use to another mode following the mobility management intervention

		Kikko-Man		Kawasaki-Jyuukou		Akashi City		Total	
		n = 31		n = 43		n = 25		n = 99	
Travel modes before mobility management	Car commuters	6	(19%)	1	(2%)	1	(4%)	8	(8%)
	Commuters using cars and other modes	0	(0%)	0	(0%)	2	(8%)	2	(2%)
Travel mode changes after mobility management intervention		Bicycle: 5 Motorbike: 1		Bicycle: 1		Railway: 3		Railway: 3 Bicycle: 6 Motorbike: 1	

The analysis of commuting behavior change using data obtained from 43 respondents who commuted by bicycle or motorbike at the first survey showed that five bicycle or motorbike commuters (12%) became train commuters after the policy intervention. This implies that the intervention of communicative workplace mobility management led to commute changes from both car to public transport and bicycle/motorbike to public transport.

CONCLUSION

We conducted a survey to verify the effects of communicative mobility management targeting commuter transport, that is, a one-shot travel feedback program for commuters to companies. The most important finding was that the travel feedback program, which asked recipients to make a behavior plan about how to change their commuting mode from car to another pro-environmental travel mode, was effective. Although such a program has demonstrated to be more effective at changing discretionary trips than commutes (Fujii & Taniguchi, 2005), no study had shown that it is effective at changing commutes for which the subjective cost of behavioral change (c.f. Loukopoulos, et al. 2004) might be higher than for other trips, such as discretionary trips. Because our program was a "one-shot" program, its implementation cost was no greater than that of programs with several steps that have been implemented in many cities in different countries (c.f. Gärling & Fujii, 2004). For recipients, the program looked like a "questionnaire survey" that was distributed with complementary information on public transport or bicycle commuting. Those conducting mobility management strategies might expect an aggregate reduction in car use and aggregate increase in more sustainable travel modes with a feasible monetary budget by conducting a one-shot travel feedback program targeting commuting trips.

We also found that the effectiveness of the program differed across companies. This might be due to differences in location. A limited number of car commuters changed their commute mode at a company that had low accessibility to a railway station and residential areas. In contrast, 12% and 19% of the car commuters changed their commute mode at companies that were accessible from railway stations and arterial roads. In addition, commuters at a company that was within walking distance to a railway station tended to use the railway as an alternative commute mode to car, while those at a company that was farther from a railway station tended to use bicycles. Therefore, the type of commute behavior modification caused by the travel feedback program seems to depend on the accessibility of alternative travel modes.

Transportation policy makers may believe that it is difficult to change commute behavior without any economic incentives/disincentives or changes in the level of service of their transportation systems. However, our data clearly indicate that commute behavior can be modified from car use to a sustainable travel mode via a simple communicative intervention that provides information about public transportation and giving people the opportunity to rethink their commute behavior for contributing environmental problems, as was predicted by the abovementioned model that incorporates determinants of behavioral intentions to perform various pro-environmental behaviors.

COMMUNICATIVE PROGRAMS TARGETING AT NEW RESIDENTS

In the previous section, we described a travel feedback program for commuting travel behavior change, and showed the empirical results of the test of its effectiveness. Yet, workplace is, of course, one among various locations for communicative measures. Actually, it has been discussed, as described above, that there are three typical locations to implement such communicative measures, i.e., residential areas, schools, and workplaces. Although communicative measures in residential areas have shown to be effective in changing people's attitude and travel behavior, the method demands typically high cost because mobility management conductors should make contact with different residents through home visit or postal mail. Therefore, development of a cost-effective and efficient method is strongly called for.

In literatures on travel behavior and psychology, it has been discussed that "habit of car use" is a critical factor to prevent people's behavior modification from car use into other modes (c.f. Fujii & Gärling, 2007; Verplanken, 1994; 1997). Such discussion implies that individuals who have a strong habit of car use are not likely to modify their behavior. It is thus expected that communicative measures targeting those without car-use habit would be much more effective than measures targeting those with strong car use habit. These discussions imply that communicative measures could much more effectively influence travel attitude and behavior of new residents who have just moved in than those of old residents, since new residents have not yet developed a travel habit for their new residential area. In addition, the new residents would tend to have a motivation to get various types of information concerning their new residential area.

In almost all cities in Japan, new residents who have just moved in usually would visit city office for moving-in notification. For mobility management conductors who try to promote environmentally sustainable transportation modes and decrease car use, this new residents' visit to the city office can be regarded as an excellent opportunity to contact with them. Differently from typical communicative measures for residents, mobility management conductors do not have to make contact with residents in different places, and what they have to do is just prepare communicational tools and distribute them to the visitors to the city hall. This implies that communicative measures for new residents that provide informational tools for newcomers from city office are expected to be highly cost-effective among mobility management measures. The objective of this study is to test communicative mobility management measures for new residents giving informational tools to newcomers visiting the city office. Thus, we conducted two experiments to test the effectiveness of communicative mobility management measures targeting new residents through 2 field experiments.

METHOD

An experiment in this study was conducted in Ryugasaki city (population is approximately 80,000), and another was conducted in Takasaki city (population is approximately 300,000). Ryugasaki city is located in the direction of the northeastern part of Tokyo; in this city, there are two railway lines operated by Japan Railway and Kanto tetsudo, several route bus lines, and community bus lines operated by city government. Takasaki city is located in the direction of the northern part of Tokyo; in this location, there are also two railway lines operated by Japan Railway and Jyoshin-dentetsu, several route bus line operated by four different bus companies, and a community bus line operated by city government. The procedures for both experiments were as following:

Step 1): A questionnaire (wave 1) was handed off to new residents who visited the city office to submit their moving-in notification and they were asked to fill in the questionnaire at the moment.

Step 2): Immediately after we received the completed questionnaire from the new residents, we handed off to them the "bag for newcomers" that includes a pamphlet for introducing them to the city, a leaflet on big hospitals and garbage collection in the city, that were typical items to be distributed to new residents in any Japanese cities. It should be noted that the bag usually does not typically include any information on public transport (PT) in Japan. In the experiments, an informational kit about the PT system in the area was also included in the bag. The kit was composed of a bus route map, a bus time table, an informational sheet about a way to use the local bus system and a bus craft postcard as a small gift. Note that the new residents, who were randomly selected, received a bag which did not include any informational kit on PT. They were regarded as the control group in the experiments, and the others were regarded as the experimental group.

Step 3): Six month after the wave 1 survey was conducted, a questionnaire was distributed (wave 2) to new residents in both experimental and control groups. The measurements of both wave 1 and wave 2 are shown in Table 4.

RESULTS

In the experiment of Ryugasaki city, we distributed the questionnaire in wave 2 to 104 respondents of wave 1, and collected 46 (21 in the experimental group, 25 in the control group). Table 5 and Figure 3 show that the ratio of frequency of car use in the experimental group to that of the control group in wave 1 (1.35) was decreased by 22.6% in wave 2 (1.04). This result indicates that frequency of car use in the experimental group decreased in 6 months later as compared to the control group. It was also found that the frequency of bus use for the experimental group substantially increased (818.7%) from wave 1 to wave 2 as compared to that for the control group, and the frequency of train use in the experimental group was also substantially increased (231.8%) from wave 1 to wave 2 as compared to that for the control group.

Table 4. Measurements of both wave 1 and wave 2 questionnaires and endpoints of scales

Variable	Measurements	Scale antipodes
Date of moved in	When did you moved in the city?	Year, month, date
behavioral intention to use public transport	Do you intend to use train and bus in the future?	No / Yes (five-point scale)
Difficulty of public transport use	Do you think that it is difficult to use train or bus in the city?	No / Yes (five-point scale)
convenience of public transport	Do you think that the train or bus in the city is convenience?	No / Yes (five-point scale)
Frequency to use car	How often do you recently use a car in the city?	frequency per month
Frequency to use bus	How often do you recently use a bus in the city?	frequency per month
Frequency to use train	How often do you recently use a train in the city?	frequency per month

In the experiment of Takasaki city, we distributed the questionnaire in wave 2 to 281 respondents of wave 1, and collected 136 (108 in the experimental group and 28 in the control group). As can be seen in Table 6 and Figure 4, the frequency of bus use for the experimental group increased from wave 1 to wave 2 by approximately threefold as compared to that for the control group, and the frequency of railway use for the experimental group increased from wave 1 to wave 2 by approximately double than that for the control group.[1] Regarding car use, a slight increase in its frequency for the experimental group was obtained as shown in Table 6, but the statistical t-test, did not indicate that this was significant.

---

[1] Note that there were several samples in which the frequency of each travel mode use was remarkably high (over 30 times / month). Because these samples would have a large effect on the mean value of frequencies, we replicated analyses after modifying the frequency data which was over 30 times/month into 30 times. The result was that the direction of the findings did not change, although the size of the difference between wave 1 and wave 2 became less salient.

Table 5. Mean (M) and standard deviation (STD) for behavioral measures in the Ryugasaki city

		Wave 1		Wave 2	
Frequencies of car use	N	M	SD	M	SD
Control group (a)	21	14.7	13.7	20.3	12.5
Experimental group (b)	16	19.8	12.7	21.2	13.1
(b) / (a)		1.35		1.04	
Frequencies of bus use	N	M	SD	M	SD
Control group (a)	21	1.50	4.64	0.52	0.81
Experimental group (b)	16	0.93	2.34	2.66	7.62
(b) / (a)		0.62		5.08	
Frequencies of train use	N	M	SD	M	SD
Control group (a)	21	4.32	9.73	2.06	5.22
Experimental group (b)	16	2.54	7.64	2.80	7.57
(b) / (a)		0.59		1.36	

N: Number of samples.

Table 6. Mean (M) and standard deviation (STD) for each behavioral measure, in the Takasaki city

		Wave 1		Wave 2	
Frequencies of car use	N	M	SD	M	SD
Control group (a)	27	24.6	11.1	20.5	13.3
Experimental group (b)	96	24.3	10.4	22.3	11.1
(b) / (a)		0.99		1.09	
Frequencies of bus use	N	M	SD	M	SD
Control group (a)	27	3.08	8.45	1.26	2.88
Experimental group (b)	96	1.09	4.04	1.40	4.11
(b) / (a)		0.35		1.11	
Frequencies of train use	N	M	SD	M	SD
Control group (a)	27	3.30	8.59	1.93	5.83
Experimental group (b)	96	3.39	7.50	3.79	7.64
(b) / (a)		1.03		1.96	

Table 7 shows means and standard deviation for each administered psychological measure, and p values of the t-test (wave 1 vs. wave 2 survey) for the experimental group standardized by the control group. No significant differences were found.

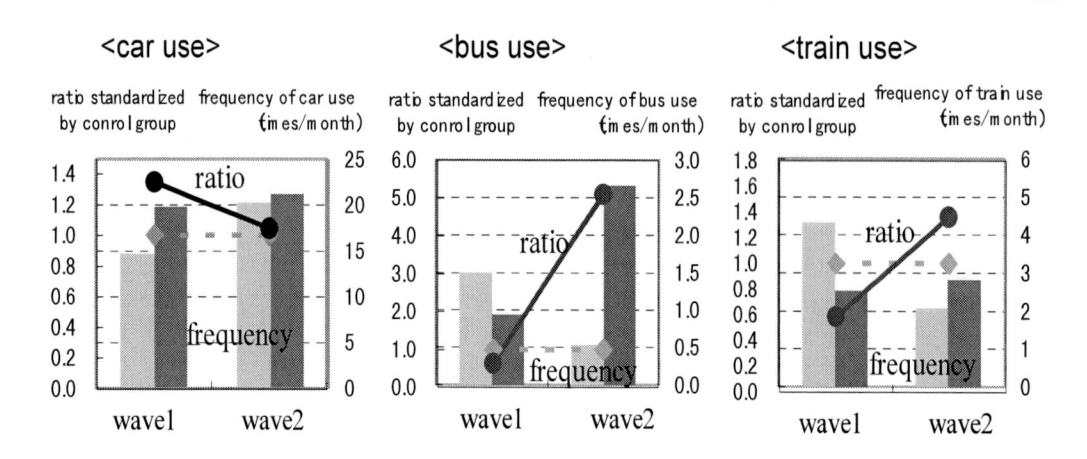

Figure 3. Mean value standardized by control group and frequencies of car, bus, and train use in Ryugasaki city.

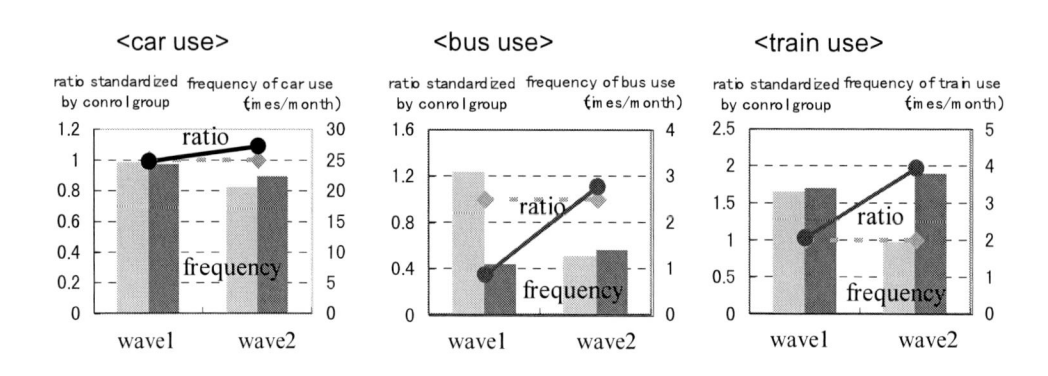

Figure 4. Mean value standardized by control group and frequencies of car, bus, train use in Takasaki city.

CONCLUSION

In this section of the experiments, we assumed that the psychological intervention targeting the new residents who had just moved in would be effective for car-user-reduction behavior and promotion of public transport use such as bus and train. To test this measure, we implemented 2 experiments in 2 different Japanese cities. The results show a substantial effectiveness of this measure in the promotion of public transportation. New residents who received a kit of public transportation information such as time tables and route maps substantially increased their frequency in using bus and train, from approximately 2 times to 8 times, compared to new residents who did not receive it. It was also shown that car use decreased, at least in Ryugasaki city. It can be noted that we did not find significant psychological effects of this intervention. This might be because the informational kit was designed to distribute information about public transportation rather than to persuade to not use participants' cars.

Implementation of mobility management measures targeting the new residents would not be difficult for city government, because they usually already distribute a "bag for newcomers". What they should additionally do is just prepare the informational kit about public transportation and include it in the bag. So, it can be said that mobility management targeting the new residents would be cost-effective, at least, to promote public transport use.

In addition, after the project was implemented in this study, the Ryugasaki city government decided that they are going to add the bus route map and timetable to their "newcomer's bag" as a part of the informational kit of public transport distributed in the city.

These results demonstrated that distributing the information kit on public transportation in an area to new residents is highly effective for mobility management measure that can promote environmental sustainable transport such as the public transport system.

Table 7. Mean (M) and standard deviation (SD) for each psychological measure, and *p* values of the t-test (wave 1 vs. wave 2 survey) for the experimental group standardized by the control group

	Ryugasaki city						Takasaki city					
	Wave1			Wave2			Wave1			Wave2		
behavioral intention to use public transport	N	M	SD	M	SD	P	N	M	SD	M	SD	P
Control group	25	3.36	1.25	3.16	1.34		27	3.22	1.50	3.33	1.14	
Experimental group	21	3.00	1.61	2.95	1.40	0.326	108	3.32	1.41	3.31	1.23	0.180
Difficulty of public transport use	N	M	SD	M	SD	P	N	M	SD	M	SD	P
Control group	25	3.16	1.14	3.28	1.06		27	3.00	1.30	2.96	1.32	
Experimental group	20	3.00	1.26	3.20	1.24	0.402	106	3.16	1.22	3.18	1.17	0.340
convenience of public transport	N	M	SD	M	SD	p	N	M	SD	M	SD	P
Control group	25	3.20	0.96	2.72	1.24		27	2.96	1.02	3.15	1.20	
Experimental group	19	2.95	1.08	2.16	1.17	0.118	105	2.84	1.19	2.86	1.31	0.108

GENERAL CONCLUSION

For achieving an environmentally sustainable society, an environmental policy aimed at promoting efficient pro-environmental behaviors that leads to reductions of CO_2 emissions is strongly called for. Nowadays, the effectiveness of CO_2 reduction measures is largely different across different types of pro-environmental behavior. As abovementioned, environmental engineering research has demonstrated that car-use-reduction behavior is one of the most effective in CO_2 reduction, especially for those who drive in daily life. The amount of CO_2 reduction by car-use-reduction behavior is from 5 times to 300 times larger than that produced by other types of pro-environmental behavior such as recycling and reduction of gas or electric use. However, this fact is not yet well known to the public, and even to environmental researchers and practitioners including environmental policy makers.

With this in mind, we firstly described a model to explain behavioral intention of multiple types of pro-environmental behavior. Results from testing the model revealed that people with the goal of reducing CO_2 emissions likely implement types of pro-environmental behavior that they believe are easy and highly effective, as compared to behaviors believed to be difficult and ineffective. Thus, we concluded that providing information regarding the actual effectiveness of CO_2 reduction by car-use-reduction behavior, and information about how to reduce car use (such as information about alternative mode's information), are indispensable for promoting car-use-reduction behavior that are objectively effective in CO_2 reduction.

Therefore, we suggested that travel feedback programs to provide such information could successfully reduce car use. The two application studies of the program were described in this chapter. One is the program for commuting behavior, and the other is for the new residents arriving into the city. The field experiments for these two types of program showed that they could actually promote environmental sustainable travel modes use as alternatives to car driving. Thus, the authors suggest to practical environmental policy makers to apply travel feedback programs developed based on theories and empirical findings of environmentally psychological research into actual environmental policy. In addition, the authors would also like to suggest to environmental psychologists to perform further research for obtaining knowledge that could be used for developing more efficient environmental policy making. Such a research would be aimed at, for example, understanding who are likely to change their travel behavior or what interventions are effective for specific types of situations and targets. As the general direction and purposes of our research described in this chapter were determined while considering the engineering findings such as objective effectiveness in CO_2 reduction, the behavioral scientific research for environmental policy should also consider what is seriously called for in practical environmental policy making throughout the world.

REFERENCES

Brög, W. (1998) Individualized marketing: Implications for TDM. CD-ROM of the *Proceedings of the 77th Annual Meeting of Transportation Research Board*.

Chen, X.P. Au, W.T., & Komorita S.S. (1996) Sequential choice in a step-level public goods dilemma: The effects of criticality and uncertainty, *Organizational Behavior and Human Decision Process* 65, 37–47.

Fujii, S. (2006) Environmental concern, attitude toward frugality, and ease of behavior as determinants of pro-environmental behavior intentions, *Journal of Environmental Psychology*, 26, 262-268.

Fujii, S., & Gärling. T. (2007) Role and acquisition of car-use habit. In T. Gärling and L. Steg (Eds.), *Threat from Car Traffic to the Quality of Urban Life: Problems, causes, and solutions* (pp. 235- 250). Amsterdam: Elsevier.

Fujii, S., & Ohta, H (2006) Comparative analysis of the determinants of pro-environmental behavioral intentions for travel and non-travel behaviors. CD-ROM of proceedings of *Transportation Research Board 85th Annual Meeting*, Washington, USA.

Fujii, S. & Ohta, H. (2008, September) Objective and subjective effectiveness of pro-environmental behavior, Presented at the *Workshop on Current Issues of Environmental Psychology in Japan*, at Hokkaido University, Japan.

Fujii, S., & Taniguchi, A. (2005) Reducing family car use by providing travel advice or requesting behavioral plans: an experimental analysis of travel feedback programs, *Transportation Research D.*, 10, 385-393.

Fujii, S. & Taniguchi, A. (2006) Determinants of the effectiveness of travel feedback programs—a review of communicative mobility management measures for changing travel behavior in Japan. *Transport Policy, 13*, 339-348.

Gärling, T., & Fujii, S. (2004) Travel behavior modification: Theories, methods, and programs. *Resource paper for the 11th IATBR conference*, Kyoto, Japan, August 16–20, 2006.

Gollwitzer, P. M. (1996). The volitional benefits of planning. In P. M. Gollwitzer & J. A. Bargh (Eds), *The Psychology of Action: Linking Cognition and Motivation to Behavior*. pp. 287–312. New York: Guilford Press.

Hirose, S. (1995). *Social Psychology of Environment and Consumption*. Nagoya, Japan: Nagoya University Press (in Japanese).

Jones, P. (2003, August) Encouraging behavioral change through marketing and management: What can be achieved? *Paper Presented at the 10th International Conference on Travel Behaviour Research*. Lucerne, Switzerland.

Locke, E.A. (1968). Toward a theory of task motivation and incentives. *Organizational Behavior and Human Performance, 3*, 157–189.

Loukopoulos, P., Jakobsson, C., Gärling, T., Schneider, C.M., & Fujii, S. (2004). Car-user responses to travel demand management measures: goal setting and choice of adaptation alternatives. *Transportation Research D, Transport and Environment, 9*, 263–280.

Olson. M. (1965). *The logic of collective action*. Cambridge, MA: Harvard University. Press.

Rose, G., & Ampt, E. (2001). Travel blending: An Australian travel awareness initiative, *Transportation Research, 6D*, 9–110.

Strobe A. & Frey B.S. (1982). Self-interest and collective action: The economics and psychology of public goods. *British Journal of Social Psychology, 21*, 121–137.

Taniguchi, A., Hara, F., Takano, S., Kagaya, S., & Fujii, S. (2003). Psychological and behavioral effects of Travel Feedback Program for travel behavior modification. *Transportation Research Record, 1839*, 182–190.

Verplanken, B., Aarts, H., Van Knienbertg, A., & Van Knienberg, C. (1994). Attitude versus general habit: Antecedents of travel mode choice. *Journal of Applied Social Psychology, 24*, 285-300.

Verplanken, B., Aarts, H., & Van Knippenberg, A. (1997). Habit, information acquisition, and the process of making travel mode choices. *European Journal of Social Psychology, 27*, 539-560.

Chapter 9

ALTRUISM AND BEYOND: THE MOTIVATIONAL BASES OF PRO-ENVIRONMENTAL BEHAVIOR

Verónica Sevillano[*]
Universidad Nacional de Educación a Distancia, Spain
Juan I. Aragonés
Universidad Complutense de Madrid, Spain
P. Wesley Schultz
California State University, San Marcos, USA

ABSTRACT

There is a rich body of psychological research that has examined the motivational bases of pro-environmental behavior. In essence, why is it that individuals engage in behaviors that are beneficial to the natural environment? One commonly-used approach for understanding pro-environmental behavior is to treat it as a specific form of prosocial behavior, motivated by altruistic concerns. This approach has allowed researchers to test hypotheses and development models that draw from the prosocial literature. While the results from this line of work have been fruitful, it seems clear that there are different motivational bases that underlie pro-environmental behavior beyond altruism. In this chapter, we review the existing research from a broader motivational framework, drawing on the models proposed by Batson (1994) and by Fiske (2004). Our review examines the motivations of egoism, altruism, collectivism, and principlism. Finally, we focus on two theoretical perspectives that attempt to integrate different motivational bases: Value-Belief-Norm Theory, and the Inclusion Model.

---

[*] Correspondence: Verónica Sevillano, currently at Princeton University, e-mail: vsevilla@princeton.edu. This chapter was partially supported by the Fulbright Program and funding from the Spanish Ministry of Science and Innovation to the first author.

INTRODUCTION

Psychological research on environmental issues has increased considerably in recent years. Studies have examined a range of issues, from specific actions like recycling and water conservation, to broader societal issues like global warming and resource depletion (as summarized in Part 1 of this book). Consistent throughout psychological research is the focus on the individual, and studies have examined topics like environmental concern, values, connectedness to nature, time orientation and worldviews (many of these are summarized in Part 2 of this book). Implicit in the psychological approach is the view that understanding individual-level processes will help to illuminate group-level and societal-level patterns of behavior. In this chapter, we explore research on *why* individuals engage in pro-environmental behavior.

Over the last 30 years, psychological studies of environmental issues have made considerable progress. Contributions to this research have come from around the world, primarily from Europe and North America, but with many seminal contributions from researchers in Asia, Latin America and Australia. One theme throughout these studies is "protection" and taking care of nature. That is to say, nature deserves moral consideration and actions that are taken by the individual with the intention of benefiting nature can be regarded as pro-social. Environmental attitudes and behavior have also been linked with issues of justice, peace and equality, and the large-scale advocacy for environmental protection is widely viewed as a social movement (Castells, 1997).

It has been argued that many social problems result from individuals pursuing their individual self interests, without taking into account the consequences for others (Batson, 1994; Hardin, 1968; Messick & Brewer, 1983; Van Lange & Joireman, 2008). The study of motives for acting in the public good, or for the benefit of others has a long history in social science (McClintock, 1972; Messick & McClintock, 1968; Van Lange De Cremer, Van Dijk, & Van Vugt, 2007). In using the term *public good* we mean, along with Batson (1994), *the welfare of some person or persons other than oneself* (p. 603). In this broad definition, we include such behaviors as resource conservation, recycling or volunteering. A more frequently used term has been *pro-social behavior:* a *broad category of actions that are defined by society as generally beneficial to other people and to the ongoing political system* (Schroeder, Penner, Dovidio & Piliavin, 1995; p.15). Although both terms are virtually interchangeable in meaning, the *pro-social behavior* label has been traditionally applied to social interaction contexts, and *public good* to issues of resource consumption. Pro-social behavior has been characterized as a behavior that: a) *intends* to help others; b) is defined by *society*; and c) benefits *other(s)* (Schroeder et al., 1995).

Why do People Act in the Public Good?

Traditionally, the set of pro-social behaviors (helping, altruism) studied has been related to the type of action done by the agent and the type of consequences for the agent. However, some authors have focused instead on the underlying motivations that lead to behavior (cf., Batson, 1991; Schwartz, 1977). Indeed, a number of psychological frameworks have been provided for classifying and studying the motivational underpinnings of pro-social behavior.

Altruism and Beyond: The Motivational Bases of Pro-environmental Behavior

In this chapter, we use the work of Batson (1994) as a broad motivational framework from which to approach environmental behavior. Our goal here is not to advocate one motivational framework in preference to another, but rather to use the Batson framework as a starting point for classifying and reviewing the research on pro-environmental behavior.

Table 1. Acting in the public good: motivational bases in environmental research

Motivational base (Batson, 1994)	Contributing factors	Environmental Research
Egoism	Mood Protection: Relieving bad moods (Guilt, Sadness) Non Social Rewards: Money Health	Kals, Schumacher & Montada (1999); Kaiser (2006); Kaiser, Schultz, Berenguer, Corral-Verdugo & Tankha (2008) Stern, Dietz & Kalof (1993)
	Attribution of responsibility Empathy and sympathy	Eiser, Reicher & Podpadec (1995) Shelton & Rogers (1981); Schultz (2000); Sevillano, Aragonés & Schultz (2007); Berenguer (2007)
Altruism	Social norms	Cialdini, Reno & Kallgren (1991); Schultz, Nolan, Cialdini, Goldstein & Griskevicius (2007)
Collectivism	Social value orientation	Van Vugt, Meertens & Van Lange (1995); Cameron, Brown & Chapman (1998); Joireman, Lasane, Bennett, Richards & Solaimani (2001); Gärling, Fuji, Gärling & Jakobsson (2003); Joireman, Van Lange & Van Vugt (2004)
	Personal norms	Heberlein & Black, (1976).Van Liere & Dunlap (1978); Black, Stern & Elworth (1985); Stern, Dietz & Black (1986); Hunecke, Blöbaum, Mathies & Höger (2001); Joireman, Lasane, Bennett, Richards & Solaimani (2001); Gärling, Fuji, Gärling & Jakobsson (2003); Nordlund & Garvill (2003); Clark, Kotchen & Moore (2003)
	Personal values	Stern, Dietz & Kalof (1993); Schultz & Zeleny (1998); Schultz, Gouveia, Cameron, Tankha, Schmuck & Franek, M. (2005)

In the Batson (1994) framework, there are four motivational bases for acting for public good: Egoism; Altruism; Collectivism; and Principlism. As with all motivational frameworks, the focus is on the underlying reasons for behavior, and not on the impact or outcome of the behavior. Acting for public good is egoistically motivated if the ultimate goal is to increase the actor's own welfare, whereas the ultimate goal of altruistically motivated behavior is to increase the welfare of one or more persons other than oneself. Collectivist motivation is present when the ultimate goal is to increase the welfare of a group or a larger collective. Finally, the ultimate goal of principlism is to uphold a moral standard or ideal (Batson, 1994).

In the following sections, we review the psychological research regarding environmental concern and behavior. We will review environmental research that has conceptualised pro-environmental behavior as prosocial behavior in order to avoid overlapping with other chapters in this book. In structuring our review, we will follow Batson's motivational bases for acting in the public good as a frame to organize research related to environmental issues (see table 1). We will focus particularly on two theoretical models: the Value-Belief-Norm Theory (Stern, Dietz, Abel, Guagnano & Kalof, 1999); and the Empathy Model (Schultz, 2002), though several other perspectives are also discussed.

EGOISM: *PROTECTING MY ENVIRONMENT*

Acting in the public good in a self-interested way has been related to several factors including social learning, mood protection and non-social rewards.

Social learning. Social learning theories that introduce inter-personal processes in the classical and instrumental conditioning paradigms, include processes such as reciprocity and social rewards and costs (Fiske, 2004). To the best of our knowledge, there is no research relating these processes and environmental research to the theoretical pro-social framework.

Mood protection. Mood protection, maintaining or improving one's mood, is repeatedly found as a factor that contributes to helping behavior (Cunningham, Steinberg & Grev, 1980; Eisenberg, 1991; North, Tarrant & Hargreaves, 2004). In this sense, pro-social behavior can be explained by attending to emotional rewards for the self. The principal exponent of this explanation is the Negative-state Relief Model of helping. This model, outlined by Schaller and Cialdini (1988), states that people avoid feeling distress for others' suffering by behaving in a pro-social manner. From this perspective, the ultimate goal of a pro-social behavior is to reduce the helper's distress. Although to our knowledge, no studies have directly examined environmental behavior as an avoidance of guilt, there has been some research focusing on such feelings in other theoretical areas. Extending the Planned Behavior Theory, Kaiser, Schultz, Berenguer, Corral-Verdugo and Tankha (2008) studied anticipated feelings of guilt and embarrassment related to pro-environmental behavior. They reasoned that feelings of guilt about not behaving in a pro-environmental manner would be related to pro-environmental intention in individualistic cultures (United States, Spain), whereas feelings of anticipated embarrassment would predict pro-environmental intention in collectivistic cultures (India, Mexico). Although they failed to find differences in the type of feelings (guilt vs embarrassment), they showed that when taking these feelings into account, the explanatory power of the Planned Behavior Theory for environmental conservation was increased. Similarly, Kals, Schumacher and Montada (1999) found that feelings of guilt due to one's own insufficient nature protection, amongst other emotions (indignation about insufficient nature protection, anger about too much nature protection, emotional affinity towards nature), predicted pro-environmental willingness.

Non-social rewards. Clearly, when a non-social reward (e.g. money) provides an explanation for pro-social behavior, that behavior cannot be characterised as altruistic. This sort of reward (save money, better health) has been proposed as an explanation of pro-environmental behavior carried out by people who are not very committed to the environmental movement. These people would be impelled by the motivation to protect their self-interest which can lead to environmental protection (Schultz, 2001). An example of this self-interest motivation would be the NIMBY *(Not In My Back Yard!)* response (see Devine-Wright's chapter, this volume). In this vein, Stern et al. (1999)'s Value-Belief-Norm Theory distinguishes between egoistic, altruistic and biospheric value orientation on environmental quality. Egoistic value orientation is rooted in worries about the impact of environmental problems on health and the monetary cost of environmental protection. When the main concern about environmental problems is the repercussion on people in general, an altruistic value orientation is implicated. Finally, a biospheric value orientation is related to the negative impact that the environmental situation has on living beings and nature. This model will be developed in more detail further on in this chapter.

Although some environmental research has applied strongly egoistic and individualistic approaches as rational-choice-based models (i.e. Theory of Planned Behavior; see Schultz & Estrada-Hollenbeck, 2009) or the Behavior Modification Approach (Geller, 1987), this research is not included here because it does not belong to the scope of pro-social behavior literature.

ALTRUISM: *PROTECTING YOUR ENVIRONMENT*

Altruistic motivation to take action in the public good is related to the attribution of processes such as responsibility and empathy.

Attribution of responsibility. Behaving to benefit others, without any positive consequence for the self, is related to the type of attributions that individuals make. Altruistic behavior is, in particular, based on attributions of responsibility to the self (Darley & Latané, 1968). In environmental research, Eiser, Reicher and Podpadec (1995) found that people who attributed global warming to individual behavior were associated with perceiving the consequences of global warming as disastrous, yet controllable by individual action. Indeed, denying responsibility for environmental problems has consistently been found to predict non pro-environmental actions (Kals & Maes, 2002).

Empathy and sympathy. Apart from any possible self rewards, defined social norms, personal norms or general values, other-oriented altruistic behavior is concerned with believing in co-responsibility between people (Fiske, 2004). This *true* altruism has been studied mainly in relation to empathetic and sympathetic feelings which tend to facilitate helping behavior.

In general, most authors have defined empathy in relation to the responses of an individual who observes the sentiments of another (Preston & de Waal, 2002). Hoffman (2000) defines empathy as *any process where the perception of the object's state generates a state in the subject that is more applicable to the object's state or situation than to the subject's own prior state or situation* (p. 4). According to Eisenberg (2002), empathy could lead both to sympathy and personal distress. Therefore, both may stem from empathy.

Sympathy is the *emotional response stemming from the apprehension or comprehension of another's emotional state or condition* (p. 33) and it is related to feelings of sorrow and concern, whereas personal distress is *a self-focused, aversive affective reaction to the apprehension of another's emotion* (p.33) and is related to feelings of discomfort and anxiety. Finally, empathy is the *emotional response stemming from the apprehension or comprehension of another's emotional state, similar to what the other person is feeling or would be expected to feel* (p. 34).

Empathic responses have been regarded as developed responses because of the demands inherent in group living (Preston & de Waal, 2002). Furthermore, empathic responses have been proposed as instrumental responses for the formation and maintenance of social bonds (Anderson & Keltner, 2002). However, a lack of empathic responses has been connected, amongst other things, with autistic disorders, psychopathic personalities (Mealey & Kinner, 2002) and food disorders like nervous anorexia (Preston & de Waal, 2002).

The experimental manipulation of empathy has generally been conducted by using experimental instructions that induce the adoption of another's perspective - *perspective-taking* or *role-taking instructional sets*.

The study of empathy applied to environmental concern was first attempted by Shelton and Rogers (1981). The authors tested whether it was possible to protect non-human life forms by inducing empathy and fear. In particular, they examined the effect of empathy and fear on the attitude towards whales. The theoretical framework of this study was the *theory of motivation for protection* by Rogers (1976; quoted in Shelton & Rogers, 1981). According to this theory, the motivation for self-protection in the face of danger has its origin in fear. Extending this self-protection theory to the protection of others also involves the empathy construct.

The authors carried out an experiment in which they manipulated the degree of harm provoked to whales (high/low), the efficacy of the protection response [1] (high/low), and empathy (high/low). Empathy was induced with instructions for adopting the whales' perspective. The stimuli were 4 audiovisual scenes with fragments of documentaries on whales from *National Geographic* and the non-governmental organisation *Greenpeace*. The dependent variable consisted of 5 items evaluating the general intention to help to save whales and to give time and money to *Greenpeace*. The three variables studied (degree of harm, efficacy of the response and empathy) produced a significant effect on pro-environmental behavioral intentions.

In a later article, Schultz (2000) studied empathy with nature resorting to theory from the field of altruism and empathy, and proposed that the type of environmental concern a person shows is related to the degree with which he/she feels interconnected with nature. The author conducted an experiment, using the induction of empathy with the environment, so as to manipulate the degree of inclusion with nature. He found that participants who had seen an image of an animal harmed in nature, in a perspective-taking experimental condition, showed higher biospheric concern with nature than participants in an objective condition. More recently, Sevillano, Aragonés and Schultz (2007) studied the effect that dispositional empathy has on environmental concern. This research will be reviewed in depth at a later point in the manuscript (see also Berenguer, 2007).

---

[1] The efficacy of response does not refer to the personal response of participants but to the efficacy of *Greenpeace* in the protection of whales.

The study of emphatic responses to animals and living beings is a logical correlate of our relationship with nature. Batson (1994) states that pro-environmental metaphors often use a sort of *personalization* for motivating actions for the public good (*Mother Earth* or *dying rivers;* p.608). Along these lines, Epley, Waytz and Cacioppo (2007) have proposed a three-factor theory of *anthropomorphism*. They define anthropomorphism as *the tendency to imbue the real or imagined behavior of non-human agents with human-like characteristics, motivations, intentions or emotions* (p. 864). They focus on three psychological determinants for explaining when people anthropomorphize: the accessibility and applicability of anthropocentric knowledge, the motivation to explain and understand the behavior of other agents, and the desire for social contact and affiliation (Epley et al., 2007). Research related to pets has revealed that pet owners give as reasons for owning pets: *I would be lonely without my pet,* or *My pet helps me get through hard times* (Staats, Sears & Pierfelice, 2006). It could be argued that those reasons show the desire for social contact and affiliation outlined by Epley et al. (2007) as one of the psychological determinants of anthropomorphism.

COLLECTIVISM: *PROTECTING OUR ENVIRONMENT*

Collectivistic motivation for acting in the public good is related to three areas of psychological research: Social Norms, Social Value Orientation, and Group Identity.

Social Norms. Social norms are socially prescribed expectations about appropriate behavior in a specific situation. In the context of altruism research, the focus has been on the social norm of reciprocity and social responsibility. Given that these social norms are rooted in social interaction contexts, they have not been applied to environmental research. Nevertheless, the social influence of norms on environmental behavior has been addressed by some authors with promising success (Cialdini, Reno & Kallgren, 1991; Nolan, Schultz, Cialdini, Goldstein & Griskevicious, 2008).

Social Value Orientation. Pro-environmental behavior has often been regarded as a *social dilemma*. Social dilemmas are characterized by two properties: 1) Each individual receives a higher pay-off for a socially defecting choice (e.g. using all the energy available) than for a socially cooperative choice, no matter what the other individuals in society do; 2) All individuals are better off if they cooperate than if they defect (Dawes, 1980; p. 169).

The first conceptualization of the decision to contaminate or to impoverish environmental resources in terms of a dilemma was described by Hardin (1968). In his article, the author describes a situation where a group of people share limited natural resources. In the allegory, each person in the group has 10 sheep and they share grazing land. If every individual were to increase his/her number of sheep, the consequence would be personal gain and detriment to the common wealth. *The commons dilemma,* as Hardin called this situation, occurs because rationality dictates that each person increase his number of sheep to increase his individual wealth, whilst the common wealth - the pasture land - becomes depleted (Dawes, Delay & Chaplin, 1974).

The commons dilemma has been considered as a generalisation of *the prisoner's dilemma* and it has been pointed out that the decisions concerning optimal decisions either for the individual (to the detriment of group gain) or for the group (to the detriment of personal gain) are related to this dilemma (Dawes et al., 1974). More explicitly, Dawes, McTavish and

Shaklee (1977) elaborated pro-environmental behavior (or non pro-environmental) in terms of *the prisoner's dilemma*, as follows:

> Each individual's rational self-interest to exploit the environment, pollute, and (in some countries) overpopulate, results in the collective effect being worse for everyone than if each individual exercised restraint (p. 1).

Other types of social dilemma frameworks have been applied to pro-environmental behavior: *Public goods games* and *resources dilemma* (Parks, 1994). The former requires that some members of a group collaborate in the provision of a common good that can be used by all members of the group (contributors and non-contributors): the dilemma lies in the decision to make use of the common good, yet not to contribute anything (Parks, 1994). Thus, if everyone decided to act in this way, the common good would run out. The latter dilemma lies in the conservation of a shared good (contrary to the previous game, the common good already exists) and which can be used by all members (Parks, 1994). Individual rationality would seem to dictate that one accumulate the maximum amount possible of the common good. As in the previous case, the generalisation of this behavior would deplete this resource. The common dilemma previously mentioned would fit into this second type.

In accordance with the terminology for dilemmas research, individuals who choose to engage in pro-environmental behaviors are considered *cooperators* (e.g., light harvesting) and *competitors* those with non pro-environmental practices (e.g., heavy harvesting) (Gifford & Hine, 1997).

One of the factors that can affect individual behavior in social dilemmas are their personal beliefs and values: *Social Values* (Parks, 1994; Kramer, McClintock & Messick, 1986) or *Social Motives* (Liebrand, 1984). A *social value* refers to preferences consistently carried out that give a specific distribution of results for oneself and others (Kramer, McClintock & Messick, 1986). A *social motive* is a general tendency or individual orientation to behave in a specific way, driven by a valued outcome. *Individualism* (maximize own gain), *competition* (maximize relative gain), *cooperation* (maximize joint gain) and *altruism* (maximize other's gain) are amongst the social values that have been proposed (Parks, 1994). Just as social values can affect the way we behave, these values can also affect the way we expect others to behave.

In one of Liebrand's studies (1984) on the problem of resource conservation, the social motives of individuals (*individualism, competition, cooperation*, and *altruism*) were assessed along with their effect on the behavior of individuals in a dilemma. The author found that competitive individuals were those who appropriated most resources, followed by the individualists, whilst the altruists and the cooperators were those who appropriated fewer resources. Liebrand (1984) concluded that people's social motives influence the way they behave in social dilemmas.

In a recent paper, Van Lange and Joireman (2008) include two more social motives (egalitarianism and aggression) and two temporal orientations (short-term orientation and future orientation) relevant to decision-making in social dilemmas. In general, pro-social (egalitarianism, altruism and cooperation) and future orientation elicit more collectively beneficial outcomes.

Within environmental research, social value orientation studies have been mainly applied to transport choice issues. Van Vugt, Meertens and Van Lange (1995) showed that pro-social individuals prefer to choose public transport (a collective well-being option) in a computerized commuter situation, whereas pro-self individuals prefer to choose their private car (a personal convenience option). Similar results were found by Cameron, Brown and Chapman (1998) about supporting a program to reduce transport pollution. The authors also hypothesized that perceiving personal costs (for pro-selfs) and environmental benefits (for pro-socials) would mediate the relationship between social value orientation and support for the program (send letters of support). However, although they found the predicted mediator for pro-self individuals (perceived personal costs), they failed to find the proposed mediator for pro-social individuals (perceived environmental benefits). The difficult task of delineating why pro-socials act in the public good is evident from these results.

Taking into account the temporal dimension (considerations of future consequences) together with the social dimension (social value orientations) in pro-environmental political behavior, Joireman, Lasane, Bennett, Richards and Solaimani (2001) found that the relationship between considerations of future consequences (CFC) and pro-environmental intention was mediated by perceived personal, social and biospheric consequences of environmental conditions. However, the relationship between social value orientation (pro-self or pro-social individuals) and pro-environmental intention was not mediated by perceived personal, social, or biospheric consequences of environmental conditions. More recently, the important role of CFC was confirmed in the context of commuting preferences (Joireman, Van Lange & Van Vugt, 2004). Similarly, other authors have found that pro-social individuals place more importance on social consequences and less on personal consequences, whilst pro-self individuals follow the opposite pattern (Gärling, Fujii, Gärling & Jakobson, 2003).

As previously mentioned, research on value orientations and pro-environmental behavior has been conducted in relation to the use of means of transport. Some of the failures in this research could be due to having focused on conduct which depends partly on macro-social factors (e.g., the existence of infrastructures) and psychological factors (e.g., habit). The consideration of other types of pro-environmental behavior may help to clarify the role of value orientations and their possible mediators.

Group Identity. Belonging to a group increases the probability of helping members of that group, when membership is salient (Fiske, 2004). Although some studies have used identity concepts, they have generally not been integrated into the altruism field (Social Cohesion, Uzzell, Pol & Bádenas, 2002; Regional identity, Carrus, Bonaiuto & Bonnes, 2005; Environmental identity, Clayton, 2003).

PRINCIPLISM: *PROTECTING THE ENVIRONMENT*

Personal norms. Shalom Schwartz developed a model of altruistic behavior based on internalised moral norms. This approach was denominated as *normative influences on altruism* (Schwartz, 1977). Altruistic behavior topics in general social psychology textbooks include this model together with research on social norms, emphasizing the term *norm* (Smith & Mackie, 2007), with research on personal values, emphasizing the term *moral* (Fiske, 2004). We shall follow the latter since, on one hand, moral norms do not imply socially mediated sanctions or rewards and, on the other hand, moral considerations apply.

Schwartz (1977) describes three non-mutually-exclusive explanations of pro-social acts: arousal of emotion (empathy), activation of social expectations (social norms), and activations of self-expectations (personal norms). He focused on the latter because he argues that pro-social behavior is altruistic only to the extent that internal norms motivate it. From his perspective, an internal norm is the self-expectation or specific action in given situations that are constructed by the individual (Schwartz, 1977). The moral norm is experienced as a feeling of moral obligation when it is activated. The model proposes an ordered sequence of norm activation, a feeling of obligation, and possible defences against the activated obligation preceding altruistic behavior. The norm activation phase is influenced by *Awareness of Consequences* (AC)[2]. AC is the tendency to be aware that personal potential acts may have consequences for the welfare of others (Schwartz, 1968). The relationship between norm and behavior could be diluted by *Responsibility Denial* (RD)[3]. RD is the individual tendency to accept rationales for denying responsibility for the consequences of one's behavior (Schwartz, 1977). Thus, personal norms and pro-social behavior would be related if people: a) were aware of the consequences that their behavior has for others which would activate their personal norm; b) and people would not engage in denial processes about their responsibility which would not neutralize their feeling of moral obligation about the behavior involved. It is of interest that the theoretical model developed by Schwartz applies to any behavior motivated by a feeling of moral obligation. Therefore, any pro-environmental behavior motivated by a feeling of moral obligation, regardless of whether it benefits others, could be studied within this model.

Environmental research has applied this model for the last 30 years. The pioneers were Heberlein & Black (1976) with their studies on the purchase of lead-free gasoline. They measured attitudes -differing on the level of specificity- towards environmentalism, beliefs about air pollution, beliefs about lead-free gasoline, and the personal obligation to buy lead-free gasoline. On this last (more specific) level, they included five items involving guilt, pride and the feeling of personal obligation to go out of one's way to purchase lead-free gasoline (e.g. *If your were to drive across town, over 10 blocks out of your way to buy lead-free gasoline instead of buying regular gas at a more convenient place, how do you think you would feel?*). In addition, they used a single-item indicator of personal norm *(How much personal obligation do you feel to purchase lead-free gasoline?)*. Their dependent variable was the actual lead-free gasoline purchase (self-reported and observed). They found a high correlation between the two types of measure and behavior ($r = .50$ and $r = .59$ for five items measure and single-item personal norm, respectively). Despite promising results, Schwartz (1977) warned of two methodological issues that prevented him from making conclusions about direction of causation: the dependent variable was partly composed of a self report; and lead-free gasoline purchase was a recurrent behavior (so, instances of that behavior had preceded norm assessment). That is, the norms may have been inferred from behavior (Schwartz, 1977).

Following this research, several others have used the Norm-Activation Model in the context of environmental behavior: yard burning (Van Liere & Dunlap, 1978); energy consumption (Black, Stern & Elworth, 1985), and participation in green electricity program

---

[2] Originally, AR and RD were conceptualised as a personality variable by Schwartz (1977).
[3] Previous to Schwartz's (1977) paper, this variable was called *Ascription of Responsibility*. This author (1977; p. 230) comments that by changing the label he was trying to emphasize a defensive tendency, not a spontaneous tendency.

(Clark, Kotchen & Moore, 2003). Methodological considerations are important in the application of Schwartz's model. Some environmental research has failed to achieve proper methodology to secure causal relationships between personal norms and behavior. In this sense, questionnaires applied at one and the same time to measure personal norms and related behavior should be avoided.

Different extensions of Schwartz's original model have been proposed. For example, Stern, Dietz and Black (1986) extended the individual Norm-Activation Model to the social level (industry and government). Thus, instead of focusing on the individual making the judgment about her/his own behavior, they focus on the organizations (industry) producing environmental hazards (e.g. hazardous chemical waste). The authors measured the extent to which people are aware of the negative consequences of chemical hazards used in industry, the ascription of responsibility to industry by individuals, and individual commitment behavior (writing to legislators about chemical wastes). The posterior development of this proposal and related research will be explained in detail in another section.

Another proposal is the modified Norm-Activation Model by Hunecke, Blöbaum, Matthies and Höger (2001) in the domain of travel mode choice. Because of difficulties differentiating Schwartz's construct of the norm activation model applied to pro-environmental behavior, the authors propose a model in which awareness of consequences and ascription of responsibility are considered together. This ascription of responsibility has been operationalized as the causal effects of personal behavior on environmental problems and that causal relation is contained in the awareness of consequences construct. The main point is that awareness of consequences regards the consequences of individual behavior on the environment. In addition, constructs from the Theory of Planned Behavior (TPB) were included (subjective norm, and perceived behavior control). So, it is proposed that awareness of consequences, subjective norms and perceived behavior control predict the ecological personal norm. Results confirmed the outlined model and showed that the ecological personal norm was the best predictor of public transport use.

Personal values. The aims with a universal character that guide our conduct are denominated personal values. Personal values are one of the motivational sources for exercising pro-social behavior.

The theory with the greatest impact on pro-environmental research has been developed by Schwartz et al. (Schwartz, 1992; Schwartz & Bilsky, 1991). These authors defined values as *concepts or beliefs pertaining to desirable end states, transcending specific situations, guiding selection or evaluation of behavior, which are ordered by relative importance* (Schwartz, 1992; p. 4). In accordance with the conceptualisation of values, the authors propose that the values express the type of goal or motivational concern. They thus establish 11 primary motivational types with a series of specific associated values:

- Self-direction (freedom, creativity, independence, choosing one's own goals, curiosity and self-respect);
- Stimulation (an exciting life and a varied life);
- Hedonism (pleasure and enjoying life);
- Achievement (ambitious, influential, capable, successful, intelligent and self-respectful);

- Power (social power, wealth, authority, preserving my public image and social recognition);
- Security (national security, reciprocation of favors, family security, sense of belonging, social order, health and cleanliness);
- Conformity (obedience, self-discipline, politeness and honouring parents and elders);
- Tradition (respect for tradition, devout, accepting my lot in life, humble and moderate);
- Spirituality (a spiritual life, meaning in life, inner harmony and detachment);
- Benevolence (helpful, responsible, forgiving, honest, loyal, mature love and true friendship); and
- Universalism (Equality, unity with nature, wisdom, a world of beauty, social justice, broad-mindedness, protecting the environment and a world at peace).

These motivational types can be structured in two basic dimensions: *openness to change* versus *conservation*; and *self-enhancement* versus *self-transcendence*. The first dimension expresses the tension between following personal intellectual and emotional interests in unknown directions, and conforming to traditions and preserving status. The second dimension refers to the opposition between self-interest and the welfare of others.

The model proposed by Stern et al. (1999) has been the one to make most use of Schwartz's model of values. In particular, Stern et al. hypothesize three value orientations (self-interest, altruism towards other humans, and altruism towards other species) underlying the norms and beliefs on the environment. These three orientations would have been formed by several values from Schwartz's proposal. Specifically, the orientation of egoistic value would have been made up of the Self-Enhancement values (Achievement and Power); the orientation of the altruistic value and of the biospheric value would have been composed of the Self-Transcendence values (Universalism and Benevolence).

The importance of values in relation to pro-environmental behavior from a cross-cultural perspective has been pointed out by Schultz and Zelezny (1999) and by Schultz, Gouveia, Cameron, Tankha, Schmuck and Franek (2005).

In the following sections, we will describe theoretical approaches that have been rooted in prosocial literature: Value-Belief-Norm Theory (Stern et al., 1999); and the Inclusion Model (Schultz, 2002).

VALUE-BELIEF-NORM THEORY

Schwartz's contributions in the field of altruism have been used most directly in pro-environmental research in the Value-Belief-Norm Theory (Stern et al., 1999; Stern, 2000). If, at the start, Stern et al.'s investigations centered on the moral norm activation model of Schwartz (Stern, Dietz, & Black, 1986), respecting pioneer investigations such as those of Heberlein and Black (1976) and Van Liere and Dunlap (1978), it was the value concept, taking as a reference the trans-cultural investigation of Schwartz's (1994) values, that finally culminated in the VBN theory.

Altruism and Beyond: The Motivational Bases of Pro-environmental Behavior 173

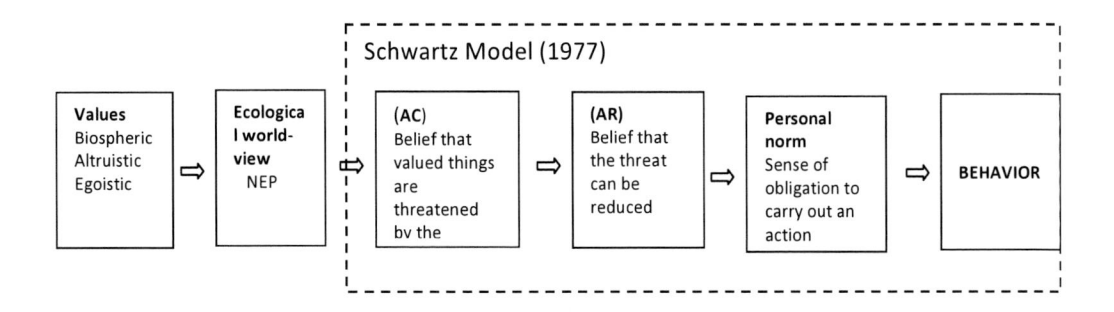

```
                        ┌─────────────────────────────────────────────────────────────┐
                        │ Schwartz Model (1977)                                        │
┌──────────┐  ┌──────────┐│┌──────────┐  ┌──────────┐  ┌──────────┐                   │
│ Values   │  │Ecologica ││ (AC)     │  │ (AR)     │  │Personal  │                   │
│Biospheric│⇒ │l world-  │⇒│Belief that│⇒│Belief that│⇒│norm      │⇒ │ BEHAVIOR │
│Altruistic│  │view      ││ valued   │  │the threat│  │Sense of  │                   │
│Egoistic  │  │NEP       ││ things   │  │can be    │  │obligation│                   │
│          │  │          ││ are      │  │reduced   │  │to carry  │                   │
│          │  │          ││ threatened│  │          │  │out an    │                   │
│          │  │          ││ by the   │  │          │  │action    │                   │
└──────────┘  └──────────┘│└──────────┘  └──────────┘  └──────────┘                   │
                        └─────────────────────────────────────────────────────────────┘
```

Figure 1. Graphic representation of the VBN Theory

This theory attempts to explain environmental concern at different levels: from the behavior in the personal sphere to any action of a participative nature designed to improve the quality of the environment. It is concerned with the variability in pro-environmental behavior across individuals. The theory is framed around five concepts that are sequentially related: personal values; ecological worldviews; awareness of consequences; ascription of responsibility; and personal norms (see Figure 1).

In relation to values, Stern (2000) proposes three value orientations: biospheric, altruistic and egoistic. These value orientations are made up of values originating from the theory of universal values proposed by Schwartz (1992, 1994). Thus, at the start, Stern et al. (1999) recognize that biospheric and altruistic orientations form part of Schwartz's Self-Transcendence dimension, and they relate the egoistic orientation to this author's Self-Enhancement dimension

Table 2. Relationship between theoretical proposals: Batson (1994), Stern, Dietz & Kalof (1993) and Schultz (2000)

Acting for the public good	Acting for environment	
Motivational base Batson (1994)	Value Orientations Stern, Dietz & Kalof (1993)	Valued Objects Schultz (2000)
1. Egoism	1. Egoistic	-Myself -My lifestyle -My future -My health
2. Collectivism 3. Altruism	2. Altruistic	-Children -All people -Neighbours -Family
4. Principlism	3. Biospheric	-Plants -Birds -Animals -Aquatic life

The second concept corresponds to the ecological world-view held by people. The authors conceptually define worldviews as beliefs corresponding to person-environment relations while they are operatively defined in the New Ecological Paradigm (NEP) developed by Dunlap, Van Liere, Mertig & Jones (2000).

The remaining concepts are the result of incorporating the three components of Schwartz's model on altruism: the belief that environmental conditions threaten things that a person values (AC) and the belief that the person him/herself can act to reduce the threat (AR); finally, a personal norm emanates from this responsibility which stimulates a person to act.

The theory refers on two occasions to altruism. First, when it mentions values that can motivate behavior, *altruism* being one of them. Secondly, when it refers to the classical model of pro-social behavior proposed by Schwartz (1977) expressed in the third, fourth and fifth concepts, as shown in Figure 1.

This theory fits into the most classical tradition of social psychology suggested by Kurt Lewin, where personal variables – pro-environmental values and beliefs – are related directly to the social situation which would allow a norm to be activated if the situation is perceived as threatening and action is positively considered.

On many occasions the VBN theory has been represented in graphic form only, indicating the links between preceding and consequent variables, as in Figure 1. However, the relation between variables is rather more complex because there are also non-sequential relations of preceding variables with the remaining ones. Multiple regression analyses with which authors test the theory constantly reiterate these relations (Stern, Dietz, Abel, Guagnano & Kalof, 1999; Steg, Dreijerink & Abrahamse, 2005). Furthermore, although the theory includes three different value orientations, there would appear to be no consensus with respect to their role in relation to other concepts involved. Whilst Stern (2000) implies in his work that altruism, in particular, is the most important value when explaining the relations between the five concepts dealt with in the theory, Steg et al. (2005), affirm that biospherism has the most influential role in explaining pro-environmental conduct, whereas altruism has no influence at all in this research.

This theory has inspired a series of studies defining beliefs about adverse consequences (ACs) from value orientations. Amongst these studies, Schultz (2000) proposes 3 types of valued objects on which people base their environmental concern (egoistic, altruistic and biospheric) which correspond to the value orientations proposed in the VBN theory. The egoistic value objects are composed of elements such as: myself, my future, my life style and my health; altruistic value objects are composed of elements such as: all people, my children, neighbours and children; biospheric value objects include things like: animals, plants, marine life and birds. The relationship between Batson (1994), Stern, Dietz and Kalof (1993), and Schultz (2000)'s proposals is showed in table 2. Paying attention to valued objects means that the three last concepts of the theory could explain pro-environmental behavior without necessarily referring to the values themselves and to the ecological worldview. Sevillano and Aragonés (2009) identified the three types of environmental concern proposed by Stern, Dietz and Kalof (1993) in open ended responses to the question *What is the environmental problem that concerns you the most and why* (used in Schultz, 2000). Content analysis on participants' responses was conducted. Responses were coded attending to the object suffering the environmental problem. Table 3 shows mentioned objects (water, family, aliments), ascribed category of the objects (natural elements, gregarious man, daily life), and type of environmental concern (biospheric, altruistic, egoistic). Biospheric concern is mainly formed by Natural Surroundings and Natural Species' categories (frequency of mention, 34 and 20, respectively). Altruistic concern is uniquely related to Gregarious Man category (20). Finally, egoistic concern is mainly related to Individual Man category (42).

More recent research in the VBN framework has brought forth new questions. Snelgar (2006) observes that there are four nonorthogonal dimensions and not three, when looking at environmental concern: egoism, altruism, animals and plants. Thompson & Barton (1994) have organised beliefs in another way. They suggest two dimensions: one, denominated "anthropocentrism", corresponding to the subordination of nature to human needs, similar to the egoistic and altruistic orientations of the VBN theory. The other is "Ecocentrism", which involves attributing value to Nature in itself and is roughly equivalent to Stern's biospheric orientation. In an attempt to combine both these positions, Amérigo, Aragonés, De Frutos, Sevillano and Cortés (2007) have observed how the ecocentric dimension referred to by Thompson and Barton can in turn be sub-divided into two aspects: one corresponding to the valuation of nature in itself, equivalent to Stern's biospherism; and another corresponding to an individual valuation of the positive effects of nature on the self, which they have called "egobiocentrism".

Therefore, from the results of their factorial analyses, environmental beliefs would be organised into three dimensions: anthropocentrism, the dimension based on the instrumental value of the environment for human beings, whether egoistic or altruistuic; biospherism, the dimension that values the environment for its own sake; and egobiocentrism, which corresponds to an individual valuation of the positive effects that nature has on the self. The first two are similar to those suggested by Stern; however, the last dimension more closely reflects the personal relation of an individual with the natural environment, similar to connectedness to nature. Finally, values and, amongst them, altruism, are consequently of interest in research, yet they require further investigation both from the psychological and cultural points of view.

The ecological worldview is the second concept that considers the theory and this concept is systematically operationalized with the NEP scale. This decision may be one of the weaknesses in the theory, even though this measure is one of the most contrasted in this field of study, because the NEP defines a determined ecological vision of the world, thus complicating the application of other measures that might offer alternative ways of confronting this problem.

Another aspect not contemplated in the theory is the fact that the moral norm activated from AC and AR beliefs is held by people prior to their activation (Hopper & Nielsen, 1991). This fact would seem to mean that the relations between beliefs and the activated moral norm are more complex than their supposedly linear associations, because there can be differences in the intensity with which people hold their moral norm before situations, or in the ease with which situations make the norm available once their beliefs are activated.

Despite the fact that these reflections may well improve certain procedural aspects of this theory, it should be recognized, as Stern (2000) himself reminds us, that it has been proved on numerous occasions, explaining almost 30% of the target behavior variance. This would seem to indicate an interesting potential when designing programs of environmental implication on both micro-social and macro-social levels.

Table 3. Objects harmed by environmental problems and type of environmental concern

Type of environmental concern	Category	Mentioned Objects	Frequency
Biospheric Concern	Natural elements	Water; Air; Sky; Stars; Moon; Sun	6
	Vegetation	Trees; Green places; Woods; Plants; Vegetation	14
	Ozone layer hole	Polar caps; Poles; ozone layer; Atmosphere	13
	Climate	Climate	5
	Natural surroundings	Ecosystems; Habitats; Surroundings; Environment; Earth; Planet; Terraqueous globe; Nature	34
	Natural species	Marine species; Natural species; Living species; Animal species; Animals; Species; Natural life; Living beings	20
Altruistic Concern	Gregarious man	Family; World; Countries; Population; Peoples; Human race; The whole world; Human lives; Human species; Humans	14
Egoistic Concern	Human Aspects	Stress; Mood; Ears; Eyes; Skin; Lungs	9
	Individual Man	Man; Us; Person; Human being; Health	42
	Daily life	Aliments; Quality of life; Life conditions; Daily situations	4

Source: Sevillano & Aragonés (2009).
Note: 14 objects were not classified. N = 116 participants.

INCLUSION MODEL

In recent extensions of the empathy model to pro-environmental attitudes and behaviors, researchers have built on the psychological principles of self-expansion. There is a growing body of research showing that individuals differ in the extent to which they include nature in the cognitive representation of self. While there are large individual differences in these cognitive representations of self, an evolutionary perspective suggests that the relation of human beings to nature is based on a biological need in the human species predisposing us to be in contact with other living beings (Bell, Fisher, Baum & Greene, 1996). The biophilia hypothesis (Wilson, 1984) claims that there is a biological inclination to learn and retain positive responses towards certain natural aspects. The most famous studies in relation to this orientation are those conducted by Ulrich on the therapeutic effects of natural environments (e.g. Ulrich, 1984).

In the literature on environmental concern, the study of the self in relation to nature is a consequence of the attention paid to the premises and declarations of the environmental movement, as well as the study of the affective component of environmental concern. One example of this line of reasoning can be found in Bragg (1996), who provides a framework for the *ecological self*. The central aspect of the ecological self would be the experience of an amplified self, which includes all life forms. The author finds theoretical support in cross-cultural investigation on the self concept.

Bragg (1996) focuses on the distinction between the *independent vision of the self*, typical of the American and western European cultures, and the *interdependent vision of the self*, typical of Asian, African, Latin American and southern European cultures (cf., Markus & Kitayama, 1991). The independent vision of the self includes a concept of the "I" as an autonomous, independent person. Acquiring independence is the construction of the self as an individual whose behavior is organised and who makes sense of his existence mainly by reference to his own thoughts, feelings and actions, more than by reference to the thoughts, feelings and actions of others. The interdependent vision of the self means having a vision of the I as part of a social relation and recognising that one's behavior is determined, is contingent and is largely organised by the perception of the thoughts, feelings and actions of others in the relation. In accordance with Markus and Kitayama (1991), the interdependent vision of the self is related to a philosophical monist tradition which affirms the belief that human beings "are made" of the same material as the rest of nature and therefore it is assumed that the relation between the self and the other, or between subject and object, is much closer. In particular, Bragg (1996) characterises the ecological self as the relation between the self and the rest of the natural world.

While Bragg's (1996) article is largely conceptual, other authors have attempted to measure constructs similar to the ecological self. Amongst these are the *emotional affinity with nature* proposed by Kals, Schumacher and Montada (1999), the *sentiment of unity with the natural world* proposed by Mayer and Frantz (2004), and the inclusion model proposed by Schultz (2002).

Kals, Schumacher and Montada (1999) define emotional affinity with nature as a positive sentiment of inclination towards nature, made operative using a scale of 4 sub-scales containing 4 items each: *love of nature, feelings of freedom, feelings of security and feelings of unity with nature*. Experiences and contact with natural surroundings have been proposed as one of the possible origins of this feeling. Emotional affinity with nature is established as a variable that affects the realisation of pro-environmental behavior. Research by Kals, Schumacher and Montada (1999) attempts to predict pro-environmental behavior from the emotional affinity construct with nature and from the indignation caused by insufficient protection of the environment. The results show that the feeling of emotional affinity with nature and also the indignation caused by insufficient protection of the environment each predict different types of pro-environmental behavior. Also, past experiences in nature and time spent in natural surroundings predicted this feeling of emotional affinity with nature.

Mayer and Frantz (2004) developed a scale for measuring the feeling of unity with the natural world. This scale is called the *Connectedness to Nature Scale* (CNS) and has 14 items. The authors report a reliability coefficient of $\alpha = .84$, and a factorial structure consisting of one factor alone which accounts for 38% of the explained variance. The scores on this scale show a significant positive correlation ($r = .44$) with pro-environmental behavior, with the *perspective-taking* sub-scale of the IRI (Interpersonal Reactivity Index; Davis, 1983) for the measurement of empathic tendencies, with the *biospheric concern* sub-scale of Schultz's (2000) measure of environmental motives. In a later study, Olivos, Aragonés and Amérigo (2009) found that the same scale correlated positively with *egobiocentrism* (Amérigo et al., 2007), which corresponds to an individual valuation of the positive effects of nature on the self.

A third perspective based on the empathy model and self expansion can be found in Schultz's inclusion model. The model conceptualizes pro-environmental conduct as pro-social conduct, and models behavior through value orientations (egoistic, altruistic, biospheric) to link the inclusion of nature in the individual's self with his/her type of environmental concern. Schultz proposes that the type of environmental concern shown by a person is related to the level of inclusion of nature—that is, the cognitive representation of the self. Using this framework, the author predicts that taking the perspective of a natural object would lead to an expanded sense of self and therefore result in higher levels of biospheric concern (Schultz, 2000). To test this hypothesis, pictures were shown of harmed animals (e.g. a seal caught in a fishing net, an eagle on a smokE factory smokestack) and animals in nature (e.g. a caribou on a hill, gorillas in a forest) and of human beings in nature (e.g. a woman meditating on a beach, a painter beside a lake). The experimental tasks were to remain objective when looking at the pictures, or to adopt the perspective of the subject in the pictures (through the instructions). The dependent variables were the scores in biospheric, altruistic and egoistic concern.

The results showed that people who viewed a harmed animal whilst adopting the animal's perspective scored higher in biospheric concern and altruistic concern, than those who remained objective when observing the harmed animal. No differences were found in the biospheric and altruistic concerns manifested by participants observing the pictures with animals or humans in nature. One result not altogether satisfactory was that there was no experimental effect on egoistic concern, either because of the type of picture or the type of instruction. Although the author did not make any prediction, it might have been plausible to expect that the score in egoistic concern is lower when adopting the perspective, as against remaining objective, and when adopting the perspective observing a harmed animal, as against observing it objectively.

In a subsequent investigation, Sevillano, Aragonés and Schultz (2007) furthered the previous findings by studying the moderating role of dispositional empathy on the effect of a perspective-taking manipulation on environmental concerns. The same methodology was used to manipulate the perspective of participants and the same pictures were used as stimuli. The results were that participants who had viewed a harmed animal from the animal's perspective, showed higher levels of biospheric concern. They also found that participants in such a situation (perspective-taking and harmed animal) showed lower levels of egoistic concern. That is, participants who viewed a harmed animal from the animal's perspective scored higher in biospheric concern but lower in egocentric concern. In addition, dispositional empathy affected the type of environmental concern that people showed. In particular, personal distress resulted in lower levels of biospheric concern and higher levels of egoistic concern.

Finally, Sevillano, Aragonés and Schultz (2007) showed that the affective dimension of personal distress moderated the relationship between an experimental pro-environmental situation (kind of task X kind of image) and both biospheric and egoistic environmental concerns. This moderating effect was found specifically in participants with low levels of dispositional empathy (personal distress). When asked to remain objective while viewing an image of a harmed animal, low empathy participants scored lower in egoistic concerns and higher in biospheric concerns. There was no moderating effect for perspective-taking. The failure to find the predicted interaction could be explained in that the comparison group for the multiple regression analysis was a no-instruction, animal-in-nature condition. Thus, there was no difference between taking the perspective of a harmed animal and giving no instruction. Nevertheless, the bias of the effect was theoretical.

The results for dispositional empathy suggest that the discomfort and anxiety level that people feel in response to needy targets may play a role in understanding the kind of environmental concern expressed by participants. The relationship between personal distress and environmental concern may come from a differential conceptualization of *parallel* and *reactive outcomes,* following the *affective outcomes* of an empathic situation, proposed by Davis (1996). A *parallel outcome* is "an actual reproduction in an observer of the target's feelings". A *reactive outcome* is defined as "affective reactions to the experiences of others which differ from the observed effect" (p.18). Following this distinction, *parallel outcomes* would be more *self-centered* reactions (e.g. distress), whereas *reactive outcomes* would be more *other-oriented* (e.g. concern for others). High tendency to feel distress was related with a high score in egoistic concern (*self-centered*) and a low score in biospheric concern (*other-oriented*). So it could be inferred that participants with a tendency to feel stress in empathic situations are normally concerned with environmental problems that affect them personally, and less concerned with environmental problems that affect all living things.

Conclusion

Applying results of the research on altruism to pro-environmental behavior, converting it to *responsible ecological behavior,* has given rise to numerous studies over the last 20 years. In this way, these studies have relied on a solid theoretical basis.

The choice of the motivational basis of altruistic behavior as the backbone of this chapter has served to group together different investigations in one and the same theoretical section. It has also served to provide a vision of the whole of a growing field.

References

Amérigo, M., Aragonés, J.I., De Frutos, B., Sevillano, & Cortés, B. (2007). Underlying dimensions of ecocentric and anthropocentric environmental belief. *The Spanish Journal of Psychology, 10,* 97-103.

Anderson, C., & Keltner, D. (2002). The role of empathy in the formation and maintenance of social bonds. *Behavioral and Brain Sciences, 25,* 1, 20-21.

Batson, D. C. (1991). *The altruism question: Toward a social-psychological answer.* Erlbaum Hillsdale, NJ.

Batson, D. C. (1994). Why act for the public good? Four answers. *Personality and Social Psychology Bulletin, 20,* 5, 603-610.

Bell, P. A., Fisher, J. D., Baum, A., & Greene, T. C. (1996). *Environmental psychology* (4th ed.). Orlando, FL: Harcourt Brace & Company.

Berenguer, J. (2007).The effect of empathy in Pro-environmental attitudes and behaviors. *Environment & Behavior, 39,* 2, 269-283.

Black, J. S., Stern, P. C., & Elworth, J. T. (1985). Personal and contextual influences on household energy adaptations. *Journal of Applied Psychology, 70,* 3-21.

Bragg, E. A. (1996). Towards ecological self: deep ecology meets constructionist self theory. *Journal of Environmental Psychology, 16*, 93-108.

Cameron, L. D., Brown, P. M., & Chapman, J. G. (1998). Social value orientations and decisions to take proenvironmental action. *Journal of Applied Social Psychology, 28*, 2, 675-697.

Carrus, G., Bonaiuto, M., & Bones, M. (2005). Environmental concern, regional identity, and support for protected areas in Italy. *Environment & Behavior, 37*, 2, 237-257.

Castells, M. (1997). *The information age: Economy, society and culture* (V.2) Oxford, UK: Blackwell.

Cialdini, R. B., Reno, R. R., & Kallgren, C. A. (1991). A focus theory of normative conduct: recycling the concept of norms to reduce littering in public places. *Journal of Personality and Social Psychology, 58*, 6, 1015-1026.

Clark, C. F., Kotchen, M. J., & Moore, M. R. (2003). Internal and external influences on pro-environmental behavior: participation in a green electricity program. *Journal of Environmental Psychology, 23*, 237-246.

Clayton, S. (2003). Environmental identity: a conceptual and an operational definition. In S. Clayton & S. Opotow (Eds.), *Identity and the natural environment. The psychological significance of nature* (pp. 45-66). Cambridge, Massachusetts: MIT press.

Cunningham, M. R., Steinberg, J., & Grev, R. (1980). Wanting to and having to help: separate motivations for positive mood and guilt-induced helping. *Journal of Personality and Social Psychology, 38*, 181-192.

Darley, J. M., & Latané, B. (1968). Bystander intervention in emergencies: Diffusion of responsibility. *Journal of Personality and Social Psychology, 8*, 377-383.

Davis, M. H. (1983). Measuring individuals' differences in empathy: evidence for a multidimensional approach. *Journal of Personality and Social Psychology, 44*, 113-126.

Davis, M. H. (1996). *Empathy: a social psychological approach*. Boulder, CO: Westview Press.

Dawes, R. M. (1980). Social dilemmas. *Annual Review of Psychology, 31*, 169-193.

Dawes, R. M., Delay, J., & Chaplin, W. (1974). The decision to pollute. *Environment and Planning A, 6*, 3-10.

Dawes, R. M., McTavish, J., & Shaklee, H. (1977). Behavior, communication, and assumptions about other people's behavior in a commons dilemma situation. *Journal of Personality and Social Psychology, 35*, 1, 1-11.

Dunlap, R., Van Liere, K., Mertig, A., & Jones, R. (2000). Measuring endorsement of the new ecological paradigm: A revised NEP scale. *Journal of Social Issues, 56*, 425-442.

Eisenberg, N. (1991). Meta-analytic contributions to the literature on prosocial behavior. *Personality and Social Psychology Bulletin, 17*, 273-282.

Eisenberg, N. (2002). Distinctions among various modes of empathy-related reactions: a matter of importance in humans. *Behavioral and Brain Sciences, 25*, 33-34.

Eiser, J. R., Reicher, S. D., & Podpadec, T. J. (1995). Global changes and local accidents: Consistency in attributions for environmental effects. *Journal of Applied Social Psychology, 25*, 1518-1529.

Epley, N., Waytz, A., & Cacioppo, J. (2007). On seeing human: a three-factor theory of anthropomorphism. *Psychological Review, 114*, 864-886.

Fiske, S. T. (2004). *Social beings: a core motives approach to social psychology*. Wiley.

Gärling, T., Fujii, S., Gärling, A., & Jakobson, C. (2003). Moderating effects of social value orientation on determinants of proenvironmental behavior intention. *Journal of Environmental Psychology, 23,* 1-9.

Geller, E. S. (1987). Applied behavior analysis and environmental psychology: from strange bedfellows to a productive marriage. In D. Stokols & I. Altman (Eds.), *Handbook of Environmental Psychology* (Vol. 1, pp. 361-387). New York: Wiley.

Gifford, R., & Hine, D. (1997). "I'm cooperative, but you're greedy": some cognitive tendencies in a commons dilemma. *Canadian Journal of Behavioral Science, 29,* 257-265.

Hardin, G. (1968). The tragedy of the commons. *Science, 162,* 1243-1248.

Heberlein, T. A., & Black, J. S. (1976). Attitudinal specificity and the prediction of behavior in a field setting. *Journal of Personality and Social Psychology, 33,* 474-479.

Hoffman, M. L. (2000). *Empathy and moral development: Implications for caring and justice*. New York: Cambridge University Press.

Hopper, J. R., & Nielsen, J. M.(1991). Recycling as altruistic behavior: Normative and behavioral strategies to expand participation in a community recycling program. *Environment & Behavior, 23,* 195-220.

Hunecke, M., Blöbaum, A., Matthies, E., & Höger, R. (2001). Responsibility and Environment: Ecological norm orientation and external factors in the domain of travel mode choice behavior. *Environment & Behavior, 33,* 830-852.

Joireman, J. A., Lasane, T. P., Bennett, J., Richards, D., & Solaimani, S. (2001). Integrating social value orientation and the consideration of future consequences within the extended norm activation model of pro-environmental behavior. *British Journal of Social Psychology, 40,* 133-155.

Joireman, J. A., Van Lange, P. A. M., & Van Vugt, M. (2004). Who cares about the environmental impact of cars? Those with an eye toward the future. *Environment & Behavior, 36,* 187-206.

Kaiser, F.G. (2006). A moral extension of the theory of planned behavior: Norms and anticipated feelings of regret in conservationism. *Personality and Individual Differences, 41,* 71-81.

Kaiser, F.G., Schultz, P.W., Berenguer, J., Corral-Verdugo, V., & Tankha, G. (2008). Extending planned environmentalism: Anticipated guilt and embarrassment across cultures. *European Psychologist, 31,* 288-297.

Kals, E., & Maes, J. (2002). Sustainable development and emotions. In P. Schmuck & P.W. Schultz (Eds.), *Psychology of sustainable development* (pp. 61-78). Norwell, MA: Kluwer Academic Publishers.

Kals, E., Schumacher, D., & Montada, L. (1999). Emotional affinity toward nature as a motivational basis to protect nature. *Environment & Behavior, 31,* 2, 178-202.

Kramer, R. M., McClintock, CH. G., & Messick, D. M. (1986). Social values and cooperative response to a simulated resource conservation crisis. *Journal of Personality, 54,* 3, 576-592.

Liebrand, W. (1984). The effect of social motives, communication and group size on behavior in a n-person multi-stage mixed motive game. *European Journal of Social Psychology, 14,* 239-264.

Markus, H. R., & Kitayama, Sh. (1991). Culture and self: implications for cognition, emotion, and motivation. *Psychological Review, 98*, 2, 224-253.

Mayer, F. S., & Frantz, C. M. (2004). The connectedness to nature scale: a measure of individuals´ feeling in community with nature. *Journal of Environmental Psychology, 24*, 503-515.

McClintock, C. G. (1972). Social motivation—a set of propositions. *Behavioral Science, 17*, 438-454.

Mealey, L., & Kinner, S. (2002). The perception-action model of empathy and psychopathic "cold-heartedness". *Behavioral and Brain Sciences, 25*, 20-21.

Messick, D. M., & Brewer, M. B. (1983). Solving social dilemmas: A review. In L. Wheeler & P. Shaver (Eds.), *Review of personality and social psychology* (Vol. 4, pp. 11–44). Beverly Hills, CA: Sage.

Messick, D. M., & McClintock, C. G. (1968). Motivational bases of choice in experimental games. *Journal of Experimental Social Psychology, 4*, 1-25.

Nolan, J., Schultz, P.W., Cialdini, R. B., Goldstein, N. J., & Griskevicious, V. (2008). Normative social influence is undetected. *Personality and Social Psychology Bulletin, 34*, 913-923.

Nordlund, A., & Garvill, J. (2003). Effects of values, problem awareness, and personal norm on willingness to reduce personal car use. *Journal of Environmental Psychology, 23*, 339-347.

North, A. C., Tarrant, M, & Hargreaves, D.J. (2004). The effects of music on helping behavior: a field study. *Environment & Behavior, 36*, 266-275.

Olivos, P., Aragonés, J.I., & Amérigo, M. (2009). *The connectedness to nature scale and its relationship with environmental beliefs and identity.* Manuscript submitted for publication.

Parks, C. D. (1994). The predictive ability of social values in resource dilemmas and public goods games. *Personality an Social Psychology Bulletin, 20*, 4, 431-438.

Platt, J. (1973). Social traps. *American Psychologist, 28*, 641-651.

Preston, S. D., & de Waal, F. B. M. (2002). Empathy: its ultimate and proximate bases. *Behavioral and Brain Sciences, 25*, 1-20.

Schaller, M., & Cialdini, R. B. (1988). The economics of the empathic helping: support for a mood-management motive. *Journal of Experimental Social Psychology, 24*, 163-181.

Schroeder, D. A., Penner, L. A., Dovidio, J.F., & Piliavin, J. A. (1995). *The psychology of helping and altruism: Problems and puzzles.* McGraw-Hill New York

Schultz, P. W. (2000). Empathizing with nature: the effects of perspective taking on concern for environmental issues. *Journal of Social Issues, 56*, 391-406.

Schultz, P. W. (2001). Assessing the structure of environmental concern: concern for self, other people, and the biosphere. *Journal of Environmental Psychology, 21*, 1-13.

Schultz, P. W. (2002). Inclusion with nature: The Psychology of human-nature relations. In P. Schmuck & P.W. Schultz (Eds.), *Psychology of sustainable development* (pp.61-78). Norwell, MA: Kluwer Academic Publishers.

Schultz, P. W., & Estrada-Hollenbeck, M. (2008). The USE of theory in applied social psychology. In L. Steg, A. P. Buunk & T. Rothengatter (Eds.), *Applied social psychology: Understanding and managing social problems* (pp. 28-56). Cambridge: University Press.

Schultz, P. W., Gouveia, V. V., Cameron, L., Tankha, G., Schmuck, P., & Franek, M. (2005). Values and their relationship to environmental concern and conservation behavior. *Journal of Cross-cultural Psychology, 36,* 457-475.

Schultz, P. W., Nolan, J. M., Cialdini, R. B., Goldstein, N. J., & Griskevicius, V. (2007). The constructive, destructive, and reconstructive power of social norms. *Psychological Science, 18,* 429-434.

Schultz, P. W., & Zelezny, L. (1998). Values and pro-environmental behavior. *Journal of Cross-Cultural Psychology, 29,* 4, 540-558.

Schwartz, S. H. (1968). Words, deeds, and the perception of consequences and responsibility in action situations. *Journal of Personality and Social Psychology, 10,* 232-242.

Schwartz, S. H. (1977). Normative influences on altruism. In L. Berkowitz (Ed.), *Advances in Experimental Social Psychology.* (Vol. 10, pp. 221-279). New York: Academic Press.

Schwartz, S. H. (1992). Universals in the content and structure of values: theoretical advances and empirical tests in 20 countries. In M. P. Zanna (Ed.), *Advances in experimental social psychology.* (Vol. 25, pp. 1-65). New York: Academic Press.

Schwartz, S. H. (1994). Are there universal aspects in the structure and contents of Human Values? *Journal of Social Issues, 50,* 19-45.

Schwartz, S. H., & Bilsky, W. (1991). Toward a psychological structure of human values. *Journal of Personality and Social Psychology, 53,* 550-562.

Sevillano, V., Aragonés, J. I., & Schultz, P. W. (2007). Perspective taking, environmental concern, and the moderating role of dispositional empathy. *Environment & Behavior, 39,* 689-705.

Sevillano, V., & Aragonés, J. I. (2009, June). *Los problemas ambientales y su correspondencia con la preocupación ambiental.* Paper presented at the XXXII CIP (Congreso Internacional de Psicología). Guatemala. [Environmental problems and their correspondence to environmental concern]

Shelton, M. L., & Rogers, R. (1981). Fear-arousing and empathy-arousing appeals to help: the pathos of persuasion. *Journal of Applied Psychology, 11,* 366-378.

Smith, E. R., & Mackie, D. M. (2007). *Social psychology* (3rd. ed.). New York: Psychology press.

Snelgar, R. S. (2006). Egoistic, altruistic and biospheric environmental concerns: Measurement and structure. *Journal of Environmental Psychology, 26,* 87-99.

Staats, S., Sears, K., & Pierfelice, L. (2006).Teachers' pets and why they have them: an investigation of human animal bond. *Journal of Applied Social Psychology, 36,* 1881-1891.

Steg, L., Dreijerink, L., & Abrahamse, W. (2005). Factors influencing the acceptability of energy policies: A test of VBN theory. *Journal of Environmental Psychology, 25,* 415-425.

Stern, P. C. (2000). Toward a coherent theory of environmentally significant behavior. *Journal of Social Issues, 56,* 407-424.

Stern, P. C., Dietz, T., Abel, T., Guagnano, G. A., & Kalof, L. (1999). A value-belief-norm theory of Support for social movements: The case of environmentalism. *Human Ecology Review, 6,* 81-97.

Stern, P. C., Dietz, T., & Black, J. S. (1986). Support for environmental protection: the role of moral norms. *Population and Environment, 8,* 3-4, 204-222.

Stern, P. C., Dietz, T., & Guagnano, G. A. (1995). The New Ecological Paradigm in social-psychological context. *Environment & Behavior, 27*, 723-743.

Stern, P. C., Dietz, T., & Kalof, L. (1993). Value orientations, gender, and environmental concern. *Environment & Behavior, 27*, 723-743.

Thompson, S., & Barton, M. (1994). Ecocentric and anthropocentric attitudes toward the environment. *Journal of Environmental Psychology, 14,* 149-157.

Ulrich, R. S. (1984). View through a window may influence recovery from surgery. *Science, 224,* 420-421.

Uzzell, D. L., Pol, E., & Bádenas, D. (2002). Place identification, social cohesion, and environmental sustainability. *Environment & Behavior, 34,* 26-53.

Van Lange, P. A. M., De Cremer, D. Van Dijk, E., & Van Vugt, M. (2007). Self-interest and beyond: Basic principles of social interaction. In A. W. Kruglanski & E. T. Higgings (Eds.), *Social psychology: Handbook of basic principles* (2nd ed., pp. 540–561). New York: Guilford.

Van Lange, P.A.M., & Joireman, J.A. (2008). How we can promote behavior that serves all of us in the future. *Social Issues and Policy Review, 2,* 127-157.

Van Liere, K., & Dunlap, R. (1978). Moral norms and environmental behavior: An application of Schwartz's norm activation model to yard burning. *Journal of Applied Social Psychology, 8,* 174-188.

Van Vugt, M., Meertens, R. M., & Van Lange, P. A. M. (1995). Car versus public transportation? The role of social value orientations in a real-life social dilemma. *Journal of Applied Social Psychology, 25,* 3, 258-278.

Wilson, E. O. (1984). *Biophilia.* Cambridge: Harvard University Press.

In: Psychological Approaches to Sustainability
Editors: V. Corral-Verdugo et al.

ISBN 978-1-60876-356-6
© 2010 Nova Science Publishers, Inc.

Chapter 10

EQUITY AND SUSTAINABLE LIFESTYLES

Victor Corral-Verdugo[*]
Departamento de Psicología, Universidad de Sonora, Mexico
**Cirilo H. García-Cadena, Laura Castro,
Iván Viramontes and Rafael Limones**
Facultad de Psicología, Universidad Autónoma de Nuevo León, Mexico

ABSTRACT

Equity is an essential psychological dimension of sustainability. This human behavioral characteristic is defined as a tendency to distribute -in a fair way- resources, power and benefits among people, avoiding bias or favoritism. Equitable actions, consequently, imply dealing with and treating fairly and equally all concerned, regardless of social, economic and demographic differences. The opposite tendency, inequity, is recognized as one of the fundamental causes of the current environmental crisis. The unequal distribution of power and resources among people induces social and ecological conflicts and problems, including violence, famine, social discrimination, consumerism, waste of resources, war, and degradation of natural resources. Social and economic inequities permeate interpersonal relations but also interactions between communities and nations. However, these inequities are not alone in inducing environmental and social problems: gender, age, sexual orientation, racial, and ethnic inequities are also partially responsible for the environmental dilemma the world currently faces. Therefore, sustainable development promoters argue that equity actions should be encouraged in order to conserve the socio-physical environment. Although most societies display inequity as a prevalent lifestyle, there are reasons to suppose that equity is intrinsic to human nature. In most of our evolutionary history as species, homo-sapiens have been equitable, as anthropological evidence shows. Inequity seems to be a recent acquisition of our mental and behavioral repertoire. Previous research had indicated that pro-ecological

---

[*] This study was funded by CONACyT (Grant 48466). Correspondence to Victor Corral-Verdugo, Departamento de Psicología, Universidad de Sonora, Rosales y Luis Encinas, S/N, Hermosillo, Sonora, 83000, Mexico. E-mail: victorcorral@sociales.uson.mx.

actions, austere consumption, and altruistic behaviors are manifestations of sustainable lifestyles (SLS). In this chapter we tested the assumption that equity is also a component of SLS. Two-hundred-and-fifty Mexican participants responded to an instrument containing scales that assessed the self-report of equitable, austere, pro-ecological, and altruistic behaviors; additionally, they provided information regarding their demographic characteristics. Results were processed within two structural models. The first model revealed that socio-economic status (indicated by schooling level and economic income) negatively affected the display of equitable actions. The second model produced high and significant relations between the four behavioral factors, which were subsumed by a higher-order factor that we identified as SLS. Such a result seems to confirm that equity is a sustainable lifestyle. These findings and the literature are considered for suggesting future research and interventional strategies aimed at developing equitable tendencies and sustainable lifestyles in people.

INTRODUCTION

Iniquity is one of the most evident manifestations of lack of sustainability in human societies. The unequal distribution of resources and benefits among people negatively affects all kind of social functioning, including the spheres in which economically affluent individuals live and prosper (Talbert, 2008; De Botton, 2005). Every social problem we could imagine is propitiated –at least partially- by inequity: Poverty, injustice, delinquency, violence, war, social discrimination, common dilemmas, and, undoubtedly, the serious environmental crisis the world currently faces. All of those problems have roots in an unequal distribution of resources, power and risks among social and demographic groups (Shiva, 2000; Talbert, 2008; Vlek, 2000).

Not long time ago, experts pointed to two fundamental causes of environmental degradation: overpopulation and consumerism (Oskamp, 2000). More recently, Ehrilch & Ehrilch (2004) argued that inequity is a third source of ecological disturbance, being as serious as the former ones. The Ehrlichs stress the fact that a minority of the human population is responsible for most of the world's pollution, global warming, exhaustion of resources, and the loss of biodiversity on Earth. It is clear that richer societies possess a major capability for exploiting natural resources, which explains how inequity in the concentration of economic and technological power plays a preeminent role in the current environmental crisis. Yet, economic inequity is not alone in inducing trouble to Earth's ecosystems: Gender, age, racial, and ethnic inequities are also potent inhibitors of sustainable development in societies throughout the world (Clayton, 2000; Haynes, 2007).

Consumerism is a well known correlate of inequity. People in non-equitable communities try to differentiate themselves from the rest of their fellows, and the preferred way of achieving this goal is by consuming at excessive levels (Brown & Cameron, 2000). This discrepancy in levels of consumption not only leads to inequity but also to unexpected outcomes for the consumerist person. De Botton (2005) shows that non-equitable societies induce a "status anxiety" to their citizens because they are afraid of being non-successful and also because there are a lot of things to envy in such societies. Of course, the less privileged will try to balance the situation and, as inequity grows, the more likely would be that social conflicts and environmental problems arise in the form of crime, violence and social instability (Talbert, 2008). In more of this, Zizzo and Oswald (2001) showed an interesting phenomenon regarding the negative consequences of inequity; in their experiment, participants were willing to pay to reduce the earning of others, especially if these earnings were associated to wealth and inequity. The consequence is that everybody, even the affluent individual is negatively affected by a lack of equity.

The definition of Sustainable Development (WCED, 1987) implicitly alludes the idea of both an intra and an inter-generational equity. This means that a sustainable society shares equitably its resources among its members in the present but also looks for a balance between the benefits that current generation could obtain and the benefits for people in the future (Pol, 2002). Evidently, the idea of intergenerational solidarity has to be based on equitable and egalitarian practices in the present, by guaranteeing that all individuals have access to resources that meet their needs in every possible way.

Equity also impinges on the balance between human wellbeing and the integrity of ecosystems; that is why equity has been related to the *interdependence* ecological principle: the idea that the global functioning of an ecosystem depends on the equilibrium between its elements (Capra & Pauli, 1995). This applies not only to the biological ecosystems but to human ecology as well; an unbalance in the access to resources –experienced by one or more elements of the system- compromises the survival of the entire structure. It is clear, from this perspective, that the more the inequity a human ecology experiences, the more the risk for social disturbances or for a collapse in its functioning.

EQUITY, EQUALITY, FAIRNESS AND EQUITABILITY

The term *Equity* is defined by the Merriam-Webster Online dictionary (2009) as "Justice according to natural law or right; specifically: freedom from bias or favoritism. Something that is equitable." Equitability, in turn, is defined as "Dealing fairly and equally with all concerned." A related term is "egalitarianism", which the Merriam-Webster dictionary conceives as "A belief in human equality, especially with respect to social, political and economic rights and privileges." Therefore, equity, fairness, and equitability are close to being synonymous. That is why Le Grand (1991, p. 8) establishes that "It is difficult to find phrases incorporating the terms equity or equitable where their replacement by fairness or fair, or by justice or just, would significantly alter the sense or the phrase."

However, a clearer distinction is found between equity and equality ("the quality or state of being equal"). Le Grand establishes that *equality* has a descriptive component –two things are equal and so they are recognized and described- while *equity* is a normative (i.e., conventional) concept leading to what is conceived to be right. Equality does not necessarily imply equity, or equity equality. For example, the situation in which three salesmen receiving 50%, 30%, and 20% of money from a product's sale, undoubtedly reflects an unequal distribution. But suppose that such distribution was decided as a function of each individual's percentage of sales of the product. Now, the decision seems to be based on equity (and fairness). Of course, there are reasons for equity other than pure effort or personal merit. As the above-mentioned definition suggests, the "natural" law or right identifies the mere fact of being human as a merit for being a recipient of the equitable distribution of benefits.

Equality, in its more literal sense, can be contrasted against *sociodiversity*, a fundamental characteristic of sustainable human ecologies. In order to be diverse, a social system should be constituted from different (therefore, unequal) elements. Socio-diversity implies a variety of individual, social and cultural traits such as gender, age, race, ethnicity, cultural practices, religions and so forth (Bonnes & Bonaiuto, 2002). Alternatively, equity, as a sustainable principle, considers a fair and equitable distribution of benefits among people, regardless of such differences. However, diversity is respected and stimulated in sustainable societies (Corral-Verdugo, Bonnes, Tapia, Fraijo, Frías & Carrus, 2009). In other words, a sustainable society stimulates both equity and sociodiversity –a form of inequality. Yet, equity and egalitarianism are not conflicted with each other in the search for a sustainable society.

INEQUITY AND ITS CONSEQUENCES

Equity has to do with the sharing of power and wellbeing among individuals in a social group, but also with the sharing of those privileges among communities and among countries. In non-equitable societies the richer have more power and wellbeing than the poorer, and this unbalance also negatively affects women before men, children and the elderly before adults, and the ethnic, racial and sexual-orientation minorities before their corresponding majorities.

Richer countries use their power against less privileged counterparts (Ehrlich & Ehrlich, 2004), so that people in poorer nations have to face not only the consequences of the internal (national) inequity but also the effects of a global non-equitable distribution of power. The underprivileged experience the worst environmental degradation (Evans, Juen, Corral-Verdugo, Corraliza & Kaiser, 2007) and, because of the intervention of corrupt regimes in their countries, they receive the toxic waste from the richer nations (Adeola, 2000). Citizens of underdeveloped countries are also less happy than people in wealthy nations, since the former do not meet their basic needs (Veenhoven, 2006). In the end, this general unbalance generates a climate that propitiates violence, anxiety, injustice, and environmental damage; in other words: non-sustainability (De Botton, 2005; Renner, 2005; Talbert, 2008). Therefore, the pursuing of a more sustainable way of living has to include the development of equitable behavioral styles in human societies. This is not an easy task.

Social equity is usually assessed by considering the distribution of resources or the access that people has to them. One measure is the *Gini* coefficient –after Corrado Gini who developed it- (Talbert, 2008), which indicates how much the economic income deviates from an equitable distribution; zero means a perfect equitable distribution and 1 indicates a maximum inequity. Countries in northern Europe –as Sweden and Denmark, but also Slovenia- have the highest levels of socio-economic equity in the world, with Ginis between .25 and .28. South Africa reaches a .73 Gini and U.S.A. scores .40 (Aliber, 2002; Eurostat, 2007; United Nations, 2008). It is not surprising that nations with higher standards of equity have also higher levels of self-reported subjective wellbeing or happiness (Veenhoven, 2006; see also Bechtel & Corral-Verdugo chapter in this book).

Although it is known that equity correlates with happiness and personal wellbeing, most countries in the world exhibit significant degrees of inequity. Moreover, the unequal distribution of resources also characterizes the world as a whole. The access and enjoyment to resources is unequally distributed at the local, regional and international levels. Fifteen percent of the world population consumes 71% of the annual production (Brown & Cameron, 2000); 80% of the income is concentrated in a 15% of the population, while a single country (USA) gets the 29% of the world income, with just a 4.6% of the planet population (Ehrlich & Ehrlich, 2004). Yet, the United States have no acceptable equity levels.

In most countries men enjoy more privileges, prestige and power tan women. Even in the developed world it is rare to find women in the highest spheres of politics and organizational activity. In these countries, the male-female unbalance in domestic labor, unequal salary and sexual harassment persists (Lorber, 2001). In other regions women struggle for surviving; raising their children; and coping with poverty, war, racial tensions, the dominant male culture and social exclusion (Haynes, 2007). Worldwide, women produce between sixty and eighty percent of the food; however, they only own a fifteen percent of the land (Gardner & Prugh, 2008). Gender inequity also affects the environmental dilemma: In countries where women are allowed to participate in family planning decisions, they decide to have two or less children, since they are more conscious than men of their own needs and capacities (Engelmann, 2008). Increasing the level of education for women decreases the number of children they decide to have (Oystein, 2002). Therefore, the best family planning policy implies facilitating their educational opportunities. However, fifteen percent of Mexicans consider that investing in girls' education is worthless (De la Torre, 2006).

Ageism is another instance of inequity. This is manifested as a differential treatment to persons in reason of their age. Older people experience discrimination in several areas of social functioning, including job, family decisions and health services. Elder (2005), for instance, points out that older people with acute coronary syndrome are treated differently to younger patient. But this discrimination also impacts on the young. Even in the western liberal nations children are considered incapable of making appropriate decisions. Etim (2004) shows the extreme case of discrimination against children in Africa: He states that, in spite of the Universal Declaration of Human Rights, many people still treat young people as *sub-human*. This affects the provision of health care, social intervention, employment, etc., to younger people. The situation is so dramatic that the Nigerian Constitution explicitly grants citizenship to children in function of birth, instead of age.

EQUITY AS A POTENTIAL OF HUMAN NATURE

According to the above mentioned, inequity seems to be the rule rather than the exception, throughout the world. The historical record shows that most civilizations were – and are- based on an unequal distribution of power and resources, which was manifested as slavery, tyranny, gender oppression, discrimination against minorities, and extreme poverty along with ostensive richness. If equity is a key component of more sustainable ways of living, then the tendency to be equitable should be promoted. Is this ideal possible?

Before attempting to answer that question, a previous one should be posited: Is there an egalitarian/equitable tendency existing in human nature? This issue has paramount importance because the lack of evidence showing that equity is a human propensity would truncate any possible intervention. It is not possible to develop (equity) actions if the potency for their realization (propensity to be equitable) is not present as a capacity in human nature.

The prevalent anthropological view establishes that, in prehistoric times, equity was the rule rather than the exception, as characterizing human societies (Gowdy, 1998; Lee, 1998). In fact, some authors agree with the idea that human inequity is a relatively recent phenomenon. Gowdy (1998) establishes that humankind has lived a 99% of its existence under egalitarian and equitable conditions. Hierarchies have apparently existed anytime, but they were not notorious until the Neolithic. A distribution of tasks based on gender existed but this did not lead to predominance of men over women. Age was not considered a clue for discrimination against the elderly, who were treated with respect, and valued because of their experience.

For most of their evolution, humans lived in genetically-related small groups, a condition that facilitated cooperation and egalitarianism. As the domestication of animals and the foundation of cities appeared, human conglomerates grew significantly and the relations between individuals became increasingly complex. Levels of cooperation, coordination and division of labor rose as never before, which led to the establishment of highly marked hierarchies (Richerson & Boyd, 1999). The bigger the group, the more hierarchical and non-egalitarian resulted. Since bigger societies tend to dominate over the smaller, egalitarian societies succumbed before the non-egalitarian and inequity became the norm. According to this perspective, inequity emerged from the complexity of human relations, as much as most causes (consumerism, overpopulation, absence of cooperation) of non-sustainability (Boyd, Gintis, Boyles & Richerson, 2003; Richardson & Boyd, 1999).

The beginning of non-equitable communities also coincided with the emergence of the market, a significant dependence on technology, private property, and the depredation of natural resources (Lee, 1998). All these particular conditions were subsumed by civilization, leading to the apparition of slavery, the establishment of dominant castes (kings, tyrants, priesthood classes) and all kind of inequity that has reached us until present times; but this is recent history. Since for most of our time as species, humans have been predominantly egalitarian and equitable, the conclusion is that these tendencies are implicit in human nature: humans have the potential for being equitable and egalitarian in their inter-relations.

EQUITY AND SUSTAINABLE LIFESTYLES

There are a limited number of studies investigating the relationship between equitable actions and other psychological dimensions of sustainability. In one of those studies, Frías, Corral, Cáñez, Cázares, Islas, Escamilla & Valenzuela (2002) developed and administered a *sexism* scale, which included items discriminating against-women. They also administered instruments assessing anthropocentrism and pro-ecological behavior. These latter variables correlated negatively, while sexism and anthropocentrism covaried in a positive way. The findings suggest that an inequitable gender vision is indicator of a non-sustainable tendency, since such a vision is associated to beliefs in the predominance of humans over other species and, indirectly, negatively affects people's engagement in pro-environmental behaviors.

In spite of those interesting results, this study did not include the assessment of equity in a way that reveals general equitable actions (in addition to gender issues); it neither measured additional sustainable behaviors other than pro-ecological activities. If the establishment of inequity as a norm in human relations coincided with the aggravation of ecological problems, then equity should be a buffer against non-sustainable actions and their effects. In other words: there should be a link between equity and the protection of the socio-physical environment, in a way that equity predisposes people to engage in more sustainable ways of living.

In order to demonstrate that this assumption has realistic grounds it is necessary to prove that equity significantly correlates with sustainable behaviors (SBs). SBs are the kind of activities people engage in to preserve the environment and its resources (Corral-Verdugo & Pinheiro, 2004). Since the environment encompasses not only its natural resources but also the world of human institutions, culture and artifacts, SBs are organized as actions intended to protect both the natural and the human resources. In correspondence with this characterization, at least three sets of behavior are mentioned as "sustainable" actions in terms of their effects on the socio-physical environment: Pro-ecological actions, frugal –or austere- patterns of consumption, and altruistic behaviors (Corral-Verdugo, Tapia, Fraijo, Mireles & Márquez, 2008).

Pro-ecological actions refer to those activities aimed at the conservation of the physical environment including recycling, reuse, composting, water and energy conservation, ecosystems' protection, pro-environmental lobbying, etc. (Kaiser, 1998; Thøgersen, 2004). Although the performance of these behaviors has a positive effect on human living conditions –equity included- they are primarily intended to minimize the negative influence of human activity on Earth's physical ecosystems.

Austerity (also called frugality) involves a lifestyle that implies the responsible consumption of products and a light-living style, which results in a reduced ecological footprint (Iwata, 2001; Fujii, 2006). Austerity reduces luxury and superficial consumption; avoids consumerism and promotes respect for nature and its resources. A reduced consumption or frugal lifestyle also promotes a more equitable use of products among people (Chokor, 2004).

Altruism can also be considered a component of sustainable actions. It is implicit in a more sustainable way of living, since implies acting with the purpose of producing positive impacts on the needs of other persons (Pol, 2002). Schultz (2001) establishes that altruism is a fundamental component of the motivation originating and maintaining environmentally protective actions. Several other authors consider sustainable or proenvironmental conducts as altruistic behavior (Ebreo, Hershey & Vinning, 1999; Hooper & Nielsen, 1991; Schultz, 2001; see also Sevillano, Aragonés & Schultz chapter in this book).

A number of authors use the term "sustainable lifestyles (SLS)" to refer to those actions intended to preserve the natural and social resources of our planet (CSD, 2004; Corral-Verdugo et al, 2008). The SLS notion was generated from conjugating the definitions of "sustainability" and "lifestyles". Chaney (1996) defines lifestyles as patterns of action that differentiate people from other individuals, establishing that those patterns satisfy individual and social needs and desires. In turn, sustainability is defined as the lifestyle that meets the needs of people living in the present without compromising the needs of future generations (WCED, 1987). Thus, sustainable lifestyles are defined as patterns of action used by people to affiliate and differentiate themselves from other individuals; those patterns: a) satisfy basic needs, b) provide a better quality of life, c) minimize both the use of natural resources and the emission of contaminants and d) do not compromise the needs of the future generations (CSD 2004).

What kinds of actions characterize a SLS? According to Corral-Verdugo *et al* (2008), SLS are based on altruistic, austere and pro-ecological actions, exhibited by individuals as idiosyncratic and relatively permanent patterns of behavior. In other words, sustainable lifestyles are constituted by sustainable behaviors that characterize an individual's enduring way of living. These authors offer evidence supporting their proposal in an empirical study showing that such actions were significantly interrelated. In their paper's conclusions, the authors suggest that equity actions (treating other persons in an equitable manner, regardless of their gender, age, race, and social status) should be an additional component of the SLS. However, they did not offer empirical evidence supporting this idea; so, we were interested in testing it in a study, which is described in the next section of this chapter.

In addition to the above, the psycho-environmental literature suggests that some socio-demographic variables affect sustainable behavior. For instance, economic income is inversely related to pro-ecological behavior and frugal consumption: the more the income, the less the effort in protecting the physical environment and the more the consumerism (see Aitken, McMahon, Wearing & Finlayson, 1994; Berger, 1997). Age has also been mentioned as a significant correlate of sustainable actions, with older people being more sustainably-oriented than younger individuals (Domina & Koch, 2002). If equity is a sustainable behavior it is possible that these socio-demographic variables also affect equity.

By considering these antecedents, we developed an empirical study aimed at: a) corroborating the presence of a SLS factor constituted by austerity, altruism and pro-ecological behavior; b) demonstrating that equity actions are also a component of sustainable lifestyles and; c) demonstrating that socio-economic status and age affect SLS.

METHOD

Participants

250 individuals (208 females and 42 males), aged 16 through 78 years old, were interviewed. They were selected from representative (low, middle and higher) socio-economic zones at the city of Hermosillo, Mexico, according to the classification of the Mexican census bureau (INEGI, 2000).

Measures

The instruments included self-reported measures investigating: 1) *Austerity* in actions such as buying the strictly necessary, the reuse of clothing, taking meals at home, etc., which were reported using a 5-point likert-options of response (0 = totally agree...4=totally disagree), this instrument was designed by Corral-Verdugo and Pinheiro (2004); 2) *Altruism,* as the self-report of nine behaviors manifesting concern for other people, such as visiting sick persons at hospitals, contributing financially with the Red Cross, providing money to the homeless, etc. (Tapia, Corral-Verdugo, Fraijo & Tirado, 2006), in a 4-point response options (0=never...3=always); 3) *Pro-ecological behavior*, using a reduced version of Kaiser's (1998) scale, which included thirteen items such as the self-report of reuse, recycling, energy conservation, etc.; and 4) *Equity*, with a scale elaborated especially for this study, which included six items indicating behaviors such as providing equal educational opportunities for girls and boys, and treating subordinates as equals, etc., using response options from 0 (totally disagree) to 4 (totally agree). The authors of scales 1, 2, and 3 reported evidence of reliability and validity for their measures. These instruments have also been administered and validated in the studied Mexican population. In addition, we investigated demographic variables of participants: age, economic income and schooling level. The latter two variables were used to constitute a socio-economic status (SES) aggregated factor.

Procedure

Participants were approached and their informed consent to participate in this study was obtained. Everyone accepted to respond to the instruments, which were administered at their households' living room. It took about 20 minutes to respond to these instruments.

Data Analysis

Univariate statistics for the used scales and their items were obtained, as well as Cronbach's alphas indicating the scales' internal consistency. An exploratory factor analysis of the equity scale was conducted in order to test its dimensionality (i.e., how many factors constitute it). Then, using structural equations, a model in which socio-demographic variables (age, and socio-economic status) predicted equity was tested. Finally, a confirmatory factor analysis (CFA) was specified and tested to estimate the level of interrelations produced by the four sustainable constructs. The CFA produces factor loadings or *lambdas*, which are the relations between *first-order factors* and their observed indicators (items of a scale, in this case). High and significant *lambdas* (i.e., factor loadings) evidence convergent construct validity for the assessed constructs (see Corral-Verdugo & Figueredo, 1999). It is also possible to estimate *second- (or higher-) order factors* as the result of high and significant ($p<.05$) interrelations among first-order factors (Bentler, 2006). Thus, higher-order factors are constituted from first-order factors in the same way that these first-order factors are constructed from their observed indicators within a factor analysis. For instance, equity, altruism, pro-ecological behavior and austerity, if sufficiently enough interrelated, should produce a higher-order construct indicating a pro-sustainability tendency. The hypothesis in our study was that the interrelations among the four factors would be high and significant enough to produce the second-order factor of sustainable lifestyles (SLS). In order to conduct the CFA, the items of every first-order factor were parceled into three indicators for each assessed construct. A *parcel* is the mean of two or more randomly chosen (from the total set of items conforming the scale) items of a construct. This procedure simplifies the process of data analysis in the context of structural equation modeling, because a small number of indicators are used in specifying the assessed factors (Little, Cunningham, Shahar, & Widaman, 2002). In this case, we randomly distributed the total number of items corresponding to each factor into a minor number of indicators or parcels used to construct the factors. In addition, goodness of fit indicators (*chi-squared*, practical goodness of fit indices, *RMSEA*, etc.) were obtained to reveal whether or not the data support the adequacy of the hypothesized factor structure and the pattern of presumed interrelations between factors (Bentler, 2006).

Table 1. Univariate statistics and reliability of scales

Scale/items	Mean	SD	Min.	Max.	Alpha
Equity					.62
My partner (wife/husband) has the same rights I have at home.	3.53	1.00	0	4	
At work, I treat my subordinate fellows like my equals.	3.42	0.90	0	4	
Children in my home have the same rights that adults in making important decisions.	2.63	1.41	0	4	
In my family, men and women have the same cleanup chores.	3.19	1.19	0	4	
I treat rich and poor people equally.	3.53	0.80	0	4	
In my family, girls and boys have the same educational opportunities.	3.76	0.60	0	4	
Altruism					.69
Donates clothing to poor people.	2.22	0.87	0	3	
Assists a person in need.	2.21	0.79	0	3	
Contributes financially with the Red Cross.	2.26	0.82	0	3	
Visits the sick at hospitals/homes.	1.16	1.01	0	3	
Guide persons asking for direction.	2.38	0.72	0	3	
Provides some money to homeless.	1.92	0.95	0	3	
Participates in fund-collection rallies	0.92	1.10	0	3	
Donates blood	0.49	0.75	0	3	
Cooperates with colleagues.	2.28	0.83	0	3	
Austerity					.62
Does not buy a new car if old one is functional.	2.99	1.33	0	4	
Wears same clothing.	3.01	1.10	0	4	
Wouldn't buy jewelry.	2.46	1.52	0	4	
Buys lots of shoes.	2.42	1.40	0	4	
Buys more food than needed.	2.65	1.46	0	4	
Uses most earnings for buying clothing.	2.73	1.28	0	4	
Always takes meals at home.	2.60	1.32	0	4	

Table 1. (Continued)

Scale/items	Mean	SD	Min.	Max.	Alpha
Rather walks than drives.	2.61	1.43	0	4	
Reuse notebooks and paper.	1.87	1.45	0	4	
Likes living lightly.	2.24	1.53	0	4	
Pro-environmental behavior					.70
Waits until having a full load before laundry.	2.17	0.98	0	3	
Drives on freeways at speeds under 100 kph.	1.75	1.22	0	3	
Collects and recycle used paper.	0.86	1.02	0	3	
Brings empty bottles to a recycling bin.	0.74	1.08	0	3	
Points out unecological behavior to someone.	1.34	0.99	0	3	
Buys products in refillable packages.	1.50	0.93	0	3	
Buys seasonal produce.	2.59	0.61	0	3	
Reads about environmental issues.	1.18	0.86	0	3	
Talks with friends about environmental problems.	1.19	0.90	0	3	
Turns down air conditioning when leaving place.	2.60	0.76	0	3	
Look for ways to reuse things.	1.77	0.94	0	3	
Encourages friends and family to recycle.	0.91	1.13	0	3	
Conserves gasoline by walking or bicycling.	1.28	1.06	0	3	

RESULTS

Univariate statistics and Cronbach's alphas are shown in Table 1. The austerity scale produced a .69 alpha, and a mean = 2.5 (values ranged 0-4); in turn, the instrument assessing altruism generated a .62 alpha, and a mean = 1.7 (range of values; 1-3). In the case of the pro-ecological behavior scale, the alpha was .70 and its means equaled 1.52; while the equity scale produced a .61 alpha (mean = 3.5, from values ranging 0-4). Responses to the equity scale revealed a balanced level of agreement for most of the items. The items showing the higher agreement levels for this scale were "In my family, girls and boys have the same educational opportunities" (mean=3.76), "My partner (wife/husband) has the same rights I have at home" and "I treat rich and poor people equally" (mean= 3.53, for these two scales). The lowest level of agreement was for the item "Children in my home have the same rights than adults in making important decisions" (mean=2.76).

Since the equity scale had not been previously analyzed in terms of its dimensionality, an exploratory factor analysis (principal components) was conducted with its items. Results revealed a unidimensional solution indicated by an eigenvalue > 1 associated to the first component, a salient factor from the *scree test,* and high loadings on a single factor (see Table 2). Therefore, we concluded that this scale was unidimensional.

A covariance matrix was computed for the scales indicating the sustainable lifestyles factor. This matrix shows significant relations between factors (see Table 3), which resulted especially high between austerity and pro-ecological behavior, between equity and austerity, and between pro-ecological behavior and altruism. Lower –still, significant- covariances resulted between altruism and equity, between pro-ecological behavior and equity, and between austerity and altruism.

The first structural model specified the equity factor as affected by socio-economic status (SES) and age. Results of this model revealed that only SES had a significant, and negative, effect on equity. Goodness of fit indicators for this model are shown in the bottom of figure 1, revealing that the data supported the tested model. A closer view to the matrix of correlations, utilized to test this model, indicated that economic income produced the highest negative correlations with the equity items "At work, I treat my subordinate fellows like my equals" ($r= -.22$, $p<.05$) and "In my family, girls and boys have the same educational opportunities" ($r=-.32$, $p<.05$).

Table 2. Factor analysis (principal components) of the equity items.
A single factor was retained

Items	loadings
1. My partner (wife/husband) has the same rights I have at home.	.50
2. At work, I treat my fellows like my equals.	.63
3. Children in my home have the same rights that adults have in making important decisions.	.43
4. In my home, men and women have the same cleanup duties.	.62
5. I treat rich and poor people the same way.	.75
6. In my family, girls and boys have the same educational opportunities.	.67

Eigenvalue for component one = 2.26; explained variance = 37.8%.

Table 3. Matrix of covariances among equity, austerity, altruism, and pro-ecological behavior

	Equity	austerity	altruism	pro-ecol.
Equity	--------			
Austerity	.52*	-------		
Altruism	.36*	.26*	-------	
Pro-ecological behavior	.29*	.65*	.51*	-------

* $p<.05$

In the subsequent model, we tested the hypothesis that the four dispositional factors are subsumed by the SLS second-order factor. The correlations between equity, altruism, pro-ecological behavior and austerity generated the sustainable lifestyles factor, as expected. The goodness of fit indicators – at the bottom of figure 2- evidence the adequacy of this model.

CONCLUSION

This chapter reviewed the potential role played by equity in the constitution of sustainable lifestyles. Equity is conceived as a tendency to distribute -in a fair way- resources, power and benefits, among people, avoiding bias or favoritism.

Equity and equality are not synonymous. Equity, as a sustainable lifestyle, assumes the existence of differences among individuals, accepting, in fact, the advantages that diversity provides to human societies (Bonnes & Bonaiuto, 2002). Yet, inequity is also based on inter-individual differences, generating a condition in which few people concentrate most of the resources and power (Talbert, 2008). Therefore, human differences offer both a dark and a bright facet and people have to choose between socio-diversity –as a sustainable characteristic- and inequity –a non-sustainable tendency. The survival of our species depends, at least partially, on this decision.

Inequity is manifested in gender, social, demographic, political and economic aspects and it very likely correlates with every kind of social problems experienced by humankind, including war, famine, social violence, poverty and discrimination. In addition, inequity is a correlate of environmental degradation and a cause of unhappiness (Veenhoven, 2006; Vlek, 2000).

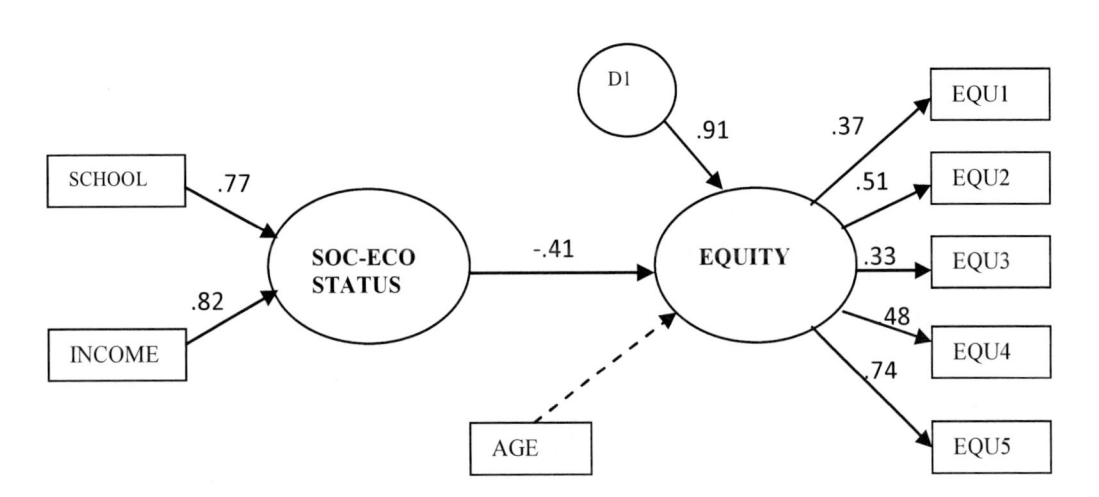

Figure 1. A model of structural relations between equity and socio-demographic variables. All structural coefficients are significant (p <.05), excepting the one indicated by the dotted arrow. Goodnes of fit: X^2 (19 df) = 43.4, p = .001; NNFI = .88, CFI = .91; RMSEA = .07. Equity R^2 = .17.

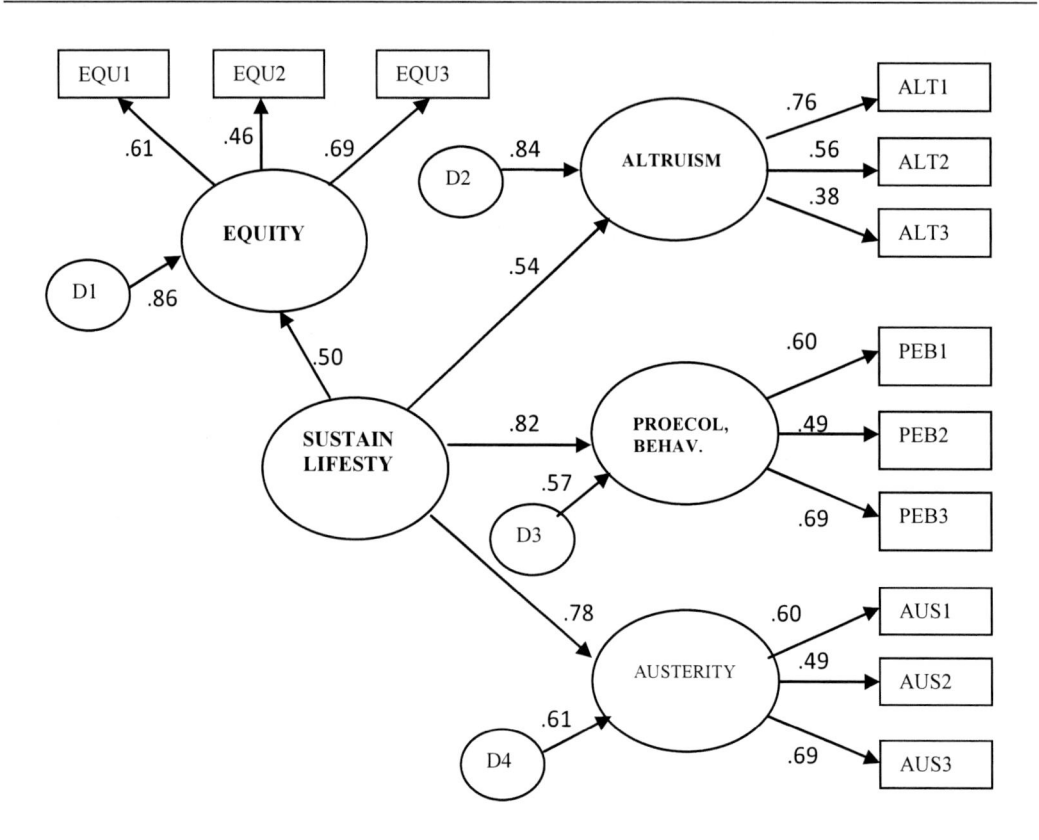

Figure 2. Relations between equity and sustainable lifestyles. All structural coefficients are significant (p <.05). Goodnes of fit: X^2 (47 df) = 109.4, $p < .001$; NNFI = .88, CFI = .90; RMSEA = .07. Equity R^2 = .25, Altruism R^2 = .29, Proecological Behavior R^2 = .68, Austerity R^2 = .62.

Prehistoric societies were essentially equitable, as most foraging communities are in present days. A feature of these groups –in addition to their being equitable- is their reduced size. Most of humankind's existence (around a 99%) was characterized by an equitable lifestyle, which supports the idea that equity is an intrinsic trait of human nature (Gowdy, 1998). This finding offers hope to the idea of a sustainable future for humankind, based – among other things- on a more equitable distribution of resources. In addition, it offers clues to interventional strategies aimed at developing equitable lifestyles in people and their communities.

Although a limited effort in research has been invested in studying the relationships between equity and other psychological dimensions of sustainability, data seem to indicate that equitable behavior is significantly linked to pro-ecological behavior, austerity and altruism. Equity is also negatively related to anthropocentric beliefs and sexism (Frías et al, 2002).

In this chapter, we presented a study aimed at investigating the links between equity and sustainable lifestyles (SLS). Its results suggest that SLS consist of austerity, altruistic and pro-ecological actions, as previous research indicate (Iwata, 2001; Corral et al, 2008). Moreover, equity seems to belong in this set of sustainable practices. Since equity correlated significantly with those sustainable behaviors there is reason for including equitable actions as additional indicators of SLS, as Corral-Verdugo et al (2008) suggested. These authors discussed the impossibility of reaching a sustainable human development without granting everybody's access to natural resources and an equitable treatment to every person, regardless of her/his gender, ethnic and cultural characteristics (see also Winter, 2000). Such argument seems to be supported by our data.

We administered a brief instrument, allowing responses from 0 (totally disagree) to 4 (totally agree) to five items assessing equitable actions. The scale produced an acceptable – yet not entirely satisfactory- internal consistency (likely due to the small number of items), and a one-dimensional solution (i.e., the items revealed a single "equity" factor). The results pointed to a balanced level of agreement for most of its items, with means of responses around 3 and higher, which indicates that respondents are more equitable (or, at least, they conceived themselves as equitable) than otherwise. The highest levels of equity were found among the actions indicating gender equity, while the lowest corresponded to age equity. This suggests that, although Mexican people have started to accept the idea of equity among men and women, they are still somehow reluctant to concede more rights and privileges to children.

As anticipated, the socio-economic factor affected negatively the display of equity behaviors- The SES explains 17% of the variance in equity. This result leaves room for an 83% of variance explained by additional factors on this variable. The result also indicates that economic affluence instigates inequity, at least partially. Since equity is an important sustainable lifestyle, our data suggest that higher-socio-economic classes should be a special target for pro-sustainability campaigns. Economic income produced the highest negative correlations with the equity items "At work, I treat my subordinate fellows like my equals" and "In my family, girls and boys have the same educational opportunities," meaning that –at least in the studied population- more affluent people tend to be slightly less equitable with subordinates and with girls, than less wealthy individuals.

Age did not correlate with equity. The level of equitable actions varied regardless of participants' age. This result partially contradicts findings from previous research regarding other indicators of sustainable lifestyle, like pro-ecological actions (Domina & Koch, 2002) and altruism (List, 2004). These studies suggest that older individuals are more pro-ecological and altruistic than the younger. Further research is needed to corroborate these findings and to include additional demographic predictors of equity.

The main result of our study indicates that equity is a part of sustainable lifestyles. By correlating with pro-ecological actions, austerity, and altruism, equity constitutes a fundamental component of the actions intended to protect the physical and social resources of the world (Corral-Verdugo *et al*, 2008). The SLS factor explained 25% of equity actions, 29% of altruism, 68% of pro-ecological behaviors and 62% of austerity; a substantial amount of predicted variance if we consider that it comes just from a set of behaviors. Economic factors such as SES also play a role in explaining equitable tendencies. As a whole, all these results would characterize an equitable person as someone interested in others' wellbeing (altruistic), frugal in his/her consumption of products and prone to practicing pro-ecological behaviors. Less educated and poorer people are more equitable than richer and more educated persons.

Of course, most variance of equity remains unexplained. Future research has to include dispositional (motives, beliefs, skills, values, intentions, etc.), and contextual (physical and normative) factors as potential predictors of equitable actions, looking for an increased explanatory power of equity and SLS models.

Our results also suggests the need of implementing psycho-environmental interventions aimed at promoting pro-environmental actions (reduced consumption of products, pro-ecological actions) as well as pro-social conducts (equitable and altruistic behaviors), trying to integrate these actions within a set of sustainable lifestyles. Past research offers evidence regarding the importance of SLS as an integrative and necessary set of behaviors in pursuing the goals of sustainability (see Corral-Verdugo *et al*, 2008). Every component of SLS is crucial in achieving such goals; however, results apparently will be unsatisfactory if a particular kind of (altruistic, pro-ecological, equitable, austere) behavior is promoted in isolated ways. Pro-ecological and austere actions induce positive effects in the physical components of the environment, while equitable and altruistic behaviors are more effective in promoting pro-social outcomes. Thus, the promotion of sustainability should include the practice and integration of these four crucial components of sustainable lifestyles in order to guarantee that benefits reach the two (physical, social) environmental levels. The investigation of factors other than the demographic ones could also define interventional strategies for the development of conservationist behaviors at both environmental levels.

REFERENCES

Adeola, F. (2000). Cross-national environmental injustice and human rights issues. *American Behavioral Scientist, 43*, 686-706.

Aitken, C., McMahon, T., Wearing, A., & Finlayson, B. (1994). Residential water use: Predicting and reducing consumption. *Journal of Applied Social Psychology, 21,* 611–619.

Aliber, M. (2002). *Poverty eradication and sustainable development*. Cape Town, Sudáfrica: HRSC Press.

Bentler, P.M. (2006). *EQS, Structural Equations Program Manual*. Encino, CA: Statistical Software, Inc.

Berger, I. (1997). The demographics of recyling and the structure of environmental behavior. *Environment & Behavior, 29*, 515-531.

Bonnes, M., & Bonaiuto, M. (2002). Environmental psychology: from spatial-physical environment to sustainable development. In R.B. Bechtel & A. Churchman (Eds.), *Handbook of Environmental Psychology* (pp. 28-54). New York: Wiley.

Boyd, R., Gintis, H., Boyles, S. & Richerson, P. (2003). The evolution of altruistic punishment. *Proceedings of the National Academy of Sciences of The United States of América, 100*, 3531-3535.

Brown, P. & Cameron, L. (2000). What can be done to reduce overconsumption? *Ecological Economics, 32,* 27-41.

Capra, F & Pauli, P. (1995). *Steering business toward sustainability*. New York: The United Nations University.

Chaney, D. (1996). *Lifestyles*. Londres: Routledge.

Chokor, B. (2004). Perception and response to the challenge of poverty and environmental resource degradation in rural Nigeria: Case study form the Niger Delta. *Journal of Environmental Psychology*, 24, 305-318.

Clayton, S. (2000). Models of justice in the environmental debate. *Journal of Social Issues, 56*, 459-474.
Corral-Verdugo, V., Bonnes, M., Tapia, C., Fraijo, B., Frías, M., & Carrus, G. (2009). Correlates of pro-sustainability orientation: the Affinity Towards Diversity. *Journal of Environmental Psychology. 29*, 34-43.
Corral-Verdugo, V. y Figueredo, A.J. (1999). Convergent and divergent validity of three measures of conservation behavior: The multitrait-multimethod approach. *Environment & Behavior*, 31, 805-820.
Corral-Verdugo, V. & Pinheiro, J. (2004). Aproximaciones al estudio de la conducta sustentable [Approaches to the study of sustainable behavior]. *Medio Ambiente y Comportamiento Humano*, 5, 1-26.
Corral-Verdugo, V., Tapia, C., Fraijo, B., Mireles, J. & Márquez, P. (2008). Determinantes psicológicos de los estilos de vida sustentables. *Revista Mexicana de Psicología 25*, 313-327.
CSD. Centre for Sustainable Development (2004). *"Every little bit helps..." Overcoming the challenges to researching, promoting and implementing sustainable lifestyles.* CSD. University of Westminster, U.K.
De Botton, A. (2005) *Status Anxiety.* Londres: Penguin Books.
De la Torre, C. (2006). *El derecho a la no discriminación en México* [Right to non-discrimination in Mexico]: Mexico City: Porrúa.
Domina, T. & Koch, K. (2002). Convenience and frequency of recycling. Implications for including textiles in curbside recycling programs. *Environment & Behavior, 34*, 216-238.
Ebreo, A., Hershey, J., & Vining, J. (1999). Reducing solid waste: Linking recycling to environmentally responsible consumerism. *Environment & Behavior, 31*, 107-135.
Ehrlich, P. & Ehrlich, A. (2004). *One with Niniveh. Politics, Consumption and the Human Future.* Washington, DC: Shearwater Books.
Elder A.T. (2005) Which benchmarks for age discrimination in acute coronary syndromes? *Age & Ageing. 34*, 4–5.
Engelman, R. (2008). *More: Population, Nature and what Women Want.* Washington, DC: Island Press.
Etim, E. (2004). *Development systems and young people in human rights, policy and participation.* Surulere, Nigeria: Center for Development Action International Head office.
Eurostat Data (2007). Retrieved August 2008 from: http://epp.eurostat.cec.eu.int.
Evans, G., Juen, B., Corral, V., Corraliza, J.A. & Kaiser, F. (2007). Children´s crosscultural environmental attitudes and self-reported behaviors. C*hildren, Youth and Environment, 17*, 128-143.
Frías, M., Corral, V. Cánez, G., Cázares, M., Islas, M.J., Escamilla, B. & Valenzuela, R. (2002). Relaciones entre machismo, antropocentrismo y conducta pro-ambiental en estudiantes universitarios [Relations between machismo, anthropocentrism and pro-environmental behavior in undergraduates]. In A. Terán & A.M. Landázuri. (Eds.), *Sustentabilidad, Comportamiento y Calidad de Vida.* Mexico City: UNAM.
Fujii, S. (2006). Environmental concern and ease of behavior as determinants of pro-environmental behavior intentions. *Journal of Environmental Psychology, 26*, 262-268.
Gardner, G. & Prugh, T. (2008). Seeding the sustainable economy. In Starke, L. (Ed.), *State of the World.* New York, W. W. Norton & Company.

Gowdy, J. (1998). Introduction: back to the future and forward to the past. En J. Gowdy (Ed.), *Limited wants, unlimited means.* Washington, DC: Island Press.

Haynes, K. (2007) Moving the gender agenda or stirring chicken's entrails?: where next for feminist methodologies in accounting? Universities of Leeds: *White Rose Research Papers.* Working paper number 27.

Hooper, J.R. & Nielsen, J.M. (1991). Recycling as altruistic behavior: Normative and behavioral strategies to expand participation in a community recycling program. *Environment & Behavior, 23,* 195-220.

INEGI (2000). *Sistema de Consulta para la Información Censal* (SCINCE) [Census Information Consulting System]. Mexico City: Instituto Nacional de Geografía e Informática.

Iwata, O. (2001). Attitudinal determinants of environmentally responsible behavior. *Social Behavior and Personality, 29,* 183-190.

Kaiser, F. (1998). A general measure of ecological behavior. *Journal of Applied Social Psychology, 28,* 395-442.

Lee, R. (1998). Foreword. In J. Gowdy (Ed.), *Limited wants, unlimited means.* Washington, DC: Island Press.

Le Grand, J. (1991). *Equity and choice: an essay in economics and applied philosophy.* London: Harper Collins.

List, J. (2004). Young, selfish, and male: field evidence of social preferences. *The Economic Journal.*

Little, T., Cunningham, W., Shahar, G., & Widaman, K. (2002). To parcel or not parcel: exploring the question, weighing the merits. *Structural Equation Modeling: A Multidisciplinary Journal, 9,* 151-173.

Lorber, J. (Ed.) (2001), *Gender Inequality: Feminist Theories and Politics.* Los Angeles: Roxbury.

Merriam-Webster Online Dictionary (2009). Retrieved on January, 2009, from: http://www.merriam-webster.com/dictionary/

Oskamp, S. (2000). A sustainable future for humanity? *American Psychologist, 55,* 496-508.

Oystein, K. (2002). Education and fertility in Sub-Saharan Africa. *Demography, 39,* 233-250.

Pol, E. (2002). The theoretical background of the City-Identity-Sustainability Network. *Environment & Behavior, 34,* 8-25.

Renner, M. (2005). Security redefined. In Brown, L. (Ed.), *State of the World 2005: Global Security.* Washington, DC: World Watch Institute.

Richerson, P.J. & Boyd, R. (1999). Complex Societies: The evolutionary origins of a crude superorganism. *Human Nature, 10,* 253-289.

Schultz, P.W. (2001). The structure of environmental concern. Concern for self, other people, and the biosphere. *Journal of Environmental Psychology, 21,* 327-339.

Shiva, V. (2000). *Protect or plunder? Understanding intellectual property rights.* Londres: Zed Books.

Talbert, J. (2008). Redefining progress. In Starke, L. (Ed.), *State of the World.* New York, W. W. Norton & Company.

Tapia, C., Corral-Verdugo, V., Fraijo, B. & Tirado, H. (2006). Factores disposicionales de la conducta sustentable: prueba de un modelo estructural [Sustainable behavior dispositional factors: testing a structural model]. In AMEPSO (Eds.), *La Psicología Social en México,* Vol. X. Mexico City: AMEPSO.

Thøgersen, J. (2004). A cognitive dissonance interpretation of consistencies and inconsistencies in environmentally responsible behavior. *Journal of Environmental Psychology, 24*, 93-103.

United Nations (2008). *United Nations, Gini Coefficient.* Retrieved September 2008 from: http://www.scribd.com/doc/328232/United-Nations-Gini-Coefficient.

Veenhoven, R. (2006). Is life getting better? How long and happy people live in modern society. *European Psychologist*, 10, 330-343.

Vlek, C. (2000). Essential psychology for environmental policy making. *International Journal of Psychology, 35*, 153-167.

WCED: World Commission on Environment & Development (1987). *Our Common Future.* Oxford, U.K.: Oxford University Press.

Winter, D. (2002). (En)Gendering sustainable development. In P. Schmuck & P.W. Schultz (Eds.), *Psychology of Sustainable Development.* Norwell, Massachusetts: Kluwer.

Zizzo, D. & Oswald, A. (2001). Are People Willing to Pay to Reduce Others' Earnings? *Annales d'Economie et de Statistique*, Special Issue, July 2001, 39-65.

In: Psychological Approaches to Sustainability
Editors: V. Corral-Verdugo et al.
ISBN 978-1-60876-356-6
© 2010 Nova Science Publishers, Inc.

Chapter 11

TIME PERSPECTIVE AND SUSTAINABLE BEHAVIOR

Jose Q. Pinheiro[*]
Universidade Federal do Rio Grande do Norte, Natal, Brazil
Victor Corral Verdugo
Universidad de Sonora, Mexico

ABSTRACT

Achieving sustainable development (SD) ideals requires the consideration of a temporal component in people's psychological functioning. According to the definition of SD, a sustainable lifestyle meets the needs of *present* and *future* generations without compromising the integrity of natural resources. Thus, for people, a *time perspective* is crucial for engaging in behaviors aimed at protecting the socio-physical environment. Psychological time is a dimension of consciousness; the way we provide order to our life experience. The interest of psychology in time arises from the fascination that this physical dimension has always exerted on the human mind. As a consequence, the area of time perception is one of the oldest among the topics of scientific psychological research. Time perspective is another important research area, which deals with the way people divide the continuous flow of experiences in time frames: past, present and future, in order to provide coherence to their lives. According to theory and investigation results, a number of individuals exhibit a biased time perspective; some of them "live" in the past, others are only concerned about the present, while others mainly focus on the future. Zimbardo and Boyd (1999) suggest five time perspectives: 1) negative past, 2) positive past, 3) fatalistic present, 4) hedonistic present and 5) Future. Positive past captures events or perceptions from the past that are linked to happy situations. Conversely, the negative past enhance painful, unpleasant memories. The present hedonistic perspective is common in persons who are prone to enjoy "here-and-now" situations, without concern for the past or the future. Alternatively, the fatalistic present implies living today at the expense of fate or others' will. Finally, future orientation bias characterizes persons who are good in setting and achieving goals, planning strategies and meeting obligations.

---

[*] Correspondence should be addressed to Jose Q. Pinheiro. E-mail: pinheiro@cchla.ufrn.br

These time perspectives are included in Zimbardo's Time Perspective Inventory (ZTPI) one of the most important instruments assessing time orientation in psychological research. These particular time orientations have been proved to affect the way people perceive time and act in situations like risky driving and drug consumption. The question is: How do this set/group of time perspectives relate to environmentally sustainable lifestyles? In this chapter, we discuss how time perspective is theoretically linked to sustainable actions. In addition, we present and discuss results from a study conducted to investigate the way the proposed five time orientations influence sustainable behavior. Three hundred individuals responded to the ZTPI and to a scale assessing self-reported water conservation. Responses to the items were processed within a confirmatory factor analysis revealing that future orientation positively and significantly covaries with that sustainable behavior, while the two present orientations negatively correlate with water conservation. Neither type of past orientation covary with water conservation. These results seem to confirm the assumption that future orientation is a crucial temporal component of sustainable behavior. Yet, the importance of the positive past (and, likely, of the present) should not be discarded.

INTRODUCTION

Time plays a central role in our lives and psychological research has given temporal matters some of the attention they deserve. Scarcely included in traditional studies of perception, social relations, and other topical areas, temporal issues have more recently been enriched by the consideration of contextual aspects of human behavior. Ecological approaches to person-environment relationships, in particular, consider time as part of the physical world (for example, in the metrics of duration or repetition of a given experience) and/or as a subjective element (for example, in attribution of meaning to the experience of time). Enlarging the focus of analysis beyond the person and towards the context implies the consideration not only of a larger scale in terms of socio-spatial elements of the environment, but also of a broader and extended temporal scope (Stokols, Misra, Runnerstrom, & Hipp, 2009).

We perceive a time scale in our relations with the environment and we act accordingly to it. To change any temporal feature of a person-environment interaction – sequence, rhythm or duration, for example – would unavoidably change the whole meaning of such experience. As Gibson (1979) puts it, we react to changes and continuities, within a time frame in general situated between seconds and years; we are capable of observing the change of position of a chair in a room, but not the slow erosion of a mountain or the slight differences between two frames of a movie. Another good illustration of the presence of time in ecologically oriented approaches to people-environment relationships is Barker's (1968) concept of *behavior setting*, for it includes both spatial and temporal limits (see also Wicker, 1987). Because we are much more culturally oriented towards space than time, it is common to think of a football field as a behavior setting, while the truly behavior setting is the football *match*, not the *field*; the unity people-environment, no the portion of physical space.

Other "classics" of the area may be mentioned. Tuan (1977), and the experiential (temporal) difference between *space* and *place*. The several instances of the presence of time in our relationship with the built environment Sommer (e.g., 1972) has brought to our attention. Hall's (1983) *chronemics*, a typology of culturally established manners of handling time according to which people may belong (and act accordingly) to *monochronic* or *polichronic* cultures. The latest versions of Bronfenbrenner's bioecological model that incorporates temporal features into his traditional systems (Bronfenbrenner & Morris, 2006). The classification of temporalities proposed by Werner, Altman and Oxley (1985), according to which time is conceived as *linear* (continuum past-present-future), *cyclic* (daily periods, for instance), or *spiral cyclic* (a combination of the first two).

A recent review about the presence of ecological perspective in environmental psychology has identified as one of the six principles of such analysis "the unfolding and articulation of person-environment dynamics over time" (Winkel, Saegert, & Evans, in press). Meanwhile, the advent of the notion of *sustainability* is pushing temporal matters even deeper into the study of pro-environmental behavior and ecologically sustainable lifestyles. *To sustain* implies time *per se*, for it means to get something and to continue on *maintaining/holding* it. The commitment to keeping Earth's current resources available for future generations (WCED, 1987) has been labeled *inter-generational solidarity* (Pol, 2002), a concept which necessarily involves the temporal gap between current and future generations. Investigators of pro-environmental commitment willing to include sustainability dimensions in their studies are challenged to develop theoretical constructs and methodological strategies that embrace such "temporal bridge" within people's minds (Pinheiro, 2005, 2006). *Time perspective* (TP) is one of these concepts and we shall focus the remaining of the chapter on it.

TIME PERSPECTIVE

When Lester Brown (1981) wrote his pioneering work, *Building a sustainable society*, he decided to include an anonymous quote that read, "We have not inherited the Earth from our fathers, we are borrowing it from our children", which happened to become popular and being converted into the slogan of T-shirts illustrated with the picture of planet Earth. Paradoxical as it may sound to our logic, the statement probably made immediate sense to those sustainably aware. Researchers dedicated to the study of people's environmental commitment were not that quick in appropriating the idea, maybe because *future* was not a relevant category in that scenario.

Recently, we took part in an international investigation that involved colleagues of 18 nations and a total of 3232 respondents, who were asked to evaluate environmental problems at three spatial levels – local, national, global – and at two time frames: today and in 25 years (Gifford et al., 2009). For our purposes here, it is important to mention that spatial optimism ("things are better here than there") was found in the assessments of current environmental conditions in 15 of 18 countries, but not in the assessments of the future. All countries except one exhibited, on average, temporal pessimism ("things will get worse") in the assessments at all three spatial levels. Such findings challenge explanations because, among other reasons, we do not know how time orientation interacts with political affairs, cultural issues or other characteristics of the respondents' environmental autobiographies.

Despite the complaint that "temporal qualities are part of the meaning and experience of activities but are often ignored by researchers" (Werner, Brown, & Altman, 2000, p. 205), there has been important efforts towards the conceptualization of people's experience of time. In this beginning of a new millennium, one can find at least two theoretical and instrumental propositions related to the psychological organization of time, which may prove useful for the investigation of intergenerational solidarity, condition for sustainability. We refer to the scale *Consideration of Future Consequences*, or CFC (Strathman, Gleicher, Bonninger, & Edwards, 1994) and, more specifically, to *Zimbardo's Time Perspective Inventory*, or ZTPI (Zimbardo & Boyd, 1999), for it is the instrument used in the investigation reported here.

Acknowledging a Lewinian heritage amplified in their model, Zimbardo and Boyd (1999) say that

> TP is the often nonconscious process whereby the continual flows of personal and social experiences are assigned to temporal categories, or time frames, that help to give order, coherence, and meaning to those events. These cognitive frames may reflect cyclical, repetitive temporal patterns or unique, non-recurring linear events in people's lives (Hall, 1983). They are used in encoding, storing, and recalling experienced events, as well as in forming expectations, goals, contingencies, and imaginative scenarios. Between the abstract, psychological constructions of prior past and anticipated future events lies the concrete, empirically centered representation of the present. (pp. 1271-1272)

According to this conception, the ZTPI was intended to be a reliable instrument for use in documenting how time determined attitudes and cognitive styles influence our lives. It reflects several years of research of its authors and contains items in Likert format covering five dimensions or (sub)scales developed during such validation period: past-negative, past-positive, present-hedonistic, present-fatalistic, and future. These dimensions are detailed below, in specific sections, where part of the literature related to ZTPI applications is presented. Even though much has been learned about time functioning of individuals and groups in relation to several themes of research, underlying psychological processes and interconnections with other constructs wait for a better understanding.

In theory, a balanced time perspective allows individuals to flexibly use time orientations, switching temporal frames between past, future and present in accordance with its pertinence to available resources, perceived demands and other appraised personal and social aspects of each situation. Therefore, people sometimes are present-oriented, while in other times they tend to the future or to the past. In contrast, when there is a tendency to habitually overemphasize a particular orientation when making decisions, a cognitive temporal "bias" appears towards that specific time orientation (past, present or future).

THE FUTURE TIME PERSPECTIVE

Future-oriented persons are achievers; they like to plan strategies, and meet their long-term obligations. They also tend to avoid risky situations and behaviors, visualize and formulate future goals that influence their present decisions and judgments. These individuals are conscious, self-controlled, organized, creative, reliable and responsible (Zimbardo & Boyd, 2008).

The concept of *Consideration of Future Consequences* (CFC) is also studied within the framework of time perspective. This concept alludes how people are influenced by the immediate versus the distal consequences of their behavior (Strathman, Gleicher, Bonninger & Edwards, 1994). Some individuals, with a clear future orientation, are able to delay the rewards resulting from their acts; while the more present-oriented ones prefer obtaining such rewards immediately, regardless of the fact that, in the future, their value could increase (Siegel, 2005). CFC always refers the capacity that people have to visualize future events that are affected by present behavior, and the way in which individuals are able to influence forthcoming times. Research results indicate that CFC is linked to a series of variables such as pro-environmental attitudes, the ability to persuade others, healthy lifestyles, and a number of pro-environmental behaviors (Benoit & Strahtman, 2004; Joireman, Anderson & Strathman, 2003; Strathman et al, 1994). Strathman et al (1994) developed a 12-item scale in order to assess CFC, which has been used to investigate future orientation and its behavioral and psychological correlates.

CFC and future orientation are a component of the so called "executive functions" by neuropsychologists. These functions refer the ability to identify a goal, formulate a plan to fulfill the goal, perform the actions according to the plan, evaluate the consequences of those actions, and change/adjust behavior in correspondence with the results (Godefroy, 2003). Executive functions are organized in the frontal lobes, the most distinctively human zone of the brain, and are considered a crucial capacity for behavioral regulation, self-control, decision making, and problem solution (Strayhorn, 2002). All these activities are intimately linked to the future perspective and, according to some authors, are essential for the development of sustainable lifestyles (Geller, 2002; Corral-Verdugo, Frías & González, 2003; Wall, Devine-Wright, & Mill, 2007). Alternatively, antisocial individuals present a deficit in executive functions (Brower & Price, 2001; Valdez, Nava, Tirado, Frías & Corral-Verdugo, 2005), which confirm the importance of developing a future orientation as a basis for pro-social and pro-environmental behaviors.

Psycho-environmental research seems to confirm the presumed link between sustainable behavior and time orientation. As anticipated, future is the key piece. Strathman et al (1994), in a pioneer study, found that the consideration of future consequences was associated to recycling behavior. Joreiman, Van lange, Van Vugt, Wood, Vander Leest and Lambert (2001) reported that individuals scoring high in the CFC scale exhibited a higher willingness to support public transportation systems, which are less pollutant than private cars. Ebreo and Vining (2001) also used this scale and found that future orientation was higher in recyclers than in non-recyclers. According to these studies, CFC makes people feel more convinced of and affected by the long-term benefits of their sustainable behavior. One more study by Joreiman et al (2004) found that responses to the CFC scale correlated with the preference to commute using public transportation. These authors conclude that a future orientation may be more important than a pro-social orientation in shaping these preferences. A recent study conducted in Mexico (Corral-Verdugo, Bonnes, Tapia, Fraijo, Frías & Carrus, 2009) revealed a positive correlation between the CFC and pro-ecological behavior, as assessed by Kaiser's (1998) scale. Their results indicate that future orientation is linked to a set of sustainable behaviors, not only to isolated environmentally-protective actions.

The use of the ZTPI has produced similar results regarding the relationship between future orientation and sustainable behavior. Corral-Verdugo and Pinheiro (2006) reported a positive covariation between the future orientation sub-scale of the ZTPI and water conservation behaviors reported by Mexicans. This finding suggests that conservationists have a more future-oriented perspective. A previous study by these authors (Corral-Verdugo

& Pinheiro, 2004) had shown that future orientation is positively associated to both pro-environmental behavior and to a series of pro-sustainable dispositional variables such as pro-ecological deliberation, pro-environmental competency, austerity and altruism. Milfont and Gouveia (2005), in Brazil, expanded this relation to a series of environmental attitudes; they found that future orientation is positively linked to pro-ecological attitudes and negatively related to attitudes favorable to the utilization and waste of natural resources. Besides, Martín, Hernández and Ruiz (2007), in Spain, found a positive relationship between future orientation, as assessed by the ZTPI, and the ecocentrism items of Thompson and Barton's (1994) scale.

Additional results show that future orientation is not only related to pro-ecological behavior and attitudes but also to pro-social behavior. This would confirm the pro-sustainable attribute of this time perspective. Zimbardo, Keough & Boyd (1997), for instance, found that future orientation inhibited risky car-driving behaviors; this effect has also been found in regard to drug consumption (Keough, Zimbardo & Boyd, 1999; Wills, Sandy & Yaeger, 2001), and pathological gambling (Hodgins & Engel, 2002). Also, Joreiman et al (2003) found that the consideration of future consequences was negatively associated with risky behaviors for others and for oneself, and also with aggressive behaviors.

The future time perspective was the main reason we initially approached ZTPI and its related studies. Besides, this dimension seems to be the "ideal" one, for it is linked to valued aspects of life, such as good academic performance, healthy functioning, and – important in the context of this chapter (and book) – sustainability. However, it is unconceivable that a person would live exclusively focused in the future; human life is lived in the present time. Delaying gratification to extremes may be psychologically (and even physically) harmful to someone if gratification never occurs in his/her life. In this respect, Zimbardo and Boyd (1999) had a footnote that presented a very interesting contrast between future and present orientations. They said:

> It is only from the perspective of future orientation that the decision to smoke can be seen to have a negative consequence: the future development of lung cancer. If judged solely through the lens of present oirentation, smoking is just a pleasurable activity without articulated future consequences. In the context of present orientation, smoking may actually be the "right" decision, because it may lead to pleasure, however short lived. (p. 1272)

The Present Time Perspective

As mentioned before, the present orientation includes hedonistic and fatalistic components. The present-hedonistic perspective occurs in individuals who are prone to enjoy here-and-now situations, disregarding the past or forthcoming events. These people are sensual, look for immediate gratification, and are not interested in future rewards. They are also impulsive and sensation-seekers, feel attracted by risky situations, tend to be happy and non-concerned. Alternatively, the present-fatalistic orientation implies living today at the expenses of chance (fate). Free will and self-control are not important for individuals biased by this time perspective. Some behavioral traits exhibited by present fatalistic people are, both, a lower self-esteem and emotional stability, anxiety, unhappiness, depression, unconsciousness, and irresponsibility (Zimbardo & Boyd, 2008).

The negative influence of present orientation on sustainable behavior seems to overpass its possible positive influence. Zimbardo and Boyd (2008) recommend moderate levels of present hedonism to be happy and pro-social. The positive effects of the present perspective should include a propensity to sustainable behavior, which the authors consider to be a relevant consequence of time orientation. Unfortunately, besides the desirable traits of the hedonistic present (happiness and friendliness), it includes, as well, negative characteristics: risk proneness and sensation-seeking that are also important components of antisocial and criminal personalities (Siegel, 2005). This kind of present orientation shares with the fatalistic one other undesirable traits, such as the lack of consideration for future consequences, and a deficit in self-control (Strathman *et al*, 1994). Of course, the fatalistic present only includes negative traits, and nothing good in terms of sustainable behavior is expected from this time orientation.

In this regard, Corral-Verdugo and Frías (2006) reported a positive correlation between anti-environmental actions (maltreating plants and animals, littering) and antisocial behavior (fighting, arguing, cheating), in addition to positive associations between all these behaviors, antisocial personality-traits and the present orientation perspective. Besides, Milfont and Gouveia (2005) found that the fatalistic present negatively influenced attitudes favorable to environmental preservation; although they also found that the hedonistic present was negatively associated to utilitarian attitudes regarding the use of natural resources.

The present-fatalistic individuals present a psychological characteristic that is antagonistic to sustainable behavior: the so-called *external locus of control*. This trait is defined as the belief on the external control of own behavior, which make people to assume that their behavior, and its consequences, depend on chance, fatality, God, or powerful others (Rotter, 1966). In opposition, the internal locus of control characterizes individuals who consider themselves as being in control of their own behavior and its consequences. Present-fatalistic oriented people are high on external locus of control. Smith-Sebasto and Fortner (1994) found that individuals with an internal locus of control tended to engage in pro-environmental behaviors. Also, Allen and Ferrand (1999) showed that the internal locus of control positively and indirectly predicted pro-ecological behavior through a state they called "sympathy" –a form of altruism- which affected, in turn, pro-ecological behavior. Hwang, Kim and Jeng (2000) reported that the internal locus of control significantly influenced the intention to act pro-environmentally. Therefore, these results apparently indicate that external locus of control inhibits sustainable behavior. Since this is a trait of fatalistic-present individuals, the findings suggest that avoiding such a time perspective is a good idea, not only because of the unhappiness it propitiates, but also due to its negative environmental effect.

Present orientation also impacts on the social consequences of behavior that may be important/relevant to sustainable lifestyles. The carefree nature of present-hedonistic persons leads them to neglect others' and own wellbeing, by –for example, getting involved in behaviors such as exceeding speed limits and drunk driving (Zimbardo et al, 1997). Lacking consideration of the consequences of their behavior makes people to be poorly concerned about other's wellbeing, in spite of their friendly attitude (Zimbardo & Boyd, 2008). Moreover, present-fatalistic individuals are neither conscious, nor considerate or committed with others. That is why it is hard to expect a significant number of altruistic responses from them (Zimbardo & Boyd, 2008).

The Past Perspective

The psychological past contains two perspectives: one oriented towards happy, joyful memories (positive past) while the other is biased towards sad or painful events (negative past). Positive past captures events or perceptions from already gone times that are associated to joyful situations, which –according to Zimbardo and his collaborators- allows people to adequately face difficult events in the present. People exhibiting a bias towards this orientation are thankful, conscious, creative, friendly, and non-depressive. Positive-past individuals tend to be happy. Conversely, those with a negative-past orientation focus on painful, unpleasant memories, from events that experienced or -they think, happened to them. Negative-past persons tend to be anxious, non-considerate, depressive, apathetic and little friendly.

Corral-Verdugo, Fraijo and Pinheiro (2006) suggest that those oriented to such a time perspective do not consider the future consequences of their behavior; therefore, it is difficult to expect a sustainably-oriented tendency in their daily actions. However, these authors also indicate that since these individuals are not prone to wasteful, risky and hedonistic behaviors (for instance, those resulting from over-consuming natural resources that characterize present-oriented people), an anti-environmental attitude is not expected in these persons. In Milfont and Gouveia's (2005) study, the negative past correlated neither with preservation nor with utilization (of resources) attitudes. Positive past resulted linked to preservation attitudes, in a positive way. Yet, their study only considered attitudes as correlates of negative-past orientation, so that a replication is needed by investigating the relationship between sustainable *behaviors* and the positive past. If, as Zimbardo and Boyd (2008) argue, this type of time propensity characterizes individuals experiencing psychological wellbeing, and if such wellbeing is a correlate of sustainability (Gardner & Prugh, 2008), then it is expected that the positive past contribute to a sustainable orientation. An additional aspect involving the past and its positive influence on the environment is Chipeniuk's (1995) finding revealing that past experiences and childhood memories of contact with nature have repercussions on present conservationist behavior. Therefore, investigating the way in which positive and the negative past influence sustainable behavior is a pending task, which would complement the previously studied links between the present and future orientations and pro-environmental behavior.

TIME PERSPECTIVE AND SUSTAINABLE BEHAVIOR

Zimbardo and Boyd (2008) suggest that a combination of time orientations would allow people to enjoy plentiful lives, get satisfaction and personal enhancement. The resulting psychological state could be interpreted as "happiness" or, at least, a tendency towards happiness. The suggested combination involves high levels of positive past and moderately high levels of hedonistic present and future orientation. Due the behavioral and psychological correlates (proneness to happiness, responsibility, consciousness, pro-sociality, etc.) of those orientations such a recommendations makes sense. Both, the negative past and the fatalistic present should be avoided since they do not provide any good either for the individual (unhappiness) or her/his social group (anti-environmental and antisocial consequences).

However, a fundamental question is whether the remaining (and desired) time orientations correlate with the adoption of more sustainable lifestyles. In other words, we want to know whether the bias for a particular time perspective orient more towards sustainability than other perspectives, or whether the "balance" between the "positive" orientations lead individuals to being more pro-ecological and pro-social. Since the diverse time orientations do not always influence the same behaviors, it would be necessary to elucidate if the positive aspects of the past, the present and the future induce sustainable actions, or –alternatively- if only the future is implicated, as the sustainable development definition suggests.

In this regard, Corral-Verdugo, Fraijo and Pinheiro (2006) conducted the only study (as far as we know) integrating the three time orientations in relation to sustainable behavior. They found that future-oriented individuals tended to be more water conservationists at their households than non-future-biased people. The present (both fatalistic and hedonistic)-oriented wasted more water, while the past oriented were not affected in their water consumption by their time perspective. These findings contradict the idea of a beneficial effect of the positive past in inducing sustainability. However, as previously indicated, it is necessary to replicate these findings in order to elucidate the role played by the positive past in the induction of sustainable actions. One more study (Pinheiro, 2006) had shown that positive past and future were positively related to ecocentric and anthropocentric environmentalism, but negative past did not covary with either pro-environmental indicator; fatalistic and hedonistic present were positively correlated to individualism, as expected.

As a whole, results from these studies show that including the time perspective concept in the analysis of sustainable behavior makes sense. They also indicate that a substantial knowledge regarding individual differences, cultural attributions towards every type of time perspectives, and related matters, is necessary.

The ZTPI was conceived to general use in psychological research including time among the dimensions to be considered. Our interests in the instrument have always been associated to its potential implications for the study of sustainable lifestyles and intergenerational solidarity. Apparently limited to the future time perspective, such interests seem to be, in fact, better served by the whole set of time perspectives contained in ZTPI, since the flexible switching of temporal frames may be the best expression of a balanced lifestyle. With such approach in mind, we planned the investigation detailed below.

METHOD

Participants

Three hundred Mexicans living in the city of Hermosillo, participated in this study. They were 160 females and 140 males, selected from zones that, according to the Mexican Census Office (INEGI, 2000) were representative of high, middle, and low socio-economic classes. Households were randomly selected from each zone. The zones were selected and maps of these neighborhoods were obtained from local authorities. The selection of households involved the use of these maps in which every premise was represented. All premises were assigned a number, and a list of random numbers was used to select 100 households. 50% of them were low-class homes, while 40% constituted middle-class homes and the additional 10% were high-class households. The individuals investigated in each home were the housewives, a male adult, and a young man/woman aged 12-18 years old. The age mean for the total sample was 31.8 (SD=13.3) years. 46% of them reported a family monthly income between 0 and 600 U.S. dollars, 26% had an income between 600 and 2000 dollars and only 15% reported earnings between 2000 and more than 3000 dollars per month. The mean of educational level for this sample was 11.9 (SD=4.9) completed grades at school.

Instruments

We utilized the Zimbardo's Time Perspective Inventory (ZTPI, Zimbardo & Boyd, 1999) for this study. The ZTPI assesses individual differences in terms of attitudes believed to identify persons of past, present or future orientation. This inventory identifies tendencies towards a Hedonistic Present, a Fatalistic Present, a Positive Past, a Negative Past, and Future Orientation, as described in the introduction of this chapter. We administered a Spanish version of the entire set of 56 items constituting the ZTPI. The items are assessed on a 5-point Likert scale; according to *how characteristic* each statement is of the respondent.

In order to investigate sustainable behavior (water conservation in this specific case) we asked participants to self-report the frequency with which they engaged in actions such as conserving water while washing dishes, brushing teeth, or washing their car(s) during the last week. Finally, participants were asked to provide demographic information, including age, family monthly income, and schooling.

Procedure

Participants were approached and their informed consent to participate in this study was obtained. Everyone accepted to respond to the instruments. Both the ZPTI and the water conservation items were administered in the households' living room. It took about 20 minutes to respond to these instruments.

Data Analysis

Cronbach's alphas, as indicators of internal consistency, as well as univariate statistic for each scale and their items were obtained. A confirmatory factor analysis model (CFA) was specified in order to test both the factor structure of the ZTPI and the covariances between time perspectives and water conservation. Items of the ZPTI were parceled into three indicators per tested construct (hedonistic present, fatalistic present, negative past, positive past and future orientation). A parcel is the mean or two or more randomly chosen items of a construct (Little, Cunningham, Shahar, & Widaman, 2002). In this case, we randomly distributed the total number of items corresponding to each factor into three indicators (the parcels). Goodness of fit indicators (chi-squared, practical goodness of fit indices, RMSEA, etc.) were also obtained from the CFA. These indicators reveal whether or not the data support the adequacy of the hypothesized factor structure and the pattern of presumed covariances between factors (Bentler, 2006). Six factors were pre-specified within the CFA. These were the five time dimensions and the water conservation factor. In addition, differences between demographic groups (gender, age) in terms of time perspectives were assessed, as well as regarding to water conservation practices.

Table 1. Reliabilities and univariate statistics of used scales

Scale/items	N	mean	(SD)	Min	Max	Alpha
Hedonistic present		3.01	(1.18)	1	5	.71
1. I believe that getting together with one's friends to party is one of life's important pleasures.	292	3.33	(1.18)	1	5	
2. I do things impulsively	293	3.32	(3.31)	1	5	
3. When listening to my favorite music, I often lose all track of time.	293	3.53	(1.04)	1	5	
5. Ideally, I would live each day as if it were my last	292	3.58	(0.99)	1	5	
6. I make decisions on the spur of the moment.	292	3.07	(1.25)	1	5	
7. It is important to put excitement in my life.	293	3.22	(1.16)	1	5	
8. I feel that it's more important to enjoy what you're doing than to get work done on time.	293	3.31	(1.06)	1	5	
9. Taking risks keeps my life from becoming boring.	293	3.00	(1.25)	1	5	
10. It is more important for me to enjoy life's journey than to focus only on the destination	291	3.14	(1.18)	1	5	
11. I take risks to put excitement in my life.	293	2.51	(1.26)	1	5	
12. I often follow my heart more than my head.	291	2.69	(1.18)	1	5	
13. I find myself getting swept up in the excitement of the moment.	291	2.80	(1.22)	1	5	
14. I prefer friends who are spontaneous rather than predictable.	293	2.54	(1.23)	1	5	
15. I like my close relationships to be passionate.	293	2.39	(1.26)	1	5	
Fatalistic present		2.89	(1.19)	1	5	.72
1. Fate determines much in my life	292	2.92	(1.25)	1	5	
2. Since whatever will be will be, it doesn't really matter what I do	293	3.63	(1.10)	1	5	
3. It takes joy out of the process and flow of my activities, if I have to think about goals, and products.	293	2.79	(1.14)	1	5	
4. You can't really plan for the future because things change so much.	289	2.93	(1.22)	1	5	

Table 1. Continued

Scale/items	N	mean	(SD)	Min	Max	Alpha
5. My life path is controlled by forces I cannot influence	293	3.64	(1.21)	1	5	
6. It doesn't make sense to worry about the future, since there is nothing that I can do about it anyway.	293	2.63	(1.16)	1	5	
7. Life today is too complicated; I would prefer the simpler life of the past.	293	2.62	(1.24)	1	5	
8. Spending what I earn on pleasures today is better than saving for tomorrow's security.	293	2.62	(1.24)	1	5	
9. Often luck pays off better than hard work.	293	2.32	(1.21)	1	5	
Positive past		2.98	(1.21)	1	5	.65
1. Familiar childhood sights, sounds, smells often bring back wonderful memories	293	3.38	(1.23)	1	5	
2. It gives me pleasure to think about my past.	292	3.67	(1.20)	1	5	
3. On balance, there is much more good to recall than bad in my past.	293	3.90	(0.97)	1	5	
4. I enjoy stories about how things used to be in the "good old times."	293	2.46	(1.26)	1	5	
5. Happy memories of good times spring readily to mind.	293	2.82	(1.36)	1	5	
6. I get nostalgic about my childhood.	293	2.57	(1.25)	1	5	
7. I find myself tuning out when family members talk about the way things used to be.	293	2.60	(1.26)	1	5	
8. I like family rituals and traditions that are regularly repeated.	292	2.88	(1.19)	1	5	
9. Life today is too complicated; I would prefer the simpler life of the past	293	2.62	(1.24)	1	5	
Negative past		2.98	(1.24)	1	5	.74
1. I often think of what I should have done differently in my life.	293	3.10	(1.22)	1	5	
2. My decisions are mostly influenced by people and things around me.	293	3.49	(1.19)	1	5	
3. Painful past experiences keep being replayed in my mind.	292	2.82	(1.28)	1	5	
4. I've taken my share of abuse and rejection in the past.	293	3.58	(1.22)	1	5	
5. The past has too many unpleasant memories that I prefer not to think about.	293	2.99	(1.23)	1	5	
6. I've made mistakes in the past that I wish I could undo.	293	2.89	(1.31)	1	5	
7. Things rarely work out as I expected.	292	2.56	(1.30)	1	5	

Table 1. Continued

Scale/items	N	mean	(SD)	Min	Max	Alpha
8. It's hard for me to forget unpleasant images of my youth.	292	3.15	(1.30)	1	5	
9. Even when I am enjoying the present, I am drawn back to comparisons with similar past experiences.	293	2.73	(1.09)	1	5	
10. I think about the bad things that have happened to me in the past.	293	2.58	(1.28)	1	5	
11. I think about the good things that I have missed out on in my life.	293	2.93	(1.27)	1	5	
Future orientation		3.24	(1.18)	1	5	.70
1. I believe that a person's day should be planned ahead each morning.	293	3.35	(1.22)	1	5	
2. If things don't get done on time, I don't worry about it.	293	2.93	(1.30)	1	5	
3. When I want to achieve something, I set goals and consider specific means for reaching those goals.	293	3.52	(1.18)	1	5	
4. Meeting tomorrow's deadlines and doing other necessary work comes before tonight's play.	293	3.70	(1.15)	1	5	
5. It upsets me to be late for appointments.	293	3.81	(1.08)	1	5	
6. I meet my obligations to friends and authorities on time.	293	3.64	(1.05)	1	5	
7. I take each day as it is rather than plan it out.	293	2.94	(1.18)	1	5	
8. Before making a decision, I weigh the costs against the benefits.	293	2.59	(1.16)	1	5	
9. I complete projects on time by making steady progress.	291	2.49	(1.04)	1	5	
10. I make lists of things to do.	292	2.81	(1.34)	1	5	
11. I am able to resist temptations when I know that there is work to be done.	293	3.29	(1.19)	1	5	
12. I think about the bad things that have happened to me in the past.	291	3.12	(1.19)	1	5	
13. There will always be time to catch up on my work.	293	3.12	(1.31)	1	5	
Water conservation						.62
1. Conserved water while washing dishes	293	4.66	(6.60)	0	25	
2. Conserved water while brushing	293	8.42	(8.04)	0	30	
3. Conserved water while washing hands	293	9.02	(0.65)	0	70	
4. Conserved water while washing his/her car	293	7.14	(9.38)	0	56	

Table 2. Factor loadings (lambda matrix) between the five time-perspective subdimensions, the water conservation scale and their parcels/indicators

Indicators	Future	Hedo-pres	Fatal-pres	Negat-pas	Posit-pas	Watcons
Future 1	.75					
Future 2	.74					
Future 3	.55					
Hedo-present 1		.46				
Hedo-present 2		.79				
Hedo-present 3		.72				
Fatal-present 1			.73			
Fatal-present 2			.52			
Fatal-present 3			.58			
Negative past 1				.65		
Negative past 2				.73		
Negative past 3				.74		
Positive past 1					.40	
Positive past 2					.50	
Positive past 3					.70	
Water consrv 1						.34
Water consrv 2						.65
Water consrv 3						.57
Water consrv 4						.62

RESULTS

Table 1 shows the reliability and univariate statistics of the ZTPI. Respondents reported a remarkably balanced time perspective, generating similar means for the five orientations. Yet, future and present hedonistic perspectives scored slightly higher (means 3.24 and 3.01, respectively) than the remaining orientations (2.89 for fatalistic present and 2.98 for both types of past perspective). The Cronbach's alphas were .65 and higher for the five subdimensions of the ZTPI, while the water conservation items produced a .62 alpha.

Tables 2 and 3 contain the *lambda* and the *phi* matrices, respectively, resulting from the confirmatory factor analysis on the data. The *lambda* matrix is the correlation between factors and their corresponding indicators. In this case, it exhibits the factor loadings between the five time perspectives and their parcels, as well as the loadings between the water conservation factor and its items. All these loadings were salient and significant, revealing convergent construct validity. The *phi* matrix, in turn, indicates the covariances between the analyzed factors. The highest inter-factor associations were for the negative and positive pasts (.74), the hedonistic and fatalistic presents (.70), fatalistic present and negative past (.63), and positive past and future orientation (.62). Both, the hedonistic (-.18) and fatalistic present (-.29) covaried significantly and negatively with water conservation, while the future resulted positively linked to this sustainable behavior (.20). Neither type of past orientation covaried significantly with water conservation. Goodness of fit indicators ($N=280$; $X^2= 256$ [134 $d.f.$], $p<.001$); $NNFI=.90$, $CFI=.91$; $RMSEA=.05$) seems to support the adequacy of this model.

Table 3. Covariances (*Phi* matrix) between the time perspective sub-scales and water conservation. Results from a confirmatory factor analysis (method = ML)

	Future	Hedon-pres	Fatal-pres	Negat-past	Posit-past	Wat-conserv
Future	-					
Hedon-pres	.07	-				
Fatal-pres	-.38*	.70*	-			
Negat-past	.12	.42*	.63*	-		
Posit-past	.62*	.33*	.31*	.74*	-	
Wat-conserv	.20*	-.18*	-.29*	-.10	-.10	-

* Significant covariances ($p <.05$). Goodness of fit of the CFA: N=280; $X^2= 256$ (134 $d.f.$), $p<.001$; NNFI=.90, CFI=.91; RMSEA=.05.

CONCLUSION

Time perspective seems to be a significant determinant of sustainable behavior. People act either pro or anti-environmentally –or simply, do not act- depending on their particular time orientation. As in previous research results, our study found that people biased towards a future perspective are prone to practice sustainable behaviors. Besides confirming this relation, we were also interested in investigating possible links between present and past perspectives and sustainable behavior. Based on ideas suggesting a link between positive past and socially responsible behavior and also a correlation between hedonistic present and such a behavior (Zimbardo and Boyd, 2008) we analyzed the covariations between those time perspectives and a measure of water conservation. We failed in finding the expected covariances: positive past did not correlate with water conservation and the hedonistic present significantly correlated with that conservationist behavior but in a negative way. In summary, the present-oriented individuals were more motivated to waste water, the future-oriented were conservationist and the past perspective did not affect respondents' inclinations toward sustainable acting.

Yet, although neither the positive past nor the hedonistic present were positively related to water conservation, concluding that the only time perspective inducing sustainable practices is the future could be an inexact summary of our results. In this study, the correlation between positive past and future orientation was high and salient ($r = .62, p <.05$). There was no correlation between the future and negative past perspectives. This could imply that the positive past indirectly influences conservation behavior through future orientation. In addition, results from this study show that the fatalistic present relates positively to the negative past. We can easily interpret reasons for this correlation: depending on how I conceive my past as bad/negative, I can only expect the same thing going on in present times. Alternatively, if my past was good and brings me peace of mind in present/current times, I am apt to think and dream about my future (which could include thinking about the need to conserve my environment). Thus, the time perspective implicated in sustainable acting is not only limited to future orientation, since this is highly influenced by a positive past, and probably by present positive experiences.

Some final comments have to be added in order to clarify our findings and ideas regarding the time perspective notions proposed by different authors. One of these comments have to do with the fact that the ZTPI and CFC approaches here mentioned were used somewhat interchangeably, while Joreiman and Strathman (2005) state they do not know how the 2 instruments relate to each other: "Thus, future research should begin to compare the relative impact of the two scales, their underlying mechanisms, and the boundary conditions that determine when each construct does and does not impact behavior. When combined, studies addressing these issues will also help to highlight the relative advantages of each scale." (p. 328). We agree with these authors' conclusions and suggest the conduction of future studies –especially in the area of sustainable behavior- aimed at elucidating those mentioned relative advantages and differences between the ZTPI and CFC approaches.

In this chapter we emphasized the subjective representation of time (time perspective, or TP), but we do not dichotomically diminish the importance of the study of the "external" time. We prefer to understand the distinction objective/subjective as a continuum that ranges from phenomena that are observable by outsiders through those only perceptible to the person in question. Each approach presents strengths and weaknesses that may influence conclusions about person-environment relationships (Winkel et al., in press).

The theoretical status of studies on time perspective in relation to sustainable behavior is yet preliminary because these studies are very recent and complex. In regard to this, Pinheiro's (2006) results suggest, for instance, that *affective* underlying links between some of the temporal perspectives may be stronger than the chronological aspect itself. In association to it, we must say that there is much to be known about time perspective implications for sustainable lifestyles from a psychological perspective, (e.g.: moral & affective basis of *delay* of gratification).

Also, the psycho-socio-cultural aspect impinging on both the time perspective and people's pro-social action has to be considered. Let's take as example the personal time perspective in a group interaction in which this perspective must be larger, more extended than the person-alone version. As an illustration of this, Wiesenfeld (1996) suggests the existence of a "we" notion among collectivistic cultures, such as the Latin American. According to this author, the ''we'' implies a set of processes such as membership, inclusion, identity, feeling of belonging, and an emotional bond or sense of community which *do not seem to vary across time* and within members of the community. These processes, by the way, result in protective behaviors positively impacting on individuals and their socio-physical environment.

Finally, clear imbrications of time perspective and sustainable behavior with the positive psychology approach are present (see Bechtel and Corral-Verdugo, this volume), which should be exhaustively studied. Positive Psychology suggests that some time perspectives are predominant in happy people, but also that this people tend to be sustainably-oriented. Thus, a link between being happy, being conservationist and "using" a biased time perspective should exist. For sure, environmental psychologists will explore this and other interesting links between positive psychological characteristics/behaviors and the varied facets constituting individuals' time perspective.

REFERENCES

Allen, J. A., & Ferrand, J. L. (1999). Environmental locus of control, sympathy and proenvironmental behavior. *Environment & Behavior, 31,* 338-353.

Barker, R.G. (1968). *Ecological psychology: concepts and methods for studying the environment of human behavior.* Stanford, CA: Stanford University Press.

Benoit, W. L., & Strathman, A. (2004). Source credibility and the Elaboration Likelihood Model. In J. Seiter & R. Gass (Eds.), *Perspectives on persuasion, social influence, and compliance-gaining.* Boston: Allyn & Bacon.

Bentler, P. M. (2006). *EQS, Structural Equations Program Manual.* Encino, CA: Statistical Software, Inc.

Bronfenbrenner, U., & Morris, P. A. (2006). The Bioecological Model of human development. In R. M. Lerner & W. Damon (Eds.), *Handbook of child psychology: Theoretical models of human development* (6th ed., Vol. 1, pp. 793-828). Hoboken, NJ: John Wiley & Sons.

Brower, M. C. & Price, B. H. (2001). Neuropsychiatry of frontal lobe dysfunction in violent and criminal behavior: a critical review. *Journal of Neurology, Neurosurgery and Psychiatry, 71,* 720-726.

Brown, L. R. (1981). *Building a sustainable society.* New York: Norton.

Chipeniuk, R. (1995). Childhood foraging as a means of acquiring competent cognition about biodiversity. *Environment & Behavior, 27,* 490-512.

Corral-Verdugo, V., Bonnes, M., Tapia, C., Fraijo, B., Frías, M., & Carrus, G. (2009). Correlates of pro-sustainability orientation: the Affinity Towards Diversity. *Journal of Environmental Psychology, 29,* 34-43.

Corral, V, Fraijo, B. & Pinheiro, J. (2006). Sustainable behavior and time perspective: present, past, and future orientations and their relationship with water conservation. *Interamerican Journal of Psychology, 40,* 139-147.

Corral-Verdugo, V. & Frías, M. (2006). Personal normative beliefs, antisocial behavior, and residential water conservation. *Environment & Behavior, 38,* 406-421.

Corral-Verdugo, V., Frías, M. & González, D. (2003). On the relationship between antisocial and anti-environmental behaviors: An empirical study. *Population and Environment, 24,* 273-286.

Corral-Verdugo, V. & Pinheiro, J. (2004). Aproximaciones al estudio de la conducta sustentable [Approaches to the study of sustainable behavior]. *Medio Ambiente y Comportamiento Humano, 5,* 1-26.

Corral-Verdugo, V. & Pinheiro, J. Q. (2006). Sustainability, future orientation and water conservation. *European Review of Applied Psychology, 56,* 191-198.

Ebreo, A. & Vining, J. (2001). How similar are recycling and waste reduction? Future orientation and reasons for reducing waste as predictors of self-reported behavior. *Environment & Behavior, 33,* 424-448.

Gardner, G. & Prugh, T. (2008). Seeding the sustainable economy. En Starke, L. (Ed.), *State of the World.* New York, W. W. Norton & Company.

Geller, E. S. (2002). The challenge of increasing pro-environment behavior. En R.B. Bechtel & A. Churchman (Eds.), *Handbook of Environmental Psychology.* New York: Wiley.

Gibson, J. J. (1979). *The ecological approach to visual perception.* Boston: Houghton Mifflin.

Gifford, R., Scannell, L., Kormos, C., Smolova, L., Biel, A., Boncu, S. et al. (2009). Temporal pessimism and spatial optimism in environmental assessments: an 18-nation study. *Journal of Environmental Psychology, 29*(1), 1-12.

Godefroy, O. (2003). Frontal syndrome and disorders of executive functions. *Journal of Neurology, 250,* 1-6.

Hall, E. T. (1983). *The dance of life - the other dimension of time.* New York: Anchor.

Hodgins, D. C., & Engel, A. (2002). Future time perspective in pathological gamblers. *Journal of Nervous and Mental Disease, 190,* 775–780.

Hwang, Y.H., Kim, S.I. & Jeng, J.M. (2000). Examining the causal relationships among selected antecedents of responsible environmental behavior. *Journal of Environmental Education, 31,* 19-25.

INEGI (2000). *Sistema de Consulta para la Información Censal* (SCINCE) [Census Information Consulting System]. Mexico City: Instituto Nacional de Geografía e Informática.

Joireman, J., Anderson, J., & Strathman, A. (2003). The aggression paradox: Understanding links among aggression, sensation seeking, and the consideration of future consequences. *Journal of Personality and Social Psychology, 84,* 1287-1302.

Joreiman, J. & Strathman, A. (2005). Further study of behavior in the context of time. In A. Strathman and J. Joreiman (Eds.), *Behavior in the Context of Time.* New York: Routledge.

Joireman, J. A., Van Lange, P., Van Vugt, M., Wood, M., Vander Leest, T., & Lambert, C. (2001). Structural solutions to social dilemmas: a field study on commuters' willingness to fund improvements in public transit. *Journal of Applied Social Psychology, 31,* 504-526.

Kaiser, F. (1998). A general measure of ecological behavior. *Journal of Applied Social Psychology, 28,* 395-442.

Keough, K., Zimbardo, P., & Boyd, J. (1999). Who is smoking, drinking, and using drugs? Time perspective as a predictor of substance use. *Basic and Applied Social Psychology, 21,* 149-164.

Little, T., Cunningham, W., Shahar, G., & Widaman, K. (2002). To parcel or not parcel: exploring the question, weighing the merits. *Structural Equation Modeling: A Multidisciplinary Journal, 9,* 151-173.

Martin, A., Hernández, B. & Ruiz, C. (2007). Variables predictoras de la norma personal en transgresiones de las leyes medioambientales [Predictors of personal norms in environmental-law transgressions]. *Medio Ambiente y Comportamiento Humano, 8,* 137-157.

Milfont, T. L., & Gouveia, V. (2005). Time perspective and values: An exploratory study of their relations to environmental attitudes. *Journal of Environmental Psychology, 26,* 72-82.

Pinheiro, J. Q. (2005, June 29). *Time perspective as a psychological corollary of solidarity between generations.* Communication presented at Interamerican Congress of Psychology, Buenos Aires, Argentina.

Pinheiro, J. Q. (2006). El tiempo en las relaciones persona-ambiente: alfabetización para la sostenibilidad [Time in person-environment relationships: literacy for sustainability]. In

M. Amérigo & B. Cortés (Eds.), *Entre la persona y el entorno. Intersticios para la investigación medioambiental* (pp. 13-41). La Laguna, Santa Cruz de Tenerife: Resma.

Pol, E. (2002). The theoretical background of the City-Identity-Sustainability Network. *Environment and Behavior, 34*(1), 8-25.

Rotter, J. B. (1966). Generalized expectancies for internal versus external control of reinforcement. *Psychological Monographs, 80* (1, full issue, 609).

Siegel, L. J. (2005). *Criminology: The Core* (2nd. Edition). Belmont, CA: Waldsworth/Thomson Learning.

Smith-Sebasto, N. J. & Fortner, R. W. (1994). The environmental action internal control index. *Journal of Environmental Education, 25*, 23-29.

Sommer, R. (1972). *Design awareness*. San Francisco: Holt, Rinehart & Winston.

Stokols, D., Misra, S., Runnerstrom, M. G., & Hipp, J. A. (2009). Psychology in an age of ecological crisis – from personal angst to collective action. *American Psychologist, 64*(3), 181-193.

Strathman, A., Gleicher, F., Boninger, D. S., & Edwards, C. S. (1994). The consideration of future consequences: Weighing immediate and distant outcomes of behavior. *Journal of Personality and Social Psychology, 66*, 742-752.

Strayhorn, J. M., Jr. (2002). Self-control: theory and research. *Journal of the American Academy of Child and Adolescent Psychiatry, 41*, 7-16.

Thompson, S.C.G. & Barton, M. (1994). Ecocentric and anthropocentric attitudes toward the environment. *Journal of Environmental Psychology, 14*, 149-157.

Tuan, Y-F. (1977). *Space and place: the perspective of experience*. Minneapolis: University of Minnesota Press.

Valdez, P., Nava, G., Tirado, H., Frías, M., & Corral, V. (2005). Importancia de las funciones ejecutivas en el comportamiento humano: implicaciones en la investigación con niños. En M. Frías & V. Corral (Eds.), *Niñez, adolescencia y problemas sociales* (pp. 65-81). México: CONACYT-UniSon.

Wall, R., Devine-Wright, P. & Mill, G. (2007). Comparing and combining theories to explain proenvironmental intentions. *Environment & Behavior, 39*, 731-753.

Werner, C. M., Altman, I., & Oxley, D. (1985). Temporal aspects of homes: a transactional perspective. In I. Altman & C. M. Werner (Eds.), Home Environments (pp. 1-32). New York: Plenum.

Werner, C. M., Brown, B. B., & Altman, I. (2000). Transactionally oriented research: examples and settings. In R. B. Bechtel & Arza Churchman (Eds.), *Handbook of Environmental Psychology* (2nd ed, pp. 203-221). New York: John Wiley & Sons.

Wiesenfeld, E. (1996). The concept of "we": a community social psychology myth? *Journal of Community Psychology, 24*, 337–346.

Willis, T., Sandy, J. & Yaeger, A. (2001). Time perspective and early-onset substance abuse: a model based on stress-coping theory. *Psychology of Addictive Behaviors, 15*, 118-125.

Wicker, A. W. (1987). Behavior settings reconsidered: temporal stages, resources, internal dynamics, context. In D. Stokols & I. Altman (Eds.), *Handbook of Environmental Psychology* (pp. 613-653). New York: Wiley.

Winkel, G., Saegert, S., & Evans, G. W. (in press). An ecological perspective on theory, methods, and analysis in environmental psychology: advances and challenges. *Journal of Environmental Psychology*; DOI:10.1016/j.jenvp.2009.02.005.

World Commission on Environment and Development (WCED, 1987). *Our Common Future*. Oxford: Oxford University Press. (also available at http://www.ourcommonfuture.org/)

Zimbardo, P. & Boyd, J. (1999). Putting time in perspective: a valid, reliable individual-differences metric. *Journal of Personality and Social Psychology, 77*, 1271-1288.

Zimbardo, P. & Boyd, J. (2008). *The time paradox. The new psychology of time that will change your life*. Nueva York: Free Press.

Zimbardo, P., Keough, K. & Boyd, J. (1997). Present time perspective as a predictor of risky driving. *Personality and Individual Differences, 23*, 1007-1023.

In: Psychological Approaches to Sustainability
Editors: V. Corral-Verdugo et al.

ISBN 978-1-60876-356-6
© 2010 Nova Science Publishers, Inc.

Chapter 12

PROMOTING PRO-ENVIRONMENTAL COMPETENCY

Blanca Fraijo-Sing, Victor Corral-Verdugo, César Tapia-Fonllem and Daniel González-Lomelí*

Departamento de Psicología, Universidad de Sonora, Mexico

ABSTRACT

Human behavior has to be *effective* in order to become sustainable. Effectiveness is a dimension of human psychology that makes possible both people's adaptation and their problem-solving processes. Environmental crises pose a variety of problems that individuals have to effectively deal with by using their behavioral capacities. *Efficiency* is one of such capacities, implying the generation of a product or result by minimizing resources and wastes. Environmental *affordances* also induce effective behaviors by offering problem-solution clues to humans and other animals; that is why environmental psychologists suggest the design of environments containing pro-environmental affordances. Environmental *knowledge* allows handling information with regard to ecological problems and also information that permits taking advantage of natural resources. Knowledge has to be transformed into *skills* to effectively impact the environment. Pro-environmental skills are significant determinants of sustainable action and they are one of the two basic components of *pro-environmental competency* (PEC), the requirements asking for environmental conservation being the second component. Thus, PEC is defined as "the possession of skills responding to pro-ecological requirements." Those requirements are demands that social groups set in order to guarantee the protection of environmental resources. People also develop self-imposed pro-environmental requirements in the form of norms, values, motives and beliefs. The pertinent literature shows that developing PEC in citizens increases the likelihood of their engaging in sustainable behaviors. In this chapter, we present a structural PEC model specified with data generated from a study with Mexican children. The model assumes

---

* Correspondence to Blanca Fraijo-Sing, Departamento de Psicología, Universidad de Sonora, Rosales y Luis Encina, S/N, Hermosillo, Sonora, 83000, Mexico. E-mail: bfraijo@sociales.uson.mx.

that pro-environmental competency results from high and significant interrelations among pro-environmental skills, knowledge, motives, beliefs and behaviors. These interrelations are presumably influenced by appropriately-designed educational programs, which integrate pro-environmental demands (requirements) with conservationist skills. An environmental education program aimed at promoting water conservation was designed and tested. Children did not exhibit pro-environmental competency prior to implementing the educational intervention, as manifested by low levels of their environmental requirements and skills, as well as by almost-zero correlations between those variables. After implementing the program, PEC coherently emerged as a second-order factor linking requirements with skills. PEC saliently and significantly predicted water conservation behaviors and the levels of pro-environmental skills, knowledge, motives, beliefs and behaviors significantly increased as a consequence of the program. Implications of these results for the development of successful environmental-education strategies and for the promotion of sustainable behaviors are discussed.

INTRODUCTION

According to a number of psycho-environmental authors (Geller, 2002; Corral-Verdugo and Pinheiro, 2004; MEA, 2005), sustainable behavior consists of *effective* actions intended to protect the socio-physical environment. In order to be effective, a behavioral action should result in an expected –or required- product or a problem solution. The effective component of sustainable behavior is manifested through the solution of environmental problems. The cited authors argue that having a pro-environmental predisposition (i.e., awareness and positive attitudes and motives towards the environment), although necessary, is not sufficient enough to fulfill the goals of sustainability. In addition, people have to be pro-environmentally skilled or competent (Corral-Verdugo, 2002; Geller, 2002), that is: they should be effective in their daily pro-social and pro-ecological actions.

Effectiveness has –since a long ago- been a topic of interest for environmental psychologists (De Young, 1996; Frick, Kaiser & Wilson, 2004; Gifford, 2007; Steele, 1980, for instance). Psychologists have elaborated varied concepts for explaining how humans –and other animals- get adapted to their environments. One of these concepts is *efficiency*, the generation of a product or result by minimizing resources and waste. Efficiency is an indicator of effectiveness, the former being manifested through reduced resource-consumption while meeting the needs of a vital process (Hardin, 1993). Sustainable actions are characterized by efficiency since they avoid waste, decrease unnecessary consumption and, simultaneously, satisfy people's needs. For most human sustainable behaviors, being efficient requires training and a self-inhibition of consumerist impulses (Jackson, 2008).

One additional concept, related to effectiveness, is *affordances*, which was created by Gibson (1979). This author believed that environmental objects and situations contain clues that induce effective responses in animal organisms. A fruit's color, texture and consistency, for instance, *afford* responses in animals such as picking up and eating (the fruit). These properties of the perceptual system, which Gibson called "affordances," helped humans to become the outstanding species they are now, because, by using their extremely well developed perceptual system of affordances, humans have indiscriminately exploited natural resources. This produced a positive result because our species has survived and prospered thanks to human's mental capacity, including the ability to perceive environmental affordances. Unfortunately, this has also resulted in environmental depredation.

If affordances have been instrumental in the origin and maintenance of environmental problems, they should also produce the opposite effect: serving as clues for conservation behavior, since this behavior is considered to be a set of effective actions (i.e., behavior solving environmental problems). In fact, some authors establish that affordances stimulating sustainable behaviors could be generated, for instance, by using environmental design that induces environmentally-protective actions (Hormuth, 1999; Kurz, 2000).

Thus, effective behavior is a cause for both environmental depredation and protection. As we will further discuss, personal and normative factors generated in everybody's social environment could make the difference in regard to the decision made by individuals, concerning the use of their capacities either for depredating or for protecting the environment.

Environmental knowledge is also an important factor in the generation of effective behavior. Humans have mastered the planet thanks to the information they possess regarding how to use and exploit environmental resources. Of course, an individual's environmental knowledge should firstly be transformed into *skills* in order to his/her being able to operate in the environment. Those skills, in turn, could be integrated into complex behavioral capabilities, which psychologists call *competencies*. Knowledge, skills and competencies constitute psychological capacities that make possible obtaining benefits from the environment (Corral-Verdugo, 2001). As in the case of affordances, the more environmental knowledge and skills an individual possesses, the more likely her/his being environmentally competent for extracting and using natural resources. Therefore, the more the potential for causing environmental damage, as well.

If environmental affordances, knowledge, skills and competencies have been instrumental in the origins of the environmental dilemma, there are reasons for presuming that these human capacities might also be used for environmental conservation (Geller, 2002). So far, a gap exists between *environmental competencies* (i.e., the aptitude for taking advantages from natural resources) and *pro-environmental competencies* (i.e., the capacity to solve environmental dilemmas), and this gap should be minimized or nullified. Environmental competencies should not be necessarily anti-ecological (neither anti-social, by the way). People could make their skills for obtaining vital resources compatible with their aptitude for conserving the environment (Bonnes & Bonaiuto, 2002; Corral, Bonnes, Fraijo, Tapia, Frías & Carrus, 2009). This compatibility synthesizes a good deal of the sustainable development ideals, and implies that pro-environmental competency is a key factor in the solution of ecological problems.

School is, doubtlessly, one of the best settings for developing pro-environmental competency and children and young people are special targets in this task. Environmental education programs should be well served by interventional strategies aimed at developing pro-environmental competency in these sectors of the population. However, as Uzzell (1999) argues, environmental education, as currently designed and implemented, does not lead to action competence. Thus, environmental educators need to understand what pro-environmental competency is, and also need to include the development of this capacity in young people as an especial goal of their interventional strategies.

By considering all the above, the purpose of this chapter is double: On the one hand, we intend to review research related to the topic of pro-environmental competency as a determinant of sustainable behavior, trying to generate a conceptual model of this human capacity. On the other hand, we are interested in presenting and discussing an empirical study, which was aimed at developing pro-environmental competency in children. This study will be used to illustrate possible ways to developing effective sustainable behavior in environmental education scenarios.

ENVIRONMENTAL KNOWLEDGE AND SKILLS

Environmental knowledge has to do with the amount and quality of information an individual has regarding his/her surroundings. This also includes information about environmental problems and their solutions. It is assumed that higher levels of environmental knowledge lead to a higher environmental concern and interest for solving ecological problems. Laurian (2003), for instance, establishes that information concerning community environmental problems is necessary for raising a collective participation in solving those problems. In turn, Meinhold and Malkus (2005) show that environmental knowledge moderates the attitudes-behavior relationship, so that this knowledge is an indirect determinant of pro-environmental acting. Environmental knowledge has also be considered a precursor of pro-environmental skills, since a person cannot develop problem-solving skills if she/he has no information regarding those problems and the manners he/she could face them in an effective way (Corral-Verdugo, 1996; Day, 2004).

Yet, the levels of environmental knowledge remain quite low throughout the world, regardless of the educational efforts and pro-environmental campaigns and programs conducted everywhere (Pooley & O'Connor, 2000). Cutter-Mackenzie and Smith (2003) criticize the emphasis of environmental campaigns on the promotion of pro-ecological attitudes and values, which has resulted in neglecting the provision of information about environmental problems and their solutions. The standardization of environmental education programs, especially in out-of-school scenarios, is an additional problem, since these programs assume that the recipients of information are homogeneous in personal characteristics such as demographic variables and previous level of knowledge. Under these circumstances information is provided to everyone, regardless of those differences (Mosler & Martens, 2007). A way of dealing with this problem is providing *tailored information* (TI) to produce the expected impact in every individual or social group, regardless of their personal characteristics. TI is an approach using data about a particular person or group, relating to an expected specific product, so that the most appropriate information meeting the needs of that person or group can be determined (Kreuter, Farrell, Olevitch, & Brennan, 1999; Abrahamse, Steg, Vlek & Rothengatter, 2007). Evidently, children require tailored information in their environmental education programs, which should lead to necessarily implementing diagnostic studies before designing interventional strategies.

A number of environmental education researchers assume that providing information will result in knowledge, which, in turn, will produce pro-environmental behavior. These researchers study people's knowledge levels, guessing that if individuals are rational agents, and if they are aware of environmental problems and their solutions, they will behave accordingly, acting pro-environmentally (Hill, 2008). However, this is not necessarily true. Research experience has showed that in spite of the notorious effort invested in providing environmental knowledge to people in diverse regions of the planet, the results have not been the expected (Frick, Kaiser & Wilson, 2004; Harland & Staats, 2001; Pooley & O'Connor, 2000; Kollmuss & Agyeman, 2002). The Hines, Hungerford & Tomera (1986) meta-analysis produced a correlation of $r = .29$ between environmental knowledge and a combined measure of attitude, intention and pro-ecological behaviors; but Frick et al (2004) found only a 6% of predictive power of environmental knowledge on pro-environmental behavior. Chu, Lee, Ko, Shin, Lee, Min & Kang (2007), in a study with Korean children, found very low correlations between environmental knowledge and pro-ecological actions. These authors conclude that attitudes are better predictors of sustainable behavior. In more of this, Kempton, Boster & Hartley (1995) report that the average knowledge of environmentalists and anti-environmentalists does not differ from each other, regardless of the fact that the two groups showed polarized attitudes regarding environmental topics.

The above does not imply that environmental knowledge is useless. It only means that this knowledge is insufficient to produce the expected sustainable actions. We cannot anticipate a change in people's behavior by simply providing them with information, since their motives and other psychological prerequisites are also necessary to induce such a change. Yet, "insufficient" doe not means "unnecessary." An effective pro-environmental behavior is unviable without information regarding ecological problems, their origins and possible solutions. Thus, in order to act effectively, people first have to know the nature of the problems they face; second, they have to know the best procedures allowing them to cope with those problems, and finally they have to apply those procedures in an effective way (Corral-Verdugo, 1996; Frick *et al*, 2004).

Now, with regard to environmental skills, since more than a quarter-of-century ago, their importance as determinants of pro-environmental actions has been recognized. Smith-Sebasto and Fortner (1994), for instance, reported that pro-ecological skills are significantly related to environmentally protective behavior, and Boerschig and De Young (1993) established that skills for specific acting should be incorporated as goals in environmental education programs. Hines *et al*. (1987), in their famous meta-analysis, concluded that pro-environmental skills are significant predictors of pro-ecological behavior. Corral-Verdugo (1996), in a study conducted in Mexico, found that reuse and recycling skills were direct (and also indirect) determinants of those pro-environmental behaviors. Skills not only directly affected reuse and recycling but also had an indirect influence on those behaviors, mediated through conservation motives. Pro-environmentally skilled individuals were the most motivated for conserving the environment, and this motivation reinforced conservationist practices. Martinportugués, Canto & Hombrados (2007), in Spain, found that socio-economic status influenced the acquisition of waste-separation skills: the poorer were more effective than the richer in displaying those capacities. In addition, Bustos, Flores, & Andrade (2004) reported that water conservation skills significantly and positively influence the practice of water conservation behaviors in residential settings, as Corral-Verdugo (2002) also found.

Pro-environmental skills are so important in educational programs that developing these capacities is central to the Environmental Education (EE) definition (UNESCO, 1987). Internationally, a number of educational systems consider pro-environmental skills as requisites in their curricular schemes (Chu *et al*, 2007; Grodzinska-Jurczak, Bartosiewicz & Twardowska, 2003). Reports in the relevant literature include experiences and recommendations for developing these skills in varied scenarios such as the training of mining engineers (Van Berker, 2000), children at schools (Jiménez-Aleixandre, 2002), farmers (Curry & Winter, 2000), and employees in varied productive enterprises (Ramus, 2002), among many others.

One limitation of pro-environmental skills is their *invariance*. An invariant behavior is always performed the same way before any circumstance; in other words, this skilled behavior does not change even if the stimuli instigating it do change (Corral-Verdugo, 2001). Since environmental problems change constantly, the solving-problem effective responses should change as well, producing versatile sets of skills in response to environmental conservation requirements.

One more limitation is that most skill-training strategies focus more on tasks and its efficient nature, than on the *requirements* (i.e, demands, challenges) established for achieving efficient behavior (Corral-Verdugo, 2001). It is rare finding systems for skill training that integrate motivational factors, normative demands, values and attitudes to facilitate pro-ecological action (Boyatzis, 1982). This integration is important since people need incentives and goals for displaying their skills in addition to be merely trained to possess these skills. As much as knowledge is insufficient to guarantee the development of skills and behaviors, skills are not sufficient enough for displaying effective behaviors: the individual has to be willing and motivated to engage in those behaviors (De Young, 1996). A capacity of higher level than skills is required to make sure the emergence of sustainable behaviors. Such a capacity produces *variant* (i.e., changing) responses before changes in environmental conditions, also integrating motivational factors and additional dispositional variables as requirements for sustainable actions. This capacity is called *pro-environmental competency*.

PRO-ENVIRONMENTAL COMPETENCY

Environmental competency (EC) is the general capacity to effectively responding in a stimulant manner before environmental opportunities (Steele, 1980). Pedersen (1999), by considering this definition, states that EC is about environmental learning, in a way that the individual gets adapted to her/his surroundings; but he also considers that this competency could lead to environmental conservation. White (1959) had defined competency as an "organism capacity to effectively deal with the environment," implying that a competent individual is, necessarily, skilled in dealing with problems in his/her surroundings. Yet, for White, competency was not just a bunch of skills possessed by the organism, since he recognized a motivational component implicit in that capacity. A competent person not only exhibits skills, but also feels predisposed to display them in response to a requirement or demand. Additional authors agree with the idea that competency involves the display of psychological dimensions other than merely skills in problem-solving situations (Boyatzis, 1982; De Young, 1996; Corral-Verdugo, 2002; Homburg & Stolberg, 2006). Our model of pro-environmental competency considers those additional components.

EC implies recognizing situational affordances that make adaptive responses possible (Gibson, 1979). Situations are made from sets of *adaptive problems*, which sometimes function as demands, and some more as challenges (see Hill et al.'s chapter, this volume). In any case, in order to produce an adaptive response it is necessary that the environment affords clues and that the organism recognizes those clues. Consequently, the individual would act, solving a problem, obtaining a benefit or avoiding a negative situation.

As in other instances of effective behavior, these aspects indicate that the human ability to deal with environmental challenges has two facets: one that is able to produce environmentally destructive behaviors, while the other might result in sustainable actions. Hill (2008) suggests that a key for understanding the difference between these two facets is found in the type of adaptive problems faced by people, and the way these problems are perceived. Since the EC notion conceives environmental problems as challenges or demands requiring effective actions for environmental conservation, human abilities or skills are expected to respond in the direction of environmental preservation while also avoiding ecologically destructive behaviors. In order to illustrate how EC becomes pro-environmental, let's clarify what pro-environmental competency is.

Corral-Verdugo (2002, p. 535) defines *pro-environmental competency* (PEC) as "...the capacity to effectively responding to environmental conservation requirements." EC consists of a set of skills that are displayed before problems faced by individuals. However, according to this author, in identifying a competency, solving-problem skills are as important as the demands and challenges for environmental conservation that the individual encounters. In other words, possessing environmentally protective skills is useless if conservationist requirements are no present. Homburg and Stolberg (2006), and Homburg, Stolberg & Wagner (2007), in illustrating this situation, claim that the remedy and control of environmental problems could only be achieved by combining the personal "responsibilities" (i.e., requirements) with the (environmental) capacities that individuals are able to display. "Responsibilities" would include environmental norms and values as well as perceived stressors resulting from environmental deterioration. Thus, according to Hamburg and its collaborators, a competency implies the capacity to responding effectively before the assumed environmental responsibilities.

Environmental motives, attitudes and beliefs are psychological factors functioning as personal pro-environmental requirements (Corral-Verdugo, 2002). When Steele (1980) talks about "responding in a stimulant and effective way," he refers –as White (1959) does- to the fact that competencies include a motivational component. Boyatzis (1982) also considers a motivational element in these capacities, adding personal traits, self-image, social roles and individual and social knowledge, as well as situational factors demanding effective environmental actions, as requirements for effective action. More recently, Uzzell (1999) claims that, in order to be successful, an environmental education strategy intended to stimulate competent actions should consider the social, cultural and political context to facilitate participation and change. All of this means that pro-environmental requirements are to be found both at the individual (motives, beliefs, attitudes), and at the social (values, norms, access to resources) levels.

Another important aspect to consider in understanding the notion of competencies is its versatile character: These capacities allow individuals to adapt their effective actions to changes in environmental problems and demands. Unlike skills, which are mostly invariant, competencies can vary. A skill manifests itself the same way under any circumstance, while competencies adequate (i.e., change) their effective behaviors in response to environmental changes and problems. Such a property makes competencies to be ideal for facing one of the most distinctive traits of the ecological crisis: its changing nature. As the United Nations (UNEP, 2002) established, the next thirty years will be as crucial as the last 30 years were in shaping our environmental future. Old problems will persist and new challenges will be generated as heavier demands for natural resources are produced. These new demands and challenges will require novel solutions to emerge from pro-environmentally competent citizens. Providing individuals with a stock of basic pro-environmental skills is necessary. Moreover, teaching how to apply those skills before changing requirements and demands, and how to produce new abilities in response to variations in environmental problems is also necessary (Corral-Verdugo, Varela & González, 2004).

Corral-Verdugo (2002), in an empirical study, found that water conservation skills significantly correlated with a series of dispositional factors (perceptions, attitudes and motives regarding water consumption) and with situational factors (access to water), both identified as "pro-environmental requirements." The skills-requirements correlation allowed his modeling a higher-order factor, which he identified as "pro-environmental competency." This factor, in turn, directly and saliently predicted water conservation behaviors. Therefore, the idea that PEC indicates a correspondence between pro-environmental requirements and skills found empirical support in these data. Incidentally, these findings also support the pertinence of the environmental education goals, as defined by UNESCO (1987). A diagnostic study on pro-environmental competency in children (Fraijo, 2002) had revealed low levels of environmental knowledge and skills, moderate levels of pro-ecological motives and higher scores of pro-environmental beliefs. Water conservation behaviors assessed in Fraijo's study did not inter-relate, nor did the dispositional variables. No correlation between these dispositional variables and the conservationist behaviors was either found. Thus, no evidence of competency in these children emerged. The author concluded that an interventional program is required to raise the levels of pro-environmental skills, requirements and behaviors and that such a program should also result in significant interrelations among those variables in order to produce the expected PEC.

STUDY'S GOAL AND HYPOTHESES

Since environmental competency is a key psychological factor in the development of sustainable behavior, we were interested in testing a model of PEC in elementary-school students. Children are a special target for environmental education programs and we wanted to know if generating such a higher-order capacity would be possible by using an educational strategy. Based on Corral-Verdugo's (2002) model, PEC was conceived as a latent variable emerging from the correlation between pro-environmental skills and requirements. Thus, in addition to assessing those skills, we measured environmental motives, beliefs and knowledge.

The study's general objective was to demonstrate that an educational interventional strategy would induce water conservation competency, a latent variable constructed from significant correlations between pro-environmental skills and its requirements for conserving water. Water conservation is one of the most important sustainable behaviors in view of the growing planetary scarcity of that vital liquid and its contribution to human existence and wellbeing (Bergkamp & Sadoff, 2008). In our study, three phases were considered: 1) Diagnostic evaluation, 2) Intervention, and 3) Impact evaluation. The specific objectives for the diagnostic evaluation were: 1a) to estimate the levels of pro-environmental beliefs, knowledge, motives, skills and behavior among the studied children; and 1b) to assess possible inter-relations among those variables, so that they indicate the presence of PEC. For the interventional phase the aim was 2a) to develop water conservation competency by implementing an environmental education program. Finally, for the impact evaluation phase, the objectives were: 3a) to estimate the presence of water conservation competency resulting from the interventional program, 3b) to replicate the PEC model (Corral-Verdugo, 2002) at the end of the intervention and, 3c) to determine the impact of the environmental education program on children's capacities and behaviors.

The hypotheses were: 1) water conservation competencies, assessed as skills responding to pro-environmental requirements (knowledge, beliefs and motives) will not be present in children before the interventional program; 2) the implementation of an environmental education program will result in the development of water conservation competencies.

METHOD

Participants

Diagnostic and Impact phases. One hundred and eighteen first-graders at two elementary randomly-selected schools in Hermosillo (N=60) and Ciudad Obregón (N=58), Mexico, participated in this study. Seventy three children were females and the rest were males; their age ranged between 6 and 7 years old.

Intervention phase. Fifty-nine children, out of the total 118, participated in this phase. A half of participants were randomly assigned into one experimental group, while the remaining were part of the control group. The experimental group received a 40-hour environmental-education course consisting of information regarding water issues, the training in water conservation skills, and the promotion of favorable attitudes towards water conservation.

Instruments

Two instruments were used; one was a questionnaire consisting of five scales administered to all children, the other was an observational recording of water consumption at home.

Questionnaire. This instrument consisted of four scales and a set of items indicating demographic variables.

Beliefs regarding water conservation. This scale measures beliefs concerning water availability on the planet and in the city, ideas regarding water renewability, the "falsity" that water is scarce and the need of imposing limits to the use of this resource. The instrument allows responses from 0 (do not agree) to 4 (completely agree).

Knowledge of water topics. This scale assesses basic information on uses of water, its physical states, and its sources of pollution. Correct responses are graded as 1, while the incorrect ones receive 0.

Water conservation skills. The scale measures effective responses to water conservation questions. Problems such as how to wash cars and dishes, water gardens, take a shower, wash hands, brush tooth, and drinking, by saving water, are asked. Correct water conservation options are graded as 1, so that no limits are imposed on the number of effective possible ways to conserve water that children are able to indicate.

Motives for conserving water. These items include reasons for conserving and consuming water, the difficulty in having access to water, and the personal commitment to conserve water and the environment. Students indicated how much did they agree with those reasons in a 0 (do not agree) to 4 (completely agree) scale.

The demographic information obtained included, age, gender, family size and income.

Observational recording of water use. This instrument measures five basic activities in which water is consumed. Activities are observed and registered by an adult, related to the participant child, during three days at home. Frequency (of use of toilet, and of water drinking, for instance) and time (invested in washing dishes, and in taking a shower, for instance) are recorded. Table 4 shows the observations considered in the observational recording.

Procedure

Diagnostic phase. The informed consent to participate was obtained from parents, teachers and schools' principals. Children were told the aims and the importance of the study, asking for their cooperation. An invitation letter and the informed consent form were delivered to parents, also asking for their cooperation to fill out the observational recording sheets. Children were individually interviewed in order to administer the questionnaire.

Intervention phase. The educational program was designed and conducted by considering results obtained in the diagnostic phase. The main instructional aspects were identified; those were related to teaching water conservation practices in personal hygiene, physiological and home cleanup activities involving water use. The educational program included: a) general objective, b) development of thematic units, c) identification of competencies and sub-competencies for each unit, d) design of activities, e) a list of materials, f) design of evaluations, g) estimation of time required for conducting the program and its activities, and h) the dates for the intervention. Every activity was followed by an evaluation conducted during the instructional process.

Data Analysis

Cronbach's alphas indicating internal consistency of the used scales were computed, and univariate analyses for individual variables (questionnaire items, behavioral observations) were obtained. Confirmatory factor analyses were conducted to obtain indicators of convergent construct validity for the used scales. Before the intervention, the model of pro-environmental competency was specified and tested using structural equations through the EQS statistical software (Bentler, 2006). In this model, five first-order factors (knowledge, skills, beliefs, motives, and water consumption) were specified. Based on Fraijo's (2002) results, no significant interrelations among these first-order factors were expected, indicating a lack of pro-environmental competency in the pre-intervention phase. Using statistical contrasting (*Student's t, chi-squared*) in the diagnostic phase, we verified that groups were not significantly different in demographic variables, levels of pro-environmental skills and requirements, to make sure that the impact evaluation reflected the expected changes in competencies as a result of the intervention.

Table 1. Univariate statistics and Cronbach's alphas of the used scales in the diagnostic phase of the study

Scales/Items	Diagnostic Evaluation					
	N	Mean	SD	Min.	Max.	Alpha.
Water Ecological Beliefs						00
Water never will exhaust	118	1.9	1.9	0	4	
Water lacks in the city	118	2.5	1.8	0	4	
Water will exhaust in a long time	118	2.6	1.8	0	4	
Water will exhaust if we don't care	118	3.2	1.5	0	4	
Use water when need it	118	1.7	1.9	0	4	
Raise water bill to conserve it	118	2.2	1.9	0	4	
Water Knowledge						.35
Watering plants	118	.16	.36	0	1	
Water as steam	118	.22	.44	0	1	
Water as a liquid	118	.16	.37	0	1	
Water as a solid	118	.28	.45	0	1	
Water pollution	118	.27	.45	0	1	
Conservation skills						.69
In washing a car	118	.88	.67	0	3	
In watering plants	118	.50	.62	0	3	
In taking a shower	118	.71	.55	0	2	
In washing dishes	118	.84	.71	0	3	
In tooth-brushing	118	.82	.53	0	2	
In washing hands	118	.75	.55	0	2	
In drinking water	118	.56	.51	0	2	
Conservation Motives						.39
Other persons conserve water	118	2.9	1.6	0	4	
It is difficult having access to water	118	3.2	1.4	0	4	
Likes conserving water	118	3.6	.90	0	4	
Want people to conserve water	118	3.6	.90	0	4	
Family conserves water	118	3.5	1.1	0	4	
Water Consumption						.48
Minutes washing dishes	118	5.7	4.0	0	20	
Minutes tooth-brushing	118	2.3	1.7	0	12	
Minutes washing sidewalk	118	1.7	1.8	0	12	
Times went to the toilet	118	2.5	1.3	0	5	
Minutes washing hands	118	2.2	1.3	0	7	

In order to assess significant differences between the diagnostic evaluation and the impact evaluation, *t*-tests were conducted, revealing a possible effect of the educational program on the experimental group. These differences were also assessed by contrasting the performance of the experimental group against the control students after implementing the program. Again, the PEC model was evaluated after the intervention, based on the five first-order factors interrelations; these interrelations were assumed to indicate the presence of the pro-environmental competency second-order factor. Implicit in this analysis was the hypothesis testing of an effect of the educational program on the emergence of PEC in the studied children.

RESULTS

Diagnostic Evaluation

Table 1 shows the internal consistency of the instruments administered before the intervention program. The only scale exhibiting an acceptable reliability level was the one assessing pro-environmental skills (alpha = .69). The remaining produced alphas of lower (and unacceptable) level. In addition, the means of the scale items are below the average level (i.e., the medium point between the maximum and the minimum scores). The observational recording showed that children invested around two minutes in tooth-brushing and washing their hands while letting water running. This time increased up to an average of five minutes in washing dishes. Children also exhibited a minimum knowledge regarding water issues, and low levels of conservation skills. Their pro-ecological beliefs ranged from low to moderate, while the levels of motives were high. Table 2 includes results of the confirmatory factor analysis performed on the scales' data. Factor loadings were not significant ($p < .05$) in all cases, revealing a lack of convergent validity in every assessed factor.

This result was confirmed in the structural equation model, which produced non-significant loadings (indicated by dotted arrows in figure 1) of scales' items on their first-order factors: beliefs, motives, skills and water consumption. The structural model also revealed an absence of factor interrelations, since the structural influence of pro-environmental competency on its first-order factors is not manifested. This also indicates that PEC has not been integrated as a behavioral capacity in the studied children. Goodness of fit indicators revealed a lack of correspondence between the data and the presumed model of interrelations.

Impact Evaluation

As Table 3 shows, the internal consistency of the used scales increased after the treatment, indicating a significant improvement in their reliability. Scores from the knowledge, beliefs, and skills scales also increased substantially after the implementation of the educational program. A confirmatory factor analysis revealed that all loadings connecting the five factors with their corresponding items were high and significant (see Table 4).

Table 2. Lambda (λ) matrix of factor loadings from the diagnostic evaluation

Variables	F1	F2	F3	F4	F5
Water never will exhaust	.53*				
Water lacks in the city	.20				
Water will exhaust in a long time	-.18				
Water will exhaust if we don't take care	.39*				
Raise water bill to conserve it	44*				
In washing a car		.44*			
In watering plants		.41*			
In taking a shower		.50*			
In washing dishes		.70*			
In tooth-brushing		.60*			
In washing hands		.75*			
In drinking water		.43*			
Other persons conserve water			.44*		
It is difficult having access to water			.01		
Likes conserving water			.48*		
Want people to conserve water			.37*		
Family conserves water			.52*		
Watering plants				.03	
Water as steam				.25*	
Water as a liquid				.30*	
Water as solid				.78*	
Water pollution				.08	
Minutes washing dishes					.88*
Minutes tooth-brushing					.25*
Minutes washing sidewalk					.02
Times went to the toilet					.15
Minutes washing hands					.36*

* Significant (p <.05) loadings.
F1 = Beliefs, F2 = Skills, F3 = Motives, F4 = Knowledge, F5 = Water consumption.

Figure 2 exhibits the PEC structural equation model results after the implementation of the educational program. This model shows practical goodness of fit, indicating that the data support the theoretical model of relations between water conservation competency and its first-order factors. The significant interrelations between pro-ecological skills, knowledge, motives and beliefs made possible the emergence of the PEC second-order factor, as predicted. PEC negatively influenced water consumption, indicating that the higher the pro-environmental competency, the lower the water use. The "treatment" variable added to this model was included as a means to increase the variability of the data, so that the total sample (experimental and control groups) were considered in this analysis. The values for this variable were 1 (being part of the experimental group) and 0 (being part of the control group). A high, significant and positive structural coefficient was produced from the treatment variable on PEC, indicating that this competency was significantly higher in those children receiving the environmental education program.

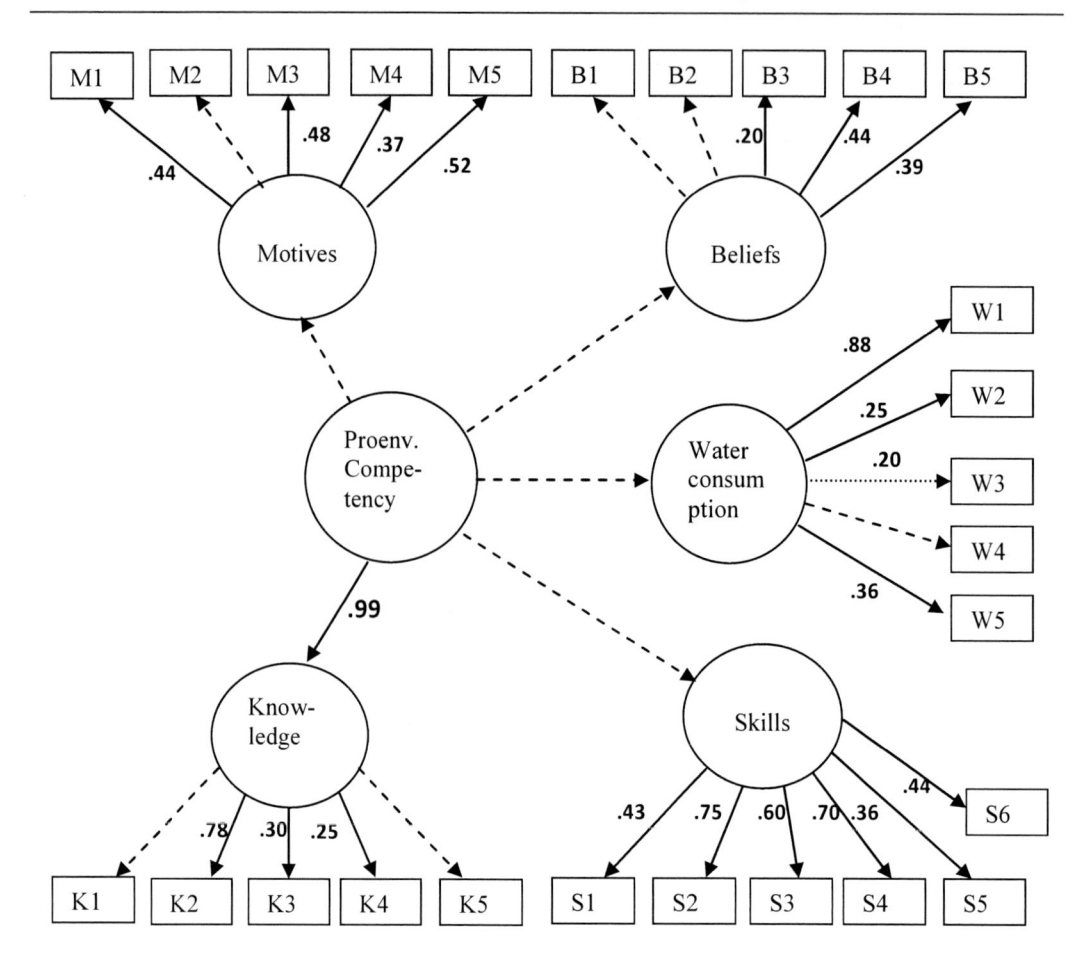

Figure 1. Diagnostic evaluation results of the PEC model. Dotted arrows indicate non-significant ($p > .05$) factor loadings and structural coefficients. Goodness of fit: $X^2 = 363.88$ (94 df), $p=.003$; $NNFI=.68$, $CFI=.71$, $RMSEA=.05$.

Table 5 shows significant differences between the diagnostic and impact evaluations of children's performances and dispositional pro-environmental variables. Those differences manifested as increased levels of beliefs, knowledge and skills after the treatment, and a lower consumption of water. The variability of skilled responses also increased as a consequence of the educational program. Maximum levels of skills rose from 3 (in the diagnostic phase) to 4 (after the treatment), implying a more diversified set of effective responses before water conservation requirements. Pro-ecological motives did not change after the intervention (they were already high before the program implementation). The differences between the control and experimental groups, after implementing the educational program, are shown in Table 6. Levels of beliefs, motives, skills and knowledge are significantly higher in the experimental group. Unexpectedly, no significant differences between treatment and control groups appeared in water consumption, since the control group decreased their water consumption (from mean=3.13 to mean=2.42) almost as much as the experimental group did (from 3.14 to 2.09).

Table 3. Univariate statistics and Cronbach's alphas of the used scales after the treatment phase*

Scales/Items	\multicolumn{5}{c}{Impact evaluation}				
	N	Mean (SD)	Min.	Max.	Alpha.
Water Ecological Beliefs					.87
Water never will exhaust	59	2.1(1.7)	0	4	
Water lacks in the city	59	2.5(1.8)	0	4	
Water will exhaust in a long time	59	2.6(1.8)	0	4	
Water will exhaust if we don't care	59	3.2(1.5)	0	4	
Use water when need it	59	2.4(1.7)	0	4	
Raise water bill to conserve	59	2.2(1.8)	0	4	
Water Knowledge					.77
Watering plants	59	.50 (.49)	0	1	
Water as steam	59	.54(.50)	0	1	
Water as a liquid	59	.55(.50)	0	1	
Water as a solid	59	.62(.48)	0	1	
Water pollution	59	.49(.50)	0	1	
Conservation Skills					.94
In washing a car	59	2.3(1.5)	0	4	
In watering plants	59	1.7(1.2)	0	4	
In taking a shower	59	1.3(.70)	0	2	
In washing dishes	59	2.1(1.6)	0	4	
In tooth-brushing	59	1.4(.60)	0	4	
In washing hands	59	1.2(.70)	0	2	
In drinking water	59	1.2(.70)	0	2	
Conservation Motives					.88
Other persons conserve water	59	2.3(1.8)	0	4	
It is difficult having access to water	59	2.4(1.8)	0	4	
Likes conserving water	59	2.8(1.7)	0	4	
Want people to conserve water	59	2.9(1.6)	0	4	
Family conserves water	59	2.7(1.8)	0	4	
Water Consumption					.59
Minutes washing dishes	59	3.1(1.2)	0	20	
Minutes tooth-brushing	59	1.1(1.2)	0	6	
Minutes washing sidewalk	59	0.4(1.5)	0	10	10
Times went to the toilet	59	2.4(1.4)	0	4	
Minutes washing hands	59	1.3(1.5)	0	8	

*Results reflect responses obtained from the experimental group.

Table 4. Lambda (λ) matrix of factor loadings from the impact evaluation. Results reflect responses obtained from the experimental group

Variables	F1	F2	F3	F4	F5
Water never will exhaust	.64				
Water lacks in the city	.76				
Water will exhaust in a long time	.74				
Water will exhaust if we don't take care	.80				
Raise water bill to conserve it	.66				
In washing a car		.95			
In watering plants		.92			
In taking a shower		.88			
In washing dishes		.93			
In tooth-brushing		.83			
In washing hands		.83			
In drinking water		.81			
Other persons conserve water			.66		
It is difficult having access to water			.66		
Likes conserving water			.90		
Want people to conserve water			.84		
Family conserves water			.82		
Watering plants				.62	
Water as steam				.79	
Water as a liquid				.59	
Water as solid				.61	
Water pollution				.56	
Minutes washing dishes					.63
Minutes tooth-brushing					.84
Minutes washing sidewalk					.47
Times went to the toilet					.34
Minutes washing hands					.51

F1 = Beliefs, F2 = Skills, F3 = Motives, F4 = Knowledge, F5 = Water consumption.
All factor loadings are significant ($p < .05$).

Table 5. Mean differences in assessed variables, before and after the treatment in the experimental group

	Diagnostic Evaluation		Impact Evaluation		t	$Pr < t$
Variables	Mean	SD	Mean	SD		
Beliefs	1.8	0.7	2.5	1.4	2.12	.0001
Knowledge	0.2	0.2	0.6	0.3	10.8	.0001
Skills	0.7	0.3	1.6	0.9	4.80	.0001
Motives	3.4	0.68	3.0	0.9	1.03	N.S.
Consumption	2.2	0.97	1.4	1.4	1.00	.0001

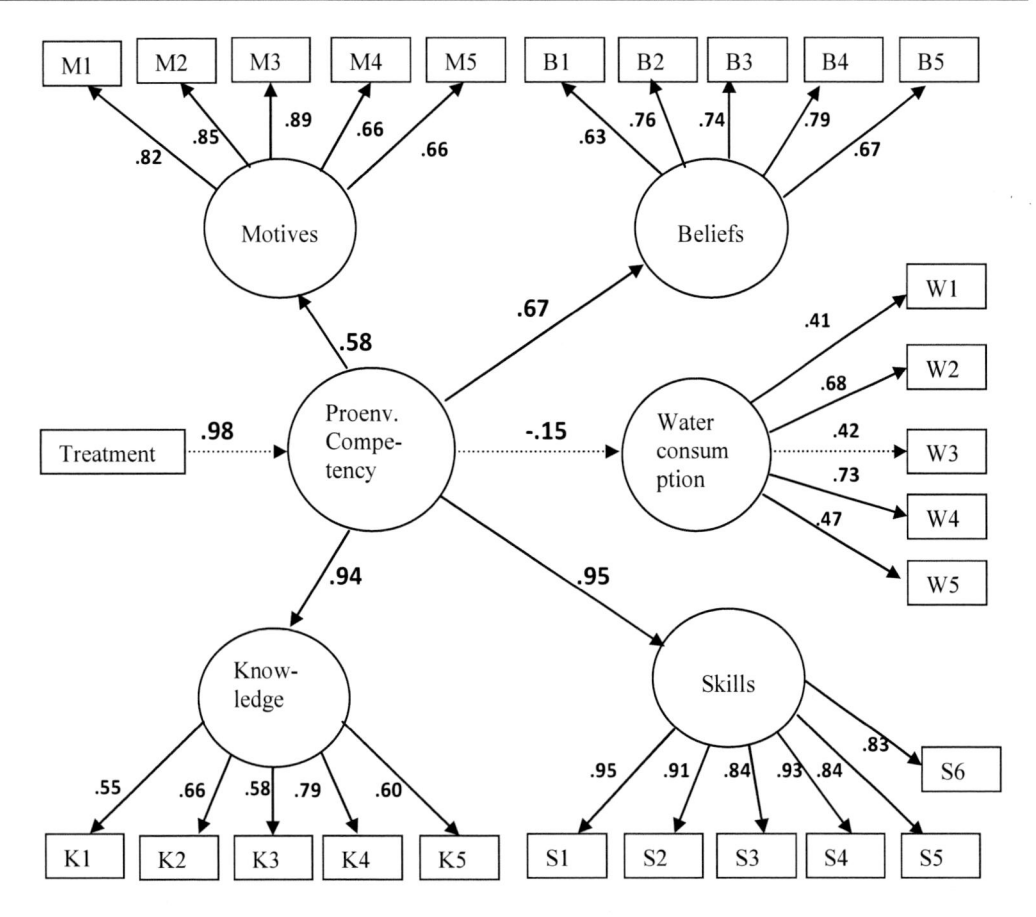

Figure 2. The PEC structural model after the program implementation. All factor loadings and structural coefficients are significant ($p < .05$). Goodness of fit: $X^2 =$ 479.78 (294 df), $p<.001$; $NNFI=.91$, $CFI=.92$; $RMSEA=.06$.

CONCLUSION

This chapter discussed the importance of *effectiveness* as a relevant psychological dimension of sustainable behavior. To be sustainably-oriented, people have to be able to perform environmentally protective behaviors when facing pro-environmental requirements or demands. The conjunction of sustainable demands and abilities produce pro-environmental competency (PEC), one of the main goals of environmental education (Uzzell, 1999; UNESCO, 1987). Pro-ecological capacities are manifested as a set of skills (and their precedent environmental knowledge), while environmental requirements include personal pro-ecological motives, norms, attitudes and beliefs, as well as social and educational demands, among others. As a result, PEC manifests as versatile and effective problem-solving behaviors responding to environmental challenges and problems.

Since children are a special target for environmental education programs, we developed an educational strategy aimed at inducing pro-environmental competency in elementary school students. In evaluating results of its implementation we were based on Corral-Verdugo's (2002) PEC model, which he tested with an adult population without any educational intervention. In our study, we considered a diagnostic phase, assessing the levels of water conservation knowledge, skills, beliefs, motives, as well as children's water consumption at home. After this evaluation, an educational program was designed and implemented, and a subsequent impact evaluation was conducted.

The diagnostic evaluation was important in generating information for the intervention plan. Results from this phase showed that, in absence of environmental education training, low values of ecological knowledge, skills and beliefs were the norm, and a poor internal consistency was found in students' responses to our instruments. A low convergence of items responses on their corresponding factors revealed a lack of validity for the instruments before the intervention. Also, a disintegrated set of pro-environmental skills and requirements made not possible the emergence of a water conservation competency, since the correlations between behavioral capacities (i.e., skills, knowledge) and their demands (i.e., beliefs, motives) were not present. Therefore, we conclude that this competency was inexistent before the implementation of the educational program.

We had hypothesized these results, following Fraijo's (2002) findings regarding the lack of pro-environmental competencies in children. We had also considered Anthony and Cohler's (1987) suggestion regarding the need of developing competency in children initiating their elementary school. According to these authors, generating environmental capacities at this level is relatively simple –as our experience instructed us- since children are able to reason, remember and practice conservationist skills and related information provided by an appropriate environmental education program. According to research results obtained in children (Phillips, Scarr & McCartney 1987; Houlares & Oden, 1990; Howes, 1990) the implementation of programs propitiating the development of behavioral capacities positively influences children's future success, their social and emotional competency and their verbal and intellectual development. Our results add pro-environmental competency to that list of positive outcomes. Nevertheless, since children differ from older individuals, we decided to design a tailored-information based program (Mosler and Martens, 2007) by considering the specific instructional needs that the diagnostic evaluation provided us.

Table 6. Mean differences in assessed variables between the experimental and control groups (impact evaluation)

	Experimental group		Control group		t	Pr < t
Variables	*Mean*	*SD*	*Mean*	*SD*		
Beliefs	3.3	0.6	1.5	1.4	8.63	<.0001
Knowledge	0.9	0.1	0.3	0.1	17.7	<.0001
Skills	2.5	0.2	1.9	0.5	24.7	<.0001
Motives	3.5	0.4	3.0	1.6	7.34	<.0001
Consumption	2.0	1.3	2.4	1.6	-1.2	N.S.

As the impact evaluation demonstrated, an increase in pro-ecological beliefs, motives, knowledge and skills, and a decrease in water consumption resulted in the experimental group after the implementation of the environmental education program. Skills resulted more diverse from the impact evaluation: children reported a higher number of possible effective solutions to water conservation requirements, as a consequence of their participation in the educational program. This is indicative of an important feature of pro-environmental competency: its versatility (Corral-Verdugo *et al*, 2004), which supports our PEC theoretical model. The experimental group also produced higher scores in beliefs, motives, knowledge and skills than the control group, as the impact evaluation demonstrated. Unexpectedly, the levels of water consumption were reduced almost equally in both groups, despite the fact that one group did not receive the environmental education training. We assume that the decreased consumption of water in the control group responded to their awareness of being investigated. Of course, it is likely that the experimental group also reasoned equally.

Very importantly, the educational program generated significant interrelationships among the studied variables, which made possible the emergence of the PEC factor in the impact evaluation phase. Therefore, we concluded that, in order to develop pro-environmental competencies, instructional programs have to guarantee coherence in teaching/training capacities, dispositional variables and behaviors. This coherence means that a correspondence should exist between the provision of skills and the specification of pro-ecological requirements. For instance, when instructing on how to conserve water in watering plants (skills), teachers also have to explicitly declare the problem to solve, and the conditions, procedures and tools for performing that task (information); the criteria or goal to reach (i.e., how much water to consume when performing the task); the positive reasons and outcomes related to engaging in such conservation behavior (motives); the social ideas that support water conservation (beliefs and norms); and related issues.

As Hungerford, Peyton & Wilke (1980) and the UNESCO (1987) established, the design and implementation of programs to generate environmental knowledge, skills, awareness, and participation are fundamental for the integral development of children. This impact goes beyond the purely intellectual aspects, implying positive attitudes, cooperation values, and abilities resulting in a view of nature as something to be respected. In the end, this process favors the formation of pro-environmentally competent and committed citizens.

Finally, although the assessment of children's' behavioral capacities and tendencies represent a thorough and complicate task, the implementation of objective and accurate measures of pro-environmental competency is still incomplete. These measures are integral and necessary in the development of educational programs, and improving their efficiency in assessing children's competency is a pending subject that environmental psychologists and educators should consider in prospective studies.

REFERENCES

Abrahamse, W., Steg, L., Vlek, C., & Rothengatter, J. A. (2007). The effect of tailored information, goal setting and feedback on household energy use, energy-related behaviors and behavioral determinants. *Journal of Environmental Psychology, 27*, 265-276.

Anthony, E J. & Cohler, B.J. (1987). *The invulnerable child.* New York: Guilford.

Bentler, P.M. (2006). *EQS 6 Structural Equations Program Manual.* Encino, CA: Multivariate Software Inc.

Bergkamp, G. & Sadoff, C. (2008). Water in a sustainable economy. En L. Starke (Ed.), *State of the World. Innovations for a Sustainable Economy.* New York: W.W. Norton & Company.

Boerschig, S. & De Young, R. (1993). Evaluation of selected recycling curricula: Educating the green citizen. *Journal of Environmental Education, 24*, 17-22.

Bonnes, M., & Bonaiuto, M. (2002). Environmental psychology: from spatial-physical environment to sustainable development. In R.B. Bechtel & A. Churchman (Eds.), *Handbook of Environmental Psychology* (pp. 28-54). New York: Wiley.

Boyatzis, R. E. (1982). *The competent manager*. New York: John Wiley.

Bustos, M., Flores, L.M. & Andrade, P. (2002). Motivos y percepción de riesgo como factores antecedentes a la conservación de agua en la ciudad de México [Motives and risk perception as water conservation antecedents in Mexico city]. In AMEPSO (Ed.), *La Psicología Social en México*, Vol. 9. Mexico: AMEPSO.

Chu, H., Lee, E., Ko, H., Shin, D., Lee, M., Min, B., & Kang, K. (2007). Korean Year 3 Children's Environmental Literacy: A prerequisite for a Korean environmental education curriculum. *International Journal of Science Education, 29*, 731-746.

Corral-Verdugo, V. (1996). A structural model of reuse and recycling behavior in Mexico. *Environment and Behavior, 28*, 665-696.

Corral-Verdugo, V. (2001). *Comportamiento Proambiental [Pro-environmental Behavior]*. Santa Cruz de Tenerife, Spain: Editorial Resma.

Corral-Verdugo, V. (2002). A structural model of pro-environmental competency. *Environment & Behavior*. 34, 531-549.

Corral-Verdugo, V., Bonnes, M., Tapia, C., Fraijo, B., Frías, M., & Carrus, G. (2009). Correlates of pro-sustainability orientation: the Affinity Towards Diversity. *Journal of Environmental Psychology, 29*, 34-43.

Corral-Verdugo, V. & Pinheiro, J. (2004). Aproximaciones al estudio de la conducta sustentable [Approaches to the study of sustainable behavior]. *Medio Ambiente y Comportamiento Humano, 5*, 1-26.

Corral-Verdugo, V., Varela, C., & González, D. (2004). O papel da Psicología Ambiental na promoçao de competencia pró-ambiental [The role of environmental psychology in promoting pro-environmental competency]. In E. Tassara, E. Rabinovich & M.C. Guedes (Eds.), *Psicología e Ambiente*. Sao Paulo, Brazil: EDUC.

Curry, N. & Winter, M. (2000). European briefing: the transition to environmental agriculture in Europe: learning processes and knowledge networks. *European Planning Studies, 8*, 107-121.

Cutter-Mackenzie, A., & Smith, R. (2003). Ecological literacy: the 'missing paradigm' in environmental education (part one). *Environmental Education Research, 9*, 497-524.

Day, J. (2004). *Connections: Combining Environmental Education and Artwork in the Primary Grades for Sustainability*. Tesis inédita de maestría en Educación. Phoenix, AZ: University of Phoenix.

De Young, R. (1996). Some psychological aspects of a reduced consumption lifestyle: The role of intrinsic satisfaction and competence motivation. *Environment & Behavior, 28*, 358-409.

Fraijo, B. (2002). La educación proambiental basada en competencias proecológicas [Environmental education based upon pro-ecological competencies]. In V. Corral-Verdugo (Ed.), *Conductas Protectoras del Ambiente*. Mexico: Consejo Nacional de Ciencia y Tecnología (CONACyT).

Frick, J., Kaiser, F.G. & Wilson, M. (2004). Environmental knowledge and conservation behavior: Exploring prevalence and structure in a representative sample. *Personality and Individual Differences, 37*, 1597-1613.

Geller, E.S. (2002). The challenge of increasing pro-environment behavior. In R.B. Bechtel and A. Churchman (Eds.), *Handbook of Environmental Psychology*. New York: Wiley.

Gibson, J.J. (1979). *The ecological approach to visual perception*. Boston: Houghton Mifflin.

Gifford, R. (2007). *Environmental psychology: principles and practice (4th Ed)*. Colville, WA: Optimal Books.

Grodzinska-Jurczak, M., Bartosiewicz, A. & Twardowska, A. (2003). Evaluating the impact of a school waste education programme upon students', parents' and teachers' environmental knowledge, attitudes and behavior. *International Research in Geographic and Environmental Education, 12*, 106-122.

Hardin, G. (1993). *Living without limits: ecology, economics, and population taboos*. New York: Oxford University Press.

Harland, P., & Staats, H. (2001). Striving for Sustainability via Behavioral Modification at the Household Level: Psychological Aspects and Effectiveness. In D. de Vuyst, L. Hens, & W. de Lannoy (Eds.), *How Green is the city? Sustainability Assessment at the Local Level*. New York: Columbia University Press.

Hill, D. (2008). *Situational control of pro/antienvironmental behavior*. Unpublished doctoral dissertation. Tucson, AZ: University of Arizona.

Hines, J.M., Hungerford, H.R., & Tomera, A.N. (1986). Analysis and synthesis of research on responsible environmental behavior: A meta-analysis. *Journal of Environmental Education, 18*, 1-18.

Homburg, A. & Stolberg, A. (2006). Explaining pro-environmental behavior with a cognitive theory of stress. *Journal of Environmental Psychology, 26*, 1-14.

Homburg, A., Stolberg, A. & Wagner, U. (2007). Coping with global environmental problems. Development and first validation of scales. *Environment & Behavior, 39*, 754-778.

Hormuth, S. (1999). Social meaning and social context of environmentally relevant behavior: shopping, wrapping and disposing. *Journal of Environmental Psychology, 19*, 277-286.

Hungerford, H., Peyton, R., & Wilke, R. (1980). Goals for curriculum development in environmental education. *Journal of Environmental Education*, 11, 42-47.

Houlares, J., & Oden, S. (1990). *A follow-up study of Head Start's role in the lives of children and families*. Interim Report. Ypsilianti, MI: High/Scope Educational Research Foundation.

Howes, C. (1990) Can the age of entry into child care and the quality of child care predict adjustment in kindergarten? *Developmental Psychology*, 26, 292-303.

Jackson, T. (2008). The challenge of sustainable lifestyles. In Starke, L. (Ed.), *State of the World*. New York, W. W. Norton & Company.

Jiménez-Aleixandre, M.P. (2002). Knowledge producers or knowledge consumers? Argumentation and decision making about environmental management. *International Journal of Science Education, 24*, 1171-1190.

Kempton, W., Boster, J.S., & Hartley, J.A. (1995). *Environmental Values in American Culture*. Cambridge, MA, MIT Press.

Kollmuss, A., & Agyeman, J. (2002). Mind the Gap: why do people act environmentally and what are the barriers to pro-environmental behavior? *Environmental Education Research, 8*, 239-260.

Kreuter, M. W., Farrell, D., Olevitch, L. & Brennan, L. (1999). *Tailored health messages: Customizing communication with computer technology.* Mahwah, NJ: Lawrence Erlbaum.

Kurz, T. (2000). The psychology of environmentally sustainable behavior: fitting together pieces of the puzzle. *Analysis of Social issues and Public Policy, 2*, 257-278.

Laurian, L. (2003). A prerequisite for participation. Environmental knowledge and what residents know about local toxic sites. *Journal of Planning Education and Research, 22*, 257-269.

Martinportugués, C., Canto, J. & Hombrados, M.I. (2007). Habilidades pro-ambientales en la separación y depósito de residuos sólidos urbanos [Pro-environmental skills in solid waste separation and disposition]. *Medio Ambiente y Comportamiento Humano, 8*, 71-92.

MEA (2005). *Millennium ecosystem assessment synthesis report.* Retrieved February 21, 2009 from www.millenniumassessment.org.

Meinhold, J., & Malkus, A. (2005). Adolescent environmental behaviors. Can knowledge, attitudes, and self-efficacy make a difference? *Environment & Behavior, 37*, 511-532.

Mosler, H., & Martens, T. (2007). Designing environmental campaigns by using agent-based simulations: Strategies for changing environmental attitudes. *Journal of Environmental Management, 88*, 805-816.

Pedersen, D. (1999). Dimensions of environmental competence. *Journal of Environmental Psychology, 19*, 303-308.

Phillips, D.A., Scarr, S., & McCartney, K. (1987). Dimensions and effects of child care quality: The Bermuda Study. In D.A. Phillips (Ed.), *Quality in child care: What does research tell us?* Washington, DC: National Association for the Education of Young Children.

Pooley, J., & O'Connor, M. (2000). Environmental education and attitudes. *Environment & Behavior, 32*, 711-723.

Ramus, C. (2002). Encouraging environmental innovative actions: what companies and managers must do. *Journal of World Business, 37*, 151-164.

Smith-Sebasto, N.J. y Fortner, R.W. (1994). The environmental action internal control index. *Journal of Environmental Education, 25*, 23-29.

Steele, F. (1980). Defining and developing environmental competence. *Advances in Experimental Social Processes, 2*, 225-244.

UNEP -United Nations Environment Programme (2002). *Synthesis Global Environment Outlook 3.* Retrieved August 2008 from the site: http://www.grida.no/geo/geo3/english/pdfs/synthesis.pdf.

UNESCO (1987). Environmental education in the light of the Tblisi Conference. Paris: UNESCO.

Uzzell, D. (1999). Education for Environmental Action in the Community: new roles and relationships. *Cambridge Journal of Education, 29*, 397-413.

Van Berker, R. (2000). Integrating the environmental and sustainable development agendas into mineral education. *Journal of Cleaner production, 8*, 413-423.

White, R. V. (1959). Motivation reconsidered: The concept of competence. *Psychological Review, 66*, 297-333.

In: Psychological Approaches to Sustainability
Editors: V. Corral-Verdugo et al.

ISBN 978-1-60876-356-6
© 2010 Nova Science Publishers, Inc.

Chapter 13

EMOTIONS AND PRO-ENVIRONMENTAL BEHAVIOR

César Tapia-Fonllem[*], *Victor Corral-Verdugo*
Departamento de Psicología, Universidad de Sonora, Mexico

Claudia Gutiérrez-Sida
Universidad Veracruzana, Mexico

José Mireles-Acosta
Universidad Autónoma de Sinaloa, Mexico

Hugo Tirado-Medina
Universidad Autónoma de Nuevo León, Mexico

ABSTRACT

Emotions are a fundamental component of human psychological functioning, yet the study of their contribution in explaining a number of behavioral facets (sustainable behavior included) has been traditionally neglected. Evolutionary and environmental psychologists stress the role played by emotions as factors facilitating human adaptive behaviors. Affective responses resulting from evolved emotions afford and incite approaches to nutritional objects, wellbeing and sex, and avoidance from danger and physical harm. These feelings promote pleasure, displeasure, activation, and related states making the survival of individuals possible. The question is whether or not emotions conduce to sustainable behaviors, which are conceived as adaptive actions allowing the long-term survival of our species. According to the pertinent literature there is a positive response to such a question: sustainable behaviors are clearly influenced by *affective-emotional* factors; nonetheless the emphasis of most explanatory models is only on the *rational* determinants of such behaviors. Previous research shows that affinity towards nature, happiness, satisfaction, empathy, interest in nature, biophilia, and affinity towards bio and socio-diversity are positive emotional states promoting sustainable actions.

---

[*] This chapter was funded by the Mexican Council of Science of Technology (CONACyT, grant 48466. Correspondence: César Tapia-Fonllem, Naranja 41, Residencial Villa California, Hermosillo, Sonora, 83114, Mexico. E-mail: ctapiaf@itson.mx.

Although some negative emotions, such as personal distress and fear, sometimes inhibit sustainable behaviors, others, as guilt, shame and indignation due to insufficient environmental protection seem to promote pro-ecological activities. Emotions also influence intentions to act in sustainable ways. Since these intentions induce pro-environmental behavior, the effect of emotions on sustainable actions is both direct and indirect. A study was conducted to illustrate the way emotions influence pro-environmental behaviors. Four-hundred and fifty-five individuals living in three Mexican cities responded to an instrument assessing pro-environmental intentions, pro-ecological behavior, emotional interest in nature, feelings of indignation due to environmental deterioration, and affinity towards biodiversity. The three latter factors constituted a second-order latent variable, which we labeled "environmental emotions." A structural equation model revealed that pro-environmental intentions affect pro-ecological behavior, as expected, yet the influence of emotions on pro-ecological behavior was higher than the one promoted by intentions. The combined effect of emotions and intentions explained slightly more than half of pro-environmental behavior variance. The second-order emotional factor significantly influenced pro-environmental intentions in addition to its affecting pro-ecological behavior. Thus, the effects of these emotions on conservationist actions were both direct and indirect, as expected. Implications of these findings are discussed.

INTRODUCTION

The dominant approach in studying pro-environmental behavior seems to derive from a "rational-man model" (RMM). Such an approach is used in most theories and models in sustainable behavior research, as the Planned Action Theory (Ajzen, 1991), the Norm Activation Theory (Schwartz, 1973), and the Subjective Expected Utility Model (Kahneman, 2003), among others. According to Hill (2008), RMM's core assumptions are that most behaviors fall under voluntary control and, if the "system" (i.e., the organism) is provided with a correct combination of information, a logical and rational output should be produced. As a consequence, information is assumed to modify the central attributes of values, beliefs, attitudes and personal norms, which affect the intention to act (as Ajzen, 1991, stipulates). In turn, intention, as a rational process, should initiate pro-environmental (and other) behaviors.

Although RMM models are objective, straightforward and adequate explanations of people's sustainable conduct, there seems to be something missing in their premises and composition: These models assume that humans act primarily guided by reason although this does not always happen. The fact that intention to act explains around a third of pro-environmental behavior variance (Bamberg & Möser 2007) leads to ask where the explanation to the remaining two thirds is. Emotions are good candidates to account for, at least, a fraction of that unexplained variance (Pooley & O'Connor, 2000; Vinning & Ebreo, 2002).

Human psychological functioning consists of emotions, cognitions and behaviors, as practically everybody acknowledges. This tripartite composition covers the vast array of mental and behavioral activities characterizing human psychology. Emotions are not only an important component of human mind but also a relevant element influencing behavior and cognition while, at the same time, being affected by these two latter psychological facets (Nolan, 2002).

Sustainable actions are behaviors based on decisions (for instance, on intentions to act and other motivational indicators), that is why determining the rational and emotional aspects guiding pro-environmental decisions is so important. A number of environmental-psychology authors agree with this explanation. Kals, Schumacher, & Montada (1999), for instance, argue that pro-ecological behavior (PEC) should not be only considered as a result of rational processes. Factors such as emotional affinity towards nature, interest in nature, and guilt and indignation due to insufficient environmental protection are examples of PEC non-rational explanatory processes. Vining and Ebreo (2002) point to evidence showing that emotions drive sustainable actions through motivational processes, which are not necessarily rational. Thus, for a growing number of authors, one problem with the RMM explanatory scheme is its neglecting the role that emotions play in sustaining psychological functioning and instigating behavior, sustainable actions included. Emotions, as well as cognitions, are linked to motivation and, as it is known, a motivational component is required for guiding attitudes, beliefs, intentions, knowledge and skills towards more sustainable behaviors (Corral-Verdugo, 1996; Darner, 2009). Moreover, motivation directly and substantively affects pro-environmentally acting (Clark, Kotchen, & Moore, 2003; Corral-Verdugo, 1996). Since affective states are among the most powerful instigators of motivation, cognitions, and actions, the role played by emotions in sustainable behavior should be considered in its explanatory models.

Intention is also an important explanatory factor of behavior, which is included in models of sustainable behavior. As indicated by recent studies, emotions play a role in the development of pro-environmental intentions in both the implicit (Korpela, Klemettilä & Hietanen, 2002; Schultz, Shriver, Tabanico, & Khazian, 2004) and the deliberate (Carrus, Passafaro, & Bonnes, 2008; Hine, Marks, Nachriener, Gifford, & Heath 2007) levels. These studies acknowledge the importance of intentions as determinants of behavior, as much as the rational models do. However, the alternative models complement the purely cognitive explanation of pro-environmental behavior by adding affective predictors of sustainable behavior.

Despite the emphasis of the Theory of Planned Action on the cognitive components of intentions, some authors suggest that intention, will or deliberation contain more dimensions than a purely rational element. In this regard, Kane (1996, p. 26) recognizes three different facets of will and deliberative acts: a) one representing *desiderative or appetitive will*, which is translated into the expression "what I want, desire or prefer to do;" b) another, implying *rational will*, which is classical in psychological models, as manifested in "what I choose, decide or intend to do;" and c) *striving will*, manifested in "what I try, endeavor or make an effort to do."

As it can be observed, there is a correspondence of this classification with the tripartite ordering of psychological factors (emotions, cognitions, and behavior), which is also reflected in matters of will. Somehow, this classification impacts the ways diverse researchers assess intention as determinant of sustainability. For example, Perugini and Baggozzi's (2004) Goal-Directed Behavior (GDB) Model incorporates non-rational aspects into Ajzen's (1991) Planned Action Theory. According to Carrus et al. (2008) the GDB model would be particularly useful in studying sustainable behaviors since it includes affective elements in the form of *anticipated emotions*. These would be the affective counterparts of behavioral intentions, which result in a distinction between "desire" and "intention", as Perugini and Bagozzi establish, and between "desiderative" and "rational" will, as Kane (1996) suggests.

Carrus et al. (2008) study is an example of the benefits of specifying emotional variables as indirect predictors of sustainable behavior. These authors demonstrated that anticipated negative emotions correlate with the desire of engaging in pro-environmental actions. Anticipating unpleasant feelings resulting from environmental deterioration may lead individuals to conservation activities. According to these authors, this conservationist desire also correlates with pro-environmental intentions, which would reveal that affections and cognitions are not opposed to each other but, on the contrary, they operate in the same direction, inciting sustainable behavior.

The effect of emotions on pro-environmental behavior could also be direct (i.e., non-necessarily mediated through intentions). A number of studies have demonstrated that experiencing direct contact with nature generates positive emotional reactions towards nature, which in turn may result in pro-environmental behaviors (Finger, 1994). Other positive emotional states, such as happiness and satisfaction due to behaving pro-environmentally seem to directly influence the determination to act more sustainably (Brown & Kasser, 2005; De Young, 1996; Iwata, 2001). There is also evidence that some negative emotional states - generated from anticipating one's engagement in anti-ecological behaviors- could result in pro-environmental actions (Kaiser & Shimoda, 1999, for instance). Affective orientations toward life (*Biophilia*) and toward biodiversity are added to the list of emotions significantly predicting sustainable behavior (Serpell, 2004; Corral-Verdugo, Bonnes, Tapia, Fraijo, Frías & Carrus, 2009).

Unfortunately, the investigation of the effect of affective states on sustainable behavior is still scarce. Pooley and O'Connor (2002) state, in an explicit way, that one of the reasons explaining the limited success of interventions aimed to develop pro-environmental behavior is the emphasis placed on the cognitive determinants of pro-ecological action. According to these authors, the absence of affective-emotional determinants in pro-environmental behavior predictive models is a cause of their limited explanatory power.

Iozzi (1989), in turn, establishes that emotion is the entry point to environmental education because if students do not develop an emotional affinity towards the environment and its conservation, their involvement in pro-environmental behaviors will be unlikely. In more of this, Littledyke (2006) affirms that a central challenge for environmental education is how to encourage and develop in children a sense of relationship with the environment, which may translate into pro-environmental behavior. For Littledyke the perception of such relationship involves cognitive and affective dimensions. That is why he suggests that an understanding of environmental relationship may be complemented by a love of and respect for nature with feelings of interconnectedness with living things that can lead to environmental conservation.

Moreover, Vining and Ebreo (2002) assure that the role played by emotions has been largely ignored –with few exceptions- in studies and interventions in conservation behavior. This omission of affective factors is not surprising if we consider that researchers in cognitive psychology and neurosciences paid little attention to emotions during the last century (Damasio, 1998a). Fortunately, a growing interest in the role played by emotions in behavior is detected nowadays in psychology and in related disciplines –as neurosciences (Damasio, 2005; Nolan, 2002) and sociology (Schilling, 2002). Damasio (1998b), a leading neuroscientist, mentions that the interaction between human emotions and reasoned decisions represents a key research area in future investigations on pro-environmental behavior.

THE IMPORTANCE OF EMOTIONS

Is it true that responsible behaviors (including environmental conservation actions) might only be achieved by "rational" psychological means? During a substantial period of time, emotions were considered an unreliable source of thoughts, attitudes, and behavior. According to thinkers of the "Enlightening era" that dominated the 18th and the 19th centuries, reason was the only medium to establishing "...truths, which were ubiquitous, universal, timeless, and independent of the vagaries of the emotions." (Schilling, 2002, p. 13). Descartes, who exerted a major influence on Western philosophy and science, claimed that the essence of humankind was our ability to think, while emotions were things done by our bodies. Descartes' dualism manifested in the form of a "good" rationality and a "bad" sentiment or impulsiveness (Toulmin, 1990). Max Weber's (1930) argument is also illustrative: according to him, the power of individual social actors resides in their self-control, under the direction of values, and against distracting impulses and emotions. Descartes and Weber were not alone in thinking of emotions as something to be tamed and fought against. This explains why emotions were largely ignored as a scientific subject in psychology, sociology and neuroscience. In fact, even in present times most branches of science dealing with the explanation of human behavior neglect the role that emotions play in socially responsible actions as is the case of sustainable behaviors.

But, is it true that emotions are unreliable and "bad" for human decisions? In present days few would answer positively to that question. Of course, the Enlightening thought ignored the fact that all actions, and reason itself, require emotions if successful actions or reasons are to be achieved (Barbalet, 2002). Thus, there should be good "reasons" explaining why we have emotions, and why we still use our feelings as instigators of behavior. Evolutionary psychologists claim that they have the answers to these questions: they think emotions are adaptive psychological processes, which evolved in responding to environmental challenges faced by our ancestors. According to Orr (2008, p. 820) humans "possess emotions because of good evolutionary reasons." Feelings resulting from evolved emotions afforded and incited (and still they do) approaches to nutritional objects, sex, and situations producing wellbeing, and avoidance from danger and harm. Emotions are also at the base of *intuition*, a rapid, holistic information-processing of which the recipient is unaware (Sadler-Smith & Sparrow, 2008). This human capacity is important in making decisions within uncertain environments where key variables and their interrelationships are difficult to identify (Priem, Rasheed, & Kotulic, 1995; Sadler-Smith & Sparrow, 2008). Intuitions are as non-rational as emotions are.

Clearly, affective responses are part of an evolved mechanism making possible the survival of organisms. The pertinent question is whether or not affects and emotions are conducive to sustainable behaviors, which are conceived as adaptive actions that shall allow the survival of our species (Tonn, 2007).

Emotions promote pleasure, displeasure, activation, and related sates. These states are manifested as corporal changes, and can be reduced into a small set of responses, which Ekman, Sorensen & Friesen (1969) initially classified as happiness, sadness, fear, surprise, anger and annoyance, being widely accepted as *fundamental emotions*. Ekman *et al* (1969) argue that emotions are innate; also that they are found in every human group regardless of their culture, and that they do not include additional emotions as sub-elements. More recently, Ekman (1999) has included fun, scorn, joy, pain, enthusiasm, guilty, pride in achievement, satisfaction, relief, sensorial pleasure and shame as basic and universal emotions.

The evolved nature of emotions as fear, happiness or anger seems obvious because they permit both avoiding danger and approaching what is beneficial for the organism. In other cases, such as the instances of pride or guilt, this advantage is less evident. Yet, for evolutionary psychologists there is always an evolved mechanism explaining the existence of every basic emotion. For instance -according to them- shame and guilt are present in human psychological structure because, in their absence, the temptation to cheat or deceive on others would be much higher and, although in the short term deceiving or cheating might result in benefits, the long-term risks (i.e., being caught) are not worthy since they do not compensate for those benefits (Trivers, 1985). Therefore, feeling shame or guilt from behaving inappropriately is more advantageous than feeling nothing.

Does the "evolved advantages" of emotions translate into sustainable actions? In other words, is it possible that some emotions incite environmental conservation while others inhibit anti-environmental actions? A positive answer to these questions is fundamental for guaranteeing the long-term survival of humankind. Emotions are inseparable from the whole human psychological structure, and this structure is the only we have to successfully face all sorts of situations challenging the continued existence of our species.

Fortunately, evidence seems to show that this is the case. For instance, Kaiser & Shimoda (1999) found that guilt functions as a mechanism inhibiting anti-ecological behavior. Individuals try to avoid their engaging in such behavior in order to prevent themselves from being embarrassed or feeling guilty. Moreover, Kaiser, Schultz, Berenguer, Corral-Verdugo, & Tankha (2008) report that anticipated guilt and embarrassment predict pro-environmental intentions, both in individualistic and collectivistic cultures, demonstrating that this is a universal phenomenon. These evolved emotions, although negative, serve both purposes of individual and collective preservation.

In more of this, happiness, one of the most positive emotions, is significantly related to altruism (Schroeder, Penner, Dovidio & Piliavin, 1995; Van de Vliert & Janssen, 2002), also to a decreased consumption of resources (Brown & Kasser, 2005), and to equitable (Veenhoven, 2006) and pro-ecological behaviors (Brown & Kasser, 2005; see also Bechtel & Corral-Verdugo chapter in this book). Emotional affinity towards nature (i.e., feeling as being one with nature), and the interest in nature predisposes individuals to conservation actions (Kals et al., 1999); a general affinity towards life and nature –recognized as "biophilia"- also biases behavior in the direction of resources conservation (Serpell, 2004). Moreover, Corral-Verdugo et al. (2009) report that liking socio and biodiversity correlates with sustainable actions. These instances, among others, which will be commented in subsequent sections of this chapter, demonstrate the crucial importance of emotions in the development of pro-environmental behaviors. They also offer hope for finding environmental-problem solutions by developing interventions based on affective and rational strategies.

By the way, sometimes emotions exert a negative influence on pro-environmental behavior. A number of negative emotions decrease the ability to engage in sustainable actions. Rochford and Blocker (1991), for instance, found that emotions (i.e., fears) resulting from environmental hazards negatively correlate with ecological activism: the more the effort a person invests in controlling his/her fears about a future environmental disaster (pollution, hurricanes, floods, etc), the less the time (s)he will invest in successfully coping with that problem. The negative effect of some emotions is also reported in regard to pro-social behavior. One example is provided by Eisenberg, Losoya & Spinrad (2003) who show that personal distress may result in avoiding the assistance to needy persons. That is, distress sometimes inhibits altruistic actions.

ENVIRONMENTAL EMOTIONS AND PRO-ENVIRONMENTAL BEHAVIOR

Environmental emotions are a fundamental mechanism if we consider the course of human evolution and its adaptation to continuous change. As suggested by Carrus et al. (2008), environmental concern –and its implicit emotions- may be conceived as essential features of present societies because these features lead human groups to act for guaranteeing their future survival. Thus, emotions serve as a mechanism guiding human behavior towards forthcoming -and, sometimes, uncertain- times, which makes emotions a basic mental ingredient of sustainable actions.

Although research on environmental emotions is not amongst the most reported in the literature, their importance in the context of human-environment relations is widely acknowledged (Kals & Maes, 2002; Kals et al, 1999; Hinds & Sparks, 2008). In considering such importance, Schultz (2000) and Sevillano, Aragonés & Schultz (2007) found that empathizing with nature (taking the perspective of an animal in pain, for instance) increases the levels of connection with nature and, most importantly, this empathy results in pro-environmental behaviors. Empathy also positively affects altruistic behaviors (Eisenberg et al, 2003), so that its effects are detected in different levels of sustainable behavior. Empathy and perspective taking for animals and other living beings are instances of *environmental emotions*. Affinity towards nature, satisfaction, happiness, feelings of indignation due to environmental deterioration, guilty, shame, biophilia, and affinity towards diversity are additional instances.

The causal flow between positive environmental emotions and pro-environmental behavior is reciprocal: Hartmann and Apaolaza-Ibáñez (2008) found that the benefits of consuming environmentally friendly products include a positive emotional state, which is experienced as "satisfaction." De Young (1996) had previously reported a similar finding. Bechtel & Corral-Verdugo (see final chapter in this book) also argue that happiness might be both a cause and effect of sustainable actions.

Affect seems to be an important predictor of environmental attitudes (Pooley & O'Connor, 2000), which, in turn, indirectly affect pro-ecological behaviors. Kals et al. (1999) also show a direct influence of affective states on pro-environmental actions: emotional affinity towards nature predicts conservationist behaviors such as using public transportation and supporting ecologist organizations. According to these authors, emotional affinity is, in turn, predicted by exposure to natural environments.

A related thought led to postulating the "Biophilia Hypothesis", the idea that human beings have an innate affinity towards life and nature (Wilson, 1995). Wilson argues that the natural world continues influencing human mind through the close and enduring relations we have with such natural world. Since technological development has been so fast –in evolutionary terms- human adaptation to modern environments has to be substantially generated before our being aware that an affinity towards those environments appear. It is clear that humankind is emotionally biased towards nature (Kaplan, 2000) so that a long time will pass before we develop a preference for built and technological environments. Therefore, we still need being in –and with- nature, and this need manifests as emotional affinity towards other living organisms.

Kals et al. (1999) suggest that environmental emotions may manifest in diverse ways: as *emotional affinity* towards nature (EAN), as *indignation* due to an insufficient effort to conserve the environment, or as an *interest* in nature. AEN can be understood as a feeling of unity with nature; indignation would manifest as emotional discomfort resulting from ecological deterioration and insufficient conservationist effort, while interest for nature involves both liking a direct contact with natural settings and the knowledge acquired from such a contact. In their study, Kals et al. reported that those three affective factors accounted for almost half of pro-environmental behavior variance. They also assessed the impact of a direct contact with nature on EAN, and found that almost forty percent of this emotional affinity was explained by the direct contact with nature. This result stresses the importance of environmental education activities such as foraging (recollection of –especially vegetal- specimens), open-space activities, and hiking and camping out of cities (Chipeniuk, 1995).

In related studies, Kals (1996) and Montada & Kals (1995) examined the emotional assessments presupposing attributions of responsibility for environmental protection. Those attributions included *self-blame* due to an insufficient environmental-conservation effort, *indignation* due to others' limited conservation effort, and *anger* resulting from the use of extreme environmentally protective measures. These three emotions were highly related to people's willingness to get involved in pro-environmental actions such as energy conservation, use of public transportation, pro-environmentally political activities, funding nature protection activities, and actively promoting conservation actions, among others (Kals, 1996).

Hind and Sparks (2008) confirm Kals' and Montada's group findings, pointing to some connections between affective and cognitive processes in the effects that these psychological facets have on pro-environmental behavior. These authors found that an emotional connection with the environment increases people's willingness to act pro-ecologically, which, in turn, results in more sustainable acting. More recently, Corral-Verdugo et al. (2009; see also Bonnes et al chapter in this book) added an element to the list of environmental emotions: *affinity towards diversity* (AD). According to these researchers, AD implies a preference for variety in both the living forms and the socio-cultural manifestations that characterize the environment. Thus, individuals would have a predisposition towards bio and socio-diversity that, according to these authors, has evolved along with human's biophilic tendencies (Wilson, 1995) and related environmental preferences (Kaplan, 2000). The emotional component of AD is present in the *liking* or *preference* (in this case, for diversity) component characterizing affective responses. That is, when a person emotionally evaluates an object, event or situation, she/he always displays a liking or disliking reaction towards those stimuli (Fridja, 1986) and this is what results from AD in regard to bio and socio-diversity. In their studies, Corral-Verdugo et al. found that AD significantly correlates with indignation feelings caused by environmental deterioration, and also with a series of indicators of pro-sustainability orientation, including future orientation, altruism and pro-ecological behavior.

Additional studies conducted by Corral-Verdugo and his group (Corral-Verdugo, Tapia, Fraijo, Mireles & Márquez (2008) and Corral-Verdugo, Tapia, Frías, Fraijo & González (2009), have reported that indignation feelings caused by environmental deterioration, along with emotional connection with nature and affinity towards diversity, correlate with sustainable lifestyles. These studies show that some affective-emotional factors are highly predictive of environmentally protective behaviors, such as a reduced consumption of products and pro-ecological behaviors.

All of these considerations and research review stimulated our testing a model of relations between environmental emotions, intentions to act, and pro-environmental behavior. We expected that the rational component of intentions would significantly correlate with environmental emotions and, also, that both intentions and emotions would saliently and significantly affect pro-environmental behavior. One particular question in this study was whether emotions would surpass the effect of intentions. One more question was whether or not the rational and emotions processes add their influence, working in combination towards the same (pro-environmental) end. In any case, what we expected was that a combined rational-emotional model would explain more pro-environmental behavior variance than a solely rational-based explanation of such sustainable behavior.

METHOD

Participants

Two hundred and sixty eight individuals living at two cities (Hermosillo, population = 7000,000 inhabitants; Huatabampo, population = 70,000 inhabitants) in the Mexican Sonora State; and one hundred and eighty seven living in the city of Monterrey (population= four million inhabitants), Nuevo Leon State, Mexico, participated in this study. Therefore, the total number of participants was 455. Three hundred were females and 155 were males. The average age was 35.38 years (SD = 14.30; minimum = 12, maximum = 71), with a mean of 11.5 years (SD = 5.8) of schooling. Forty percent of this sample self-classified as low socio-economic class, thirty six percent as middle class, while twenty four percent stated they were high class. Participants were selected from zones of their cities that, according to the Mexican Census Office (INEGI, 2000), were representative of high, middle, and low socio-economic classes. Households were randomly selected from each zone; three individuals from each house responded to the used research instruments. These individuals were the housewife, a male adult, and young man/women aged 12-18 years old. All accepted to participate.

Instruments

A scale assessing *feelings of indignation* due to environmental deterioration (Corral-Verdugo et al. [2008] "Feelings of Indignation" scale), which includes situations such as "watching jammed and polluted streets" or "watching my neighbors wasting water", was also used. Respondents had to rate their reaction before each situation, using the following scale: 0="I feel indifference", 1="I feel slightly bad myself".... to 5="I feel so bad that I'd try to prevent someone from doing it by all means". Corral-Verdugo et al (2008) reported a .92 alpha for this scale.

Three items assessing *Affinity towards biodiversity* from the ATD scale (Corral-Verdugo et al., 2009) were used. These were the items positively worded, by the authors, that considered preference for animal and plant variety ("I like many kinds -species- of animals," "I like visiting zoos," "The more the variety of plants, the better for me"). Participants were asked to express their views on biodiversity on a four-step scale, ranging from 0="Does not apply to me", 1="It almost does not apply to me", 2= "It partially applies to me", to 3="It totally applies to me." The authors reported a .68 Cronbach's alpha for the total scale.

Emotional interest in nature, as manifested in people's liking direct contact with natural elements (plants, animals, open spaces), was measured using four items developed by Corral-Verdugo et al. (2008), who, in turn, were based on the proposal by Kals et al. (1999). "Feels happy when in contact with nature" and "Plants and trees make me being in good mood" are examples of this scale, which is responded by considering options ranging from 0= "does not apply to me" to 3 "it totally applies to me." The authors reported a .89 Cronbach's alpha for this scale.

Eight items selected from Kaiser's (1998) *General Environmental Behavior* (GEB) scale were also administered. Participants were asked to report the frequency (on a scale ranging from 0="never" to 3="always") of their engaging in behaviors such as collecting and recycling used paper, buying products in refillable packages, or turning down the air conditioning when leaving home. Kaiser and Wilson (2000) obtained a reliability coefficient of .72 for this scale. The internal consistencies of the measures for the current study are reported in the results section.

Finally, six items from a scale of *intention to act* developed by Corral-Verdugo et al. (2008) were used. They assessed respondent's willingness to engage in behaviors such as recycling, participating as voluntary in conservationist actions, and water conservation behaviors. They responded to these items by considering a four-option scale ranging from 0 (never) to 4 (4) always. A .80 alpha was previously reported from administering this instrument.

Procedure

Participants were approached, the purpose of the research was explained to them and their informed consent to participate was obtained. The information was collected at the living room of their households in a 30-minute interview.

Data Analysis

Univariate statistics (means, standard deviations, frequencies) were obtained for every item used in the study. In addition, the scales' reliability (internal consistency) was estimated by computing Cronbach's alphas. A *t*-test did not reveal significant differences in means between Sonora and Nuevo Leon participants in terms of the administered scales. Therefore, we decided to conduct further statistical analysis by considering the total sample as belonging to the same (Mexican) population.

A structural equation model (SEM) was specified and tested. In this model, three emotional factors were constructed from the interrelations from their respective indicators: "Emotional interest in nature," "Feelings of indignation due to environmental deterioration," and "Affinity towards biodiversity". These three first- factors constituted a second-order latent variable, which we labeled "Environmental emotions (EE)." Thus, the EE factor was assumed to subsume the interrelations among the first-order latent variables. In addition, "Intentions to act pro-environmentally" and "pro-environmental behavior" were specified as factors also resulting from their corresponding indicators interrelations. In short, this component of the process of specification constituted the *measurement model* of SEM (Bentler, 2006), which is basically a confirmatory factor analysis. By estimating the relationships between factors and their corresponding indicators (items), the convergent validity of measures could be assessed. High and significant factor loadings indicate such validity.

The second component of the SEM was the structural model, which includes the estimation of presumably causal relations between factors. In this model, "intention to act" was specified as affecting pro-environmental behavior, while "Environmental emotions" was assumed to affect both the intention to act and pro-environmental behavior. Goodness of fit indicators (X^2, *NNFI, CFI, RMSEA*) were also obtained in order to evaluate the adequacy of the specified theoretical model.

RESULTS

Table 1 shows the univariate statistics and reliability coefficients (Cronbach's alphas) for items and scales used in this study. In all cases, but one, alphas are equal to or higher than .73. The three affinity-towards-biodiversity items produced a .60 alpha. The analysis of participants' responses to items revealed that the most frequently self-reported pro-environmental behaviors were reuse of products, conservation of gasoline by walking or bicycling and pointing out unecological behavior to someone; in turn, the most *intended* actions resulted to be buying environmental friendly products and conserving water at home. Watching someone hurting a person or animal and watching factories dropping wastes were the causes of the highest levels of indignation; while the four items of the scale of emotional interest in nature and the three ATD items resulted with similar (and high levels) of response. In general, respondents exhibited most agreement with emotional interest in nature and affinity towards biodiversity items, followed by intentions to act, feelings of indignations, and, finally, pro-environmental behaviors.

Figure 1 is a representation of the specified and tested structural model. Rectangles represent the observed indicators (items) and ovals indicate their corresponding latent variables (factors). Salient and significant (p<.05) factor *loadings* were obtained in all measurement models, indicating convergent construct validity for every assessed factor. The interrelations among feelings of indignation, emotional interest in nature, and affinity towards diversity resulted high and significantly enough to allow the emergence of the second-order factor "Environmental emotions." According to the results of the structural model, EE significantly affected both the intention to act pro-environmentally and pro-ecological actions. Since those intentions also influence pro-ecological behavior, the effect of EE on this behavior was both direct and indirect. Clearly, the structural coefficient of environmental emotions on pro-environmental behavior (.55) was higher than the one resulting from intentions on that behavior (.27). The value of R^2 estimated from the influence of environmental emotions on intentions to act was .23, while the value of R^2 in the case of the combined influence of emotions and intentions to act on pro-environmental behavior was .52. Goodness of fit indicators are reported in the legend of figure 1. Although the p value of X^2 resulted significant, the practical goodness of fit indicators ($NNFI =. 90$; $CFI = .91$) could be considered acceptable. The value of $RMSEA$ was .05.

Table 1. Univariate statistics and reliability of scales

Scale/items	Mean	SD	Min.	Max.	Alpha
Pro-environmental behavior					.82
Keeps and recycle used paper	1.08	1.11	0	3	
Brings empty bottles to a recycling bin	1.08	1.11	0	3	
Points out unecological behavior to someone	1.71	1.08	0	3	
Reads about ecological topics	1.32	1.01	0	3	
Talks with friends about environmental problems	1.40	0.99	0	3	
Look for ways to reuse things.	1.89	1.05	0	3	
Encourages friends and family to recycling	1.26	1.14	0	3	
Conserves gasoline by walking or bicycling	1.64	1.16	0	3	
Intention to act					.73
Participating as voluntary in conservationist action	1.66	1.04	0	3	
Buying environmental friendly products	2.28	0.92	0	3	
Using energy efficient systems at home	2.55	0.76	0	3	
Conserving water at home	2.57	0.81	0	3	
Recycling paper	2.30	0.94	0	3	
Cooperating with an ecologist organization	1.74	1.01	0	3	
Feelings of indignation					.80
Watching someone cutting off a tree	2.29	1.27	0	5	
Watching someone littering	2.82	1.20	0	5	
Watching someone hurting a person or animal	3.28	1.17	0	5	
Watching factories dropping wastes	2.88	1.32	0	5	
By watching jammed or smog-polluted streets	2.48	1.25	0	5	
Watching neighbors wasting water	2.85	1.27	0	5	

Table 1. Univariate statistics and reliability of scales

Scale/items	Mean	SD	Min.	Max.	Alpha
Emotional interest in nature					.87
Feels happy in contact with nature	2.56	0.70	0	3	
Plants and trees make her/him being in good mood	2.62	0.68	0	3	
Open places produce a wellbeing feeling	2.62	0.69	0	3	
Contact with plants at patio make him/her feel good	2.52	0.75	0	3	
Affinity towards biodiversity					.69
Likes many kinds (species) of animals	2.10	1.09	0	3	
Likes visiting zoos	2.27	0.92	0	3	
The more the variety of plants, the better for him/her	2.48	0.86	0	3	

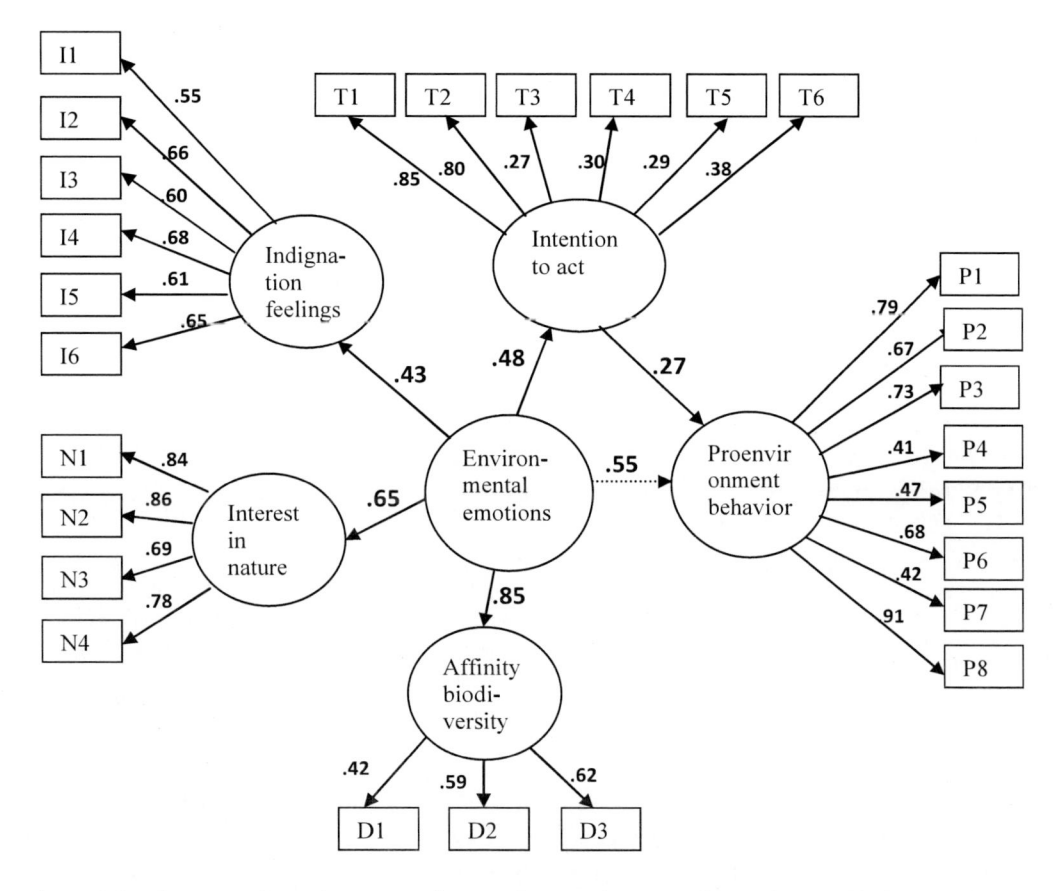

Figure 1. Environmental emotions as predictors of pro-environmental intentions and behavior. Models' goodness of fit: $X^2=$ 665.14 (314 df), $p<.001$; NNFI=.90, CFI=.91; RMSEA=.05. Intentions' $R^2=.23$; Proenvironmental behavior's $R^2=.52$.

CONCLUSION

Emotions are a crucial component of the human psychological structure. Despite the past undeserved fame of emotions as unlikely drivers of socially responsible actions –sustainable behavior included- we now know that affective responses are as important as rational-analytical processes in inciting pro-social and pro-ecological activities.

Emotions serve the substantive purpose of individuals' survival by rewarding their approach to safe, nutritious, and sexual situations, and by punishing their exposition to harmful events. In doing this, emotions make the struggle for life more likely successful by adding psychological tools to the arsenal of behavioral adaptive capacities (Carrus et al., 2008; Orr, 2008). One question that remains unanswered is whether emotions, along with other human capabilities, will permit the survival of the human race (see Tonn, 2008). The current environmental dilemma represents one of the most significant threats to human existence. Is it possible that our affects, as adaptive responses, make us to successfully cope with such dilemma? One way of responding this question is looking at the relationships between emotions and sustainable behavior.

Emotions affect both behavior and some of its most important determinants: attitudes, motives, skills, and intentions to act. Therefore, explanatory models of pro-environmental behavior should include emotional factors as determinants of people's conservationist actions, if a realistic representation is to be achieved (Pooley & O'Connor, 2002; Vining & Ebreo, 2002). Purely rational predictors of these actions explain only a fraction (a third of the variance in most cases) of their variation. Moreover, human decisions are based on affective states in addition to rational aspects that people consider in any course of action.

The empirical study presented in this chapter was intended to illustrate how rational and emotional processes interrelate and influence sustainable actions. Two scales assessing positive emotions towards nature (emotional interest in nature and affinity towards biodiversity), combined with a measure of indignation due to environmental deterioration, were administered to Mexicans living in three northern cities. The scales showed an acceptable (yet, improvable, in the case of the ATD items) reliability level, as well as evidence of convergent construct validity, as reflected in Cronbach's alpha values and the statistical significance of *lambda* loadings on their corresponding latent variables. Those psychometric properties were also exhibited by measures assessing intentions to act pro-environmentally and the self-report of pro-ecological behavior.

When analyzing responses to the scales' items we found that the levels of environmental emotions reported by respondents were high, especially in regard to emotional interest in nature and affinity towards biodiversity. Although feelings of indignation due to anti-environmental behaviors were not as high as the other assessed emotions, they were saliently exhibited by participants in this study. These were the expected results: emotional interest in nature reflect individuals' preferences for natural features of the environment (Kaplan, 2000), while affinity towards biodiversity biases those preferences towards plant and animal variety (Corral-Verdugo et al, 2009). It is also likely that these marked emotional responses reflect a biophilic tendency (Wilson, 1995). Feelings of indignation, in turn, manifested a marked concern for the status of the environment, as well as a negative emotional reaction, as Montada and Kals (1995) and Kals et al. (1999) found in their studies.

The interrelations among the three scales assessing affective responses produced a second-order factor that we identified as "environmental emotions (EE)." As expected, these emotions significantly correlated with pro-environmental intentions. This finding replicates results from previous studies conducted by our research team (Corral-Verdugo et al., 2008; 2009), which seems to confirm that rational and affective factors work together in inducing pro-environmental predispositions (i.e., environmental emotions, intentions to conserve the environment). The combined influence of emotions and intentions explained more than a 50% of pro-environmental behavior variance, a substantially higher percentage than the variance predicted by purely rational models of sustainable actions. Although intentions to act significantly predicted the self-report of conservation behaviors -confirming the well known link between the deliberative rational component of human decision making and pro-environmental behaviors (Bamberg and Möser, 2004)- environmental emotions produced a higher influence on this behavior than did intentions.

We detected some limitations in our illustrative study. One of them is the use of verbal measures of emotional states. Those measures are pertinent ways of assessing rational-analytical processes, since language derives from related information-processing mechanisms, while emotions result from different (synthetic, holistic) processes, which are not necessarily linked to language. Undoubtedly, language might express or describe emotional states but only in a limited way; that is why a number of authors (Cacioppo, Bernston, Larsen, Poehlmann, & Ito, 2000; Mendes, McCoy, Major, & Blascovich, 2008, for instance) use alternative (psycho-physiological, behavioral, etc.) assessments of emotions, different from verbal measures. Thus, further studies would be benefited by the use of alternative, non-verbal measures of environmental emotions. This limitation also affects the assessment of pro-environmental behavior. Self-reports are known to be biased indicators of actual behavior (Corral-Verdugo, 1997); people usually report a higher involvement in pro-ecological actions than they actually do. Therefore, the use of measures alternative to self-reports of behavior is also recommended.

Nonetheless, our findings seem to represent a big deal of actuality. Emotions, being integral to human psychological repertoire are a fundamental piece to consider in evaluating people's orientation towards more sustainable lifestyles. These results suggest that affective responses are not only crucial in guaranteeing individuals' survival but also in ensuring humankind long-term permanence on this planet. In facing the serious environmental dilemma produced by human behavior and mental dispositions, emotions undoubtedly will play a relevant role.

REFERENCES

Ajzen, I. (1991). The theory of planned behavior. *Organizational Behavior and Human Decision Processes, 50*, 179-221.

Bamberg, S. & Möser, G. (2007). Twenty years after Hines, Hungerford, and Tomera: A new meta-analysis of psycho-social determinants of pro-environmental behavior. *Journal of Environmental Psychology, 27*, 14-25.

Barbalet, J.M. (2002). Why emotions are crucial? In J.M. Barbalet (Ed.), *Emotions and Sociology* (pp.1-9). NY: Blackwell.

Bentler, P.M. (2006). *EQS 6 Structural Equations Program Manual*. Encino, CA: Multivariate Software Inc.

Brown, K.W. & Kasser, T. (2005). Are Psychological and Ecological Well-being Compatible? The Role of Values, Mindfulness, and Lifestyle." *Social Indicators Research, 3,* 49–68.

Cacioppo, J., Bernston, G., Larsen, J., Poehlmann, K., & Ito T. (2000). The psychophysiology of emotion. In: M. Lewis & J. Haviland-Jones (Eds.), *Handbook of emotion.* 2 (pp. 173–191). New York: Guilford Press.

Carrus, G., Pasafaro, P. & Bonnes, M. (2008). Emotions, habits and rational choices in ecological behaviours: The case of recycling and use of public transportation. *Journal of Environmental Psychology, 28,* 51-62.

Chipeniuk, R. (1995). Childhood foraging as a means of acquiring competent cognition about biodiversity. *Environment & Behavior, 27,* 490-512.

Clark, Kotchen, & Moore (2003). Internal and external influences on pro-environmental behavior: Participation in a green electricity program. *Journal of Environmental Psychology, 23,* 237-246.

Corral-Verdugo, V. (1996). A structural model of reuse and recycling behavior in Mexico. *Environment and Behavior, 28,* 665-696.

Corral, V. (1997). Dual "realities" of conservation behavior: Self-reports and observations of reuse & recycling behavior. *Journal of Environmental Psychology, 17, 135-145.*

Corral-Verdugo, V., Bonnes, M., Tapia, C., Fraijo, B., Frías, M., & Carrus, G. (2009). Correlates of pro-sustainability orientation: the Affinity Towards Diversity. *Journal of Environmental Psychology, 29,* 34-43.

Corral-Verdugo, V., Tapia, C., Fraijo, B., Mireles, J. & Márquez, P. (2008). Determinantes psicológicos de los estilos de vida sustentables [Psychological determinants of sustainable lifestyles]. *Revista Mexicana de Psicología, 25,* 313-327.

Corral-Verdugo, V., Tapia, C., Frías, M., Fraijo, B. & González, D. (2009). Orientación a la sostenibilidad como base para el comportamiento pro-social y pro-ecológico. [Pro-sustainability orientation as a basis for prosocial and proecological behaviors]. *Medio Ambiente y Comportamiento Humano, 10,* 5-25.

Damasio, A. (1998a). Emotion in the perspective of an integrated nervous system. *Brain Research Reviews, 26,* 83-86.

Damasio, A. (1998b). Emotion and reason in the future of human life. In B. Cartldedge (Ed.), *Mind, brain and the environment: The Linacre Lectures 1995-96* (pp. 57-71). New York: Oxford University Press.

Damasio, A. (2005). Emotion and the human brain. *Annals of the New York Academy of Sciences, 935,* 101-106.

Darner, R. (2009). Self-determination theory as a guide to fostering environmental motivation. *Journal of Environmental Education, 40,* 39-49.

De Young, R. (1996). Some psychological aspects of a reduced consumption lifestyle: The role of intrinsic satisfaction and competence motivation. *Environment & Behavior, 28,* 358-409.

Eisenberg, N., Losoya, S. & Spinrad, T. (2003). Affect and prosocial responding. En R. Davidson, K. Scherer & H. Goldsmith (Eds.), *Handbook of Affective Sciences.* New York: Oxford University Press.

Ekman, P. (1999) Basic emotions. En T. Dalgleish and T. Power (Eds.) *The handbook of cognition and emotion* (Pp. 45-60). New York: John Wiley & Sons.

Ekman, P., Sorenson, E. R. & Friesen. W. V. (1969). Pan-cultural elements in facial displays of emotions. *Science, 164*, 86-88.

Finger, M. (1994). From knowledge to action? Exploring the relationships between environmental experiences, learning, and behaviour. *Journal of Social Issues, 50*, 141-160.

Fridja, N. (1986). *The Emotions*. Cambridge, UK: Cambridge University Press.

Hartmann, P. & Apaolaza-Ibáñez, V. (2008). Virtual nature experiences as emotional benefits in green-product consumption: The moderating role of environmental attitudes. *Environment & Behavior, 40*, 818-842.

Hill, D. (2008). *Situational control of pro/antienvironmental behavior*. Unpublished doctoral dissertation. Tucson, AZ: The University of Arizona.

Hinds, J., & Sparks, P. (2008). Engaging with the natural environment: the role of affective connection and identity. *Journal of Environmental Psychology, 28*, 109-120.

Hine, D., Marks, A., Nachreiner, M., Guifford, R. & Heat, Y. (2007). Keeping the home fires burning: Te affect heuristic and wood smoke pollution. *Journal of Environmental Psychology, 27*, 26-32.

INEGI (2000). *Sistema de Consulta para la Información Censal* (SCINCE) [Census Information Consulting System]. Mexico City: Instituto Nacional de Geografía e Informática.

Iozzi, L. A. (1989). What research says to the educator. Part one: Environmental education and the affective domain. *Journal* of *Environmental Education*. 20(3), 3–9.

Iwata, O. (2001). Attitudinal determinants of environmentally responsible behavior. *Social Behavior and Personality, 29*, 183-190.

Kahneman, D. (2003) A perspective on judgment and choice: Mapping bounded rationality. *American Psychologist, 58*, 697-720.

Kaiser, F. (1998). A general measure of ecological behavior. *Journal of Applied Social Psychology, 28*, 395-442.

Kaiser, F., Schultz, P.W., Berenguer, J., Corral-Verdugo, V. & Tankha, G. (2008). Extending planned environmentalism. Anticipated guilt and embarrassment across cultures. *European Psychologist, 13*, 288-297.

Kaiser, F., & Shimoda, T. (1999). Responsibility as a predictor of ecological behaviour. *Journal of Environmental Psychology, 19*, 243-253.

Kaiser, F., & Wilson, M. (2000). Assessing people´s general ecological behavior: A crosscultural measure. *Journal of Applied Social Psychology, 30*, 952-978.

Kals, E. (1996). Are proenvironmental commitments motivated by health concerns or by perceived justice? En L. Montada y M. Lerner (Eds.), *Current Societal concerns about justice*. Nueva York: Plenum.

Kals, E., & Maes, J. (2002). Sustainable development and emotions. In P. Schmuck, & W. P. Schultz (Eds.), *Psychology of sustainable development* (pp. 97–122). Norwell, MA: Kluwer Academic Publishers.

Kals, E., Schumacher, D. & Montada, L. (1999). Emotional affinity toward nature as a motivational basis to protect nature. *Environment & Behavior, 31*, 178-202.

Kane, R. (1996). *The Significance of Free Will*. New York: Oxford University Press.

Kaplan, S. (2000). Human nature and environmentally responsible behavior. *Journal of Social Issues*, 56, 491-508.

Korpela, K., Klemettilä, T. & Hietanen, J.K. (2002). Evidence for rapid affective evaluation of environmental scenes. *Environment and Behavior*, 34, 634-650.

Littledyke, M. (2006). Science education for environmental awareness: approaches to integrating cognitive and affective domains. In E. Manolas (Ed.) *Proceedings of the 2006 Naxos International Conference on Sustainable Management and Development of Mountainous and Island Areas* (pp. 254-268). Heraklion-Crete, Greece: University of Crete.

Mendes, W., McCoy, S., Major, B., & Blascovich, J. (2008). How attributional ambiguity shapes physiological and emotional responses to social rejection and acceptance. *Journal of Personality and Social Psychology, 94*, 278-291.

Montada, L., & Kals, E. (1995). Perceived justice of ecological policy and proenvironmental commitments. *Social Justice Research, 8*, 305-327.

Nolan, R.J. (2002). Neuroscience and psychology. Emotion, cognition, and behavior. *Science, 298*, 1191-1194.

Orr, D. (2008). The psychology of survival. *Conservation Biology, 22*, 819-822.

Perugini, M., y Bagozzi, R. P. (2004). The distinction between desires and intentions. *European Journal of Social Psychology, 34*, 69–84.

Pooley, J., & O'Connor, M. (2000). Environmental education and attitudes. *Environment & Behavior*, 32, 711-723.

Priem, R. Rasheed, A. & Kotulic, A. (1995). Rationality in strategic decision processes, environmental dynamism and firm performance. *Journal of Management, 21*, 5, 913-929.

Rochford, E.B., & Blocker, T.J. (1991). Coping with "natural" hazards as stressors: The predictors of activism in a flood disaster. *Environment & Behavior, 15*, 143-164.

Sadler-Smith, E. & Sparrow, P. (2008). Intuition in organizational decision making. In G. Hodginkson, & W. Starbuck (Eds.), *The Oxford Handbook of Organizational Decision Making* (pp. 305-324). New York: Oxford University press.

Schilling, C. (2002). The two traditions in the sociology of emotions. In J.M. Barbalet (Ed.), *Emotions and Sociology* (pp.10-32). NY: Blackwell.

Schroeder, D.A., Penner, L.A., Dovidio, J.F., & Piliavin, J.A. (1995). *The psychology of helping and altruism: Problems and puzzles*. New York: McGraw-Hill.

Schultz, P. W. (2000). Empathizing with nature: The effects of perspective taking on concern for environmental issues. *Journal of Social Issues, 56*, 391-406.

Schultz, P. W., Shriver, C., Tabanico, J. J. & Khazian, A. M. (2004). Implicit connections with nature. Journal of Environmental Psychology, 24, 31–42.

Schwartz, S. H. (1973). Normative explanations of helping behavior: A critique, proposal, and empirical test. *Journal of Experimental Social Psychology, 9*, 349–364.

Serpell, J.A. (2004). Factors influencing human attitudes to animals and their welfare. *Animal Welfare, 13*, 145-151.

Sevillano, V., Aragonés, J.I., & Schultz, P.W. (2007). Perspective taking, environmental concern, and the moderating role of dispositional empathy. *Environment & Behavior, 39*, 685-705.

Tonn, B. (2007). Futures sustainability. *Futures, 39*, 1097-1116.

Toulmin, S. (1990). Theology in the context of the university. *Theological Education, 26*, 51-65.

Trivers, R.L. (1985). *Social Evolution*. Menlo Park, CA: Benjamin/Cummings.

Van de Vliert, E., & Janssen, O. (2002). "Better than" Performance Motives as Roots of Satisfaction Across more and Less Developed Countries. *Journal of Crosscultural Psychology, 33*, 380-397.

Veenhoven, R. (2006). Is life getting better? How long and happy people live in modern society. *European Psychologist*, 10, 330-343.

Vining, J., & Ebreo, A. (2002). Emerging theoretical and methodological perspectives on conservation behavior. In R.B. Bechtel & A. Churchman (Eds.), *Handbook of Environmental Psychology* (pp. 541-558). New York: Wiley.

Weber, M. (1930). The protestant ethic and the spirit of Capitalism (1905). London: Allwn and Unwin.

Wilson, E. (1995). Biophilia and the Conservation Ethic. En S. Keller & E. Wilson (Eds.), *The Biophilia Hypothesis*. Washington, DC: Island Press.

PART III:
CONTEXTUAL DETERMINANTS OF SUSTAINABLE BEHAVIOR

Chapter 14

CONTEXTUAL INFLUENCES ON SUSTAINABLE BEHAVIOR

Dawn Hill[*], *Aurelio José Figueredo and W. Jake Jacobs*
University of Arizona, USA

ABSTRACT

Studies of Proenvironmental behavior (PEB) commonly take a person-centered approach, assuming that the primary determinants of behavior are a person's attributes. Hence, PEB studies typically measure attitudes, values, intentions, knowledge, altruism, environmentalism, etc. – all of which reside in the individual and all of which are posited to cause pro/anti-environmental behavior. Although the empirical base is substantial, person-factors often do not predict behavior well and the posited close relationship between intention and behavior is rarely demonstrated. One reason for this is that part of the "causal" story is missing – the causal role played by context (setting/situation). Hence, the present chapter focuses on various contexts that present to-be-solved adaptive problems and that display affordances, cues, and stimuli that guide adaptive behavior. The Theory of Planned Behavior (TPB) represented the "person-factor" approach; however, we suspected the TPB in isolation would not sufficiently explain behavioral choices. In our study, instead of measuring behavioral intention in a contextual vacuum, we presented each behavioral choice within the context of written multidimensional vignettes. Each context consisted of physical settings as well as theoretically driven dimensions of social situations. We systematically varied the social dimensions to "cue" specific adaptive problems, on the assumption that person-by-context relationships provide more stable and externally valid predictions of PEB than intentionality alone. Settings accounted for a significant proportion of variance in both pro- and anti-environmental behavior. Traditional theory, such as TPB, did not predict context-specific behavior; however, components of the theory did predict behavior in the aggregate. We conclude that attending to the context in which environmental behavior occurs provides a better basis for predicting, understanding, and affecting changes in PEB.

---

[*] Correspondence: Dawn Hill. E-mail: dawnh@u.arizona.edu.

INTRODUCTION

As is obvious from other chapters in this volume, Proenvironmental Behavior (PEB) (or sustainable behavior) attracts significant attention from many scientific researchers and disciplines. Prevailing theoretical approaches often assume that person factors such as attitudes, values, beliefs, etc, are the best predictors of PEB or proenvironmental intention (Bamberg, 2003; Clark & Finney, 2007; Corraliza & Berenguer, 2000; Ewert & Baker, 2001; Garling, Fujii, Garling & Jakobsson, 2003; Harland, Staats & Wilke, 1999; Hwang, Kim & Jeng, 2002; Schultz & Zelenzy, 1998; Staats, Harland & Wilke, 2004; Thogersen & Olander, 2006; Valle, Reis, Menezes & Rebelo, 2004; Widegren, 1998; Zarakovskii, Medvedev & Polesterova, 2000). Taken in the aggregate, most researchers assume that person factors adequately characterize concern, affinity toward the environment, indignation, interest and, of course, intention to act in a proenvironmental way (Bamberg, 2003; Clark & Finney, 2007; Fransson & Garling, 1999; Garling et al, 2003; Kals et al, 1999; Mainieri et al, 1997).

Although PEB research rests on several foundational theories,[1] the Theory of Reasoned Action (Ajzen & Fishbein, 1980) and its successor, the Theory of Planned Behavior (TPB) (Ajzen & Fishbein, 1980) dominate the action. The deceptively simple TPB[2] has been empirically validated across topics such as leisure participation, sexual behavior, driving, health-related practices, taking vitamins, class attendance, academic achievement, weight loss, and PEB (see Mannetti, Pierro & Livi, 2004 and Oreg & Katz-Gerro, 2006 for specific citations). The theory states that the best predictor of real-world behavior is behavioral intention – a composite of *attitudes, subjective norms* and *perceived behavioral control*, all principally considered to be person attributes. Its widespread use reflects the view that person attributes cause PEB.

There are pressing concerns about this view. The most urgent pure question is why proenvironmental intentions do not lead to PEB more consistently. An equally important theoretical question is why the field lacks adequate causal specification of PEB. Most of the literature identifies person/ dispositional attributes that *correlate* to PEB and essentially assume that these correlates "cause" PEB. Unfortunately, intention, as measured normally, often correlates with real-world behavior[3] 0.30 or less (Blanchard, Kupperman, Sparling, Nehl, Rhodes, Corneya, Baker & Rupp, 2008; de Brujin, Kroeze, Oenema & Brug, 2008; Kerner & Grossman, 1998; Rice, Kovac, Kraft & Moan, 2008; Staats et al, 2004). Moreover, "appropriately measured"[4] intentions typically accounts for less than 30% of the variance of future behavior (Ajzen, 1991; Armitage & Connor, 2001; Sheeran, 2002; Sheeran & Orbell, 1998; Sheppard, Hartwich & Warshaw, 1988). These facts suggest that targeting

---

[1] Decision and Choice Theory (Hogarth, 1987) and its extensions like Subjective Expected Utility (Prospect Theory - Kahneman and Tversky 1982, Kahneman 2003), Schwartz's Norm Activation Theory (Schwartz, 1977), Social Comparison Theory (Masters & Smith, 1987), Social Learning Theory (Bandura, 1977), and the Theory of Normative Conduct (Cialdini, Kallgren and Reno, 1991).

[2] Its underpinnings are complex and often misunderstood.

[3] Not self-described behavior but real-world behavior as it actually unfolds and measured in the world – the former results in higher correlations, which do not typically exceed 0.55 (Boyd & Wandersman, 1991; White et al, 2008).

[4] Ajzen and Fishbein (2005) specify that intentions can be predictive if they are appropriately measured by ensuring "compatibility" between intention and the behavioral object. Meta-analytic studies cited to support this claim. Although this empirical evidence may be true, a construct that is supposed to be the "closest cognitive antecedent of actual behavior" (pg 188) which accounts for only 20-30% of the variance doesn't convince us its useful to predict behavior.

proenvironmental intention as a means to increase PEB may be, at best, only partially effective. There are equally pressing applied questions, such as, how can one change person attributes in a way that produces greater proenvironmental intention? Twenty years of education designed to increase environmental knowledge as a means to affect intention have not had strong effects (Frick et al, 2004; Kollmus & Agyeman, 2002; Pooley & O'Conner, 2000).

One portion of the PEB research paradigm that seems missing is serious consideration of the influence of context (setting/situation) – the "environment" – on behavior. Thousands of social psychological experiments illustrate that contextual variables dramatically influence the structure of behavior. Although the authors of some of those experiments explain the behavioral change as if some person attribute has changed, deeper inspection reveals the results show strong person-context interactions.

Psychologists from a few sub-disciplines acknowledge the importance of contextual influences on behavior (e.g., Figueredo, Jacobs, Burger, Gladden & Olderbak, 2008; Funder, 2006; Furr & Funder, 2004; Kelley, Holmes, Kerr, Reis, Rusbult & Van Langue, 2003; Mischel, 2004). Some have studied these interactions for years (e.g., Zimbardo, 2004). One prominent psychologist even claims there is a "false dichotomy" between person and context attributes. For him, behavior is but one part of a system composed of the person, context[5] and behavior (Funder, 2006). As the personality literature makes clear, context strongly influences – and more often than not overrides – dispositional person attributes. Surely, Environmental Psychology must incorporate that fact.

Hence, a shortcoming of PEB research is the assumption that person characteristics carry the lion's share of causal weight which remains largely uninfluenced across contexts. It follows that predictions about PEB that depend on context-independent assessments of person attributes (i.e. self report questionnaires) may starkly mislead. Moreover, modifying person attributes may not modify the real target, PEB.

Some PEB researchers understand there are "situational constraints and facilitators of behavior" (Kaiser & Gutscher, 2003, pg 586); they often argue the "perceived behavioral control" component in the TPB paradigm captures contextual influences sufficiently. This idea assumes that contextual influences carry less causal weight than person characteristics. The view ignores the fact that affordances, cues, and stimuli in settings/situations make salient, guide, transmit, and set the occasion for the "appropriate" behavior (Baum, 2005; Gibson, 1966; Macrae, Hood, Milne, Rowe &Mason, 2002; Malott & Trojan Suarez, 2003; Perkins, Dougher, Greenway, 2007; Wittenbrink, Judd & Park 2001; Zimbardo, 2004). Although many studies, both experimental and correlational, in literatures such as basic learning theory, personality theory, and social psychology, demonstrate this fact, the role of context as an independent and direct causal contributor has not yet been tested in PEB research.

With this in mind, the study presented in this chapter empirically investigates the role of contexts that contain cues and stimuli indicating the presence of adaptive problems and the presence of affordances that can guide solutions to those problems. We included TPB constructs to determine if they reliably predict self-described behavioral decisions in distinct contexts.

---

[5] He uses the term situation; however, to remain consistent with our operational definition context was inserted here.

THEORY OF PLANNED BEHAVIOR

TPB assumes the best predictor of behavior is behavioral intention – a composite of *attitudes, subjective norms* and *perceived behavioral control*. The model asserts that people arrive at *intentions* through a "reasoned action" approach – which follows from beliefs about performing a behavior, regardless of whether or not those beliefs map to the real world veridically (Ajzen, 1991; Ajzen & Fishbein, 1980)[6]. Beliefs provide the cognitive foundation from which attitudes, perceived social norms, and perceptions of control and, ultimately, intentions follow.

Consider the following examples. Kaiser and Gutscher (2003) examined the prediction that there is a direct correlation between perceived behavioral control (PBC) and self-reported PEB. They reported that, if PBC is *specifically* applied, then it predicts self-reported environmental behavior, however, when applied more generally, it does not. Lam (1999) used TPB to predict intention to reduce water usage and intention to install water-saving appliances in Taiwan. The TPB explained 41% of the variance in intention to reduce usage and 24% of the variance in intention to install water-saving appliances. Mannetti et al (2004) tested TPB with recycling, which accounted for 33% of the variance in recycling intention. Clark & Finney (2007) used TPB along with a few other person factors to predict water conservation intention in Blagoevgrad, Bulgaria. However, the TPB constructs did not predict intention to conserve water well, by only adding an additional 10% variance to their model. Pouta and Rekola (2001) tested TPB and derived beliefs supporting attitudes in predicting proenvironmental intention. They found that TPB predicted "Willingness To Pay" intention "reasonably well" supporting forest restoration[7]. Our point here is that TPB studies in the PEB domain typically explain anywhere from 30 to 70% of the variance in behavioral intention, however, intention only occasionally leads to behavior.

SETTING/SITUATIONAL CONTROL

Although the terms "context" and "situation" commonly appear in the literature, and at times serve as explanatory constructs, we have not found specific methods permitting us to operationalize either construct. Given our interest in contextualized behavior, we began working on this problem several years ago. Briefly, we argued:

> "An *environment* is the full set of adaptive problems an individual of a given species faces across development, independent of time (that is, the full set of adaptive problems that individual faced, is facing, and will face). A *context* is the subset of extant adaptive problems that the individual is facing. A *setting* is a subset of the context: the adaptive problems originating from the abiotic (nonliving) environment. A *situation* is also a subset of the context: In contrast to a setting, however, a *situation* consists of the subset of adaptive problems originating from biotic (living) sources." (Figueredo et al, 2008; p. 25)

---

[6] Interestingly, they state that beliefs can be irrational (Ajzen & Fishbein, 2005; p 153).
[7] Their findings are too complex/nuanced to state herein.

This view treats context as an inclusive construct denoting the full set of adaptive problems and affordances an environment might present to an individual.[8] In contrast, a setting consists of sensed "nonliving" objects and entities as well as the sensed adaptive problems, affordances, and contingencies provided by them in an extant context. These are the objects and entities that one might find comprising a cognitive map of an immediate environment (e.g., McNaughton, Battaglia, Jensen, & Moser, 2006; Wagatsuma & Yamaguchi, 2007). Similarly, a situation consists of extant living entities, including conspecifics as well as the sensed adaptive problems, affordances, and contingencies provided by them. We reserve the term "social situation" to include extant conspecifics, the sensed adaptive problems provided by them, and the sensed affordances and contingencies that might lead to solutions of that set of adaptive problems.

Although the standard social sciences often use the term 'situation' globally as a referent to the "environment" or "context", that tradition has created theoretical concern:

"Although social psychologists have emphasized the importance of the situation[9], they have been less successful in its conceptualization... [T]here is no universally accepted scheme for understanding what is meant by a situation. It does not even appear that there are major competing schemes, and all too often the situation is undefined". (Kenny et al, 2001; p.129)

Evidence points to the power of both settings and situations to moderate and sometimes mediate behavior. The idea is that behavior is not unconstrained, but the cues (Figueredo et al, 2006) supported by affordances (Gibson, 1966) that the organism detects prompt some conception of to-be-solved problems. Cues and affordances can be either evolutionarily instilled or learned over developmental time through experience, thus creating a behavioral or experiential history. Any given setting or situation will have only a subset of cues, affordances, and contingencies that are relevant *at that time*, and thus frame the full set of adaptive problems in a specific way. It is certainly the case that an individual cannot keep "in mind" all relevant salient cues, information, past experience, motivations, goals, etc. and carry them point to point, context to context, while behaving in the world. Therefore, it is crucially important to account for the sensed context when assessing behavior.

PEB researchers have not ignored the power of the setting/situation completely. Some acknowledge that context or at least external forces impinge on and constrain behavior. Some use the idea of externalities to explain the recognizable discontinuity between intention and behavior. The predominant perspective is, however, that contextual forces merely act to facilitate or inhibit person attributes (i.e. intentions).

Consider these studies. Schultz & Oskamp (1996) used "effort" as a behavioral moderator. They argued the amount of effort required to behave functions as an impediment to action (a behavioral barrier) and that overcoming higher behavioral barriers requires strong attitudes. They did not consider effort as a contextual variable outside the TPB paradigm; instead they treated effort as a constituent of perceived behavior control. This was, nevertheless, a step toward recognizing other determinants of behavior. Diekmann & Preisendorfer (1998) developed a "low-cost hypothesis of environmental consciousness" and

---

[8] Conceiving this as "outside" the individual is a misnomer because there is an intimate relationship between the perceiver and the perceived – they cannot be separated. However, for definitional purposes it is easier to denote it in this fashion.
[9] The term situation is used here globally to refer to context/environment.

tested its effects. They described a greater correlation of attitude and behavior in shopping and recycling contexts versus energy and transport contexts (the former having lower cost than the latter). Derksen and Gartrell (1993) implicitly acknowledged contextual constrains when they maintained that environmental attitudes affect recycling behavior only in communities with easy access to a structured recycling program. Corraliza and Berenguer (2000) examined relations between situational[10] "constraints" and person-centered variables by asking one question for each of 16 environmental actions: "my immediate physical environment facilitates/inhibits my carrying out the following action". They classified all the possible situations using a single dimension of conflict or consistency. Their results were mixed and although a noteworthy attempt, was unsatisfactory because *immediate physical environment* is vague and not descriptive of any real context. Kollmuss and Agyman (2002) hypothesize that primary motives such as altruistic and social values are often covered up by more immediate, selective motives, which evolve around one's own needs (e.g. being comfortable, saving money and time), which they interpret as PEB constraints, however they did not test that hypothesis. Cialdini, Reno & Kallgren (2000); Kallgren, Reno & Cialdini (2000); Reno, Cialdini & Kallgren, (1993) have all shown that people litter if there is litter in their surroundings but do not litter if their surroundings are litter-free. Although many consider this "normed-behavior" (again causal in itself), another interpretation is that environmental cues conveyed an acceptable, context dependent, way to behave, irrespective of individual "person attributes".

Potter, Dwyer & Lemming (1995) demonstrated complete contextual mediation in the PEB domain. Grounded in Functional Analytic methodology, these authors demonstrated that changing environmental contingencies through an integrative, supportive, coherent infrastructure drastically reduced environmental-code violations and specifically repeat violators. Each change addressed contextual components – none attempted to change violators' person attributes. The impact of this program insists we consider relations between situational infrastructure and PEB both within naturalistic and laboratory-based contexts. To do so we must recognize, acknowledge and empirically act on *specified differences* between current psychological conceptualizations and how Functional Analysts use situational control. TPB theory and its cousins consider behavioral variability to be noise, error or another as-yet-unmeasured or controlled person attribute. The Functional Analyst considers behavioral variability to result from contextual influences (Cooper et al, 2007). That simple difference in perspective changes the way we approach PEB.

EVOLUTIONARY RELEVANT CONTEXTUAL CUES

Examining influences of settings/situations requires identifying influential attributes of contexts. Evolutionists consider contexts as a conduit for presenting to-be-solved adaptive problems. The question then becomes, what is an *adaptive* problem and how do those adaptive problems overlap with PEB?

Evolutionary theory provides ultimate means and Functional Analytic (radical behaviorist) principles provide proximate mechanisms to produce contextualized behavior.

---

[10] This was their terminology – should have been "setting" to be consistent with operational definitions in this study.

By this perspective, past experience provided by an evolutionary history (base-rates) and a developmental history (experience), interacting with extant contingencies structure the form and probability of current behavior. Proximate mechanisms rely heavily on a basic three-term contingency (antecedent-behavior-consequence, Lehman & Geller, 2004). Phylogeny and ontogeny both operate through selectionist principles. Gene immortality lies at the basis of both the ultimate and proximate mechanisms (Dawkins, 1976). Simply put, organisms behave and reproduce, genes combine (or copies get passed on in new and varying combinations) that influence behavior, which simultaneously interacts with the environment; the *combination* that best solves adaptive problems in the *current context* will tend to be preserved. Then, when organisms behave and reproduce; genes combine and/or are copied and the cycle begins again. Through its cyclical nature, natural selection, which includes sexual and social selection (Miller, 2000; Nesse, 2007) takes place. Through this cycle, exant behavior finds its root in a successful behavioral history.

For our purposes, what is important is how behavior and how unconscious forces define salient contextual cues in the PEB domain which translate into gene immortality. We suggest that solving an adaptive problem increases the probability of using the same solution (behavioral tactic) upon the next encounter of the problem (reinforcement). Moreover, we suggest that, for modern humans, two major classes of to-be-solved adaptive problems involve situations.

The first involves reproductive success directly. Although we assume that a suite of mating strategies exist, we also assert that implementation of those strategies (tactics) leading to a short or long-term mating or relationship opportunity are reinforced. To do so, one must sense the adaptive problem(s) and act on it. The sensitivity to and the strategies used to solve this set of adaptive problems depends on Life History Strategy, evolutionarily base-rates, and behavioral history. Nevertheless, the presence of reproductive opportunities will influence the organization of behavior.

The second involves reproductive success indirectly. Humans must navigate non-mating social situations as well, solving the adaptive problems inherent in them. Successful solutions will ultimately lead to reproductive (either direct or indirect) opportunities by enhancing status and other means (Dawkins, 1976). Social norms, which prescribe appropriate tactics in social situations, strongly predict PEB (Schneider & Sundali, 1999; Uzzell et al, 2002). Importantly, social norms gain their power through "social pressure" (Buss & Kenrick, 1998), selecting for – and more importantly against – specific contextually bound behavioral tactics.

Shackelford (2006), recently suggested that determining the historical, developmental and situational[11] forms of contextual input processed by psychological mechanisms are important because those items guide human behavior. He recognized the use of social pressure in PEB this way:

> "Social pressure by valued others in the local population to adopt long-term recycling behaviors may prove to be a useful means to encouraging mass durable and generalizable recycling behavior". (Shackelford, 2006; p. 1555)

By this view, social pressure is subjective selective pressure one puts on him/herself (largely unconsciously) to mimic and/or behave similar to high status individuals. In so doing,

---

[11] This is his term, to be completely comprehensive "setting" should also be included.

the individual increases his or her own fitness. Hence, adaptively relevant contextual cues are those conveying any opportunity to enhance fitness because doing so leads to greater direct or indirect reproductive success. Impressing a potential mating target or remaining consistent with context-dependent social norms can override or negate individual person attributes.

MAIN HYPOTHESIS

If the person attribute view is correct, then the TPB constructs will 1) account for the largest share of variance in PEB across settings and situations and 2) the pattern of person-factor effects on PEB will be consistent across environmental settings and situations. If a contextual view is correct, then 1) contextual factors will account for the larger share of variance in PEB, and 2) this dominance will persists across multiple specific settings and situations.

METHOD

Overview

An on-line website administered questionnaires to investigate the person-by-context relationship. Written vignettes depicted the contextual components and TPB questions captured person factors. The dependent variable was the behavioral choice to the vignettes.

Participants

Three hundred forty subjects, self-selected from a large undergraduate subject pool, voluntarily participated in the study. They received four (4) experimental credits toward their experimental participation requirements.

Measures

Social Desirability Scale – Balanced Inventory of Desirable Responding (BIDR) Scale (Paulus, 2002). This scale, which measures self-deceptive enhancement and impression management, controlled for socially desirable responding. Egoistic bias is "a self-deceptive tendency to exaggerate one's social and intellectual status" and moralistic bias is a "self-deceptive tendency to deny socially-deviant impulses and claim sanctimonious, 'saint-like' attributes" (Paulus, 2002). There were 40 questions total using a 7-point Likert scale from -3 to +3 on agreeing/disagreeing with the statements.

Attitude Questions – This scale measures a person's overall evaluation of a given item or behavior. Specific behavioral items were taken from the GEB scale (Kaiser, 1998) that directly related to environmental actions depicted in the vignettes. Two sets of questions were asked; the first rated the statements as far as how *very good to very bad* they were and the second rated the statements as how *very appropriate to very inappropriate* they were. Other questions related to health, exercise, and purchasing products made with child labor (other setting themes described below). There were additional control questions to reduce task demand effects. The thirty two questions used a 7-point, -3 to +3, Likert scale.

Perceived Behavioral Control – This measures how easy or difficult a given behavior is to perform (Ajzen, 1991). Twelve questions were created, divided into two sets with six questions per set. The first set explicitly asked how *easy/difficult* the behavior was to perform on a 7-point Likert scale from -3 to +3. The second set used a *strongly agree to strongly disagree* 7-point Likert scale from -3 to +3 creating two questions per category. The second set questions began with, "Nothing can be done to…"

Subjective Norms – This measures a person's belief about whether other people (such as friends, neighbors, relatives or other in-group members) think he or she should engage in the specified behavior. Fifteen questions, all beginning with "Most people important to me…", were used that related to setting themes. The 7-point Likert scale (-3 to +3) ranged from strongly agree to strongly disagree.

Intention Questions – This is the outcome component of the TPB and measures how much someone intends to complete the behavior. Each of the 14 items were rated on 7-point (-3 to +3) *strongly agree to strongly disagree* Likert scale.

All questions assessing TPB constructs related specifically to each setting. This tactic was used to be consistent with Ajzen and Fishbein's (2005) reformulation of TPB addressing a) how *general* attitudes may not predict *specific* behaviors and b) why this may be the case. These authors concluded it is important to ensure that, when assessing relations between attitudes and behavior, those attitudes map *specifically* to the behavior of interest.

Vignettes

Each written vignette denotes a unique context with both setting and situational components. There were six different settings; four environmental and two non-environmental:

- Recycling – Neighborhood Program
- Water – Landscaping (Ecological Restoration)
- Energy – Clothes Drying
- Fuel – Car Rental
- Child Labor
- Health

We included the non-environmental vignettes for two reasons. First, certain settings may be perceptibly or adaptively indistinguishable from others, which may or may not fall along environmental lines. For example, perhaps the health and the recycling settings will produce similar behavioral choice patterns, whereas water and energy will not. That result would be taxonomically important. Secondly, if situational aspects influenced the behavioral choice more than settings; having only environmental vignettes would be a confound. Alternatively, detecting differential responding to environmental and non-environmental vignettes would produce useful results for both PEB researchers and other psychologists interested in creating taxonomies of context.

Three situational dimensions varied within *each* vignette: Social norm salience, cost and mating-target orientation. Descriptions of what the neighborhood, friends or some in-group is like and/or doing conveyed social norms. Costs were either monetary or "effort" costs[12]. We purposely depicted monetary costs vaguely as "free", "expensive" or "inexpensive" because actual monetary values may be confounding. Ten dollars is expensive to some students but not others, depending on their socioeconomic status. Therefore, vague terms make cost relevant to the subjects' current conception of expensive/ inexpensive. More or less behavioral effort (caloric cost) in the vignette depicted effort. Mating target was portrayed as a potential mate that may or may not be environmental and/or support health or child labor practices.

Conceivably each setting contains eight possible vignettes after varying the three situational dimensions; the total behavioral landscape is 48 cells (8x3x2). Each subject rated 24 out of 48 possible vignettes. There were four versions of the vignettes, each with a different order to control for order effects.

The vignettes mapped out a portion of the behavioral landscape that touched context-relevant nuances; a snippet of a typical tradeoff that is made moment to moment as a person navigates through life[13]. Similarly, the vignettes were a first step in taxonomizing contexts from an evolutionary perspective for PEB-relevant study. The vignettes presented equivalently structured scenarios; however, they contained purposefully pointed differences to convey specific adaptive problems – all the while being similar for good experimental control. Furthermore, the vignettes purposely pitted competing adaptive problems against one another, thereby mandating a trade-off when making behavioral choices[14].

Research Design

Subjects used a web-based experimental signup system developed by the University of Arizona. Upon receiving signup notification, we sent an instructional email alerting the subject to the survey website. Subjects accessed the survey from any web-available computer. They did not have to complete the entire survey at one time; they could exit and reenter as many times as they wished. The survey contained 24 vignettes and all the questionnaires described above. Subjects responded to the vignettes before all other measures to ensure the questionnaires did not bias their vignette responses.

RESULTS

Scale Inter-item Reliabilities

Table 1 lists Cronbach's alpha reliability coefficients. They were computed using PROC CORR in SAS software version 9.2 (SAS Institute, 2002). There was no standard criterion for

---

[12] This study was part of a larger study using other person-factors related to evolutionary theory. Cost was relevant within that framework; space constraints limited further elaboration herein.

[13] The vignettes were pilot tested determining if there would be variability in responding (since they are similar within contextual categories).

non-inclusion; however, an alpha of 0.70 and above is considered good inter-item reliability. Some of the TPB alphas were less than desirable. There were one to three items for each TPB constructs for each setting (recycling, child labor, etc). The TPB constructs paralleled how TPB is used in PEB studies. All attitudes alphas were good except three, which were slightly below 0.70 (none below 0.63). For subjective norms, two items were dropped (one subjective norm item about water and another subjective norm item about health) due to poor performance. Only one item remained for the water subjective norm construct and thus no alpha was computed. The alpha for the health subjective norm increased from 0.494 to 0.648, which is within tolerable range. Perceived behavioral control (PBC) constructs all have poor alphas. There were two items per setting. Dropping any one item would have required a corresponding drop in all other "like" items across settings; for example, questions 1-6 and 7-12 largely mirrored each other providing two items per setting. Considering it wasn't clear which item contributed to the low alpha and secondly given PBC is typically measured unsystematically, no PBC items were dropped. Intentions had good alphas except for energy and water (0.20 and 0.49 respectively). Intentions were measured in this study as they are in other PEB research; therefore, the reason reliabilities are low is unclear. Intention questions all related specifically to the settings.

Dependent Variables

The first behavioral choice question required choosing from a dichotomous option answering "what would you do", and the second question asked subjects, "How certain are you that you would actually choose to do what you indicate above?" on a five point "not at all certain" to "absolutely certain" scale. The two behavioral responses were combined to create one response on a 10-point scale. The scale was unfolded so that the lowest score (1) is consistently the least pro-environmental response and the highest score (10) is the most pro-environmental. Suppose that choice "a" is the most pro-environmental option. Choosing "a" with "absolute certainty" translated into a rating of 10, choosing "a" with "not at all certain" translated to a 6, choosing "b" with "not at all certain" translated to a 5, and "b" with "absolute certainty" translated to a 1.

This particular design created "missing data" in the dependent variable. The response burden was too heavy for subjects to properly distinguish all 48 vignettes. However, it was important to obtain data for all 48 vignettes even though *each subject* could not rate all 48. Therefore to accomplish appropriate statistical analyses, it was essential to determine if the responses would reduce into smaller composites. Furthermore, if settings could reduce that would enlighten possible taxonomic relationships amidst contexts. This determination was handled by contrast coding using SAS.

The vignettes were a crossed design of situational dimensions (social norms, mating target orientation, cost) by settings (recycling, car/fuel, ecological restoration, clothes drying, child labor and health). Therefore two separate contrast coding regimes were implemented; the first on the situational dimensions and the second on settings. For dimensions, contrasts were created determining which dimensions contributed to the behavioral choices. Similarly, contrasts were created determining if the settings could be combined. R^2 for this model was

---

[14] Space constraints prohibited including an example.

0.73, accounting for a large share of the variance in behavioral choice and was statistically significant ($p<0.001$).

Table 1. Inter-item Consistencies (Cronbach's alphas)

Measures	Cronbach's Alpha
Theory of Planned Behavior Constructs	
Attitudes Recycling	0.868
Attitudes Energy	0.643
Attitudes Water	0.631
Attitudes Fuel	0.646
Attitudes Child Labor	0.773
Attitudes Health	0.734
Subjective Norm Recycling	^
Subjective Norm Energy	^
Subjective Norm Water*	^
Subjective Norm Fuel	^
Subjective Norm Child Labor	^
Subjective Norm Health*	0.648
Perceived Behavioral Control Recycling	0.541
Perceived Behavioral Control Energy	0.314
Perceived Behavioral Control Water	0.291
Perceived Behavioral Control Fuel	0.220
Perceived Behavioral Control Child Labor	-0.138
Perceived Behavioral Control Health	0.095
Intentions Recycling	^
Intentions Energy	0.200
Intentions Water	0.490
Intentions Fuel	0.742
Intentions Child Labor	0.879
Intentions Health	0.762

* Additional Item dropped for further analyses due to low Cronbach alpha.
^ Only one item – no alpha computed.

Situational Dimension Reduction – Unexpectedly, social norms being high or low did not make a statistical difference in the behavioral choices. However, cost as high/low and mating target being for or against the setting theme remained intact as valid situational dimensions. This resulted in a dimensional reduction from eight to four. That social norms did not make a statistical difference was surprising and unexpected; there exists a substantial literature regarding social norms effects. An explanation to support this result is the subjects were from a college student sample and therefore the social norms depicted in these vignettes may not have been sufficiently potent to override the effect of mating target orientation or cost.

Setting Reduction – Recycling and fuel/car rental were combined; clothes drying and child labor were combined. Ecological restoration and health each remained separate settings. The clothes drying setting had behavioral mean choice ratings and standard deviations quite low; this sample did not choose to dry their clothes on a clothes line over a machine dryer.

This is not surprising given this young student sample. Most of these subjects likely have never been exposed to line-drying clothes given their mean age of 19. Similarly, the child labor setting had similar low means and standard deviations in the choice ratings; most did not support purchasing items made with child labor. This is also not surprising; our culture largely does not support using child labor, regardless of the "lures" in a situation that may seemingly condone it (i.e. short-term mating target support). Hence because both settings were consistently rated (low means and standard deviations) they were statistically combined. As expected, ecological restoration was not combined with other environmental settings, offering evidence that all environmental problems/contexts cannot be deemed and treated the same.

The 48 dependent variables were reduced to 16; a cross of two situational dimensions; 1) cost: high or low 2) mating target orientation: yes or no (meaning for or against PEB or Health), by four settings; a 4x2x2 design. Bivariate correlations were run to determine if the 16 contexts were orthogonal and if not, how much they were correlated; most correlations remained substantial within but *not* across settings. Interestingly, within setting the correlations weren't as high as might be expected. This indicates that each specific setting/situational configuration had differential, systematic effects on the behavioral choice.

Due to multicollinearity among vignettes of "like" setting, it was important to control for shared variance in the model statements when testing TPB constructs. Properly dealing with this dilemma was described in a study by Jones and colleagues (2007), who noted that researchers typically perform separate statistical analyses with all independent variables on *each* of the correlated dependent variables. However, this treatment is statistically flawed because it might incorrectly detect significant effects when there truly aren't any, thus creating Type I errors. Instead, the four co-linear vignettes were treated as converging indicators of a single common factor (Gorsuch, 1983; Jones, Figueredo, Dickey & Jacobs, 2007). The common factor created for each setting is "behavior in the aggregate" because combining four vignettes into one averaged the situational aspects.

Each model statement testing person factors began with the single unit-weighted common factor, estimated as the mean of each setting-by-situation configuration (Gorsuch, 1983). This controlled for the influence of the common factor variance by entering it as the first predictor variable when separate regression analyses were conducted on the unique variance associated with the independent variables (i.e. person factors). This allowed direct examination of the person factor effects specifically on the situational configurations controlling for the overlap in variance among them.

Person Factors (Independent Variables)

TPB items were all scored such that a high score resulted in being proenvironmental, supporting health regimes, and/or supporting/buying products using child labor[15]. The BIDR social desirability scale was disaggregated and the sub-scales of impression management (IM) and self-deceptive enhancement (SDE) were used individually.

---

[15] This was done because the child labor behavioral choices were coded as a high score (10) meant subjects would buy products using child labor. This may seem counter-intuitive; however, this coding direction was necessary given a priori predictions. Coding direction needed to remain consistent.

Table 2. Proportion of Variance Estimates; Total and Partitioning by Source

RECCAR^		RECCARLY		RECCARHY		RECCARLN		RECCARHN	
Source	R^2	Source	R^2	Source	R^2	Source	R^2	Source	R^2
		RECCAR	0.645	RECCAR	0.540	RECCAR	0.717	RECCAR	0.636
SD	0.043	SD	0.005	SD	0.014	SD	0.003	SD	0.013
TPB*	0.213	TPB*	0.004	TPB*	0.012	TPB*	0.008	TPB*	0.006
Subtotal	0.256	Subtotal	0.654	Subtotal	0.566	Subtotal	0.728	Subtotal	0.655
Error	0.744	Error	0.346	Error	0.434	Error	0.272	Error	0.345
Total	1.000	Total	1.000	Total	1.000	Total	1.000	Total	1.000

ER^		ERLY		ERHY		ERLN		ERHN	
Source	R^2	Source	R^2	Source	R^2	Source	R^2	Source	R^2
		ER	0.642	ER	0.716	ER	0.741	ER	0.681
SD	0.008	SD	0.001	SD	0.004	SD	0.003	SD	0.002
TPB*	0.176	TPB*	0.010	TPB*	0.015	TPB*	0.009	TPB*	0.008
Subtotal	0.184	Subtotal	0.653	Subtotal	0.735	Subtotal	0.753	Subtotal	0.691
Error	0.816	Error	0.347	Error	0.265	Error	0.247	Error	0.309
Total	1.000	Total	1.000	Total	1.000	Total	1.000	Total	1.000

Health^		HealthLY		HealthHY		HealthLN		HealthHN	
Source	R^2	Source	R^2	Source	R^2	Source	R^2	Source	R^2
		Health	0.655	Health	0.663	Health	0.653	Health	0.582
SD	0.003	SD	0.000	SD	0.008	SD	0.005	SD	0.001
TPB*	0.031	TPB*	0.014	TPB*	0.008	TPB*	0.005	TPB*	0.015
Subtotal	0.034	Subtotal	0.669	Subtotal	0.679	Subtotal	0.663	Subtotal	0.598
Error	0.966	Error	0.331	Error	0.321	Error	0.337	Error	0.402
Total	1.000	Total	1.000	Total	1.000	Total	1.000	Total	1.000

CDCL^		CDCLLY		CDCLHY		CDCLLN		CDCLHN	
Source	R^2	Source	R^2	Source	R^2	Source	R^2	Source	R^2
		CDCL	0.682	CDCL	0.539	CDCL	0.616	CDCL	0.424
SD	0.027	SD	0.003	SD	0.006	SD	0.009	SD	0.013
TPB*	0.135	TPB*	0.010	TPB*	0.010	TPB*	0.025	TPB*	0.017
Subtotal	0.162	Subtotal	0.695	Subtotal	0.555	Subtotal	0.650	Subtotal	0.454
Error	0.838	Error	0.305	Error	0.445	Error	0.350	Error	0.546
Total	1.000	Total	1.000	Total	1.000	Total	1.000	Total	1.000

^ Results shaded in gray is an average of the four specific dimensions within content type; behavior in the aggregate.
* All main effects and interaction terms from this person factor model was collapsed together in this composite.
SD: BIDR Social Desirability Scale; Impression Management and Self Deceptive Enhancement combined.
RECCAR: Combination of Recycling and Energy/Fuel (Car Rental).
ER: Water (Ecological Restoration).
Health: Health.
CDCL: Combination of Energy (Clothes Drying) and Child Labor.
LN: Low Cost, Mating Target not supporting PEB, Child Labor or Health.
LY: Low Cost, Mating Target supporting PEB, Child Labor or Health.
HN: High Cost, Mating Target not supporting PEB, Child Labor or Health.
HY: High Cost, Mating Target supporting PEB, Child Labor or Health.

Table 3. Theory of Planned Behavior Person Factors by Situation GLM significante Tests

	RECCAR^			RECCARLY			RECCARHY			RECCARLN			RECCARHN		
	b	F	p	b	F	p	b	F	p	b	F	p	b	F	p
RECCAR	n/a	n/a	n/a	0.97	607.38	0.0001	0.93	404.75	0.0001	1.02	862.93	0.0001	1.07	603.19	0.0001
IM	**0.51**	**18.39**	**0.0001**	-0.16	3.52	0.0616	-0.14	4.33	0.0383	0.11	2.19	.1397	**0.19**	**5.90**	**0.0157**
SDE	-0.16	0.49	0.4863	0.14	1.23	0.2681	-0.17	5.80	0.0166	0.11	0.94	0.3334	**0.43**	**6.72**	**0.0100**
ATTitude	**0.28**	**42.76**	**0.0001**	0.11	0.10	0.7494	-0.17	0.24	0.6234	-0.06	1.76	0.1850	0.12	1.53	0.2176
Subject Norm	-0.28	0.21	0.6503	0.06	0.00	0.9957	0.16	0.65	0.4206	-0.20	0.20	0.6518	0.00	0.18	0.6698
Perc Beh Cont	**0.18**	**16.24**	**0.0001**	0.02	0.49	0.4853	-0.10	1.83	0.1769	0.24	0.05	0.8184	-0.16	0.90	0.3441
Intention	**0.52**	**29.42**	**0.0001**	-0.09	1.13	0.2876	-0.08	0.93	0.3362	0.07	1.17	0.2799	0.10	1.03	0.3100
ATT*SN	0.02	0.55	0.4584	0.00	0.26	0.6071	-0.16	1.18	0.2773	0.16	1.67	0.1972	-0.01	0.28	0.5979
ATT*PBC	-0.12	0.06	0.8107	-0.02	0.11	0.7387	0.14	2.71	0.1005	**-0.15**	**5.15**	**0.0239**	0.02	0.15	0.6962
SN*PBC	0.11	0.33	0.5632	0.02	0.55	0.4599	-0.12	0.01	0.9159	0.00	0.44	0.5061	0.10	1.67	0.1972
ATT*SN*PBC	**0.11**	**4.13**	**0.0429**	-0.04	0.94	0.3325	0.08	2.21	0.1378	-0.01	0.13	0.7166	-0.02	0.14	0.7097

	ER^			ERLY			ERHY			ERLN			ERHN		
	b	F	p	b	F	p	b	F	p	b	F	p	b	F	p
ER	n/a	n/a	n/a	0.87	603.76	0.0001	1.05	868.75	0.0001	1.04	974.95	0.0001	1.04	710.96	0.0001
IM	0.14	2.11	0.1468	-0.23	0.86	0.3538	0.00	1.51	0.2202	**0.30**	**3.90**	**0.0492**	-0.08	0.03	0.8566
SDE	-0.20	1.04	0.3078	0.08	0.09	0.7600	-0.36	3.87	0.0500	-0.02	0.02	0.9021	0.29	1.66	0.1981
ATTitude	**0.57**	**37.74**	**0.0001**	**0.36**	**6.20**	**0.0133**	0.00	4.29	0.0390	-0.27	0.99	0.3103	-0.09	0.11	0.7386
Subject Norm	**0.14**	**6.17**	**0.0135**	0.01	1.59	0.2086	0.19	1.14	0.2869	-0.20	2.09	0.1494	0.00	2.12	0.1464
Perc Beh Cont	**0.43**	**18.13**	**0.0001**	0.05	0.04	0.8391	-0.06	**4.52**	**0.0342**	0.04	3.51	0.0620	-0.04	0.01	0.9269
Intention	**0.41**	**8.02**	**0.0049**	-0.06	0.34	0.5584	-0.17	3.40	0.0661	0.03	0.17	0.6821	0.20	3.12	0.0784
ATT*SN	-0.05	0.01	0.9436	-0.09	1.15	0.2846	-0.14	1.55	0.2136	0.13	0.41	0.5227	0.08	2.25	0.1343
ATT*PBC	-0.04	0.01	0.9212	-0.03	0.06	0.8050	-0.10	0.64	0.4258	0.13	1.38	0.2402	0.00	0.00	0.9581
SN*PBC	0.01	0.52	0.4728	0.00	0.16	0.6915	0.00	1.25	0.2650	0.08	0.44	0.5097	-0.10	0.53	0.4665
ATT*SN*PBC	0.03	0.21	0.6467	0.01	0.06	0.8116	0.04	0.75	0.3883	-0.09	3.61	0.0582	0.04	0.45	0.5013

	HEALTH^			HEALTHLY			HEALTHHY			HEALTHLN			HEALTHHN		
	b	F	p	b	F	p	b	F	p	b	F	p	b	F	p
HEALTH	n/a	n/a	n/a	0.95	641.05	0.0001	1.03	664.89	0.0001	1.04	628.78	0.0001	0.97	467.69	0.0001
IM	0.18	0.05	0.8160	-0.03	0.22	0.6360	0.02	1.22	0.2698	-0.07	0.27	0.6000	0.07	0.77	0.3816
SDE	-0.38	0.84	0.3609	0.02	0.02	0.8882	**-0.59**	**6.54**	**0.0110**	**0.44**	**4.40**	**0.0368**	0.13	0.05	0.8287
ATTitude	-0.12	0.43	0.5133	0.04	0.06	0.8021	0.12	3.46	0.0639	-0.30	0.08	0.7775	0.15	1.42	0.2347
Subject Norm	-0.31	1.08	0.2992	0.24	3.01	0.8036	0.18	0.94	0.3336	0.17	0.03	0.8736	-0.56	0.10	0.7464
Perc Beh Cont	-0.04	1.13	0.2881	**0.34**	**6.73**	**0.0099**	0.35	0.43	0.5142	-0.30	0.34	0.5594	**-0.38**	**4.90**	**0.0276**
Intention	**0.47**	**7.79**	**0.0055**	0.18	2.34	0.1274	0.00	0.00	0.9460	0.06	0.20	0.6574	-0.24	3.11	0.0787
ATT*SN	0.08	0.03	0.8617	-0.04	0.56	0.4542	-0.08	0.03	0.8651	-0.10	0.04	0.8485	0.21	0.33	0.5668
ATT*PBC	0.02	0.00	0.9898	-0.06	0.38	0.5584	-0.20	2.42	0.1210	0.18	3.33	0.0691	0.07	0.02	0.8932
SN*PBC	0.13	0.14	0.7057	0.02	0.00	0.9816	-0.16	0.85	0.3562	0.13	0.20	0.6529	0.27	0.17	0.6786
ATT*SN*PBC	-0.04	0.17	0.6845	0.00	0.01	0.9224	0.04	0.34	0.5621	0.07	0.93	0.3364	-0.11	1.71	0.1919

	CDCL^			CDCLLY			CDCLHY			CDCLLN			CDCLHN		
	b	F	p	b	F	p	b	F	p	b	F	p	b	F	p
CDCL	n/a	n/a	n/a	1.05	732.82	0.0001	1.12	397.52	0.0001	0.90	572.77	0.0001	0.93	254.69	0.0001
IM	**-0.67**	**9.24**	**0.0026**	-0.12	2.19	0.1395	-0.16	3.07	0.0806	-0.16	0.00	0.9668	**0.44**	**7.68**	**0.0059**
SDE	0.33	1.51	0.2203	-0.08	0.70	0.4043	-0.26	1.54	0.2160	**0.43**	**8.56**	**0.0037**	-0.10	0.04	0.8403
ATTitude	**0.66**	**42.75**	**0.0001**	-0.08	0.67	0.4147	0.17	0.08	0.7738	-0.32	0.05	0.8156	0.24	0.20	0.6515
Subject Norm	0.31	0.37	0.5433	-0.12	0.28	0.5969	-0.21	0.11	0.7378	0.20	.17	0.6825	0.12	0.20	0.7499
Perc Beh Cont	0.07	1.20	0.2745	**0.00**	**5.38**	**0.0209**	-0.37	0.08	0.7802	0.51	0.05	0.8170	-0.15	2.98	0.0850
Intention	**0.23**	**3.91**	**0.0487**	-0.11	1.45	0.2288	-0.13	0.89	0.3451	0.10	0.98	0.3234	0.14	1.21	0.2729
ATT*SN	0.21	2.05	0.1531	-0.12	1.25	0.2646	-0.18	0.69	0.4068	0.11	0.22	0.6425	0.18	1.62	0.2040
ATT*PBC	0.14	1.57	0.2111	0.16	1.66	0.1991	**-0.27**	**4.15**	**0.0424**	**0.41**	**16.63**	**0.0001**	-0.30	2.84	0.0932
SN*PBC	-0.12	0.00	0.9607	0.00	0.42	0.5198	0.15	0.02	0.8999	-0.22	2.04	0.1538	0.07	1.72	0.1902
ATT*SN*PBC	-0.09	1.00	0.3190	0.03	0.15	0.6970	0.11	1.23	0.2676	-0.11	2.68	0.1023	-0.03	0.06	0.8010

Items in bold are statistically significant at the p<0.05 level.

^ Results shaded in gray should be interpreted with caution – they combine all four content factors together, thus collapsing dimensions.

IM: Impression Management Subscale of BIDR Social Desirability Scale.

SDE: Self Deceptive Enhancement Subscale of BIDR Social Desirability Scale.

RECCAR: Combination of Recycling and Energy Fuel (Car Rental).

ER: Water (Ecological Restoration).

CDCL: Combination of Energy (Clothes Drying) and Child Labor.

LN: Low Cost, Mating Target not supporting PEB, Child Labor or Health.

LY: Low Cost, Mating Target supporting PEB, Child Labor or Health.

HN: High Cost, Mating Target not supporting PEB, Child Labor or Health.

HY: High Cost, Mating Target supporting PEB, Child Labor or Health.

The TPB person factors was an all inclusive model of main effects and interactions except for intention; intention (when asked specifically what one's intention is) is typically treated as a dependent variable in most studies using TPB and isn't theoretically meant to interact with the three causally preceding terms. Therefore intention was not included in any interaction term. Construct ordering is depicted in Table 3. Finally, aside from the setting common factor included first in each model statement, IM and SDE were included next in the model statements to control for their effects. IM was included before SDE because most of these situations deal with social issues where impression management should dominate.

Table 2 outlines the amount of variance accounted for (R^2) for each vignette; partitioning the variance for the common setting factors, social desirability and the TPB person-factor model. There are two separate areas to focus attention. First are the common factors highlighted in gray and second are the 16 specific situations all shown in white.

Common Factor Variance – The left side of Table 2 lists each common factor by setting (in gray). Recall the common factors are the average of the four vignettes containing unique situational configurations. Consolidating in this manner can be conceived as "behavior in the aggregate" because a number of contexts were averaged together. It is important to keep this in mind as a fruitful way to predict aggregated behavior because it may be difficult to predict any one person's behavior in every unique context (although ultimately that should be the goal of psychological science). The TPB person factor model performed well in the RECCAR, ER and CDCL common factors, by accounting for 21% of a total 26% amount of variance, 17.6% of a total 18.4% amount of variance, and 14% of a total 16%, respectively. TPB did not hold up well in the Health common factor. Therefore, if one is interested in predicting environmental behavior in the aggregate (i.e. consolidating many contexts to predict behavior on average), then TPB paradigm could be used as a close approximation. However, with regard to health/exercise contexts TPB may not be as precise in predicting behavioral aggregates.

Situational Factor Variance – The overarching theme among the specific situational vignettes (the non-shaded vignettes in Table 2), is the setting common factors are accounting for the largest share of variance. In addition, it is also clear that the dimensional aspects of the unique situations are not accounting for much variance. For example, referencing RECCARLY, the total model variance is 65.4% and the common factor is accounting for 64.5% of that variance. The remaining 0.9% of variance is divided between the social desirability constructs, TPB person factors and also the unique contribution of the situational dimensions. Finally, TPB person factor model did not perform well in any of these unique situations. The most variance explained was in the CDCLLN vignette, accounting for 2.5% of the variance.

A larger picture emerges when viewing Table 3, which display significance tests for the items in the model statements. There are some significant effects of person factors, however, caution is necessary when interpreting the results as described below.

Common Factor Settings

Environmental Settings – Attitude, PBC and intention were all positively associated with proenvironmental behavior in both environmental common factor settings (see Table 3 for significance). Specifically in the Ecological Restoration common factor, subjective norm was also significant and positively associated with PEB. Therefore, when considering behavior in the aggregate, TPB does offer sufficient explanatory power. Notably, in RECCAR, attitude was correlated 0.32 with the averaged behavior choice, however intention was only correlated 0.42 with the averaged behavior choice. In ER, attitude was correlated 0.31 with the averaged behavioral choice but again, intention was only correlated 0.31 with the average behavioral choice. Even further, when evaluating specific situations, intention is *never statistically significant*. Although attitude correlations are noteworthy, intention correlations are less than desirable. Nevertheless, TPB constructs, as measured specifically to the setting, was predictive of behavior in the aggregate for the environmental settings.

Impression Management (IM) was statistically significant in the RECCAR common factor (F=19.48, p<0.0001). People with higher IM recycled and chose to conserve fuel. It is interesting that IM was not a significant factor in the ER common factor. It could be that recycling is more directly associated with "environmentalism", thus people who are prone to socially desirable responding may do so in a more "obvious" context, whereas with ecological restoration "environmentalism" may not be quite as obvious.

Health Setting – In this common factor, only intention was statistically significant (F=8.00, *p*=0.005). Higher intentions to exercise, in general, lead to choosing the exercise program. However the correlation between intention and the behavioral choice was modest (0.16), although statistically significant (*p*=0.0026).

CDCL Setting – According to these results intention is statistically significant (F=3.90, p=0.049) and attitude is statistically significant (F=42.72, p>0.0001). This is an odd combination to try and discern the TPB constructs, however, especially considering the coding direction for the child labor vignettes and items; a higher score meant subjects supported child labor practices[16]. Furthermore, to follow methodological convention from the combination of recycling and fuel/car rental, all clothes drying items in the TPB scales were combined with the child labor TPB items. Theoretically, however, this doesn't make logical sense. For example, attitudes about energy do not overlap in any theoretical way with attitudes about child labor. Furthermore, in order to follow Ajzen and Fishbein's (2005) doctrine of utilizing specific attitudes and intentions to predict specific behavior, the energy questions for both constructs were specific about using a clothes dryer. The attitude questions asked how good/bad and how appropriate/ inappropriate it was to use a clothes dryer[17]. As already noted, a younger student sample may not understand the level of energy used by a clothes dryer since they may not have relative experience with energy savings of line-drying. This resulted in *positive attitudes* associated with using a clothes dryer, even though this was necessarily recoded as bad for the environment.

Interestingly IM was statistically significant (F=9.81, p=0.002). The negative relationship (b-weight = -0.49) occurred due to coding direction for the child labor vignettes. People with higher impression management purchase products with child labor more and use the clothes dryer more. This relationship was predicted.

---

[16] This was done because of behavioral predictions made a priori by the authors. In order to make the direction consistent across all situations with all person factors it was necessary to code all child labor items in this fashion.

[17] Given specific mapping the correlations among this and the behavioral choices should have been very high, however, they were not.

Conclusion

This study 1) tested the degree to which there may be contextual influence on PEB and 2) determined that TPB person factors alone are insufficient to account for the behavioral data. Settings accounted for most of the variance in behavioral choices and this pattern remained reliable across situations regardless of setting type. Furthermore, TPB person factors contributed little to the explained variance in any of the situations measured. This fact is inconsistent with the foundational assumption that TPB person factors contribute significantly to behavior, independent of context.

The results of the TPB analysis still tell a compelling story. Most of the TPB person factors were not statistically significant in specific situations – and there was substantial variability in those that were. Given that TPB is perceived as a known, predictive paradigm (at least with regard to intention), it may be surprising to some that it did not predict context-specific behavior.

More specifically, this study illustrated that settings influenced behavioral choices more than either situations or person factors. This was an unexpected but informative result. Humans are social creatures and driven to navigate the social landscape to their reproductive advantage. Hence, it was surprising the situational components did not account for a larger share of variance. Certainly research investigating specific situational dimensions may be taxonomically meaningful. Moreover, the fact that some settings could be combined and some could not is a very important finding. This result supports the idea that each proenvironmental setting should be studied in isolation and/or paired in such a way that these effects can be systematically disentangled. Finally, there may be other relevant person factors that should be studied in combination with contexts that we discuss more specifically below.

Situational Dimensions

We chose situational dimensions such as social norms, mating target orientation and cost as evolutionarily meaningful cues in an attempt to identify factors that influence behavior, specifically PEB. That social norms did not contribute to the situational variance surprised us. Humans have affinities to belong to in-groups, to impress and be swayed by peers, neighbors, friends, co-workers (anyone they admire), to become a part of a group, and/or to emulate it (Alexander, 1987; Bettencourt & Hume, 1999; Cialdini & Goldstein, 2004; Cohen, 2003; Conover & Feldman, 1984; Dovidio & Gaertner, 1999; Heaven, 1999; Hogg & Abrams, 1988; Ridley, 1996; Turner, 1991).

Although we prefer to face the data directly, perhaps the social norm manipulation in this study was too weak/not perceptible, or that, given the subjects were without real-world home ownership experience, these manipulations were not adaptively relevant as situational cues. For example in the recycling, ecological restoration and clothes drying situations, the neighbors were the social norm reference group. To our subjects, this could mean neighbors in a student dorm. Hence, the reference group may be too weak and not perceived as an adaptive problem to solve. Dorm neighbors may not be a group to impress or emulate. Similar arguments might be mounted against each of the scenarios. Another explanation is that their personal norms may have competed against the depicted social norms; personal norms were not measured in this study to determine if that was the case. There is substantial empirical support concerning the salience and influence of social norms to dismiss them entirely as relevant cues. Interestingly, however, it has been shown in another PEB study that young people are not attracted to obeying social norms (Frías-Armenta, Martín & Corral-Verdugo, 2009). Future studies attempting to taxonomize situations must use better manipulations to cast this construct properly, testing its capacity to influence situations. Perhaps verbal vignettes are not sufficient to invoke social norms realistically, calling for research focused on behavior unfolding in the natural world to properly flesh out those effects.

The presence of situation-specific mating opportunities affected subjects' behavioral choice. Specifically testing this notion, we created two groups, one with all mating target N's (not supporting the setting theme) and a second with all mating target Y's (supporting the setting theme). The mean behavioral choice ratings of these groups differed significantly (t=-9.53, p<0.000; two-tailed test), and were consistent in the direction of mating target orientation. This result lends support that reproductive opportunities has situational relevance which augment behavior.

There is some suggestion that cost is an important situational cue, however, its relations to person and/or contextual factors remain unclear. This may be due to our conception of the cost construct. We gave it no monetary amounts, and the effort spectrum was loose. Clearly, we should consider other kinds and various ranges of costs.

Table 4. Global Proportion of Variance Estimates

Source	R^2
Situation	0.013
Setting	0.163
Person	0.098
Setting X Situation	0.008
Situation X Person	0.069
Setting X Person	0.244
Setting X Situation X Person	0.131
Subtotal	0.726
Error	0.274
Total	1.000

Other Personal Costs?

Essentially none of the TPB person factors explained situation specific behavior. Perhaps other person factors, not included in this study, may account for more variance in the behavioral choices or help us understand what makes various contextual features adaptively important. For example, Table 4 displays the variance accounted for by the various sources (setting, situations, and persons). Settings have an R^2 of 16%, situations 1%, and persons

10%. Clearly, person factors cause systematic differential responding in this study. Moreover, the setting-by-person interaction accounts for 24% of the variance. Finally, the three-way interaction of setting-by-situation-by-persons explains 13% of the variance, supporting the point that these factors, taken as a whole, permit better behavioral predictions.

Overall, context matters for PEB specifically, and behavior in general. Humans use context-specific cues to determine appropriate behavioral tactics (i.e., solve adaptive problems). Clearly, settings carried the lion's share of variance and as such influenced the behavioral choices in these vignettes. It is unlikely 'simple' framing effects produced these differences, because the situations were the same *except for* the dimensional configurations. Casting framing effects as cues to specific adaptive problems makes these dimensional differences "meaningful" due to perceiving the adaptive problem in different ways. Therefore, these types of inconsistent results were expected, at least across the TPB paradigm. Although some topics remain unclear, the main finding is that including contextual variables within behavioral studies get researchers accurate behavioral predictions. Furthermore, studying person-by-context interactions is a key to understanding and predicting PEB. As investigations such as move forward, researchers can begin to create a taxonomy of contexts and consider person factors in light of various contextual effects upon them.

REFERENCES

Ajzen, I., & Fishbein, M. (2005). The influence of attitudes on behavior. In D. Albarracín, B.T.
Johnson, M.P. Zanna, (Eds): *The handbook of attitudes*, pp. 173-221. NJ, US: Lawrence Erlbaum Associates Publishers.
Ajzen, J. (1991). The theory of planned behavior. *Organization Behavior and Human Dimension Processes, 50,* 179-211.
Ajzen, I., & Fishbein, M. (1980). *Understanding Attitudes and Predicting Social Behavior.* Englewood Cliffs, New York: Prentice Hall.
Alexander, R.D. (1987). *The biology of moral systems.* Hawthorne, NY. Aldine de Gruyter.
Armitage, C.J., & Connor, M. (2001). Efficacy of the theory of planned behavior: A meta-analytic view. *British Journal of Social Psychology, 40(4),* 471-499.
Bamberg, S. (2003). How does environmental concern influence specific environmentally related behaviors? A new answer to an old question. *Journal of Environmental Psychology, 23(1),* 21-32.
Bandura, A. (1977). *Social learning theory.* Englewood Cliffs, NJ: Prentice-Hall.
Baum, W.M. (2005). *Understanding behaviorism: Behavior, culture and evolution.* Oxford: Blackwell Publishing.
Bettencourt, B.A., & Hume, D. (1999). The cognitive contents of social group identity: Values,
emotions and relationships. *Journal of Social Psychology, 29(1),* 113-121.
Blanchard, C.M., Kupperman, J., Sparling, P., Nehl, E., Rhodes, R.E., Corneya, K.S., Baker, F., & Rupp, J.C. (2008). Ethnicity and the theory of planned behavior in an exercise context: A mediation and moderation perspective. *Psychology of Sport and Exercise, 9(4),* 527-545.

Boyd, B., & Wandersman, A. (1991). Predicting undergraduate condom use with the Fishbein and Ajzen and the Triandis attitude-behavior models: Implications for public health interventions. *Journal of Applied Social Psychology, 21(22),* 1810-1830.

Buss, D. M., & Kenrick, D. T. (1998). Evolutionary social psychology (4th ed.). In D. T. Gilbert, S. T. Fiske, & G. Lindsey (Eds.). *The handbook of social psychology* (vol. 2, pp. 982–1026). New York: Oxford University Press.

Clark, W.A., & Finney, J.C. (2007). Determinants of Water Conservation Intention in Blagoevgrad, Bulgaria. *Society and Natural Resources, 20(7),* 613-627.

Cialdini, R.B., & Goldstein, N.J. (2004). Social influence: compliance and conformity. *Annual Review of Psychology, 55(1),* 591-621

Cialdini, R.B., Kallgren, C.A., & Reno, R.R. (1991). A focus theory of normative conduct. In L. Berkowitz (Ed.) *Advances in Experimental Social Psychology. Vol 24,* (pp 201-234).

Cialdini, R.B., Reno, R.R., & Kallgren, C.A. (2000). A focus theory of normative conduct: Recycling the concept of norms to reduce littering in public places. *Journal of Personality and Social Psychology, 58(6),* 1015-1026.

Cohen, J.E. (2003). Human population: The next half century. *Science, 302(5648),* 1172-1175.

Conover, P.J., & Feldman, S. (1984). Group identification, values and the nature of political beliefs. *American Politics Quarterly, 12(2),* 151-175.

Cooper, J.O., Heron, T.E., & Heward, W.L. (2007). *Applied Behavioral Analysis.* Pearson/Merrill-Prentice Hall, NJ.

Corraliza, J.A., & Berenguer, J (2000). Environmental Values, Beliefs and Actions A Situational Approach. *Environment and Behavior, 32(6),* 832-848.

Dawkins, R. (1976). *The selfish gene.* New York: Oxford University Press.

de Brujin, G., Kroeze, W., Oenema, A., & Brug, J. (2008). Saturated fat consumption and the Theory of Planned Behaviour: Exploring additive and interactive effects of habit strength. *Appetite, 51(2),* 318-323.

Derksen, L., & Gartrell, J. (1993). The social context of recycling. *American Sociological Review, 58(3),* 434-442.

Diekmann, A., & Preisendörfer, P. (1998). Environmental Behavior: Discrepancies between aspirations and reality. *Rationality and Society, 10(1),* 79-102.

Ewert, A., & Baker, D. (2001). Standing for where you sit: An exploratory analysis of the relationship between academic major and environment beliefs. *Environment and Behavior, 33(5),* 687-707.

Figueredo, A.J., Jacobs, W.J., Burger, S.B., Gladden, P.R., & Olderbak, S.G. (2008). The biology of personality. In Terzis, G., & Arp, R., (Eds.), *Information and the Biological Sciences.* Cambridge, MA: MIT Press, in press.

Figueredo, A.J., Hammond, K.R., & McKiernan, E.C. (2006). A Brunswikian evolutionary developmental theory of preparedness and plasticity. *Intelligence, 34(2),* 211-227.

Fransson, N., & Garling, T. (1999). Environmental Concern: Conceptual definitions, measurement methods, and research findings. *Journal of Environmental Psychology, 19(4),* 369-382.

Frías-Armenta, M., Martín, A., & Corral-Verdugo, (2009). Análisis de factores que influyen en el desarrollo de conductas ambientales y en la conducta anti-ecológica. *Interamerican Journal of Psychology, 43,* 278-286.

Frick, J., Kaiser, F.G., & Wilson, M. (2004). Environmental knowledge and conservation behavior: Exploring prevalence and structure in a representative sample. *Personality and Individual Differences, 37(8)*, 1597-1613.

Funder, D.C. (2006). Towards a resolution of the personality triad: Persons, situations and behaviors. *Journal of Research in Personality, 40(1)*, 21-34.

Furr, M.R., & Funder, D.C. (2004). Situational similarity and behavioral consistency: Subjective, objective, variable-centered, and person-centered approaches. *Journal of Research in Personality, 38(5)*, 421-447.

Garling, T., Fujii, S., Garling, A., & Jakobsson, C. (2003). Moderating effects of social value orientation on determinants of proenvironmental behavior intention, *Journal of Environmental Psychology, 23(1)*, 1-9.

Gibson, J. J. (1966). *The senses considered as sensory systems.* Boston: Houghton-Mifflin.

Gorsuch, R.L. (1983). *Factor Analysis.* Hillsdale, NJ: Lawrence Erlbaum

Harland, P., Staats, K., & Wilke, H. (1999). Explaining proenvironmental intention and behavior by personal norms and the theory of planned behavior. *Journal of Applied Social Psychology, 29(12)*, 2505-2528.

Hogarth, R.M. (1987). *Judgment and Choice (2nd Ed.)* Chichester, UK: Wiley.

Hoggs, M., & Abrams, D. (1988). *Social identifications: A social psychology of intergroup relations and group processes.* London: Routledge.

Hwang, Y., Kim, S., & Jeng, J. (2002). Examining the causal relationships among selected antecedents of responsible environmental behavior. *Journal of Environmental Education, 31(4)*, 19-25.

Jones, D.N., Figueredo, A.J., Dickey, E.D., & Jacobs, W.J. (2007). Relations among individual differences in reproductive strategies, sexual attractiveness, affective and punitive intentions, and imagined sexual or emotional infidelity. *Evolutionary Psychology, 5(2)*, 387-410.

Kahneman, D. (2003) A perspective on judgment and choice: Mapping bounded rationality. *American Psychologist, 58(9)*, 697-720.

Kahneman, D., & Tversky, A. (1982). The psychology of preferences. *Scientific American, 246*, 160-173.

Kaiser, F. (1998). A general measure of ecological behavior. *Journal of Applied Social Psychology, 28(5)*, 395-422.

Kaiser, F., & Gutscher, H. (2003). The Proposition of a General Version of the Theory of Planned Behavior: Predicting Ecological Behavior. *Journal of Applied Social Psychology, 33(3)*, 586-603.

Kallgren, C.A., Reno, R.R., & Cialdini, R.B. (2000). A focus theory of normative conduct: when norms do and do not affect behavior. *Personality and Social Psychology Bulletin, 26(8)*, 1002-1012.

Kals, E., Schumacher, D., & Montada, L. (1999). Emotional affinity toward nature as a motivational basis to protect nature. *Environment and Behavior, 31(2)*, 178-202.

Kelley, H.K., Holmes, J.G., Kerr, N.L., Reis, H.T., Rusbult, C.E., & Van Langue, P.A.M. (2003). *An atlas of interpersonal situations,* Cambridge University Press: UK.

Kenny, D.A., Mohr, C.D., & Levesque, M.J. (2001). A social relations variance partitioning of dyadic behavior. *Psychological Bulletin, 127(1)*, 128-141.

Kerner, M.S., & Grossman, A.H. (1998). Attitudinal, social and practical correlates to fitness behavior: A test of the theory of planned behavior. *Perceptual and Motor Skills, 87,* 1139-1154.

Kollmuss, A., & Agyeman, J. (2002). Mind the Gap: why do people act environmentally and what are the barriers to pro-environmental behavior? *Environmental Education Research, 8(3),* 239-260.

Lam, S. 1999. Predicting intentions to conserve water from the theory of planned behavior, perceived moral obligation, and perceived water right. *J. Appl. Social Psychol. 29(5),*1058–1071.

Lehman, P.K., & Geller, S. (2004). Behavior analysis and environmental protection: accomplishments and potential for more. *Behavior and Social Issues, 13(1),* 13-32.

Macrae, C. N., Hood, B. M., Milne, A. B., Rowe, A. C., & Mason, M. F. (2002). Are you looking at me? Eye gaze and person perception. *Psychological Science, 13(5),* 460-464.

Mainieri, T., Barnett, E., Valdero, T., Unipan, J., & Oskamp, S. (1997). Green buying: The influence of environmental concern on consumer behavior. *The Journal of Social Psychology, 137(2),* 189-204.

Malott, R.W., & Trojan Suarez, E.A. (2003). *Principles of behavior (5th ed.).*Upper Saddle River, NJ: Prentice-Hall.

Mannetti, L., Pierro, A., & Livi, S. (2004). Recycling: Planned and self-expressive behavior. *Journal of Environmental Psychology, 24(2),* 227-236.

Masters, J.C., & Smith, W.P. (1987). Social comparison, social justice and relative deprivation: *Theoretical and policy perspectives.* Vol 4. Hillsdale, NJ: Lawrence Erlbaum Associates, Inc.

McNaughton, B.L., Battaglia, F.P., Jensen, O., Moser, E.I., Moser, M. (2006). Path integration and the neural basis of the 'cognitive map.' *Nature Reviews Neuroscience, 7(8),* 663-678.

Miller GF. (2000). *The mating mind: how sexual choice shaped the evolution of human nature.* New York: Doubleday.

Mischel, W. (2004). Toward an integrative science of the person. *Annual Review of Psychology, 55(1),* 1-22.

Nesse, R.M. (2007). Runaway social selection for displays of partner value and altruism. *Biological Theory 2(2),* 1-13.

Oreg, S., Katz-Gerro, T. (2006). Predicting proenvironmental behavior cross-nationally: Values, the theory of planned behavior, and value-belief-norm theory. *Environment and Behavior, 38(4),* 462-483.

Paulus, D.L. (2002). Socially desirable responding: The evolution of a construct. In H.I. Braun, D.N. Jackson, D.E. Wiley (Eds.). *The role of constructs in psychological and educational measurement,* pp.49-69. Mahway NJ: Erlbaum.

Perkins, D.R., Dougher, M.J., Greenway, D.E. (2007). Contextual control by function and form of transfer of functions. *Journal of the Experimental Analysis of Behavior, 88(1),* 87-102.

Pooley, J.A., & O'Connor, M. (2000). Environmental education and attitudes: Emotions and beliefs are what is needed. *Environment and Behavior, 32(5),* 711-723.

Potter, L.E., Dwyer, W.O., & Lemming, F. (1995). Encouraging proenvironmental behavior: The environmental court as a contingency manager. *Environment and Behavior, 27(2),*196-212.

Pouta, E., & Rekola, M. (2001). The Theory of Planned Behavior in Predicting Willingness to Pay for Abatement of Forest Regeneration. *Society and Natural Resources, 14(2)*, 93-106.

Reno, R.R., Cialdini, R.B., & Kallgren, C.A. (1993). The transsituational influence of social norms. *Journal of Personality and Social Psychology, 65(1)*, 104-112.

Rice, J., Kovac, V., Kraft, P., & Moan, I.S., (2008). Predicting the intention to quit smoking and quitting behaviour: Extending the theory of planned behaviour. *British Journal of Health Psychology, 13(2)*, 291-310.

Ridley, M. (1996). *The origins of virtue*. London, Viking Press.

Schneider, S., Sundali, J (1999). Curbside Recycling: Does it Promote Environmental Rsponsibility? In M. Foddy and M. Smithson (Eds.), Resolving social dilemmas: Dynamic, structural, and intergroup aspects. Philadelphia, PA : Psychology Press pp. 253-262

Schultz, P., & Oskamp, S. (1996). Effort as a moderator of the attitude-behavior relationship: General environmental concern and recycling. *Social Psychology Quarterly, 59(4)*, 375-383.

Schultz, P., & Zelezny, L. (1998). Values and proenvironmental behavior: A five-country survey. *Journal of Cross-Cultural Psychology, (29)4*, 540-558.

Shackelford, T.K. (2006). Recycling, evolution and the structure of human personality. *Personality and Individual Differences, 41(8)*, 1551-1556.

Sheeran, P. (2002). Intention-behavior relations: A conceptual and empirical review. In W. Stroebe & M. Hewstone (Eds.) *European Review of Social Psychology*, pp 1-36. Chichester, UK: Wiley.

Sheeran, P., & Orbell, S. (1998). Do intentions predict condom use? Meta-analysis and examination of six moderator variables. *British Journal of Social Psychology, 37(2)*, 231-250.

Sheppard, B.H., Hartwick, J., & Warshaw, P.R. (1988). The theory of reasoned action: A meta-analysis of past research with recommendations for modifications and future research. *Journal of Consumer Research, 15(3)*, 325-343.

Staats, H., Harland, P., & Wilke, H. (2004). Effecting Durable Change: A Team Approach to Improve Environmental Behavior in the Household. *Environment and Behavior, 36(3)*, 341-367.

Thögersen, J., Olander, F. (2006). To what degree are environmentally beneficial choices reflective of a general conservation stance? *Environment and Behavior, 38(4)*, 550-569.

Uzzell, D., Pol, E., Badenas, D. (2002). Place Identification, social cohesion, and environmental sustainability. *Environment and Behavior, 34(1)*, 26-53.

Valle, P.O.D., Reis, E., Menezes, J., & Rebelo, E. (2004). Behavioral determinants of household recycling participation. *Environment and Behavior, 36(4)*, 505-540.

Wagatsuma, H. & Yamaguchi, Y. (2007). Neural dynamics of the cognitive map in the hippocampus. *Cognitive Neurodynamics, 1(2)*, 119-141.

White, K.M, Robinson, N.G., Young, R., Anderson, P.J., Hyde, M.K., Greenbank, S., Rolfe, T., Keane, J., Vardon, P., & Baskerville, D., (2008). Testing an extended theory of planned behaviour to predict young people's sun safety in a high risk area. *British Journal of Health Psychology, 13(3)*, 435-448.

Widegren, O. (1998). The new environmental paradigm and personal norms. *Environment and Behavior, 30(1)*, 75-100.

Wittenbrink, B., Judd, C. M., & Park, B. (2001). Spontaneous prejudice in context: Variability in automatically activated attitudes. *Journal of Personality & Social Psychology, 81(5)*,815–827.

Zarakovskii, G.M., Medvedev, V.I., & Polesterova, N.A. (2000). Comprehensive study of environmental consciousness of high school students. *Human Physiology, 26(5)*, 612-620.

Zimbardo, P.G. (2004). A situationist perspective on the psychology of evil: Understanding how good people are transformed into perpetrators. In A. Miller (Ed.), *The social psychology of good and evil: Understanding our capacity for kindness and cruelty*. New York: Gilford.

In: Psychological Approaches to Sustainability
Editors: V. Corral-Verdugo et al.

ISBN 978-1-60876-356-6
© 2010 Nova Science Publishers, Inc.

Chapter 15

WHY DO PEOPLE FAIL TO ACT?
SITUATIONAL BARRIERS AND CONSTRAINTS ON PRO-ECOLOGICAL BEHAVIOR

Rui Gaspar de Carvalho[*], *José Manuel Palma-Oliveira*
Faculdade de Psicologia e Ciências da Educação, Universidade de Lisboa, Portugal
and *Victor Corral-Verdugo*
Universidad de Sonora, Mexico

ABSTRACT

The lack of success in dealing with the inconsistency between positive attitudes and ecological behaviors, and in explaining why people fail to act pro-environmentally is still widespread in practice and research. In our view, this has to do with three main reasons: 1) A positivity fallacy - the belief shared by many researchers and practitioners that as long as people have the right (or positive) attitudes, intentions, skills, information, etc., the right pro-ecological action should follow; thus, they disregard the importance of *negative* determinants in explaining the attitude-behavior inconsistency. 2) Lack of a psychological level of explanation; even when negative determinants are considered, the psychological explanation is often disregarded or incompletely identified, with most of the factors identified being socio-economical, or urban planning and architectural, etc. However, factors explaining why people fail to act can also be viewed within a psychological level of explanation, with behavior considered to be the result of an interaction between contextual variables and psychological processes. 3) Underestimation of the unconscious processes influence; contextual effects on behavior can be mediated not only by conscious perception but also by cognitive processes of which people are not aware of. Given these reasons, a model of psychological barriers and constraints is proposed (DN-Work model; "Didn't work") trying to integrate negative determinants

---

[*] Correspondence: Rui Gaspar DE Carvalho (C/A Jose Manuel Palma), Faculdade de Psicologia e Ciências da Educação, Universidade de Lisboa, Alameda da Universidade, 1649-013 Lisboa, Portugal. E-mail: rui.carvalho@campus.ul.pt

within a psychological explanatory model of pro-ecological behavior. This model aims to represent a process view regarding how a conflict between pro-ecological and anti-ecological behavioral goals can be produced, given the presence of two types of barriers and constraints: a) perceived barriers and constraints, and b) unconscious barriers and constraints. We briefly present two studies based on this model. These studies address habit accessibility as an unconscious behavioral barrier on ecological decisions to buy organic products, mediated by the effect of behavioral-goals activation from the situation.

INTRODUCTION

The Positive Fallacy

Being "positive" in life is not always a good thing, especially if you work in the field of Environmental Education and Behavior Change. Many projects in this area are biased by a "positivity fallacy", i.e. the belief that as long as people develop the right attitudes, intentions, skills, information, etc., the right pro-ecological behavior should follow. However, as informed by the social sciences literature, an inconsistency exists between attitudes and behaviors, with cross-country studies showing high levels of ecological concern but, at the same time, low levels of ecological action (e.g. Ferreira Marques, Palma-Oliveira, Marques, & Ferreira 1995). In our view, one of the causes of such inconsistency is an underestimation of the factors working as barriers and constraints to ecological behavior change and to the promotion of pro-ecological behavioral goals (i.e. factors which increase the attitude-behavior inconsistency). Hence, the "right" factors do not seem to be enough to promote behaviors consistent with one's positive attitudes, beliefs, etc.

This "positivity fallacy" is also evident in research on ecological behavior regarding models that intend to identify the "positive determinants" of action (i.e. factors that when present can promote a new behavior or increase the strength of an existing one.) Consequently, the barriers and constraints on pro-ecological behaviors are seen as *lacking factors*, i.e. factors that influence pro-ecological behavior in a negative way, due to absence or weak influence of a positive determinant or "right" factor. One example is provided by Stern, Dietz, Abel, Guagnano, & Kalof's (1999) Value-Belief-Norm Model, in which it is implicit that, if people lack altruistic personal values or an ecocentric orientation towards nature, for example, pro-ecological behavior should not develop. Other models are more explicit regarding these negative factors, as it is the case of Kollmuss and Agyeman's (2002) model identifying the lack of internal incentives, environmental consciousness, external possibilities and incentives, and the negative or insufficient feedback about behavior.

One problem with this view is that it fails in acknowledging the fact that people's behavior is influenced by situations. Even if people have a strong intention to behave in a pro-ecological way, the situation can be perceived as inhibitive (Corraliza & Berenguer, 2000), leading to inaction. In this sense, models and projects based on a "positivity fallacy" only identify "what people are supposed to do" given the right factors – prescriptive view - but not "what people actually do" when they are in a certain situation – descriptive view. Identifying "what people actually do" implies identifying the reasons why people fail to act pro-ecologically, being this the aim of our chapter.

The Need for a More Integral Analysis of Behavior

A number of behavioral models try to explain why people fail to act. However, most of the negative factors analyzed so far are non-psychological in nature (e.g. socio-economic). These factors are seen as having their influence outside the person's intention or will and are represented as a direct effect of situations on people's behavior. Thus, no matter how strong the commitment to perform a behavior is, how positive the ecological attitude is, or how responsible a person feels in its performance, the situation can directly inhibit behavior.

One example, presented in the literature as a situational barrier to recycling behavior, is garbage-containers spatial accessibility (Schultz, Oskamp & Mainieri, 1995). The less spatially accessible (i.e. the more distant) the waste disposal facilities are, the lower the probability that people will separate at home and dispose the waste in the right recycling bins. This problem appears to be more related to design and urban planning issues than to people's "fault" and can be labeled as a "blame it on the situation" effect, as manifested in the literature regarding ecological behavior. In addition, this approach does not explain why when people's dispositions and the situation are both facilitative (e.g. spatially accessible containers + positive attitudes and intentions; etc.), people still do not behave in the "right way." Thus, the approach provides an incomplete account of the interaction between situations and psychological processes.

Additional examples pertaining the negative effect of situations on pro-ecological behavior are the influence of exterior temperature on domestic energy consumption levels (Olsen, 1981); the inadequacy of infra-structures, like ergonomic features and transportation network planning, on different ecological behaviors (Kollmuss & Agyeman, 2002); the influence of place of residence and other demographic variables on driving behavior (e.g. Tanner, 1999); and the absence of income on purchasing energy-efficient devices (Constanzo, Archer, Aronson & Pettigrew, 1986). These factors correspond to levels of explanation from disciplines other than psychology (economy, sociology, architecture, etc.), thus the situation's effect on behavior is not assessed within a psychological level of explanation. Our criticism is not intended to imply that non-psychological factors and psychological variables should not be assessed together when an attitude-and-behavior-change intervention is designed. What we alert is that by assessing only these non-psychological factors, researchers and practitioners are often prevented from seeing them through a "psychological lens" (as lay people usually do) and implicitly dismiss their importance and explanatory power.

One illustration of this case comes from Gardner and Stern's (2002; Stern & Oskamp, 1987) causal model of resource-consumption behavior. These authors identify internal and external psychological and non-psychological "limiting factors" which prevent people from acting based on their pro-ecological attitudes. Such factors are classified ranging from the highest level of causality (variables with the strongest influence on behavior) to the lowest, respectively: 1) resource-use or resource-saving behavior; 2) attention, and behavioral commitment; 3) knowledge; 4) attitudes and beliefs; 5) values and worldviews; 6) external incentives and constraints; and 7) household background. External and internal barriers can be found within these levels, with their influence being higher for high-cost or difficult actions (i.e. stronger influence as attitude-behavior inconsistency factors). Thus, for example, an inconsistency between attitudes (level 4) and behavior (level 1) could be due to internal barriers like absence of the necessary behavioral knowledge (level 3) or the absence of either attention or behavioral commitment (level 2). In opposition, the influence of external barriers is higher on household background (7) and external incentives and constraints (6) levels, which can inhibit the development of positive values and worldviews (level 5), and both attitudes and beliefs (level 4). According to Gardner and Stern (2002), these external barriers can be associated with people's socioeconomic background, available technology, economic forces, inconvenience, etc.

A problem with these models is that, more than identifying all the possible psychological and non-psychological explanatory factors and how they *independently* affect behavior, we researchers should consider their effect in a synergistic way. In other words, we should analyze how situations and psychological processes interact to influence behaviors, in order to increase the models' explanatory power. One example of this was given by Talarowsky (1982) in a study on water conservation during a drought situation. This study showed that when residents considered that the drought was due to environmental reasons, they tended to conserve water within the limits proposed by the authorities. However, when they thought that individual consumption was the cause of water scarcity, the limits on consumption average were exceeded. The latter allowed the attribution of others' responsibility implying a belief such as: "(...) if the crisis is due to other people's behavior, then my behavior will not alter much the situation and it is better to continue using water because if I don't, others will do it in my place" (Palma-Oliveira & Gaspar de Carvalho, 2004, p.5; Palma-Oliveira & Correia dos Santos, 1998).

Thus, the non-psychological behavioral barriers and constraints can also be seen in a psychological level of explanation, because a perceptual component is involved. Accordingly, one of the main psychological principles regarding how people interact with their environment is that we are the "builders" of our own reality (Smith & Mackie, 1995). People can construct their own reality through social and cognitive processes and thus, some aspect of people's environment can work as a behavioral barrier if people perceive that aspect in such a way. In other words, the limiting non-psychological factors (Gardner & Stern, 2002) which are present in the situation can have their effect on behavior mediated by perception-based processes, translated into an interaction between psychological factors and the situation.

BARRIERS AND CONSTRAINTS ON ECOLOGICAL BEHAVIOR

Perceptual Factors

Situational factors negatively affecting behavior through the mediation of perceptual processes are called *perceived barriers and constraints*. They can be considered "true" negative determinants of action, since they do not correspond to an absence or weak influence of a positive determinant. Accordingly, in the example regarding garbage containers accessibility, a barrier/constraint could be the perceived cost and difficulty in performing the behavior, in terms of mental effort, time, motivation level, and degree of discomfort in the performance of behavior (Gaspar de Carvalho & Palma-Oliveira, 2004; Kollmuss & Agyeman, 2002). A study by Diekmann and Preisendörfer (1992) supports this idea, showing that small-effort behaviors like recycling are performed more frequently than large-effort behaviors like car use reduction, with this difference being attributed to the perceived costs vs. benefits.

Another example comes from the Theory of Planned Behavior (Ajzen, 1991), which apart from analyzing two positive behavioral determinants (attitude and subjective norm), identifies a process which is similar to the costs/benefits analysis, named "perceived behavioral control" (PBC; Ajzen, 1991). The idea is that since there are many behavioral constraints that may limit volitional control, it is useful to analyze people's perception of these constraints, which serves as a "proxy" for actual control of their behavior, to the extent that these perceptions are close to reality (Ajzen, 2002). Hence, a low PBC functions as a negative determinant because the individual can perceive that behavior is not under her/his control and that there are strong external constraints impeding its performance, decreasing the intention to perform it. Other studies in Environmental Psychology use similar concepts, like for example, perceived behavioral barriers (Mckenzie-Mohr, 2000), perceived behavioral costs (Kollmuss & Agyeman, 2002) or perceived difficulty (De Young, 1988-1989). These perceptions can be seen as a product of expectancy or perceived likelihood of reaching a goal (e.g. "How likely is that I separate residues at home?") and goal value (e.g. "How important is for me to separate residues at home?") (Förster, Liberman & Friedman, 2007).

Apart from the expectancy/value assessments, other types of perceptions of the situation exist as, for instance, biased perceptions due to the influence of beliefs. For example: someone has a belief that water-scarcity problem resolution depends on technology and that someday a successful and non-expensive way to use water from glaciers, atmosphere or another source will be found. Beliefs like this, that according to Thompson and Barton (1994) are based on an anthropocentric orientation, will function as limiting factors to conserve water because individuals will expect ecological problems to be solved through technological improvements and not through individual and societal behavioral change. If people add to this a belief that, in spite of what is said in the media about environmental problems, water is an abundant resource (Biel & Garling, 1995), the need of water conservation will be minimized and underestimated (see Corral-Verdugo, 2002).

Another type of *perceived barriers and constraints* refers to perceptions about the self and one's own behaviors. In this regard, research has shown that the tendency to break social norms, or antisocial behavior (conceptualized in terms of the perception of how frequently people engage in antisocial actions), can inhibit water conservation. Anti-ecological behavior can be seen as an instance of more general antisocial behavior (Corral-Verdugo, Frias-Amenta, Gonzalez-Lomelí, 2003; Corral-Verdugo & Frías-Armenta, 2006). Also, we can include the perceptions regarding other people, translated into the influence of explicit cognitive representations working as *perceived barriers and constraints*, such as: stereotypes regarding environmentalists (Stoll-Kleemann, 2001), attitudinal ambivalence (Costarelli & Colloca, 2004), anti-environmental subjective norms (Schultz, Oskamp & Mainieri, 1995) or anti-environmental attitudes (Palma-Oliveira & Garcia-Marques, 1988).

As a conclusion, we can see that perception-based factors are important because by analyzing them we can identify the underlying factors characterizing a certain context and behavior (Suárez, 1998). Moreover, there is idiosyncrasy in these factors, since what might be a barrier for one person might not be for another. Consequently, different perceptions might imply different interventions to change attitudes and behaviors and they should be assessed.

These perceptions do not occur in a situational void and even when they are biased in some way, they are still associated with one or more situationally perceived characteristics (e.g. recycling behaviors of relevant people; availability and price of organic products in a supermarket shelve; location of a garbage disposal facility; amount of litter in a public space, etc.). We perceive these situational characteristics in a broad way from the most concrete to the most abstract levels, including not only the context's physical features and tangible aspects but also those characteristics associated with social environments and events happening in there, like other people's behaviors and attitudes, for example. By identifying these perceived barriers and constraints, we try to bring the situation back to the study of barriers and constraints on ecological behavior, yet within a psychological level of explanation.

A SITUATION-BASED APPROACH ON ECOLOGICAL BEHAVIOR

An example of a model that acknowledges the influence of the situation as mentioned, is provided by Tanner (1999) based on the Ipsative Theory of Behavior (e.g. Frey, 1989). Although still including some non-psychological factors (the "objective constraints") it represents an evolution compared to the previous examples, because it goes beyond the "positivity fallacy" and explicitly considers an analysis of pro-ecological behavior negative determinants based on the situation. According to this author, there are three classes of constraints, which are conceived as internal and external conditions inhibiting the performance of an action: 1) *Ipsative constraints* – internal factors that prevent the activation of a particular behavioral alternative from occurring, i.e. the action can only be performed if the individual remembers to perform it, implying the assessment of a limited number of alternatives and without considering the pro-ecological option in them; 2) *Subjective constraints* – perceived factors that inhibit preference for a particular behavioral alternative or willingness to act; these constraints entail beliefs regarding what is possible or not, desired or not, or allowed or not, so that they can eliminate behavioral options based on that assessment; 3) Objective constraints – external factors that prevent the performance of a particular behavior alternative from occurring, which are independent from individuals' perception (lack of opportunities, mental and physical disabilities; low income; influence of legal and political institutions; etc.).

Apart from this model, methodological approaches have also been used to assess the situation's effect on behavior (e.g. Kaiser & Keller, 2001). Still, as in the previous example, they are mainly descriptive and do not explain how the situation can affect behavior through the mediation of psychological processes. Nevertheless, they consider some "invisible" factors scarcely identified in research (ipsative constraints; Tanner, 1999; implicit situational factors; Kaiser & Keller, 2001), which should be more profoundly studied. This study should be complemented with a process view, to understand how contexts can inhibit or constrain people's behavior, outside their awareness and conscious control.

The "Invisible" Factors

Situation's effect on behavior can be mediated not only by perception-based processes but also by cognitive processes of which people are not aware of, which can work as *unconscious barriers and constraints*. Accordingly, since the 1960's, research in social psychology has increasingly demonstrated the relative automaticity of social behavior and the influence of cognitive and motivational factors outside people's awareness on behavior (Bargh, 1997). These factors are rarely considered in both Environmental Education and Behavioral Change projects and in models of barriers and constraints on ecological behavior, and when they are, they are not explicitly identified as such.

To be clear on how the automatic processes affect behavior, it is important to understand what we mean by "unconscious" and "conscious" processes and the differences in the way they are initiated to influence social behavior. Conscious processes are mental acts which we are aware of, that are intentional, effortful and controllable (Bargh & Chartrand, 1999). In a different way, for a process to be automatic and unconscious, it has to be effortless and to occur when a set of preconditions are in place (conditional automaticity), without any conscious choice or guidance from that point on (Bargh, 1997). Hence, the category of *unconscious barriers and constraints* can include cognitive representations of the world (e.g. attitudes), which can increase the probability of anti-ecological behaviors to occur in an automatic and unintended way, given the presence of certain environmental cues. These barriers/constraints produce their effect without people being aware of them and can influence across different contexts and behaviors (i.e. they are "universal"), as long as the activating cues are stable across those contexts and behaviors. The same does not happen with *perceived barriers and constraints,* which often are behavior or domain specific and idiosyncratic (e.g. McKenzie-Mohr & Smith, 1999; Black, Stern & Elworth, 1985).

One example of *unconscious barriers and constraints* refers to the influence of implicit anti-ecological attitudes on ecological behaviors, with research showing that they can be more predictive of ecological behavior than explicit attitudes (e.g. Vantomme, Geuens, De Houwer & De Pelsmacker, 2005), which are more prone to social desirability effects. Research shows that a behavior can be associated to various attitudes supporting it, depending on the individual or situation; and yet the attitude that appears to support a behavior (explicit attitude) is not always the one most related to it (Palma-Oliveira & Gaspar de Carvalho, 2004). The attitude with the highest impact on behavior will be the one with the highest cognitive accessibility (as demonstrated in the MODE model; Fazio, 1990). Therefore, if an implicit anti-ecological attitude exists and is stronger (i.e. more accessible) than other attitudes influencing a certain behavior, it will affect behavior in accordance with its cognitive accessibility.

Apart from attitudes, other cognitive representations can have an automatic effect on behavior, such as stereotypes, norms and habits. However, there is a gap in ecological-behavioral research regarding these variables, since most studies report the influence of explicit factors (e.g. Stoll-Kleemann, 2001) and only a few communicate the implicit effect (e.g. Vantomme et al., 2005). We will get back to this point and report our own research regarding this implicit effect on ecological behaviors and specifically to what concerns the effect of habit accessibility.

Summarizing, we argue in favor of an explanatory approach considering *unconscious barriers and constraints*, given that these variables can affect behavior without people being aware of, and thus cannot be analyzed through traditional perception-based measures (e.g. questionnaires)[4] and dealt with in attitude and behavioral change programs. In order for their relevance to be more explicit, we need to show how they relate with perceived barriers/constraints and with behavioral goals, in influencing pro-ecological acting. Moreover, we should demonstrate how these types of barriers and constraints relate to behavioral goals. We will refer to these aspects next.

WHY PEOPLE FAIL TO ACT? - A MODEL PROPOSAL

The research field of negative barriers and constraints is defined as the study of the "I don't understand why it didn't work" factors, which are considered among the main causes of unsuccessful Environmental Education and Behavioral Change projects (Palma-Oliveira & Gaspar de Carvalho, 2004). These factors can be included in what we call the *DN-Work model* ("didn't work"), which we will present here. This model has three main principles: 1) barriers and constraints are not defined in terms of the "lack" of strength or absence of positive factors -what we call the "lack factors"- but as psychological factors independent from these; 2) their influence depends on psychological processes interacting in different levels and ways with situational features, and is mediated by the activation of behavioral goals[2] (Bargh & Chartrand, 1999); and 3) their influence can occur in different degrees of awareness and conscious mediation.

In the first part of the model (see figure 1) the situation is considered as having an effect on behavior given the presence of *limiting factors*, with this category including either path: 1) the situational characteristics that activate psychological barriers and constraints, through the mediation of conscious/intentional processes or 2) the situational cues that activate psychological barriers and constraints, with reduced consciousness and through unintentional and automatic processes. Consequently, we call the psychological barriers and constraints, which are activated through the first "path", *perceived barriers and constraints*; while the psychological barriers and constraints which are activated through the second "path" are the *unconscious barriers and constraints*.

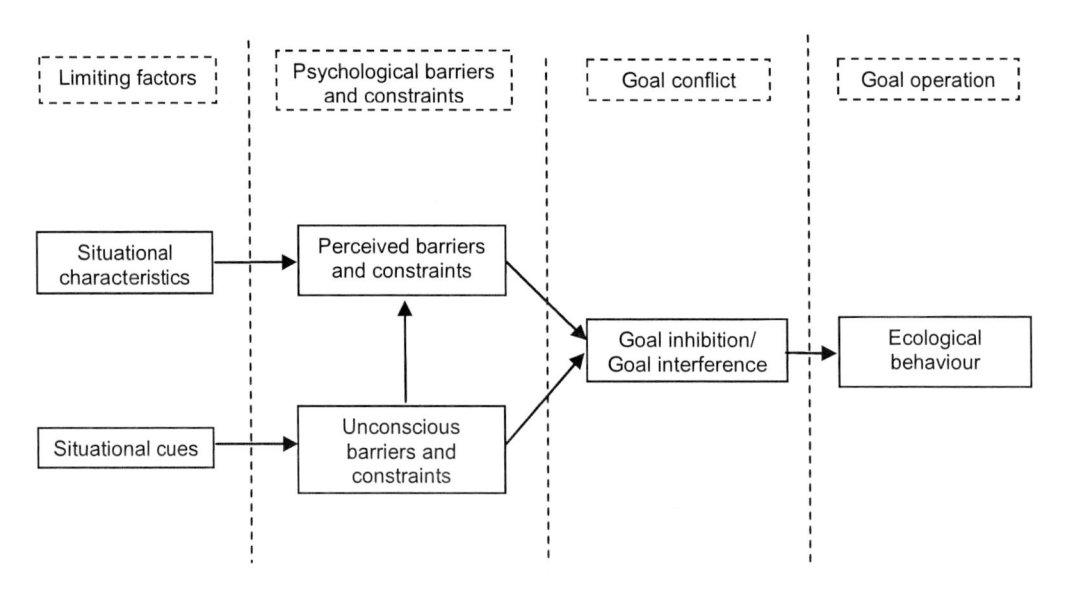

Figure 1. DN-Work model of barriers and constraints on ecological behavior.

We make a distinction between the two types of situational limiting factors, for the purpose of making clear our explanation of the different psychological processes involved in each path. However, there is some overlap between "characteristics" and "cues", given that the same limiting factor can sometimes work as one or another, or both. For example, watching a neighbor watering the front lawn works as a situational characteristic by eliciting the belief that there is water abundance and therefore, conservation is not an urgent matter (thus, constraining the behavioral goal of water conservation). At the same time, this event can work as a situational cue to activate the implicit norm of spending as much water as we want in watering the lawn, given that it is the behavior that most people engage in at that neighborhood (thus, facilitating the anti-behavioral goal of spending water).

Additionally, there are situations in which different processes are elicited not by the same limiting factor but by different limiting factors. One example regards the behavior of buying non-organic products such as non-organic milk. On one side, the organic milk high price can work as a perceived barrier/constraint to not buy organic, eliciting a high perceived cost and incommodity in performing that behavior. On the other side, the presence of non-organic milk familiar brands can activate the non-organic milk buying habit, which can inhibit an intentional organic milk buying goal and increase the probability of performing in accordance with a non-organic milk buying goal. We will get back to this example later on.

Regarding the concept of psychological barriers and constraints on pro-ecological behavior, we define them as factors that can: 1) lower the activation strength of pro-ecological goals and/or increase the activation strength of anti-ecological goals – *behavioral constraints*; 2) elicit the activation of an anti-ecological goal and inhibit the activation of pro-ecological goals – *behavioral barriers*. This distinction refers to the magnitude of the effect. If a factor has a weak-to-moderate effect, it works as a *behavioral constraint* by means of a *goal interference effect* - hampering with pro-ecological behavioral goals (i.e. pro-ecological actions can still occur, although with reduced frequency or effectiveness). If this factor has a strong effect, it works as a *behavioral barrier* by means of a *goal inhibition effect* - inhibiting pro-ecological behavioral goals (i.e. facilitating anti-ecological behavioral goals, meaning that pro-ecological actions cannot occur).

We make this distinction between barriers and constraints, and in terms of the effect's magnitude, since most of the times in the real world ecological decisions are associated with a conflict between pro-ecological and anti-ecological behavioral goals (e.g. decision between having a cooperative or competitive behavior; Garcia-Marques & Palma-Oliveira, 1989). Which goal "wins" this conflict[3] depends on the situation where behavior is expected to occur, but also on how barriers and constraints interact. Accordingly, anti-ecological goals are expected to be stronger when there is an inhibition effect in addition to an interference effect, i.e. when barriers and constraints "work" together. This is supported by the Goal Systems Theory (Kruglanski, Shah, Fishbach, Friedman, Chun, & Sleeth-Keppler 2002), which claims that accessible goal alternatives or "background" goals (e.g. anti-ecological) can either pull away resources from a focal goal by reducing its activation strength and goal commitment or facilitate its activation, depending on what is activated and the context in which it happens. The negative effect can happen even when the activation of alternative goals is subliminal (priming) by: undermining the commitment to the focal goal, hampering progress toward the goal, hindering the development of effective means for goal pursuit and dampening participant's emotional responses to positive and negative feedback about their goal striving efforts (Kruglanski et al., 2002; Shah & Kruglanski, 2003).

Unrealistic optimism about environmental degradation (Hatfield & Job, 2001) or uncertainty about resource's level of availability and about how many people are cooperating in a pro-ecological way (Biel & Garling, 1995; De Young, 1999) can be considered *behavioral constraints*. This is because they reduce the level of goal commitment (Kruglanski et al., 2002) and the strength of a pro-ecological goal intention like "I intend to save water while taking a shower", which causes a *goal interference effect*. In a different way, the high accessibility of an anti-ecological habit (Gaspar de Carvalho, 2009) or its perceived benefits in terms of comfort (Kollmuss & Agyeman, 2002) can work as barriers by facilitating the activation of an anti-ecological goal such as "spend much water while taking a shower" and inhibition of a pro-ecological goal ("conserve water while taking a shower"), which causes a *goal inhibition effect*.

Apart from interacting with goals, *unconscious barriers and constraints* might show their effect also indirectly, through their influence on *perceived barriers and constraints*. An example of this is the cognitive inaccessibility of pro-ecological/cooperative behavioral options in a social dilemma situation (with the anti-ecological/competitive options being more accessible; Biel & Garling, 1995; Palma-Oliveira & Gaspar de Carvalho, 2004; Tanner, 1999). Such a cognitive inaccessibility can affect behavior as an unconscious barrier and/or constraint. This can be due to the work of an information-processing heuristic which does not take into account all the behavioral options but only some of them, based, for example, on some criteria habitually used in similar decisions (Palma-Oliveira, 1995). These cognitive options of inaccessibility can promote a perceived lack of opportunities to behave in a pro-ecological way, which work as a perceived barrier/constraint. Some Environmental Education and Behavioral Change projects and psychological models attribute this to the lack of opportunities presented by the situation where the person is in, when in fact this perceived lack of opportunity might result from cognitive processes.

As in any new theoretical model, although the DN-Work model is based on theories and studies supporting its fundamental claims, there is still not enough research on its specific predictions. Given this gap, we will next present research assessing the least studied category of the model and the processes involved in its influence on ecological behavior: *unconscious barriers and constraints*.

HABITS AS UNCONSCIOUS BARRIERS AND CONSTRAINTS

Given the lack of success and efficacy in dealing with factors that can explain the attitude-behavior inconsistency, our research aims to demonstrate the effect of habit as a negative determinant of such inconsistency, trying to overcome the positivity fallacy identified before. Moreover, habit is considered to be an *unconscious barrier* since it is a mental representation having an effect outside people's awareness and conscious control. Thus, habit is a true psychological negative determinant of behavior, resulting from an interaction between situational and psychological processes.

Habits are distinct from other forms of repeated automatic behavior (e.g., body reflexes) because the former are goal-directed automatic behaviors that are mentally represented (as knowledge structures; Higgins 1989) and can be triggered by environmental cues (Aarts, Verplanken & van Knippenberg 1998; Verplanken, Aarts & van Knippenberg 1997). Thus, a pre-condition for them to be performed automatically is the existence of an active goal due to the presence of relevant environmental cues. The situation can activate the behavioral goal and behavior is performed automatically following that activation. This is because there is a goal-action cognitive link and for that reason activating the goal automatically elicits the action (Aarts & Dijkterhuis, 2000).

For example, the development of a habitual domestic behavior of separating garbage for recycling, starts with a goal intention such as "I intend to recycle", which is associated with a behavioral goal like "separate garbage for recycling". The first times this behavior is performed involve effort, time and a set of behavioral steps (e.g., categorize the material; choose to which container it should go; etc.) and consume cognitive resources. However, with frequent co-activation of the behavioral goal and action over time, this effort, time, number of behavioral steps and resources consumption are reduced and behavior is performed automatically upon activating the goal. This automatic behavior can then occur either upon the presence of the relevant cues (e.g. recycling containers at home) without people being aware of it or through a conscious activation of the behavioral goal (i.e. upon thinking on recycling the waste). Accordingly, research shows that regardless of the source of activation, these two "paths" (Bargh & Chartrand, 1999) can elicit the same automatic behavior (see Aarts & Dijksterhuis, 2000, experiment 2).

Apart from this positive effect, habits can also negatively influence ecological attitude and behavioral change programs, outside of people's awareness, upon the presence of relevant cues. Moreover, even if people are aware of their habits activation, this might not be sufficient to prevent it from occurring, since once the goal is activated automatic behavior is expected to occur. In this regard, we performed 2 experimental field studies (Gaspar de Carvalho, 2009) to assess how certain characteristics of the decisional context can elicit automatic habitual behavior by activating the relevant mental goal-action link, and how this could influence pro-ecological decisions to buy organic food.

STUDY 1

In the first study, we aimed to test the assumption that by exposing people to the means that allow achieving a behavioral goal, we can increase the probability of goal attainment (Kruglanski et al., 2002; Shah & Kruglanski, 2003), i.e. that people automatically behave or decide according with their goals. For example, if we habitually buy non-organic milk, when we are in the supermarket's milk section, the presence of the non-organic brand X that we habitually buy (the mean to attain our milk buying goal) can automatically elicit the milk buying goal, and the associated milk buying behavior (buy brand X) can follow. This can occur without people being aware that this process was the cause of their behavior or without a conscious intention to engage in it (Aarts & Custers, in press).

Following from this, we aimed to test if in the presence of two types of means associated with either the goal to buy organic milk or to buy non-organic milk, people would choose significantly more a mean from the first type, in a list with various products (means) of both types. This is because the means of the first category co-occurred more often in the past with the goal of buying non-organic milk, in a stable context (i.e. given their non-organic milk buying habit).

However, given the situational dependence of goal activation (Kruglanski et al., 2002), we predicted that this would only happen in a familiar choice context. This is because in this context the cues that habitually elicit the non-organic milk buying habit are present (e.g. familiar brand). In a different way, if the choice context is new and unknown, there are not familiar cues that could activate the buying non-organic milk habit and therefore the probability of goal activation should be similar for both organic and non-organic milk buying. Thus, regarding the example given before, if the non-organic brand X that we habitually buy (i.e., mean) is not present, then our choice will follow a decision process not directly related to our habit (e.g., product appearance).

METHOD

Participants and Procedure

Eighty students from the University of Lisbon and other individuals were either given credits for their participation or volunteered to participate respectively. To participate they had to fulfill the criteria of buying food products for domestic consumption at least once per week. For this reason, the students that participated were requested to bring in their parents or friends that fulfilled these criteria, if they did not.

The sample consisted mainly on young adults, with an overall mean age of 28.16 years old (SD=10.52; Min=19; Max= 54) and the majority having a high school degree (60%) or a university degree (27.50%). A questionnaire (see description below) portrays them as frequent shoppers, shopping for food on an average of twice a week (M=2.10; SD = 1.28). Also, the sample is characterized by a low percentage of reported organic food products bought in general (M=12.33%; SD = 19.85) and medium intention to buy organic food in the future (M=3.44; SD = 1.78), portraying them as habitual non-organic food buyers.

Participants were asked to take part in a web-based study on "Health and Consumption in Portugal." After providing their informed consent, they responded to a small questionnaire containing the following items: a) socio-demographic and purchase behavior items; and b) future intention to buy organic products (1-7 Likert type scale; from Ajzen, 2002). Subsequently, they performed one of two online shopping simulations to choose milk, from a list of 12 organic and non-organic products chosen by means of a pre-test, which included price, brand and a picture of the product. One task - *familiar context* - had national brands known to the participants (representing familiar means to attain their milk buying goal), while the other - *new context* - had foreign brands, unfamiliar to them.

In these we maintained price and organic and non-organic products availability constant among them, in a proportion of .66 non-organic products and .33 organic products. This was because these aspects usually work as post-hoc justifications for not behaving in a pro-environmental way and for non-organic products buying habits maintenance. We aimed to argue against these justifications, by showing means familiarity as a psychological dimension which determines choice, independently from price and availability. A representation of the goal system involved in these two tasks can be seen in figure 2.

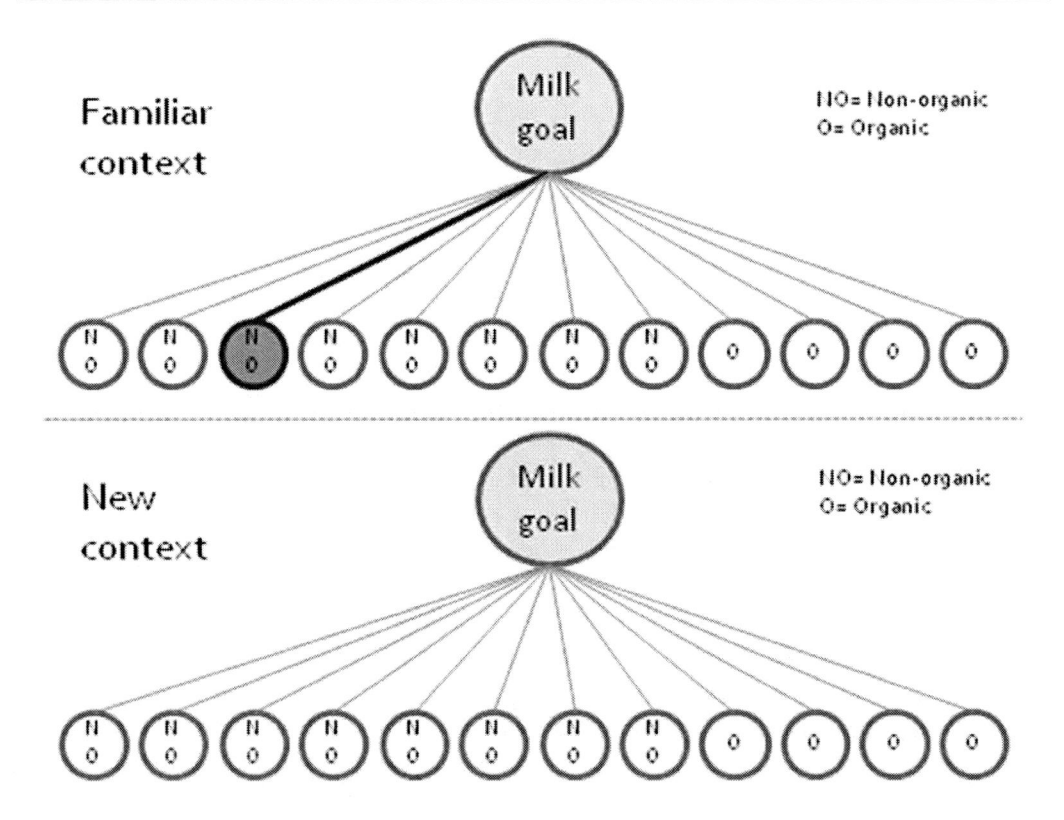

Figure 2. Goal-means structure representation for each type of context manipulation.

RESULTS

Fisher's Exact test results regarding the differences in the choice of non-organic milk between the familiar and new context (see Table 4), showed that a higher proportion of non-organic products chosen in the familiar context (.95) compared to the new context (.68) (p=.002; Fisher's exact test).

These results show that the situation's influence on behavior is not direct but mediated by psychological processes going beyond price and availability of organic food, which usually are considered to be the main reasons underlying the decision to buy organic food (from a pre-test we performed). In fact, differences in results were explained by familiarity (a psychological dimension) rather than those socio-economic factors, with significantly more non-organic milk being chosen than the expected proportion in the familiar context but not in the novel context. Thus, exposing people to the relevant familiar behavioral means (6 non-organic products out of 12) activated the goal associated with the habitual behavior, which in turn biased choices toward a habitual mean (1 out of 6 non-organic products). This shows the situation's influence on behavior, mediated by a psychological process (familiarity).

STUDY 2

While study 1 aimed to demonstrate the effect of means priming, study 2 aimed to also show the effect of goal accessibility associated with the habitual behavior, i.e. a high goal accessibility before the choice situation is expected to bias the subsequent choice toward a habitually chosen mean (Kruglanski et al., 2002). This was done either by priming the goal in a behavioral simulation or dividing the participants into weak vs. strong habit participants (the latter expected to have a higher chronic accessibility; Higgins, 1996),

The choice situation was again manipulated in terms of familiarity but, instead of the categories of non-organic and organic milk, there were non-organic milk - habitual product - and non-organic orange juice - non-habitual product. Our aim was to not only replicate the familiarity effect but also to demonstrate that habitual behavior can still occur in a new context, with more habitual than non-habitual products chosen, as long there is a high goal accessibility (either through priming or habit strength), based on the prediction that *strong accessibility can compensate for weak applicability* (Higgins & Brendl, 1995).

METHOD

Participants and Procedure

One hundred and sixty students from the University of Évora, Portugal and other participants were either given credits for their participation or volunteered to participate respectively (same criteria as in study 1). The sample consisted mainly of young adults, with an overall mean age of 25.53 years old (SD=7.56; Min=18; Max= 60) and the majority having a high school degree (56.90%) or a university degree (33.10%). There was an overall moderate milk buying habit strength (M=4.27; SD=1.42), which was significantly higher than the orange juice buying habit strength (M=2.41; SD=1.37) ($t_{(159)}$=12.00; p<.000).

Participants were asked to take part in a web-based study on "Health and Consumption in Portugal." After providing their informed consent, participants were requested to write a brief description of their behavior in a certain situation (goal priming): *"Imagine that you need to go shopping for the week's breakfasts or lunches in your house and in order to do that you go to the nearest supermarket/local store. Once you get there, you decide to buy bread and milk. Please describe what you would do from the time you arrive at each product section in the supermarket/local store, until the time you choose what you want to take, writing in the space below the options available in there and the way you make your choice for each of the two products."* The participants in the irrelevant buying goal accessible condition performed the same task but with milk being substituted by water. In this, only the milk goal had the opportunity to be attained, given that the subsequent task had a list of milk and orange juice products to choose from. The idea here is that, priming stimulates or activates the stored knowledge (Higgins, 1996), thus providing people with a behavioral goal (buy milk) should increase its accessibility (and consequently, the mental representation of the associated habit) and therefore, the probability of automatically choosing milk when opportunity arises. After this, participants performed two online shopping tasks (within-participants) with a choice of milk and orange juice with national brands (familiar context) and foreign brands (new context), in a way similar to study 1). A representation of the goal system involved in these two tasks can be seen in Figure 3.

Finally, they performed a questionnaire in which reported their non-organic products buying habit by responding to the Self Report Habit Index (1-7 Likert type scale; Verplanken & Orbell, 2003), which allowed to create the weak- vs. strong-habit participant groups based on the first and last quartile.

RESULTS

McNemar's test results regarding the differences between decisions in the familiar and new context when the target goal was accessible (see table 1) showed a significantly higher percentage of participants which revised their choice, by choosing the non-habitual product (orange juice) in the new context and the habitual product (milk) in the familiar context (23.75%) compared to the opposite revision (3.75%) (p=.001; McNemar). For the accessible irrelevant goal results showed a significantly higher percentage of participants which revised their choice, by choosing the non-habitual product in the new context and the habitual product in the familiar context (32.5%), compared to the opposite revision (6.25%) (p=.000; McNemar). Moreover, in this condition there was a higher choice consistency for the habitual (38.75%) than for the non-habitual products (22.5%) between contexts, although this difference was marginally significant.

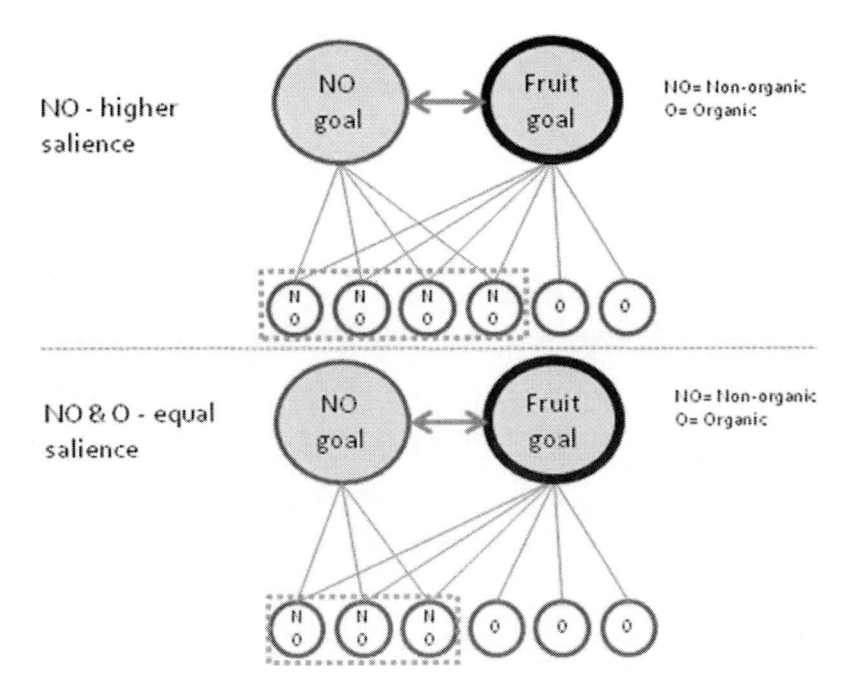

Figure 3. Goal-means structure representation for each type of context manipulation.

Table 1. Differences in frequencies between decisions in the new and familiar context for the goal priming manipulations with McNemar's test

		Target goal			
		New context		McNemar (A/D)	McNemar (B/C)
		Non-hab.	Hab.		
Familiar context	Non-hab.	29	3	n.s.	p=.001
	Hab.	19	29		
		Irrelevant goal			
		New context		McNemar (A/D)	McNemar (B/C)
		Non-hab.	Hab.		
Familiar context	Non-hab.	18	5	p=.087*	p=.000
	Hab.	26	31		

As expected, the majority of the strong-habit participants chose the habitual product consistently between contexts (58.97%; p=.000; McNemar). The weak habit participants chose more the habitual product in the familiar context and the non-habitual product in the new context (45%; p=.002; McNemar) than otherwise. Given their weak habit, their mental representation was inferred to be more unstable than for the strong habit participants and thus they are more affected by contextual changes. At the same time, they are "aided" by the context, with the weak chronic accessibility being compensated by the context familiarity.

On one side, this shows that habits can have an effect across situations (strong habits effect) and that their power is sometimes underestimated. On the other side, our goal priming seems to have failed and even resulted in an almost opposite pattern, with less consistency in the habitual products chosen when the milk goal was primed (compared to the control condition). One explanation is that the goal priming might have elicited a monitoring process in which some participants compared the options available with their milk buying habit. If a weak match between habit and the available means in the decision task was perceived, they chose more the non-habitual product. Thus, a contrast effect might have occurred because the priming was supraliminal and they were aware that their habits were brought to mind (Dijksterhuis, Chartrand & Aarts, 2007).

CONCLUSION

Most of the Environmental Education and Behavior Change projects and models regarding ecological behavior are still biased by a "positivity fallacy", i.e. the belief that as long as people have the right attitudes, intentions, skills, information, etc., the right pro-ecological behavior should follow. However, the social sciences literature shows that there is an inconsistency between attitudes and behaviors in this regard and that the difficulty in changing behaviors is being underestimated. One reason for this to occur is that the factors working as barriers and constraints to ecological behavior are not analyzed and dealt with. In this regard, a behavioral analysis that includes the "negative" determinants should be performed.

Models studying the negative determinants of pro-environmental behavior consider that most barriers and constraints are non-psychological. Even those models acknowledging the importance of psychological barriers and constraints only see a part of the big picture. This is because they do not consider the effect of automatic processes occurring outside people's awareness and consciousness, which mediate the effect of situations on behavior.

In our studies we aimed to fill these identified gaps through the DN-Work model, concerning the effect of barriers and constraints on pro-ecological behavior. This model specifies some conditions for their influence to take place, presenting psychological processes as mediators of situational influences on behavior, and transcending the incomplete and sometimes erroneous consideration of a direct influence of the former on the latter. Accordingly, this chapter presented two examples from empirical research showing that habit - defined as a goal-dependent automatic behavior – can work as a negative determinant of ecological behavior, outside people's awareness and control. These studies demonstrated that automatic habitual behavior can be elicited by situational features (the means in the choice context) or by chronic accessibility, which determined the subsequent behavior in the decision making tasks. Additionally, some control over the habitual choice is possible, although habitual behavior awareness (study 2) seems to be necessary. This has evident implications for the development of Environmental Education and Behavior Change projects because habit can work as an *unconscious barrier* by making anti-ecological goals stronger and more accessible, without the mediation of consciousness.

Thus, our model and studies suggest that the investigation of pro-ecological behaviors should be conducted not only by considering the different levels of individuals' analysis (person, group, society, world) but also by considering the different levels of the situation where behavior occurs (Pinheiro, 2009). This means that the situation should be approached from the most concrete level of analysis regarding physical features and tangible aspects, up to the most abstract level considering those characteristics and events associated with social environments, like other people's behaviors, attitudes, etc. One common error in this regard is the assessment of people's habits (at the individual level) as only determined by the social environment (e.g. neighbors; family living in the same house) and/or the city environment (e.g. urban planning). Often, this implies missing the influence of psychological processes in a more concrete level of the situation (the "psychological context"), in terms of the elicitation of automatic behaviors from certain situational cues. Only by matching these different levels of ecological-behavior analysis and considering the different influences associated with them, we can "bring back" the situation to the psychological study of barriers and constraints impinging on ecological behavior.

Although the viewpoint presented in this chapter (i.e., the study of negative determinants) seems like a pessimistic approach to the study of ecological behavior, we think this is actually an optimistic perspective. In fact, by identifying factors increasing the inconsistency between positive attitudes and ecological behaviors, we will be able to design interventions focusing on these factors and increase the success and efficacy of attitude behavior change programs. On the contrary, it is the design of interventions including only positive determinants and involving an incomplete explanatory level of the psychological processes involved that makes us pessimistic regarding the promotion of ecological behaviors and their maintenance in the long run.

As Corral-Verdugo (2001; pg. 149) states: "Given the complexity of ecological problems, it is better to respond in a plastic than in a rigid way". This plasticity can be developed by increasing people's environmental competency (Corral-Verdugo, 2002; see also Fraijo-Sing *et al*, in this book) in a way that individuals are enabled to resist the influence of barriers and constraints on ecological behavior. Whenever they are or are not able to perceive/identify those barriers and constraints by themselves, strategies aimed to increase people's competence in dealing with them should be developed (Gaspar de Carvalho & Coutinho de Faria, 2003).

Other negative determinants still need to be identified and the processes involved should be assessed with various methodologies. Nevertheless, the model here described and its associated research can be a starting point to answer, from a psychological perspective, an unfortunately understudied question in pro-ecological behavior research: why do people fail to act?

REFERENCES

Aarts, H. & Custers, R. (in press). Habit, action and consciousness. In W. P. Banks (Ed.), *Encyclopedia of consciousness*. Oxford, UK: Elsevier Ltd.

Aarts, H & Dijksterhuis, A. (2000). Habits as knowledge structures: Automaticity in goal-directed behavior. *Journal of Personality and Social Psychology, 78*, 53-63.

Aarts, H., Verplanken, B. & van Knippenberg, A. (1998). "Predicting behavior from actions in the past: Repeated decision making or a matter of habit?" *Journal of Applied Social Psychology, 28* (15), 1355-74.

Ajzen, I. (1991). The theory of planned behavior. *Organizational Behavior and Human Decision Processes, 50*, 179-211.

Ajzen, I. (2002). Residual effects of past on later behavior: habituation and reasoned action perspectives. *Personality and Social Psychology Review, 6*, 107-122.

Bargh, J. (1997). The automaticity of everyday life. In R.S. Wyer Jr. (Ed.), *The automaticity of everyday life: Advances in social cognition* (vol.10, pp. 1-61). Mahwah, NJ: Erlbaum.

Bargh, J. & Chartrand, T. (1999). The unbearable automaticity of being. *American Psychologist, 54*, 462-479.

Biel, A. & Gärling, T. (1995). The role of uncertainty in resource dilemmas. *Journal of Environmental Psychology, 15*, 221-233.

Black, J., Stern, P. & Elworth, J. (1985). Personal and contextual influences on household energy adaptations. *Journal of Applied Psychology, 70*, 3-21.

Constanzo, M., Archer, D., Aronson, E. & Pettigrew, T. (1986). Energy conservation behavior: the difficult path from information to action. *American Psychologist, 41*, 521-528.

Corral-Verdugo, V. (2001). *Comportamiento proambiental: Una introducción al estudio de las conductas protectoras del ambiente* [Proenvironmental behavior: An introduction to the study environmental protection behaviors]. Santa Cruz de Tenerife, Spain: Editorial Resma.

Corral-Verdugo, V. (2002). A structural model of pro-environmental competency. *Environment & Behavior, 34*, 531-549.

Corral-Verdugo, V. & Frías-Armenta, M. (2006). Personal normative beliefs, antisocial behavior, and residential water conservation. *Environment & Behavior, 38*, 406-421.

Corral-Verdugo, V., Frias-Amenta, M. & Gonzalez-Lomelí, D. (2003). On the relationship between antisocial and anti-environmental behaviors: An empirical study. *Population and Environment, 24*, 273-286.

Corraliza, J.A. & Berenguer, J. (2000). Environmental values, beliefs and actions: A situational approach. *Environment & Behavior, 32*, 832-848.

Costarelli, S. & Colloca, P. (2004). The effects of attitudinal ambivalence on pro-environmental behavioral intentions. *Journal of Environmental Psychology, 24*, 279-288.

De Young, R. (1988-1989). Exploring the difference between recyclers and non-recyclers: The role of information. *Journal of Environmental Systems, 18*, 341-351.

De Young, R. (1999). Tragedy of the commons. In D. E. Alexander and R. W. Fairbridge (Eds.). *Encyclopedia of Environmental Science*. Hingham, MA: Kluwer Academic Publishers.

Diekmann, A & Preisendörfer, P. (1992). Persönliches Umweltverhalten. Diskrepanzen zwischen Anspruch und Wirklichkeit. *Kölner Zeitschrift für Soziologie und Sozialpsychologie, 44*, 226-251.

Dijksterhuis, A., Chartrand, T. & Aarts, H. (2007). Effects of Priming and Perception on Social Behavior and Goal Pursuit. In John A. Bargh (Ed.), *Social psychology and the unconscious: The automaticity of higher mental processes*. New York: Psychology Press.

Fazio, R. (1990). Multiple processes by which attitudes guide behavior: The MODE model as an integrative framework. *Advances in Experimental Social Psychology, 23*, 75-109.

Ferreira Marques, J., Palma-Oliveira, J.M., Marques, J.F. & Ferreira, M.B. (1995). Subgroup comparisons. In C. Levy-Leboyer, M. Bonnes, K. Pawlik, J. Ferreira Marques and J. Chase (Eds.), *The Psychological and Social Determinants of Environmental Attitudes and Behaviors: International comparison*. Brussels: EU Project Report.

Förster, J., Liberman, N. & Friedman, R. (2009). Seven principles of goal activation: A systematic approach to distinguishing goal priming from priming of non-goal constructs. *Personality and Social Psychology Review*, 11, 211-233.

Frey, B.S. (1989). Ipsative and objective limits to human behavior. *Journal of Behavioral Economics, 17*, 229-248.

Garcia-Marques, L. & Palma-Oliveira, J. (1989). A exaustão de recursos e a acção colectiva: a psicologia desnecessária e a necessidade da psicologia. [Resources exhaustion and the collective action: the unnecessary psychology and the necessity of psychology.] *Terra Solidária, 20*, 23-26.

Gardner, G.T. & Stern, P.C. (2002). *Environmental problems and human. behavior* (2nd ed.). Boston, MA: Pearson Custom Publishing.

Gaspar de Carvalho, R. (2004). Concepção de projectos de Educação Ambiental [Conception of Environmental Education Projects]. In Escola Profissional do Montijo (Ed.), *Manual do curso de "Animadores de Educação Ambiental*. Montijo, Portugal: EPM-IEFP.

Gaspar de Carvalho (2009). *Consistent... me? Barriers and Constraints on Pro-environmental Behavior*. (Submitted) PhD dissertation in Social Psychology. Lisbon: University of Lisbon, Faculty of psychology and Educational Sciences.

Gaspar de Carvalho, R. & Coutinho de Faria, J. (2003). Say hello to E.T.!: Beyond Environmental Education towards Environmental Training. In T. Craig (Ed.), *Crossing boundaries- The value of interdisciplinary research*. Aberdeen: The Robert Gordon University.

Hatfield, J. & Job, R.F. (2001). Optimism bias about environmental degradation: The role of the range of impact of precautions. *Journal of Environmental Psychology*, 21, 17-30.

Higgins, T. (1989). Knowledge acessibility and activation: Subjectivity and suffering from unconcious sources. In J.S. Uleman & J.A. Bargh (Eds.), *Unintended Thought* (pp.75-123). New York: Guildford Press.

Higgins, T. (1996). Knowledge activation: Accessibility, applicability, and salience. In E.T. Higgins and A.W. Kruglanski (Eds.), *Social psychology: Handbook of basic principles* (pp. 133-168). New York: Guilford Press.

Higgins, T. & Brendl, M. (1995). Accessibility and applicability: Some" activation rules" influencing judgment. *Journal of Experimental Social Psychology*, 31, 218-243.

Kaiser, F. & Keller, C. (2001). Disclosing situational constraints to ecological behavior: A confirmatory application of the mixed Rasch model. *European Journal of Psychological Assessment*, 17, 212-221.

Kollmuss, A. & Agyeman, J. (2002). Mind the gap: why do people act environmentally and what are the barriers to pro-ecological behavior? *Environmental Education Research*, 8, 239-260.

Kruglanski, A., Shah, J., Fishbach, A., Friedman, R., Chun, W. & Sleeth-Keppler, D. (2002). A theory of goal systems. In M. Zanna (Ed.), *Advances in Experimental Social Psychology*, (pp. 331-376). New York: Academic Press.

McKenzie-Mohr, D. (2000). Fostering sustainable behavior through community-based social marketing. *American Psychologist*, 55, 531-537.

McKenzie-Mohr, D. & Smith, W. (1999). *Fostering sustainable behavior: An introduction to community-based social marketing*. Gabriola Island B.C.: New Society Publishers.

Olsen, M.E. (1981). Consumer's attitudes toward energy conservation. *Journal of Social Issues*, 37, 108-131.

Palma-Oliveira, J. M. (1995). *The differences and similarities between a person and a walkman: experiments in person and a consumer memory*. PhD dissertation in Psychology. Lisbon: Faculdade de Psicologia e de Ciências da Educação da Universidade de Lisboa.

Palma-Oliveira, J.M. & Correia dos Santos, S. (1998). *Análise do consumo doméstico de água em Portugal- Uma experiência de campo para promoção da conservação da água*. [Analysis of water domestic consumption in Portugal - A field study to promote water conservation]. Lisbon: Quercus-Inag (MA).

Palma-Oliveira, J.M. & Garcia-Marques, L. (1988, May). *Os dilemas sociais e as atitudes na promoção de estratégias de conservação de energia* [Social dilemmas and attitudes in the promotion of energy conservation strategies]. Paper presented at the "Seminar on Environmental Conservation." Sevilla, Spain.

Palma-Oliveira, J.M. & Gaspar de Carvalho, R. (2004). Environmental education programs construction: some conceptual and evaluation guidelines. *Discursos: Língua, Cultura e*

Sociedade – Número especial: Global Trends on Environmental Education (pp. 19-35). In U.M. Azeiteiro, M.J. Pereira, W. Leal-Filho, S. Caeiro, P. Bacelar-Nicolau, F. Morgado, & F. Gonçalves (Eds.). Lisbon: Universidade Aberta.

Pinheiro, J.Q. (2009, January). Terræ Incognitæ, tempo e sustentabilidade: fronteiras abertas para uma psicologia do global. [Terræ Incognitæ, time and sustainability: open frontiers towards a psychology of the global] *Paper presented at the X Environmental Psychology Congress*. Lisbon, Portugal.

Schultz, P.W., Oskamp, S. & Mainieri T. (1995). Who recycles and when?: a review of personal and situational factors. *Journal of Environmental Psychology, 15*, 105-121.

Shah, J. & Kruglanski, A. (2003). When opportunity knocks: Bottom-up priming of goals by means and its effects on self-regulation. *Journal of Personality and Social Psychology, 84*, 1109–1122.

Smith, E. & Mackie, D. (1995). *Social psychology*. New York: Worth.

Stern, P., Dietz, T., Abel, T., Guagno, G. & Kalof, L. (1999). A Value, Belief, Norm Theory of Support for Social Movements: The Case of Environmentalism, *Human Ecology Review, 6*, 81-97.

Stern, P. & Oskamp, S. (1987). Managing scarce environmental resources. In D. Stokols & I. Altman (Eds.), *Handbook of Environmental Psychology* (pp. 1043-1088). New York: Wiley.

Stoll-Kleemann, S. (2001). Barriers to nature conservation in Germany: A model explaining opposition to protected areas. *Journal of Environmental Psychology, 21*, 369-385.

Suárez, E. (1998). Problemas ambientales e soluciones conductuales [Environmental problems and behavioral solutions]. In Aragonés J.I., Amérigo M. (Eds.), *Psicologia Ambiental* (pp. 303-327). Madrid: Ediciones Pirámide.

Talarowsky, F. (1982). *Attitudes toward and perceptions of water conservation in a Southern California community*. Unpublished study.

Tanner, C. (1999). Constraints on environmental behavior. *Journal of Environmental Psychology, 19*, 145-157.

Thompson, S.C.G. & Barton, M. (1994). Ecocentric and anthropocentric attitudes toward the environment. *Journal of Environmental Psychology, 14*, 149-157.

Vantomme, D., Geuens, M., De Houwer, J. & De Pelsmacker, P. (2005). Implicit attitudes toward green consumer behavior. *Psychologica Belgica,* Vlerick Leuven Gent Working Paper Series 2005/31.

Verplanken, B., Aarts, H. & van Knippenberg, A. (1997). Habit, information acquisition and the process of making travel mode choices. *European Journal of Social Psychology, 27*, 539-560.

Verplanken, B. & Orbell, S. (2003). Reflections on past behavior: A self-report index of habit strength. *Journal of Applied Social Psychology*, 33 (6), 1313-1330.

In: Psychological Approaches to Sustainability
Editors: V. Corral-Verdugo et al.
ISBN 978-1-60876-356-6
© 2010 Nova Science Publishers, Inc.

Chapter 16

COMMUNITY SUSTAINABILITY: ORIENTATIONS AND IMPLICATIONS FROM ENVIRONMENTAL COMMUNITY PSYCHOLOGY

Esther Wiesenfeld and Euclides Sánchez*
Instituto de Psicología, Universidad Central de Venezuela

ABSTRACT

Sustainable development (SD) is a topic of interest that transcends geographic and disciplinary borders. Environmental psychology is one of the disciplines that, for over a decade, has been interested in this topic, approaching it from diverse theoretical and methodological perspectives. Pol and collaborators, who are among the pioneers in the study of SD in environmental psychology, propose a model in which social identity and appropriation occupy a central place, vindicating in this way the importance of the psychosocial dimension for SD. Taking this component into account, and based on a proposal for an environmental community-psychology interested in promoting community sustainability, we emphasize the importance of delimiting SD projects in communities, because of the advantages this represents for the development of such social organizations. We also highlight the protagonist roles that members of the community, as well as other social actors linked to these contexts, must play as interpreters of the living conditions and as managers of the transformations that are required to improve their conditions with sustainability criteria. Based on these considerations, this chapter argues in favor of the conceptual and methodological principles that support the implementation of community sustainability projects and describes an intervention case that illustrates the application of these concepts.

---

* Correspondence concerning this chapter should be addressed to Esther Wiesenfeld: email esther.wiesen@gmail.com

INTRODUCTION

Globalization has been thought of as a revolution on an international scale. It has caused all sorts of reactions, from adhesion to the rejection of its associated effects. Those who reject it, blame it for the increase of poverty, environmental degradation and social inequality. One of the most accepted proposals for confronting these problems has been the formulation of a development model based on sustainability.

Background to this model can be traced back to 1972 at the United Nations Conference on Human Environment held in Stockholm, where the relationships between environmental degradation and economic growth were discussed (Dietz, York & Rosa, 2008).

This event was followed by the analysis about the unsustainability of the planet, conducted by the International Union for the Conservation of Nature (IUCN), the United Nations Environment Programme (UNEP), and the World Wildlife Fund (WWF) (1980) in their *World Conservation Strategy* publication. Also by the United Nations (UN) sponsored World Commission on Environment and Development (WCED, 1987) led by Gro Harlem Brundtland, in "Our Common Future", known as the *Brundtland Report*. This publication was a milestone which placed the environment at the heart of a model of sustainable development (SD) that was driven by three goals: economic security, ecological integrity, and social equity. These widely shared goals continue to be relevant nowadays.

Wide dissemination of this report, together with contributions from events sponsored by international agencies, contributions from academic and government sectors and civil society aimed at achieving SD, created a new discourse that penetrated all spheres of society (Sheddon, Howarth & Norgaard, 2006). As Pol (2002a) states, it has been politically convenient to include DS in virtually any working agenda that hopes to have an impact on society. At present, the concept of DS is used in almost any field (economic, social, political, humanistic, environmental sciences), context (local and global, rural and urban, industrialized and developing), and sphere (private, government, non-government, academic, community).

This widespread coverage has resulted in numerous definitions of SD, which represent different ways of interpreting it and dealing with it. The various international events in which SD has been discussed have played a key role in this proliferation. In this sense, while the Brundtland Report emphasized the environmental component of SD, the Rio Summit, also known as the Earth Summit (United Nations Conference on Environment and Development [UNCED], 1992) highlighted the social component. In this event the participating countries prioritized (a) the fight against poverty, poor public health and population dynamics; (b) attention to vulnerable groups (women, children, indigenous populations and precarious human settlements); and (c) the application of a model based on the education, consciousness raising and organization of those involved. These three topics correspond to the *what*, the *who* and the *how* of SD.

Subsequently, in the Habitat II City Summit held in 1996 in Istanbul, Turkey, (Second United Nations Conference on Human Settlements Habitat II, 1996), the *where* of SD was particularly important. To this end, the represented states pledged to prioritize the problems of housing and habitat of the inhabitants at precarious human settlements and to generate proposals for overcoming poverty. The importance of participation, training and strengthening of these sectors for the management of development was also recognized. The Istanbul Summit stressed the impossibility of sustainability while the majority of the population had inadequate food, education and housing, as evidenced by poverty indicators at that time.

At the time of this summit 1% of the world's richest people had incomes equivalent to those of the poorest 57%. In Latin America and the Caribbean, 43.5% of the population was poor and 19% was in extreme poverty (United Nations Development Programme [UNDP], 2001). The concentration of poverty was noted as particularly critical in precarious urban settlements and in developing countries and was identified as a serious obstacle for the survival of their inhabitants and for SD (Urban 21, 2000). In this sense, the urban slum dwellers are the most impoverished urban population worldwide, the most dependent on local ecosystems for their survival, and hence the most damaged by their deterioration (Vilches, Gil Pérez, Toscano & Macías, 2008a). Their elevated growth rate, similar to that of the general urban population (UN Habitat United Nations Human Settlements Programme, 2006; Worldwatch Institute, 2007/2008), has led to calling the XXI century the *"urban millennium...of slums"* (Hayden, 2008, p. 12); and according to the results of the study "The Urban Age", conducted by the London School of Economics (Burdet y Sudjic, 2008), it constitutes an enormous challenge for society. In the case of Latin America and the Caribbean, more than 75% of its population is urban and its growth implies an increase in the number of urban poor (United Nations Population Fund [UNFPA], 2007, 2008; Fay, 2005; Demian, 2008).

This situation prompted the incorporation of human settlements, particularly in developing countries, as a permanent theme in the meetings of the SD Committee. Likewise, the UN rated the problem as a developmental emergency and agreed to integrate poverty and environmental concerns as priority in development policy, planning and investments (UNDP, 2008).

With this purpose, representatives of 189 countries, members of the UN, endorsed the "Millennium Declaration", an agreement in which they pledged to coordinate efforts to build a safer, richer and fairer world, aims that are similar to those of the Brundtland Report. They also formulated an action plan designed to reduce the number of people living in extreme poverty (income of less than one dollar a day) by the year 2015 to half of what it was in 1990. For Latin America and the Caribbean this would require reducing the number of poor people to 10.5 million, equivalent to half of the poor in 1990, that is: 21 million (Trigo, 2004).

Eight key objectives, known as the Millennium Development Goals, were proposed to achieve this goal. They consisted of reducing income poverty, hunger, disease, lack of adequate shelter and exclusion, and promoting gender equity, health, education, shelter, security and environmental sustainability by 2015, with emphasis on developing countries. This approach endorsed the social dimension of sustainability as a priority and subordinated the environmental dimension to it. Because of the differences between and within countries, the local scale of SD was also vindicated, by facilitating the integration of SD principles into the policies and programs of each country. UN-Habitat in the implementation of the Habitat Agenda, the Declaration on Cities and other Human Settlements in the New Millennium and the Millennium Development Goal 7, agreed on the need of incorporating government, regional and local authorities, civil society and the private sector in achieving these objectives.

These efforts have borne some fruit, namely improved macroeconomic indicators, global decline of the number of people living in extreme poverty, fall in the proportion of people in the world suffering from malnutrition and hunger; increased awareness of the environmental impact of some development projects, the emergence of new interdisciplinary fields and alternative paradigms (Sheddon et al. 2006), the incorporation of national policies with goals aimed toward sustainability, and the formalization of international agreements (Economic Commission for Latin America and the Caribbean [ECLAC], 2006).

In the case of Latin America, ECLAC estimated that the 2003-2007 period as the best five-year period in the last 40 years in terms of reducing poverty and increasing gross domestic product. Indeed, in 2007 the percentage of the poor had decreased to 35.1% and that of the extreme poor to 12.7% (Rosales, 2007).

Despite the reduction of poverty, it still remains high. In fact, World Bank statistics show that the number of people living in extreme poverty -that is, a dollar per day or less- had increased from 1.200 millions in 1987 to 1500 in 2007 and was expected to reach 1900 millions by 2015, and that 50% of world population lived with less than two dollars per day (The World Bank Group, 2004; UNFPA, 2008; Vilches, Gil Pérez, Toscano & Macías, 2008b). According to Sen & Kliksberg (2007) the richest 10% own 85% of international wealth, whereas half of overall population only owns 1%.

In Latin America, poverty still remains above 36%, which is equivalent to 195 million people. With respect to extreme poverty, although the percentage dropped from 18.6% in 1980 to 13.4 % in 2007, the absolute number increased from 62 millions to 71 millions. Furthermore, the inequity in income distribution between the different socioeconomic strata increased in this decade (Corporación Latinobarómetro, 2007; ECLAC, 2008, 2009).

As suggested by the previous data, achievements have lagged behind expectations. Weaknesses have been reported in relation to the integration of environmental concerns with economic and decision-making sectors, the consolidation of strategic plans for implementing SD at national and local levels, the success of participation in the redistribution of power in society and in the adoption of sustainable patterns of production and consumption. Likewise, developing countries have not enjoyed the expected economical and technical assistance (Rees, 2002, Sheddon et al., 2006).

Even though the poverty rate decreased in Latin America, recent data from the Economic Commission for Latin America and the Caribbean (ECLAC) report that out of 18 Latin American countries that were analyzed, only 7 will be able to reach the goal of reducing poverty in half by 2015, which, according to its authors, indicates that the high inequality rates in the region threaten the reduction of poverty (Trigo, 2008).

The aforementioned deficiencies have been attributed to factors such as ineffective institutions and a general lack of political will on the part of governments and citizens at multiple scales (Sheddon et al., 2006), but also to unexpected changes at the scientific, political, economical and international levels, that are beyond the control of SD.

A third interpretation attributes these shortcomings to the heterogeneity of perspectives that promote SD, which is reflected in the innumerable conceptual approaches developed by academics and other sectors, as we will now see.

SUSTAINABLE DEVELOPMENT: ONE CONCEPT, MANY MEANINGS

The best known definition of SD comes from the Brundtland Report, according to which SD is *"The development that satisfies the basic needs and aspirations for a better life of the present population, without compromising the capacity of future generations for satisfying their needs and aspirations"* (Brundtland, 1987, p. 22).

Since then, the numerous definitions that have been formulated reflect the diversity of ways of understanding and dealing with the constituent elements of SD, and the ideological, political and epistemological positions that sustain them. In general, conceptualizations about SD can be grouped into the categories that are presented in Table 1.

The categories and contents are not related to specific disciplines or sectors, but we can identify common threads among the contents of some categories, which group them into two major trends. On the one hand, we have the traditional trend (in regional, scientific, economical and political terms) associated to developed countries, the "hard" sciences, sectors with power, and the global impact of SD. On the other hand are the SD approaches aimed toward developing countries, with contributions from human and social sciences, with an interest in socio-economically disadvantaged sectors, that vindicate local development, particularly of precarious urban communities, that vindicate the participation of the inhabitants in their processes of social and environmental transformation, as well as their training and strengthening through academic and non academic strategies.

Pol (2002a) connects the first trend to powerful sectors, interested in promoting production and consumption for economic growth, and the second with ecological movements that defend the conservation of the environment as a positive social value of SD.

Sheddon et.al (2006) identify similar trends in the academic world. The first is represented by proponents of what they call a mainstream, conventional version of SD, to whom they attribute a fragmented vision of the production of knowledge, centered on technology, individualism and economicism (Robinson, 2004). This knowledge is based on quantitative and generalizable representations of human environmental relations, whose political expression is the pathway to development.

The second is attributed to critical academic sectors, supporters of social constructivist perspectives, for whom knowledge comes from social interaction (Robinson, 2004), and is subject to the contingencies of the context in which it occurs. It is based on qualitative studies and questions development promoted by the state. (Dryzek, 1999).

From this second perspective, some scientists that are critical of the traditional view of SD propose pluralism as an effective way to generate discourses and practices of SD that recover the local context, without losing sight of an integrated, global approach (Cabrera 2005; Moser, 2003; Pinheiro, 2002; Pol, 2002b). Pluralism summons debates that lead to transdisciplinary and holistic knowledge and approaches that address SD in all its complexity (Vilches, Gil Pérez, Toscano & Macías 2008c).

Table 1. Examples of Categories of SD Conceptualizations

Category	Contents
Dimensions of SD	Environmental, ecological, economical, political, social, institutional, psychological, ethical
Notion of development in SD	Preservation of the environment, green development, economic growth, welfare, satisfaction of needs, quality of life, security, equity, freedom, happiness
Contribution to SD	Theoretical, methodological, applied, technological
Model of SD	Traditional, dominant or alternative democratic
Approach to SD	Fragmented, integral
SD Methodological strategies	Quantitative, qualitative
Types of knowledge to deal with SD	Scientific, technological, from everyday life
Disciplines most related to SD	Environmental, economic, social, political, psychological, health sciences,
Emerging disciplines oriented towards SD	Ecological economy, political ecology, sustainable architecture, ecological democracy, environmental and community psychology
Disciplinary orientation	Uni disciplinary, Inter disciplinary, cross disciplinary, trans disciplinary
Indicators for assessing the scope of SD	Rejection of SD indicators for considering it an open and uncertain process, creation of indicators that vary according to the areas that SD refers to (i.e.: the ratio of human welfare to overall environmental impact, measures of capability in the environmental and sustainability sciences)
Political conditions for SD	Democracy, governability, citizenship
Social conditions	Participation, education, training, organization, health
Environmental conditions	Recovery of biodiversity, prevention of climate change, water conservation, recycling of solid waste, stopping deforestation, preservation of natural resources, stopping ecological degradation
Institutional conditions	Articulation within and between institutions, strategic alliances, reduction of bureaucracy
Economical conditions	Reduction of economical inequalities within and between societies
Psychosocial conditions	Reflexivity, empowerment, consciousness raising, subjective wellbeing, psychological restoration, happiness, environmental altruism, cooperation, place identity, appropriation and attachment
Psycho-environmental conditions	Pro environmental competencies and dispositions (aptitudes, beliefs, norms, attitudes, values, knowledge, skills), pro environmental behaviors (recycling, resources conservation, reduced consumption)
Ethical conditions	Justice, equity, altruism
Generational delimitation of SD	Within or between generations

Table 1. (Continued)

Category	Contents
Spatial scale of SD	Global, regional, national, local, community, human settlements
Delimitation of the concept of SD	Closed or open, precise or ambiguous
Actors of SD	Government officials, civil society members, nongovernmental organizations, communities, academics, private sector, multinational corporations, philanthropic foundations
Modes of relationship between actors of SD	Authoritarian, horizontal
Roles of the actors	Advocate, facilitator, researcher, practitioner, activist
Degree of involvement of SD actors	Inexistent, occasional, permanent
Styles of governability for SD	Hierarchical, deliberative, participative

These two trends represent extreme poles in many ways of conceiving SD, whose heterogeneity hinders agreements that could guide coordinated actions towards sustainability (Naredo & Rueda, 1997). This heterogeneity has been linked to uncertainty, confusion, ambiguity (Williams & Millington, 2004), which for authors such as Pol (2002) can be beneficial when it allows meeting points, even though no necessarily agreement, between opposing interests. In this manner, sectors that are interested in promoting production and consumption for economic growth, as well as ecological movements that defend the preservation of the environment, can agree in conceiving SD as a positive social value.

However, from our point of view, after more than two decades of the term's definition in the Brundtland Report (1987), this ambiguity is an obstacle when it comes to developing strategies and implementing actions to solve problems of unsustainability here and now, that is, at a local level in the present, for later projection to a global scale. If we add that we are almost two decades away from the Rio Summit 1992, when countries pledged to move beyond rhetoric to action, and placed the fight against poverty as a priority, such ambiguity is unacceptable.

Referring to this ambiguity, Naredo and Rueda (1997) state that:

> ...the lack of results inherent to the purely rhetorical use of the term "sustainable" has continued too long... the growing dissatisfaction that this situation has created is multiplying the criticisms of the aforementioned conceptual ambiguity, and entreating ever more strongly the search for precisions that would make the goal of "sustainability" operative...Because as long as the target is ambiguous there will be no effective practical action, no matter how much the prevailing pragmatism tries to look for shortcuts by refining the instruments before setting the goals..." (Naredo & Rueda, 1997, p.1)

According to the above authors, the conceptual ambiguity of SD is not solved by proposing more exhaustive definitions, but through the reasoning we adopt to examine the concept of SD. We interpret Naredo and Rueda's proposal of incorporating alternative analytical systems as the contribution that different disciplines can offer to SD, in so far as each one is based on specific principles that emphasize aspects of SD not looked upon in a unidisciplinary approach. Thus, the object of SD will by amplified when the significance of dimensions relevant to the disciplines is highlighted, and the knowledge that is produced will be enriched when the methodological strategies that are appropriate to these dimensions -and are a part of these disciplines- come into action. This interpretation coincides with Sheddon's et al. (2006) proposition to revitalize SD from conceptually plural research.

From this point of view, Environmental Community Psychology (ECP) is one of the disciplinary fields that, with its emphasis on environment and community, can provide important knowledge to SD, as we will explain later in this chapter.

Dietz and Stern (2008) believe that, due to poverty conditions, people do not associate the improvement of their quality of life with the solution of environmental problems, and we can assume that even less so with the long-term consequences of these problems. However, authors such as Sadan and Churchman (1996) and Wint (2002) consider that it is possible to foster the link between basic needs and environmental problems, many of them associated to poverty, through tools such as community strengthening.

According to Sadan and Churchman (1996) community strengthening allows the expansion of the definition of the limits of a person's world, usually restricted to the private sphere, by identifying the community as his/her necessary social reference space, and what happens there as a product of collective responsibility. It means moving from the individual to the community. Eid (2003) adds that thinking of oneself as part of a collective also encourages principles of equity, justice, among others.

Community participation has been widely considered the fundamental process in achieving these goals. Not only the solutions of problems pertaining to the collective are mentioned among its virtues, but also the promotion of other processes such as strengthening, social identity, sense of community, which in turn ensure the continuity of community participation (Churchman & Sadan, 2004; Pol, 1998, 2002b; Sánchez, 2000; Wiesenfeld & Sánchez, 2002).

THE ENVIRONMENTAL AND SOCIAL COMPONENTS OF SUSTAINABLE DEVELOPMENT AND ENVIRONMENTAL COMMUNITY PSYCHOLOGY

As previously noted, ECP is a discipline that has the potential to contribute to SD with the knowledge it has produced -and can produce- regarding the environmental and social dimensions of SD. Especially because this knowledge explains the person-environment transactions in the community context, which is an appropriate scale to understand the psychological processes involved in the community's relationship with the environment. These processes are also transferable to the larger scale of society (Wiesenfeld, 2001, 2003; Wiesenfeld & Giuliani, 2005) as we will explain further.

Environmental Psychology (EP) studies human-environment transactions in everyday life, emphasizing the understanding of the psychosocial processes involved in these transactions. When we say "psychosocial processes," we mean psychological processes that take place in the realm of intersubjectivity, in networks of subjectivities that are structured in and are influenced by culture. In this sense, EP's purpose is to understand these transactions in order to produce theory and to guide the development of actions aimed at increasing pro-environmental behaviors. Community Social Psychology (CSP), in turn, is particularly interested in understanding the role played by psychosocial processes in the development of the community, with the dual purpose of producing knowledge and empowering its members to exercise control in the actions, programs or projects aimed at solving the problems of their physical and social surroundings (Rappaport, 1977; Chavis & Newbrough, 1986). Furthermore, and it has been so since its origin in Latin America, CSP prioritizes working with poor communities, especially those of informal human settlements, which are the specific focus of concern for SD in relation to poverty.

Thus, the integration of EP and CSP into what we have called ECP recognizes the community as the meaning and destination of its mission, which directly links the discipline to the goal of SD. Indeed, if we consider that SD aspires to satisfy the needs of community's present and future generations, especially the needs of poor communities and, consequently, improve their quality of life, it can be concluded that EP and CSP agree with this purpose.

When we refer to the community, we understand it as the intermediate level between the individual and society as a whole, as an adequate level, due to its size and complexity, to understand human-environmental transactions, to encourage and consolidate psychosocial processes, and to facilitate actions that optimize these transactions, contributing in this manner to the improvement of the communities' quality of life and sustainability. As pointed out by Eid (2003), the recent awareness about the importance of the community, has made it the purpose, the goal and the means for SD.

To approach its object of study, ECP is guided by the following principles (Sánchez & Wiesenfeld, 2002):

a. Promotion of equitable relations between the actors involved in the management of the community that seeks to solve its environmental and social problems. ECP acknowledges the existing imbalances between social sectors, but uses strategies that encourage the participation of the multiplicity of positions in creating solutions to problems.
b. Recognition of the various meanings that social actors elaborate on the selected situation (problems, resources, needs), which allows them to problematize and raise consciousness on "what it is" directing them to "what it could be"
c. Promotion of the negotiation of the plurality of interpretations, to formulate and execute projects that meet different needs and interests.
d. Promotion and/or strengthening of social and emotional links between the members of communities.
e. Encouragement of community participation in the management of the selected situations, by understanding them and making them their own.
f. Development of the resources of the community and other actors outside the community (such as researchers), so that its members get stronger and assume greater control of their surroundings.
g. Systematization of the knowledge generated by this type of participatory experiences that enriches the ECP discipline.
h. Application of this knowledge, so as to establish as a practice the cycle of reflection, action, theorization, and action.

To fulfil these principles, the understanding and optimization of human-environmental transactions in community settings cannot be achieved independently from the social, political, and economical processes of the context in which these transactions occur. Neither can they be achieved without establishing multilateral alliances, based on the convergence of objectives between actors. This convergence can be achieved through the mediation of ECP, which encourages the production of different versions of the problems to be tackled, the systematization and problematization with different actors, seeking agreements within and between the groups of actors. To the extent that each player understands the rationale behind the projects, it is possible for them to make them their own and participate jointly in their (re)design, execution and evaluation.

The aforementioned principles are based on the theoretical corpus of social constructionism and the methodological corpus of qualitative research and qualitative participatory action research (Jiménez, 2002; Lincoln, 2001; Sánchez & Wiesenfeld, 2002; Wiesenfeld, Sánchez & Cronick, 2002).

On social constructionism, because it is a framework that postulates the constitution of reality or, in the context of this chapter, the constitution of the socio-environmental problems of the community in relation to SD, from the perspectives that different key actors contribute to its definition (Guba & Lincoln, 2005; Gubrium & Holstein, 2008). This viewpoint stimulates the plural production of knowledge and the requirement of the different subjects' active presence in its development.

On qualitative research, on the one hand, because it stresses the importance of the participants' configurations in defining the problem to be tackled, and because it establishes that the research or intervention design will evolve as the problem becomes more precisely defined. On the other hand, because qualitative research requires that the selection or construction of methods not only envisages their adequacy to the problem being studied, but also their ability to converge with the cultural values of the context, and their capacity to not impinge on the participants' patterns of structuring experiences. Meanwhile, qualitative participatory action research concurs with the postulates described above, but adds the conceptualization of the participant as an operator with the resources to intervene, together with the researcher, in the fundamental decisions of the intervention or research. In addition, the strategies that emerge for the achievement of SD by public policies or other actions, have the virtue of legitimizing the plurality of actors that intervene, because they are the result of the diversity of viewpoints, reflected and negotiated through participation.

From our point of view, these bases provide a framework to guide the formulation and execution of SD projects and to systematize their results, thus responding to the call to move beyond rhetoric on to action and to meet the demand for conceptual and methodological precision of the SD model.

These views have been widely accepted in CSP, but not in EP; we therefore think that the proposed disciplinary link will help to enrich EP theoretically and methodologically and to increase its social relevance. In the words of Sánchez and Wiesenfeld (2002, p. 23):

> The development of EP from the constructionist framework, and from Participatoy Action Research and Qualitative Research as research strategies, will enrich the discipline by expanding its vision of the object of study, expanding its knowledge production means, and designing projects for the optimization of the human-environment relationship. All this, moreover, in a framework of holistic conceptualization of the environment, and of sustainability of the social change that is promoted, by recognizing groups or communities as subjects that are responsible for change management.

In synthesis, we believe that this way of working with communities helps to build community sustainability, as seen from local praxis, which, as we stated previously, is where it becomes meaningful, because it is aimed at satisfying the needs that, according to those involved, ensure and improve their living conditions. This is a necessary prerequisite to consider the survival of future generations.

The previous considerations guided a qualitative participatory action research project about SD, which we will refer to forthwith.

CASE STUDY

The experience to be described is based on research sponsored by a government agency in several Venezuelan states, in which one of the authors of this chapter was involved as a consultant.

First we will present some background that led to the research proposal, then how the development of the SD programs was conceived and designed by its planners, and finally we will illustrate the application of some of the principles of ECP that have been mentioned, and their implications for SD.

Background

The research originated with the request made by the strategic planning team of a ministry (we call it "client team") to a government agency from another ministry which we will call "research team". The client team is responsible for the design of sustainable development projects and is composed of engineers, architects, urbanists, veterinarians, and ecologists. The research team carries out studies in areas related to the social development of the Venezuelan population and is composed of social scientists and professionals of other disciplines.

The client team's request was to investigate how the inhabitants of several of the country's states would greet development programs aimed at sustainability that targeted these areas. Given this request, an interview of the client team was proposed to the research team, in order to ascertain their plans for SD, the bases that supported their proposals, how they would be put into practice, the conception they had of the processes and actors involved in these plans, the forms of relationship they had had with the members of the target communities, and the expectations they had about the requested research. With this proposal to the research team, besides obtaining information about the points in question, a conversational context with the client team was encouraged, which stimulated critical reflection about the development programs that were being planned. In addition, they would get to know the client team's disposition to take into account the diversity of meanings about development and quality of life that existed in the communities. It was hoped, in this way, to facilitate a future meeting between the client and the residents so that both visions could come face to face, be problematized, and encourage negotiations on the program contents where they did not coincide.

These three objectives correspond to some ECP principles, particularly the first three, which we can summarize as the need to know, interchange, confront and negotiate the viewpoints of different actors, without favoring some viewpoints over others, that is, on an equitable plane.

The interview lasted about three hours, with six members of the client team and three of the research team. The interviewees' answers are identified by the codes CTC (client team coordinator) and CTM (client team member).

About the Origin and Objectives of the Programs

One of the coordinators of the client team expressed that the first program, around which the team responsible for the development plan was formed, was elaborated by an architect and an engineer. He identified the environmental dimension as the core of this development plan, as they hoped the interventions would not alter components of the physical surroundings. To this end, they proposed the creation of a strategic plan of self-sustainable integral endogenous development programs, which, they trust, can be executed when the communities get organized for that purpose:

> The idea was born within the Ministry, which is responsible for the strategic plans of planning and development. A group of professionals coordinated by an architect and an engineer designed the first tentative program, which acted as a base for the formation of the current team that is responsible for the development program (CTC).
> It fits here perfectly, as we are interested in creating an environmental equilibrium in the entire region, and to do so we are obliged to consider all the variants that could endanger the ecology, the flora, the fauna and the region's current great beauty (CTC).
> The program consists of developing a strategic plan for self-sustainable programs of endogenous development in the states...This will allow the consolidation of existing human settlements towards a better quality of life..., that is the essence of the projects. ...So our goal is to develop this axis as it should be done, in an integral way...and then the organization of the communities for production (CTC).
> Stil..., our work. because it is an articulating work, that is, work that is at the top, does not have the ability to um! get into the radio, television, the media, so that people could have information about this development... (CTC).

Interpretation

Although the development plan is conceived as a comprehensive plan, the procedural sequence described by the client team shows that planning is done "from above", without prior diagnosis of the needs and resources of the target communities, which is a fundamental requirement of community psychosocial work. It also reveals the role of the planner as expert, as "the one who knows" what is right for the community, and assumes that community participation is a process that is triggered in cascade by the offers of plans for development. The secondary role of the community is accentuated when the need to inform it is recognized after structuring the development plan.

ABOUT THE DEFINITION OF COMMUNITY NEEDS

They acknowledge that it is frequent for people to express basic needs of employment, health services, but they rate them as common relative to other needs that will come forth as a result of the intervention with the development plan.

> ...and once they are carried out, the development programs in which the communities are integrated in cooperatives, production centers, they have to get to know this for other needs to arise, if they don't know about it they are going to ask for the basic things: what I want to have here is a dispensary, what I want to have here is, who do I sell my milk to, who what's it called, who am I going to work for. Do you understand? What I need is a salary in order to support my children. So, these aspects are going to show up like this, because it's logical, because these are the people's needs (CTM).

Interpretation

It is interesting that, though the client team accept the basic character of the needs they anticipate in people, they devaluate them compared to what the planner conceives as what the product of the intervention should be through the plan. In this sense, they also underestimate the subject's creative potential for generating different meanings about his/her needs, by considering them a consequence of the execution of the plan. It also draws attention that the planner remains unalterable, as he/she is not perceived as an agent capable of change resulting from the exchange between his/her points of view and those of the community. This absence is another expression of the traditional conception of the role of the planner.

ABOUT THE CENTRAL ACTOR IN DEVELOPMENT

They emphasize that the communities targeted by the programs are central actors, but the type of relationship that the planners will establish with the community is not specified, nor the roles will the community play.

> Evidently the key actor here is the productive communities, the people that produce. That is the central actor towards whom all this work is directed. We are articulators of this function and...and our central objective is man, we make eco-development plans, not physical plans in the abstract, as it has always happened, that build great dams and we don't know who will benefit from them; which farmers are being supported, no one knows. They know how much the dam costs, how much the profits will be, what investments are going to be made, but they don't know for what purpose, what direction development is taking. This is what distinguishes our work from the way development has been carried out previously (CTM).

Interpretation

The community appears as a general referent (the community, people, the people), decontextualized, which allows us to think *about* it, rather than *with* it. Acting with it implies acknowledging community as a singular entity, in a specific context, with particular historical and cultural referents and with concrete potentials for development.

ABOUT THE APPROPRIATION OF THE PROGRAMS BY THE COMMUNITY

It is assumed that once the programs are handed over to the community, "in the hands of the people", there is an identification with the project and an appropriation of it, such that the community itself will impel its execution. This is attributed to the endogenous nature of the programs, which is understood as if "they [the programs] will reproduce themselves, they have their own internal capacity to continue".

> For the first time, the Venezuelan State has a policy to make these programs concrete. And in these projects, the word endogenous itself means that they will reproduce themselves, that they have the endogenous ability to work. So I see that in this sense we must go from the bottom upwards. Each program will come from the people's sinews, this is a novel idea in Venezuela, this had never happened before; things here went from the top towards the bottom. Once you put these programs in the people's hands, the program belongs to them, they will be the first to make it work (CTM).

Interpretation

The planner sees the appropriation as a product that is generated after the event, as an effect of the intervention, and not as a process that must begin from the subject's involvement in the construction of the object, in this case of the development programs.

ABOUT THE PLANNER'S COMMITMENT IN THE PROGRAM DEVELOPMENT PROCESS

The planner restricts his responsibility to the stage of program content formulation and to its cross-sector articulation.

> Don't forget that we establish the general guidelines; the specific tasks are not up to us...We have to hand out the organizational standards but not the organization itself (CTC).

Interpretation

This assumes that the phases of the projects are independent from each other, ignoring the feedback that occurs between the different moments of the planning stage and the different times of the execution phase. The planner separates himself from knowledge that could change the definition of the programs because of the effects they are generating.

ABOUT THE TIES WITH OTHER ACTORS OUTSIDE THE COMMUNITY

The planner describes the existence of local development programs as an obstacle, such as mayors' offices or governors' offices, which he believes should act in accordance to the central development plan.

> What are the obstacles for developing, carrying out the project? We consider that we need to create an articulation system, which is our role and...this process of articulation leads us to the need that for this plan to succeed, a structure must be created to bring cohesion to all the plans, in every region. What are the obstacles? That these structures are separated at the moment, the political structures with the specific interests of each State, where we still haven't been able to work, as you could say, coherently, we have worked from above, since the governors have particular plans that don't correspond, the mayors' offices have them also, they are closed systems, that it is necessary that the planning and development institute function as an articulator to open, that this program may penetrate them, and get them to understand that...not for each mayor's office and that everyone will benefit as a whole (CTM).
>
> The plan must be flexible, but one must be inflexible in applying it (CTC).
>
> Let me clarify something important, what is going on is that we are in electoral processes, we are in the process of political changes, that we don't know how they are going to be generated, and that Venezuela has suffered the illness that political changes are changes that have always paralyzed the existing developments. Venezuela has lived from paralysis to paralysis for not having had central plans, [plans] of continuity (CTC).

Interpretation

By conceiving the diversity of perspectives expressed in the specific programs that are developed in the localities as a limitation, the historical and cultural particularities inherent to contexts are negated. Just as the community needs are defined from above and outside, the same seems to happen to local projects. The national-local articulation does not refer to generating mechanisms to reduce successful local projects to the central plans, but rather to form the central plan based on the qualities of the local plans.

Besides, the approach we are criticizing ignores the richness of the constructive exchange that is generated in horizontal relationships between national planners and local agents, and threatens the continuity of successful programs and of SD, because it underestimates the knowledge and motivation the locals have about the importance of their region's resources for themselves and for other generations.

Conclusion

According to the previous case analysis, SD is conceptualized from the expert action of the planner. It is he/she who indicates the community's needs, the means to satisfy them and the way to interact with the community and other actors that are important for the success of the plan.

Development, coming from the planner, travels the route of program imposition, undermining the notion of SD in its social component. It imposes the cognitive structure of the planner onto the plan, denying the community's participation with their viewpoints and actions that could influence the decisions made about the plan, which is a basic principle of the ECP we propose. By denying the intervention of the community, the synergy between community knowledge and expert knowledge is excluded, as well as the opportunity for changing the particular conceptions of the groups of actors that are important to the development plan.

From the ECP perspective, on the contrary:

1. By assuming needs or problems as meanings that are constructed in the planner-community dialogue, the existence of the planner's preconceptions about what people want is acknowledged, but it is postulated that those preconceptions are transformed in the light of the new formulations that are made at the planner-community encounter and operation modes. This is a key operation of SD.
2. By recognizing the importance of community needs and of development plans or programs that local decision makers (such as mayors) have, diversity is valued as an energizer of SD resignification. But this creative scenario for SD is possible when the central planner-local agents and communities relationships are handled horizontally, ensuring the flow of production of alternative meanings about the development programs. This exchange of new versions helps the development program to change and to adjust to the new requirements that are created as the relationship between the different actors evolves. Rather than imposition, the negotiation of conceptions and operations modes is a key operation of SD.
3. But ECP also emphasizes the role of the community's social resources or capital for development. Thus, just as needs are conceived in construction, so can the community social capital be amplified with new additions that enhance the community agent's contribution to development.
4. By looking at the link between community and SD in this way, that is, as a process that grows stronger in the entire continuum of the relationship and not as an isolated result of the planner's intervention, the appropriation of the programs by the community agent is ensured. This is because it achieves congruence between planning and community needs, and the resources of both of them, in a dynamic plan of recurrent changes that refine the development plan with the positions of the variety of actors that are involved.

These guidelines are part of the agenda that we hope will orient the successive phases of the study. It should be mentioned that the following phase consisted of a qualitative research study with residents of several localities selected for the study, as well as local authorities and other key informants such as teachers, doctors, chroniclers, and community leaders. 160 interviews were conducted, between individual interviews and focus groups. The study's objectives were specified from successive conversations with the client team and they were negotiated according to the guidelines that have been mentioned. The objectives varied depending on the type of informant, but in general terms they referred to: a) needs, aspirations, resources, membership and roots of the community, b) community organization and participation, c) conception of quality of life, d) meaning of sustainable development and progress, e) willingness and strategies to promote development. Consistent with the above approach, the results were shared with the communities and local authorities, as well as with the client team.

The discussion with community members hoped to foster a collective consciousness about the possibilities of development, starting from the solution of their own problems and analyzing the potentialities offered by the formulated programs. The discussion with the client team is encouraging and we hope that the development that is achieved will materialize in the direction of community sustainability of the localities where the program implantation is foreseen, whether they are new programs emerging from the communities, or designed by the planners but adapted to the requirements of the communities, based on a more complex and enriched conception of their problems.

We hope, lastly, that the experience and guidelines we have presented will help to transcend the considerations about SD from discourse to praxis, and to conceptually and methodologically clarify the social dimension of Sustainable Development.

REFERENCES

Brundtland, G. H. (1987). Our common future (Report of the World Commission on Environment and Development, WCED). Oxford, UK: Oxford University Press.

Burdet, R. & Sudjic, D. (2008) The Endless City. London: Phaidon.

Cabrera, J. L., (2005) ¿Qué es el desarrollo sustentable? Consideraciones a partir del Programa Valle Verde del Río Lurín. disPerSión. Revista Electrónica del Instituto Psicología y Desarrollo. Página 1-11 Año II, Número 4, www.ipside.org/dispersion archivo http://www.ipside.org/dispersion/2005-4/4_cabrera.pdf.

Chavis, D. y Newbrough, J. (1986). The meaning of 'community' in Community Psychology. *Journal of Community Psychology, 14*(4), 335-340.

Churchman, A. & Sadan, E. (2004). Public participation in environmental design and planning. In C. Spielberg (Ed.), Encyclopedia of applied psychology (pp. 793-800). Oxford: Elsevier.

Corporación Latinobarómetro. (2007). Informe Latinobarómetro 2007. Retrieved August 8, 2008, from www.der.oas.org/INFORME%20LB%202007.PDF.

Demian, A. (2008). Pobreza en América Latina. Retrieved March 28, 2009, from biblioteca.iiec.unam.mx/index.php?option=com_content&task=vi.

Dietz, T. & Stern, P. (2008). Public participation in environmental assessment and decision making. Retrieved January 10, 2009, from http://www.iisd.ca/publications_resources/sust_devt2008htm

Dietz, T., York, R. & Rosa, E. (2008). Ecological democracy and sustainable development. Retrieved April 29, 2009, from http://sedac.ciesin.columbia.edu/openmeeting/dowloads/1006029486_presentation_tdietz_riopaper.doc

Dryzek, J. (1999). Transnational democracy. *The Journal of Political Philosophy* 7 (1), 30-51.

Economic Commission for Latin. America and the Caribbean (ECLAC). (2006). Sustainable Development Latin American and Caribbean Perspectives. Retrieved January 11, 2009, from www.blackwell-synergy.com/doi/abs/10.1111/j.1477-8947.2006.00162.x

Economic Commission for Latin America and the Caribbean (ECLAC). (2008). Social Panorama of Latin America 2008. Retrieved March 20, 2009, from http://www.eclac.org/publicaciones/xml/3/34733/PSI2008-SintesisLanzamiento.PDF

Economic Commission for Latin America and the Caribbean (ECLAC). (2009). New Statistical Yearbook for Latin America and the Caribbean, 2008. Retrieved March 20, 2009, from http://www.eclac.cl/cgibin/getprod.asp?xml=/publicaciones/xml/7/36327/P35327.xml&xsl=/dype/

Eid, Y. (2003). Sustainable urban communities: History defying cultural conflict. En G. Moser, E. Pol, Y. Bernard, M. Bonnes, J. Corraliza y M. Giuliani (Eds.). *People, Places and Sustainability* (p. 83-93). Alemania: Hoegrefe & Huber Publishers.

Fay, M. (Ed.) (2005). The Urban Poor in Latin America (Directions in development). Washington, USA: The World Bank.

Guba, E. & Lincoln, Y. (2005). Paradigmatic controversies, contradictions, and emerging confluences. In N. Denzin & I. Lincoln (Eds.), *The Sage Handbook of qualitative research* (pp. 191-215). Thousand Oaks, CA: Sage Publications.

Gubrium, J. F. & Holstein, J. A. (2008). The constructionist mosaic. In J. A. Holstein & J. F. Gubrium (Eds.), *Handbook of construccionist research* (pp. 3-10). New York: The Guilford Press.

Hayden, T. (2008). El estado del planeta. National Geographic España. Madrid: RBA.

International Union for the Conservation of Nature (IUCN), United Nations Environment Programme (UNEP) & World Wildlife Fund (WWF). (1980). World Conservation Strategy: Living resources conservation for sustainable development. Retrieved January 12, 2009, from http://www.nssd.net/references/KeyDocs/IIEDa24.htm

Jiménez, B. (2002). Which kind of sustainability for a social environmental psychology? En P. Schmuck & W. Schultz. (Orgs.), *Psychology of sustainable development* (pp. 257-276). Boston: Kluwer Academic Publishers.

Lincoln, Y. (2001). Engaging sympathies: relationships between action research and social constructivism. En: P. Reason y H. Bradbury (Eds.). *Handbook of Action Research* (pp.124 – 132). Gran Bretaña: Sage.

Moser, G. (2003). La psicología ambiental en el Siglo XXI. *Revista de Psicología de la Universidad de Chile, XII* (2), 11-17.

Naredo, J. M. & Rueda, S. (1997). "La ciudad sostenible": Resumen y conclusiones. Retrieved March 30, 2005, from http://habitat.aq.upm.es/cs/p2/a.010.html

Pinheiro, J. Q. (2002). Comprometimento ambiental: Perspectiva temporal e sustentabilidade. In J. Guevara & S. Mercado (Eds.), Temas selectos de psicología ambiental. México: UNAM, Greco, Fundación Unilibre.

Pol, E. (1998). Evoluciones de la psicología ambiental hacia la sostenibilidad: tres propuestas teóricas y orientaciones para la gestión. In D. Páez & S. Ayestarán (Eds.). *Los*

Desarrollos de la Psicología Social en España (pp. 105 – 120). Madrid, España: Infancia y Aprendizaje

Pol, E. (2002a). Environmental management: A perspective from environmental psychology. In R. Bechtel y A. Churchman (Eds.). *Handbook of Environmental Psychology* (pp. 55 – 84). New York, USA: John Wiley and Sons.

Pol, E. (2002b). The theoretical background of the city-identity-sustainability research network. *Environment &Behavior 34* (1), 8-25.

Rappaport, J. (1977). *Community Psychology (Values, Research and Action).* Nueva York, EE. UU. : Holt, Rinehart y Winston.

Rees, E. W. (2002). Globalization and sustainability: Conflict or convergence? *Bulletin of Science, Technology and Society 22* (4), 249-268.

Robinson, J. (2004). Squaring the circle? Some thoughts on the idea of sustainable development. *Ecological Economics 48* (4), 369-384. Retrieved January, 10, 2009, fromhttp://www.infra.kth.se/courses/1H1142/Squaring_the_circle%20.pdf

Rosales, O. (2007). Facilitación del Comercio para PYMEs Latinoamericanas. Retrieved January 11, 2009, from www.eclac.org/comercio/noticias/paginas/6/31926/Osvaldo_Rosales.pdf

Sadan, E. & Churchman, A. (1996). *Global sustainability and community empowerment.* In M. Gray (Ed.), Evolving environmental ideals-changing way of life, values and design practices (IAPS 14) Proceedings of the 14 Conference International Association for People-Environment Studies (IAPS) (pp.184-192). Stockholm.

Sánchez, E. (2000). *Todos con la esperanza: la continuidad de la participación comunitaria.* Caracas, Venezuela: Comisión de Estudios de Postgrado, Universidad Central de Venezuela.

Sánchez, E., & Wiesenfeld, E. (2002). El construccionismo como otra perspectiva metateórica para la producción del conocimiento en psicología ambiental. En J. Guevara y S. Mercado (Eds.). *Temas Selectos de Psicología Ambienta* (pp. 9 - 30). D.F., México: GRECO, UNAM, Fundación Unilibre.

Second United Nations Conference on Human Settlements (Habitat II). (1996). Istanbul, Turkey. Retrieved January 6, 2005, from www.un.org/conferences/habitat/

Sen, A. & Kliksberg, B. (2007). Primero la gente. Barcelona, Es: Deusto.

Sheddon, C., Howarth, R. B. Norgaard, R. B. (2006). Sustainable development in a post-Brundtland world. *Ecological Economics 57* (2), 253–268. Retrieved January 10, 2009, from www.elsevier.com/locate/ecolecon.

The World Bank Group (2004), Millenium Development Goals 2004. Retrieved December 10, 2008, from web.worldbank.org/data

Trigo, C. A. (2004). Pobreza y desigualdad en América Latina. *Futuros, Revista Trimestral Latinoamericana y Caribeña de Desarrollo Sustentable 2*,1-2. Retrieved January 10, 2009, from www.revistafuturos.info/futuros_8/pobreza1.htm

United Nations Conference on Environment and Development (UNCED) (1992). The Earth Summit. Retreived January 5, 2009, from http://www.un.org/geninfo/bp/enviro.html

United Nations Development Programme (UNDP) (2001). Annual Report. Retrieved January 7, 2009, from http://www.undp.org/dpa/annualreport2001/

United Nations Development Programme [UNDP]. (2008). Endpoverty Millenium Development Goals. Retrieved March 30, 2009, from http:// www.un.org/ millenniumgoals/2008high level/sgstatement.shtml

UN-Habitat United Nations Human Settlements Programme (2006). World Urban Forum (WUF) III. Retrieved January 8, 2009, from http://ww2.unhabitat.org/

United Nations Population Fund (UNFPA). (2007). State of world population 2007. Unleashing the potential of urban growth. Retrieved January 11, 2009. from http://www.unfpa.org/swp/2007/english/introduction.html

United Nations Population Fund (UNFPA). (2008). Reaching Common Ground. Retrieved January 11, 2009, from http://www.unfpa.org/swp/2008/en/index.html

Urban 21. Global Conference on the urban future (2000). Berlin Declaration on the Urban Future. Retrieved January 8, 2009, from www.agenda21-treffpunkt.de/archiv/00/sv/urb21bdec.doc

Vilches, A., Gil Perez, D., Toscano, J.C. & Macías, O. (2008 a). Urbanización y sostenibilidad. Retrieved March 31, 2009, from http://www.oei.es/decada/accion20.htm

Vilches, A., Gil Pérez, D., Toscano, J.C. & Macías, O. (2008b). Reducción de la pobreza. Retrieved March 31, 2009, from http://www.oei.es/decada/accion01.htm

Vilches, A., Gil Pérez, D., Toscano, J.C. & Macías, O. (2008c). La sostenibilidad como [r]evolución cultural, tecnológica y política. Retrieved March 31, 2009, from http://www.oei.es/decada/accion000.htm

Wiesenfeld, E. (2001). La problemática ambiental desde la perspectiva psicosocial comunitaria: hacia una psicología ambiental del cambio. *Medio Ambiente y Comportamiento Humano, 2*(1), 2-20.

Wiesenfeld, E. (2003). La psicología ambiental y el desarrollo sostenible: ¿cuál psicología ambiental ? ¿cuál desarrollo sostenible ?. *Estudios de Psicología, 8*(2), 253-261.

Wiesenfeld, E. & Giuliani, F. (2005). La psicología ambiental comunitaria: una vía para el desarrollo sostenible. En E. Tassara, E.P. Rabinovich, M.C. Guedes M.C (Eds.). *Psicología en Ambiente* (pp. 389 – 408). São Paulo, Brasil: EDUC.

Wiesenfeld, E. Sánchez, E. & Cronick, K. (2002). Participatory action research as a participatory approach to addressing environmental issues. In R. García Mira, J. M. Sabucedo & J. Romay Martínez (Eds.), Culture, enviromental action and sustainability (pp.85-100). Gottingen, Germany: Hogrefe and Huber Publisher.

Williams, C. C. & Millington, A. C. (2004). The diverse and contested meanings of sustainable development. *The Geographical Journal 170* (2), 99-104.

Wint, E. (2002). Sustainable communities, economic development and social change: two case studies of 'Garrison communities' in Jamaica. *Journal of Community, Work and Family, 5* (1), 83-101.

World Commission on Environment and Development [WCED]. (1987). Our Common Future. Oxford, England: Oxford University Press.

Worldwatch Institute (2007/2008). The Worldwatch Institute Annual Report: Innovation for a sustainable world. Retrieved January 8, 2009, from http://www.worldwarch.org/system/files/annual_Report_2007_2008.pdf

Chapter 17

PLACE ATACHMENT AND THE SOCIAL ACCEPTANCE OF RENEWABLE ENERGY TECHNOLOGIES

Patrick Devine-Wright[*]
School of Geography, University of Exeter, United Kingdom

ABSTRACT

Renewable energy technologies are a vital component of governmental responses to the climate change threat. However, despite high levels of public support for an increase in the use of renewable energy, specific projects have often met with resistance by local residents, a phenomenon often dubbed 'NIMBYism' (Not In My Back Yard) by policy makers, industrialists and media commentators. In this chapter, I argue that the NIMBY concept is an unhelpful way of explaining public responses to technology projects, and an alternative explanation is proposed, drawing from theoretical and empirical literature in Environmental Psychology on the concept of place attachment. From this perspective, local opposition is reconceived as a form of place-protective action, arising when technology projects disrupt pre-existing place attachments and threaten place-related identity processes. This proposal is empirically investigated by means of a case study of a proposed offshore wind farm in North Wales, UK, drawing on both qualitative and quantitative data, collected using in-depth interview and questionnaire methods. Results indicate how the local opposition group employed a discourse of threat to the place in their campaign against the wind farm, arguing that the turbines would 'industrialise' the area and 'fence' in the bay. Analysis of residents' responses indicated that individuals who felt strongly attached to the place were most likely to interpret the project as producing negative local outcomes, to feel negative emotions associated with the project, to indicate low levels of project support and to have undertaken oppositional behaviours such as signing petitions or writing letters to the local paper. Moreover, there was a significant positive correlation between place attachment and trust in the local opposition group, and a significant negative correlation between place attachment and trust in the development company. Conceptually, the results suggest that opposition from the

---
[*] Correspondence: Patrick Devine-Wright; e-mail: pdwright@manchester.ac.uk

residents was rooted not in so-called 'NIMBYism', but in pre-existing feelings of attachment to the place, which was strategically made use of by the opposition group to mobilise local people against the project using a discourse of threat. More practically, the results suggest the necessity of developers to take processes of place attachment into account when engaging with local residents about their project proposals.

INTRODUCTION

According to an international panel of the world's leading climate scientists, climate change is not only happening but arises as a consequence of human activities that lead to the emission of greenhouse gases (Intergovernmental Panel on Climate Change, 2007). Given that, it is important to identify what role psychological expertise can play in informing our understanding of climate change and the design of effective policies in response (Spence, Pidgeon and Uzzell, 2009). It is hard to imagine an effective response that does not pay significant attention to the domain of energy, that is to how we generate the heat and electricity needed to power our homes and workplaces, and how we use this heat and electricity for a range of everyday services upon which our quality of life is based (lighting, heating, washing, taking leisure etc.). Governments around the world are making commitments to reduce the emission of greenhouse gases and this can happen in one of two ways: by reducing energy demand (e.g. by increasing energy efficiency) or by reducing the carbon emitted per unit of energy (e.g. by increasing the use of low or zero-carbon fuel sources) (Foresight Sustainable Energy Management and the Built Environment Project, 2008). Whilst the pathway of reduced demand has received considerable research attention by environmental psychologists (see Abrahamse, Steg, Vlek and Rothengatter, 2005 for a review), far less attention has been paid to the psychological aspects of increasing the use of zero-carbon fuels. This chapter begins to address this gap.

In many developed countries, heat and electricity are created from fossil-fuel (e.g. natural gas, coal and oil) and nuclear energy sources, and distributed to locations of use through a centralised infrastructure or 'national grid'. Whilst nuclear energy does not emit carbon, concerns about safety and the storage of radioactive waste materials have led governments to seek to increase the proportion of heat or electricity generated from an alternative zero-carbon energy source: renewable energy. Renewable energy is an umbrella term describing a wide variety of sources that are non-depleting with use, including solar, wind, tidal, wave or bioenergy sources. For example, in the UK, there is a policy commitment to increase electricity derived from renewable energy sources from a current level of about 5% to 20% by 2020 (Department of Trade and Industry, 2006). Such targets necessitate that technologies generating electricity and heat from wind, sun, biomass and marine sources become commonplace, rather than 'alternative', as is currently the case. It is also likely to lead to alterations to networks of heat and electricity distribution and the introduction of low-carbon technologies such as the use of hydrogen energy for storing electricity and for transport (e.g. in electric or hydrogen vehicles). What is clear is that the energy systems in place one century from today are likely to differ significantly from those we have inherited from the 20th century era of 'hydrocarbon' economies (Rifkin, 2002).

There is a growing awareness that 'de-carbonising' a complex, large-scale technical system of energy generation, transmission and distribution is a project with important social and psychological as well as technical, economic and environmental aspects. One of the most frequently cited social aspects is that of 'public acceptance', a subject given a high priority in an authoritative multi-disciplinary review of research needs for a decarbonised energy system (Ekins, 2004). The reason why public acceptance is relevant in relation to renewable energy is that there has been significant local opposition, both in the UK and internationally, to development proposals. What makes such local opposition somewhat puzzling is the fact that numerous UK and European opinion polls have indicated public support for more renewable energy in principle (McGowan and Sauter, 2005), and the apparent 'social gap' (Bell, Gray and Haggett, 2005) between general societal support and specific local opposition is a critical issue influencing the trajectory of renewable energy development. If countries such as the UK are to be successful in meeting policy targets of a four-fold increase in electricity generated from renewable energy sources in little over a decade of time, then deepening understanding of the dynamics of acceptance and opposition is an important issue for research.

SOCIAL RESEARCH ON ENERGY TECHNOLOGIES

Over recent years there has been a rapid expansion in research on what is commonly labelled 'public perceptions' of energy technologies. This literature includes studies best characterised as market research, employing opinion polling of large-scale representative samples seeking to describe people's beliefs, as well as more theoretically driven academic studies, informed by a diverse set of social and human sciences, including sociology, social and environmental psychology, human and cultural geography and political science. Opinion polls have studied general beliefs or attitudes towards renewable energy, stimulated by policy concerns such as climate change, energy security and support for nuclear power (e.g. Poortinga, Pidgeon and Lorenzioni, 2006). This literature has shown consistently high levels of public support for increasing renewable energy, both in the UK and across Europe (e.g. Eurobarometer, 2006), albeit shaped by socio-demographic characteristics such as levels of education, age and political beliefs. For example whilst generally supported, it is the case that older, more politically conservative individuals are less likely to support specific low carbon technologies such as wind turbines (McGowan and Sauter, 2005).

Contrasting with these opinion polls seeking to capture general attitudes to energy, many studies have focused upon beliefs about specific energy projects, typically through case study research, using smaller samples of respondents and questionnaire survey methods. Recent research has investigated a variety of technologies and resources including onshore and offshore windfarms (e.g. Loring, 2007), biomass power plant (e.g. Upham and Shackley, 2006), hydrogen energy for transport and renewable energy storage (e.g. O'Garra, Mourato, and Pearson, 2005; Sherry-Brennan, Devine-Wright, and Devine-Wright, forthcoming), electricity pylons for transmitting renewable energy (e.g. Devine-Wright and Devine-Wright, 2006a) and the capture and storage of carbon underground (e.g. Shackley, McLachlan and Gough, 2005). Whilst the majority of these studies focus upon public beliefs about large-scale technology projects, a growing minority have focused upon acceptance of smaller-scale low carbon technologies for energy generation and storage, including solar photovoltaic panels, micro-wind turbines, and micro-scale combined heat and power plant (e.g. Sauter and

Watson, 2007) sometimes developed through community-based, rather than utility-led initiatives (e.g. Walker and Devine-Wright, 2008).

Perhaps unsurprisingly, the rapid growth of research in this area has produced a less than coherent body of literature, with researchers employing a confusing array of constructs to describe human responses, from public perceptions to social representations, each with varying disciplinary, epistemological and methodological implications. The term 'public acceptance' is itself problematic, since exactly what constitutes 'public' is rarely made explicit, and 'acceptance' has a stronger foundation in normative policy agendas for rapid implementation, rather than any particular social science theory. Perhaps in consequence, in energy research, acceptance is typically defined by its opposite - most studies focus upon the reasons people give for objecting to a given technology or project, typically informed by the NIMBY concept (Not In My Back Yard, Dear, 1992), rather than investigating support (Burningham, Barnett, and Thrush, 2007). This emphasis upon objection overlooks whether acceptance should be conceived uni-dimensionally or multi-dimensionally, for example whether acceptance is the absence of resistance, or acceptance and resistance separate social phenomena, to which one should add the position of 'indifference', that is those individuals who have no particular opinion with regards to a technology or project. From a psychological perspective, this fails to clarify whether 'acceptance' is best conceived as a positive belief or evaluation, as a favourable affective response, as an action of a particular kind, as a combination of these or something else entirely, such as a discourse or narrative. These alternative conceptions of acceptance also raise the question of level of analysis: whether acceptance should be researched at the intra-personal level, the inter-personal level, the socio-cultural level or somehow spanning all levels of analysis.

Methodologically, most studies have adopted an empirical approach, quantifying public responses using tools such as questionnaire surveys (e.g. Warren, Lumsden, O'Dowd, and Birnie, 2005). However, the use of opinion polls, particularly within market research studies, has been strongly critiqued (e.g. Wolsink, 2007), particularly by advocates of a more constructivist epistemology (e.g. Haggett and Smith, 2004; Ellis, Barry, and Robinson, 2007) who have instead recommended the study of discourse, using qualitative methods such as the Q-Sort. In contrast, other researchers have advocated a mixed-method approach combining qualitative and quantitative approaches (e.g. Devine-Wright, 2005; Toke and Haggett, 2006).

Early energy research studies assumed the determinants of public opposition to reside in the assumed 'characteristics' of the technologies involved (such as noise or visual aspects of wind turbines; smells and noise aspects of biomass plant), whose effects upon individuals were assumed to follow directly from spatial proximity (i.e. the closer a person's home to a site of technology development, the more negative their attitudes would be; e.g. Priestley and Evans, 1996). But this rather techno-centric, environmentally determinist approach to research has been challenged as overlooking important aspects of how each project proposal is *emplaced* in a specific socio-environmental context - a place with which local people often have important symbolic and affective bonds known as place attachments or place identities (Devine-Wright, forthcoming). Given the magnitude of changes to localities caused by the development of large-scale energy projects such as wind farms, it is therefore necessary to address how theory on the phenomenon of disruption to place attachments may be useful in shedding light on the dynamics of public acceptance of energy technologies. Therefore, the remainder of this chapter focuses upon these issues more deeply, beginning with a review of the most commonly used psycho-spatial concept to describe public resistance: 'NIMBYism'.

NIMBYSM AS A PSYCHO-SPATIAL EXPLANATION FOR LOCAL OPPOSITION

NIMBYism (Not In My Back Yard) has been used to refer to opposition to a diverse array of technologies or facilities, including waste dumps, gas pipelines and, more recently, wind farms (Burningham et al., 2007).

'In plain language ... [NIMBYs are] residents who want to protect their turf. More formally, NIMBY refers to the protectionist attitudes of and oppositional tactics adopted by community groups facing an unwelcome development in their neighbourhood... residents usually concede that these 'noxious' facilities are necessary, but not near their homes, hence the term 'not in my back yard' (Dear 1992, p288).

The NIMBY concept is used both to describe and explain aspects of public response. NIMBY is used as a label, almost exclusively pejoratively, to describe the kinds of people who oppose development, assuming the beliefs they hold to be akin to 'it is OK somewhere else, just not around here' (Burningham, 2000). The concept has been used by journalists, academics, policy makers and industrialists in often emotive ways to undermine local opposition to particular developments. For example, in a recent UK newspaper article, it was argued that *'Wind farms (are) now trapped in planning hell by local NIMBYs. NIMBYs can't be allowed to put a block on wind farms'* (Toynbee, 2007). Secondly, as an explanatory term, NIMBY presumes opposition to be motivated by a combination of selfishness, irrationality and ignorance (Burningham et al., 2007).

The NIMBY concept locates the causes of energy conflicts in the characteristics of people living spatially proximate to technology projects, yet conflict may also be engendered by a range of more contextual factors, from national energy policies, engineering designs and planning procedures to industry practices. This tendency to blame local residents for causing conflict has led to numerous academic critiques of the descriptive and explanatory assumptions underlying the NIMBY concept. Planning experts have noted with irony that the use of the NIMBY label itself can undermine democratic planning processes (Warburton, 2005). Sociologists have challenged the validity of 'deficit' views of public responses (i.e. that local opposition is really caused by deficits of knowledge and rationality, Petts, 1997) by illustrating contexts where members of the public were highly informed, and by advocating the adoption of a more pluralist definition of expertise. Policy makers' advocacy of 'reasoned debate' on energy technologies simplifies distinctions between 'fact' and 'myth' obscures areas of scientific disagreement and marginalises subjective and affective responses (Devine-Wright and Devine-Wright, 2006). Others have challenged the presumed negativity of local opposition, arguing that controversies over new technologies have a social value in signalling political or technical problems that may have been overlooked at earlier stages of technology development (Bauer, 1995).

Across the social sciences, academics have challenged the 'rational actor' model of the person intrinsic to the 'NIMBY' concept, which assumes that human behaviour is fundamentally motivated by self interest; instead the importance of beliefs about fairness and justice have been stressed (Hunter and Leyden, 1995). Political scientists have warned that the provision of incentives can increase rather than decrease local opposition, if symbolically regarded as a bribe by local people (Bell et al., 2005). Psychologists have argued for a more complex approach to public responses involving the interplay between diverse contextual, social and psychological factors (Devine-Wright, 2005). Finally, empirical studies have found little support for the spatial proximity assumptions embedded in NIMBYism (e.g. Wolsink, 2000; Warren et al., 2005), instead typically finding consistency between local and non-localised beliefs - more 'Not In Anyone's Back Yard' or 'In Everyone's Back Yard' than 'NIMBY' (e.g. Wolsink, 2000). In summary, most academics would agree with the following conclusion:

> 'We have three reasons for not using this term [NIMBYism]...it is generally used as a pejorative...it may not be accurate...this label leaves the cause of the opposition unexplained' (Kempton, Firestone, Lilley, Rouleau and Whitaker, 2005, pp. 124-5)

However, what is now required is the proposition of alternative conceptual frameworks to guide research - *'there is a need to develop a research agenda for understanding the role of subjectivity in wind energy debate'* (Ellis, Barry and Robinson, 2006, page 22). Geographers and sociologists have concluded that locating the causes of energy conflict in the characteristics of particular individuals is a fruitless exercise. Instead, some advocate the study of institutional functioning (e.g. Wolsink, 2007), while others emphasise the need to analyse 'discourses of objection' (Ellis et al., 2006), that is how 'NIMBYism' is socially produced through the discourses employed by protagonists in conflict (Burningham, 2000). Whilst both perspectives are useful, rejection of the NIMBY concept does not, in principle, invalidate the legitimacy of explanations at the level of individuals rather than institutions or socio-cultural discourse.

It is argued here that explaining public responses to energy technology projects is best achieved not by reductionist accounts affirming the significance of any one particular level of analysis or disciplinary approach, but by re-conceiving 'public perceptions' as socially embedded, dynamic and evolving beliefs held by individuals who are emplaced within physical-spatial-social contexts. It follows that deepening our understanding of public acceptance requires the construction of a conceptual framework that encompasses psychological explanations, but is nested within an interdisciplinary perspective that combines non-psychological aspects of facility sitting: environmental, technological, political, institutional and economic. Whilst this interdisciplinary perspective is beyond the scope of this particular chapter, I argue that the concept of place, which by definition encompasses both objective/material aspects and subjective/socio-psychological aspects, can form one useful building block in developing this interdisciplinary perspective.

PUTTING ENERGY TECHNOLOGIES INTO PLACE

Place is *'one of the trickiest words in the English language, a suitcase so overfilled that one can never shut the lid'* (Hayden, 1995, p112). It is an historic concept traceable to the work of Aristotle (*topos,* Sime, 1986), of interest to architects, geographers, sociologists, planners and psychologists, and researched from several epistemological approaches (Patterson and Williams, 2005). A common principle is that 'place' is distinct from more general concepts such as 'space' or 'environment' in reflecting a location of varying size or scale that is imbued with meanings and emotions by individuals or groups of people (Tuan, 1977; Farnum, Hall and Kruger, 2005; Zeisel, 2005).

From seminal contributions in the late 1970s (human geography: Relph, 1977; Tuan, 1977; psychology: Canter, 1977; architecture: Norburg-Schultz, 1980), place research has developed into a number of discrete strands. In environmental psychology, researchers have investigated concepts such as *place identity* (connections between the self and particular environments, Proshansky, Fabian, and Kaminoff, 1983); *place attachment* (emotional bonds between person and environment, Altman and Low, 1992) and *place satisfaction* (cognitive evaluations of place quality, Stedman, 2003). In human and cultural geography, there has been interest in *sense of place* (a conscious awareness of locatedness and distinctions between places: Tuan, 1980) and, more recently, in place as a socially constructed nodal point within a complex web of social interactions which may stretch over local, regional and national boundaries (Massey, 1995; Milligan, 2003). Interweaving these strands is a persistent interest in a particularly kind of place: the home (Easthorpe, 2004).

Environmental psychology is the sub-discipline within psychology that investigates the transactions between individuals and particular environments (Altman and Rogoff, 1987), with 'place' as a key concept (e.g. Bonnes and Seccharioli, 1995). However, few environmental psychologists to date have focused upon infrastructural or technological aspects of place, instead focusing upon structural aspects such as housing and public space. Although some social psychologists have studied public beliefs about specific energy sources, including both nuclear power and renewable energy (e.g. Poortinga, Pidgeon, and Lorenzioni, 2006), the risk perception perspective has typically overlooked the relevance of place in shaping public responses. For example, Huits, Midden and Meijnders' (2007) analysis of a proposed carbon storage facility in the Netherlands investigated local residents' attitudes (defined instrumentally in terms of perceived costs and benefits) towards carbon storage 'near and far' away and emotional responses to carbon storage 'in this area', without considering if 'this area' might constitute a place with which respondents felt emotionally attached.

Energy research studies have addressed spatial aspects of public responses, even though not drawing upon the concept of place directly, through a recurring emphasis upon the 'proximity hypothesis' (Devine-Wright, 2005), assuming that the objective distance between an individual's residence and the site of technology development is a key determinant of that individual's level of acceptance. This has led to studies examining public responses amongst residents living at different spatial distances from the site, assuming such responses to be different, an assumption about which there is conflicting evidence, with several studies showing elevated levels of public support at closer proximity to technology projects (e.g. Warren et al., 2005). However, whilst levels of familiarity are likely to be a factor shaping public responses, such familiarity is unlikely to be solely derived from direct experience, conceived as a function of spatial distance from existing developments. Rather, familiarity arises from both mediated and direct experience, and is therefore as much an outcome of socio-cultural processes such as social representations (e.g. exposure to media sources and interpersonal communication).

Wester-Herber (2004) advocated that studies should take account of 'local attachment to a specific geographical place' (p109) and not be blind to locational aspects of person-technology interactions. She argued that the siting of hazardous or unwanted facilities such as landfill dumps or industrial sites not only implicates issues of health and safety, but also changes to the aesthetics of the landscape, with such changes potentially stigmatising places and inducing local opposition. Wester-Herber focused upon 'underlying concerns' lying behind land-use conflicts, proposing that the guiding principles of place-identity, drawn from environmental psychology research, can be affected in a negative way by facility siting. Although specific to the siting of energy technologies, Wester-Herber's analysis hints at a potential alternative to the NIMBY explanation in which local opposition may be explained using place theory.

In energy research specifically, several studies have proposed that the concept of 'place' is useful for deepening our understanding of technology siting. Empirically, Vorkinn and Riese (2001) showed the importance of place attachment (defined as 'human bonding to a specific physical environment', page 249) in explaining public beliefs about a proposed hydropower project in Norway. They found that the more attached local residents felt towards the affected areas, the more the residents felt negative beliefs about the proposal. Issues of place were also emphasised in Kempton et al.'s (2005) empirical study of public responses to proposed offshore wind energy development in the USA, noting how local opposition was founded in particular beliefs about the ocean as a 'special place that should be kept natural and free from human intrusion' (page 119). More conceptually, van der Horst (2007), drew on Wester-Herber (2004) to claim that people who 'derive a more positive sense of identity from particular rural landscapes are likely to resist such potential developments, especially if they live there (page 2705). Finally, Brittan (2001) stressed how wind energy developments disrupt 'sense of place' by imposing standardised devices that undermine 'local character' and people's sense of being at home. All of these studies point in a similar direction – that considering theory of place may yield insights that help explain public responses to energy technology projects.

DISRUPTION TO PLACE ATTACHMENT AND THREAT TO PLACE IDENTITY

Brown and Perkins (1992) define place attachment as *"positively experienced bonds, sometimes occurring without awareness, that are developed over time from the behavioural, affective, and cognitive ties between individuals and/or groups and their socio-physical environment"* (p 284). A series of studies have explored place attachment over the past two decades, teasing out aspects such as the strength of connection between person and location, which correlates with length of dwelling (Brown and Perkins, 1992), such that leaving that place might be upsetting, disruptive and avoided (Fried, 2000; Brown, Perkins and Brown, 2003); the typically positive (although sometimes negative, Manzo, 2005) valence of this bond; the empirically distinct sub-dimensions of social and physical/spatial aspects, the relative weight of each which vary (Hidalgo and Hernandez, 2001), and links between place attachment and action, both at individual and collective levels (Stedman, 2002; Brown, Perkins and Brown, 2003; Manzo and Perkins, 2006).

There has been consistent interest in the psychological consequences of disruption to place attachments. Disruption has one of two pathways: resulting from the person deciding to leave a particular place that they feel attached to (e.g. students leaving home for the first time to go to University: Chow and Healey, 2008) or from a place changing due to social, environmental or economic circumstances (e.g. Dixon and Durrheim, 2000). The literature suggests that along both pathways, change can lead to feelings of displacement (Fullilove, 1996), grief and loss (Fried, 2000). Brown and Perkins (1992) draw attention to the manner in which such change challenges people's ability to cope, resulting in feelings of helplessness and anxiety: change which *'becomes so great that humans must work hard to define the thread of continuity or stability in life; at times change may feel overwhelming'* (page 282). Scholars have focused upon environmental as well as human-induced place change, ranging from the sudden shock of burglary (Brown and Perkins, 1992) to more prolonged forms of change including the impacts of relocation due to demolition of residential housing schemes (Fried, 2000), responses to neighbourhood decline (Brown, Perkins and Brown, 2003), organisational change (Milligan, 2003) and aspects of intergroup conflict (Dixon and Durrheim, 2000; Possick, 2004). Alike in rural and urban areas, whether through natural or human causes, the literature suggests that abrupt changes, whether through relocation or alteration to the physical aspects of places can disrupt existing place attachments and lead to negative emotional responses as individuals and groups struggle to cope, feeling a sense of loss and, sometimes, grief.

Associated with, yet distinct from the concept of place attachment is the concept of place identity, which refers to the ways in which certain locations can contribute to the identity of individuals and groups (Proshansky et al., 1983; Bonaiuto, Breakwell and Cano, 1996; Twigger-Ross and Uzzell, 1996; Devine-Wright and Lyons, 1997; Knez, 2005). Whilst there is some confusion in the literature about the relationship between place attachment and place identity, here they are considered to be closely associated, yet conceptually distinct aspects of person-environment relations, one referring to emotional bonds, the other to aspects of the self. It is presumed that locations to which an individual feels attached are also likely to be important for engendering a positive sense of identity and that change to a place can impact upon place identities as well as place attachments. It may also be the case that the distinction between attachment and identification is purely temporal – that attachment precedes identification over time (Hernandez, Hidalgo, Salazar-Laplace and Hess, 2007).

Place identity research has drawn on theories from social psychology, for example identity process theory (IPT, Breakwell, 1986; 1992), assuming that individuals are motivated to create and maintain a positive sense of identity, guided by four principles: continuity over time, distinctiveness, self-efficacy and self-esteem (Breakwell, 1986, 1992). Empirical studies of place identity applying IPT are diverse, encompassing studies of local identity in London (Twigger Ross and Uzzell, 1996), places symbolic of national identities in Ireland (Devine-Wright and Lyons, 1997) and climatic aspects of urban identities in Sweden (Knez, 2005). A central element of IPT is a focus upon how individuals respond to identity threats. For example, Bonaiuto, Breakwell and Cano (1996) investigated people's responses when beaches in the UK were labelled as polluted by the European Union. Measuring identity at both local and national-levels, they showed that the stronger the local identity of residents, the less polluted local beaches were believed to be, and the stronger the national identity, the less polluted national beaches were believed to be. In both cases, this was interpreted as forms of coping response to place identity threat in which individuals denied attributions of pollution to their local environment in order to protect a sense of place-related identity distinctiveness. Applying a similar conceptual approach, Speller (1999) focused upon the consequences of a very different form of disruption - the forced relocation of a former mining community in the UK. Her longitudinal, mixed-method study suggested that identity principles may be threatened not just by changes to the descriptive labelling of places, but by the physical change of relocation, challenging the sense of continuity with the past, with many residents finding it difficult to cope with the novel, unfamiliar surroundings of the new village, the differences between the old terrace houses and new *cul de sacs* increasing the sense of privacy but reducing social contact and sense of community.

Stedman's (2002) analysis of place identity in a lakeside area of Wisconsin, USA is useful in showing how proposals to make physical changes to place can lead to specific behavioural responses. He operationalised 'sense of place' through symbolic meanings and evaluations, which were used to predict behavioural intentions, adopting a socio-cognitive perspective. Using regression analysis, Stedman indicated that behavioural intentions to protect the lake (i.e. willingness to vote for new laws or join/form a protest group to campaign against new development) were explained by high levels of place attachment, low levels of 'place satisfaction' and the holding of particular symbolic beliefs about the place: that the lake was 'up north', a place 'to escape from civilization' (page 571) rather than a place symbolised more socially as a 'community of neighbours' (page 570).

Stedman's findings, alongside those of Speller (1999) and Bonaiuto et al. (1996) suggest that disruption or threat to person-place bonds can arise from diverse causes: negative labelling, proposals for physical changes and actual relocation. Each can threaten place identities and disrupt place attachments, inducing coping responses varying from denial (Bonaiuto et al., 1996) to behavioural resistance (Stedman, 2002). It is this possibility of behavioural resistance that suggests a useful link could be made between so called 'NIMBY' type public responses to the siting of renewable energy technologies, and the phenomena of disruption to place attachments and threat to place identities. However, before exploring this in more detail, it is necessary to capture the socially constructed nature of shared beliefs about change to existing places, since Stedman's perspective cannot account for the origin of place-related meanings such as 'up North' or 'community of neighbours'. As he himself recognised: '*the source of cognition is a relative mystery using this framework and data. More research is needed on the source of symbolic meanings*' (2002, p. 577).

To do this requires a shift in analytic gaze away from the individual as the sole point of reference towards a multi-level approach, premised on the assumption that knowledge about place change is collectively constructed through interactions among individuals and between individuals and the institutionalised structures that make up society (Wagner and Hayes, 2005). Social representations theory (Moscovici, 2000) provides such an approach, addressing aspects of content, process and power in the construction of social knowledge, encompassing individual and social aspects of identity processes (Moloney and Walker, 2007), that are rendered via processes of anchoring (the connecting of new ideas to familiar knowledge) and objectification (the making concrete of abstract ideas). It is also useful for understanding how change to the context of individuals' lives can lead to perceptions of threat, implicating identity processes (Timotijevic and Breakwell, 2000).

Social representations theory offers a useful approach to explain how proposals to change a place can engender communication amongst local residents about the impacts of change upon the physical environment as well as upon the individuals and groups who live, work or visit the place, leading to the adoption of specific attitudes to change proposals and to specific behavioural responses. Research informed by social representations theory can investigate how proposed changes to places are interpreted (via anchoring and objectification), evaluated (as threat or opportunity), contested (amongst individuals and between individuals and organisations, mindful of the unequal power relations between different actors) and actively responded to, both through individual and collective actions. Applying the theory alongside the notion of place-identity to the study of disruption has the potential to extend social representations theory, which to date has typically neglected the 'emplacement' of social phenomena (Gieryn, 2000).

To progress these aspects and provide a basis for future research, a framework for understanding individual responses to place change has been proposed that comprises multiple levels of analysis, ensuring the emplacement of the individual in social and spatial contexts, and possesses multiple stages to explain responses over time (Devine-Wright, forthcoming). This framework connects environmental psychology theory on place with social psychological theory on social representations and identity processes. The stages include becoming aware, interpreting change, evaluating change as threat or enhancement, coping responses and, in certain circumstances, behavioural resistance or support (see figure 1).

These stages were investigated in a mixed-method empirical study of public responses to offshore wind energy in a case study project in North Wales, UK.

Becoming aware
What kind of place change will occur?

Interpreting
What are the implications of change for this place?

Evaluating
Will the outcomes of place change be positive or negative?

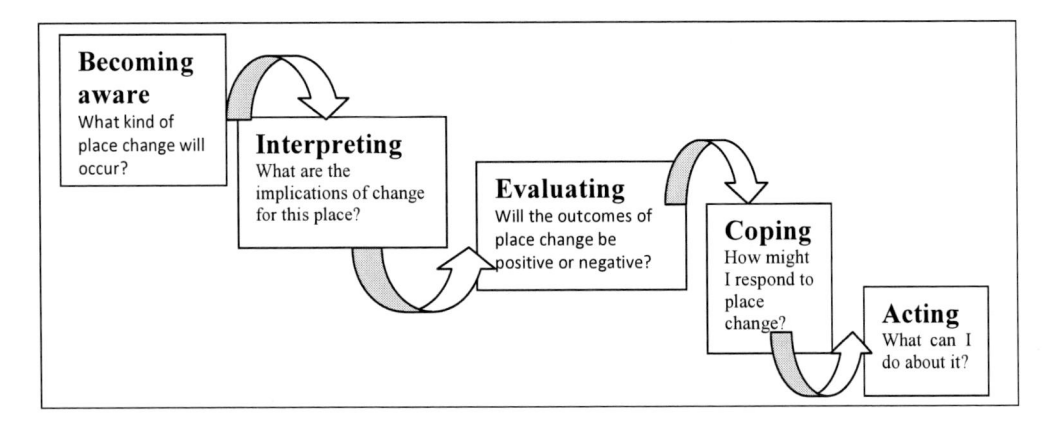

Coping
How might I respond to place change?

Acting
What can I do about it?

Figure 1. Stages of psychological response over time to place change.

METHOD

Context: Place and Project

The study was conducted in Llandudno, a seaside town in North Wales situated opposite the proposed site of an offshore wind farm. Llandudno is an important holiday resort, receiving 20% of Welsh national tourist income (Haggett, 2008). In 2001, the town had a population of approx 20,000, and a substantial minority (26%) of residents over 65 years of age, indicating its importance as a retirement location. The project is an offshore wind farm called 'Gwynt y Mor' that will install about 250 turbines, each over 100m tall, approximately 9 miles out to sea. Some local residents set up an opposition group called 'Save Our Scenery', arguing that the wind farm will damage tourism. Whether local residents adopted ways of thinking propagated by the opposition group or the developer was investigated in the study.

Procedure and Sample

The research employed a mixed method research design, involving in-depth interviews with key organisations, group discussions with local residents and a questionnaire survey. As regards the survey, 250 questionnaires were distributed to residents using a 'drop and collect' procedure, involving repeat visits to each household to personally drop off and later collect a completed survey. 219 completed questionnaires were returned, a response rate of 87.6%. Respondents' average age was 61.11 (SD = 15.44), 46% were female and the average length of local residence was 21.45 years (SD = 17.40). The sample is representative of the local population in consisting of predominantly older individuals, although the proportion of those working full and part time is slightly lower than in Llandudno more generally.

Measures

Both interviews and focus groups followed a standardised schedule drawn up by the project team. Discussions were recorded and transcribed before coding was undertaken using a standardised template and analysed using MAXQDA qualitative software. Thematic analysis was undertaken to identify manifest and latent themes (after Joffe and Yardley, 2004). The survey began with a section on place, capturing representations of Llandudno, using a free association task, and levels of attachment, using a standardised 8 item scale (Hidalgo and Hernandez, 2001) that had a high level of reliability (alpha = 0.94), and with a five point response format from 1 (weak attachment) to 5 (strong attachment). Following this, emotional response to the project was measured using 11 specific forms of affect (e.g. happy, proud, threatened), with responses scored between 1 (not at all) to 5 (extremely). Attitude to the project was measured using two items (e.g. *I support the Gwynt y Mor offshore wind farm*), which correlated highly (r = 0.74, n = 201, p <.01), with scores between 1 (weak support) and 5 (strong support). Representations of the project were measured using items mixing positive and negative outcomes from local to national and beyond, with responses between 1 (strongly disagree) and 5 (strongly agree). Behaviour was measured using items capturing the frequency of undertaking certain actions (e.g. writing a letter to the paper in support/opposition, signing a petition against/in favour). The items were clustered into composite measures of 'supportive' and 'oppositional' behaviour where a high score means a greater frequency of undertaking such action.

RESULTS

The structure of the section follows the different stages of the framework. At the outset, place-related meanings are analysed; then each stage of the framework is described, focusing upon interpretation, evaluation and coping/acting - drawing upon both qualitative and quantitative data.

1. Place-Related Symbolic Meanings

Analysis of free association data indicated that Llandudno was predominantly interpreted by the residents in terms of visual aesthetics, emphasising the place's scenic beauty linked to its coastal situation and environmental features, which provide its distinctive qualities as a tourist resort. In the first free association, the most frequently mentioned thematic categories were about aesthetic beauty (21%), pleasant living (13%), holiday resort (12%) and coastal features (11%). The rankings of themes illustrated the predominance of aesthetic beauty in the meaning of the place, since it was the most common thematic category in each of the first three free associations. The second most commonly ranked category in Llandudno was coastal features, ranked 4th in the first free association, 2nd in the second and 2nd in the third free association. Thematic references for 'aesthetic beauty' included words or phrases such as 'beautiful view of the bay', 'picturesque' and 'stunning location'; while 'coastal features' included references to 'seaside', 'bay', 'promenade' and 'horizon'.

2. Interpreting Change: Representations of the Project and Levels of Trust

The content of social representations was investigated using qualitative data from the interviews, focus groups, and quantitative data from the survey.

2a. The Perspective of the Local Opposition Group

In the interview, two representatives of the group spoke at length about the character of the place. They stressed local distinctiveness, describing Llandudno as 'unique' and known as the 'Queen of Resorts' – *'We are the premier resort of Wales. Tourism is our number one industry. The reason is of course the, the scenery more than anything else'*. Aside from stressing natural beauty (in a similar manner to the free associations of residents), they also emphasised the historical continuity of the place: *'There's so much history and heritage attached to it; it's a very special area and people have a deep love for it and we don't want to see it spoiled and we're happy to share it with other people'*.

They made clear there preference was for opposing change: *'we want to preserve that for future generations ... we want to keep it that way'*. The most salient change evident was the wind farm proposal: *'What they want to do now is to industrialise our scenery ... We're on about the impact on our visual and the people who come here don't ... are getting away from industrialisation. They want to come here and see nature in its raw, you know'*. The natural beauty of the location is contrasted with the 'industrialisation' of the wind farm proposal, constructed as a significant threat to the future of a place: *'So there's a tipping point, there's a tipping point. And that's what's happening with this area and you fence in that bay, it's another nail in the coffin'*.

2b. The Perspective of Local Residents

Analysis of group discussions indicated that the wind farm proposal was predominantly represented in terms of its size and scale. For example:

> Roger: 'This one, there's 250 [wind turbines], and they're the tallest in the world. People should know that. They're actually 50 feet taller than Blackpool Tower, 565 feet high, Npower's [the developer] figures and information'.

These comments indicate how the size and scale of the project is conveyed by claims of the turbines being both numerous and gigantic (e.g. 'the tallest in the world'). In terms of processes of representation, objectifying the turbines by comparing them to a familiar regional landmark, Blackpool Tower, provides an efficient means of communicating their scale, and in a credible, trustworthy manner – quoting the company's own data. The size and scale of the project was interpreted as a significant threat to the town, with one person commenting:

> Roger: 'This is a tourist resort. People have been flocking here since 1842 because it's such an area of outstanding natural beauty. This is undeniable. You stand outside and look. And, to put the largest wind farm in Europe, as this one is meant to be, right out there, just a few miles in front of that bay is to me monstrously damaging to the area, to the environment that it professes to be saving. That's what I think'.

Here the wind farm is interpreted as posing a threat to a place constructed as a beautiful and historic tourist resort, with an emphasis upon aesthetic beauty similar to the free association data. By representing the wind farm as 'monstrously damaging', it is asserted to be alien to Llandudno as a place. The use of such a metaphor is characteristic of resistance to new technologies (e.g. Kronberger and Wagner, 2007). The reason for the concern is conveyed by arguments about the restorative character of the place:

> John: 'Apart from the population of Llandudno, and the million, two million people that visit this town every year, you can say what you like, they come for the centre of beauty, they come from largely industrial towns to get away from industrial landscapes, and in this case, to see a beautiful, open, natural seascape.... They come here, if only for a day, to get away from it, to go back feeling refreshed and regenerated and the soul is stronger for it. They don't want to see more industry when they get here'.

The contradiction in symbolic meaning between a 'natural' place and an 'industrial' wind farm supports Markova's (2003) emphasis upon oppositional dyads in social representation. These have been shown in the literature to be relevant to energy technology controversies, notably argumentation over 'facts' and 'myths' in debate on wind energy (Devine-Wright and Devine-Wright, 2006) and the contrast between 'industrial' or 'man-made' energy technologies and 'natural' or 'wild' places in contexts of local opposition (e.g. Kempton et al., 2005). They also echo the contradiction between 'up north' and the proposed housing in Stedman's (2002) study.

Questionnaire data was analysed to establish the degree to which certain aspects of these interpretations were widely shared amongst local residents. The analyses indicate a consistent trend - that Llandudno participants typically adopted negative beliefs about the project's outcomes, and placed more trust in the local opposition group in comparison to the company proposing the project or the government decision-making body.

Table 1. Descriptive statistics for Llandudno participants

	M	SD
Place attachment	4.40	0.74
Interpreting change		
Perceived outcomes of the project		
Create an eyesore	3.82	1.42
Fence in the bay	3.53	1.50
Industrialise the area	3.43	1.37
Damage tourism	3.41	1.50
Reduce property values	3.22	1.43
Help meet national policy targets	3.05	1.35
Tackle climate change	2.97	1.34
Have a positive impact on wildlife	2.59	1.39
Provide jobs	2.46	1.20
Levels of trust		
In the developer	1.94	0.98
In the opposition group	3.39	1.16
In the Government	1.82	0.98
Evaluating change		
Emotional response to the project		
Sceptical	3.02	1.47
Threatened	2.46	1.58
Angry	2.40	1.58
Frustrated	2.37	1.60
Hopeful	2.33	1.36
Shocked	2.11	1.42
Happy	1.73	1.19
Attitude to the project	2.79	1.51

To quantitatively investigate links between place attachment and interpretations of the project, bivariate correlations were performed (see Table 2). These indicated a generally positive correlation between strength of place attachment and negative outcomes in Llandudno and a lack of correlation in Llandudno between place attachment and positive outcomes.

2c. Levels of Trust and Links to Place Attachment

The explanation that the adoption of negative interpretations of the project arose from the influence of the opposition group is supported by data on levels of trust (see tables 2 and 3). In terms of links with place attachment, there was a significant, positive relation between place attachment and levels of trust in the opposition group for Llandudno participants ($r = .164$, $n=185$, $p<.025$), and significant, negative relations between place attachment and trust in the project developer ($r = -.166$, $n=192$, $p<.021$) and the Government decision-making body ($r = -.153$, $n=190$, $p<.035$).

Table 2. Bivariate Correlations with Place Attachment

	Llandudno
Interpreting change	
Perceived outcomes of the project	
Create an eyesore	0.20**
Fence in the bay	0.20**
Industrialise the area	0.20**
Tackle climate change	-0.07
Help meet national policy targets	-0.12
Provide jobs	0.00
Positive impact on wildlife	-0.05
Reduce property values	0.13
Damage tourism	0.13
Levels of trust	
In the developer	-0.15*
In the opposition group	0.19*
In the Government	-0.14
Evaluating change	
Emotional response to the project	
Angry	0.19*
Threatened	0.17*
Sceptical	0.14
Hopeful	-0.11
Happy	-0.15
Frustrated	0.09
Shocked	0.08
Attitude to the project	-0.16*
Coping/Acting	
Supportive behaviour	-0.03
Opposition behaviour	0.22**

Note: Values with asterisks indicate significant correlation with place attachment.
** significant at $p < .01$; * significant at $p < .05$.

3. Evaluation: Emotional Responses, Attitude to the Project and Links with Place Attachment

Emotional responses and attitudes of local residents to the wind farm were captured using data from the questionnaire. Bivariate correlations indicated positive relations between strength of attachment with Llandudno and feeling angry, threatened and sceptical (see table 3). To investigate the relation between place attachment and attitude to the project, 1 way ANOVA was used with the sample subdivided into groups of high (score of 4 or higher), medium (2.5-3.5) or low (below 2) levels of project support. For Llandudno respondents, this analysis showed a significant effect of attachment upon project support ($F(2) = 3.65$, $p < .028$), with post-hoc Scheffe tests indicating weaker place attachment for those with high project support in comparison to those with low project support (means of 4.17 and 4.49, $p <.05$).

4. Behavioral Responses to the Project and Links with Place Attachment

Descriptive data for self-reported behavioural responses indicate that action was relatively infrequent. Signing a petition against the project was undertaken by 38.8% of Llandudno participants and was the most frequently enacted behaviour. Analysis of links between behaviour and place attachment (see Table 3) found a significant relation between attachment and oppositional behaviour, but not supportive behaviour, for Llandudno participants. They more they felt attached to the place, they more they reported engaging in oppositional behaviour.

CONCLUSION

This chapter aimed to deepen understandings of public responses to large-scale zero-carbon technologies for energy generation, having identified a dearth in psychological research to date. This gap was addressed by advocating a place-based approach as an alternative to the commonly cited 'NIMBY' concept. A novel perspective upon disruption to place attachment and threat to place identity was proposed, drawing upon theories of identity and social representations, with a framework proposed that conceives disruption as a process unfolding in a series of stages involving identification, interpretation, evaluation and forms of coping response, including behaviour.

The framework was applied in a mixed-method case study of residents' responses to a proposed offshore wind farm in a town called Llandudno in North Wales. Drawing on qualitative data from interviews and free association tasks, it was shown that both project opponents and local residents represent the local place in terms of natural beauty, an escape for tourists from nearby cities. Analysis revealed how the wind farm was interpreted as a threat, with its 'industrial' scale contradicting the 'natural' beauty of the place. Questionnaire analyses for place attachment align with this explanation. Correlations between place attachment and negative interpretations of project outcomes (objectified as an 'eyesore' that would 'fence in the bay'), negative evaluations of the project in terms of emotional responses (including anger and threat) and attitudes, as well as oppositional behaviours (such as signing petitions or writing letters), suggest how the project was experienced as a threat to identity for those with strong attachment to the place, leading to negative attitudes to the project and oppositional behaviour. Findings from mixed methods were triangulated to suggest a consistent pattern of disruption to place attachment.

Strength of attachment with Llandudno was associated with opposition to the wind farm and founded in place-related symbolic meanings, supporting previous research (Vorkinn and Riese, 2001; Stedman, 2002). Both in this and Stedman's study, development proposals are interpreted to threaten the character of places constructed as locations to escape from urban life. These suggest that oppositional symbolic meanings (Markova, 2003) between place-related 'nature' and development-related 'industry' underlie many contexts where local residents engage in place-protective behaviours. These are places where many people choose to live or to holiday in order to escape from cities and to provide restoration from stress and fatigue (cf. attention restoration theory, Kaplan and Kaplan, 1989), leading to strong bonds of attachment. The results suggest that development proposals will be less likely to encounter local opposition if they are sited away from places represented as 'natural' and 'restorative' by visitors and locals alike. They also suggest that offshore wind farms may be just as controversial as onshore projects, since the places affected by change do not cease at the water's edge but include the view of the horizon as much as Victorian façades on a promenade.

The importance of the local social context in shaping the behavioural responses of individuals is presumed by the perspective taken on interpretations of change and by the data on trust. Social representations theory assumes that powerful interests will seek to shape how individuals make the unfamiliar familiar (Moloney and Walker, 2007). The results are illuminating in suggesting how efforts to encourage local support by the developer have met with either indifference or opposition, whereas negative ways of representing the project, focusing predominantly upon local, place-relevant aspects propagated by the opposition group (e.g. to 'fence in the bay') have been more widely adopted. Perhaps the power to influence interpretations of the project arose more from perceived 'insideness', and less from organisational size or resources, with the developer and government regarded as 'outsiders' to the place, to be distrusted accordingly.

Since the data collected was not longitudinal, temporal ordering of stages of responses cannot be evidenced by the study. Indeed, the order of stages may be less linear than represented in figure 1, with different forms of coping linking back to interpretation and evaluation as responses evolve over time. Nor can causal relations between trust and interpretations of change be presumed from questionnaire data. Secondly, the study has taken strength of place attachment as a given, yet it too is likely to evolve over time, shaped by the communications of different groups that focus explicitly or implicitly upon 'threats' to the character of a place arising from proposals for change. Finally, the study indicates the advantages to be gained from triangulating mixed-methods findings rather than relying upon a single methodology.

In conclusion, the findings suggest that a place-based, mixed-method approach to researching public responses to energy projects offers some value in providing an alternative to the 'NIMBY' explanation, drawing upon the phenomena of disruption to place attachment and threat to place identity to deepen understanding of public responses. However, it should not be presumed that place attachment inevitably leads to resistance to place change. Rather, future studies should be aware of the diverse positions that local residents can adopt in response to development proposals, and to study contexts where changes are more widely supported or even ignored. In doing so, research can serve the twin aims of furthering theory on place attachment and place identity, whilst at the same time producing policy-driven research outputs that demonstrate the contribution psychology can make towards addressing climate change.

ACKNOWLEDGMENTS

To my colleagues Yuko Howes, Hannah Devine-Wright and to the entire project team, survey distributors and all participants; and to the funding agency: Research Councils' Energy Programme/Economic and Social Research Council (ref: RES-125-25).

REFERENCES

Abrahamse, W., Steg, L., Vlek, C. and Rothergatter, T. (2005). A review of intervention studies aimed at household energy conservation. *Journal of Environmental Psychology*, 25, 273-291.

Altman, I. and Low, S. (1992). *Place Attachment*. New York: Plenum Press.

Altman, I. and Rogoff, B. (1987). World Views in Psychology: Trait, Interactional, Organismic, and Transactional Perspectives. In D. Stokols and I. Altman (Eds.) *Handbook of Environmental Psychology*, John Wiley and Sons: Chichester, pp. 7-40.

Bauer, M. (1995). Towards a functional analysis of resistance. In M. Bauer (Ed.) *Resistance to new technology: nuclear power, information technology and biotechnology*. Cambridge University Press: Cambridge.

Bell, D., Gray, T. and Haggett, C. (2005). The 'Social Gap' in Wind Farm Policy Siting Decisions: Explanations and Policy Responses, *Environmental Politics*, 14, 460-477.

Bonnes, M. and Secchiaroli, G. (1995). *Environmental Psychology: a psycho-social introduction*. Sage: London.

Breakwell, G.M. (1986). *Coping with threatened identities*. London: Methuen.

Breakwell, G.M. (1992) Processes of self-evaluation: efficacy and estrangement. In G.M. Breakwell (Ed.) *Social psychology of identity and self-concept*. Surrey: Surrey University Press.

Brittan, G. (2001). Wind, Energy, Landscape: reconciling nature and technology. *Philosophy & Geography*, 4, 171-178.

Brown, B., Perkins, D.D. (1992). Disruptions to Place Attachment. In I. Altman and S. Low (Eds.) *Place Attachment* (pp. 279-304). New York: Plenum.

Brown, B., Perkins, D.D. and Brown, G. (2003). Place attachment in a revitalizing neighbourhood: Individual and block levels of analysis. *Journal of Environmental Psychology*, 23, 259-271.

Burningham, K. (2000). Using the Language of NIMBY: A topic for research not an activity for researchers. *Local Environment*, 5, 55-67.

Burningham, K., Barnett, J. and Thrush, D. (2007). *The limitations of the NIMBY concept for understanding public engagement with renewable energy technologies: a literature review*. Manchester: Manchester Architecture Research Centre, University of Manchester.

Canter, D. (1977). *The Psychology of Place*. London: Architectural Press.

Dear, M. (1992). Understanding and Overcoming the NIMBY Syndrome. *Journal of the American Planning Association*, 58, 288-300.

Department of Trade and Industry (2006) *The Energy Challenge. Energy Review Report 2006*. Department of Trade and Industry, London.

Devine-Wright, P. (2005). Beyond NIMBYism: towards an integrated framework for understanding public perceptions of wind energy. *Wind Energy, 8,* 125-139.

Devine-Wright, P. (forthcoming) Rethinking Nimbyism. *Journal of Community and Applied Social Psychology.* DOI: 10.1002/casp.1004

Devine-Wright, P. and Devine-Wright, H. (2006). Social representations of intermittency and the shaping of public support for wind energy in the UK. *International Journal of Global Energy Issues, 25,* 243-256.

Devine-Wright, P. & Lyons, E. (1997). Remembering Pasts and Representing Places: The construction of National Identities in Ireland. *Journal of Environmental Psychology, 17,* 33-45

Dixon, J. and Durrheim, K. (2000). Displacing place identity: A discursive approach to locating self and other. British Journal of Social Psychology, *39,* 27-44.

Easthorpe, H. (2004). A Place Called Home. *Housing, Theory and Society, 21,* 128-138.

Ekins, P. (2004). Step changes for decarbonising the energy system: research needs for renewables, energy efficiency and nuclear power. *Energy Policy, 32,* 1891-1904.

Ellis, G., Barry, J and Robinson, C. (2006). Renewable energy and discourses of objection: towards deliberative policy making. Summary of main research findings. Queen's University Belfast. ESRC grant reference: 000-22-1095. Available at the following website: http://www.qub.ac.uk/research-centres/REDOWelcome/filestore/Filetoupload,40561,en.pdf

Ellis, G., Barry, J. and Robinson, C. (2007). Many ways to say no, different ways of saying yes: Applying Q-methodology to understand public acceptance of wind farm proposals. *Journal of Environmental Planning and Management, 50,* 517-551.

Eurobarometer (2006). *Attitudes towards energy.* Available at: http://ec.europa.eu/public_opinion/archives/ebs/ebs_247_en.pdf [last accessed 1st June 2009].

Farnum, J., Hall, T. and Kruger, L.E. (2005). Sense of Place in Natural Resource Recreation and Tourism: An Evaluation and Assessment of Research Findings. Gen. Tech. Rep. PNW-GTR-660. Portland, Oregon: USDA.

Fried, M. (2000). Continuities and Discontinuities of Place. *Journal of Environmental Psychology, 20,* 193-205

Foresight Sustainable Energy Management and the Built Environment Project (2008). Final Project Report. London: Government Office for Science.

Fried, M. (2000). Continuities and Discontinuities of Place. *Journal of Environmental Psychology, 20,* 193-205

Fullilove, M.T. (1996). Psychiatric implications of displacement: Contributions from the psychology of place. *American Journal of Psychiatry,* 153, 1516-1523.

Gieryn, T. (2000). A Space for Place in Sociology. *Annual Review of Sociology, 26,* 463.

Haggett, C. (2008). Over the Sea and Far Away? A Consideration of the Planning, Politics and Public Perception of Offshore Wind Farms. *Journal of Environmental Policy & Planning,* 10, 289-306.

Haggett, C. and Smith, J.L (2004). *Tilting at windmills? Using Discourse Analysis to Understand the Attitude-Behaviour Gap in Renewable Energy Conflicts.* Paper presented at the British Sociological Association Annual Conference, March 22-24, University of York.

Hayden, D. (1995). *The Power of Place: Urban Landscapes as Public History.* Cambridge, MA: Mitt Press.

Hernández, B., Hidalgo, M.C, Esther Salazar-Laplace, M., and Hess, S. (2007). Place attachment and place identity in natives and non-natives. *Journal of Environmental Psychology, 27,* 310-319.

Hidalgo, M.C., & Hernandez, B. (2001). Place attachment: conceptual and empirical questions. *Journal of Environmental Psychology, 21,* 273-281.

Huits, N. Midden, C.J., and Meijnders, A. (2007). Social acceptance of carbon dioxide storage. *Energy Policy,* 35, 2780-2789.

Intergovernmental Panel on Climate Change (2007). *Climate Change 2007: Synthesis Report.* Geneva: Author.

Joffe, H., & Yardley, L. (2004). Content and thematic analysis. In D. F. Marks & L. Yardley (Eds.), *Research Methods for Clinical Health Psychology* (pp. 56-68). London: Sage.

Kaplan, R., & Kaplan, S. (1989). *The experience of nature: a psychological perspective.* New York: Cambridge University Press.

Kempton, W., Firestone, J., Lilley, J., Rouleau, T. and Whitaker, P (2005) The Offshore Wind Power Debate: Views from Cape Cod. *Coastal Management, 33,* 119-149.

Knez, I. (2005). Attachment and identity as related to place and its perceived climate. *Journal of Environmental Psychology, 25,* 207-218.

Loring, J. (2007). Wind energy planning in England, Wales and Denmark: Factors influencing project success. *Energy Policy, 35,* 2648-2660.

Manzo, L. (2005). For better or for worse: Exploring multiple dimensions of place meaning. *Journal of Environmental Psychology, 25,* 67-86.

Manzo, L. and Perkins, D. (2006). Finding Common Ground: The importance of place attachment to community participation in planning. *Journal of Planning Literature, 20,* 335-350.

Massey, D. (1995). 'The conceptualisation of place', In D. Massey and P. Jess (Eds.) *A Place in the World? Places, Cultures and Globalisation (*pp. 87-132). Oxford: Open University Press.

Marková, I. (2003). *Dialogicality and social representations: The dynamics of mind.* Cambridge: Cambridge University Press.

McGowan, F. and Sauter, R. (2005). *Public Opinion on Energy Research: A Desk Study for the Research Councils.* Sussex Energy Group, SPRU, University of Sussex.

Milligan, M. (2003). Displacement and Identity Discontinuity: The Role of Nostalgia in Establishing New Identity Categories. *Symbolic Interaction,* 26, 381-403.

Moloney, G. and Walker, I. (2007). Introduction. In G. Moloney and I. Walker (Eds.) *Social Representations and Identity: Content, Process, and Power.* Hampshire: Palgrave Macmillan, pp. 1-8.

Moscovici, S. (2000). *Social Representations: Explorations in Social Psychology.* London: Polity Press.

Norburg-Schultz, C. (1980). *Genius Loci: Towards a Phenomenology of Architecture.* New York: Rizzoli.

O'Garra, T., Mourato, S. and Pearson, P. (2005). Analysing awareness and acceptability of hydrogen vehicles: a London case study. *International Journal of Hydrogen Energy, 30,* 649-659.

Patterson, M.E. and Williams, D.R. (2005). Maintaining research traditions on place: Diversity of thought and scientific progress. *Journal of Environmental Psychology, 25,* 361-380.

Petts, J. (1997). The public-expert interface in local waste management decisions: expertise, credibility and process. *Public Understanding of Science*, 6, 359-381.

Poortinga, W., Pidgeon, N., and Lorenzioni, I. (2006). Public perceptions of nuclear power, climate change and energy options in Britan: Summary of findings of a survey conducted during October and November 2005. School of Environmental Science, University of East Anglia.

Possick, C. (2004). Locating and relocating oneself as a Jewish Settler on the West Bank: Ideological squatting and eviction. *Journal of Environmental Psychology*, 24, 53-69.

Priestley, T., & Evans, G. W. (1996). Resident perceptions of a nearby electric transmission line. *Journal of Environmental Psychology*, 16, 65-74.

Proshansky, H., Fabian, H.K. and Kaminoff, R. (1983). Place identity: physical world socialisation of the self. *Journal of Environmental Psychology*, 3, 57-83.

Relph, E. (1977). *Place and Placelessness*. London: Pion.

Rifkin, J. (2002). *The Hydrogen Economy*. Oxford: Polity Press.

Sauter, R. and Watson, J. (2007). Strategies for the deployment of micro-generation: Implications for social acceptance. *Energy Policy*, 35, 2770-2779.

Shackley, S., McLachlan, C., and Gough, C. (2005). The public perception of carbon capture and storage in the UK. *Climate Policy*, 4, 377-398.

Sherry-Brennan, F., Devine-Wright, H. and Devine-Wright, P. (forthcoming) Public understanding of Hydrogen: A theoretical approach. *Energy Policy Special Issue on Hydrogen Energy*.

Speller, G. (1999). *Residential re-location, place and threats to identity processes*. Unpublished PhD Thesis, Department of Psychology, Surrey: University of Surrey.

Spence, A., Pidgeon, N. and Uzzell, D. (2009). Climate change – psychology's contribution. *The Psychologist*, 22, 112-115.

Stedman, R. (2002). Toward a social psychology of place: predicting behaviour from place-based cognitions, attitude, and identity. *Environment and Behaviour*, 34, 561-581.

Stedman, R. (2003). Is it really just a social construction? The contribution of the physical environment to sense of place. *Society and Natural Resources*, 16, 671-685.

Timotijevic, L. and Breakwell, G.M. (2000). Migration and threat to identity. *Journal of Community and Applied Social Psychology*, 10, 355-372.

Toke, D. and Haggett, C. (2006). Crossing the great divide: using multi-method analysis to understand opposition to windfarms. *Public Administration*, 84, 103-120.

Toynbee, P. (2007). NIMBYs can't be allowed to put a block on wind farms. *The Guardian Newspaper*, January 5, p31.

Twigger-Ross, C.L. and Uzzell, D. (1996). Place and identity processes. *Journal of Environmental Psychology*, 16, 205-220.

Tuan, Y.F. (1977). *Space and Place: The perspective of experience*. Minneapolis: University of Minnesota Press.

Tuan, Y.F. (1980). Rootedness versus sense of place. *Landscape*, 24, 3-8.

Upham P. and Shackley, S. (2006). Stakeholder opinion of a proposed 21.5MWe biomass gasifier in Winkleigh, Devon: implications for bioenergy planning and policy. *Journal of Environmental Policy and Planning*, 8, 45-66.

Van der Horst, D. (2007). NIMBY or not? Exploring the relevance of location and the politics of voiced opinions in renewable energy siting controversies. *Energy Policy*, 35, 2705-2714.

Vorkinn, M. & Riese H. (2001). Environmental Concern in a Local Context: The Significance of Place Attachment. *Environment and Behaviour, 33,* 249-263.

Wagner, W. and Hayes, N. (2005). Everyday Discourse and Common Sense: The Theory of Social Representations. Hampshire: Palgrave Macmillan.

Walker, G. and Devine-Wright P. (2008). Community Renewable Energy: What does it mean? *Energy Policy, 36,* 497-500.

Warren, C.R., Lumsden, C., O'Dowd, S. and Birnie, R.V. (2005). 'Green on Green': Public Perceptions Wind Power in Scotland and Ireland. *Journal of Environmental Planning and Management, 48,* 853-875.

Wolsink, M. (2000). Wind power and the NIMBY-myth: institutional capacity and the limited significance of public support. *Renewable Energy, 21,* 49-64.

Wolsink, M. (2007). Planning of renewables schemes: deliberative and fair decision-making on landscape issues instead of reproachful accusations of non-cooperation. *Energy Policy, 35,* 2692-2704.

Zeisel, J. (2005). Inquiry by design: environment/behavior/neuroscience in architecture, interiors, landscape, and planning. New York: W.M.Norton & Company.

In: Psychological Approaches to Sustainability
Editors: V. Corral-Verdugo et al.

ISBN 978-1-60876-356-6
© 2010 Nova Science Publishers, Inc.

Chapter 18

CULTURAL BACKGROUND AND ENVIRONMENTAL CONTEXT OF WATER PERCEPTION AND USE

Gabriel Moser[*]
Université René Descartes, France

Oscar Navarro
Groupe de Recherche sur l'Amérique Latine, MSH - Alpes, Grenoble, France

Eugenia Ratiu
Université René Descartes, France

Karine Weiss
Université de Bourgogne, Dijon, France

ABSTRACT

Water preservation needs a worldwide commitment to strategies towards sustainable development with the participation of all actors concerned. This chapter, built on the results of three field researches on the perception and use of water in different cultural contexts, proposes a model of the relation to water based on social representations. The first research deals with peoples' perceptions of and behaviours toward the use of water resources. It focuses on quality, quantity, access, and daily use of water as well as the perception of others' behavior in Italy, France, India and Mexico. Results show differentiated perceptions of water issues among participants. In terms of prospective, the populations differ with respect to their view of the future: those who are most pessimistic about other peoples' behavior are also the most reluctant to engage in water-saving behavior. The second research tackles the social representations of water of farmers, city-dwellers and aboriginals in Colombia. The words "life" and "health" appear to be a central reference. However, city dwellers and farmers have a functional and economic vision of water, whereas for the aboriginals, the "ecological values" are prominent, thus integrating water into the territory and nature itself. These differences are attributed to the

---

[*] Correspondence : Gabriel Moser, e-mail : gabriel.moser@parisdescartes.fr

socio-cultural and ideological framework of the different groups. The third research looks at values and social representations in relation with water conservation behaviours. It is based on the assumption that the resolution of the dilemma between individual short-term behaviour and the need of collective action depends on cultural values, accessibility to water and water perception. In the six sample cities (Brasilia, Djakarta, Madrid, Ouagadougou, Osaka and Munich), the social representation of water is shaped according to respective values. Identitarian ecological values lead to a dynamic, global vision, whereas a limited utilitarian representation is founded on spatial and temporal proximity. The consciousness of the problematic of water is linked to causal attributions which in turn determine the behaviour through the perceived efficiency of individual and/or collective control. The integration of the findings of these different investigations leads us to propose a tentative model of water perception taking into account cultural and societal backgrounds as well as different environmental and social contexts, in order to look at the conditions of water use and preservation behaviors in the light of sustainability.

Water "impregnates our cells and our thought, our vocabulary, and our imaginary"
Bouguerra, 2003, p. 26.

INTRODUCTION

Water is currently one of the main concerns worldwide. As a limited resource and due to unequal access, it is considered as a major political and geo-strategic issue. In the light of sustainability it is urgent to address the problem and confront its relative scarcity and quality. And this is a matter of authorities, industrials, farmers as well as a matter of individual behaviors. At the individual level, relations to water are dependent on essentially two aspects: (1) values and the environmental and societal context in which people live, and thus their environmental concerns, and (2) the accurate perception of the water cycle and the perceived solidarity of others.

Cultural theory (Douglas & Wildawsky, 1982) states that individual belief systems exist that organize our view of nature and the environment. Four different myths of nature have been identified: nature benign, nature ephemeral, nature tolerant/perverse and nature capricious. Research has shown how these values are linked with preferences in environmental matters. They are, for instance, related to evaluations of environmental policies, (Steg & Sievers, 2000) and risk perception (Lima & Castro, 2005). On the other hand, research concerning ecological values and attitudes has identified an increased interest in the environment, which Dunlap & Van Liere (1978) named as the *"New Environmental Paradigm"* (NEP). Subsequently, the so-called NEP scale has become a widely used measuring instrument in research on sustainable behaviour (Dunlap & Van Liere, 1978; Dunlap et al., 2000). These approaches have in common that they hypothesize a wide range of commitments to sustainable behaviours based essentially on environmental values and attitudes, regardless of the individual's relation to a specific aspect. Furthermore, one can ask if these identified worldviews are equally shared in different cultures and ideologies.

In fact, environmental concerns and attitudes towards environmental matters differ widely from one country to another (Schultz & Selezny, 1999) and studies as the one by Guifford et al. (2009) show quite different prospective views among various countries across the world. Different attitudes towards water use and conservation are likely to be rooted in peoples' cultural backgrounds and specific environmental contexts. For instance, Franzen (2003) found that environmental concern is strongly related to a country's economic development. The less developed a country is, the lower the concern. Conversely, Dunlap, Gallup & Gallup (1993) found more environmental concern in Latin American countries than in the highly developed North America. But this may be only one aspect of the influence of the social, economical and environmental context on people's water conservation behavior.

While solidarity and the sharing of vital resources are indispensable practices (Sironneau, 1996), several analyses have shown individualistic behavior in the presence of limited resources ("tragedy of the commons"; Hardin, 1968; Thompson & Stoutemeyer, 1991; and "social dilemmas"; Dawes, 1980). The emergence and preservation of relations conducive to sustainable development are slowed down or fostered by individual and environmental factors. As regards to natural resources, we know that the types of conduct fostering their preservation are related to peoples' knowledge about both the long term effects and the perceived efficacy of individual actions, and finally, to a functional or ecological view of the environment (Dunlap & Van Liere, 1978; Stern & Oskamp, 1987), the latter being influenced by the social uncertainty about the conduct of others as well as by the environmental uncertainty regarding the levels of excessive use and deterioration of the resource (Biel & Gärling, 1995). Furthermore, the temporal and the spatial perspectives appear to structure the perceptions of natural resources (Dawes and Messick, 2000).

Grob (1995) argues that the best predictors of behaviours towards water include environment-related attitudes and values, amplified by perceived control, personal commitment and the extent to which a person is physically and/or emotionally affected by these aspects. In the literature, the perception of risks (the resource being polluted or otherwise damaged) has been shown to be a driving force in certain behaviours conducive to preservation (Rogers, 1983, Gardner & Stern, 1996).

WATER AS AN OBJECT OF SOCIAL REPRESENTATION

The economic, political and social conflicts it raises make water a social object *par excellence*. Water is loaded with symbolism and representation, which ensue from societal and cultural particularities and may condition not only one's perception of it, but also one's behavior towards it. Water is a fundamental element in religion and in artistic creation; also, it is present in everyday metaphors. Due to the place of water in our everyday lives and to the symbolism it inspires, water is an object of social thought. As a social object, the representation of water is imbedded in the social context and constitutes a set of cognitive systems enabling the interpretation of the social and physical world leading to specific behaviors towards it.

Social representations as social thoughts have shown their relevance and pertinence in approaching the interaction of people with their physical and social environment (Moscovici, 1988). They can be understood as cognitive sets including opinions, information (knowledge), and beliefs (convictions) (Moliner, Rateau, and Cohen-Scali, 2002), enabling the construction, organization, and communication of social knowledge. They include the genesis of knowledge, its adaptation, and its being rooted in the socio-cultural framework, as well as the use of such knowledge in social exchanges. Social representations refer to a type of knowledge that is socially shared and elaborated in the course of social exchanges. These representations are in a privileged position between ideology and praxis. They are affected both by the normative co-actions of society and/or groups (values, history, and collective memory) and by circumstantial co-actions which are determined by the physical context, by the social position of individuals, their repertoires of conduct, and by the opportunities to take action. Ideology is a key dimension which guarantees the stability of social representations. Social practices enable to update social representations in the social context and eventually their transformation. By virtue of their normative character, that is, their strong relation with social norms and beliefs regarding social events, social representations are "guides for action" (Abric, 1994).

Ecological behavior is shaped by individuals' relations with natural resources as well as by the societal context, and in particular by environmentally-related values. Also, the question remains open: How these factors relate to each other and how they lead to a particular behavior. In other words, what is the relationship between practices on the one hand and the ideological context on the other?

The representations of water in different societal contexts constitute interpretative filters of reality and normative means for orientating both individual and collective behaviors. We know that environmentally-related perceptions, attitudes and behaviors vary from country to country, as they are modulated by the prevailing environmental circumstances, most notably the condition of the resource and the societal context, i.e. culture, values, regulations, infrastructure and opportunities to take action (Lévy-Leboyer, Bonnes, Chase, Ferreira-Marques and Pawlik, 1996). A person's relationship to the environment develops as a result of his or her experience, values, aspirations and preferences. The social representations of water inform the organization and structuring of reality as well as its conceptualization; they take the shape of a coherent cognitive system that structures the subject's world in such a way that he or she can apprehend it and act upon it. This system "flows from the individual's personality traits, his or her past or present experience in regard to the environment (and hence her or his belonging to a culture or a sub-cultural network) and finally of his or her anticipation of future events" (Codol, 1969). It builds up and evolves as a result of the individual engaging in social relations (Moscovici, 1989). As a system for the interpretation of the world, it becomes a means of information and a way of developing attitudes towards the object of a representation. In respect to water, the representations are even more important as its potential pollutions cannot be perceived and identified as such; as a matter of consequence, they may lead to opposed interpretations (Moser, 1984). It follows that already at the level of perception an interpretation/evaluation of the context comes into play: Water is perceived as being linked to sets of activities, conducts and meanings (Gibson, 1979). In this sense it has been shown that farmers' social representations of the earth condition their practices (Weiss, Moser & Germann. (2006), and that their ideological position is consistent with their way of farming and using pesticides (Michel-Guillou & Moser, 2006).

What are the factors that contribute to the adoption of an ecologically sound behavior, and how do they interrelate in different cultures where the environmental and societal conditions differ fundamentally? Which types of behavior and which strategies of adjustment towards water are being chosen (individual protections, economical and discriminating consumption of water, environmental activism), how do they differ as a result of perceived water quality and envisaged usages, of the levels of environmental and social uncertainty concerning the utilization of the resource, and how do they impact on the perception of opportunities for individual and/or institutional control?

This chapter is based on three different international researches looking at perception and water use in various societal contexts.

- The first research, *"Water use in contrasting environmental contexts"* (Bonnes, M., Moser, G., Sinha, J. & Corral-Verdugo, V., 2006), was designed to establish a multicultural questionnaire on water issues in the light of sustainability. Its test in four different countries permits to look at the use and perception of fresh water resources and at the water conservation behaviour in these countries.[1]
- The second research, *"Cultural identity and representation of water"* (Navarro, 0., 2008; 2009), analyses specifically the social representations of three different groups of users, city dwellers, peasants and aboriginals in Colombia.[2]
- The third research, *"From social representations to behavior"* (De Vanssay, B., Ratiu, E., Casal, A., Colbeau-Justin L., Porto de Lima, C. & Weiss K. (1998) is particularly concerned with values, on the one hand, and diagnosis and awareness of water problems, on the other hand. It is based on interviews with different actors in relation to water in Europe, Asia and Latin America.[3]

In a concluding section, the integration of the results of these different investigations leads to propose a tentative model of water perception taking into account cultural and societal backgrounds as well as different environmental and social contexts, in order to look at the conditions of water use and preservation behaviors in the light of sustainability.

WATER USE IN CONTRASTING ENVIRONMENTAL CONTEXTS

This first study enables to assess the divergences and similarities in fresh water perceptions, beliefs and use across different cultural contexts.

Sample and Methodology

A questionnaire was built on the basis of the qualitative data previously collected in an exploratory phase. The arguments that emerged in participants' spontaneous discourses about fresh water were used to build a series of statements (items) investigating different aspects of

---

[1] Research funded by ICSU *(International Council for Scientific Unions)* Grants Program 2004 and IUPSYs *(International Union of Psychological Science)*.
[2] Doctoral thesis « *L'eau comme enjeu : Territoire, Identités et Conflits d'usages* [Water as a stake : Territories, Identities and Conflicts of everyday practices] », Navarro, O., Paris Descartes University and Laboratory of Environmental Psychology, 2006
[3] Project funded by "*Agence de Bassin Seine-Normandie - Académie de l'Eau*" n° 9697086 and 9797012 under the scientific supervision of B. de Vanssay

water use, perception of water issues, and attitudes/beliefs towards global changes problems in general.

The study was conducted in nine sites (Paris, Brest, New Delhi, Patna, Rome, Cagliari, Monterey, Hermosillo, La Victoria) located within four countries: France, India, Italy and Mexico.

A total of 759 participants responded to the questionnaire: 196 in France, 154 in India, 248 in Italy and 162 in Mexico. Participants were 375 (49.4%) males and 384 (50.6%) females. Their age ranged from 18 to 84 years (mean = 38.7). In particular, 255 (33.6%) were between 18 and 29 years old, 260 (34.3%) were between 30 and 45 years old, and 244 (32.1%) were over 46 years old. Among the whole sample, 61 (8.1%) had completed primary/elementary schools, 123 (16.2%) had completed junior high school, 206 (27,1%) had completed high school and 369 (48,6%) had a university degree. 410 (54%) were married, 314 (41.4%) single, and 34 (4.6%) divorced. Furthermore, participants were asked to categorize themselves as: "poor", "rich", or "neither poor nor rich". 145 (19.1%) defined themselves as poor, 120 (15.8%) as rich and 495 (65.1%) neither poor, nor rich.

The questionnaire was originally drafted in English and then translated into 4 different languages corresponding to the countries involved in the research. The questionnaire was administered to people living in the above-mentioned cities from July to September 2005.

Access to Water

Which are the particular conditions of water access (accessibility of water, periodicity of access, perception of water quality, etc.) in the four different countries?

Patterns of water access: In Europe the whole sample (100%) has access to tap water. In Mexico 56% have access to tap water and 41% to tap water plus other types of supply. In India 58% have access to tap water plus other types of supply, and 40% have only access to water from a well. How good or bad is that access to water? People could choose one or more of the following answers: *"No problem", "I have constant access"; "Water is scarce during certain months"; "Water is not available during certain hours".* In France everybody has constant access to water. In Italy 6 % of the respondents experience water scarcity during certain hours and/or months. For India only half of the respondents and for Mexico only 60% of the respondents have constant access to water.

Quality of water: People were asked to evaluate the quality of each kind of water they get. Results showed that on the overall our sample rated water as of moderately good quality (*mean*=2.3 *sd*= 0,448; on a scale ranging from 1 to 3). Statistically significant differences were found among participants concerning the way they judge quality of water from municipal taps ($F_{(3.689)}$ = 29.536; p>.001). Participants from Europe gave better judgments on water from municipal taps compared to participants from India and Mexico (France: mean = 2.50; sd = *.39884; Italy:* mean = 2,46; sd = *.35017;* .India: mean = 2.23; sd = *.50019, and Mexico;* mean = 2.14; sd = *.50203).*

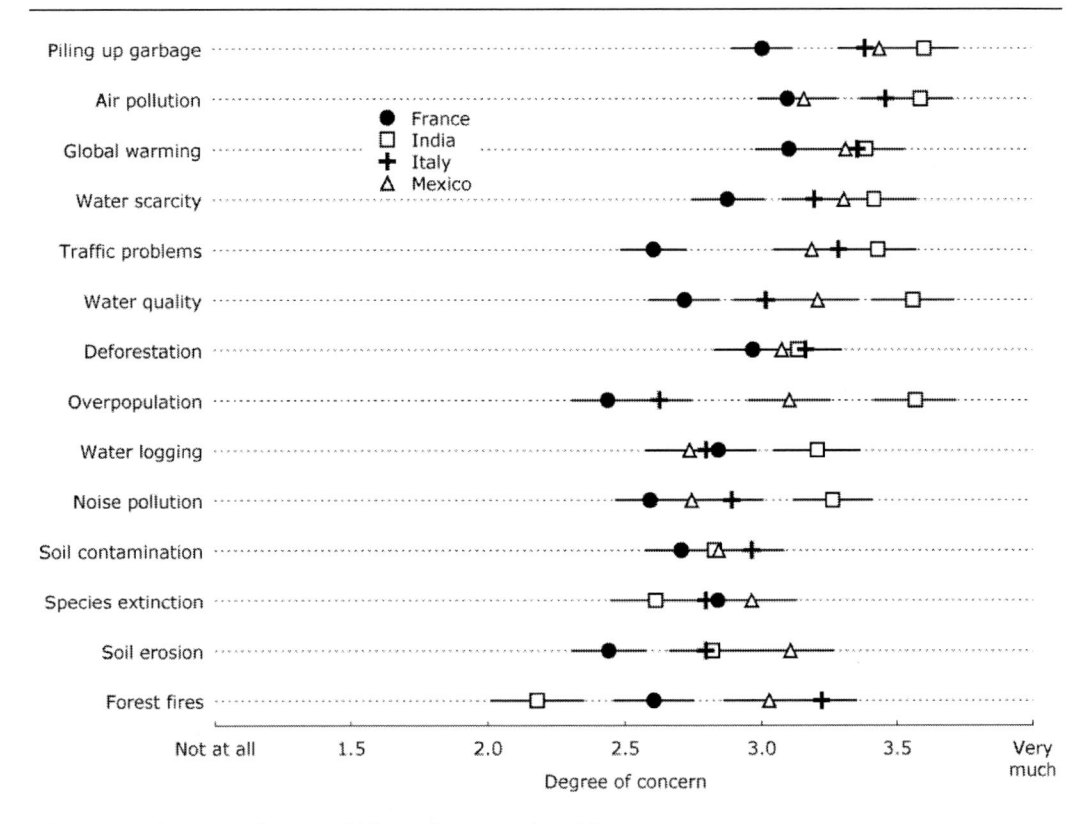

Cultural Background and Environmental Context of Water Perception and Use 367

Figure 1. Relevance of water within environmental problems.

Perception of Water Issues

Europeans do not consider water as an unlimited resource (85% do not believe in eternal water resources), whereas 42 % of the Indians and 36 % of Mexicans tend to do so. Similarly, Europeans tend to think that water quality will be worse in the future (55% do so), whereas much more Indians (85%) and Mexicans (70%) think that water quality will be worse in the future, being thus more pessimistic than Europeans about future water quality.

Relevance of water within environmental problems: Participants were asked to indicate how seriously they felt to be personally affected by a series of relevant environmental problems, including water problems. These items were specifically built in order to investigate whether people feel that each of the listed environmental problems may affect them *"Very seriously", "Seriously", "Not so seriously"* or *"Not at all."*

Water scarcity is a relatively serious issue for the Indian, Italian and Mexican respondents, but not such an important issue for the French respondents. The same relative importance can be observed for the quality of water, Indians and Mexicans being most concerned, French less (Figure 1).

On the whole, waste disposal (*piling up garbage*), *air pollution* and *global warming* are ranked among problems by which people feel to be very seriously affected, while *soil erosion*, *forest fires* and *species extinction* are ranked among problems by which people feel to be relatively less affected. Nevertheless, water scarcity ranks only 4th and poor water quality ranks 7th.

Spatial and temporal dimensions of water issues: People were asked to express their opinion about problems concerning water availability, quality and consumption in relation to a spatial and a temporal dimension as well as its stability over time. These items were specifically built in order to investigate whether people believe that water problems are peculiar to their own country, region, city and neighborhood, or rather more generalized.

A Principal Component Analysis (PCA) performed on the 14 items composing the scale, revealed a two-factor structure, which reflects the spatial and the temporal dimensions by which items were mainly inspired. The two factors explain 46.9% of variance and resulted as non-correlated with each other: r (F1F2) = -.05. The first factor seizes the specificity of water problems in relation to the spatial dimension and is composed of 4 items. The second factor accounts for the perceived changing of water problems in a temporal perspective (expected worsening of water quality and quantity through time) and is composed of 6 items. Scores of items composing each factor have been aggregated and results show that on average people do not perceive water problems as specific to their neighborhood, city, region or country, but rather as generalized, while they perceive that water problems were less serious in the past and will get worse in the future. Compared to French, Indian and Mexicans, the Italians tend to perceive water problems as more specific to their country (and thus less generally diffused). However, all countries differ from each other in regard to the pessimistic views of future trends of water problems. Indians in particular are the most pessimistic, followed by Mexicans, Italians and French.

WASTING WATER AND ATTRIBUTIONS OF RESPONSIBILITY

Own behavior versus other people's behavior. More than three quarters of the respondents declare that they are careful about water use. But the figures are quite different from one country to another. In France and India, respectively 82 % and 86% declare to save water, whereas in Mexico there are only 76% and in Italy 64%. Most ecological behaviors - water saving behaviors included - could be performed for many reasons, which are not necessarily ecological (Kaiser, 1998). Indeed, the reasons for engaging in water-saving behaviors may be quite different from one country to another: A necessity for India, for instance, or a lack of trust in the authorities in Italy or Mexico.

By what means do the different respondents save water? Rankings based on means and standard deviations on a list of possible behaviors showed that those most frequently performed by the whole sample were: *"Not letting taps running uselessly", "Machine washing clothes only with full load", "Not dropping garbage into a river"* and *"Not letting children waste water".*

Italians engage least in conservation behavior and at the same time are most suspicious about other people's anti-ecological behavior. Only one Italian out of five thinks that other people are saving water. In France they are one out of three, in Mexico 40% and in India more than 50%. Water saving behaviors have important collective implications. Indeed, the individual effectiveness in conserving water depends upon the extent to which other people also decide to conserve water. Hence, perception of others' behaviors may help in understanding how much people feel that their efforts are shared with others, and thus how much these efforts are worth making.

Attribution of responsibility: What are the respondents' beliefs about who wastes more water and how much citizens and institutions care about water supply and water quality? Respondents had to indicate their agreement/disagreement on a four point scale (*completely agree, partially agree, partially disagree, completely disagree*) with a series of statements: *Village people waste water, Women are more careful to save water, Rich people waste much more water than poor ones, Generally children waste more water than adults, Industries waste water, Municipal service does not care about water supply, Those who do not have to pay for water waste more water, The poor save more water, Men tend to save water more than women, People think that they have the right to use as much water as they can, Municipal service does not care about water quality, Very few people really care to conserve water, Agriculture wastes water, People think that others, not they, waste water, People believe that government must supply as much water as they need, Urban people waste more water than rural people.*

A Principal Component Analysis (PCA) performed on the 16 items composing the scale, revealed a two-factor structure, in which the first factor gathers items concerning institutional and organizational responsibilities (municipality / government) and people's lack of concern for saving water. Factor two integrates water waste/preservation by specific social categories (poor/rich, men/women, villagers/townspeople, agriculture/industries, etc.). The two factors explain 34.4% of variance and are modestly correlated with each other: (F1F2) = .22. Scores of the items composing each factor were aggregated and results showed how on average people of the whole sample agreed with the idea that institutions have the responsibility to conserve water (M= 1,7) and disagree (at least partially) with the ideas that specific social categories (like, poor, rich, children, or villagers) were responsible of wasting water (M=2,2).

However, statistically significant differences emerged among the four countries regarding the two factors. Univariate Analysis of Variance and Post Hoc tests showed three groups of countries which differed in a statistically significant way for responses provided to items of these two factors. French participants perceived the lowest institutional responsibility in saving water compared to Italians and Mexicans on the one hand and to Indians on the other hand. However, Mexicans and Indians are similar in that they perceive that specific categories are particularly responsible for saving/wasting water, while French and Italians are less likely to indicate specific categories as responsible for water saving/wasting.

In conclusion, it appears clearly that in each of the countries investigated, the context of access to water is different. While Europeans have unlimited access to high quality water, both Mexico and India experience shortage and water of poor quality. Furthermore, in India and Mexico there are social disparities in access to water. When one looks at the perception of water issues by the different respondents, it is obvious that scarcity of water is an issue for those who experience it directly or indirectly.

Differentiated water quality perception among participants of the four countries has to be seen as a relatively adequate judgment. It is indeed consistent with other studies that show that the lay assessment of environmental conditions is strongly accurate when compared to expert assessments of environmental quality (Gifford, Scannell, Kormos, Smolova, Biel, et al., 2009).

In terms of prospective, the different populations differ with respect to their view of the future: Indians and Mexicans tend to consider water as an unlimited resource whereas Italians and French are conscious of its increasing scarcity. On the other hand, the latter are less preoccupied by the degradation of the water quality. Overall, the relative pessimism about the future is consistent with other findings, like the one reported by Dunlap, Van Liere, Mertig, & Jones (2000) who show that environmental problems are rated as more threatening to one's health over time.

The differentiated access to water, the experience of scarcity and/or of poor water quality, and the perception that others do or do not waste water contribute to favor or, on the contrary, to impede the commitment to water conservation behavior. Social confidence is indeed important for those who engage in sustainable behavior. These results show that those who are most pessimistic about other people's behavior, the Italians, are also the most reluctant to engage in water saving behavior.

CULTURAL IDENTITY AND SOCIAL REPRESENTATION OF WATER

The purpose of this study was to identify the constitutive elements of the representations of water among social groups that are differentiated by their identification to the territory on which they live, by their respective cultural contexts, and by their use of the water resource (Navarro, 2008; 2009).

Sample and Procedure

The Sierra Nevada de Santa Marta, a region that is a theater of permanent conflicts regarding water, is the highest coast side mountain range in the world. It is located in the northern area of Colombia and was declared a biosphere patrimony by UNESCO in 1979. It supplies water to the different inhabitants of the northern slope of the Sierra Nevada de Santa Marta.

Three different groups of inhabitants have been interviewed: 76 citizens (university students, employees, merchants, and housewives of different neighborhoods and residential areas of the city of Santa Marta), 66 peasants of the region, composed of 24 inhabitants of the middle mountain and belonging to an association of ecological agriculture and 42 workers from banana farms, and 59 native Indians belonging to the three families of the Sierra Nevada de Santa Marta ("Kogis", "Wiwas", and "Arhuacos"). The common point among the participants is that they live in the same region and share the same water resources; yet, they differ in their lifestyles, history and in the importance they give to water.

In order to elicit their representations of water, participants were asked to think about water and to emit the words "coming to their minds". This free evocation and association task permits to have access to the semantic field related to water (Vergès, 1994 p. 235). The spontaneous and projective character of this technique enables to access the elements that make part of the semantic universe of water. A corpus of 775 words was obtained of which 320 were different words, which is an average of 3.9 words per person. A lexicographic analysis ("prototypical analysis") of the produced words, crossing two indicators, was undertaken: the frequency of appearance of the words and their evocation rank. These indicators offer two types of information: firstly, a collective dimension revealed by terms that are highly consensual, and secondly, an individual dimension which is the result of statistics based on the order of evocation of a specific word by each participant.

Inside each group of individuals, we found strongly consensual elements (central elements) and elements that are less shared by the group (peripheral elements). The common vision of the group of a given object is based on consensual opinions. Such opinions are not the result of random convergences, but are shared by all the individuals and have qualities that enable to define the object (Moliner, Rateau & Cohen-Scali, 2002). The peripheral cognitions do not only acquire their meaning through their relation with the central elements, but conversely they enable to interpret the meaning given by the group to the central cognitions. Social representations are made up of elements (cognitions) articulated among them, they are "socio-cognitive sets organized in a specific manner and managed by proper functioning rules" (Abric, 1994 p. 8). According to Guimelli (1994), social representations need to be considered as an organized entity around a central nucleus.

The Differentiated Representation of Water

The analysis and interpretation of the data are based on the relative frequency and the rank of each element's evocation. Those elements which, on average, have a high frequency and a low rank of appearance (that is, which are first evocated) constitute the central nucleus of the social representation. In other words, a characteristic is considered central (outstanding, important), if it has been evoked first and is evoked by a large number of participants.

The words that make up the central (frequency ≥ 15 and average range <2.9) zone represent 29% of total evocations. In this zone we find the elements belonging to the central nucleus of the social representation of water, i.e. those that constitute the core of the representation of water, since they organize the relations between all the cited elements. Of the four central words (life, health, balance, thirst and cleanness) the first two represent 25% of the evocations. They refer to the normative dimension of water and by themselves define what "water" is. The three remaining words evoke two types of relation regarding the object: "balance" denotes an integral vision of water in the ecological sense, and the remaining two, "thirst" and "cleanness", refer to the utilitarian aspect of water.

As expected, differences among the groups distinguished by their socio-cultural (ideological) frames and their life environment emerge: the central words "life" and "health" are proportionally evoked by the same amount of people in each group. They define a type of universal social (or collective) representation of water, based on *thémata* or on binary differentiators (life/death, health/diseases).

It is in relation to the other evocations that substantial differences can be found (see Figure 2). For example, proportionally more natives evoked the word "nature" as well as the word "welfare". And this group was alone to evoke the word "balance". The words "cleanness, thirst, freshness, hygiene, purity, and hydration" (utilities and uses of water), were more evoked by townspeople, especially the last three, quoted respectively by 90%, 89% and 86% of this group.

Beyond the consensus around two central elements, "life" and "health", it appears that there are two distinctive types of representations among the three groups studied. The representation of the urban populations contains additional functional elements expressing the "utility" and the "usefulness" of water ("thirst" and "cleanness"). On the other side, aboriginals evoke the term "balance" as an important element of their social representation of water. At the same time, their social representation does not contain any utilitarian element, which permits to speak about an ecologist representation of water. Peasants furnish a social representation which is, in its normative aspects, limited to the core elements, "life" and "health". The fact that the evoked peripheral elements denote essentially the use and economical benefits of water to the detriment of ecological values makes this representation essentially utilitarian.

In conclusion, given the existence of different central nuclei among inhabitants of a same territory, there are obviously different social representations of water among users of the same resource. In this sense, there are similarities between the social representation of water of townspeople and peasants since they share the same logic of the elements' sense that constitute it, expressed in what can be called a "utilitarian" model, contrary to the "ecological" model of the natives. The total absence of economic values as well as the absence of words referring to the use of water by natives confirms this difference. This differentiation is the result of the impact of the life environment (rural/urban and high/medium mountain) and of the technological facilities that determine the relation to water, but also of the socio-cultural framework in reference to the socioeconomic and ideological (beliefs, norms, and values) conditions. A "utilitarian" representation brings with it an instrumented perception of the resource, likely to generate egocentric behaviors towards water consumption and, concomitantly, a weak personal commitment to its responsible management. On the opposite, an "ecological" representation conceiving water as an integral element of nature, along with a global perception of the water cycle, generates more commitment, more responsibility, and the conviction that one's actions impact on the preservation of the resource.

	Citizens average range		Peasants average range		Natives average range	
	< 2.9	≥ 2.9	< 2.9	≥ 2.9	< 2.9	≥ 2.9
≥ 15	Life health **thirst** cleanness		Life health		Life balance health	welfare nature
< 15	freshness nature	Hygiene welfare purity needs hydration	welfare source of life thirst bath needs drink energy	care for water freshness cleanness peace happiness	mother durability	

Figure 2. Comparison of water SR prototypes by the three groups of users.

VALUES, SOCIAL REPRESENTATIONS, AND WATER CONSERVATION

The study purported to establish the representations of water and the corresponding practices in different ideological and societal settings, in order to identify the resulting types of specific relations to water (de Vanssay, Ratiu, Casal, Colbeau-Justin, Porto de Lima, & Weiss (1998). As in the two previous studies, the multicultural approach is meant to highlight the role of cultural contexts as well as of the modalities of accessing and managing water, and to identify their respective effect on behaviors towards water.

Sample and Procedure

Since the study was exploratory, the data were elicited by way of semi-directive interviews with a heterogeneous sample of 18 witnesses, in the ethnological sense of the term, per selected site (water professionals, public authorities, members of ecological NGOs, health professionals, industrialists, technical and administrative staff, teachers, mothers, persons with at least one small child). The interviews addressed various aspects of the relation to water: water as heritage (a common good) at local, national and global levels; household water and the associated public service; water as a product (packaged water) and its qualities as compared to those of tap water and natural water; water as an element linked to issues of health, well-being and living conditions; water and associated risks at local, national and global levels; the usages of water and the resulting conflicts (industrial and agricultural production in conflict with the provision of drinking water, health and well-being, the aesthetic quality of the countryside and the functioning of the ecosystem. The interviews were transcribed *in extenso* and subjected to a content analysis using the same analytical grid for all sites of investigation.

The sites span a range of contrasting conditions in terms of geography, climate and culture as well as in terms of access to water. Their choice was guided by the local environmental conditions, as reflected in levels of environmental pollution and/or (permanent, periodical or occasional) climatic characteristics that are more or less favorable to effective water management. These environmental characteristics, whose effects (i.e. direct exposure to a polluted environment, scarcity of water, poor water quality, shortfalls of provision) and their inherent risks, are experienced daily or occasionally; as such they are likely to impact the relationship to water.

Beyond the settings in France (Rennes, Limoges, Bordeaux and the Paris Region), we have, on the European continent, looked at the situations in Munich and Madrid, where the supply of high-quality water is abundant. In Asia, Jakarta and Osaka are at opposite ends of the spectrum of levels of development and ways of life: The Japanese emphasis on a hygienic way of life is culturally opposed to traditional forms of conduct encountered in the Indonesian culture. In both cities, high rates of population growth threaten the quality of the environment. As regards Africa, Ouagadougou is a typical example of supply problems, combining steadily growing levels of urban density with endemic water shortages. For South America, Brasilia exemplifies the difficulties of a planned city to coexist with its spontaneous outgrowths. Like Jakarta and Ouagadougou, Brasilia is characterized by massive socio-economic inequalities in terms of access to good-quality tap water.

Values and Societal Context

The water-related values which we have been able to identify in these different settings can be arranged into two clusters: on the one hand, there are the European and Far-Eastern sites in Paris, Bordeaux, Limoges, Rennes, Munich, Madrid and Japan; on the other hand, there are the Third World sites in Ouagadougou (Burkina Faso), Brasilia (Brazil) and Jakarta (Indonesia). The first cluster is essentially characterized by an aesthetic and identitarian view, and affection for water as heritage. The aesthetic view is concerned not only with water as a part of the natural environment, but also with water in the city (fountains, waterways), symbolizing a connection to nature. At the other end of the spectrum, the Third World sites are characterized by an essentially instrumental and ethical view. The instrumental view is expressed by the utilitarian relation to domestic water (food, drink, bodily hygiene). The ethical references operate in the context of access to water. Indeed, the social inequalities, and in particular the inequalities in terms of access to water, lead interviewees to invoke ethical values in discussing the sharing of domestic water resources. In Brasilia and Jakarta, this is completed by the expression of hedonistic values that are either related to religion (Jakarta) or based on personal wealth.

The expressions of water-related values enable the identification of two types of social representations of water (see Figure 3): while the first consists of a global ecological, aesthetic and identitarian representation, relating to water in all its manifestations, the second consists of a fragmented and functional representation that is limited to domestic water and related to the conditions under which water is accessed.

How are these two opposed representations connected to the individual's relations to water and in particular to its perception?

aesthetic and identity values	**functional and ethical values**
ECOLOGICAL and global representation	FACTUAL and fragmented representation

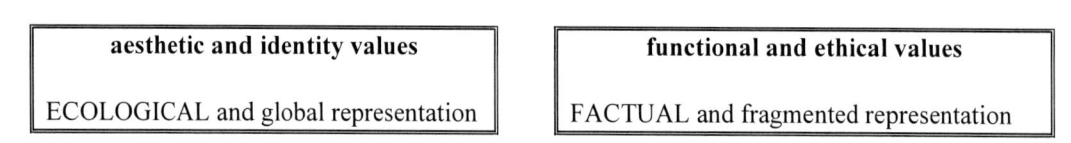

Figure 3. Values and social representations.

perception of a quantitative and/or qualitative evolution	⟶ ENVIRONMENTAL UNCERTAINTY
perception of water as an immutable resource	⟶ ENVIRONMENTAL CERTAINTY

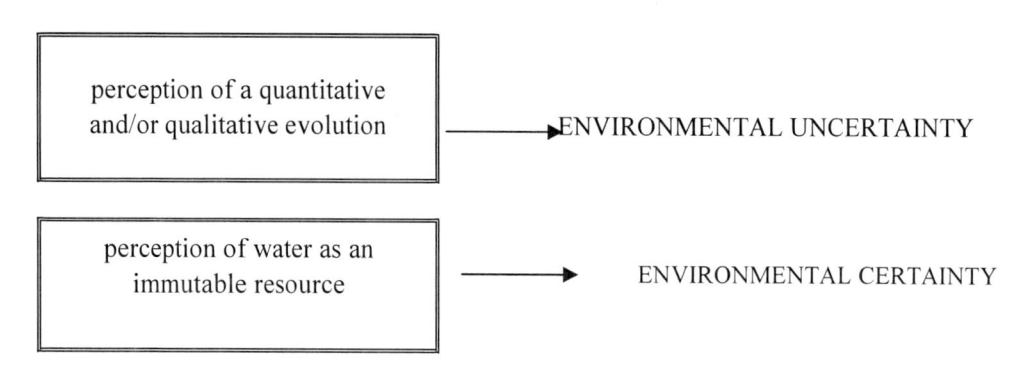

Figure 4. Perception of the resource and environmental confidence.

Relations to Water

Both the perception of changes in the state of water and the elaboration of a diagnosis of its current and future situation are abetted by the acceleration of changes in certain regions and by the emergence of break-downs that put the spotlight on such deteriorations and changes. This is particularly true for Rennes and Madrid, where quality or supply break-downs have occurred. The awareness of certain categories of people (environmental activists, water and health professionals) and the presence of emotional relations to water combined with aesthetic and identitarian values (France, Germany, Spain, Japan) accelerate the perception of such qualitative and/or quantitative changes. The presence of these values is dependent on the abundance and accessibility of water and a high-quality water environment, characteristic of the European and Japanese sites and of the living standards of the privileged classes in developing countries. The perception of changes and their irreversibility was observed more frequently amongst those who hold global ecological representations (water and health professionals, members of environmental associations) than among those adhering to fragmented representations. Besides, the functional relation lowers peoples' attentiveness to changes in the natural environment that go with modifications in the state of water. A functional relation to water was observed more frequently amongst the disadvantaged segments of the population who are exposed to inequalities in terms of access to water, particularly in the developing countries. It entails a tendency to focus on individualistic short-term solutions and often imply a habituation to such unstable conditions (Ouagadougou, Jakarta, and Brasilia). Moreover, the perceived abundance of the resource or of financial means leads to an over-consumption of water, grounded in the desire to maintain the levels of personal comfort and pleasure that are related to the seemingly unlimited availability of water (Brasilia). Temporary restrictions (Madrid) give rise to water-saving behavior; however, they fade out as soon as a return to relative abundance is perceived.

The types of relations to water which we have identified can be classified under two headings: on the one hand, there is a perception of water as a perpetual and unchanging resource, opposed to an awareness of qualitative and/or quantitative changes; on the other hand, there is an attitude of environmental certainty, opposed to environmental uncertainty. The groups of countries which we have defined in respect of their societal values can be found here, regardless of the individual features of relations to water which are determined by the respective social positions (cf. Figure 4). The European and Japanese sites are characterized by environmental uncertainty and an awareness of ongoing changes, whereas the Third World sites of the sample regard water as a permanent and unchanging resource, which goes along with environmental certainty.

The types of behavior towards water are shaped by these particular relations. The perceptions of efficiency, of control and individual vulnerability, of skills and means which may be brought into play individually or socially (level of development, financial means), of environmental and social uncertainty (perception of the behavior of others and of the presence of active minorities, of levers and target publics) all combine to shape the particular relations to water.

In addition, their evolution over time triggers a dynamic that informs behavioral adjustments (conservation, transformation or blocking off). In turn, such adjustments are modulated by individual variables such as level of education, professional activity, temporal, emotional and identity dimensions (temporal horizon, ability to project, memories, emotional attachment, spatial identity), and by the person's perceived levels of personal vulnerability and control. Finally, these are completed by the individual's chosen way of life, and on the basis of his or her values (environmental ethics / consumerism; altruism / egotism).

Overall, it appears clearly that the societal and ideological context, through values, and the environmental context of people's experience of water are essential dimensions for the building up of representations of water.

The conditions of access to water obviously participate in the representation of water. Thus, ethical values prevail in the light of inequitable access to bad water quality, and fragmented views of the resource go along with a utilitarian approach to water and environmental certainty. At the opposite, identitarian values go along with a more global vision of the water cycle and, consequently, also environmental uncertainty.

A Model of Relations to Water

The local specifics and their effect on consumers' behavior help to bring to light the conditions that are conducive to the espousal of sustainable behavior, and to the development of a better understanding of the place and role of the social representations of water. On this basis, we can distinguish four consecutive levels of factors, organized around social values, and operating as determinants of behavior towards water:

(1) contextual characteristics and value systems;
(2) social representations of water;
(3) awareness of water-related issues and elaboration of a diagnosis;
(4) enacted behaviors (cf. Figure 5).

Contextual Characteristics and Value Systems

The environmental and societal contexts are the foundation from which the relations to water arise and evolve.

Beyond the level of the environment, general geo-climatic conditions and features of the water resource (quantity and quality) incidents of change also come into play. The perceptibility of changes in the state of water is subject to the temporary and spatial scales of the phenomena that condition the renewal and the quality of water as well as to instances where the eco-system breaks down.

At the societal level, we can distinguish the ideological dimensions and the available information about water (ideological system, collective memory, information, and underlying values) on the one hand and, on the other hand, those aspects that are to do with the development level of the economic, institutional and technical frameworks that shape the specific every-day conditions for accessing water. Each culture has its own, unique way of viewing—natural elements and the "commons" (unchanging / changing; renewable / exhaustible; controllable / uncontrollable) resources as well as the place of humans in the natural environment, and to ascribe certain values to them. For example, the fusion with

Cultural Background and Environmental Context of Water Perception and Use 377

nature in the Far East contrasts strongly with the idea – linked to Christianity and productivism – of Man's supremacy in the West.

environmental context
climatic conditions
characteristics of the resource
water quality
temporal and spatial scale
of water supply

INDIVIDUAL
temporal horizon
environmental ethic
lifestyle
affective attachment

societal context
ideological system
collective memory
available knowledge
institutional framework
conditions of access to water

REPRESENTATIONS OF WATER

Conceptual Representation
water within the ecological system
fragmented vision / global vision

Ideology and values
identity / ethics
functionality / aestheticism

PERCEPTION OF THE STATE OF WATER

Unchanging state in the long-term

Perceptions of quantitative and/or qualitative evolution

Awareness
Recognition of the problem

Habituation
Absence of awareness

Causal attributions

DIAGNOSIS OF THE STATE OF WATER

environmental certainty / uncertainty

social certainty / uncertainty

PERCEPTION OF THE POSSIBILITIES TO CONTROL THE SITUATION

control unconceivable
fatalism
habituation

perceived ineffectiveness of individual and institutional control

individual control perceived as efficient

collective and/or institutional control perceived as efficient

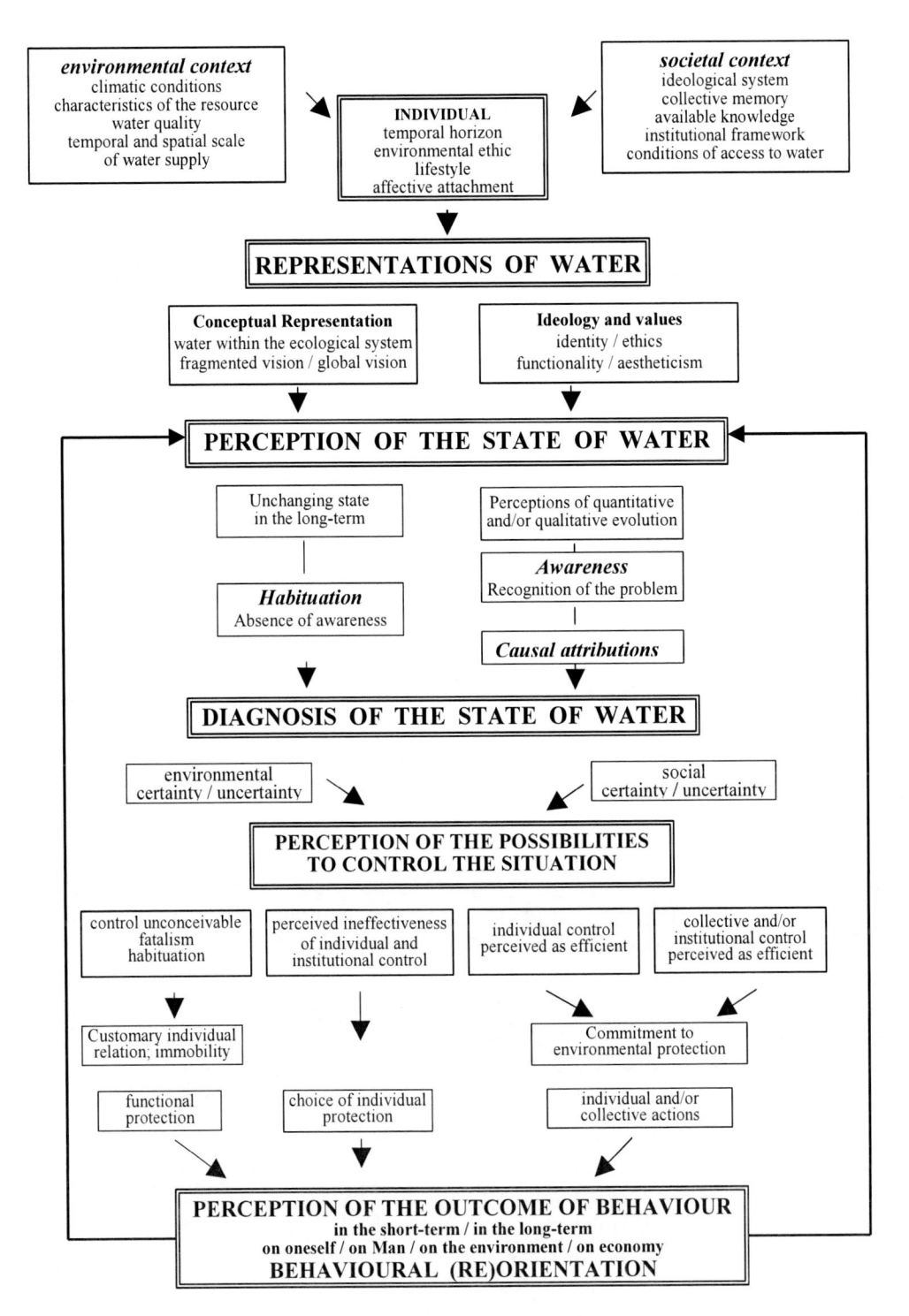

Customary individual relation; immobility

Commitment to environmental protection

functional protection

choice of individual protection

individual and/or collective actions

PERCEPTION OF THE OUTCOME OF BEHAVIOUR
in the short-term / in the long-term
on oneself / on Man / on the environment / on economy
BEHAVIOURAL (RE)ORIENTATION

Figure 5. A model of relations to water in the light environmental and cultural contexts.

Elaborating a Diagnosis, Sharpening Awareness

The elaborating of a diagnosis of the state of water and its evolution precedes the process of developing awareness and identifying the issues at stake. The diagnosis proceeds essentially from the perception of the evolution of the state of water under both quantitative (renewal, exhaustion / relative stability) and qualitative (improvement, deterioration / relatively stable quality) aspects, but also from the representation of water as an unchangeable gift of God or as an everlasting natural resource, or one that is in constant evolution.

Regardless of the state of the resource (abundance or scarcity, satisfying or impaired or even dangerous quality), not noticing modifications of the supplied water induces attitudes where any of these states is seen as "normal" if it lasts, and/or if its modification is thought to be impossible. Such a perception tends to combine with habituation and an absence of attempts to raise questions about environmental issues, thus encouraging stable behaviors.

In addition, the perception of changes in the state of water is linked to a diagnosis based on temporal references that trigger comparisons between past and present situations. The prior state of water – often idealized – is reconstructed either on the basis of personal memories, or on the basis of the narrative of witnesses, and/or on the basis of material and cultural evidence. In this way, the diagnosis is modulated by an appropriation of the collective memory regarding water in all its forms. This is the case of France, Germany, and Japan, in research 3.

The difficulty to pin down indicators of modifications in the state of water and, – most importantly – to identify their consequences (proven / probable; present / future; irreversible / reversible; local / general) stands in the way of the elaboration of an objective diagnosis. The transition from risks implying immediate threats to risks of a more diffuse nature changes the conditions of perception. The development of awareness is linked to the representation of the evolution of the harmful effects (their accumulation, activation, and aggravation over time). The elaboration of a long-term diagnosis, based on an analysis of the way the system works, rather than on a factual representation of the situation, goes along with a global ecological vision, as opposed to a fragmented perception.

The development of awareness depends on the evaluation of the present state of the resource and of its comparison with an imagined future state, as well as on the identification of the causes of this situation. The reference to a temporal dimension appears to be vital for the development of awareness of the problems related to water. It emerges in the individual and collective construction of the representation of water, in particular of its essential qualities on which the evaluation of improvements and deteriorations, the recognition of the problem and the attribution of responsibility will ultimately be based.

A factual representation of the causes of the state of water is strongly influenced by the daily experience of the players and their practices. On the other hand, the reference to processes goes hand in hand with a global long-term representation of the situation. In such circumstances, the individual may anticipate what to expect unless the way the system operates is changed. In such a case, the attribution of the causes takes place at a more abstract level, i.e. the level of the relations between players who represent common or diverging interests that are compatible or incompatible with the "natural" logic of the phenomena related to water. The conflicting features of these different logics originate in the extremely dissimilar time scales involved: the very long term for natural phenomena (limits of the quantitative and qualitative renewal of water) vs. the short for economic and political action (the rhythm and nature of consumption and pollution of the natural elements, the choice of economic and environmental priorities, the electoral calendar).

The recognition of the problem seems to be facilitated by environmental variables such as the acceleration of ecological phenomena related to the quality of water, and particularly the occurrence of breakdowns that dramatize changes in the state of water and make them more perceptible. A further facilitating factor is the perception of the seriousness of the risks resulting from such changes. The threats are evaluated against the perception of the risks for life on earth and humankind and the irreversible nature of the changes in the ecosystem. This perception depends also on the types of representations of water and seems to be more frequent among holders of a global ecological vision as water and health professionals and members of pro-environmental organisations than among individuals with a fragmented view,. At the same time, one observes a rise of environmental uncertainty in rich countries, in connection with the representation of probable future threats. This uncertainty is heightened by the perception of the limitations of science and technology, and of political intervention in the face of the complexity and newness of the phenomena that are linked to long-term environmental risks. Moreover, this uncertainty feeds on the fact that the available information and the opinions held by specialists of this subject often diverge. Conversely, the situation in developing countries is characterized by the absence of a perception of the actual and real threats, combined with relative environmental certainty.

Enacted Behaviors

The behaviors that are enacted result from the perception of the possibility of control and its effectiveness. In this respect, it is possible to distinguish those who think that in quantitative and/or qualitative terms the relation to water is beyond control from those who believe that the situation can still be brought under control. The perceived impossibility to exercise control goes along with a behavioral block (action seen as impossible, fatalism, nature seen as unchanging, feelings of powerlessness vis-à-vis nature and/or the laws of the economy). Conversely, the perception of a possibility to gain control leads to a range of behaviors in line with the envisaged types of control (individual, institutional or exercised jointly by all players):

- The perception of an impossibility to act efficiently on the institutional level leads to a great number of individual protective behaviors. In this case, we witness a withdrawal into short-term individual solutions aiming to ensure the individual's personal security (filtering water or purchasing mineral water) and/or the limitation of water consumption and, in a context of scarce supplies or insufficient financial means, an option for thriftiness.
- A perception of the effectiveness of the controls exercised by institutions and/or jointly by all players, permits to envisage global solutions of environmental protection. Such a perception is based on one or more of the following aspects: a trusting/distrustful relation to the institutions in charge of water management and towards the State as the protector of the common good, combined with careful

individual behavior aiming to preserve the environment and with the possibility to put pressure on the institutions at local, national and international level.

The activities to protect the environment (careful attentiveness, lobbying the institutions in combination with individual environmentally-friendly behavior) are linked to a capacity to project and to implement lasting long-term strategies targeting the deeper causes of the state of water. They go together with a representation of the interdependence between humans and their environment. Their results and benefits – often hard to ascertain – are indirect and delayed, benefiting future generations. This type of action is buttressed by emotional commitment, aesthetic, identitarian and sometimes ethical values (responsibility towards future generations, sharing resources and commitment to a "healthy" environmental heritage). These factors bring even the smallest changes in the aquatic environment to light and are apt to sustain actions having long-term effects.

Conclusion

From the Societal to the Individual Level

Social representations represent the pivot between the environmental and societal contexts and the individual relations to water as they result from the societal position of the individual. They shape the conditions in which individuals perceive and react (or don't react) to concrete situations.

Societal and environmental contexts differ significantly between different countries, and hence by their respective cultural backgrounds and reference values. While individuals base their thinking on their own experience and prefer diagnoses and evaluations that flow from their personal experience, the ins and outs are shaped by the value system of their respective society, and hence by their environmental and societal contexts. The contextual differentiation results essentially from the awareness of the temporal dimension, between those who perceive the (mainly qualitative) evolution of the state of water and the possibility of efficient interventions, and those who do not. It is possible to distinguish between those who do as of now perceive certain problems with the quantity and/or quality of water and the aquatic environment, those who locate them in a more or less distant future, and finally those who maintain that the state of water is immutable.

This said, as the acceleration of these changes and the breakdowns of supply impact on the environment, it becomes ever more difficult for the wider public to ignore these transformations. These circumstances, as well as the fact that such incidents took place only recently, in combination with the marking of the resource and the promotion of more attentive attitudes towards it (opportunities to take action, frequent and regular advertisements reminding the public of the institutional interventions and their results) constitute contextual factors that facilitate the sharpening of awareness and the development of a (more or less sustained) personal commitment to eco-compatible behavior.

The perception of changes in the state of water, of the importance and urgency of these issues, of the efficacy of one's own action compared to those of others, as well as the capacity to project oneself into the future and to adopt an altruistic stance represent so many individual factors that pave the way to embracing sustainable behaviors. A long-term commitment of this kind reflects an optimistic and active attitude which is based on the global appropriation of the environment both in space and time. It aims to alter the course of future developments in the state of water and to preserve its life-saving properties by way of present-day activities. More than by anything else, such a wish to act is modulated by the perceived efficacy of one's own individual actions and the conviction that their aims, i.e. the survival of future generations, are legitimate (ethos focusing on access to goods that are essential to life, in opposition to the equity underpinning their commercial value).

The social representations hold a central position between the ideological and societal contexts on the one hand and the practical day-to-day relations to water on the other hand. As the link between the psychological and the social dimensions, the social representations account for the individual's interpretations of the reality in which she or he lives (Moscovici, 1989; Jodelet, 1989). The conditions under which a social representation is produced depend on the ideology, the societal values and the practices that are developed in relation to the object. The relation to water in different societal contexts which we observe here illustrates the role of ideology – highlighted by Rouquette (1996) and Rateau (2000) – in framing the production of social representations. Ideology and societal representations operate as guiding referential conditions that contribute to the social representations of "water".

An "utilitarian", "functional" representation accompanies egocentric relations to water, an instrumental perception of the resource and a weak personal involvement in sustainability. Conversely, an "identitarian" representation of water considers water as an integral element of nature and goes along with a global perception of the water cycle, a deeper commitment and potentially the conviction that one's actions have a positive impact on the preservation of the resource. This opposition between a "utilitarian", "identitarian" and an "ecological" representation of water rejoins the distinction between *"ecocentric"* and *"anthropocentric"* environmental values proposed by Gagnon-Thompson & Barton (1994) and Stern, (2000). While *ecocentric* people value nature for its own sake, *anthropocentric* people express concern about protecting the environment because of the positive effects this can have on them. Thus, both ecocentric and anthropocentric people may express concern for environmental issues, but the former are more likely to establish a link between their pro-environmental attitudes and their actual behaviours, compared to anthropocentric individuals, particularly when this involves personal or economic costs.

Thus, it appears that social representations are not only the locus of construction of the object "water" which serves to express the relations to this same object "water", but also the crucial element that must be targeted in order to promote sustainable behaviors. Certain solutions can be envisaged to counter the effects of the so-called "tragedy of the commons" and to support the sustainable use of water. They are grounded in an idea of humankind as either irreducibly egotistic or as capable of changing its relations to nature. The first view argues for coercive, normative or inciting measures to be put in place at institutional level, so as to encourage individual behaviors that don't come in conflict with the general interest and preserve the resources in the long term. This solution does not require a deep individual commitment to solving the environmental crisis; nor does it ensure that behaviors remain sustainable if the normative pressure is reduced. But the conflict between representations and enforced practices justifies the expectation that the desirable behaviors will be adopted in the long run. Besides, if the strategy counts on individuals' sense of responsibility, it is much more appropriate to target small groups and communities that can later transmit such values at their own initiative, to raise their awareness of environmental issues and to transmit ecological values to them, and to appeal to their moral feelings and ethical principles in order to encourage and maintain behaviors that are able to preserve the commons (Gardner & Stern, 1996). Transforming representations via the dissemination of knowledge, the transmission of values transcending the individual and treasuring the natural environment, the perception of control and the efficacy of the enacted behaviors-may induce deep changes in the relations to the environment and stimulate the individual to develop behaviors that are compatible with sustainable development.

REFERENCES

Abric, J-C. (1994). *Pratiques sociales et représentations.* Paris, PUF.
Bouguerra, M. L (2003). *Les batailles de l'eau. Pour un bien commun de l'humanité.* Enjeux Planète. Paris.
Biel, A. & Gärling, T. (1995). The role of Uncertainty in Resources Dilemmas. *Journal of Environmental Psychology, 15,* 221-233.
Bonnes, M., Moser, G., Sinha, J. & Corral-Verdugo, V. (2006*). Human Dimension of Global Change: Human Perceptions and Behaviour in Sustainable Water*. Research Report, Rome: University "La Sapienza", pp 70.
Codol, J.P. (1969). Note terminologique sur l'emploi de quelques expressions concernant les activités et processus cognitifs en psychologie sociale. *Bulletin de Psychologie, 23,* 63-71.
Dawes, R.M. (1980). Social Dilemmas. *Annual Review of Psychology, 31,* 169-193.
Dawes, R.M. & Messick, D.M. (2000). Social Dilemmas. *International Journal of Psychology, 35,* 111-116.
De Vanssay, B., Ratiu, E., Casal, A., Colbeau-Justin L., Porto de Lima, C. et Weiss K. (1998). *Les citadins et l'eau. Contrastes et similitudes dans le monde.* Internal report. Paris : Laboratoire de Psychologie Environnementale et Agence de l'eau Seine-Normandie, 207p.
Douglas,M. & Wildawsky, A. (1982). *Risk and culture: An essay on the selection of technological and environmental dangers.* Berkley: University of California Press
Dunlap, R. E., & Van Liere, K. D. (1978). The " New Environmental Paradigm". A proposed measuring instrument and preliminary results. *Journal of Environmental Education,* 9(4), 10-19.
Dunlap, R. E., Gallup G. H., Jr., & Gallup, A. M. (1993). Of global concern: Results of the health of the planet survey. *Environment, 35,* 7-15, 33-39.
Dunlap, R.E., Van Liere, K.D., Mertig, A.G. & Jones, R.E. (2000). Measuring Endorsement of the New Environmental Paradigm: A Revised NEP Scale. *Journal of Social Issues, 3,* 425-442.
Franzen, A. (2003). Environmental attitudes in international comparison : an analysis of the ISSP surveys 1993 and 2000. *Social Science Quarterly, 84,* 297-308.
Gagnon-Thompson, S.C. & Barton M.A. (1994). Ecocentric and anthropocentric attitudes toward the environment. *Journal of Environmental Psychology, 14,* 149-157.
Gardner, T. G., & Stern, P. C. (1996). *Environmental Problems and human behavior.* Needham Heights, Ma: Simon, Allyn & Bacon

Gibson, J. J. (1979). *An ecological approach to visual perception*. Boston: Houghton Mifflin.
Michel-Guillou, E. & Moser, G. (2006). Commitment of farmers to environmental protection: From social pressure to environmental conscience. *Journal of Environmental Psychology.* 26(3), 227-235
Grob, A. (1995). A structural model of environmental attitudes and behavior. *Journal of Environmental Psychology*, 15, 209-220.
Gifford, R., Scannell, L., Kormos, C., Smolova, L., Biel, A., Boncu, S., Corral, V., Günther, H., Hanyu, K., Hine, D., Kaiser, F., Korpela, K., Lima, L. M., Mertig, A., Garcia Mira, R., Moser, G., Passaforo, P., Pinheiro, J., Saini, S., Sako, T., Sautkina, E., Savina, Y., Schmuck, P., Schultz, W. Sundblad, E-L., & Uzzell, D. (2009). Temporal pessimism and spatial optimism in environmental assessments: An 18-nation study. *Journal of Environmental Psychology, 29*, 1-12
Guimelli, C. (Ed.). (1994). *Structures et transformations des représentations sociales*. Neuchâtel: Delachaux et Niestlé, Coll. Textes de Base en Sciences Sociales.
Hardin, G. (1968). The tragedy of the commons. *Science, 162*, 1243-1248.
Jodelet, D. (1989). *Les représentations sociales*. Paris : PUF
Lévy-Leboyer, C., Bonnes, M., Chase, J., Ferreira-Marques, J., & Pawlik, K. (1996). Determinants of Pro-Environmental Behaviours : A Five-Countries Comparison. *European Psychologist, 1(2)*, 123-129.
Lima, M.L., & Castro, P. (2005). Cultural Theory meets the community: Worldviews and local issues. *Journal of Environmental Psychology, 25,*23-35.
Michel-Guillou, E. & Moser, G. (2006). Commitment of farmers to environmental protection: From social pressure to environmental conscience. *Journal of Environmental Psychology.* 26(3), 227-235
Moliner, P. Rateau, P. & Cohen-Scali, V. (2002). *Les représentations sociales. Pratiques d'études de terrain.* PUR, Rennes.
Moscovici, S. (1988). Notes towards a description of social representations. *European Journal of Social Psychology, 18*, 211-250.
Moscovici, (1989). Des représentations collectives aux représentations sociales. *In* : D. Jodelet, *Les Représentations sociales*. Paris : PUF. 62-86
Moser, G. (1984). Water quality perception: a dynamic evaluation. *Journal of Environmental Psychology*, 4, 201-210.
Navarro, O. (2008). L'eau comme enjeu: territoire, identité et conflits d'usage. *In* : Kirat, T. and Torre, A. (Eds.) *Territoires de conflits. Analyses des mutations de l'occupation de l'espace*. Paris : éditions l'Harmattan.
Navarro, O. (2009). Représentations sociales de l'eau dans un contexte de conflits d'usage : le cas de la sierra Nevada de santa Marta, Colombie. *Cahiers Internationaux de Psychologie Sociale. 81,* 65-86.
Rateau, P. (2000). Idéologie, représentation sociale et attitude : Etude expérimentale de leur hiérarchie. *International Review of Social Psychology, 13(1),* 29-57.
Rogers, R. (1983). Cognitive and physiological processes in fear appeals and attitude change: A revised theory of protection motivation. *In*: J. Cacioppo, R. Petty (Eds.), *Social psychology: A sourcebook.* New York: Guilford Press.
Rouquette, M-L. (1996). Représentations et idéologie. *In* : J-C. Deschamps et J-L. Beauvois (Eds.). *Des attitudes aux attributions*. Grenoble : Presses Universitaires de Grenoble, 163-173.

Schultz, P.W., & Zelezny, L. (1999). Values as predictors of environmental attitudes: evidence for consistency across 14 countries. *Journal of Environmental Psychology, 19*, 255-265.

Sironneau, J. (1996). *L'eau. Nouvel enjeu stratégique mondial.* Paris: Editions Economica.

Steg, L., & Sievers, I. (2000). Cultural Theory and Individual Perceptions of Environmental Risks. *Environment and Behavior, 32* (2), 248-267.

Stern, P.C. (2000). Toward a coherent theory of environmentally significant behavior. *Journal of Social Issues, 56*, 407-424.

Stern, P. C., & Oskamp, S. (1987). Managing scarce environmental resources. *In*: D. Stokols & I. Altman (Eds.), *Handbook of environmental psychology*). New York: Wiley. 1043-1088.

Thompson, S. C., & Stoutemyer, K. (1991). Water use as a commons dilemma: The effects of education that focuses on long-term consequences and individual action. *Environment and Behavior, 23(3)*, 314-333.

Vergès, P. (1994). Approche du noyau central: propriétés quantitatives et structurales. *In*: C. Guimelli (Ed.). *Structures et transformations des représentations sociales.* Genève: Université de Lausanne et de Genève.

Weiss, K., Moser, G., & Germann, C. (2006). Perception de l'environnement, conceptions du métier et pratiques culturales des agriculteurs face au développement durable (Perception of the environment, professional conceptions and practices of farmers in favor of sustainable development). *Revue Européenne de Psychologie Appliquée, 56,* 73-81.

In: Psychological Approaches to Sustainability
Editors: V. Corral-Verdugo et al.

ISBN 978-1-60876-356-6
© 2010 Nova Science Publishers, Inc.

Chapter 19

INFLUENCE OF SOCIAL AND LEGAL NORMS ON ANTI-ECOLOGICAL BEHAVIORS

Martha Frías-Armenta[*]
Universidad de Sonora, Mexico
Ana M. Martín[†]
Universidad de la Laguna, Spain

ABSTRACT

This chapter is aimed at both analyzing current theories on normative variables related to anti-environmental behavior, and testing an explanatory model using these normative variables as determinants of such a behavior. We first review theories and factors related to the inhibition of anti-ecological conducts; then, we present and discuss results from an empirical study on the determinants of such conducts. Two-hundred and ninety-seven individuals living in the proximities of a natural protected area in a Mexican northwestern city were interviewed. An instrument was utilized to measure diverse components of legitimacy, legal deterrence, social and personal norms, emotional volatility, antisocial behavior and illegal anti-ecological behavior. Results from a structural equation model indicated that personal norm and antisocial behavior had a direct effect on illegal anti-ecological behavior; social norm produced an indirect effect on that behavior through personal norm. Deterrence also exerted its effect through social norm. Legitimacy correlated with social norm and deterrence, and emotional volatility affected personal norm. These results replicated findings from previous studies on antisocial and anti-ecological behaviors; the direct predictor of illegal behavior is personal norm, while external pressure perceived by individuals should be first internalized in order to modify, maintain and control their potentially illegal anti-ecological behavior. Emotional volatility was included in the model resulting also as a

---

[*] Correspondence: Martha Frías-Armenta, Departamento de Derecho, Universidad de Sonora, Blvd. Transversal y Rosales S/N, Hermosillo, Sonora, 83000, Mexico. E-mail: marthafrias@sociales.uson.mx.
[†] This chapter was written while the second author conducted a research study funded by the Spanish Ministry of Education and Science (I+D grant SEJ2006-11604/PSIC).

determinant of the way people integrate external pressure into their personal norms. We concluded that law and public policies should consider these results in their attempts to promote pro-ecological behavior among citizens.

INTRODUCTION

Pro-environmental behavior is defined as the set of deliberate and effective actions resulting in the protection of the environment or in minimizing its deterioration (Corral-Verdugo, 2001). Consequently, anti-ecological behavior could be defined as those actions that degrade the environment, damaging, contaminating or preventing natural resources from recovering after being extracted or exploited by human action. Then, this conduct is assumed to produce a significant, negative repercussion on the physical environment and, consequently, on human society (Corral-Verdugo & Frías-Armenta, 2006). Solutions to environmental problems have been traditionally sought in the physical sciences; however, environmental problems are mainly originated by human behavior so that those solutions should include the study of psychological variables, including beliefs, values, motives, and worldviews. Since human behavior is responsible for most of the environmental degradation nowadays experienced, something more than a physical technological solution is required (Winter, 2003).

Most explanatory models of pro-environmental behavior include cognitive variables (beliefs, norms, intentions) as predictors. The theory of Reasoned Action (TRA; Fishbein & Ajzen, 1975) has been one of the most used to predict behavior. This model, applied to pro-environmental behavior (PEB), establishes that intentions are the most immediate determinants of PEB, while intentions are a function of two variables: personal attitudes and social pressure (Ajzen & Fishbein, 1980). However, a number of studies indicate that when facing situational and perceived barriers, people does not engage in the intended behavior (see Gaspar de Carvalho et al.'s chapter in this volume), which limits the scope of the TRA model. Azjen (1985) built another approach, in the form of a "Theory of Planned Behavior" (TPB), which was based on the TRA, trying to explain action when behavioral control is incomplete. This theory includes a new variable called "perceived behavioral control" (Azjen & Madden, 1986) that predicts intentions and behavior when control is incomplete.

Yet, there is something more than reasons, intentions and self behavioral control –as personal predictors of action- in determining why people are pro-environmentally oriented. The TRA is an example of a model stressing *internal* causes of behavior. Another models focus rather on *external* determinants. For example, proponents of the Social Control Theory (SCT) argue that behavior is motivated by external consequences, in the form of punishments and rewards (Tyler, 2006a). This approach presupposes that governments and authorities can alter people behavior by manipulating social resources or by delivering punishment. Such an instrumental theory tries to secure the compliance with the law by focusing on the authorities' influence, which can be implemented by administering personal costs to rule-breaking. Therefore, the state is assumed to control societal resources and administer them to citizens in order to obtain compliance with the law. As a consequence, Social Control Theory is considered a deterrence-based perspective; it implies an economic standpoint indicating that people will break the law when the potential gains overcome the costs (Tyler, 2006a).

Alternatively, Self–Determination Theory (SDT, Deci & Ryan, 1985) indicates that self-regulated behavior is more probably *maintained* than *controlled*. This theory states that there are two kinds of intentional behaviors: one linked to intrinsic motives and other associated to extrinsic consequences (Chatzisarantis & Biddle, 1998). The extrinsic motivation is associated to external consequences, while the intrinsic refers to enjoyable and self-satisfying outcomes. Extrinsic motivation is related to externally controlled behavior and intrinsic motivation relates to autonomous action. However, the level of autonomy varies in extrinsic behavior because some extrinsic motives are self-regulated, and this is called "introjected regulation" (Moller, Ryan, & Deci, 2006). Since intrinsic motivation leads to self-regulated behavior, providing people the opportunity to make choices helps to intrinsic motivation, which in turn might result in self-regulated behavior. Apparently, autonomous motivation leads to pro-environmental behavior by facilitating the internalization of pro-environmental values (Pelletier, 2002).

TRA, TPB, SDT, and SCT are theories based on, basically, cognitive processes; however, some researchers (Hine, Marks, Nachriener, Gifford, & Heath 2007; Pooley & O'Connor, 2002; see also Tapia-Fonllem et al, and Bonnes et al chapters in this volume) argue that it is important to incorporate emotional-affective components of pro-environmental behavior in explanatory models. Emotions may change the way people act (Posner, 2001); abilities, preferences, and beliefs are sometimes modified during emotional states. Moreover, there are emotional dispositions that moderate these emotional states (Posner, 2001). In addition, it is possible both to "cultivate" emotional dispositions and to control emotions (Cacioppo & Gardner, 1999). Evolved behavioral mechanisms determine a quick and appropriate (i.e., adaptive) response accompanying an emotion. For instance, escape from an imminent physical danger is the best possible reaction. However, controlling emotional responses serves better the cause of individual's adaptation in facing social stimuli, regardless of their perceived dangerous nature.

Publicists acknowledge that emotions modify consumer preferences; therefore, if they want to increase the sales of a product they try to elicit the positive emotions related to its consumption. People, of course, seek pleasant emotions and avoid disagreeable ones. However, feelings of guilt restrain the action that produces those pleasurable emotions; thus, guilt could increase environmental conservation (Kaiser & Shimoda, 1999) in spite of its being a negative emotion. Moreover, guilt could be transformed into a moral norm and work also by controlling anti-environmental behavior (Caccioppo & Gardner, 1999; Kaiser & Shimoda, 1999). Emotions can also affect reasoning (Blanchette, 2006); thus, both positive and negative emotions could direct behavior to pro-environmental actions (see Tapia-Fonllem et al chapter, this volume, for more of this).

Additional explanations of anti-environmental behavior assume that this conduct derives from personal traits; some of those are lack of self-control, risk-seeking, sensation-seeking, and inability to delay gratification (Gottfredson & Hirschi, 1990). In more of this, the Classical Theory of Crime (CTC) establishes that crime is an uncontrolled natural human tendency to seek pleasure; also that individuals search for immediate satisfaction and that self control restrains this tendency (Muraven, Pogarsky, & Shmueli, 2006). Individual differences in self-control determine participation in criminal activities; people with low self-control are impulsive, insensitive and risk-taking (Gottfredson & Hirschi, 1990). According to this theory, people do not seek for an opportunistic situation for crime; when opportunity arises, individuals with low self-control are more likely to offend. Therefore, CTC would approach anti-ecological behavior as an unrestrained natural tendency of humans to seek pleasure by wasting natural resources, with only self-control being able to moderate this tendency (Corral-Verdugo et al., 2006).

Evolutionary psychology also tries to explain anti-ecological behavior. This approach suggests that the human desire to accumulate goods has ancestral origins, constituting a "deep" explanation of human nature (Trivers, 1971). According to this theory, the genetic success of individuals depends on two basic factors: surviving sufficiently enough time to reach reproductive age and finding a sexual partner. Human nature is conditioned to obtaining material and sexual resources to achieve those tasks, in which individuals compete for potential partners against same-sex rivals (Jackson, 2008). This sexual competition causes that individuals expand their aspirations for obtaining more and more resources because their possession guarantee reproductive success (Trivers, 1971). A problem with this tendency is that it stimulates excessive consumption and accumulation of resources to the expense of others' well-being, who can experience trouble in obtaining them. Such a tendency could result in extreme egoistic behaviors (Dawkins, 1976), which are recognized by human societies as antisocial or criminal conducts. Therefore, anti-ecological behavior (polluting, wasting resources, destroying ecosystems, etc.) could also be conceived as egoistic and antisocial behavior, since every time a person engage in it, he or she affects others' access to natural resources (Corral-Verdugo, Frías-Armenta, Fraijo, & Tapia, 2006). Consequently, evolutionary psychology establishes that the balance between egoistic and cooperative behavior could only be established by social order (i.e., law; Trivers, 1971).

For Jackson (2008), the balance between egoism and cooperation depends on social conditions like cultural rules, norms, social pressure, government, and related institutions and factors. Groups exert influence on individuals through social pressure; people behave in reference to their social group (Tyler, 2006a). Jackson also argues that government, who acts as representative of the collectivity, could regulate the tendencies towards consumerism, the waste of resources, and their just distribution, by passing and enforcing laws that promote environmentally protective conducts. Norms and laws have to prevent anti-environmental behaviors from occurring and to stimulate pro-ecological ones. For example, fiscal laws should promote the use of recycled materials in industries, their use of electricity from low or zero-carbon fuel sources, or their investing in reducing the production of polluting agents. Other laws could stimulate individual behaviors such as the use of public transportation, the participation in conservation campaigns, etc. (Starke, 2008). Implementing laws and public policies that promote pro-ecological and cooperative behavior would also be useful in alleviating environmental deterioration. However, passing laws is not enough for reaching this goal. Law itself does not lead to changes in people's behavior. Other factors impinge on individuals' compliance; therefore, it is necessary to study the effect of norms in their different manifestations (social, legal, personal), as well as the influence of related variables on pro or anti environmental behavior.

In spite of the serious environmental problems at worldwide level and their repercussions on the integrity of the human species, there are few studies analyzing why people break environmental norms and how these norms influence behavior having environmental impact. Some of the studied variables are personal and social norms, legitimacy, and deterrence (Corral-Verdugo & Frías-Armenta, 2006; Tyler, 1997; Schultz, 2002; Wenzel, 2004a; Wenzel, 2004b; Wenzel & Jobling, 2006). The aim of this chapter is to analyze current theories and normative variables related to the prediction of anti-environmental behavior.

Thus, the following sections will review presumably factors related to the inhibition of anti-ecological conducts.

LEGAL NORMS, ENVIRONMENTAL PROTECTION AND ANTI-ECOLOGICAL BEHAVIOR

Norms are beliefs about how people must act and they are enforced under the threat of a sanction or the promise of a reward (Thøgersen, 2006). Within the legal system, norms are conduct rules that impose a certain behavior (García Máynez, 2000). Legal norms are distinguished from social and moral norms, in terms of the coercive power that legal norms have. This means that the State has the power to enforce them by force, under the threat of the application of a sanction or punishment (Alvarez, 1995). In turn, social norms are subject to social disapproval and the morals of internal reproach (Santiago-Nino, 1987).

Legal and Psychological Characteristics of Illegal Anti-ecological Behavior

Anti-ecological behavior is a peculiar form of deviated action from both a legal and a psychosocial point of view. From a legal perspective the singularity of environmental transgressions are reflected in three features. To begin with, environmental law is a fragmented and difficult-to-coordinate field in many western countries. It involves administrative, civil and criminal regulations, enforced at federal, state and local levels (Parejo-Alfonso, 2008; Situ & Emmons, 2000; Tompkins, 2005). Therefore, environmental transgressions are not always crimes in the strict legal sense, although very often they incur substantial fines. Secondly, most people have difficulty in distinguishing illegal ecological behaviors from legal ones, partly because many anti-ecological behaviors become illegal only when they exceed the limits established by the law or when a specific license to carry out an action has not been obtained (Korsell 2001). Thirdly, neither is it easy to determine when an illegal anti-ecological behavior is an offense or an administrative infraction because the criterion to differentiate between them is "the degree to which [a specific behavior] seriously harms the balance of the natural systems" (Art. 325 of the Spanish Criminal Code).

From a psychosocial point of view, breaches of environmental laws also constitute a peculiar form of illegal behavior. Environmental transgressions harm both the environment and human beings but are not universally perceived as illegal, or even reproachable, as their "wrongness" is not always obvious (Korsell, 2001; Martín, Hernández, Hess, et. al., 2008). This explains why, in many cases, society prefers to refer to this type of transgression as "accidents" or "human errors" instead of crimes (Mårald, 2001). This lack of social reproach may be related to the characteristics of the consequences, sanctions, victims and perpetrators.

The consequences of environmental transgressions are not always immediate or indeed evident. In many cases, as the incident often occurs for the first time, there is frequently no precedent that enables evaluation of the actual situation and predictions of the consequences for the immediate and more distant future. Furthermore, even experts disagree in their evaluation of the harm inflicted, depending on whether or not they are involved with the interests of the different parties. This situation is worse when the punishable effect is not the harm itself but the risk of such harm occurring (Mårald, 2001).

The very severe penalties which do exist for environmental transgression are seldom imposed (Korsell 2001; Watson, 2005). This could be because environmental laws have generally been drawn up in response to extreme, catastrophic events, which are in fact infrequent (Mårald, 2001). The extremity of these events considerably raises the thresholds for specific behaviors to be considered punishable. Also the exceptional nature of these transgressions leads to the underestimation of the risks of future occurrence and the need for subsequent surveillance. Therefore, although sanctions are severe for those found responsible for ecological damage, the frequency with which the accused are found guilty of producing these wrongdoings is very low, making legal precedents scarce. Accordingly, prison sentences for environmental transgressions are very rare, and fines are the most frequently imposed sentence (Korsell, 2001; Watson, 2005). Finally, when the transgressor is a company, some fines are, in many cases, minor investments compared to the routine cost of doing business legally. Thus, breaking environmental laws becomes economically profitable (Wilson, 1986).

The victims of environmental transgressions, when compared to those of regular offenses, are not specific individuals but often a large, indeterminate group of people affected in the short or long-term. In some cases, environmental transgressions can affect present and future populations of an entire region. But, as there is no *individual* victim who feels compelled to report the incident, detection of environmental transgression depends almost exclusively on the efforts of administrations to find and sanction anti-normative behaviors (Martin, Salazar, Hess, et al., 2008).

The profile of environmental transgressors also contributes to the peculiarity of environmental offenses since environmental transgressions are often committed by people who are "radically different from ordinary criminals" (Mårald, 2001, p. 158), no matter whether the transgressor is a corporation, the military, the government or a private individual (Situ, 1998; Martin, Salazar, Hess et al., 2008). Research by Situ (1998) showed that the environmental transgressors in a New Jersey sample were ordinary people without criminal records. Their illegal behavior was motivated by saving small amounts of money. Martin, Salazar, Hess et al. (2008) replicated Situ's results in a highly protected environment and showed that most transgressions handled by the public administrations across jurisdictions were carried out mainly by individuals in the course of their personal activities regarding home care or leisure. To a lesser extent, transgressions were also committed by individuals during their work, but always in small local businesses (tourist excursion agencies, building, car repairs).

VARIABLES STUDIED IN COMPLIANCE WITH LAW AND ANTI-ECOLOGICAL BEHAVIOR AREAS

Legitimacy

Legitimacy implies two elements, power and dominance (Chriss, 2007). Power is defined as the imposition of the will of one person upon others, and domination is the probability that a command will be followed by a group of persons. An authority possesses legitimacy when a group of person bestows the right to issue commands (Chriss, 2007). This right could be based on the tradition, law, or personality. States maintain regulations by validating their authority. A validation refers to legitimating their rules in the eyes of their citizens (Chriss, 2007).

Tyler (2006a) argues that people will voluntarily comply with laws if they perceive them as appropriate and if laws are related to their personal attitudes. The voluntary observation of the law, based on attitudes, includes personal norm and legitimacy. If people follow the law is because they feel that the law is just, and the resulting predisposition is defined as *personal norm*. However, if the law is obeyed because it is perceived that the authorities that apply the law are just and they had the right to do it, legitimacy is established.

Institutions have several forms to achieve the endorsement of norms. Conventionally they use their faculty to punish or to sanction to obligate people to comply with the laws. Authorities have to possess power, which can be defined as the faculty of one person, group of persons or organizations to compel others; in this sense, the state, authorities or government have the power to coerce the inhabitants to establish social order. Nevertheless, an effective institution must recognize that power does not simply and automatically lead to submission and obedience before laws. Rather, the previous is determined by the perception about how the state institutions use or abuse power (Lee-Chai & Bargh, 2001). From this perspective, power can be defined as the capacity to exert influence on people's attitudes and conducts (Raven, 2001). Legitimacy derives from the effective use of power, and it is effective only when it changes others' behavior and if it is socially validated through a process of social influence (Haslam, 2004). In this regard, Bridgeman (2004) found that the perceived legitimacy of authorities resulted in acceptance of water conservation measures, as well as in the installation of water recycling plants, in spite of the reluctance that could be derived from this proposal.

Turner (2005) argues that the meaning of prize and sanction and other forms of control, including physical force, vary depending on the influence that they exercise. On the one hand, they can be considered legitimate forms of control if the authority has a social consensus; on the other hand, they can be perceived as coercive forms of power, if the authority is perceived as illegitimate.

The perception of authority's legitimacy is also subordinated to other variables, social identity, for example (Wenzel & Jobling, 2006). If the members of a group identify their authorities as a part of the group or as their representatives (social identity), it is more likely that they treat such authorities with respect (Tyler, 1997). Studies intended at assessing social identity and authority's perception of legitimacy have found that the subordinate members of a group evaluate more favorably their authorities if they are members of the group, and more unfavorably if they are outsiders (Tyler, 2006a; Haslam, 2004; Wenzel & Jobling, 2006).

Identifying the authority as a part of the group results in treating them with respect, benevolence and neutrality; it also grants them a great legitimacy (Tyler, 1997). Once the authority is considered as a part of the group, the subordinates will consider it more representative, with more authority and more persuasiveness. Power then is exerted as legitimate influence (Haslam, 2004).

Social and Personal Norm

Personal and social norms are also variables that have been analyzed in relation to the compliance with the law. Grasmick and Bursik (1990) operationalize the concept of personal norm as a feeling of guilt, and social norm as the loss of respect from socially valuable people (friends or acquaintances); also, personal norm has been identified as a sentiment of moral obligation (Schwarts, 1992). Schultz (2002) indicates that personal norm is like an obligation or sensitivity to act in a particular way in specific situations, as in environmental protection. Whereas social norms establish an external influence (the perception of what others are doing or what they have to do), personal norms are related to internalized self-expectations (what I should do). Social and personal norms have been related to pro-environmental behavior (Corral-Verdugo & Frías-Armenta, 2006; Schultz & Tyra, 2000; Hunecke, Blöbaum, Matthies, & Höger, 2001).

Personal norm is also defined as the moral standards of people, acquired through the internalization of social norms. This is understood as a process of self-categorization related to the identification with the group to which people attribute the norms (Wenzel, 2004a). From this point of view, social norm includes the moral standards attributed to a group, which remain external to individuals, but that can be internalized and transformed into personal norms that will guide behavior.

There are theories trying to explain the influence of social norms on people's behavior and on the compliance with norms. One of them is Self-Categorization Theory (Sigala, Burgoyne, & Webley, 1999), which proposes that the prominence of social identity depends on the context. This theory establishes that there are three levels of abstraction that can be used to categorize identity: personal identity (the being as individual), social identity (the being as member of a group), and intra-species identity (oneself as part of the human race). Each level is as valid as the subsequent (or precedent); the being is also defined as "individual" and "social member of the group." This tripartite system of classification of the being is what constitutes the base of the Self-Categorization Theory (Oakes, Haslam, & Turner, 1994).

In essence, people are prone to be influenced by whom they consider members of their relevant self-categorization. These influences mean that the points of view and behavioral tendencies of the members of the group are going to be internalized as their social convictions (Abrams & Hogg, 1990).

Thøgersen, (2006) argues that a continuum exists within the levels of internationalization of social norms; when they are superficially internalized they are called "introjected norms," and when they have a deeper processing they are identified as "integrated norms." The introjected and integrated norms form personal norms. Integrated norms are stronger in predicting behavior (Schwartz, 2002). Thøgersen, (2006) also differentiate between descriptive social norms and subjective social norms, considering the former as the perception of normal behavior while the latter refers to the group expectations about certain behavior. The norm's taxonomy proposed by Thøgersen (2006) begins with descriptive norms, followed by subjective and introjected norms, finishing with integrated norms.

Deterrence

Deterrence is defined as the threat of sanctions established to obtain compliance with the law (Wenzel & Jobling, 2006). Deterrence theory establishes that the involvement in illegal activities is determined by the likelihood that a criminal is detected or by the certainty to receive sanctions by his/her infractions, as well as by the anticipated magnitude of those sanctions (Marlowe, Festinger, Foltz, Lee, & Patapis, 2005). This theory states that an individual balances the utility of being involved in illegal behavior, assessing the gains and contrasting them against the certainty of being detected and punished, and also against the severity of the sanctions. This theory predicts that if punishment is sufficiently immediate, certain, and severe, then the antisocial conduct will change in a predictable way (Barratt, Chanteloup, Lenton, & Marsh, 2005). In addition, the theory indicates that criminal activity is evaluated assessing its costs and benefits. If the criminal activity does not compensate its risks (i.e., being detected and being severely sanctioned); that is, if the costs are higher than the benefits, this will inhibit involvement in these activities. On the contrary, if the benefits are higher, it is more likely that the potential delinquents become implicated in criminal actions (Wilson, 2004).

Pogarsky, Kim, & Paternoster (2005) suggest that deterrence can be considered as a two-stage process. In the first, the actor forms her/his perception about the risks and consequences of committing crimes; several perceptions about the certainty, the immediateness and severity of the potential sanctions are elaborated, based on the information received. In the second stage, the threat of the sanction prevents the commission of the crime from occurring. These authors argue that the process is not static but modifiable depending on the experiences of individuals. The threat of the sanction is what would actually modify the perception.

Deterrence can inhibit crime by means of three different processes (Wenzel, 2004b). The first is essentially by deterrence itself, that is, by the prospect of punishment in relation to personal or material costs, which would move the delinquent away from potential commissions of criminal acts. The second is by means of normative evaluation, wherein the sanction would increase the perception of criminal acts as morally bad. The third is by a social mediated process in which the sanctions become expensive for the individuals by the reaction of people surrounding them in their social environment. Individuals try to obtain material goods and emotional support from people in their surroundings and, if crime generates a negative perception of them, they will not be able to obtain that support.

STUDIES OF COMPLIANCE WITH ENVIRONMENTAL LAW

The conceptualization of environmental transgressions was originally constructed from theory, almost exclusively by criminologists and criminal justice scholars. However, psychological research is interested in this topic because several reasons. Firstly, studies on moral judgment of environmental transgressions allow knowing the factors that people consider important to assign/avoid punishment and/or feelings of guilt associated to these behaviors (Walton, 1985). Secondly, studies on causal explanations of environmental transgression permit determining whether the peculiarities attributed to environmental transgressions by scholars resemble lay-people's perception. Lastly, studies on the impacts of norms on anti-ecological behavior show their social support and the degree in which are consolidated as social, moral and/or personal norms. These studies display the strength or weakness of the link between people and environmental laws (Fritsche, 2002), laws which are mostly of recent creation (Mårald, 2001).

Studies on Moral Judgement of Illegal Anti-Ecological Behavior

Studies on moral judgment of illegal anti-ecological behavior show that law-enforcement officers are influenced by transgression severity, transgressor's previous records and transgressor's willingness to collaborate with authorities. This latter factor is so important that can reduce the impact of transgression severity on the decision of imposing a formal sanction (Hawkins, 1984 a & b). Transgressor's cooperation with authorities is also the most important determinant of the length of a sanction imposed to somebody found responsible for a contamination offence, together with transgression severity and the amount of harm caused (Taylor & Mason, 2002). Taylor and Mason (2002) also showed that the professionals' perception of contamination offences is extreme negative, since around two third of their participants would sentence contamination offenders to prison and almost half of them considered adequate a prison sentence of twenty years. In Spain, both lawyers and lay participants allocate offences of contamination and forest fire in the middle ranges of a severity scale, according to the offence ordering established by the Spanish Penal Code for prison sentences (De la Fuente, García-Cueto, San Luis, García, & de la Fuente, 2002; García-Cueto, García, Fuente, et al., 2003).

Nevertheless, when people compare specific transgressions occurring in their surroundings, they take into account other factors besides severity and/or criminal sentence. Hernández, Martín, Hess, et al. (2005) and Martín, Hernández & Suárez (2006) showed that participants evaluate transgressions of environmental law in relation to three dimensions. These dimensions are related to whether (illegal) construction activities are involved, whether transgressions imply a primary versus secondary environmental impact, and the extent in which these misbehaviors generate economical benefits. Martín, Hess, & Salazar (2005) verified the presence of a discriminant function, defined by the two first dimensions described above, which show how people oppose illegal constructions to transgressions against natural environment and contamination. Economical benefits defined a second discriminant function that situated contamination and transgressions against natural environment in the two ends of the continuum. Salazar, Hernández, Martín, & Hess (2006) and Martín, Hernández, Hess, et al., (2008) also found that scores in justification, indignation and severity of the consequences are the best predictors of punishment for environmental transgressions and, as illegal constructions received lower rates in all these scales, punishment assigned to illegal constructors were always comparatively lower than that assigned to contaminators and to those that harmed protected flora, fauna or natural preserves.

Studies Explaining why People Break Environmental Laws

Studies aimed at explaining why people break environmental laws can be grouped in two categories: those based on the use of neutralization techniques and those based on justifications given in conflictive interactions. Sykes and Matza's (1957) Neutralization Theory states that the guilt transgressors feel for breaking the law disappears using neutralization techniques that modify the way they perceive their behavior. Research developed from this perspective in the context of illegal anti-ecological behavior has focused in describing the neutralization techniques used by environmental transgressors and by law enforcement personnel.

Situ (1998) reported that environmental transgressors believe that their behavior is not illegal although the law states the opposite. They denied both having done any harm and the existence of any victim. Professionals in charge for arresting those transgressors neither seemed to understand why their behavior was illegal and why it had to be persecuted. The author stresses the fact that prosecutors are reluctant to fill charges against environmental offenders because of the difficulties to establish criminal intent and to prove that transgressions have serious consequences. Eliason and Dodder (1999) found that poachers believe that poaching is wrong but, simultaneously, they consider themselves general-law-abiding citizens. To justify their behavior they claimed that transgression has been a mistake or an accident; that they do not deserve sanction for breaking the law just "this time;" that they have hunted to get meat to feed their families and not to get a trophy; and that game wardens who has reported them were corrupt, the true guilty for the incident and the responsible for the whole situation.

The use of neutralization techniques by environmental-law enforcement officers also has been studied by Du Rées (2001) in Sweden. She asked these professionals why agencies in charge of environmental law enforcement do not report all companies being suspicious of committing environmental offences. Most participants justified these cases of impunity by claiming the lack of confidence in the capacity of the legal system to satisfactory dealing with environmental transgressions. They argued that transgressions do not cause a direct harm, and that the consequences were not serious. They also stated the need of safeguarding their relationship with these companies and/or with the local authorities.

The second set of studies explaining why people break environmental laws has been carried out within the framework of conflictive situations in which a norm has been broken and the transgressors are asked for the reasons of their behavior. According to previous studies on breaking non-environmental norms, transgressors use explanations during the social interaction to reduce conflict, with self-presentational purposes and as a way to avoid punishment (Fritsche, 2002). There are two studies on explanations given by transgressors to justify their illegal anti-ecological behavior to avoid punishment. In the first study, Martín, Salazar, Hess et al. (2008) studied the explanations included in the statements that environmental transgressors had presented in four public administrations during the process aimed at punishing them for breaking an environmental law in a highly environmentally-protected territory. Their results showed that the explanations mostly used by transgressors were denying the norms, reparation measures, redefining the fact, denying intention/responsibility and claiming emotional/pro-social objectives. Although there were some differences in the frequency in which each type of explanations were used, these data replicate previous findings showing that environmental transgressors consider that what they have done is not wrong. It is true that transgressors always justify their behavior to avoid sanctions, but in this case they specifically claim that there are no law regulating their behavior, that existing laws cannot be applied to their behavior, that there are mistakes in the conduction of the files or in the presentation of the case, that there are incongruent regulations and, over all, that a social norm exists that contradicts the legal norm. Indeed, the most used expression is "everybody does it" and that might be suggesting that environmental laws fail in having enough social legitimacy.

In a later study, Martín, Salazar, & Ruiz (2008) used sequential analysis (Bakeman & Quera, 1995) to conclude that when environmental transgressors start their argumentation with an explanation of a specific category (acceptance, justification, excuses and denial) they continue with the same type of explanation during their whole line of reasoning. Thus, they use argument streams that are more defensive or more conciliatory. This happens always, except in relation to the category "appealing to emotional/prosocial objectives," which function as a referentialization, as defined by Fristche (2002). When a referentialization is used, the transgressor provides information that does not appear in authorities' charges and that allows her/his to reduce her/his guilt refereeing to other norms, persons or behaviors. For example, to avoid the sanction for an illegal construction, a man stated that he built the house so that his daughter has her own home. In saying this, this person tried to redirect authorities' attention from his performing an illegal behavior to his daughter getting her own home. By using this explanation, he simultaneously has changed the person, the behavior and the norm.

A third study on explanations for environmental transgressions have been carried out by Martín, Salazar, Hess, & Hernández (2005), with the purpose of approaching naive theories of illegal anti-ecological behavior. In this case, the authors assessed the explanations that people from the general population preferred, in providing reasons for several environmental transgressions occurring in their close settings. Their results showed that the highest level of evil and unconcern for the environment were attributed to a city council that allows sewage to drain into the sea and to a hunter that shot a bird classified as member of a protected species. The draining of sewage, the unauthorized removal of volcanic gravel used for construction, and the noise caused by playing music in a bar were considered the episodes mostly producing economic benefits. Performing actions to compensate environmental harm, the ignorance of prohibitions, and believing that transgression does not cause harm to anybody, were used in a larger extent to explain illegal camping and the inadequate substitutions of windows in a historical downtown. This study also shows that, although differences resulted in the preferred explanations depending on the episode being evaluated, the highest amount of punishment was assigned when participants believed that transgressors behave in this way because they were "bad persons," because they did not care for the environment, and because they were looking for economic benefits. On the contrary, behaviors oriented to compensate environmental harm, ignoring the prohibition and the belief that the transgression does not harm anybody attenuated the punishment being assigned.

Summing up the results of the studies described in this section, it seems that people consider that illegal anti-ecological behavior is wrong in general terms and exhibits the evil of who behave in this way, but also that there are circumstances that may lead individuals, who are not really wicked, to behave illegally in environmental terms.

Studies on the Impacts of Norms on Anti-Ecological Behavior

The third set of studies on environmental transgressions is relevant in modeling compliance with environmental law, although illegality was not of interest for the authors. It includes research by Cialdini et al., and Corral-Verdugo and collaborators. Studies led by Cialdini (Cialdini, Reno, & Kallgren, 1990; Cialdini, Demaine, Sagarin et al., 2006) focus on the effects of injunctive social norms and descriptive social norms on anti-ecological behavior. Injunctive social norms involve perceptions of which behaviors are typically approved or disapproved, and are motivated by promises of reward or punishment. In turn, descriptive social norms involve perceptions of which behaviors are typically performed, and are motivated by the fact that they provide evidence of what is effective and adaptive: what most people do. The activation of either type of norm generates different behaviors (Reno, Cialdini, & Kallgren, 1993).

This research team found that making subjects focused on the frequency of an environmental transgression increases the occurrence of this behavior. In their classical study on littering, Cialdini, Reno, & Kallgren (1990) showed that people littered more onto a dirty rather than onto a clean floor. The highest level of undesirable behavior was produced when a confederate threw a paper on a dirty floor and the lowest level when the confederate dirtied a clean floor. Along the same lines, Corral-Verdugo, Frías-Armenta, Pérez, Orduña, & Espinoza (2002) found that perceiving that others (neighbors, the government, etc.) are water wasters decreases the motivation for environmental conservation and increases water consumption. Cialdini et al. (2006) reported that the activation of injunctive norms ("Please, do not remove...") was more effective in preventing the anti-ecological behavior of taking petrified wood from the Petrified Forest National Park in Arizona than activating descriptive norms ("Many past visitors have removed..."). It seems that the activation of descriptive norms increases the occurrence of both anti-ecological and pro-environmental behavior like recycling (Cialdini, 2003). These studies also show that other variables such as previous attitudes towards specific behavior, information and even sense of humor included in a message, influence pro-environmental behavior simultaneously with descriptive norms.

Corral-Verdugo and Frías-Amenta (2006) also addressed the role of personal normative beliefs in water conservation behavior. They showed that these beliefs have a positive effect on such specific behavior and that they co-vary positively with beliefs in the efficacy of environmental laws related to water conservation. However, self-reported anti-social behavior had a negative effect, and beliefs in the inefficacy of water conservation laws produced no effect.

Cialdini et al.'s research is focused on littering and the removal of petrified woods from a national park, whereas Corral-Verdugo et al. were interested in water wastage. Differences in the specific illegal anti-ecological behavior under study are relevant because the size of the impact of the explanatory variables on compliance may be different when various types of law are involved. In the study by Elffers, Van der Heijden, and Hazemans (2003) the severity of the sanction and the perceived likelihood of being sanctioned predicted self-reported compliance with the law on individual rent subsidy; yet this effect was not found with the law on agricultural chemicals. May (2005) also found these variables useful in relation to normative behavior toward the environment of marine facilities workers but not in relation to normative conduct of farmers or home builders.

More recently Martín, Hernández, & Ruiz (2007) studied the impact of deterrence variables and social norms on personal norms in breaches of several environmental laws, and Frías-Armenta, Martín, & Corral-Verdugo (in press) and Martín, Frías-Armenta, and Hernández (2009) assessed the impact of these variables on illegal anti-ecological behavior, using structural analysis. Lastly, Hernández, Martín, Ruiz, and Hidalgo (2009) also conducted a study focusing on the role of place identity in which step-way analysis were used to disclose the links between norms, environmental concern and anti-ecological behavior.

In summary, results from diverse studies show that the process of compliance with environmental law resembles the process of compliance with other laws (tax, property, etc.) in many ways, to the extent that the variables involved and some of the relationships between them are alike. These processes are characterized by the role of personal norms as the main antecedent of behavior. Deterrence variables also influence personal norms but only by indirectly affecting social norms. However, the legal and psychosocial peculiarities of illegal anti-ecological behavior are reflected in Hernández et al.'s (2009) and Martín et al.'s (2009) studies. Hernández et al. (2009) report that the scores in Thompson and Barton (1994)'s scale influenced illegal anti-ecological behavior through personal norm, whereas Martín et al. (2009) found the same results for sustainability attitudes such as ecocentrism and future orientation.

Other studies indicate that individuals who conserve the physical environment are also concerned about the social context (Corral-Verdugo, Tapia, Frías-Armenta, Fraijo, & González, in press). Anti-environmental behavior is also conceived as a kind of anti-social behavior. Antisocial and anti-environmental behavior related positively to risk seeking and lack of self-control; however, no relationship was found between these variables and pro-ecological actions (Corral-Verdugo, Tapia, Frías-Armenta, & Fraijo, 2006).

These antecedents and considerations motivated the conduction of an empirical study on the influence of social and personal norms on illegal anti-ecological behavior. Deterrence, legitimacy, antisocial behavior and emotional control were also investigated, as potential determinants of both norms and behavior. Such study is presented in the following sections.

METHOD

Participants

The sample was selected in a harbor city (Guaymas, population = 200,000), close to a natural protected area in northwestern Mexico (Sonora). Two hundred and ninety seven individuals answered to a questionnaire; 156 were females and 132 were males (9 cases resulted missing values regarding gender). Age ranged between 13 and 79 (M=25, SD=11) years.

Instruments

A questionnaire previously developed to measure illegal environmental behavior, deterrence, social norm, personal norm, legitimacy, antisocial behavior and emotional control was used. All items, excepting those related to illegal anti-ecological behavior, were developed by Martín, Hernández, and Ruiz (2007), in Spain, who in turn based their formulation mainly on Cialdini, Reno, and Kallgren (1990), Tyler (2006a&b) and Wenzel (2004a and b). Conducts referred by the questionnaire items were modified to adapt to Mexican laws. Participants responded, in a 0 to 10 scale, how often they threw toxic substances into the sea, into the natural protected area, and into a lot at the urban area; also how often they allowed sewage water spills get into the sea, washed their cars wasting water, threw garbage into the natural protected area, played music too loud so that it can be heard from the street, sold protected species, killed protected animals, destroyed endangered plants, bought or consumed marine species in close season, fished endangered marine species, and destroyed estuaries. Two types of questions were elaborated to assess these illegal environmental behaviors; one concerned present, actual behavior and the other, the likelihood of engaging in those behaviors. Perceived illegality and perceived wrongfulness of behaviors were assessed to indicate personal norm. Social norm, in turn, was assessed as indicated by the extent the majority of people and the five persons closest-to-respondents disapproved the considered illegal behaviors. Deterrence was measured by considering the severity of sanction, the likelihood of being caught and the likelihood of sanction. In addition, participants self-reported their engaging in antisocial behaviors such as fighting with others, endangering public places, stealing, etc., using the scale by Grasmick, Title, Bursick, and Arneklev (1993). Emotional volatility was assessed utilizing eight items from Raffaelli and Crockett's (2003) self-control scale. Both Grasmick et al. (1993), and Raffaelli and Crockett (2003) reported high internal consistence from these instruments.

Procedure

Participants were interviewed in their houses by previously trained psychology students, after obtaining their informed consent to participate. The interview lasted about 25 minutes.

Data Analysis

Univariate statistics were obtained as well as Cronbach's alphas to indicate internal consistency. Indexes (i.e., the average of responses to an entire set of items) were computed to represent the variables investigated. These indexes were used to create a structural equation model. Four latent variables were specified and tested: deterrence, personal norm, social norm, and illegal ecological behavior. The deterrence factor included the indexes of severity of sanction, likelihood of being caught and sanctioned. Personal norm was constructed from the indexes of perceived illegality and moral judgment; while social norm was indicated by "the majority of people" and "five closest people" disapproval indexes. Finally, the indexes of present and likely illegal behavior formed the illegal environmental behavior factor. The specified hypothetical model considered the direct and indirect effects of moral and social norm, deterrence, emotional volatility and antisocial behavior on illegal anti-ecological behavior. In addition, an indirect effect of legitimacy on such behavior through deterrence and social norm was tested. In order to estimate the pertinence of this hypothesized model, goodness of fit indicators were considered. These indicators show whether the specified relations in the model are supported by the data, and included the statistical indicator χ^2, expecting a low value, and a non-significant p value ($p > .05$) associated to this indicator. Practical indicators were also considered, including the Non-Normed Fit Index (*NNFI*) and the Comparative Fit Index (*CFI*); which should produce a value higher than .90 (Bentler, 2006). To measure the reasonable error of approximation in terms of goodness of fit, the index root mean squared error (RMSEA) was obtained, requiring a <.08 value (Browne & Cudeck, 1993).

RESULTS

Table 1 shows the alphas produced by the used scales. All of them exhibit high internal consistency. In turn, figure 1 shows the results of the tested structural model. All the proposed factors seem to evidence convergent construct validity, manifested by the high and significant values of their factor loadings. Personal norm generated a negative effect (structural coefficient = -.41) on illegal anti-ecological behavior, while antisocial behavior positively influenced (structural coefficient = .37) such an illegal behavior. The expected effect of social norm, deterrence and emotional volatility on anti-ecological actions was not demonstrated, since their structural coefficients were not significant ($p<.05$). However, social norm affected positively personal norm (structural coefficient = .51), thus exhibiting an indirect effect on illegal ecological behavior through personal norm. Deterrence influenced positively both social norm (structural coefficient = .31), and emotional volatility (structural cocfficient = .25). Emotional volatility negatively correlated with personal norm (structural coefficient = -.18) and positively with antisocial behavior (structural coefficient = .40). Legitimacy presented a positive effect on social norm (structural coefficient = .25), and on deterrence (structural coefficient = .25).

Table 1. Cronbach's alphas from the used scales

Scale	ALFA
Present behavior	.90
Future behavior	.94
Severity of sanction	.96
Likelihood of sanction	.97
Likelihood of being cough	.96
Perceived illegality	.96
Perceived wrongfulness	.94
The majority of people disapproval	.97
Five nearest people disapproval	.98
Antisocial behavior	.86
Emotional volatility	.87
Legitimacy of authorities	.98

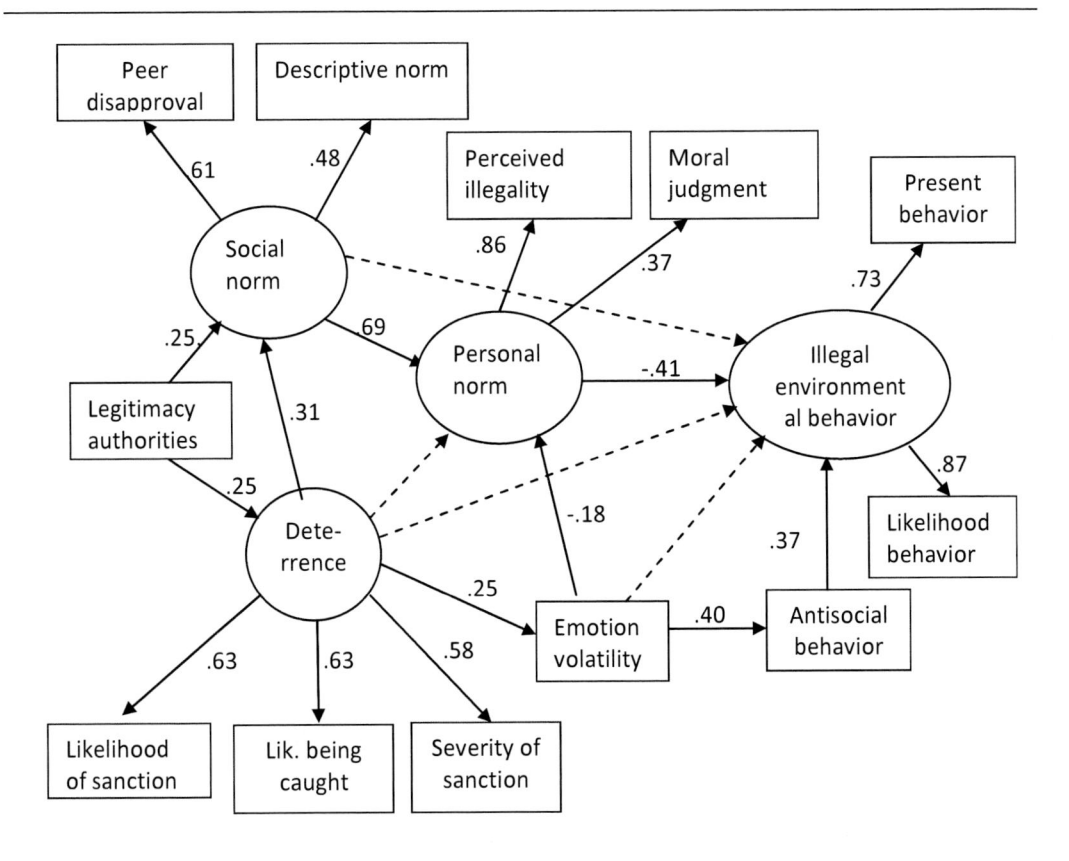

Figure 1. Structural Model of Compliance with ecological law. All factor loadings and structural coefficients are significant at $p < .05$, except those indicated by dotted arrows. Goodness of fit: N=293 $\chi^2 = 80.88$ (g.l.=43), $p < .001$; NNFI = .90, CFI = .91, RMSEA = .05. Target variable $R^2 = .29$.

The practical goodness of fit indicators met the required criterion values, evidencing the adequacy of the tested model. Although X^2 was significant ($\chi^2(43) = 80.68$; $p < .000$), probably because of the large number of participants in the study, the practical indexes demonstrated that the model adjusted to the data (*NNFI* =.90, *CFI* = .91, *RMSEA* = .05) (Bentler, 2006).

CONCLUSION

Results from our model replicated findings from previous related studies. As in those cases, personal norm was the direct predictor of illegal anti-ecological behavior. The negative effect of personal norm on such behavior implies that the higher the perceived illegality of anti-ecological behavior and the higher the corresponding moral judgment, the lower the likelihood of engaging in illegal anti-ecological behavior. This model's results also showed the importance of the internalization of social norms and the effect of emotional control on personal norm. Since social norm exerts its effects through personal norm, it is necessary to incorporate social pressure into the internal psychological structure of individuals in order to prevent illegal ecological behavior from happening. Thøgersen (2006) argues that the external pressure should be replaced by an internal pressure to modify behavior, and our data seem to support his statement. Social disapproval is important but it has to be integrated into individuals' morality in order to promote pro-ecological behavior. As in the case of Gaspar de Carvalho et al study (see their chapter in this volume), contextual factors exert their influence through psychological processes. This means that the study of the way settings and situations affect environmental behavior should necessarily incorporate intra-personal subjective variables.

In our study, deterrence had no direct effect on illegal anti-ecological behavior; meaning that solely threatening potential delinquents with punishment is insufficient to controlling their anti-ecological behavior. Self Determination Theory (SDT) assumes that autonomous choices are more likely to maintain an expected (pro-social) behavior (Moller, Ryan, & Deci, 2006) than does deterrence. Thus, an indirect effect of deterrence on behavior is expected, in the best of the cases. This indirect effect has been tested and demonstrated in previous studies (Frias-Armenta, Martín, & Corral-Verdugo, in press; Martín, Frías-Armenta, & Hernández, 2009). In the study presented in this chapter, deterrence produced a positive effect on social norm, indicating that accepting the collective norm as appropriate also implies the acceptance of penalties from breaking legal rules. Thus, deterrence could be helpful in defining what the socially incorrect is and in accepting the group pressure on disapproving what is wrong (i.e., being punished because wrongdoing, in this case). According to our data, it seems that sanction itself does not deter individual from acting antisocially or anti-ecologically; it is the group disapproval due to the received sanction what affects behavior. Previous studies had produced similar results. Pogarsky, Kim, & Paternoster (2005) concluded that it is necessary that the individual perceives the risk of group's disapproval due to the received sanction. This also seems to indicate that the social cost is more important than the legal sanction. Such explanation would support psycho-evolutionary theories stating that reputation is a key factor in explaining pro-ecological tendencies (se Hill et al chapter, this volume).

Antisocial behavior had a direct effect on illegal anti-ecological behavior, which probably implies that antisocial individuals share some psychological traits with individual who break ecological laws. This seems logical, at first glance; illegal ecological behavior is a peculiar form of anti-sociality, consisting of egoistic acts that negatively affect others' integrity, just as antisocial actions do (Corral-Verdugo & Frías-Armenta, 2006). Although anti-social behaviors and anti-ecological actions are differentiable from each other (see Corral-Verdugo et al, 2006, for a detailed explanation) there seem to be high covariation between these two instances of negative behavior.

Legitimacy positively covaried with deterrence, indicating that individuals should recognize their authorities' legal right to act, in order to consider the probability of a sanction from occurring. If a person believes that a sanction cannot be administered, it is also more likely that she or he disbelieves in their authorities' legitimacy. These authorities cannot exercise their influence or deter to potential criminals if they are not perceived as just or legitimate. In our model, legitimacy also positively correlated with social norm, implying that authorities should exhibit dependability to promote behavioral change among citizens. If the authorities are perceived as a just group they can influence the citizens and groups they govern.

Emotional volatility had no a direct effect on illegal ecological behavior, but it affected personal norm; this indicates that emotional control is necessary in integrating norms that lead to pro-ecological behavior. Our finding seems also to imply that encouraging moral judgment is a good way to promote the emotional stability of individuals. Cacioppo and Gardner (1999) argue that it is possible to "cultivate" emotional dispositions to control emotional responses.

Our model explained 29% of illegal anti-ecological behavior's variance. That means that almost one third of the variance is accounted for by personal and social norms, deterrence, legitimacy, emotion and antisocial behavior (although only personal norm and antisocial behavior had a significantly direct effect on the target variable). The original contribution of this model is its showing the significant effect of emotional stability on personal norm, an effect that should be replicated in prospective studies. It is also necessary to include additional variables in this model in order to increase its explanatory power on anti-ecological behavior.

In Social Control Theory, deterrence is the base of compliance with the law. However, our study, and others, demonstrate that the administration of sanctions or the threat of receiving a punishment are not sufficient enough for preventing illegal or antisocial behaviors from happening. Government and societies must recognize these facts and seek alternative forms of promoting pro-social and pro-ecological behaviors. Environmental Psychology, joined by Psychology & Law, and other social-science approaches surely will contribute in elucidating what those alternative forms are.

REFERENCES

Abrams, D. & Hogg, M. A. (1990). Social identification, self-categorization and social influence. *European Review of Social Psychology, 1,* 195-228.

Ajzen, I. (1985). From intentions to actions: A theory of planned behavior. In J. Kuhl & J. Beckman (Eds), *Action-control from cognition to behavior* (pp. 11-39). New York: Springer.

Ajzen, I. & Fishbein, M. (1980). *Understanding attitudes and predicting social behavior.* Eglewood_Cliffs, NJ: Prentice Hall.

Azjen, I. & Madden, T. (1986). Prediction of goal-directed behavior: Attitudes, intentions and perceived behavioral control. *Journal of experimental Social Psychology, 22,* 453-474.

Álvarez, M. (1995). *Introducción al Derecho.* México, D.F.: McGraw-Hill.

Bakeman, R., & Quera, V. (1995). *Analyzing interaction: Sequential analysis with SDIS and GSEQ.* New York: Cambridge University Press.

Barratt, M. J., Chanteloup, F., Lenton, S., & Marsh, A. (2005). Cannabis law reform in western Australia: An opportunity to test theories of marginal deterrence and legitimacy. *Drug and Alcohol Review, 24,* 321-330.

Bentler, P.M. (2006). *EQS, Structural Equations Program Manual.* Encino, CA: Multivariate Statistical Software, Inc.

Blanchette, I. (2006). The effect of emotion in interpretation and logic in a conditional task. *Memory & Cognition, 34,* 1112-1125.

Bridgeman, J. (2004). Public perception towards water recycling in California. *Journal of Water and Environment (CIWEM), 18,* 150-154.

Browne, M. W. & Cudeck, R. (1993). Alternative ways of assessing model fit. In K. A. Bollen & J. S. Long (Eds.), *Testing structural equation models* (pp. 136-162). Thousand Oaks, CA: Sage.

Cacioppo, J. T. & Gardner, W. L. (1999). Emotion. *Annual Review of Psychology, 50,* 191-214.

Chatzisarantis, N. L. D. & Biddle, S. J. H. (1998). Functional significance of psychological variables that are included in the Theory of Planned Behavior: A self-determination theory approach to the study of attitudes, subjective norms, perceptions of control and intentions. *European Journal of Social Psychology, 28,* 303-322.

Cialdini, R.B. (2003). Crafting normative messages to protect the environment. *Current Directions in Psychological Science, 12,* 105-109.

Cialdini, R.B., Demaine, L.J., Sagarin, B.J., Barrett, D.W., Rhoads, K., & Winter, P.L. (2006). Managing social norms for persuasive impact. *Social Influence, 1,* 3-15.

Cialdini, R.B., Reno, R.R., & Kallgren, C.A (1990). A focus theory of normative conduct: Recycling the concept of norms to reduce littering in public places. *Journal of Personality and Social Psychology, 58,* 1015-1026.

Corral-Verdugo, V. (2001). Comportamiento pro-ambiental. Santa Cruz de Tenerife España: Editorial RESMA.

Corral-Verdugo, V., & Frías-Armenta, M., (2006). Personal normative beliefs, antisocial behavior and residential water conservation. *Environment & Behavior, 38,* 407-421.

Corral-Verdugo, V., Frías-Armenta, M. Fraijo, B., & Tapia, C. (2006). Rasgos de la conducta antisocial como correlatos del actuar anti y proambiental. *Medio ambiente y comportamiento humano, 7,* 89-103.

Corral-Verdugo, V. Frías-Armenta, M., Pérez, F., Orduña, V., & Espinoza, N. (2002). Residential water consumption, motivation for conserving water, and the continuing tragedy of commons. *Environment Management, 30,* 527-535.

Corral-Verdugo, V., Tapia, C., Frías, M., Fraijo, B., & González; D., (in press). Orientación a la Sostenibilidad como base para el Comportamiento Pro-Social y Pro-Ecológico. *Medio Ambiente y Comportamiento Humano.*

Chriss, J. (2007). Social Control: An Introduction. Maiden, MA. USA: Polity Press.

Dawkins, R. (1976). *The Selfish Gene.* Oxford: Oxford University Press.

De la Fuente, E., García-Cueto, E., San Luis, C., García, J., & de la Fuente, L. (2002). Escalamiento subjetivo de conductas delictivas. *Metodología de las Ciencias del Comportamiento, 4,* 67-76.

Deci, E. & Ryan, R. (1985). *Intrinsic motivation and self-determination in human behavior.* London: Plenum.

DuRées, H. (2001). Can criminal law protect the environment? *Journal of Scandinavian Studies in Criminology and Crime prevention, 2,* 109-126.

Elffers, H., van der Heijden, P., & Hezemans, M. (2003). Explaining regulatory non-compliance: A survey study of rule transgression for two Dutch instrumental laws, applying the randomized response method. *Journal of Quantitative Criminology, 19,* 409-439.

Eliason, S.L., & Dodder, R.A. (1999). Techniques of neutralization used by deer poachers in the western United States: A research note. *Deviant Behavior, 20,* 233-252.

Fishbein, M. & Ajzen, I. (1975). *Belief, attitude, intention and behavior: An introduction to theory and research.* Reading, MA: Addison-Wesley.

Frías-Armenta, M. Martín, A.M., & Corral-Verdugo, V. (In press). Análisis de factores que influyen en el desarrollo de normas ambientales y en la conducta anti-ecológica. *Revista Interamericana de Psicología.*

Fritsche, I. (2002). Account strategies for the violation of social norms: Integration and extension of sociological and social psychological typologies. *Journal for the Theory of Social Behavior, 32,* 21-83.

García-Cueto, E., García, J., Fuente, L., Borges, A., Sánchez-Bruno, A., & San Luis, C. (2003). Escalamiento subjetivo de conductas delictivas en legos y expertos. *Psicothema, 15,* 638-642.

García Máynez, E. (2000). *Introducción al Estudio de Derecho.* México, D.F.: Editorial Porrúa.

Gottfredson, M. R. & Hirschi. T. (1990). *A General Theory of Crime.* Stanford, CA: Stanford University Press.

Grasmick, H. G. & Bursik, R. J., Jr. (1990). Conscience, significant others, and rational choice: Extending to deterrence model. *Law and Society Review, 24,* 837-861.

Grasmick, H., Title, C., Bursick., & Arneklev, B. (1993). Testing the core empirical implication of Gottfredson and Hirschi's General Theory of Crime. *Journal of Research in Crime and Delinquency, 30,* 5-29.

Haslam, S. A. (2004). *Psychology in the Organizations: The Social Identity Approach* (2nd ed.). London: Sage.

Hawkins, K. (1984a). Creating cases in a regulatory agency. *Urban Life, 12,* 371-395.

Hawkins, K. (1984b). *Environment and enforcement: Regulation and the social definition of pollution.* New York: Oxford University Press.

Hernández, B., Martín, A., Hess, S., Martínez-Torvisco, J., Suárez, E., Salazar, M., Ruiz, C. & Ramírez, G. (2005). Análisis multidimensional de la percepción del delito ecológico. *Medio Ambiente y Comportamiento Humano, 6,* 51-70.

Hernández, B., Martín, A., Ruiz, C., & Hidalgo, M.C. (2009). *The role of place identity and place attachment in breaking environmental protection laws.* Manuscript submitted for publication.

Hine, D.W., Marks, A.D.G., Nachriener, M., Gifford, R., & Heath, Y. (2007). Keeping the home fires burning: The affect heuristic and wood smoke pollution. *Journal of Environmental Psychology, 27,* 26-32.

Hunecke, M., Blöbaum, A., Matthies, E., & Höger, R. (2001). Responsibility and environment. Ecological norm orientation and external factors in the domain of travel mode choice behavior. *Environment & Behavior, 33,* 830-852.

Jackson, T. (2008). The Challenge of sustainable lifestyles. In L. Starke, (Ed.), *State of the World.* New York, W. W. Norton & Company.

Kaiser, F., & Shimoda, T. (1999). Responsibility as a predictor of ecological behaviour. *Journal of Environmental Psychology, 19,* 243-253.

Korsell, L.E. (2001). Big stick, little stick: Strategies for controlling and combating environmental crime. *Journal of Scandinavian Studies in Criminology and Crime prevention, 2,* 127-148.

Lee-Chai, A. Y. & Bargh, J. A. (2001). *The use and Abuse of Power: Multiple perspectives on causes of corruption.* Philadelphia, PA: Psychology Press.

Mårald, E. (2001). The BT Kemi scandal and the establishment of the environmental crime concept. *Journal of Scandinavian Studies in Criminology and Crime prevention, 2,* 149-170.

Marlowe, D. B., Festinger, D. S., Foltz, C., Lee, P. A., & Patapis, N. S. (2005). Perceived deterrence and outcomes in drug court. *Behavioral Science and the Law, 23,* 183-198.

Martin, A.M., Frías-Armenta, M., & Hernández, B. (2009). *Why ordinary people comply with environmental laws: A structural model on normative and attitudinal determinants of illegal anti-ecological behavior.* Manuscript submitted for publication.

Martín, A.M., Hernández, B., Hess, S., Suárez, E., Salazar, M.E, & Ruiz, C. (2008). Valoración social y asignación de castigo en transgresiones a las leyes de protección del medio ambiente. *Psicothema, 20*, 90-96.

Martín, A.M, Hernández, B., & Ruiz, C. (2007). Variables predictoras de la norma personal en transgresiones de las leyes medioambientales. *Medio ambiente y comportamiento humano, 18*, 137-157.

Martín, A. M., Hernández, B., & Suárez, E. (2006). Elementos críticos en la valoración social de las transgresiones medioambientales cotidianas. In J. A. Corraliza, J. Berenguer & R. Martín (Comps.), *Medio ambiente, bienestar humano y responsabilidad ecológica* (pp. 435-442). Tenerife, Spain: Resma.

Martín, A.M., Hess, S., & Salazar, M.E. (2005, September). *Criterios espontáneos en la categorización del delito ecológico.* Paper presented at the IX Congreso Nacional de Psicología Social, La Coruña (Spain).

Martín, A.M., Salazar, M.E., Hess, S., & Hernández, B. (2005, October). *Las explicaciones espontáneas sobre el delito ecológico.* Paper presented at the Convención Internacional de Psicología y Ciencias Sociales, Havanna, Cuba.

Martín, A. Salazar, M.E., Hess, S., Ruiz, C., Kaplan, M.F., Hernández, B., & Suárez E. (2008). Individual breaches of environmental laws in cases from public administration files. *Deviant Behavior, 29,* 611-639.

Martín, A.M., Salazar, M.E., & Ruiz, C. (2008). The sequential analysis of transgressors' accounts of breaking environmental laws. *The Spanish Journal of Psychology, 11*, 115-124.

May, P. (2005). Compliance motivations: Perspectives of farmers, homebuilders and marine facilities. *Law and Policy, 27*, 317-347.

Moller, A. C., Ryan, R. M., & Deci, E. L. (2006). Self-determination theory and public policy: Improving the quality of consumer decisions without using coercion. *American Marketing Association, 25*, 104-116.

Muraven, M., Pogarsky, G. Shmueli, D. (2006). Self-control depletion and the General Theory of Crime. *Journal of Quantitative Criminology, 22*, 263–277.

Oakes, P. J., Haslam, S.A. & Turner, J.C. (1994). *Stereotyping and Social Reality.* Oxford: Blackwell.

Parejo-Alfonso, L. (2008). *Código de Medio Ambiente.* Cizur Menor (Spain): Aranzadi.

Pelletier, L. G. (2002). Motivation toward the environment. In E. L. Deci and R. M. Ryan (Eds), *Handbook of self-Determination Research,* (pp. 205-232). Rochester, NY: University Rochester Press.

Pogarsky, G., Kim, K., & Paternóster. R. (2005). Perceptual change in the national youth survey: Lessons for deterrence theory and offender decision-making. *Justice Quarterly, 22*, 1-30.

Pooley, J.A. & O'Connor, M. (2000). Environmental education and attitudes. Emotions and beliefs are what is needed. *Environment & Behavior, 32*, 711-723.

Posner, E. A. (2001). Law and Emotions. *Georgetown Law Journal, 89*, 1977-1993.

Rafaelli, M. & Crockett, L. (2003). Sexual risk taking in adolescence: The role of self regulation and attraction to risk. *Developmental Psychology, 39*, 1036-1046.

Raven, B. H. (2001). Power/interaction and interpersonal influence. Experimental investigations and case studies. In A. Y. Lee-Chai & J. A. Bargh (Eds.), *The use and abuse of power: Multiple perspectives on causes of corruption.* (pp. 217-240). Philadelphia, PA: Psychology Press.

Reno, R.R., Cialdini, R.B., & Kallgren, C.A (1993). The transituational influence of social norms. *Journal of Personality and Social Psychology, 64*, 104-112.

Salazar, M.E., Hernández, B., Martín, A.M., & Hess, S. (2006). Predictores de la asignación de castigo en transgresiones de las leyes medioambientales. *Medio Ambiente y Comportamiento Humano, 7*, 103-120.

Santiago-Nino, C. (1987). *Introducción al Análisis del Derecho*. Barcelona, Spain: Editorial Ariel.

Schultz, P.W. (2002). Knowledge, information, and household recycling: Examining the knowledge-deficit model of behavior change. In T Dietz y P. Stern (Eds.), *New Tools for Environmental Protection: Education, Information, and Voluntary Measures* (pp. pp. 67-82). Washington, DC: National Academic Press.

Schultz, P. W., & Tyra, A. (2000, April). *A field study of normative beliefs and environmental behavior*. Poster presented at the meeting of the Western Psychological Association, Portland, OR.

Schwartz, S. (1992). Universals in the content and structure of values, Theoretical advances and empirical test in 20 countries. *Advances in Experimental Social Psychology, 10*, 221-279.

Schwartz, S. (2002). ¿Existen aspectos universales en la estructura y contenido de los valores humanos? In M. Ros & V. Gouveia (Eds.), *Psicología Social de los Valores Humanos*. Madrid: Biblioteca Nueva.

Sigala, M., Burgoyne, C., & Webley, P. (1999). Tax communication and social influence: Evidence from a British simple. *Journal of Community and Applied Social Psychology, 9*, 237-241.

Situ, Y. (1998). Public transgression of environmental law: A preliminary study. *Deviant Behavior, 19*, 137-155.

Situ, Y., & Emmons, D. (2000). *Environmental crime*. New York: Sage.

Starke, L. (Ed.) (2008). *State of the World*. New York, W. W. Norton & Company.

Sykes, G.M., & Matza, D. (1957). Techniques of neutralization: A theory of delinquency. *American Sociological Review, 43*, 643-656.

Taylor, D. E. (2000). The rice of the environmental justice paradigm: Injustice framing and the social construction of environmental discourses. *American Behavioral Scientist, 43*, 508-580.

Taylor, R. B. & Mason, R. J. (2002). Responses to prison for environmental criminals. Impact of incident, perpetrator and respondent characteristics. *Environment and Behavior, 34*, 194-215.

Thøgersen, J. (2006). Norms for environmentally responsible behavior: An extended taxonomy. *Journal of Environmental Psychology, 26*, 247-261.

Thompson, S.C.G. & Barton, M. (1994). Ecocentric and anthropocentric attitudes toward the environment. *Journal of Environmental Psychology, 14*, 149-157.

Tompkins, K. (2005). Police, law enforcement and environment. *Current Issues in Criminal Justice, 16*, 294-306.

Trivers, R.L. (1971). The evolution of reciprocal altruism. *Quarterly Review of Biology, 46,* 35-57.

Turner, J. C. (2005). Explaining the nature of power: A three-process theory. *European Journal of Social Psychology, 35,* 1-22.

Tyler, T. R. (1997). The psychology of legitimacy: A relational perspective on voluntary deference to authorities. *Personality and Social Psychology Review, 1,* 323-345.

Tyler, T. R. (2006a). *Why People Obey The Law*. New Jersey: Princeton University Press.

Tyler, T.R. (2006b). Psychological perspectives on legitimacy and legitimation. *Annual Review of Psychology, 57,* 375-400.

Walton, M.D. (1985). Negotiation of Responsibility: Judgments of blameworthiness in a natural setting. *Developmental Psychology, 21,* 725-736.

Watson, M. (2005). Environmental offences: The reality of environmental crime. *Environmental Law Review, 7,* 190-200.

Wenzel, M. (2004a). An analysis of norm processes in tax compliance. *Journal of Economic Psychology, 25,* 213-228.

Wenzel, M. (2004b). The social side of sanctions: Personal and social norms as moderators of deterrence. *Law & Human behavior, 28,* 547-567.

Wenzel, M. & Jobling, P. (2006). Legitimacy of regulatory authorities as a function of inclusive identification and power over ingroups and outgroups. *European Journal of Social Psychology, 36,* 239-258.

Wilson, D. P. (2004). Additional law enforcement as a deterrent to criminal behavior: empirical evidence from the National Hockey League. *Journal of Socio-Economics, 34,* 319-330.

Wilson, J. D. (1986). Re-thinking penalties for corporate environmental offenders: A view of the law reform commission of Canada's sentencing in environmental cases. *McGill Law Journal, 30,* 315-332.

Winter, D. (2003). *Ecological Psychology: Healing the Split between the Planet and self*. New Jersey: Lawrence Erlbaum Associates Publishers.

Part IV:
The Positive Psychological Impacts of Sustainable Behavior

In: Psychological Approaches to Sustainability
Editors: V. Corral-Verdugo et al.

Chapter 20

URBAN SUSTAINABILITY, PSYCHOLOGICAL RESTORATION AND SOUNDSCAPES

Sarah R. Payne[*]
University of Manchester, United Kingdom

ABSTRACT

This chapter argues that the sustainability of environments and societies are not necessarily two opposing things. Sustainable behaviour by the state, such as designing and preserving urban places that aids the environment can also have positive effects on people's physiology, affect and cognition. Sustainable planning decisions need to be based upon social outcomes as well as economic and environmental impacts. Research is presented that argues for the inclusion of urban green spaces into sustainable city planning strategies. This is to ensure urbanites' well-being, via positive psychological impacts, including offering opportunities for restoration. Psychological restoration can be considered as enhancing both the sustainability of the individual and the city by enabling a productive society. Psychological restoration tends to occur in natural environments, thus access to nearby nature is important for sustainable city planning. The experience within urban green spaces is important for achieving restoration, thus the soundscape (what can be heard) may influence the restorative experience and soundscapes are also affected by city planning strategies. Case study research of two urban parks in Sheffield, UK, is presented, identifying the role of perceived soundscapes on urban park visitors' restorative experiences. The parks varied in their sound pressure levels and types of perceived soundscapes. Participants' perceived restoration after time spent in the park significantly varied depending on the type of soundscape they perceived. Providing urban green spaces which are predominated by natural sounds, relate to visitors having a restorative experience. Overall, sustainable city designs should include urban green spaces and the resultant soundscapes should be considered. This will enable positive psychological impacts such as restoration and ensure sustainable urban communities.

---

[*] Correspondence: Sarah.Payne@postgrad.manchester.ac.uk

INTRODUCTION

Sustainability is an important aspect of our future development that relates to our current practices and behaviours. It is vital to understand how we influence the environment and what we can do to achieve sustainable practices. It is not just our behaviour towards the physical world and its ecological preservation that is important though, because a sustainable world involves a supportive and balanced environment, a prosperous economy, and social well-being (World Commission on Environment and Development, 1987). Therefore, in addition to protecting ecology and natural resources, humans' quality of life is also important.

The sustainability of bio-physical environments and societies are not necessarily two opposing things. Individuals' sustainable actions can benefit both the environment and future societies, through the protection of natural resources. Moreover, individuals' sustainable attitudes and behaviours can also be beneficial for themselves, because they are associated with increased feelings of happiness, an aspect of well-being (e.g. Brown & Kasser, 2005; Nisbet, Zelenski & Murphy, 2009). Additionally, by protecting natural environments, individuals can benefit physiologically, affectively and cognitively, because viewing or visiting these natural environments aids attention restoration (Kaplan & Kaplan, 1989), increases overall happiness and decreases negative emotions (van den Berg, Koole & van der Wulp, 2003), and aids recuperation from ill health and stress related disorders such as 'burn out' (Stigsdotter & Grahn, 2004; Ulrich, 1981). Psychological restoration and green spaces therefore enable the 'sustainability' of individuals' lifestyles. This in turn can enhance other aspects of sustainability, such as societies' productivity and economic prosperity (CABE, 2009).

For successful sustainable development, as well as individuals' own behaviours, the collective actions of society, in particular institutes and Governments are also important. Policies and practices need to be in place to support individuals' attitudes and abilities to behave sustainably. Policies and planning decisions are increasingly designed with sustainable development considerations in mind (e.g. 'The London Plan' by the Mayor of London, 2004a) and the importance of sustainability is well recognised at a global level (World Commission on Environment and Development, 1987). These higher level decisions are therefore important for societies' physical and psychological welfare. For example, urban sustainable design can support or conflict peoples own 'sustainability' by encouraging or hindering opportunities for sustainable behaviours and the positive psychological benefits that can arise, including restoration. For people living and working in urban environments (urbanites), the 'natural' environments of urban parks and green spaces can offer the opportunity for psychological restoration. The availability of urban green spaces though, is reliant on the support of state and local authorities and the value placed on green spaces in comparison to other city planning components.

Another, often neglected, consequence of urban planning is the city's soundscape. In a similar manner as landscape definitions, 'soundscape' is the accumulation of all sounds within a location, with an emphasis on the relationship between individuals', or societies', perception, understanding, action and interaction with the sonic environment. A city's design and location of its industries and transportation systems play a key part in a city's sound level; industries and transport networks are used to model sound levels across all European cities, in accordance with the European Commission (European Parliament and Council,

2002). Additionally, within a dense compact city, mixed land usage, could create a loud, noisy city for residents, creating an annoying, rather than restorative, soundscape.

This chapter therefore considers the importance of sustainable behaviour, in the form of urban planning, by the provision of urban parks, their resultant soundscapes, and their potential restorative effects for urbanites. Research relating to sustainable planning and urban parks, psychological restoration, and soundscapes are first discussed in turn, before presenting a case study from Sheffield, United Kingdom, in which the interaction between these three important concepts is innovatively explored.

SUSTAINABLE PLANNING AND URBAN GREEN SPACES

The amount of green space available in a city is dependent upon its deemed importance within any adopted sustainable planning strategies of local or state authorities. Recent guidelines have highlighted green spaces as one of seven elements contributing to making a city sustainable, both environmentally and socially (CABE, 2009). In some places (e.g. Quaggy river, Lewisham, UK, QWAG, 2009), these guidelines have been put into practice by preserving and extending green space around an urban river, so that the area can once again act as a flood plain. This prevents flash floods in the area, while at other times, a useable green space is created where natural sounds are heard (water flowing, wildlife in the reeds). However, not all sustainable planning strategies necessarily encourage the development of urban green spaces.

Compact city planning is one strategy proposed for sustainable development, which encourages high residential densities and mixed land use (Neuman, 2005). The theory is that resources are brought together into a smaller spatial area, so that people and resources have shorter transportation distances, thus less pollution is created, and energy consumption levels are reduced (Jenks, Burton &Williams, 2000). However, the sustainable success of a city, designed with a focus on urban form and density has been debated (Burton, 2003; Churchman, 1999; Jenks *et al.*, 2000; Neuman, 2005). For example, higher density communities (in student dormitories) were rated less positively, had less trust for neighbours and exhibited less helping behaviour than lower density communities (Bickman, Teger, Gabriele *et al.*, 1973). Additionally, compact cities often involve a reduction of green space and differential access, which is dictated by wealth, to the remaining green space (Burton, 2003). A compact city without urban green spaces reduces opportunities for restoration, thus hindering the well-being and satisfaction of the city's inhabitants. A compact city with high density and mixed land use is also likely to increase sound levels.

Without careful consideration the inclusion of green spaces and designs to alter density perceptions, a compact city strategy could have negative consequences on people's well-being and quality of life. Indeed, perceived high density of an area and lack of open space can have a significant negative effect on perceived residential environmental quality (Bonaiuto, Fornara & Bonnes, 2003). Moreover, open spaces can alleviate negative perceptions of dense communities, by enhancing neighbourhood satisfaction levels, more so than physical density changes (Kearney, 2006). With strategic design, green spaces can be incorporated into the sustainable developments of a city, while still achieving the same density of people, thereby maintaining positive psychological impacts. For example, a comparison was made between a traditional suburban planned community (curvilinear streets and cul-de-sacs) and a new compact city design incorporating green spaces (high density small housing lots), in Gaithersburg, Maryland, U.S.A. (Kim & Kaplan, 2004). The 'compact community' actually had more open green spaces and a higher sense of community than the traditionally planned community. Nearby nature was consistently found to be important in residents' sense of community and attachment to the place (Kim & Kaplan, 2004).

Another planning design termed 'a pattern language' (Alexander, Ishikawa & Silverstein, 1977), involves interconnecting a variety of different types of open spaces to provide a socially integrative city. Such an approach towards urban green spaces could have important sustainable benefits both environmentally and socially. The diversity and interconnectedness of urban green infrastructures provide numerous benefits: a variety of eco-habitats and ecological bridges for species to migrate (Catchpole, 2006), particularly necessary as climate change alters environments; an urban cooling effect and water surface drainage (Gill, Handley, Ennos & Pauleit, 2007); accommodate different people's demands and preferences (Urban Green Spaces Taskforce, 2002); and maximise opportunities for psychological restoration (Thwaites, Helleur & Simkins, 2005). Additionally, nearby nature alleviates stress (Grahn & Stigsdotter, 2003), reduces noise annoyance (Gidlöf-Gunnarsson & Öhrström, 2007), reduces aggressive behaviour and crime (Kuo, 2001), and provides economic benefits (CABE, 2005), as well as traditional health benefits from exercising (Cohen, McKenzie, Sehgal et al., 2007). Therefore, sustainable urban planning that incorporates green spaces has important positive psychological impacts for urban users.

The restorative benefits of urban green spaces and their soundscapes were identified as the top three reasons for visiting an urban park in Amsterdam, Holland; 'to relax', 'to listen and observe nature' and 'to escape from the city' (7 non-restorative options also presented; Chiesura, 2004). Additionally, open responses about the importance of the park, identified three key themes, described as cognitive recovery, being away from the city and spirituality. Therefore, urban green spaces are an important component of the development of sustainable cities, because they enhance urbanites psychological restoration and general quality of life; consequently, they need to be considered as part of urban sustainable planning.

Psychological Restoration

Psychological restoration is the process of recovering from attentional fatigue and enabling reflection (Herzog, Black, Fountaine & Knotts, 1997; Kaplan & Kaplan, 1989). Attentional fatigue occurs after focussing on one thing for a period of time, eventually draining aspects of the individual's cognitive resources. This makes it harder for the individual to attend to the matter at hand, while trying to block out other distractions that are competing for attention, including loud or annoying soundscapes. A fatigued state means the individual is likely to make more errors, have reduced productivity levels and incur stress (Kaplan & Kaplan, 1989; Kaplan, 1995), resulting in time off work owing to poor health. Thus, huge societal costs can incur from the collective effect of individuals existing in fatigued states (Grahn & Stigsdotter, 2003).

Restoration potentially aids the 'sustainability' of an individual's behaviour, affect, and overall well-being, as well as the sustainability of a productive society.

Four successive stages of psychological restoration have been described as part of Attention Restoration Theory (ART, Kaplan & Kaplan, 1989). These are, clearing the head, recovery of directed attention, cognitive quiet and reflection (Kaplan & Kaplan, 1989). Restoration first involves clearing information from the last task that was being attended too, so that a cognitive calm can be restored. The mind is then able to wander or concentrate on other things, instead of focussing on one thing and inhibiting all other stimuli, allowing recovery of directed attention. After recovery (the first two stages), reflection is then possible (the next two stages; Herzog et al., 1997). Reflection starts with cognitive quiet, during which, small issues from prior experiences that had not been processed are considered and any 'clutter' within cognitive thoughts are cleared. Finally, the individual can reflect on larger life issues, including priorities, possibilities, actions, goals, and how to accomplish these things. Reflection is considered a deeper benefit than recovery and could take longer to achieve and need a higher quality restorative environment, because it may be more demanding on the individual (Herzog et al., 1997). Indeed, if an individual is fatigued, recovery is significantly evaluated as more favourable and reflection less favourable than if individuals were not fatigued (Staats, Kieviet & Hartig, 2003). Therefore, it may only be possible for reflection to occur when there is no attentional fatigue or after an attentional recovery period. For a fuller and longer lasting restoration, the two cognitive benefits of recovery and reflection may require a longer restoration period than the more rapid physiological recuperation (e.g. reduced heart rate and muscle tension) that has been identified (Kaplan, 1995, Ulrich, Simons, Losito et al., 1991).

In general, natural environments are more restorative than urban environments (Hartig, Mang & Evans, 1991). Research has shown that views of natural elements, in contrast to urban elements, provide positive benefits in terms of people's physical health (Ulrich, 1984), affect, (Ulrich et al., 1991), attention (Berto, 2005; Tennessen & Cimprich, 1995), ability to cope with life issues (Kuo, 2001) and general well-being (Kaplan, 2001a). Specifically, when participants were put into a stressed state of mind (via a video), those who then watched short videos of natural environments reported significantly higher positive emotions and significantly lower anger and fear, than those who watched videos of urban environments (Ulrich et al., 1991). In other research, participants were first attentionally fatigued with a rapidly cognitive draining task, before being presented with restorative scenes (mostly containing nature) and non-restorative scenes (mostly containing urban scenes; Berto, 2005). When repeating the cognitive task, participants who viewed the restorative scenes performed significantly better than before viewing the scenes and had significantly faster reaction times than those who saw non-restorative scenes; the restorative scenes had provided attentional recovery.

Natural views from people's homes are also a significant predictor of residents' well-being, as measured by their general perceived level of distraction, perceived effective functioning, and feelings of being at peace (Kaplan, 2001a). Even views of low levels of vegetation from an apartment, increases residents' ability to cope with major life issues, goals and problems, owing to their increased attentional capabilities, compared with residents with barren views (Kuo, 2001). The latter research is one of few that have focussed upon the restorative benefits of reflection. It shows the importance of psychological restoration in everyday life and the subsequent effects this can have on individuals' economic affairs, education, safety, and situation in life by improving their ability to deal with their current situation. Furthermore, the provision of urban green spaces can aid ecological sustainability by encouraging biodiversity, which itself has been associated with increased psychological benefits such as restoration (Fuller, Irvine, Devine-Wright et al., 2007). In turn, appreciating that psychological restoration can be derived from viewing or visiting natural environments, in particular via fascination, is associated with, and may encourage pro-ecological behaviour, through desires to protect the natural features that provide the restorative experiences (Hartig, Kaiser & Bowler, 2001). Additionally, ecologically responsible behaviour and feeling connected to nature, is also associated with increased levels of happiness, as well as intrinsic values (e.g. personal growth and purpose in life) and mindfulness, which are also related to individuals' well-being (Brown & Kasser, 2005; Nisbet, Zelenski & Murphy, 2009). Overall, access to natural, restorative environments, such as urban green spaces is great for the environment and for increasing urbanites' happiness, reducing their stress, alleviating cognitive fatigue, and enabling reflection. Therefore, views of nature and access to nearby nature are important for sustainable city planning.

Four components are considered important in creating a restorative environment, Fascination, Being-Away, Compatibility and Extent (FACE; Kaplan & Kaplan, 1989), with their presence or absence determining the restorative quality of an environment (Kaplan, 1995). In general, higher levels of the four components have been identified in natural environments in contrast to urban environments (Hartig, Korpela, Evans & Gärling, 1997; Kaplan, 1995; Laumann, Garling & Stormark, 2001), hence the restorative qualities natural environments provide and the importance of green spaces in urban environments.

Fascination is akin to involuntary attention, because it is the ability of a stimulus to have attention-holding properties, without requiring much effort (Kaplan, 1995). An individual viewing a fascinating stimulus is therefore not draining the directed attentional facilities they previously used. Two types of fascination have been proposed, hard and soft (Kaplan, 1995), with the latter associated with natural environments and considered to provide a deeper level of restoration, by providing both recovery and reflection (Herzog et al., 1997).

Being-Away involves either a physical or a conceptual shift away from the present situation/problems to a different environment/way of thinking. This allows tired cognitive structures to rest while other ones are activated. Originally, Being-Away was considered an escape from specific distractions, content, or goals (Kaplan & Kaplan, 1989). More recently though, a desire to be in a specific type of place (a pull factor; Being-Away-To) rather than just the desire to escape (a push factor, Being-Away-From), has been suggested (Hammitt, 2000). Moreover, for urban green space users in Cleveland, Ohio, USA, regardless of where they lived, Being-Away-To factors were more important motivations for visiting green spaces than Being-Away-From factors (Hammitt, 2000). The reasons presented earlier for visiting urban parks in Amsterdam (Chiesura, 2004) were in a similar vein, thus highlighting the importance of green spaces in providing alternative, desired environments within a city, which can provide restoration.

Extent refers to the richness, coherency and scope of an environment that enables the individual to feel as if it is one " whole other world" (Kaplan, 1995, p173), which has explorative potential. The structure, content, and scale of the perceived elements allow directed attention to rest and recover, possibly via the use of schemas (pre-formed generalised knowledge; Kaplan, 2001b). Compatibility depends on the individuals' desires as much as the environment's features. The environment needs to be responsive enough to enable an individual's planned behaviour and for the aims of the individual to fit within the environment's capabilities. The more similar these two aspects are, then the less directed attention will be needed to resolve any incompatibilities. Potential differences can be informational (e.g. visual and acoustic cues are not congruent) or motivational (e.g. an individual's planned behaviour and what the environment offers is not congruent; Kaplan, 2001b). Compatibility therefore explicitly emphasises the person-environment interaction and the importance of an individual's frame of reference, goals, and activities in restoration.

Focussing on restoration arising from a person-environment interaction rather than a passive observation or visitation of an environment, emphasises the notion of a restorative experience instead of a restorative environment. Research has shown that individuals vary in the perceived restoration of an environment, depending on individuals' available time (hours, days, weeks), age and the type of activity to be pursued (Scopelliti & Giuliani, 2004). Places identified as restorative by individuals, varied in their FACE component levels, depending on individuals' age or available time (Scopelliti & Giuliani, 2004). For example, at weekends, people mentioned visiting places that were rated lower in Fascination, than those visited for a holiday. Therefore, not all restorative environments necessarily need to contain high levels of all four FACE components and each of the four components may provide different depths and types of restoration.

The social situation of the environment is another factor that can influence restoration. Perceived restoration, both recovery and reflection, decreased if an individual imagined walking through a natural environment with a close friend or family member (Staats & Hartig, 2004), but made no such difference for an urban environment. The results for the natural environment were only if safety was first ensured, otherwise being with another person was necessary for the natural environment to be perceived as restorative (Staats & Hartig, 2004). Social preferences may also cause variation in perceived restoration, as suggested by young people tending to mention restorative environments as ones they visited with friends, which were also environments with high Being-Away component ratings (Scopelliti & Giuliani, 2004).

Being-Away was also an important element for visiting urban parks, but this was particularly true for those who sought privacy instead of social stimulation (intimate communication; Hammitt, 2000). Therefore, the perception of an environment as restorative involves a complex array of factors; ultimately, a restorative environment is only such if it facilitates a restorative *experience* for that individual.

Importantly, people's experiences of environments are not just visually based, but are multi-sensorial; therefore, soundscapes may have an important role in producing a restorative experience. This could have significant consequences for the level of restoration achieved within urban green spaces. For example, urban parks may provide a visual appearance of nature, but their soundscapes can contain a mixture of sounds from the natural elements of the green space, alongside sounds emanating from the surrounding built environment. The impact of a soundscape on experiencing a place as restorative (e.g. an urban park), is currently unclear, because little research to date has explored this topic. Yet, it is important to consider soundscapes in the provision of urban parks and the positive benefit of psychological restoration, both of which are important for planning sustainable development.

SOUNDSCAPES

Soundscapes can have an important role in people's well-being and quality of life in both positive and negative ways, yet they are still relatively poorly understood. Like individual noises, some soundscapes can be detrimental to people's physical and mental health, causing sleep disorders, stress, hyper-tension and reduced cognitive capabilities, amongst other deleterious effects that affect both children and adults (Soundscape Support to Health, 2008; World Health Organisation, 2000). Some of these physical and cognitive health issues are the same types of problems that visits to restorative environments can help alleviate (e.g. Hartig et al., 1991). Soundscapes can also influence an individual's behaviour, because awareness of peripheral environmental cues can be limited if attention is taken up by the intensity and complexity of competing dominant stimuli information (stimulus overload theory). For example, loud traffic reduced awareness of unusual objects and increased walking speeds (Korte & Grant, 1980). High 'noise' levels can also reduce helping behaviour (Mathews & Canon, 1975; Moser, 1988), increase arousal and stress levels (Glass & Singer, 1972), and decrease a neighbourhood's perceived environmental quality (Bonaiuto et al., 2003). Therefore, if denser compact cities with mixed land usage increases city sound levels, people are likely to have large attentional demands, both acoustically and visually. This will induce fatigue and stress. Consequently, if the effect of city planning on soundscapes is not considered, urbanites may be negatively affected psychologically, alongside having limited opportunities for restorative experiences, making their cognitive capabilities, health and behaviour less sustainable over time.

Policy agendas are starting to consider soundscapes (e.g. Payne, Davies & Adams, 2009 – a project for Defra; European Parliament and Council, 2002; Mayor of London, 2004b, 2006). Noise maps of all large European cities were requested by the European Commission, to raise awareness of harmful noisy places and boost action plans to reduce sound pressure levels and preserve quiet places (European Parliament and Council, 2002). Sound levels can explain 25% of the variance in visitors' assessments of an urban park's sound quality (Nilsson, Botteldooren & De Coensel, 2007). However, the dominance of natural, human, and technological sounds within urban and suburban green spaces, in Stockholm, Sweden, were identified as better predictors of overall sound quality ratings than the sound level (Nilsson, 2007). A focus upon sound levels, therefore, does not guarantee that soundscapes will be evaluated in a positive way; the quality of the soundscape is not ensured, because appreciated sounds are not guaranteed by quiet sound levels. For example, in residential homes and urban parks in Sweden, there was no guarantee that soundscapes below 50 dB had a good perceived soundscape quality (Berglund & Nilsson, 2006; Nilsson & Berglund, 2006).

Equally, not all loud environments are disliked, with some people purposely choosing to visit places with loud soundscapes (e.g. nightclubs), or live in the hubbub and vibrant nature of a city. Moreover, maintaining a diverse range of soundscapes is likely to be important, to satisfy everyone's preferences; this could be feasible with different urban green spaces having different functions, such as a focus upon biodiversity or amenities for people.

Many current planning practices and theories, as well as psychological restoration research, tend to ignore all other sensory aspects apart from vision. Rapoport (1977, 1990) comments on the importance of all the senses in creating a variety of place types and a beneficial network of different urban forms, rather than just focussing on places' physical or social characteristics. Indeed, linking green spaces, as suggested by the pattern language (Alexander et al., 1977) may provide a visually restorative experience, but unlike landscapes, soundscapes are not bounded, sound propagates throughout the environment. Therefore, the quality of the soundscape in connected green spaces is dependent on the surrounding activities and morphology in the urban environment.

Soundscape evaluations are influenced by the context of perceived soundscapes, the associations and meanings attached to individual sound sources, and the interaction between different sounds (e.g. Guillén & López-Barrio, 2007; Guyot, Nathanail, Montignies & Masson, 2005). Laypeople describe sounds by referencing the sources that create the sounds (Dubois, 2000; Payne, Devine-Wright & Irvine, 2007) and categorise them by their semantic features, affective evaluations and expectation (Guastavino, 2007; Payne et al., 2007), which are additionally dependent on the context within which the sound is heard. Furthermore, soundscapes are not perceived or evaluated in isolation, but in conjunction with other senses. The congruency of the information provided from visual and auditory elements can influence how sounds are evaluated (Anderson, Mulligan, Goodman & Regen, 1983; Carles, Barrio & Lucio, 1999; Carles, Bernáldez & Lucio, 1992). Congruent visual and auditory information (e.g. from a park, village, or stream) received higher pleasure ratings than mean ratings of either the visual or auditory information presented separately (Carles et al., 1999).

Sounds in particular were evaluated as more pleasant when matched with congruent images, than when matched with incongruent images. Positive or negative evaluations of visual images vary depending on the in/congruence of the presented sound and the type of sound presented. For example, the addition of water sounds (natural sounds), generally increased the positive evaluation of visual images, even when it was not congruent with the image (Carles et al., 1999). However, the presentation of incongruent sounds, such as traffic (mechanical sounds) with the image of a natural environment, reduced the positive rating of the visual image (Anderson et al, 1983).

Urban green spaces may suffer from this visual-acoustic in-congruency, because sounds from the surrounding urban environment may mask natural sounds within the park, thereby reducing the overall evaluation of the green space. Indeed, the image of a city park was rated less pleasant when it was shown with an audio recording of its soundscape (Carles et al., 1999). The soundscape may remind the individual of the city's density, as suggested by frequent park visitors being more concerned with the area's perceived density than less frequent visitors (Kearney, 2006). Moreover, in relation to restoration, if an urban park's soundscape is predominated by urban sounds such as traffic, individuals may feel an inability to truly escape from the city and its soundscape. This would create only low perceived levels of the ART component, Being-Away, thus reducing the restorative experience. Conversely, the introduction of natural sounds into urban open spaces may enhance psychological restoration by providing higher levels of the ART component Fascination. Altogether, this infers that if the soundscape is not considered in conjunction with visual aspects of the space, the urban green spaces may not have the optimum restorative impact and subsequent social sustainability. Unfortunately, there has been very little research to date, that focuses on the influence of soundscapes on psychological restoration and the positive role it may play in providing sustainable urban communities.

A number of studies have focussed on describing and evaluating soundscapes within urban parks via objective acoustic measures (e.g. A weighted sound pressure levels) and subjective measures, including the perception of three broadly categorised sound types (natural, human and technological). Overall, in the same way that images of natural environments are generally preferred over urban environments (e.g. van den Berg *et al.*, 2003), natural sounds are generally preferred to all other sound types (e.g. human and mechanical), regardless of the individual's age and gender (Irvine, Devine-Wright, Payne *et al.*, 2009; Nilsson & Berglund, 2006). Links between levels of biodiversity, sound levels and perceived sounds within urban parks have also been explored (Irvine *et al.*, 2009); the predominance of natural sounds, matched the level of biodiversity, in particular bird sounds, within three different types of urban green spaces in Sheffield, UK. The loudest green space contained the least biodiversity and its soundscape was evaluated significantly less positively than the other spaces' soundscapes (Irvine *et al.*, 2009). This highlights the benefits of providing urban green spaces that can aid the sustainability of both the environment and humans, if planned appropriately.

In a large urban park, in Saga City, Japan, park users differentiated between soundscapes at a number of locations within the park, using eleven semantic differential scales, such as noisy-quiet, inactive-active (Ge & Hokao, 2004). Soundscapes varied in their levels of natural and urban sounds (Ge & Hokao, 2004). Some of these soundscapes may therefore be more restorative than other soundscapes, depending on the integration of natural and urban acoustic elements. Additionally, sounds from within the park had a positive influence on the majority of residents living near the park, because they could hear natural sounds, or were enticed by the vibrancy of sounds from events held there (although for some these also had negative impacts; Ge & Hokao, 2004). Considering soundscapes in sustainable planning is therefore important, because not only can green space soundscapes have a psychological impact on those visiting the place, but also on those living nearby. If the sound events and landscape are designed and controlled appropriately, the sustainable planning can have a positive psychological impact.

The most frequent reason (25% of 232 participants) given for people visiting five urban parks, in Milan, Italy, was because they provided 'quiet' (Brambilla, Maffei & Zambon, 2006). Additionally, in Cleveland, USA, the most important motivation for visiting an urban green space was Being-Away-To private, peaceful, and quiet places (Hammitt, 2000). These studies highlight the importance of urban green spaces' soundscapes in visitors' experiences. In addition, Being-Away-From everyday sounds, including noise stressors, may be less important than going *to* a peaceful environment in a city; potentially it is not so much the absence of negative sounds, but the presence of positively rated sounds or sounds heard at a lower sound level, that create a peaceful ambience that increases the restorative potential. For example, the urban parks in Milan which were visited in part for their 'quietness' were actually predominated by road traffic sounds and sound levels louder than 50dB(A), yet the presence of non-urban sounds and the relative quiet compared to surrounding areas may still make the park an attractive place to visit for 'quiet' (Brambilla & Maffei, 2006). Although, a perceived quiet may be achieved in such parks, a full restorative experience may still be hampered if the soundscape causes the individual to have to filter out wanted sounds from unwanted sounds, potentially adding to attentional fatigue, rather than reducing it.

Despite the number of associations that can be made between attention restoration and soundscapes, particularly within urban green spaces, the two topics have barely been combined in studies, although support for this research direction is growing. For example, psychological restoration was suggested as a potential reason for nearby green areas providing positive benefits by counteracting perceptions of residential noise, such as reduced long term noise annoyance (Gidlöf-Gunnarsson & Öhrström, 2007).

Another piece of research has considered the involvement of soundscapes in providing restorative experiences by interviewing a number of blind people about their interaction with natural environments (Shaw, Ungar & Gatersleben, 2005). The blind participants used similar terms to the four ART components (FACE) when describing natural environments, suggesting that the soundscape and other non-visual sensory aspects can help contribute to the provision of a restorative experience. Nuances in urban park visitors' categorisation of urban park sounds have been identified, depending on the level of restoration they perceive they gain from visiting urban parks (Payne et al., 2007); people who had higher perceived restorative levels distinctly separated natural sounds from all other sounds. This may emphasise the importance of natural sounds in the production of a restorative experience, compared to other sound types.

Suggestions have also been made as to the processes by which restorative soundscapes could be incorporated into urban designs, including considering the placement of human activities and how the soundscape may affect neighbouring spaces (Graham, 2004). It is evident that there are a lot of potential relationships between soundscapes, psychologically restorative experiences, and the planning of sustainable urban communities, via the inclusion of urban green spaces.

GOALS OF THE STUDY

The aim of the proceeding study is to fill some of the knowledge gaps identified above in the relationship between planning sustainable urban developments and the well-being of urbanites. Specifically, the study explores the relationship between urban parks' soundscapes, and the effect the perceived soundscape may have on visitors' restorative experiences.

METHOD

During the summer of 2007, an *in situ* questionnaire was conducted in two urban parks in Sheffield, UK, named Weston Park and Botanical Gardens. Both parks are located less than 1.5 miles from the city centre, are 0.7 miles apart from each other and have residential housing nearby. Weston Park also has a children's hospital across the road and two other hospitals nearby, as well as University buildings adjacent to the park. The park is flanked on two sides by busy roads, with heavy bus and car usage.

There are also additional green spaces across the road from Weston Park. Similarly, Botanical Gardens is located near a University, as well as several schools and a nearby hospital. It is also flanked by a busy road, but only on one side of the park, with residential gardens surrounding the rest of the park. Botanical Gardens is bigger than Weston Park (6.93 and 4.82 hectares, respectively) and has a higher percentage of amenity planting, whereas Weston Park has a higher percentage of amenity turf (R.A. Fuller, personal communication, 27th March 2008). Both parks though have a similar amount of tree canopy, water areas, singing bird species (6 and 5 different types), and overall ratio of natural to artificial covering

(80:20; R.A. Fuller, personal communication, 27th March 2008). During the research, Weston Park was undergoing a redevelopment project, which meant there were a number of workers, large mechanical equipment, and vehicles in the park during the week. In Botanical Gardens, park vehicles were often driven around, as well as the occasional, tractor driven, lawn mower.

Sound pressure levels [dB(A)] in the parks were measured on a Tenma 72-860 sound level meter, attached to a camera stand, at a height of 130cm. Measurements were made every 10 seconds for 5 minute periods, every other hour, between 10am and 7pm, at 8 or 9 locations throughout the two parks for 7 days (4 in Weston Park, 3 in Botanical Gardens). Additionally, between 10am and 7pm, the researcher stood at the parks' various exits and asked every park user leaving the park, if they could help with a questionnaire about their experience of the park (half of those asked, declined). The questionnaire lasted between 5 and 20 minutes. In each park, 200 participants answered the questionnaire, with 63% questioned on a weekday. Five participants' responses were removed due to missing data (sample size = n=395). The remaining participants ranged from 15 to at least 76 years old, with an average age of 35 to 44 years. There was approximately a 50:50 split of female and male participants.

Among other questions about their experience in the park (see Payne, 2008), participants' perceived restoration was evaluated on semantic differential scales (seven point) from disagree to agree for seven items, based on those used by Staats et al., (2003). Three items assessed recovery (*renew your energy, regain the ability to concentrate* and *reduce any tension*), and four assessed reflection (*ponder over your daily experiences, think about your relationships with others, think about important issues* and *see things in a new perspective*). The seven items created a reliable scale for attention restoration (α=.76) as did the sub scales of recovery (α=.7) and reflection (α=.69).

To identify participants perceived soundscapes, they were presented with a list of seven types of sounds, each with some examples; *Background City (e.g. background traffic), Happy People sounds, Sounds from the Surrounding Buildings (e.g. construction work), Natural sounds, Object sounds due to people in the park (e.g. bicycle), Individual Vehicle or Aircraft sounds, Sad and Angry People sounds*. These were developed from urban park users' classification of urban park sounds (Payne et al. 2007). Next to each sound type was a line marked from 0% (did not hear), to 50% (half of the time) to 100% (all of the time). Participants were asked to '*make a mark on the line which represents how much of the time you heard these types of sounds today*' while in the park. For each perceived sound type they were asked to rate its '*average volume*', on a seven point semantic differential scale ranging from *quiet* (1) to *loud* (7).

Additionally, a sound predominance value was generated by multiplying the two scores of each sound type together. For example, if a participant perceived hearing the Background City for 70% of their duration in the park, at a perceived volume level of 3, the predominance value for the sound type would be 210. Sound predominance values ranged from 0 to 700.

RESULTS

On average, participants only perceived themselves as being slightly restored when leaving the park ($\Re$=4.48, σ=1.3). There was no significant difference between the perceived level of attention restoration for participants in Botanical Gardens and those in Weston Park, $t(388)$=-.42, p>.05. There were also no significant differences between the two parks in terms of participants' age or gender (χ^2=11.05, 1.31, p>.05 respectively).

The two parks' sound pressure levels significantly differed $t(283.18)$=-4.45, p<.001; Botanical Gardens was slightly quieter [$\Re$=50.4 dB(A), ranging from 41.6 to 66.2 dB(A)] than Weston Park [$\Re$=53.1 dB(A), ranging from 46.5 to 67.2 dB(A)]. Sound levels varied more across locations within Botanical Gardens [average 15.2 dB(A) difference] than with time or being a weekday/weekend [average 11.0 dB(A) change]. Weston Park, however, only slightly varied more across locations [average 12.0 dB(A) difference], than with time or weekday/weekend [average 10.4 dB(A) change]. On average, the noisiest location for each park was at the exit adjacent to the busiest road, and the quietest locations were in secluded, less frequently used areas. The sound level in the park around the time the participant was there, had no significant relationship with the level of perceived restoration [$F(2,383)$=.58, p>.05)].

The Background City, Happy People, Surrounding Buildings, Natural, Individual vehicle/Aircraft, and Objects in the park sounds, were perceived by participants between 0 to 100% of the time. Sad and Angry People sounds were never perceived for more than half of the time spent in the park. The perceived volume of the seven sound types also ranged from quiet (1) to loud (7). The longer the time period a sound type was perceived for, the louder its perceived volume (.39<r<.65, p<.01), except for Sad and Angry People sounds (r=.26, p>.05). The majority of participants perceived Natural sounds (n=370), Happy people sounds (n=369) and Background City sounds (n=310), for an average of 63, 58 and 40% of the time respectively. Half the participants perceived Objects in the Park too (n=197) for an average of 36% of the time.

Table 1. Soundscape types, as defined by their most predominant sound types

Soundscape Type	Description
1 (n=181)	Weak Natural and Happy People sounds
2 (n=124)	Strong Natural sounds with Happy People and Object sounds
3 (n=36)	Strong Happy People sounds with Background City/Traffic and Natural sounds
4 (n=24)	Strong Buildings/Construction sounds with Background City/Traffic, as well as Natural and Happy People sounds
5 (n=21)	Strong Background City/Traffic sounds and a cacophonic soundscape

n = the number of participants who perceived the sound type.

Five different types of perceived soundscapes were established via K-means cluster analysis, from the predominance levels of each sound type, perceived by each participant. Figure 1 describes the five different soundscape types perceived by the park users. There were significant differences between the two parks as to the types of soundscapes perceived (χ^2=48.68 p<.001). Participants within Weston Park were more likely to report perceiving the soundscape types that consisted of a number of sound types, but predominated by People and Traffic sounds (soundscape type 3, 4, or 5). Conversely, participants in Botanical Gardens, were more likely to perceive the soundscape predominated by Natural sounds (soundscape type 2).

Table 2. Mean perceived level of restoration, recovery, and reflection achieved for participants who perceived each soundscape type

Soundscape Type	N	Restoration Mean	Restoration Standard Deviation	Recovery Mean	Recovery Standard Deviation	Reflection Mean	Reflection Standard Deviation
1	177	*4.31*	1.35	*4.33*	1.52	4.29	1.68
2	123	*4.75*	1.14	*4.83*	1.21	4.67	1.49
3	36	4.27	1.46	4.24	1.52	4.30	1.61
4	24	4.95	1.03	4.78	1.40	5.11	1.37
5	21	4.37	1.24	4.55	1.36	4.19	1.32
Total	381	4.49	1.29	4.52	1.42	4.46	1.59

Figures in italics indicates significant differences in mean ratings.

Three one-way ANOVAs were conducted, comparing the perceived soundscape type (1 to 5) and the level of overall perceived restoration (1 to 7), as well as perceived recovery and reflection. The soundscape type significantly affected the level of overall perceived restoration achieved [$F(4,376)$=3.29, p<.05], the level of perceived recovery [$F(4,376)$=2.91, p<.05], but not the level of perceived reflection [$F(4,376)$=2.35, p>.05]. Post hoc tests revealed the significant difference for both perceived restoration and perceived recovery was due to mean differences between soundscape type 1 and 2, (see Table 2). Participants who perceived soundscape type 2, consisting of predominant Natural sounds with Happy People and Object sounds, had a greater perceived restorative experience, in particular for recovery, than participants who perceived soundscape type 1 (weak Natural and Happy People sounds).

DISCUSION

Perceived soundscapes have some role in the level of restoration achieved within urban parks. They are a part of the whole experience which may be restorative depending on a number of contributory factors that can influence the whole restorative experience (e.g. visual aspects, time available, age, social interaction; Scopelliti & Giuliani, 2004, Staats & Hartig, 2004).

Park users perceived five different types of soundscapes within the two parks, and these significantly related to the level of restoration participants achieved. The soundscape predominated by Natural sounds, along with Happy People sounds and Object Sounds due to people, was perceived by park users who recovered the most while in the park, and had a restorative experience. As with viewing natural elements, natural sounds tend to be restorative. Perceiving only weaker predominance levels of Natural and Happy People sounds (soundscape type 1) is not as restorative as when they are more predominant, nor when they are mixed with sounds of the Background city and traffic (soundscape type 3). Designing parks to include increased amounts of natural sounds, by considering the types of vegetation planted and by attracting different wildlife may enhance the potential to have a restorative experience. However, if the sounds of the surrounding city are still quite predominant, the restorative effect may be reduced, individuals may not feel like they are 'Being-Away-From' the urban soundscape, which is a necessary component of attention restoration theory (Kaplan & Kaplan, 1989).

Botanical Gardens, was also, on average, quieter than Weston Park, with some locations having particularly quieter sound levels. This may have been expected, owing to the larger size of Botanical Gardens, which provides some areas at a greater distance away from the busy road, however, the quietest locations were at secluded locations, which were visited less frequently, and not necessarily the furthest from the roads. Moreover, other locations within the park had louder sound levels, not owing to traffic alone, but to the presence of (loud) people and nature. This was also identified by the park users, who perceived all the different types of sounds at the full range of sound levels (quiet to loud). Therefore, sound levels alone were not sufficient to identify the type of restorative experience that may be achieved in an urban park. Instead, it is the perceived soundscape types and their involvement in the perceived restoration, which also varies between the parks that is of importance. This is in agreement with research that has found that the types of sounds perceived, rather than recorded sound level, predicts the perceived sound quality of an urban park (Nilsson, 2007).

The soundscape types perceived predominantly in Weston Park were those that included predominant Background City sounds, including traffic. The design of the parks would have influenced the differences in this perception as the sound of the traffic (from similar traffic volume roads) can easily propagate through Weston Park compared to Botanical Gardens. The latter park is shielded by a large green house that runs parallel to the road, where as in Weston Park, the large museum is perpendicular to the road, and the traffic is also still visible from within the park. Additionally, the topography of Botanical Gardens (a hill on one side of the park near the road) also diffuses the traffic sound level and removes any visual cues. The design of the park is therefore an important attribute in creating a soundscape that is more restorative, thus enhancing the sustainable benefits of urban parks.

Positively, Natural and Happy people sounds were reported more by participants than any other sound types. This suggests, that although the two parks were near traffic, there was still an opportunity to 'Be-Away-To' other sound types than those they may usually hear. Natural sounds may also involve more Fascination, than the sounds of traffic, which is an important component in providing a restorative environment (Kaplan, 1995). This could also explain the relationship between restoration levels and the soundscape type predominant in natural sounds, compared to weaker levels of natural sounds. Further research into the levels of ART components for each sound type, could be useful in aiding the design and consideration of soundscapes to provide a restorative experience.

Weston Park had one soundscape that was predominated by construction sounds from the redevelopment work occurring within the park itself. Counterintuitively, people who perceived that soundscape (type 4) also had the highest mean perceived recovery level, although it was not significantly higher, owing to its small sample size. As the construction sounds were part of a redevelopment project benefiting the park, the park users' comments were about accepting these sounds, because they knew the end result was worth it. The lack of annoyance for the construction sounds and perceiving these sounds alongside other sound types expected to be heard in the park (Natural sounds) meant the restoration level achieved in the park was seemingly not hindered. This highlights the importance of the context in the perception of certain sound types and attitude towards the source of the sound, as found in other urban soundscapes (e.g. Guillén & López-Barrio, 2007).

In Weston Park, the perceived soundscape was also very complex at times (type 5), with no one sound type predominating, except for the hum of the Background City and its traffic. Although complexity is considered an important attribute of visually preferred environmental scenes (Kaplan & Kaplan, 1989), too much complexity may cause fatigue if few sounds are easily identifiable. Without some form of structure and harmony between the different sound types, too many demands may be placed on individuals' attentional capabilities. For example, trying to comprehend and filter perceived acoustic information and decide upon the aspects of the soundscape to attend to and which to block out, will require a greater amount of attention than a coherent, simplistic, non-competitive soundscape. This will prevent the individual from recovering from any fatigue and prevent them from reaching the deeper level of restoration, in the form of reflection. Indeed, reflection was not significantly related to perceived soundscape types in the urban parks, possibly due to the number of competing sound types and longer time necessary to achieve reflection.

The research showed that different places of the same place type/behaviour setting (e.g. urban parks) can have different, and similar, types of perceived soundscapes and this in turn can potentially affect restoration levels. Furthermore, the soundscape type that was related to having the most restorative experience was more likely perceived in Botanical Gardens than in Weston Park, yet on average, there was no difference in the overall perceived restoration achieved between these two parks.

Although the soundscape may have contributed to part of the restorative experience, it is only one of many elements that can influence restoration. Other aspects may have increased the restorative experience within Weston Park, such as providing a relative escape from the stresses of the academic and medical jobs that people occupy around the park. A number of attributes will aid or hinder a restorative experience, and not all the same elements will contribute to providing the same level of restoration for different people within the same or different parks. Indeed, of two gardens that were shown to vary in their restorativeness levels, the garden with the overall highest perceived restoration did not contain the highest perceived levels of all four FACE components, which are considered important for a restorative environment (Ivarsson & Hagerhall, 2008). Therefore, not all natural environments will provide the same high levels of restoration, and if urban parks are not carefully planned with regard to their design, location, surrounding activities, and subsequent soundscape, then they will not necessarily provide a restorative experience.

To understand the extent of the role of soundscapes in providing a restorative experience, a number of variables need to be considered at once, which were not considered here (see Payne, 2008 instead). Moreover, restoration was a perceived self reported measure in this research and prior fatigue levels before entering the park are also likely to influence the resultant restoration. Research into the interaction between different sound types could also be fruitful because it may play a role in the restorative quality of soundscapes, possibly with different ratios of People sounds to Background City traffic sounds being of importance, as is the case for affective evaluations of urban soundscapes (Guyot *et al.*, 2005).

Conclusion

Sustainable urban development is important for the environment and for societies. Achieving a sustainable urban environment should not necessarily involve a competition between environmental resources and human's well-being. Instead, with careful planning considerations, the two can support each other, with natural green spaces enabling psychological restoration and environmental benefits. The design of a city, its activities, and its subsequent soundscape can influence people's restorative experiences within urban green spaces. Therefore, the combination of visual, acoustic, social, and environmental aspects of a city need to be considered collectively, when planning for sustainable urban environments. It is essential that Environmental Psychologists, Architects, Landscape Designers, and Urban Planners work together, to help produce a quality environment that caters for people's needs, preferences, and health, while sustaining future environmental and societal needs (Churchman, 2002).

Acknowledgments

This research has kindly been funded by the EPSRC, University of Manchester and De Montfort University as part of a doctorate. The author would like to thank Dr Devine-Wright for reviewing an early draft of this chapter and general doctoral supervision.

References

Alexander, C., Ishikawa, S., & Silverstein, M. (1977). *A pattern language. Towns, Buildings, Construction.* New York: Oxford University Press.

Anderson, L.M., Mulligan, B.E., Goodman, L.S. & Regen, H.Z. (1983). Effects of sounds on preferences for outdoor settings. *Environment and Behavior, 15*, 539-566.

van den Berg, A.E., Koole, S.L. & van der Wulp, N.Y. (2003). Environmental preference and restoration: (How) are they related? *Journal of Environmental Psychology, 23*, 135-146.

Berglund, B. & Nilsson, M.E. (2006). On a tool for measuring soundscape quality in urban residential areas. *Acta Acustica united with Acustica, 92*, 938-944.

Berto, R. (2005). Exposure to restorative environments helps restore attentional capacity. *Journal of Environmental Psychology, 25*, 249-259.

Bickman, L., Teger, A., Gabriele, T., McLaughlin, C., Berger, M. & Sunaday, E. (1973). Dormitory density and helping behaviour. *Environment and Behavior, 5*, 465-490.

Bonaiuto, M., Fornara, F. & Bonnes, M. (2003). Indexes of perceived residential environment quality and neighbourhood attachment in urban environments: a confirmation study on the city of Rome. *Landscape and Urban Planning, 65*, 41-52.

Brambilla, G. & Maffei, L. (2006). Responses to noise in urban parks and in rural quiet areas. *Acta Acustica united with Acustica, 92*, 881-886.

Brambilla, G., Maffei, L. & Zambon, G. (2006, December). *Preserving natural quiet areas and urban parks.* Paper presented at Inter-Noise, in Honolulu, Hawaii.

Brown, K.W. & Kasser, T. (2005). Are psychological and ecological well-being compatible? The role of values, mindfulness and lifestyle. *Social Indicators Research, 74*, 349-368.

Burton, E. (2003). Housing for an urban renaissance: Implications for sound equity. *Housing Studies, 18*, 537-562.

CABE. (2009). *Hallmarks of a sustainable city.* London: Commission for Architecture and the Built Environment.

CABE. (2005). *Does money grow on trees?* London: Commission for Architecture and the Built Environment.

Carles, J.L., Barrio, I.L. & de Lucio, J.V. (1999). Sound influence on landscape values. *Landscape and Urban Planning, 43*, 191-200.

Carles, J., Bernáldez, F. & de Lucio, J. (1992). Audio-visual interaction and soundscape preferences. *Landscape Research, 17*, 52-56.

Catchpole, R.D.J. (2006). Planning for Biodiversity – opportunity mapping and habitat networks in practice: a technical guide. *English Nature Research Reports, 687*.

Chiesura, A. (2004). The role of urban parks for the sustainable city. *Landscape and Urban Planning, 68*, 129-138.

Churchman, A. (2002). Environmental Psychology and Urban Planning: Where can the twain meet? In R. Bechtel & A. Churchman (Eds.) *Handbook of Environmental Psychology.* New York: J. Wiley & Sons.

Churchman, A. (1999). Disentangling the concept of density. *Journal of Planning Literature, 13*, 389-411.

Cohen, D.A., McKenzie, T.L., Sehgal, A., Williamson, S., Golinelli, D. & Lurie, N. (2007). Contribution of public parks to physical activity. *American Journal of Public Health, 97*, 509–514.

Dubois, D. (2000). Categories as acts of meaning: the case of categories in olfaction and audition. *Cognitive Science Quarterly, 1*, 33-66.

European Parliament and Council. (2002). Directive 2002/49/EC of the European Parliament and of the Council of 25th June 2002, relating to the assessment and management of environmental noise. *Official Journal of the European Communities. L189.*

Fuller, R.A., Irvine, K.N., Devine-Wright, P., Warren, P.H. & Gaston, K.J. (2007). Psychological benefits of green space increase with biodiversity. *Biology Letters, 3*, 390-394.

Ge, J. & Hokao, K. (2004). Research on the sound environment of urban open space from the viewpoint of soundscape – A case study of Saga Forest Park, Japan. *Acta Acustica united with Acustica, 90*, 555-563.

Gidlöf-Gunnarsson, A. & Öhrström, E. (2007). Noise and well-being in urban residential environments: The potential role of perceived availability to nearby green areas. *Landscape and Urban Planning, 83*, 115-126.

Gill, S.E., Handley, J.F., Ennos, A.R. & Pauleit, S. (2007). Adapting cities for climate change: the role of the green infrastructure. *Built Environment, 33*, 115-133.

Glass, D.C. & Singer, J.E. (1972). *Urban Stress: Experiments on noise and social stressors.* New York: Academic Press.

Graham, C.S.R. (2004). *Designing landscapes for psychological restoration: adding considerations of sound.* Unpublished Master of Landscape Architecture Thesis, University of Guelph, Canada.

Grahn, P. & Stigsdotter, U.A. (2003). Landscape Planning and Stress. *Urban Forestry & Urban Greening, 2,* 1-18.

Guastavino, C. (2007). Categorisation of environmental sounds. *Canadian journal of experimental psychology, 61,* 54-63.

Guillén, J.D. & López-Barrio, I. (2007, September). *Importance of personal, attitudinal and contextual variables in the assessment of pleasantness of the urban sound environment.* Paper presented at the International Congress of Acoustics, in Madrid, Spain.

Guyot, F., Nathanail, C., Montignies, F. & Masson, B. (2005, September). *Urban sound environment quality through a physical and perceptive classification of sound sources: a cross cultural study.* Paper presented at Forum Acusticum, in Budapest, Hungary.

Hammitt, W.E. (2000). The relation between being away and privacy in urban forest recreation environments. *Environment and Behavior, 32,* 521-540.

Hartig, T., Kaiser, F.G. & Bowler, P.A. (2001). Psychological restoration in nature as a positive motivation for ecological behaviour. *Environment and Behavior, 33,* 590-607.

Hartig, T., Korpela, K., Evans, G.W. & Gärling, T. (1997). A measure of restorative quality in environments. *Scandinavian Housing and Planning Research, 14,* 175-194.

Hartig, T., Mang, M. & Evans, G.W. (1991). Restorative effects of natural environment experiences. *Environment and Behavior, 23,* 3-26.

Herzog, T.R., Black, A.M., Fountaine, K.A. & Knotts, D.J. (1997). Reflection and attentional recovery as distinctive benefits of restorative environments. *Journal of Environmental Psychology, 17,* 165-170.

Irvine, K.N., Devine-Wright, P., Payne, S.R., Fuller, R.A., Krausse, B., Gaston, K.J. (2009). Green space, soundscape and urban sustainability: an interdisciplinary, empirical study. *Local Environment, 14,* 155-172.

Ivarsson, C.T. & Hagerhall, C.M. (2008). The perceived restorativeness of gardens – assessing the restorativeness of a mixed built and natural scene type. *Urban Forestry and Urban Greening, 7,* 107-118.

Jenks, M., Burton, E. & Williams, K. (Eds.) (2000). *The compact city. A sustainable urban form?* Oxford: E & FN Spon.

Kaplan, R. (2001a). The nature of the view from home. Psychological benefits. *Environment and Behavior, 33,* 507-542.

Kaplan, S. (2001b). Meditation, restoration, and the management of mental fatigue. *Environment and Behavior, 33,* 480-506.

Kaplan, S. (1995). The restorative benefits of nature: toward an integrative framework. *Journal of Environmental Psychology, 15,* 169-182.

Kaplan, R. & Kaplan, S. (1989). *The experience of nature: A psychological perspective.* Cambridge: Cambridge University Press.

Kearney, A.R. (2006). Residential development patterns and neighbourhood satisfaction. Impacts of density and nearby nature. *Environment and Behavior, 38,* 112-139.

Kim, J. & Kaplan, R. (2004). Physical and psychological factors in sense of community. New Urbanist Kentlands and Nearby Orchard Village. *Environment and Behavior, 36,* 313-340.

Korte, C. & Grant, R. (1980). Traffic noise, environmental awareness, and pedestrian behaviour. *Environment and Behavior, 12,* 408-420.

Kuo, F.E. (2001). Coping with poverty. Impacts of environment and attention in the inner city. *Environment and Behavior, 33,* 5-34.

Laumann, K., Gärling, T. & Stormark, K.M. (2001). Rating scale measures of restorative components of environments. *Journal of Environmental Psychology, 21,* 31-44.

Mathews, K.E.Jr & Canon, L.K. (1975). Environmental noise level as a determinant of helping behaviour. *Journal of Personality and Social Psychology, 32,* 571-577.

Mayor of London. (2006). *The Mayor's Ambient Noise Strategy - progress report.* http://www.london.gov.uk/mayor/strategies/noise/docs/progress_report_20061030.pdf last accessed 3.5.09

Mayor of London. (2004a). *The London Plan. Spatial development strategy for Greater London.* London: Greater London Authority, HMSO.

Mayor of London. (2004b). *Sounder City. Highlights of the Mayor's Ambient Noise Strategy.* London: Greater London Authority, HMSO.

Moser, G. (1988). Urban stress and helping behavior: effects of environmental overload and noise on behavior. *Journal of Environmental Psychology, 8,* 287-298.

Neuman, M. (2005). The compact city fallacy. *Journal of Planning Education and Research, 25,* 11-26.

Nilsson, M.E. (2007, August). *Soundscape quality in urban open spaces.* Paper presented at Inter-Noise, in Istanbul, Turkey.

Nilsson, M.E. & Berglund, B. (2006). Soundscape quality in suburban green areas and city parks. *Acta Acustica united with Acustica, 92,* 903-911.

Nilsson, M.E., Botteldooren, D. & De Coensel, B. (2007, September). *Acoustic indicators of soundscape quality and noise annoyance in outdoor urban areas.* Paper presented at International Congress on Acoustics, in Madrid, Spain.

Nisbet, E.K.L., Zelenski, J.M. & Murphy, S.A. (2009). *Happiness is in our nature: Exploring the links between nature relatedness and subjective well-being.* Manuscript submitted for publication.

Payne, S.R. (2008, June). *Are perceived soundscapes within urban parks restorative?* Paper presented at Acoustics' 08, in Paris, France.

Payne, S.R., Davies, W.J., & Adams, M.D. (2009). *Research into the practical and policy applications of soundscape concepts and techniques in urban areas.* A report for Defra Department for Environment, Food and Rural Affairs. In preparation. www.defra.gov.uk last accessed 3.5.09

Payne, S.R., Devine-Wright, P. & Irvine, K.N. (2007, August). *People's perceptions and classifications of sounds heard in urban parks: semantics, affect and restoration.* Paper presented at Inter-Noise, in Istanbul, Turkey.

QWAG. (2009). Quaggy Waterways Action Group. Bringing an urban river to life. http://www.qwag.org.uk/home/ last accessed 3.5.09.

Rapoport, A. (1990). *History and precedent in environmental design.* New York: Plenum Press.

Rapoport, A. (1977). *Human aspects of urban form.* Oxford: Pergamon Press.

Scopelliti, M. & Giuliani, M.V. (2004). Choosing restorative environments across the lifespan: a matter of place experience. *Journal of Environmental Psychology, 24,* 423-437.

Shaw, B., Ungar, S. & Gatersleben, B. (2005, September). *Represented in a glittering array: An understanding of blind people's perceptions of natural environments.* Paper presented at Royal Geographical Society with IBG conference in London, UK.

Soundscape support to health. (2008). http://www.soundscape.nu last accessed 3.5.09.

Staats, H. & Hartig, T. (2004). Alone or with a friend: A social context for psychological restoration and environmental preferences. *Journal of Environmental Psychology, 24,* 199-211.

Staats, H., Kieviet, A. & Hartig, T. (2003). Where to recover from attentional fatigue: An expectancy-value analysis of environmental preference. *Journal of Environmental Psychology, 23,* 147-157.

Stigsdotter, U.A. & Grahn, P. (2004, October). *A garden at your doorstep may reduce stress – Private gardens as restorative environments in the city.* Paper presented at Open Space-People Space Conference, in Edinburgh, Scotland.

Tennessen, C.M. & Cimprich, B. (1995). Views to nature: effects on attention. *Journal of Environmental Psychology, 15,* 77-85.

Thwaites, K., Helleur, E. & Simkins, I.M. (2005). Restorative Urban Open Space: Exploring the spatial configuration of human emotional fulfilment in urban open space. *Landscape Research, 30,* 525-547.

Ulrich, R.S. (1984). View through a window may influence recovery from surgery. *Science, 224,* 420-421.

Ulrich, R.S. (1981). Natural versus Urban scenes: some psychophysiological effects. *Environment and Behavior, 13,* 523-556.

Ulrich, R.S., Simons, R.F., Losito. B.D., Fiorito, E., Miles, M.A., Zelson, M. (1991). Stress recovery during exposure to natural and urban environments. *Journal of Environmental Psychology, 11,* 201-230.

Urban Green Spaces Taskforce. (2002). *Green Spaces, Better Places. Final report of The Urban Green Spaces Taskforce.* London: Department of Transport Local Government and the Regions.

World Commission on Environment and Development (1987). *Our Common Future, Report of the World Commission on Environment and Development.* Published as Annex to General Assembly document A/42/427, Development and International Co-operation: Environment August 2, 1987. Oxford University Press.

World Health Organisation. (2000). *Guidelines for community noise.* Geneva: WHO.

In: Psychological Approaches to Sustainability
Editors: V. Corral-Verdugo et al.
ISBN 978-1-60876-356-6
© 2010 Nova Science Publishers, Inc.

Chapter 21

HAPPINESS AND SUSTAINABLE BEHAVIOR

Robert B. Bechtel[*]
Department of Psychology, University of Arizona, USA
Victor Corral-Verdugo
Departamento de Psicología, Universidad de Sonora, Mexico

ABSTRACT

Most studies on the psychological dimensions of sustainability focus on the cognitive, affective and behavioral determinants of sustainable actions, the former being considered as *antecedents* of the latter. Quite recently, the research interest has included the study of the psychological *consequences* of sustainability. Subjective well being or happiness is mentioned among those consequences. In fact, a number of governments consider the achievement of happiness for their citizens as a goal to reach through their sustainable-development strategies. Happiness is an elusive psychological state determined by a combination of genetic and environmental influences. Despite the contrast of theories used to explain happiness, there is a remarkable convergence of findings. There is, for example, general agreement on the high level of influence from heredity on this psychological state. There is also fair agreement on the surprisingly high level of happiness among people, on the limits of money to increase wellbeing and on the need of connectedness to other humans to keep a satisfactory level of positive psychological states. There is also agreement that the exact definition of happiness is elusive. Most authors in the area of positive psychology recommend actions to increase happiness, for instance the practice of altruistic behaviors, the acquisition of problem-solving skills, and the engagement in actions to connect with other individuals. Since sustainable actions normally result in benefits for oneself and for other persons, a link between sustainable behavior and happiness is expected. The pertinent literature shows that this is the case. Altruistic individuals get happiness from their actions, as well as individuals who practice equitable behaviors. A frugal lifestyle (living lightly, avoiding waste and overconsumption) has also been mentioned as a promoter of positive

---

[*] Correspondence concerning this chapter should be addressed to Robert B. Bechtel: Department of Psychology, University of Arizona, Tucson, AZ, 85721, USA. Email: bechtel@email.arizona.edu.

psychological states. There are, however, few studies investigating the link between pro-ecological actions and subjective wellbeing and we conducted one such study. Four hundred forty-one undergraduates taking psychology courses at American and Mexican universities responded to a questionnaire investigating pro-environmental behavior, happiness, and demographic variables. Their responses were processed within a structural equation model, which showed that pro-ecological actions significantly predict happiness: those students reporting a higher engagement in conservationist actions also tended to report higher levels of happiness. Income did not influence subjective wellbeing. No significant differences in levels of this psychological state were found across samples; also no gender differences were found. However, the explanatory power of pro-environmental behavior on happiness was three times larger in the Mexican sample, suggesting that being pro-ecological is more conducive to a positive psychological state in the Latin American country than in U.S.A. These results are consistent with the findings of a relationship between happiness and diverse indicators of sustainable behavior, and suggestive of further cross-cultural research. The main finding, however, is that engaging in sustainable actions might be subsequently added to the list of the "How of happiness."

INTRODUCTION

Sustainable development (SD) goals include the achievement of ecological, social, political and economic benefits for citizens (Moffatt, 2000). Thanks to sustainable actions, the physical environment can be restored and conserved; communities have access to education, infrastructure, employment, and justice; resources are equitably distributed, and the levels of social corruption are reduced (Gouveia, 2002). But that's not all: some governments and international groups add psychological benefits to that list, including subjective wellbeing or happiness (Talbert, 2008). Happiness is an expected consequence of sustainability, joining the rest of the indicators of sustainable development, namely: its ecological, social, political and economic consequences.

Although it may appear strange at a first glance, Australia, Canada and the United Kingdom have established the achievement of subjective wellbeing for their citizens as a national policy goal, and, in a more decisive way, the Kingdom of Bhutan (in the Himalaya) has declared that its official goal is not anymore the economic growth, assessed as "gross national product," but to increase the "gross national happiness" (Gardner & Prugh, 2008). By doing so, they intend to raise the kingdom's educational level and to fight poverty, while preserving the physical environment and the cultural traditions of their nation. For the first time in history, at least officially, people's happiness is recognized as a goal of governmental plans and programs explicitly linking subjective wellbeing to sustainability.

However, these goals are recent history. The United States Declaration of Independence established, in 1787, "the pursuit of happiness" as an unalienable human right, and the government is supposed to offer conditions guaranteeing the exercise of such right. If sustainability is one of those conditions, it is clear that, at least the US Government (as well as the above-mentioned authorities), should promote environmental conservation and sustainable lifestyles.

This has a significant implication for psychology, especially for environmental psychology, since the levels of impact of sustainability already include subjective indicators, in addition to the more "classical" socio-economic and ecological ones. Wellbeing and happiness levels should be considered in the global assessment of sustainability, and these psychological states are to be established as objectives in the strategies of national sustainable development (Talbert, 2008). This also means that sustainability is not only determined by psychological factors, as most chapters in this book show, but also that sustainability generates changes in positive psychological states, as we will try to demonstrate in this chapter. First, we will discuss some concepts associated with the psychological study of happiness.

WHAT IS HAPPINESS?

In his book on the history of Happiness, Darrin McMahon (2006) begins with the story of King Croesus who called on Solon, a sage, to ask him to find the happiest man on earth, thinking that Solon would surely find it was Croesus himself. He was surprised when Solon found it was two men already dead, and when Croesus protested that people who were dead could not be happy, he dismissed Solon as "stupid." Yet when later misfortunes came upon him, Croesus finally saw the wisdom in Solon's choice.

Now move forward a number of centuries and this dance between death and Happiness continues as the modern Terror Management Theory (Solomon, Greenberg, & Pyszczynski, 2004). This theory now has more than 200 studies. The theory was inspired by Becker's (1973) *The Denial of Death*. The fear of death is managed by the development of cultural world views, some of which promise immortality as an antidote to death. And whenever the terror of death becomes salient, the cultural view of self worth and cultural worldview is leaned on as the "management" tool that keeps us from being overwhelmed. This is the "anxiety buffer hypothesis." The more we fear death, the greater the need for reinforcing the cultural world view and self worth as anchored in that world view.

It was Martin Seligman who began the positive psychology movement that led to the study of happiness. He describes how psychology "lost its way" and did not find it until positive feelings replaced the mere absence of mental illness as a subject for study. Yet even to the present, definitions of happiness vary. Seligman (2002) used *learned optimism* and *fulfillment* as equivalent terms while Myers (1992) also used fulfillment but also "well-being" and "personal joy." Diener (2000) is credited with the use of *subjective well being* and Csikszentmihalyi (1990) introduced the concept of *FLOW*.

These studies have expanded into Existential Psychology, the psychology of human existence. While the central focus was the Happiness-death teeter totter, the larger view is now to cover *all* the questions of human existence including the question of meaning itself. As Koole, Greenberg, & Pyszczynski (2004) express it (page 497), it includes…"sexuality, human-nature relations, religion, morality, identity construction, nostalgia, culture, ideology, close relationships, group identification, disgust, ostracism, communication, decision making, goal striving," and even killing bugs (Martens Kosloff, Greenberg, Landau, & Schmader, 2007). Yet, despite this seemingly complete coverage, there are a number of other theories dealing with Happiness from different points of view.

Lykken (Lykken & Tellegen, 1996), for example, studied three thousand identical and fraternal twins and came up with the conclusion that identical twins had much the same level of subjective well being even if separated at birth. This contrasted to the fraternal twins who showed little similarity of mood or subjective well being even when raised in the same household. Lykken attributed 80% of Happiness as due to genetics. His famous quote is, "Trying to be happier is like trying to be taller." (Lykken & Tellegen, 1996, p. 188). He later compromised a little but always maintained that at least 50% of happiness was due to inheritance.

Lykken's main conclusion was that there is a "set point" for happiness and the differences between people are seen as largely due to genetic differences. The 50% mark seems to have stood up well under the test of time.

Yalom (1980) developed a form of psychotherapy that dealt with the isolation of each human from all others. This isolation was (he claimed) actually bridged by acknowledging one's own mortality. In fact, the "cure" was the recognition of one's own mortality. He pointed out that because of this isolation we can often feel more alone among a group of people than we would feel if we were actually alone.

Seligman (1998), who is credited with founding positive psychology, is also the author of *Learned Optimism*. His main thesis is that we can learn how to be happy by being more optimistic. Echoing Yalom's isolation, Seligman sees the growing depression in our culture as being due to the emphasis on "I" failing to achieve our own goals. This concentration on individualism makes failure unbearable and this can only be relieved by the "we" which other cultures already have, such as Japan. Seligman alphabetizes his technique under the rubric ABC, adversity, belief and consequences. When you encounter adversity, list the event, list your belief about why the event occurred and then list how it made you feel (consequences). After going over each of these Seligman teaches how to change them into positive elements. The beliefs are critical. *Why* did this event occur? Isn't a new interpretation possible? Dispute the negative interpretation and turn it into something positive. Somebody insulted you. It may be they weren't feeling good that day and just," took it out" on you. Maybe this kind of thing has happened before and this is just the way this person acts. The point is to get the child (or adult) to start disputing negative interpretations and to learn this as a habit. Thus, one can learn to be more positive by learning to carry this routine into daily life so it becomes automatic.

Seligman believes that happiness comes from three things, pleasure, engagement and meaning. Seeking pleasure, as opposed to becoming inundated in work or other routines, can bring momentary relief but engaging with others ends isolation and self concentration and seeking the positive meaning of all events lifts up the level of daily experience.

Myers (1992) uses "well being" as his term for happiness. He dispelled many popular notions about well being by showing that more than just a few people are genuinely happy, that wealth does not buy happiness, that tragedies erode it, that happiness springs from happy memories, that teens and elderly are not the unhappiest people, that one sex is happier than the other and many more. He concludes that three elements compose happiness: faith, hope and joy. A quote that might sum up his findings is, "The essence of happiness is pausing to savor the gift of our present moments." (Myers, 1992, p. 203).

Diener (Diener Sandvick, & Larsen, 1985) developed the most used instrument for subjective well being in the 80s and found that most people report above average SWB, in fact, 75-80 % report they are above average. Although, at the same time, when people in the

West were four times better off economically than they were forty years earlier, the SWB had not changed at all (Diener & Suh, 1997) and the very rich were below average. After many research studies it was finally concluded that wealth only contributed to happiness in a limited way. If you are poor and struggling, money can increase your satisfaction with life but beyond a certain point it ceases to have an increasing effect. Wealthy people are happier than poor people but not significantly happier than middle class (Diener, 2000; Veenhoven, 2006).

Argyle (2001) claims that there are three relatively independent elements in happiness: Satisfaction with life, positive and negative affect. Essentially one has to be satisfied with life before happiness can be claimed and there has to be a preponderance of positive over negative affect. These can be measured and the scores combined. Argyle feels that experiments are the best way to measure them.

Joy is the positive emotion most associated with happiness while satisfaction is seen as more cognitive in nature. Expression of positive emotion is seen in the Duchenne smile (Ekman & Friesen, 1975). Essentially this is a smile that uses both the upper part as well as the lower part of the face. Thus, the crinkling of the eyes along with the upcurling of the mouth expresses a happier smile than the mere lower face smile. Seeing smiles on other faces is rewarding. Women smile more than men.

Negative emotions seem to exist in greater varieties than positive. We have anger, fear, depression, disgust, boredom, being tired, frustration, anxiety (as opposed to fear) and others. Obviously a preponderance of negative feeling interferes with happiness.

Csikszentmihaly (1990) developed an entirely different approach in the concept of FLOW. When you are doing something that you are good at and this is something that is valued by others, you lose all sense of time. This is called a state of FLOW. Csikszentmihaly believes this is happiness. Some question whether it is just a form of preoccupation. FLOW may or may not be accompanied by a feeling of joy. Csikszentmihaly first thought this was experienced by experts in tennis, golf or some other sport, but it quickly became evident that FLOW was also an experience at work. In this sense the barriers between work and leisure fell away. Work no longer had to be the dreaded drudgery of the required eight hours. People could look forward to work, even prefer it. Thus, a new sense of meaning in life would include all aspects, work, play, leisure as including opportunities for FLOW.

Lyubomirsky & Tucker (1998) found that happy people are able to look at the same adverse events in more positive ways than unhappy people. She developed a short seven item Happiness scale that was later scaled down to four items. Lyubomirsky feels that the many self help books on happiness are based on non-empirically tested ideas and wrote a book that uses only scientifically tested methods for gaining happiness (Lyubomirsky 2008).

Lyubomirsky's scale contains the following questions, scored on a basis of 1 (not a very happy person) to 7 (a very happy person):

1) In general I consider myself...
2) Compared to most of my peers, I consider myself...
3) Some people are generally happy. They enjoy life regardless of what is going on, getting the most out of everything. To what extent does this characterization describe you?
4) Some people are generally not very happy. Although they are not depressed, they never seem as happy as they might be. To what extent does this characterization describe you?

The last item is reverse scored. Total score possible is 28.

Myers (1992) found that although income in Europe increased additively from 1930 to 1990, satisfaction level seemed to decline slightly. He also found that people of faith are generally happier than those without faith. His interpretation of faith is that it gives people a sense of hope and that (in a quote from Samuel Johnson) "Hope is itself a species of happiness and, perhaps, the chief happiness the world affords."

So far the earlier pioneers of happiness research have not been mentioned. Hadley Cantril (1965) did an international survey with over 23,000 participants. Bradburn (1969) developed his Happiness Scale using another survey and Campbell, Converse & Rogers (1976) did a survey at the University of Michigan. It was not until 1999 that the *Journal of Happiness Research* began publishing studies. Yet with all these studies happiness research still has a relatively low profile in psychology as a whole. There are no basic texts, for example, with a chapter on happiness. But it must be remembered that there are many books on happiness. Most of these are the "how to" kind of books, e. g. *The Art of Happiness* by the Dalai Lama and Cutler (1998).

The kind of books mentioned above, however, attempt to apply the fruits of psychological research to the measurement and understanding of happiness. Argyle, Csikszentmihaly, Diener, Lykken, Seligman and Yalum all attempt to show how psychological research illuminates happiness. Despite the contrast of theories there is a remarkable convergence of findings. There is general agreement on the high level of influence from heredity. There is also fair agreement on the surprisingly high level of happiness, on the limits of money to increase happiness and on the necessity of connectedness to other humans. There is also agreement that the exact definition of happiness is elusive.

Further, most researchers in happiness now agree that only 40% of your natural state of well-being can be increased to make you happier (Lyubomirsky, 2008). Thus, all the myriad books aiming to increase happiness have a 60% smaller target. Lyubomirsky, Scheldon & Schkade (2005) point to three sources of happiness: a genetic predisposition, circumstantial factors and the practice of activities promoting happiness.

Seligman et al (2005) ask their participants to engage in some of the following exercises promoting happiness: Writing a gratitude letter to someone that has been good to them; listing at least three positive events they experienced that day; writing about their strengths and skills; and related situations. Sonia Lyubomirsky (Lyubomirsky & Ross, 1997) resonated with the idea of doing something for others through kindness, gratitude and optimism, in order to get happiness. At the same time she finds that this should not become habitual, that the acts of kindness, gratitude and optimism must be renewed and refreshed over time or they will lose their meaning.

But an interesting question arises when trying to study happiness because with the increasingly threatened physical environment, how does the desire to preserve that environment influence happiness and, conversely, how does happiness have anything to do with being *green* (wanting to sustain the environment)? These questions are central to this chapter.

HAPPINESS AND SUSTAINABLE BEHAVIOR

As mentioned in the introduction of this chapter, achieving subjective wellbeing is one of the goals of sustainable development (Talbert, 2008). This goal assumes that feelings of wellbeing or happiness shall result from living in sustainable environments. Since these environments are a consequence of people's daily pro-environmental actions, the question is whether or not a relationship exists between being pro-environmental and being happy. According to some authors this link is not evident enough. For example, Lindenberg and Steg (2007) suggest that hedonic goals (searching for pleasure) are often opposed to pro-ecological behavior: People wishing to feel good are not expected to maintain environmentally protective behaviors among their life goals, since these behaviors imply a personal sacrifice, a decrease in consumption levels, and other factors that are supposedly antagonistic to pleasure. In fact, these authors propose that, for achieving sustainability, hedonic goals should be made incompatible with normative goals that stress responsibility for the environment. Brown and Kasser (2005, p. 349) also establish that the "Political discourse on the subject of ecological sustainability often suggests a conflict between human well-being and ecological welfare."

However, Lindenberg and Steg recognize that, occasionally, searching for comfort could lead to sustainable behaviors. In other words, some individuals would seek for pleasure and wellbeing by protecting their environment. Evidence in the literature suggests that this is a plausible case. Pelletier, Tuson, Green-Demers, Noels & Beaton (1998), for instance, found that it is more likely that men and women display pro-ecological behavior when this behavior derives pleasure and satisfaction. De Young (2000) argues that many people consider their getting involved in certain pro-environmental actions as worthwhile, due to the satisfaction and pleasure resulting from those actions. Moreover, people obtain psychological wellbeing from a direct contact with nature; thus, that such wellbeing constitutes a motivation for protecting the environment (see Kals, Schumacher & Montada, 1999) could be expected.

As authors of chapters in this book show, sustainable behavior includes altruistic, frugal, equitable, and pro-ecological actions as key components. A sustainable-oriented individual looks for the protection of the physical environment by engaging in pro-ecological and frugal behaviors and protects her/his social environment by being altruistic and equitable. If sustainability promotes happiness, there should be significant relations between positive psychological wellbeing and those sustainable actions.

In regard to the possible links between altruism and happiness, Van de Vliert, Huang & Parker (2004, p. 9) assure that altruism is about "seeking to improve the happiness of others" but also indicate that altruistically motivated action makes the actors feel good. They also suggest that happiness and altruism are "scientific twins" sharing the subjacent notion of "quality of life." As reiterated by many authors, pro-environmental behavior is altruistically motivated (see, for instance, Ebreo, Hershey & Vinning, 1999; Hooper & Nielsen, 1991).

Research data indicate that individuals experiencing happy states are more sensitive at others' needs; they also report pro-social thoughts and spontaneously help strangers in need (Schroeder, Penner, Dovidio & Piliavin, 1995). In addition, happy states negatively correlate with the need for competition in both the individual (Baron, 1990) and national levels (Van de Vliert & Janssen, 2002). Altruism makes feel people good in the long term (Schroeder et al, 1995) and leads them to experience happiness in their close relations with significant others (Buunk & Schaufeli, 1999).

The above means that although hedonism –a form of egoism- sometimes implies a successful search for wellbeing, its alternative path, altruism, is also conducive to the same end (happiness). This is an unexpected finding because egoism is the antithesis of altruism. Yet, one could be happy by combining hedonistic (egoistic) and cooperative (altruistic) ways of life. Altruism results in wellbeing states for both the author and the direct beneficiary of the altruistic act.

Austerity –also called frugality, or voluntary simplicity lifestyle- also seems to correlate with happiness. This sustainable lifestyle is manifested as a reduced consumption of products and a simple and light way of living (Iwata, 2002; Fujii, 2006). The social ideal, however, depicts austere behaviors as implying personal sacrifice and no benefit at all. This ideal is reflected in the cultural and political spheres: most government programs aimed at reducing expense and waste avoid mentioning the terms "frugal" or "austere" in their discourse. Instead, they ask citizens to generate an "improvement in the efficiency" of their production and consumption patterns (Duncan, 1999). Promoting frugality is politically incorrect.

Consuming less, however, does not mean depriving oneself from the essential, nor even the necessary. Austerity is neither equal to deprivation nor to living bad and unhappy. Moreover, a sustainable development requires an economic and consumption basis for achieving wellbeing (Inglehart & Klingemann, 2000), so that a sustainable lifestyle does not imply suppressing comfort and consumption. Yet, for some people resigning luxuries and material wellbeing could be a burden, making them reluctant to abandon them (Sober & Wilson, 1998). In a few words, austerity could be perceived as more harmful and unpleasant than beneficial for many people.

Surprisingly, as in the case of altruism, practicing frugal behaviors results in positive emotional states as psychological research seems to demonstrate. De Young (1991, 1996), in a series of studies, found that frugal actions were accompanied by internal states of satisfaction. Participants in his studies reported feelings of intrinsic reinforcement due to practicing those actions: they felt good as a result of engaging in pro-environmental behaviors, needing no one else to be administering (external) rewards to maintain their behavior. De Young (1996) identified three types of *intrinsic satisfactions*, which are relevant for sustainability: 1) *competence motivation* resulting from being able/skilled at solving environmental problems, 2) satisfaction from participating in maintaining a community, and 3) satisfaction due to practicing a frugal consumption of products. This means that the practice of an austere way of living is self-reinforced; also, that a reduced consumption produces an intrinsic reward in an intangible but powerful way. So powerful that it does not require anything external for producing its effect (De Young, 2000).

Brown & Kasser (2005) also found a relationship between frugality and wellbeing. People who voluntarily simplify their consumption patterns develop a slight, yet significant, increase in their levels of happiness. This finding is counterintuitive to what most people think, promote and practice: A voluntarily reduced consumption produces psychological wellbeing.

Now, with regard to equity, Veenhoven (2006) argues that ancient (and present) hunter-gatherer societies –which were equitable and egalitarian- used to be happier than (more inequitable) agricultural societies. However, Veenhoven establishes that we live better and happier now than in the past, but he does not clarify whether this condition obeys an improvement in equity social conditions of modern and industrialized societies or to any other situations.

In more specific aspects, Amato, Booth, Johnson & Rogers (2007) show that egalitarian married partners, who share domestic responsibilities and decision making, and exhibit gender equity attitudes, tend to be happier than non-egalitarian couples. This not only impacts on women but also on men, who report more satisfaction, less marital conflict and, also, more happiness (Chibucos, Leites & Weiss, 2005).

According to Veenhoven (2006) the happiest countries in the world are in Northern Europe (Finland, Sweden, and Iceland). Being no necessarily the richest, they are the most equitable in distribution of resources among their citizens. The unhappiest countries are all in Sub-Saharan Africa –including Zimbwawe and, the unhappiest of all: Tanzania- with the highest levels of inequity (and poverty).

People experiencing the worst from inequity, report lower levels of subjective wellbeing: the poor are unhappier than the wealthy (Veenhoven, 2006); members of minority groups are less happy than members of the majority (Gintis, 2007; Pew Research Center, 2006); and also unhappy are those who suffer from environmental injustice (Adeola, 2000). Perceiving inequity also induces psychological discomfort: It is known that conservative individuals are happier than liberals (Pew Research Center, 2006). According to Napier and Jost (2008) this happens because liberals are more concerned about the consequences of inequity in people. Perceiving inequity is a source of unhappiness; living in inequity is even worse (Veenhoven, 2006).

Finally, we have the relation between pro-ecological behavior and happiness. In a study investigating this link, Brown and Kasser (2005) found, both in adolescents and adults, that individuals with higher levels of subjective wellbeing reported a higher involvement in environmentally-protective behaviors such as turning off lights in unoccupied rooms, reusing paper and plastic bags and so forth. The correlation between subjective wellbeing and pro-ecological behavior was $r=.17$ ($p <.02$) in their study with adolescents, while in their model with adults this correlation increased up to .45 ($p <.001$). As far as we know, this is the only study investigating in a specific way the relationship between happiness and the conservation of the physical environment. No cross-cultural comparison had been conducted in this regard. That is why we were interested in replicating this finding, investigating patterns of pro-environmental behavior and the report of happiness provided by young individuals living in two countries (USA and Mexico) of different cultural background and economic developmental level.

In order to test the potential relationship between sustainable behavior and happiness, we decided to test middle-class students who would be outside the influence of wealth on happiness and to compare across two countries at least in order to explore cultural differences. Standard instruments were chosen that has already been used in happiness and sustainable behavior measures.

METHOD

Participants

Four hundred forty-one undergraduates taking psychology courses at Arizona (USA, N=221) and Sonora (Mexico, N=220) universities responded to a questionnaire investigating pro-environmental behavior and happiness. These were typical middle-class students of a state university in their late teens and early 20s. The participants were 120 males and 321 females. In the Arizona sample, the age mean was 22.02 years (3.23 SD) against an average of 21.40 years (4.68 SD) in the Mexican sample.

Instruments

Eleven items of Kaiser's (1998) General Ecological Behavior Scale (GEB) were used in this study, including the self-report of reuse, recycling, energy conservation, etc., behaviors, in a 0 (never) to 3 (always) scale. The GEB encompasses the assessment of pro-ecological and frugal (reduced consumption) activities, being considered a reliable and valid indicator of sustainable behavior, at least in terms of the protection of the physical environment. This instrument has been extensively utilized, including its English and Spanish versions, in international studies. In addition Lyubomirsky and Lepper (1999) Happiness scale was administered. This is a 4-item measure of global subjective happiness developed and validated in USA, using a 7-point (1 = not very happy... 7 = very happy) likert format of responses to items such as "In general I consider myself happy" and "Compared to most of my peers, I consider myself happy." Lyubomirsky and Lepper's reported high internal consistency for the scale, as well as evidence of convergent and discriminant validity. The participants also provided demographic information regarding their family monthly income and gender.

Procedure

Both the Arizona and Sonora students responded to instruments in their classrooms. The average time for completion was about ten minutes.

Data Analysis

We obtained univariate statistics (means, standard deviations, minimum and maximum values) as well as Cronbach's alphas from responses to the scales. Mean difference tests were computed across samples and gender, regarding levels of happiness and pro-environmental behavior effort. Finally, a structural equation model was specified and tested for each sample. In this model, "pro-environmental behavior," a factor emerging from Kaiser's GEB scale was assumed to affect "happiness", a latent variable constructed from the item interrelations of Lyubomirsky and Lepper's instrument. Since economic income is sometimes mentioned as a significant determinant of happiness, we included this variable as influencing both the happiness level and participants' engagement in pro-environmental behaviors in our model. Convergent validity was measured by considering the values of the factor *loadings* between the assessed factors and their corresponding indicators. High and significant (p <.05) *loadings* were expected as evidence of convergent validity. Goodness of fit indicators were also obtained in order to assess the adequacy of this model of relations between GEB, happiness and income.

RESULTS

Univariate results from the scales administration are shown in tables 1 and 2. We decided to drop item 4 from the Happiness scale because of its poor contribution to the internal consistency (alpha = .58) in the Arizona sample and the non-significant ($p > .05$) *loadings* it produced in both samples. In addition, only nine out of the eleven items were retained as indicators of the GEB for each sample. This decision was made because two items in both samples produced non-significant *loadings* ("Turns down air conditioning when leaving place" and "saves gasoline by walking or bicycling" in the Arizona sample; and "Collects and recycle used paper" and "Reads about environmental issues" in the Sonora sample). The alphas produced values from .66 for the GEB scale among the Mexicans, to .92 for the happiness instrument, also in the Mexican sample.

Table 1. Univariate statistics and internal consistency of scales. American sample

Scale/items	Mean	SD	Min.	Max.	Alpha
Happiness	5.35	1.04			.86
In general, I consider myself happy	5.55	0.87	1	7	
Compared to most peers, I consider myself happy	5.40	1.08	1	7	
I enjoy life, regardless of what is going on	5.11	1.17	1	7	
Pro-environmental behavior	1.61	0.81			.74
Waits until having a full load before laundry.	2.17	0.98	0	3	
Collects and recycle used paper.	1.45	0.92	0	3	
Brings empty bottles to a recycling bin.	1.86	0.96	0	3	
Points out unecological behavior to someone.	1.27	0.76	0	3	
Buys products in refillable packages.	1.39	0.69	0	3	
Buys seasonal produce.	1.78	0.74	0	3	
Reads about environmental issues.	1.55	0.82	0	3	
Talks with friends about environmental problems.	1.31	0.76	0	3	
Look for ways to reuse things.	1.78	0.72	0	3	

The levels of reported happiness were non-significantly ($p > .05$) different between the Americans (mean=5.35, sd=1.04) and the Mexicans (mean=5.41, sd=1.54). These levels were high, as expected in middle-class young individuals. As for the GEB results, and in spite of the slightly different item-composition of the scale for both samples, it can be seen that the pro-environmental effort is similar (mean = 1.61, sd =. 81, for the Arizonans; mean = 1.70, sd =. 88, for the Sonorans).

Table 2. Univariate statistics and internal consistency of scales. Mexican sample

Scale/items	Mean	SD	Min.	Max.	Alpha
Happiness	5.41	1.54	.		
In general, I consider myself happy	5.45	1.58	1	7	92
Compared to most peers, I consider myself happy	5.44	1.52	1	7	
I enjoy life, regardless of what is going on	5.34	1.52	1	7	
Pro-environmental behavior	1.70	0.88			.66
Waits until having a full load before laundry.	2.01	0.97	0	3	
Brings empty bottles to a recycling bin.	0.75	0.86	0	3	
Points out unecological behavior to someone.	1.87	0.93	0	3	
Buys products in refillable packages.	1.39	0.80	0	3	
Buys seasonal produce.	2.18	0.79	0	3	
Talks with friends about environmental problems.	1.47	0.79	0	3	
Turns down air conditioning when leaving place.	2.52	0.82	0	3	
Look for ways to reuse things.	1.68	0.83	0	3	
Conserves gasoline by walking or bicycling.	1.43	1.21	0	3	

No significant gender difference was found in either sample regarding happiness levels (mean = 5.35, sd = .89, for women; mean = 5.39, sd = .99 for men in the Arizona sample; mean = 5.36, sd = 1.43, for women; mean = 5.53, sd = 1.48, in the Sonora participants). Yet, the pro-environmental effort was higher in women (mean = 1.65, sd = .50) than in men (mean = 1.33, sd = .51, t = 4.28, p <.0001) in the Arizona sample, but non-significantly different between Sonoran women (mean = 1.51, sd = .48) and men (mean = 1.45, sd = .51; t = -.71, p = .47).

Figure 1 exhibits results of the structural model for the American sample. High and significant (p < .05) *loadings* between both factors and their corresponding indicators (i.e., items of the happiness and GEB scales) were obtained, revealing convergent construct validity. Pro-environmental behavior produced a .22, significant, structural coefficient on happiness, while family income did not influence either latent factor. In turn, figure 2 shows that the evidence of convergent validity is reproduced for the Mexican sample but also indicates that the effect of pro-environmental behavior on happiness increases in this sample (structural coefficient = .45). For the Sonorans, family income produce a slight, yet significant (p <.05), and negative effect on pro-environmental behavior, but no influence at all on happiness levels. Goodness of fit indicators are shown in the legends of figures 1 and 2, evidencing an adequate correspondence between the hypothesized relations and the data. These legends also establish that pro-environmental behavior explains 6 % of the variance in happiness among the American participants, and that this explanatory power increases up to 19 % in the Mexican sample.

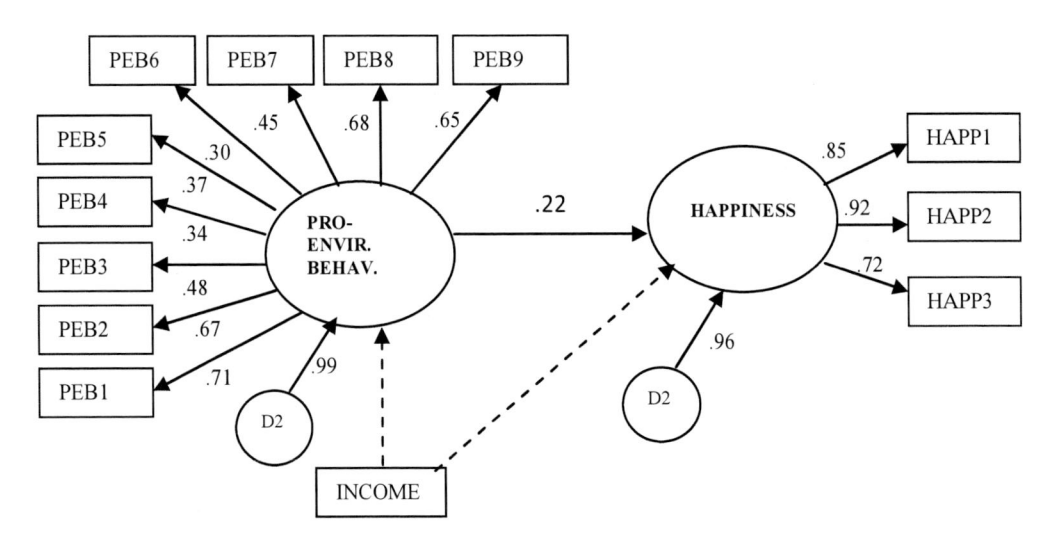

Figure 1. Structural relations between income, pro-environmental behavior and happiness (American sample). Goodness of fit: X^2= 94.2 (61 df), p=.006; $NNFI$=.91, CFI=.93; $RMSEA$=.06. Pro-ecological behavior R^2=.01; Happiness R^2=.06.

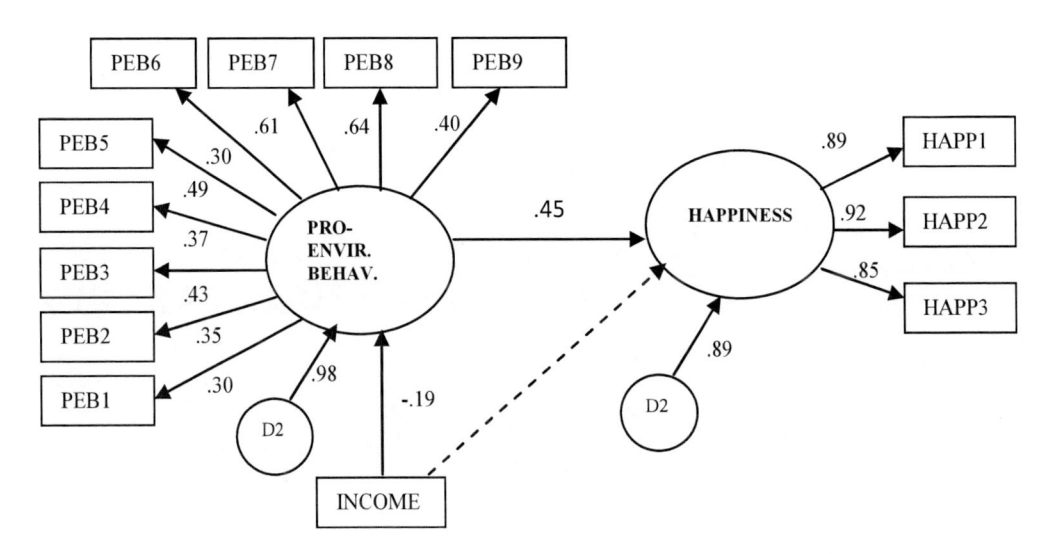

Figure 2. Structural relations between income, pro-environmental behavior and happiness (Mexican sample). Goodness of fit: X^2=109.4 (61 df), p<.001; $NNFI$=.90, CFI=.92; $RMSEA$=.06. Pro-ecological behavior R^2=.04; Happiness R^2=.19.

CONCLUSION

Unlike most chapters in this book, dealing with the *determinants* of sustainable behavior, the present writing focused on one psychological *consequence* of sustainability. For more than forty years, environmental psychologists have demonstrated that the environmental dilemma has psychological roots but also that its solutions might be found –at least partially– in a deep comprehension of human nature (Cone & Hayes, 1980; Oskamp, 2000). These psychological roots and determinants are antecedents of sustainable behavior and its particular manifestations: altruism, equity, austerity and pro-ecological actions, among others. But sustainable behavior has not only psychological causes; clearly it also has psychological consequences, happiness being one of them. Our study was aimed at investigating the link between this positive psychological state and pro-ecological behavior.

The most significant results were in the expected directions. The fact that family income did not influence happiness confirms the widespread findings that income is not related to happiness at the middle class level (Diener, 2000; Myers, 1992). The levels of self-reported happiness were high in both the American and Mexican samples, also confirming results from previous studies (Diener et al, 1985). Another expected finding was the positive correlation between happiness and pro-environmental behavior, although this turned out to be small (.22) in the American sample, as compared to the Mexicans (.45). This reflected in a large difference between the Mexican and American samples on the explained variance in happiness such that the Mexican sample had 19% of the variance in happiness explained by pro-ecological behavior vs. only 6% in the US sample. Thus, the Mexican students had three times the influence of pro-environmental behavior on psychological wellbeing. These data tend to contradict the popular notion that poorer countries have less environmental concerns and, by the way, lower levels of happiness.

Of course, our data come from a correlational research design, so that we cannot establish for sure that a causal flow from sustainable behavior to happiness is the best explanation for our results. An alternative explanation could be that happiness affects the desire for being pro-ecological, which reverses the causal flow. But, in any case, the fact is that happiness is higher in those who practice more pro-environmental behaviors. This makes appropriate the conclusion of recommending pro-environmental activities to people, in order to reach higher levels of happiness.

Interestingly, our results from the American sample replicated those obtained by Kasser & Brown (2005), with American teenagers, who found a .17 correlation between pro-ecological behavior and happiness, which is similar to that produced in our Arizona sample ($r=.22$). More interestingly yet, the magnitude of such correlation increased in both Kasser & Brown's sample of adults and in our Mexican group of young people ($r=.45$ in both cases). These results seem to imply that as age increases the association between proenvironmental behavior and happiness gets stronger; the findings also would indicate that in some cultures this association is higher than in others. We do not have a conclusive explanation for these differences. It could be that, as people get older, their happiness from being pro-ecological increases because mature individuals are more attuned with the needs of others (List, 2004) and with the preservation of the environment (Domina & Koch, 2002). Thus, for older people, engaging in sustainable actions would result in an increased feeling of satisfaction or intrinsic reinforcement, as De Young (1991; 1996) has demonstrated. We were unable to detect a moderator effect of age on the relationship between pro-ecological behavior and happiness because of the relative invariance of age in our samples, so that a future investigation with participants of diverse age is required to replicate Kasser and Brown's findings.

As for the differential influence of proecological behavior on happiness due to culture, previous research has shown that collectivistic social traditions, such as the Mexican for instance, are more oriented towards the need of others and also more concerned about the environment than individualistic traditions, as the American (see Schultz & Zelezny, 2003, for instance). It is likely that these differences would explain why Mexicans in our study got a higher level of happiness from their pro-ecological commitment. Of course, this explanation is preliminary, so that we need to test it in a further study.

The main finding, however, is that engaging in sustainable actions might be subsequently added to the list of the "How of happiness" (Lyubomirski, 2008). Since a significant amount of subjective wellbeing may be obtained from practicing pertinent behaviors, everybody should be aware of the kind of activities that lead to positive psychological states (Lyubomirski, 2008; Seligman, Steen, Park, & Peterson, 2005). Pro-ecological and pro-social actions are among those activities. Therefore, psychologists, social workers and educators, among many other professionals, should recommend the practice of daily pro-environmental behaviors as a means to get both, a sustainable environment and personal happiness.

REFERENCES

Adeola, F. (2000). Cross-national environmental injustice and human rights issues. *American Behavioral Scientist, 43*, 686-706.

Amato, P., Booth, A., Johnson, D. & Rogers, S. (2007). *Alone together: how marriage in America is changing*. Cambridge, MA: Harvard University Press.

Argyle, M. (2001) *The Psychology of Happiness, 2nd edition*. Sussex: Routledge.

Baron, R. (1990). Environmentally Induced Positive Affect: Its Impact on Self-Efficacy, Task Performance, Negotiation, and Conflict. *Journal of Applied Social Psychology, 20*, 368-384.

Becker, E. (1973) *The Denial of Death*, New York: Free Press.

Bradburn, N. (1969) *The Structure of Psychological Well Being*. Chicago: Aldine.

Brown, K.W. & Kasser, T. (2005). Are Psychological and Ecological Well-being Compatible? The Role of Values, Mindfulness, and Lifestyle." *Social Indicators Research*, 74, 349–368.

Buunk, B. Schaufeli, W. (1999). Reciprocity in Interpersonal Relationships: An Evolutionary Perspective on Its Importance for Health and Well-being. *European Review of Social Psychology, 10*, 259-291.

Campbell, A., Converse, P. & Rogers, W. (1976) *The Quality of American Life: Perceptions, Evaluations and Satisfactions*. New York: Sage.

Cantril, H. (1965) *The pattern of Human Concerns*. New Brunswick, NJ: Rutgers University Press.

Chibucos, T., Leites, R. & Weiss, D. (2005). *Readings in Family Theory*. Thousand Oaks: Sage.

Cone, J.D. y Hayes, S.C. (1980). *Environmental problems. Behavioral solutions*. Monterey, CA: Brooks Cole.

Csikszentmihaly, M. (1990). *FLOW: The Psychology of Optimal Experience*. New York: Harper & Row.

Dalai Lama & Cutler, H. (1998) *The Art of Happiness: A Handbook for Living*. New York: Penguin.

Diener, E. (2000) Subjective well-being: the science of happiness and a proposal for a national index. *American Psychologist, 55*, 34-43.

Diener, E., Sandvick, E., & Larsen, R. (1985). Age & sex effects for emotional intensity. *Developmental Psychology, 21*, 542-546.

Diener, E. & Suh, E. (1997) Measuring quality of life: economic, social and subjective indicators. *Social Indicators Research, 40*, 189-216.

De Young, R. (1991). Some psychological aspects of living lightly: Desired lifestyle patterns and conservation behavior. *Journal of Environmental Systems, 20*, 215-227.

De Young, R. (1996). Some psychological aspects of a reduced consumption lifestyle: The role of intrinsic satisfaction and competence motivation. *Environment & Behavior, 28*, 358-409.

De Young, R. (2000). Expanding and evaluating motives for environmentally responsible behavior. *Journal of Social Issues, 56*, 509-526.

Domina, T. & Koch, K. (2002). Convenience and frequency of recycling. Implications for including textiles in curbside recycling programs. *Environment & Behavior, 34*, 216-238.

Duncan, A. (1999). What is source reduction? A critique and comparative analysis of Polish and American students. *Environmental Management, 23*, 495-505.

Ebreo, A., Hershey, J., & Vining, J. (1999). Reducing solid waste: Linking recycling to environmentally responsible consumerism. *Environment & Behavior, 31*, 107-135.

Ekman, P., & Friesen, W. (1975) *Unmasking The face*. Englewood Cliffs, NJ: Prentice Hall.

Fujii, S. (2006). Environmental concern and ease of behavior as determinants of pro-environmental behavior intentions. *Journal of Environmental Psychology, 26*, 262-268.

Gardner, G. & Prugh, T. (2008). Seeding the sustainable economy. En Starke, L. (Ed.), *State of the World*. New York, W. W. Norton & Company.

Gintis, H. (2007). Economic growth and well-being: a behavioral analysis. *The Economic Journal, 117*, F455-F459.

Gouveia, V. (2002). Self, culture and sustainable development. En P. Schmuck y P.W. Schultz (Eds.), *Psychology of Sustainable Development*. Norwell, Massachusetts: Kluwer.

Hooper, J.R. & Nielsen, J.M. (1991). Recycling as altruistic behavior: Normative and behavioral strategies to expand participation in a community recycling program. *Environment & Behavior, 23*, 195-220.

Inglehart, R., & Klingemann, H.D. (2000). Genes, culture, democracy, and happiness. In E. Diener & E. Suh (Eds), *Culture and Subjective Wellbeing*. Cambridge, MA: The MIT Press.

Iwata, O. (2002). Coping style and three psychological measures associated with environmentally responsible behavior. *Social Behavior and Personality, 30*, 661-669.

Kaiser, F. (1998). A general measure of ecological behavior. *Journal of Applied Social Psychology, 28*, 395-442.

Kals, E., Schumacher, D. & Montada, L. (1999). Emotional affinity toward nature as a motivational basis to protect nature. *Environment & Behavior, 31*, 178-202.

Koole, S., Greenberg, J., & Pyszczynski, T. (2004). The best of two worlds: Experimental Existential psychology now and in the future, in *Handbook of Experimental Existential Psychology,* Greenberg, J., Koole, S., & Psyszczynski, T. (Eds) 497-504. New York: Guilford Press.

Lindenberg, S & Steg, L. (2007). Normative, gain and hedonic goal frames guiding environmental behavior. *Journal of Social issues, 63*, 117-137.

List, J. (2004). Young, selfish, and male: field evidence of social preferences. *The Economic Journal, 114*, 121-149.

Lykken, D. & Tellegen, A. (1996) Happiness is a stochastic phenomenon. *Psychological Science, 7,* 186-189.

Lyubomirski, S. (2008) *The How of Happiness.* New York, The Penguin Press.

Lyubomirsky, S., & Lepper, H. (1999). A measure of subjective happiness: preliminary reliability and construct validation.

Lyubomirsky, S. & Ross, L. (1997) Hedonic consequences of social comparison: A contrast of happy and unhappy people. *Journal of Personality & Social Psychology, 73,* 1141-1157.

Lyubomirsky, S., Sheldon, K. M., Schkade, D. (2005). Pursuing happiness: The architecture of sustainable change. *Review of General Psychology, 9,* 111-131.

Lyubomirsky, S. & Tucker, K., (1998) Indications of individual differences in subjective happiness for perceiving, interpreting and thinking about life events. *Motivation and Emotion, 22,* 155-186.

Martens, A., Kosloff, S., Greenberg, J., Landau, M. & Schmader, T. (2007). Lilling Begets Killing: Evidence from a Bug-Killing Paradigm that Initial Killing Fuels Subsequent Killing, *Personality & Social Psychology Bulletin,33,* 1251-1264.

McMahon, D. (2006) *Happiness: A History.* New York: Grove/Atlantic.

Moffatt, I. (2000). Ecological footprints and sustainable development. *Ecological Economics, 32,* 359-362.

Myers, D. (1992) *The Pursuit of Happiness.* New York: Avon Books.

Napier, J.L., Jost, J.T. (2008). Why Are Conservatives Happier Than Liberals?. *Psychological Science, 19,* 565-572.

Oskamp, S. (2000). A sustainable future for humanity? *American Psychologist, 55,* 496-508.

Pelletier, L. C., Tuson, K. M., Green-Demers, I. & Noels, K. (1998). Why are we doing things for the environment? The motivation toward the environment scale (MTES). *Journal of Applied Social Psychology, 25,* 437–468.

Pew Research Center (2006). *Are we happy yet?* Washington, DC: Pew Research Center.

Schroeder, D.A., Penner, L.A., Dovidio, J.F., & Piliavin, J.A. (1995). *The psychology of helping and altruism: Problems and puzzles.* New York: McGraw-Hill.

Schultz, P.W. & Zelezny, L. (2003). Reframing Environmental Messages to be Congruent with American Values. Human Ecology Review, 10, 126-136.

Seligman, M. (1998) *Learned Optimism: How to Change Your Mind and Your Life.* New York: Pocket Books.

Seligman, M. (2002) *Authentic Happiness.* New York, Free Press.

Seligman, M.E.P., Steen, T., Park, N. & Peterson, C. (2005). Positive psychology in progress. Empirical validation of interventions. *American Psychologist, 60,* 410-421.

Sober, E., & Wilson, D.S. (1998). *Unto others: the evolution and psychology of unselfish behavior*. Cambridge, MA: Harvard University Press.

Solomon, S., Greenberg, J. & Pyszczynski, T. (2004) The Cultural Animal: Twenty Years of Terror Management Theory and Research in Greenberg, Koole & Pysczynski (Eds.) *The Handbook of Experimental Existential Psychology*. New York: Guilford Press, 13-34.

Talbert, J. (2008). Redefining progress. In Starke, L. (Ed.), *State of the World*. New Van de Vliert, E., Huang, X. & Parker, P. (2007). Do colder and hotter climates make richer societies more, but poorer societies less, happier and altruistic? *Journal of Environmental Psychology, 24*, 17-30.York, W. W. Norton & Company.

Van de Vliert, E., Huang, X. & Parker, P. (2007). Do colder and hotter climates make richer societies more, but poorer societies less, happier and altruistic? *Journal of Environmental Psychology, 24*, 17-30.

Van de Vliert, E., & Janssen, O. (2002). "Better than" Performance Motives as Roots of Satisfaction Across more and Less Developed Countries. *Journal of Crosscultural Psychology, 33*, 380-397.

Veenhoven, R. (2006). Is life getting better? How long and happy people live in modern society. *European Psychologist, 10*, 330-343.

Yalom, I. (1980) *Existential Psychotherapy*. New York: Basic Books.

INDEX

A

ABC, 436
abiotic, 272
academic performance, 210
academics, 320, 323, 341
acceleration, 375, 379, 380
accessibility, 9, 44, 51, 52, 53, 55, 111, 152, 167, 296, 297, 298, 301, 304, 308, 310, 311, 362, 366, 375
accidents, 29, 180, 389
accountability, 106
accounting, 115, 202, 280, 284
accuracy, 63
ACE, 421
achievement, 146, 252, 270, 326, 433, 434
acid, 64
acoustic, 417, 419, 420, 426, 427
action research, 326, 327, 334, 336
activation, 40, 66, 73, 75, 114, 115, 139, 170, 171, 172, 175, 181, 184, 247, 251, 296, 300, 302, 303, 304, 305, 306, 313, 314, 378, 397
activism, 252, 264, 365
acute, 189, 201
acute coronary syndrome, 189, 201
Adams, 418, 430
adaptation, 22, 23, 38, 93, 126, 159, 225, 253, 254, 364, 387
adhesion, 318
adjustment, 142, 245, 364
administration, 403, 406, 443
adolescence, 406
adolescents, 121, 441
adult, 52, 214, 234, 241, 255, 436
adult literacy, 52
adult population, 241
adults, 93, 188, 194, 195, 196, 306, 308, 369, 418, 441, 446

adverse event, 437
advertisements, 380
advocacy, 162, 341
aesthetics, 343, 349
affective dimension, 178, 250
affective reactions, 179
affective states, 249, 250, 253, 260
Africa, 13, 24, 31, 188, 189, 202, 373, 441
African-American, 95
agent, 162, 246, 329, 332
agents, 15, 72, 80, 167, 228, 331, 332, 388
aggregates, 284
aggression, 168, 222
aggressive behavior, 210
agricultural, 373, 397, 440
agriculture, 26, 36, 127, 244, 369, 370
aid, 415, 420, 426
aiding, 425
AIDS, 5, 134
air, 24, 26, 48, 88, 113, 132, 135, 142, 146, 170, 195, 256, 367, 443, 444
air pollution, 146, 170, 367
Aircraft, 422, 423
all-electric, 77
alpha, 99, 133, 134, 135, 195, 218, 236, 256, 257, 260, 278, 280, 348, 443
alternative, 68, 69, 83, 90, 97, 146, 147, 150, 152, 158, 175, 249, 261, 300, 303, 320, 322, 323, 332, 337, 338, 340, 342, 344, 353, 354, 403, 416, 440, 446
alternatives, 31, 65, 68, 87, 113, 141, 158, 159, 300, 303
alters, 414
altruistic behavior, 11, 132, 139, 165, 169, 170, 179, 181, 186, 191, 200, 202, 253, 433, 448
ambiguity, 94, 264, 323
ambivalence, 138, 299, 313
amphibia, 138

Amsterdam, 76, 77, 79, 158, 414, 416
analysis of variance, 150
anger, 164, 252, 254, 353, 415, 437
animals, 22, 27, 114, 127, 128, 131, 133, 140, 167, 173, 174, 175, 176, 178, 190, 211, 225, 226, 253, 256, 259, 264, 399
anorexia, 166
ANOVA, 352
antagonism, 92
antecedents, 4, 8, 9, 14, 62, 63, 79, 143, 192, 222, 244, 290, 398, 433, 446
anthropological, 87, 185, 190
anthropology, 86
antisocial behavior, 13, 211, 221, 299, 313, 385, 388, 398, 399, 400, 403, 404
antisocial personality, 211
antithesis, 440
anxiety, 36, 110, 115, 166, 179, 186, 188, 201, 210, 345, 435, 437
application, 11, 73, 84, 88, 141, 158, 171, 175, 184, 314, 317, 318, 327, 389
applied psychology, 121, 333
aptitude, 227
Argentina, 222
argument, 110, 115, 136, 199, 251, 350, 396
Ariel, 407
Aristotle, 342
arousal, 170, 418
ART, 415, 419, 421, 425
articulation, 207, 330, 331
Ascription of Responsibility, 95, 170
Asia, 4, 162, 365, 373
Asian, 24, 87, 95, 177
assessment, 22, 39, 79, 84, 88, 96, 132, 170, 190, 243, 246, 261, 300, 311, 333, 369, 428, 429, 435, 442
assets, 5
assumptions, 36, 46, 88, 128, 180, 248, 341, 342
Atlantic, 449
atmosphere, 4, 21, 22, 24, 64, 299
attachment, 13, 322, 337, 343, 344, 345, 346, 348, 351, 352, 353, 354, 355, 357, 376, 405, 414, 427
attractiveness, 73, 290
attribution, 11, 165, 206, 298, 378
audition, 428
authoritarianism, 95, 130, 138
authority, 172, 391
automatic processes, 15, 301, 302, 311
automaticity, 301, 312, 313
automation, 101
automobiles, 151
autonomy, 123, 387

availability, 28, 68, 233, 300, 304, 306, 307, 368, 375, 412, 428
aversion, 48
avoidance, 6, 15, 164, 247, 251

B

back, 22, 89, 111, 122, 202, 216, 217, 300, 301, 303, 311, 318, 341, 350, 354
Bali, 17, 140
Baltic States, 93, 104
Bangladesh, 38
barrier, 26, 27, 273, 296, 297, 298, 299, 303, 304, 311
barriers, 9, 12, 19, 20, 25, 26, 28, 32, 33, 34, 37, 63, 68, 71, 246, 273, 291, 295, 296, 297, 298, 299, 300, 301, 302, 303, 304, 311, 312, 314, 386, 437
basic needs, 188, 191, 321, 324, 329
beaches, 345
behavior modification, 152, 159
behavioral change, 14, 63, 73, 74, 147, 151, 159, 271, 299, 301, 305, 402
behavioral dimension, 50, 90
behavioral dispositions, 120
behavioral effects, 159
behavioral intentions, 143, 144, 145, 152, 158, 166, 250, 313
behavioral models, 297
behavioral sciences, 3
behaviorism, 288
behaviours, 16, 27, 29, 30, 33, 34, 35, 36, 38, 41, 57, 74, 262, 337, 353, 354, 361, 362, 363, 381, 412
belief systems, 47, 49, 84, 89, 362
benchmarks, 201
beneficial effect, 213
benevolence, 90, 392
benign, 362
Bhutan, 434
bias, 11, 28, 30, 39, 179, 185, 187, 197, 205, 208, 212, 213, 276, 278, 308, 314
biodiversity, xi, 12, 17, 48, 87, 126, 127, 128, 129, 132, 137, 139, 186, 221, 248, 250, 252, 256, 257, 259, 260, 262, 322, 416, 418, 420, 428
biomass, 338, 339, 340, 358
biosphere, 4, 17, 44, 46, 97, 106, 123, 126, 128, 140, 182, 202, 370
biotechnology, 355
biotic, 89, 272
bipolar, 96
birds, 4, 174
birth, 4, 127, 189, 436
Blacks, 95
blame, 254, 297, 318, 341

blocks, 170
blood, 133, 194
bonding, 116, 344
bonds, 101, 166, 179, 340, 343, 344, 345, 346, 354
boredom, 437
borrowing, 207
Boston, 17, 41, 75, 102, 123, 139, 140, 221, 222, 245, 290, 313, 334, 383
Botanical Garden, 421, 422, 423, 424, 425, 426
bottom-up, 34
boundary conditions, 220
boys, 193, 194, 195, 196, 199
brain, 209, 262
Brazil, 20, 31, 102, 205, 210, 244, 374
breaches, 389, 398, 406
British Columbia, 104
Bronfenbrenner, 207, 221
Brussels, 313
Buenos Aires, 222
buffer, 191, 435
buildings, 36, 135, 421
bulbs, 65
Bulgaria, 272, 289
bureaucracy, 322
burglary, 345
Burkina Faso, 374
burn, 412
burning, 22, 24, 28, 170, 184, 263, 405

C

campaigns, 44, 56, 109, 110, 111, 115, 116, 119, 133, 137, 199, 228, 246, 388
Canada, 20, 24, 58, 91, 93, 408, 428, 434
cancer, 24
candidates, 248
Cape Town, 200
Capitalism, 265
caps, 176
carbon, 4, 21, 22, 24, 39, 338, 339, 343, 353, 357, 358, 388
carbon dioxide, 21, 22, 24, 357
carbon emissions, 4
Caribbean, 319, 320, 334
case study, 13, 38, 57, 337, 339, 347, 353, 357, 413, 428
cast, 115, 287
categorization, 8, 392, 403
causal attribution, 362
causal model, 74, 297
causal relationship, 171, 222, 290
causality, 297
causation, 170

Census, 202, 213, 222, 255, 263
CFA, 193, 214, 219
CFI, 53, 56, 136, 197, 198, 219, 238, 241, 257, 258, 259, 400, 401, 445
changing environment, 246, 274
cheating, 211, 252
chemicals, 397
chicken, 202
child labor, 277, 278, 279, 280, 281, 285
childhood, 212, 216
children, 12, 27, 94, 174, 188, 189, 199, 207, 225, 227, 228, 229, 232, 233, 234, 236, 237, 238, 241, 242, 243, 245, 250, 318, 329, 368, 369, 418, 421
Chile, 334
chimera, 109, 112, 118
China, 93
Chi-square, 53, 136
Christianity, 377
chronemics, 207
citizens, 12, 85, 133, 186, 225, 232, 243, 320, 369, 370, 386, 391, 395, 402, 433, 434, 440, 441
citizenship, 66, 115, 189, 322
civil society, 318, 319, 323
classes, 50, 55, 133, 190, 199, 213, 255, 275, 300, 375
classification, 192, 207, 249, 392, 422, 429
classrooms, 442
clean air, 113
clean-energy, 37
cleanup, 194, 196, 234
climate change, 4, 9, 19, 20, 21, 22, 23, 24, 25, 26, 27, 28, 29, 30, 31, 32, 33, 34, 35, 36, 37, 38, 39, 40, 41, 45, 48, 77, 87, 322, 337, 338, 339, 351, 352, 354, 358, 414, 428
close relationships, 215, 435
closure, 75
cluster analysis, 423
clusters, 374
CNS, 177
Co, 54, 77, 431
CO2, 9, 11, 61, 62, 73, 141, 142, 143, 144, 145, 147, 157, 158
coal, 22, 28, 338
codes, 328
coding, 279, 281, 285, 348
coercion, 406
cognition, 182, 221, 249, 262, 263, 264, 346, 403, 411
cognitive biases, 29
cognitive dissonance, 203
cognitive map, 273, 291, 292
cognitive perspective, 346

cognitive process, 67, 98, 254, 295, 298, 300, 304, 387
cognitive psychology, 250
cognitive representations, 176, 299, 301
cognitive set, 363, 371
cognitive style, 208
cognitive system, 363, 364
cognitive variables, 386
coherence, 6, 205, 208, 243
cohesion, 184, 292, 331
collaboration, 72, 73
collective behaviors, 364
collectivism, 91, 161
collectivism-individualism, 91
Colombia, 139, 361, 365, 370
Columbia, 104, 245
Columbia University, 245
combined effect, 12, 248
commons, 31, 39, 57, 58, 103, 105, 120, 121, 167, 180, 181, 313, 363, 376, 381, 383, 384, 404
communication, 34, 35, 38, 41, 47, 180, 181, 246, 343, 346, 364, 407, 417, 422, 435
communities, 5, 85, 87, 185, 186, 188, 190, 198, 274, 317, 321, 323, 325, 326, 327, 328, 329, 332, 333, 334, 336, 381, 411, 413, 419, 421, 434
community psychology, 12, 322
Comparative Fit Index, 53, 400
compatibility, 227, 270
competence, 50, 107, 227, 244, 246, 262, 312, 440, 448
competency, 7, 11, 14, 57, 210, 225, 227, 230, 231, 232, 234, 236, 237, 241, 242, 243, 244, 312, 313
competition, 5, 7, 168, 388, 427, 439
complement, 71, 212, 249
complexity, 50, 101, 129, 190, 312, 321, 325, 379, 418, 426
compliance, 13, 221, 289, 386, 388, 392, 393, 397, 398, 403, 404, 408
components, 6, 7, 8, 12, 13, 40, 89, 99, 100, 111, 122, 127, 137, 147, 174, 196, 200, 210, 211, 225, 230, 249, 269, 274, 276, 277, 286, 328, 385, 387, 412, 416, 417, 421, 425, 426, 430, 439
composites, 279
composition, 4, 113, 122, 129, 248, 443
composting, 191
comprehension, 166, 446
computer technology, 246
computing, 256
concentration, 24, 186, 319, 436
conception, 87, 89, 94, 96, 97, 111, 208, 273, 278, 287, 327, 329, 333
conceptual model, 227

conceptualization, 28, 83, 99, 116, 167, 179, 208, 273, 326, 364, 393
conceptualizations, 116, 274, 321
concrete, 32, 33, 35, 56, 208, 300, 311, 330, 346, 380
conditioned stimulus, 118, 119
conditioning, 111, 118, 119, 132, 135, 142, 164, 195, 256, 443, 444
condom, 289, 292
conduction, 220, 396, 398
confidence, 41, 370, 374
configuration, 281, 431
confirmatory factor analysis, 93, 122, 193, 206, 214, 218, 219, 236, 257
conflict, 5, 12, 27, 31, 35, 67, 114, 274, 296, 303, 334, 341, 342, 345, 373, 381, 395, 412, 439
conformity, 289
confrontation, 92
confusion, 64, 323, 345
Congress, 21, 222, 315, 429, 430
congruence, 332, 419
connectivity, 91
conscious awareness, 343
conscious perception, 295
consciousness, 205, 212, 273, 293, 296, 302, 311, 312, 318, 322, 325, 333, 362
consensus, 24, 93, 94, 117, 174, 371, 391
consent, 52, 193, 214, 234, 256, 306, 308, 399
consolidation, 101, 320, 328
Constitution, 189
constraints, viii, 12, 25, 66, 68, 271, 274, 278, 279, 295, 296, 297, 298, 299, 300, 301, 302, 303, 304, 311, 312, 314
construct validity, 193, 218, 234, 257, 260, 400, 444
construction, 58, 177, 314, 326, 330, 332, 342, 346, 356, 364, 378, 381, 394, 396, 422, 425, 435
constructionism, 326
constructionist, 180, 326, 334
constructivist, 321, 340
consumerism, 47, 139, 185, 186, 190, 191, 192, 201, 376, 388, 448
consumers, 58, 69, 71, 79, 103, 245, 376
consumption patterns, 440
contaminant, 13
contaminants, 191
contamination, 394
content analysis, 373
context-dependent, 276
contingency, 78, 275, 291
continuity, 43, 55, 126, 324, 331, 345, 349
control condition, 310
control group, 72, 153, 154, 155, 156, 157, 233, 237, 238, 242, 243
convergence, 95, 112, 242, 326, 335, 433, 438

conviction, 372, 381
cooking, 62
cooling, 64, 414
Copenhagen, 21
Coping, 245, 264, 352, 355, 429, 448
correlation, 94, 96, 98, 99, 114, 129, 132, 137, 170, 218, 219, 229, 232, 272, 274, 285, 337, 351, 352, 441, 446
correlations, 63, 95, 99, 196, 197, 199, 226, 229, 232, 242, 270, 281, 285, 351, 352
corruption, 405, 407, 434
cost-effective, 30, 32, 65, 70, 118, 152, 153, 157
costs, 27, 34, 35, 36, 65, 66, 68, 72, 84, 110, 112, 113, 134, 164, 169, 217, 278, 287, 299, 329, 343, 381, 386, 393, 414
cough, 400
couples, 441
covariate, 96
covering, 22, 208, 421
creative potential, 329
creativity, 171
credibility, 221, 358
Crete, 264
crime, 5, 186, 387, 393, 405, 407, 408, 414
crimes, 389, 393
criminal activity, 393
criminal acts, 393
criminal behavior, 221, 408
criminal justice, 393
criminals, 390, 402, 407
criticism, 88, 91, 131, 297
cross-country, 296
cross-cultural comparison, 441
Cuba, 37, 406
cues, 12, 269, 271, 273, 274, 275, 276, 286, 288, 301, 302, 303, 304, 305, 306, 311, 417, 418, 425
cultivation, 4
cultural character, 199
cultural differences, 441
cultural factors, 91
cultural influence, 105
cultural perspective, 90, 172
cultural practices, 188
cultural values, 326, 362
culture, 13, 17, 42, 48, 58, 96, 180, 189, 191, 252, 281, 288, 324, 364, 373, 376, 382, 435, 436, 447, 448
curiosity, 171
curriculum, 244, 245
curriculum development, 245
cycles, 7
cycling, 147
cyclones, 22, 24

D

daily living, 12
danger, 5, 20, 134, 166, 247, 251, 252, 387
data analysis, 53, 193
dead zones, 4
death, 7, 134, 371, 435
death penalty, 134
debates, 321
decision makers, 332
decision making, 73, 209, 245, 261, 264, 311, 312, 333, 435, 441
decision task, 310
decisions, 33, 36, 37, 40, 68, 71, 113, 121, 138, 167, 180, 189, 194, 195, 196, 208, 215, 216, 249, 251, 260, 271, 296, 303, 304, 305, 309, 310, 326, 332, 358, 406, 412
Declaration of Independence, 434
defects, 4, 31
defense, 88, 130
deficit, 34, 209, 211, 341, 407
deficits, 341
definition, 22, 90, 120, 126, 162, 180, 187, 205, 213, 229, 230, 271, 321, 323, 324, 326, 331, 341, 342, 405, 433, 438
deforestation, 22, 24, 26, 322
degradation, 3, 4, 6, 15, 37, 39, 88, 92, 97, 104, 126, 127, 185, 186, 188, 197, 200, 304, 314, 318, 322, 369, 386
delinquency, 186, 407
delinquents, 393, 402
democracy, 322, 334, 448
demographic characteristics, 186, 339
demographics, 57, 64, 65, 103, 200
denial, 36, 170, 346, 396
Denmark, 79, 188, 357
density, 373, 413, 419, 427, 428, 429
dependent variable, 115, 166, 170, 178, 276, 279, 281, 284
depressed, 437
depression, 210, 436, 437
deprivation, 291, 440
desert, 133
destruction, 4
detachment, 172
detection, 390
detergents, 113
deterrence, 13, 385, 386, 388, 393, 398, 399, 400, 402, 403, 405, 406, 408
developed countries, 321, 338
developed nations, 45
developing countries, 25, 49, 319, 320, 321, 375, 379
development policy, 319

deviation, 99
dichotomy, 84, 88, 92, 96, 271
differential treatment, 189
differentiation, 49, 372, 380
diffusion, 70, 80, 85
dimensionality, 193, 196
disabilities, 300
disaster, 33, 253, 264
discipline, 172, 324, 325, 326, 343
discomfort, 166, 179, 254, 298, 441
discontinuity, 273
discounting, 39
discourse, 20, 318, 333, 337, 340, 342, 439, 440
discretionary, 147, 151
discrimination, 5, 185, 186, 189, 190, 197, 201
disorder, 76
dispersion, 333
displacement, 344, 356
disposition, 10, 109, 112, 113, 117, 246, 327
dissatisfaction, 323
disseminate, 23
distraction, 415
distress, 164, 165, 178, 179, 248, 253
distribution, 50, 56, 84, 93, 168, 185, 186, 187, 188, 189, 190, 198, 320, 338, 388, 441
diversity, 6, 7, 10, 14, 89, 95, 104, 125, 126, 127, 128, 129, 130, 131, 132, 133, 136, 137, 138, 139, 188, 197, 247, 253, 254, 255, 257, 321, 326, 327, 331, 332, 414
division, 190
division of labor, 190
DNA, 28
doctors, 333
domestic demand, 45
domestic labor, 189
domestication, 190
dominance, 276, 391, 418
dominant strategy, 114
draft, 427
drainage, 414
dream, 219
drinking, 222, 233, 234, 235, 237, 239, 240, 373
drinking water, 235, 237, 239, 240, 373
drought, 26, 49, 58, 298
droughts, 22, 24
drug consumption, 206, 210
drugs, 222
drunk driving, 211
drying, 279, 280, 285, 286
dualism, 251
duality, 83, 84, 90, 96, 97
duration, 206, 422
duties, 196

E

earnings, 187, 194, 214
earth, 88, 89, 116, 123, 364, 379, 435
eastern cultures, 87
eating, 128, 226
ecological damage, 138, 390
Ecological Economics, 38, 200, 335, 449
Ecological footprint, 449
ecological restoration, 279, 281, 285, 286
ecological systems, 4, 14, 25, 89, 125, 130
ecologists, 327
ecology, 25, 85, 121, 126, 128, 137, 140, 180, 187, 245, 322, 328, 412
economic activity, 84
Economic and Social Research Council, 355
Economic Commission for Latin America, 320, 334
economic development, 45, 85, 336, 363, 441
economic growth, 6, 36, 92, 318, 321, 322, 323, 434
economic incentives, 152
economic security, 318
economic status, 9, 44, 52, 53, 94, 186, 192, 193, 196, 229
economic systems, 23, 126
economically disadvantaged, 321
economics, 85, 106, 139, 159, 182, 202, 245
ecosystem, 4, 6, 15, 86, 97, 127, 187, 246, 373, 379
ecosystems, 4, 5, 6, 7, 14, 20, 25, 26, 43, 55, 56, 88, 89, 90, 93, 101, 126, 127, 128, 139, 186, 187, 191, 319, 388
Education, 58, 75, 76, 102, 103, 104, 105, 121, 123, 202, 222, 223, 229, 244, 245, 246, 262, 263, 264, 290, 291, 296, 301, 302, 304, 310, 311, 313, 314, 315, 382, 407, 430
educational programs, 226, 229, 243
educational system, 229
educators, 227, 243, 447
egalitarianism, 168, 187, 188, 190
egoism, 161, 175, 388, 440
elaboration, 13, 278, 375, 376, 378
elderly, 188, 190, 436
elders, 172
e-learning, 138, 139
electoral process, 331
electricity, 62, 63, 75, 76, 78, 143, 145, 170, 180, 262, 338, 339, 388
elementary school, 130, 241, 242, 366
email, 278, 317, 433
e-mail, 109, 161, 337, 361
emission, 20, 36, 62, 141, 142, 191, 338
emotion, 15, 166, 170, 182, 250, 252, 262, 263, 387, 403, 437
emotional dispositions, 387, 403

Index

emotional processes, 260
emotional reactions, 250
emotional responses, 260, 264, 303, 343, 345, 353, 387, 403
emotional stability, 210, 403
emotional state, 166, 247, 250, 253, 261, 387, 440
emotions, xi, 10, 12, 15, 164, 167, 181, 247, 248, 249, 250, 251, 252, 253, 254, 255, 257, 259, 260, 261, 263, 264, 288, 342, 387, 437
empathy, 11, 96, 101, 165, 166, 170, 176, 178, 179, 180, 182, 183, 247, 253, 264
employees, 147, 230, 370
employment, 189, 329, 434
empowerment, 138, 322, 335
encoding, 208
encouragement, 38
endurance, 15, 16
energy audit, 69
energy consumption, 62, 70, 74, 77, 78, 80, 170, 297, 413
energy efficiency, 338, 356
engagement, 41, 49, 55, 65, 112, 117, 118, 119, 121, 190, 250, 355, 433, 436, 442
England, 102, 336, 357
Enlightenment, 87
enrollment, 52
enterprise, 92
enthusiasm, 252
environmental awareness, 27, 47, 264, 429
environmental change, 6, 20, 25, 26, 38, 41, 46, 47, 59, 126, 128, 231
environmental characteristics, 373
environmental conditions, 5, 6, 47, 169, 174, 207, 230, 322, 369, 373
environmental context, 45, 340, 363, 365, 376, 380
environmental crisis, xi, 3, 85, 185, 186, 381
environmental degradation, 4, 6, 15, 37, 39, 92, 104, 126, 127, 186, 188, 197, 304, 314, 318, 386
environmental effects, 180
environmental factors, 45, 85, 363
environmental impact, 29, 40, 73, 88, 102, 181, 320, 322, 388, 394, 411
environmental influences, 433
environmental issues, 19, 20, 25, 27, 28, 30, 31, 35, 38, 47, 49, 69, 94, 123, 131, 135, 162, 164, 182, 195, 264, 336, 378, 381, 382, 443
environmental movement, 165, 176
environmental policy, 78, 79, 121, 142, 147, 157, 158, 203
environmental protection, 77, 93, 129, 138, 145, 162, 165, 183, 248, 249, 254, 291, 313, 379, 383, 392, 405
Environmental Protection Agency, 75

environmental resources, 15, 88, 167, 225, 227, 315, 384, 427
environmental sustainability, 42, 59, 73, 84, 184, 292, 319
environmentalism, 66, 79, 89, 96, 107, 115, 117, 170, 181, 183, 213, 263, 269, 285
environmentalists, 115, 229, 299
EPA, 61, 75
epidemics, 5
epistemology, 340
equality, 88, 123, 162, 187, 197
equilibrium, 4, 6, 187, 328
equity, 11, 84, 101, 139, 185, 187, 188, 189, 190, 191, 192, 193, 195, 196, 197, 198, 199, 318, 319, 322, 324, 381, 428, 440, 441, 446
erosion, 206
estimating, 257
estrangement, 355
estuaries, 399
ethical principles, 382
ethics, 41, 88, 376
ethnic diversity, 95
ethnic groups, 95
ethnicity, 128, 133, 188
ethnocentrism, 130, 138
Europe, 13, 95, 139, 162, 188, 244, 339, 350, 365, 366, 438, 441
European Commission, 412, 418
European Parliament, 412, 418, 428
European Union, 78, 345
Europeans, 367, 369
Eurostat, 188, 201
evil, 293, 396
evolution, 41, 127, 129, 137, 139, 190, 200, 253, 254, 288, 291, 292, 300, 374, 375, 378, 380, 408, 450
exclusion, 319
excuse, 396
execution, 326, 329, 330, 331
executive function, 209, 222
executive functions, 209, 222
exercise, 87, 277, 284, 285, 288, 325, 342, 379, 391, 402, 434
experimental condition, 166
expertise, 338, 341, 358
exploitation, 85, 88, 111
exposure, 117, 253, 343, 373, 427, 431
external constraints, 299
external environment, 12
external influences, 180, 262
external locus of control, 91, 211
externalities, 9, 273
extinction, 3, 6, 15, 127, 128, 139, 140, 367

extreme poverty, 189, 319, 320
extrinsic motivation, 387
eye, 40, 181
eyes, 391, 437

F

facilitators, 271
factor analysis, 93, 98, 122, 193, 196, 206, 214, 218, 219, 236, 257
failure, 20, 26, 36, 72, 178, 436
fairness, 75, 187, 341
faith, 92, 436, 438
family, 25, 90, 95, 135, 159, 172, 174, 189, 194, 195, 196, 199, 214, 216, 234, 258, 311, 417, 442, 444, 446
family income, 444, 446
family members, 216
family planning, 189
famine, xi, 185, 197
FAO, 128, 139
Far East, 13, 377
farmers, 230, 329, 361, 362, 364, 383, 384, 397, 406
farming, 22, 127, 364
farms, 341, 354, 370
fat, 289
fatalism, 379
fatalistic, 11, 205, 208, 210, 211, 212, 213, 214, 218, 219
fatigue, 354, 414, 415, 416, 418, 420, 426, 429, 431
fauna, 328, 394
fear, 36, 97, 166, 248, 251, 252, 383, 415, 435, 437
fears, 252
fee, 147
feedback, 11, 63, 70, 71, 72, 74, 75, 76, 77, 78, 141, 146, 147, 150, 151, 152, 158, 159, 243, 296, 303, 331
feelings, 10, 11, 12, 29, 36, 71, 116, 121, 126, 130, 132, 137, 164, 165, 166, 177, 179, 181, 247, 250, 251, 253, 254, 255, 257, 260, 338, 344, 379, 382, 387, 394, 412, 415, 435, 439, 440
feet, 350
females, 50, 96, 130, 192, 213, 233, 255, 366, 398, 442
feminist, 202
fertility, 202
filters, 364
financial crisis, 5
fines, 50, 389, 390
Finland, 441
fire, 394
fires, 263, 367, 405
first dimension, 172, 394

First World, 21
fish, 4, 31, 88
fishing, 128, 178
fitness, 276, 291
flexibility, 6, 7, 14, 116
flood, 264, 413
flooding, 4, 28, 38
flora, 328, 394
flow, 205, 215, 253, 332, 380, 446
fluctuations, 6
focus group, 50, 333, 348, 349
focus groups, 50, 333, 348, 349
focusing, 20, 164, 171, 311, 343, 348, 354, 381, 386, 398
food, 4, 5, 25, 79, 127, 128, 139, 166, 189, 194, 305, 306, 307, 319, 374
food production, 127
food products, 306
football, 206
forest fire, 367, 394
forest fires, 367
forest restoration, 272
forestry, 36, 429
fossil, 24, 62, 338
fossil fuel, 24, 62
fossil fuels, 24, 62
fowl, 88
fragility, 94
framing, 34, 41, 67, 77, 288, 381, 407
France, 43, 44, 46, 50, 51, 52, 55, 98, 361, 366, 368, 373, 375, 378, 430
fraternal twins, 436
free association, 348, 349, 350, 353
free enterprise, 92
free trade, 85
free will, 88
freedom, 72, 75, 171, 177, 187, 322
freedoms, 52
fresh water, 43, 44, 45, 48, 365
freshwater, 44, 48
friendship, 172
frontal lobe, 209, 221
frontal lobes, 209
fruits, 438
frustration, 437
fuel, 35, 62, 63, 279, 280, 285, 338, 388
fulfillment, xi, 435
functional analysis, 355
funding, 46, 161, 254, 355
fusion, 376

G

Gallup, 20, 363, 382
gambling, 210
games, 168, 182
garbage, 143, 145, 153, 297, 298, 300, 305, 367, 368, 399
gas, 19, 22, 23, 24, 35, 36, 61, 62, 63, 75, 78, 142, 143, 145, 157, 170, 338, 341
gases, 22, 62, 338
gasifier, 358
gasoline, 135, 170, 195, 257, 258, 443, 444
GDP, 36
gender, 5, 47, 50, 52, 94, 95, 107, 131, 133, 184, 185, 188, 189, 190, 192, 197, 199, 202, 215, 234, 319, 398, 420, 423, 434, 441, 442, 444
gender differences, 107, 434
gender equity, 199, 319, 441
gene, 115, 119, 275, 289
gene pool, 119
generation, 13, 27, 29, 35, 133, 187, 225, 226, 227, 338, 339, 353, 358
generativity, 27, 40
genes, 275
genetic diversity, 127
genetics, 436
Geneva, 357, 431
geography, 85, 339, 343, 373
geology, 25, 85
geophysical, 31
Germany, 109, 139, 146, 315, 336, 375, 378
Gibbs, 103, 138
gift, 153, 378, 436
girls, 189, 193, 194, 195, 196, 199
glaciers, 299
glass, 54, 118
global climate change, 39, 74, 89, 104
global warming, xi, 4, 9, 15, 19, 20, 21, 22, 23, 25, 28, 29, 30, 33, 34, 37, 38, 39, 40, 42, 43, 64, 87, 128, 162, 165, 186, 367
Global Warming, vii, 19, 20, 22, 89
globalization, 127, 128, 318, 335
goal attainment, 305
goal setting, 69, 74, 159, 243
goal-directed behavior, 67, 112, 118, 312, 403
God, 88, 211, 378
gold, 45
goodness of fit, 193, 197, 214, 237, 258, 259, 399, 401
goods and services, 62
Gore, 23
governance, 31

government, vi, xi, 4, 23, 37, 49, 62, 92, 146, 147, 153, 157, 171, 318, 319, 320, 327, 338, 350, 354, 369, 386, 388, 390, 391, 397, 433, 434, 440
governors, 331
GPS, 63
grades, 214
grants, 189, 392
graph, 23
grass, 34, 41
gravity, 85
grazing, 167
greenhouse, 19, 20, 21, 22, 23, 24, 36, 48, 61, 75, 77, 78, 142, 338
greenhouse gas, 19, 20, 21, 22, 23, 24, 36, 61, 75, 142, 338
greenhouse gases, 20, 21, 22, 24, 36, 61, 338
Greenland, 4
grief, 344
gross domestic product, 84, 320
gross national product, 434
group identification, 435
group processes, 290
group size, 181
growth, 4, 6, 36, 45, 66, 84, 85, 88, 92, 93, 94, 96, 97, 126, 127, 318, 319, 321, 322, 323, 336, 340, 373, 416, 434, 448
growth rate, 36, 319
Guatemala, 183
guessing, 228
guidance, 27, 301
guidelines, 35, 314, 330, 332, 333, 413
guiding principles, 343
guilt, 36, 115, 164, 170, 180, 181, 248, 249, 252, 263, 387, 392, 394, 395, 396
guilty, 252, 253, 390, 395

H

habitat, 117, 318, 334, 335, 428
habituation, 312, 375, 378
handling, 87, 207, 225
hands, 217, 233, 235, 236, 237, 239, 240, 330
happiness, xi, 3, 8, 13, 14, 16, 99, 188, 211, 212, 247, 250, 251, 252, 253, 322, 412, 416, 433, 434, 435, 436, 437, 438, 439, 440, 441, 442, 443, 444, 445, 446, 447, 448, 449
Harlem, 318
harm, 166, 172, 247, 251, 389, 394, 395, 396, 426
harmful effects, 378
harmony, 172, 426
Harvard, 104, 140, 159, 184, 447, 450
harvesting, 168
Hawaii, 427

hazards, 28, 30, 33, 40, 171, 252, 264
Head Start, 245
healing, 123
health, 25, 87, 88, 119, 120, 121, 139, 140, 165, 172, 173, 174, 189, 246, 263, 270, 277, 278, 279, 280, 281, 284, 319, 322, 329, 343, 361, 370, 371, 373, 375, 379, 382, 412, 414, 418, 427, 430
health care, 189
health services, 119, 189, 329
hearing, 422
heart, 90, 215, 318, 415
heart rate, 415
heat, 4, 22, 24, 26, 54, 338, 339
heating, 62, 64, 338
hedonic, 65, 67, 77, 122, 439, 449
hedonism, 171, 211, 440
height, 422
helping behavior, 123, 164, 165, 182, 264, 430
helplessness, 345
heredity, 433, 438
heterogeneity, 129, 320, 323
high risk, 292
high school, 130, 293, 306, 308, 366
high school degree, 306, 308
higher quality, 415
high-level, 19, 21, 32, 33, 35
hip, 285
hippocampus, 292
Hispanic, 105
HIV, 131
Holland, 414
home ownership, 286
homeless, 131, 133, 192, 194
homosexuals, 131
horizon, 349, 354, 375
hospital, 421
hospitals, 133, 153, 192, 194, 421
hotels, 76
household, 9, 59, 61, 62, 63, 64, 68, 69, 70, 71, 73, 74, 75, 77, 142, 179, 243, 292, 297, 312, 348, 355, 373, 407, 436
households, 9, 52, 55, 61, 63, 64, 69, 70, 71, 72, 77, 78, 79, 142, 193, 213, 214, 256
housing, 318, 343, 345, 350, 414, 421
human actions, 26, 27, 85
human activity, 22, 92, 191
human animal, 183
human behavior, 3, 7, 15, 44, 45, 46, 48, 68, 74, 75, 128, 185, 206, 221, 251, 253, 261, 275, 313, 382, 386, 404
human brain, 262
human development, 6, 27, 52, 53, 84, 101, 138, 199, 221

human development index, 53
Human Development Report, 59
human dimensions, 38
human nature, xi, 185, 189, 190, 198, 291, 388, 446
human psychology, 15, 225, 248
human reactions, 9
human resources, 191
human rights, 52, 200, 201, 447
human sciences, 339
human values, 106, 183
human welfare, 97, 98, 322
humanity, 30, 41, 66, 84, 85, 86, 90, 202, 449
humans, 6, 10, 11, 12, 14, 15, 25, 26, 27, 28, 55, 84, 85, 87, 88, 89, 91, 92, 93, 94, 97, 101, 114, 117, 127, 129, 137, 172, 178, 180, 190, 225, 226, 248, 251, 275, 345, 376, 380, 388, 412, 420, 433, 438
Hungary, 429
hurricanes, 28, 29, 253
husband, 194, 195, 196
hydration, 371
hydrocarbon, 338
hydrogen, 338, 339, 357
hydropower, 344
hygiene, 234, 371, 374
hyperopia, 29, 30, 39
hypothesis, 45, 86, 89, 111, 117, 176, 178, 193, 197, 236, 273, 343, 435
hypothesis test, 236

I

ice, 4, 24, 25
id, 53, 55, 72, 96, 238, 280, 286, 444, 446
identical twins, 436
identification, 10, 42, 50, 61, 73, 86, 88, 90, 184, 234, 289, 330, 345, 353, 370, 374, 378, 392, 403, 408, 435
ideology, 39, 94, 96, 104, 364, 381, 435
idiosyncratic, 192, 301
IDR, 282
images, 217, 419, 420
imbalances, 325
immediate gratification, 210
immortality, 275, 435
implementation, 10, 56, 61, 70, 71, 72, 74, 78, 143, 151, 233, 236, 237, 238, 241, 242, 243, 275, 317, 319, 340
impulsive, 210, 387
impulsiveness, 251
in situ, 66, 206, 421
inactive, 420
incentive, 31, 69, 151
incentives, 42, 70, 79, 159, 230, 296, 297, 341

inclusion, 45, 91, 97, 100, 111, 116, 120, 166, 177, 178, 220, 279, 411, 413, 421
income, 47, 52, 64, 186, 188, 189, 192, 193, 196, 199, 214, 234, 297, 300, 319, 320, 347, 438, 442, 444, 445, 446
income distribution, 320
income inequality, 52
incomes, 319
independence, 171, 177
independent variable, 281
India, 24, 43, 44, 50, 51, 52, 55, 98, 164, 361, 366, 368, 369
Indian, 367, 368
Indians, 367, 368, 369, 370
indicators, 52, 53, 55, 63, 95, 111, 126, 132, 136, 193, 196, 197, 198, 199, 214, 218, 234, 236, 249, 254, 257, 261, 281, 319, 322, 370, 378, 399, 401, 430, 434, 435, 442, 443, 444, 448
indices, 53, 193, 214
indigenous, 87, 102, 318
indirect effect, 13, 385, 399, 400, 402
individual action, 37, 165, 363, 381, 384
individual differences, 40, 48, 138, 176, 197, 213, 214, 290, 449
individual perception, 55, 59
individualism, 88, 91, 92, 168, 213, 321, 436
Indonesia, 17, 24, 140, 374
induction, 13, 166, 213
industrial, 87, 88, 128, 147, 343, 350, 353, 373
industrial production, 87
industrialisation, 349
industrialized societies, 440
industry, 36, 171, 341, 349, 350, 354
inequality, 188, 318, 320
inequity, 5, 185, 186, 187, 188, 189, 190, 197, 199, 320, 441
inertia, 36
infinite, 93
influenza, 5
information age, 180
information processing, 67
information technology, 355
informed consent, 52, 193, 214, 234, 256, 306, 308, 399
infrastructure, 47, 274, 338, 364, 428, 434
inheritance, 436
inherited, 207, 338
inhibition, 13, 226, 303, 304, 385, 389
inhibitors, 13, 186
injury, vi, 76
injustice, 186, 188, 200, 441, 447
innovation, 59, 85, 161, 336
insight, 63, 73

inspection, 112, 271
instability, 187
institutional change, 85
institutions, 17, 140, 191, 300, 320, 322, 342, 369, 379, 380, 388, 391
instruction, 178
instruments, 93, 110, 116, 118, 132, 190, 192, 193, 206, 214, 220, 233, 236, 242, 255, 323, 399, 441, 442
intangible, 440
integration, 10, 41, 77, 85, 91, 97, 101, 126, 131, 132, 200, 230, 291, 319, 320, 325, 362, 365, 420
integrity, 3, 5, 6, 8, 11, 23, 89, 97, 126, 129, 187, 205, 318, 388, 402
intellectual development, 242
intellectual property, 202
intellectual property rights, 202
intentional behavior, 101, 387
intentionality, 269
interaction, 13, 122, 128, 162, 167, 178, 184, 206, 220, 251, 282, 284, 288, 295, 297, 298, 304, 321, 363, 395, 403, 407, 412, 413, 417, 419, 421, 424, 426, 428
interactions, 3, 7, 10, 15, 70, 125, 127, 128, 185, 271, 284, 288, 343, 346, 395
interdependence, 6, 7, 9, 10, 14, 15, 49, 54, 55, 56, 97, 100, 101, 104, 121, 128, 187, 380
interdisciplinary, 73, 314, 320, 342, 429
interface, 358
interference, 26, 303, 304
intergenerational, 88, 187, 208, 213
Intergovernmental Panel on Climate Change (IPCC), 20, 21, 38, 39, 338, 357
internal barriers, 297
internal consistency, 95, 99, 132, 193, 199, 214, 234, 236, 242, 256, 399, 400, 442, 443, 444
internalised, 169
internalization, 91, 101, 387, 392, 401
internationalization, 392
internet, 69, 107
interpersonal communication, 343
interpersonal relations, 185
interrelations, 44, 53, 101, 130, 193, 226, 232, 234, 236, 237, 257, 261, 442
interrelationships, 243, 251
intervention, 6, 62, 68, 69, 71, 73, 74, 110, 117, 118, 147, 148, 150, 151, 152, 156, 180, 188, 189, 226, 233, 234, 236, 238, 242, 297, 317, 326, 329, 330, 332, 355, 379
intervention strategies, 62, 68, 69
interview, 256, 327, 328, 337, 349, 399
interviews, 50, 333, 348, 349, 353, 365, 373
intrinsic motivation, 387

intrinsic value, 89, 90, 416
intuition, 251
IPCC, 20, 21, 22, 23, 24, 25, 34, 36, 39
Ireland, 24, 345, 356, 359
irrationality, 341
irrigation, 4
island, 99
isolation, 269, 286, 419, 436
Italy, 43, 44, 46, 50, 51, 55, 57, 98, 125, 130, 180, 361, 366, 368, 420
IUCN, 126, 127, 139, 318, 334

J

Jamaica, 336
Japan, 49, 93, 102, 141, 145, 146, 147, 152, 153, 159, 374, 375, 378, 420, 428, 436
Japanese, 96, 141, 153, 156, 159, 373, 375
jewelry, 194
jobs, 351, 352, 426
joining, 95, 434
Jordanian, 58
journalists, 41, 341
judge, 366
judgment, 171, 263, 290, 314, 369, 394
judgmental heuristics, 28
junior high, 366
junior high school, 366
jurisdictions, 390
justice, 88, 90, 140, 162, 172, 181, 187, 201, 263, 264, 291, 324, 341, 393, 407, 434
justification, 76, 394, 396

K

killing, 435
kindergarten, 245
King, 435
Kobe, 147
Korean, 229, 244
Kyoto Protocol, 21

L

labor, 281, 285
Labour Party, 27
lack of confidence, 395
lack of opportunities, 300, 304
lambda, 218, 260
land, 5, 24, 57, 127, 167, 189, 343, 413, 418
land use, 24, 57, 343, 413
landfill, 343

landscapes, 128, 344, 350, 419, 428
language, 119, 261, 341, 342, 414, 419, 427
large-scale, 5, 10, 13, 15, 22, 110, 115, 116, 119, 162, 338, 339, 340, 353
Latin America, 13, 95, 96, 162, 177, 220, 319, 320, 325, 334, 363, 365, 434
Latin American countries, 320, 363
Latinos, 95
laundry, 135, 195, 443, 444
law, 13, 187, 222, 386, 388, 389, 391, 392, 393, 394, 395, 397, 398, 401, 403, 404, 407, 408
law enforcement, 395, 407, 408
laws, 8, 34, 68, 87, 92, 346, 379, 388, 389, 390, 391, 394, 395, 397, 398, 399, 402, 404, 405, 406
lawyers, 394
learning, 117, 118, 119, 139, 164, 230, 244, 263, 271, 288, 436
learning process, 117, 118, 119, 244
leisure, 147, 270, 338, 390, 437
lens, 210, 297
Less Developed Countries, 265, 450
liberal, 94, 95, 189
liberty, 92
life cycle, 39, 127
life expectancy, 52
life forms, 89, 126, 137, 166, 177
life style, 101, 174
life-cycle, 62
lifespan, 430
likelihood, 30, 56, 67, 92, 97, 225, 299, 393, 397, 399, 401
Likert scale, 131, 214, 276, 277
limitation, 230, 261, 331, 379
limitations, 261, 355, 379
Lincoln, 326, 334
linear, 145, 175, 207, 208, 281, 354
linear regression, 145
links, 11, 19, 32, 48, 87, 130, 174, 198, 212, 219, 220, 222, 325, 344, 351, 353, 398, 430, 439
listening, 215
literacy, 222, 244
living conditions, 20, 191, 317, 327, 373
living environment, 130
living standard, 375
living standards, 375
lobbying, 191, 380
local authorities, 213, 319, 332, 395, 412
local community, 50
localised, 342
location, 147, 152, 153, 300, 342, 344, 347, 349, 358, 412, 423, 426
locus, 91, 211, 221, 381

Index 463

London, 39, 58, 77, 78, 121, 202, 265, 290, 292, 319, 333, 345, 355, 356, 357, 358, 404, 405, 412, 418, 428, 430, 431
Los Angeles, 202
losses, 34
love, 172, 177, 250, 349
low-level, 32, 35
lung, 210
lung cancer, 210
Lungs, 176
lying, 343

M

macroeconomic, 319
magazines, 20
magnetic, vi
mainstream, 321
maintenance, 135, 166, 179, 227, 306, 312
maladaptive, 27, 29
males, 50, 96, 130, 192, 213, 233, 255, 366, 398, 442
malnutrition, 319
management, 17, 36, 40, 42, 48, 49, 53, 59, 75, 87, 106, 140, 146, 147, 148, 151, 152, 157, 159, 182, 245, 276, 281, 284, 285, 318, 325, 326, 335, 358, 372, 373, 379, 428, 429, 435
management practices, 48
manipulation, 166, 178, 286, 307, 309
man-made, 350
manners, 207, 228
mapping, 285, 428
marital conflict, 441
market, 39, 73, 89, 104, 190, 339, 340
marketing, 78, 158, 159, 314
marriage, 181, 447
Maryland, 414
mask, 419
masking, 27
mass media, 78
Massachusetts, 17, 18, 106, 107, 180, 203, 448
mastery, 139
mathematics, 112
matrix, 196, 218, 219, 237, 240
maturation, 17
meals, 192, 194
meanings, 73, 325, 327, 329, 332, 336, 342, 346, 348, 354, 364, 419
measurement, 10, 39, 58, 61, 63, 105, 110, 112, 118, 120, 177, 257, 289, 291, 438
meat, 65, 395
media, 47, 78, 299, 328, 337, 343
mediation, 274, 288, 298, 300, 302, 311, 326
mediators, 55, 169, 311

melting, 4, 24
membership, 169, 220, 333
memory, 26, 48, 68, 314, 364, 376, 378
men, 4, 94, 99, 134, 188, 189, 190, 194, 196, 199, 369, 435, 437, 439, 441, 444
mental capacity, 227
mental health, 418
mental illness, 435
mental processes, 313
mental representation, 304, 308, 310
messages, 34, 147, 246, 404
meta-analysis, 16, 47, 57, 58, 114, 120, 121, 137, 138, 146, 229, 245, 261, 292
metabolism, 76
metaphor, 350
metaphors, 167, 363
methane, 22, 24
methodological implications, 340
metric, 140, 224
Mexico City, 138, 140, 201, 202, 222, 263
middle class, 255, 437, 446
migrants, 95
military, 390
milk, 303, 305, 306, 307, 308, 309, 310, 329
Millennium, 4, 17, 37, 41, 127, 140, 246, 319
Millennium Development Goals, 319
mineral water, 379
mining, 229, 345
Ministry of Education, 385
Minnesota, 223, 358
minorities, 131, 188, 189, 375
minority, 186, 339, 347, 441
minority groups, 441
misconception, 110
missions, 9, 19, 22, 23, 24, 36, 61, 62, 73, 75, 77, 78, 141, 142, 144, 145, 157, 158
MIT, 120, 180, 245, 289, 448
mixing, 348
mobility, 146, 147, 148, 151, 152, 157, 159
modalities, 373
modeling, 128, 132, 193, 232, 397
models, 24, 67, 74, 76, 85, 96, 101, 161, 164, 165, 178, 186, 199, 221, 247, 248, 249, 250, 257, 260, 261, 289, 296, 297, 298, 301, 304, 310, 311, 386, 387, 403
moderates, 228
moderators, 112, 408
modern society, 42, 203, 265, 450
modernization, 87
money, 35, 50, 65, 66, 70, 110, 112, 113, 131, 133, 165, 166, 187, 192, 194, 274, 390, 428, 433, 437, 438
mood, 164, 180, 182, 256, 259, 436

moral development, 90, 181
moral feelings, 382
moral judgment, 394, 399, 401, 402
moral reasoning, 90, 105
moral standards, 115, 119, 392
morality, 74, 110, 111, 114, 115, 116, 119, 402, 435
morals, 389
morning, 131, 217
morphology, 419
mortality, 436
mosaic, 334
mothers, 373
motion, 264
motives, xi, 3, 8, 10, 50, 66, 79, 84, 86, 90, 109, 110, 111, 112, 114, 115, 116, 118, 162, 168, 177, 180, 181, 199, 225, 226, 229, 231, 232, 233, 234, 236, 237, 238, 241, 242, 243, 260, 274, 386, 387, 448
mouth, 437
movement, 39, 128, 162, 435
multinational corporations, 323
multiple regression, 178
multiple regression analysis, 178
multiplicity, 325
muscle, 415
music, 182, 215, 396, 399
mutations, 383

N

NAM, 66, 67, 138, 140, 201
nation, 222, 383, 434
National Academy of Sciences, 200
National Association for the Education of Young Children, 246
national identity, 345
national policy, 351, 352, 434
national security, 172
Native American, 87
natural disasters, 28
natural environment, 111, 116, 117, 118, 119, 120, 139, 140, 161, 175, 176, 180, 253, 263, 374, 375, 376, 382, 394, 411, 412, 415, 416, 417, 419, 420, 421, 426, 429, 430
natural gas, 62, 338
natural laws, 87
natural resources, 3, 5, 6, 8, 12, 13, 17, 31, 47, 55, 84, 85, 93, 100, 113, 122, 127, 140, 167, 185, 186, 190, 191, 199, 205, 210, 211, 212, 225, 226, 227, 231, 322, 363, 364, 386, 388, 412
natural science, 85
natural sciences, 85
natural selection, 117, 275
nature conservation, 315

negative attitudes, 13, 130, 131, 132, 137, 353
negative consequences, 22, 29, 35, 69, 110, 119, 127, 171, 187, 413
negative emotions, 248, 250, 252, 337, 387, 412
negative outcomes, 31, 348, 351
negative relation, 92, 95, 285, 351
negativity, 341
neglect, 211, 251
negotiation, 325, 332
nervous system, 262
Netherlands, 61, 62, 74, 76, 78, 79, 109, 120, 343
network, 80, 297, 335, 364, 418
networking, 138
neuroscience, 251, 359
neutralization, 395, 404, 407
Nevada, 370, 383
New Frontier, 17
New Jersey, 390, 408
New Zealand, 19, 24, 27, 31, 36, 37, 38, 39, 40, 41
NGOs, 373
Nielsen, 130, 139, 175, 181, 191, 202, 439, 448
Niger, 200
Nigeria, 200, 201
nitrous oxide, 22, 24
NNFI, 53, 56, 136, 197, 198, 219, 238, 241, 257, 258, 259, 400, 401, 445
noise, 26, 146, 274, 340, 396, 414, 418, 420, 421, 427, 428, 429, 430, 431
nonconscious, 208
non-human, 46, 84, 89, 97, 137, 166, 167
non-native, 357
Non-Normed Fit Index, 53, 400
non-renewable, 49
normal, 127, 378, 393
normative behavior, 67, 390, 397
North America, 162, 363
Norway, 76, 344
nuclear, 28, 29, 338, 339, 343, 355, 356, 358
nuclear energy, 338
nuclear power, 339, 343, 355, 356, 358
nuclear reactor, 29
nuclear technology, 28
nuclei, 372
nucleus, 371
Nuevo León, 3, 185, 247
nutrients, 127
nutrition, 88

O

obedience, 172, 391
obese, 4
objectification, 346

obligate, 391
obligation, 66, 70, 72, 114, 115, 170, 291, 392
obligations, 90, 134, 205, 208, 217
observations, 74, 234, 262
observed behavior, 63
oceans, 4, 24
OECD, 62, 77
offenders, 394, 395, 408
offshore, 337, 339, 344, 347, 348, 353, 354
Ohio, 416
oil, 5, 45, 85, 338
older people, 189, 192, 446
olfaction, 428
omission, 250
online, 276, 306, 308
open space, 256, 413, 414, 419, 428, 430, 431
open spaces, 256, 413, 414, 419, 430
openness, 172
operant conditioning, 118
operator, 326
opinion polls, 339, 340
opposition, 37, 97, 118, 131, 132, 172, 211, 297, 315, 337, 339, 340, 341, 342, 343, 344, 347, 348, 350, 351, 352, 353, 354, 358, 381
oppositional behaviour, 337, 353
oppression, 189
optimism, 41, 42, 207, 222, 304, 383, 435, 438
optimization, 325, 326
oral, 105, 122, 169
orange juice, 308, 309
organic, 64, 296, 300, 303, 305, 306, 307, 308, 309
organic food, 305, 306, 307
Organisation for Economic Co-operation and Development, 77
organism, 139, 230, 248, 252, 273
overexploitation, 31, 87
overload, 69, 418, 430
overpopulation, 9, 186, 190
ownership, 118
oxide, 22, 24
oxygen, 4
ozone, 4, 21, 26, 48, 64, 176

P

packaging, 142
pain, 252, 253
paradox, 55, 222, 224
paralysis, 331
parameter, 87
parenting, 27
parents, 27, 172, 234, 245, 306
Paris, 50, 51, 77, 104, 139, 246, 365, 366, 373, 374, 382, 383, 384, 430
Parliament, 418, 428
passive, 417
pasture, 167
pathogenic, 115
pathological gambling, 210
pathways, 344
patients, 134
PBC, 272, 279, 284, 299
PCA, 368, 369
pedestrian, 151, 429
pedestrian traffic, 151
peer, 23, 24
peers, 286, 437, 442, 443, 444
penalties, 72, 390, 402, 408
penalty, 134
Pennsylvania, 106
perceived control, 47, 363
perceptions, 8, 13, 15, 38, 39, 42, 45, 46, 47, 49, 51, 53, 67, 68, 75, 146, 205, 212, 232, 272, 299, 315, 339, 340, 342, 346, 356, 358, 361, 363, 364, 365, 375, 393, 397, 404, 413, 421, 430
perceptions of control, 272, 404
perceptual component, 298
periodicity, 366
permit, 15, 252, 260, 288, 394
personal communication, 421
personal hygiene, 234
personal identity, 392
personal norms, 13, 76, 79, 101, 121, 165, 170, 171, 173, 222, 248, 286, 290, 292, 385, 392, 394, 398
personal relevance, 48
personal responsibility, 11
personal values, 169, 171, 173, 296
personal wealth, 374
personality, 28, 40, 41, 78, 114, 121, 170, 182, 271, 289, 290, 292, 364, 391
personality traits, 364
persuasion, 41, 80, 183, 221
perturbation, 26
Peru, 93, 102
pessimism, 207, 222, 369, 383
pesticides, 28, 364
pets, 167, 183
pharmaceutical, 127
Philadelphia, 292, 405, 407
Philippines, 24
philosophical, 177
philosophy, 84, 110, 202, 251
Phoenix, 244
photovoltaic, 339
physical activity, 428

physical environment, 6, 8, 10, 16, 46, 55, 57, 97, 102, 127, 128, 185, 191, 192, 200, 205, 220, 226, 244, 274, 344, 346, 358, 386, 398, 412, 434, 438, 439, 441, 442
physical force, 391
physical health, 415
physical sciences, 386
physical world, 206, 358, 363, 412
physiological, 118, 234, 261, 264, 383, 415
physiology, 411
pipelines, 341
planetary, 232
planning, 159, 189, 205, 295, 297, 311, 319, 327, 328, 331, 332, 333, 341, 357, 358, 359, 411, 412, 413, 414, 416, 417, 418, 420, 421, 427
planning decisions, 411, 412
plants, 27, 51, 54, 127, 128, 131, 133, 147, 174, 175, 211, 235, 237, 239, 240, 243, 256, 259, 391, 399
plastic, 312, 441
plasticity, 117, 289, 312
play, 12, 13, 45, 49, 64, 73, 103, 134, 179, 199, 217, 249, 251, 261, 317, 329, 338, 364, 375, 376, 412, 419, 426, 437
pleasure, 119, 171, 210, 216, 247, 251, 375, 387, 419, 436, 439
pluralism, 321
plurality, 325, 326
point like, 192
policy makers, 39, 152, 157, 337, 341
policy making, 158, 356
politeness, 172
political parties, 27
politicians, 20, 41
politics, 189, 358
polling, 339
pollutant, 209
pollution, xi, 4, 26, 28, 35, 45, 48, 87, 93, 146, 169, 170, 186, 233, 235, 237, 239, 240, 253, 263, 345, 367, 373, 379, 405, 413
poor, 4, 118, 133, 194, 195, 196, 242, 279, 318, 319, 320, 325, 366, 367, 369, 370, 373, 414, 437, 441, 443
poor health, 414
poor performance, 279
population, 4, 5, 17, 44, 45, 48, 64, 72, 93, 94, 116, 127, 130, 153, 186, 189, 193, 199, 227, 241, 245, 255, 256, 275, 289, 318, 319, 320, 321, 327, 336, 347, 348, 350, 373, 375, 396, 398
population growth, 4, 45, 127, 373
Portugal, 20, 96, 295, 306, 308, 313, 314, 315
positive attitudes, 101, 130, 226, 243, 285, 295, 296, 297, 311
positive behaviors, 55

positive correlation, 91, 137, 177, 209, 211, 337, 351, 446
positive emotions, 252, 260, 387, 415
positive mood, 180
positive relation, 90, 137, 210, 351, 352
positive relationship, 90, 210
poverty, xi, 5, 189, 197, 200, 318, 319, 320, 323, 324, 325, 429, 434, 441
poverty rate, 320
power plant, 339
power relations, 346
powers, 87
pragmatic, 118
pragmatism, 323
praxis, 327, 333, 364
precedents, 85, 390
precipitation, 24
prediction, 32, 33, 42, 178, 181, 272, 308, 388
predictive model, 100, 250
predictive models, 250
predictors, 12, 31, 38, 45, 47, 53, 78, 106, 130, 132, 140, 199, 221, 229, 249, 250, 259, 260, 264, 270, 363, 384, 386, 394, 418
pre-existing, 337
preference, 7, 24, 87, 89, 129, 131, 139, 140, 163, 209, 254, 256, 300, 349, 427, 431
prejudice, 293
premature death, 4
preparedness, 289
press, 29, 31, 36, 40, 58, 66, 75, 79, 116, 117, 120, 122, 139, 180, 183, 207, 220, 223, 264, 289, 305, 312, 398, 402, 404
pressure, 54, 65, 275, 380, 381, 383, 385, 386, 388, 401, 402, 411, 418, 419, 422, 423
prestige, 189
prevention, 322, 404, 405
prices, 69
pricing policies, 69, 78
priming, 303, 308, 310, 313, 315
privacy, 346, 417, 429
private, 31, 44, 75, 76, 92, 114, 115, 118, 169, 190, 209, 318, 319, 323, 324, 390, 420
private good, 31
private property, 92, 190
private sector, 44, 319, 323
probability, 28, 35, 113, 169, 275, 297, 301, 303, 305, 306, 308, 391, 402
problem-solving, 28, 225, 228, 230, 241, 433
problem-solving behavior, 241
problem-solving skills, 228, 433
producers, 245
production, 62, 64, 84, 87, 127, 189, 246, 320, 321, 323, 326, 328, 329, 332, 373, 381, 388, 421, 440

productivity, 412, 414
profits, 111, 329
program, 139, 141, 146, 147, 150, 151, 152, 158, 169, 170, 180, 181, 202, 226, 232, 233, 234, 235, 236, 237, 238, 241, 242, 243, 262, 274, 285, 327, 328, 330, 331, 332, 333, 448
proliferation, 318
promoter, 433
property, vi, 92, 112, 190, 202, 231, 351, 352, 398
property rights, 92
proposition, 324, 342
prosocial behavior, 75, 77, 161, 164, 180
prosperity, 412
protected area, 57, 180, 315, 385, 398, 399
protected areas, 57, 180, 315
protection, 77, 93, 111, 129, 138, 145, 162, 164, 165, 166, 177, 183, 191, 225, 227, 248, 249, 254, 291, 313, 379, 383, 386, 392, 405, 412, 439, 442
proxy, 52, 299
psychological development, 27
psychological functions, 13
psychological problems, 58
psychological processes, 13, 15, 46, 142, 208, 251, 295, 297, 298, 300, 302, 303, 304, 307, 311, 312, 324, 402
psychological states, 10, 433, 435, 447
psychological tools, 260
psychological variables, 8, 36, 131, 297, 386, 404
psychologist, 271
psychometric properties, 260
psychopathic, 166, 182
psychophysics, 28
psychophysiology, 262
psychosocial factors, 90
psychotherapy, 436
public administration, 390, 395, 406
public goods, 31, 158, 159, 182
public health, 26, 289, 318
public interest, 31
public opinion, 20, 33, 44
public policy, 406
public service, 373
public support, 71, 337, 339, 343, 356, 359
public transit, 222
punishment, 200, 386, 389, 393, 394, 395, 396, 397, 402, 403
punitive, 290
purchasing power, 52
purchasing power parity, 52
Pyszczynski, 435, 449, 450

Q

Q-methodology, 356
qualitative research, 326, 332, 334
quality of life, 62, 72, 73, 74, 79, 89, 138, 176, 191, 322, 324, 325, 327, 328, 333, 338, 412, 413, 414, 418, 439, 448
quartile, 309
Quercus, 314
questioning, 98, 101
questionnaire, 44, 50, 51, 112, 131, 147, 148, 149, 151, 153, 154, 233, 234, 306, 309, 337, 339, 340, 348, 352, 354, 365, 366, 398, 421, 422, 434, 441
questionnaires, 150, 154, 171, 271, 276, 278, 301, 348

R

race, 176, 188, 192, 260, 392
radio, 328
radioactive waste, 28, 338
rain, 4, 31, 64
rain forest, 4, 31
rainfall, 26
random, 213, 371
random numbers, 213
range, 8, 39, 66, 67, 94, 99, 117, 130, 162, 195, 279, 314, 338, 341, 362, 370, 371, 373, 379, 418, 425
ratings, 90, 280, 287, 417, 418, 419, 424
rationality, 167, 168, 251, 263, 290, 341
raw material, 91
reaction time, 415
reading, 95
reality, 4, 85, 120, 289, 298, 299, 326, 364, 381, 408
reasoning, 67, 90, 105, 176, 323, 387, 396
recall, 216
recalling, 208
reciprocity, 164, 167
recognition, 19, 145, 172, 378, 379, 436
recollection, 254
reconciliation, 97
recovery, 6, 13, 118, 119, 184, 414, 415, 416, 417, 422, 424, 425, 429, 431
recreation, 429
recycling plant, 391
recycling plants, 391
Red Cross, 131, 133, 192, 194
redevelopment, 422, 425
redistribution, 101, 320
refining, 323
reflection, 85, 112, 325, 327, 414, 415, 416, 417, 422, 424, 426

reflexes, 304
regression, 100, 145, 174, 281, 346
regression analysis, 100, 346
regular, 170, 380, 390
regulation, 28, 87, 89, 92, 209, 315, 387, 406
regulations, 34, 37, 47, 68, 73, 364, 389, 391, 396
rehabilitation, 85
reinforcement, 76, 77, 223, 275, 440, 446
rejection, 89, 94, 100, 131, 216, 264, 318, 342
relationships, 28, 47, 64, 66, 95, 121, 144, 171, 198, 206, 215, 220, 222, 246, 257, 260, 263, 269, 279, 288, 290, 318, 331, 332, 334, 398, 421, 422, 435
relatives, 277
relevance, 31, 46, 48, 101, 109, 116, 119, 287, 301, 326, 343, 358, 363
reliability, 23, 52, 53, 75, 97, 99, 132, 133, 177, 193, 194, 218, 236, 256, 257, 258, 259, 260, 278, 348, 449
religion, 8, 134, 363, 374, 435
religions, 128, 133, 188
religious belief, 106
religious beliefs, 106
René Descartes, 43, 361
renewable energy, 337, 338, 339, 343, 346, 355, 358
rent, 397
reparation, 395
replication, 74, 212
representative samples, 20, 339
reproduction, 179
reproductive age, 388
reputation, 402
research design, 71, 348, 446
reservation, 6, 111, 322, 412
residential, 49, 58, 74, 76, 78, 80, 98, 129, 138, 146, 150, 152, 221, 229, 313, 345, 370, 404, 413, 418, 421, 427, 428
residues, 299
resilience, 6, 17, 37, 39, 140
resistance, 13, 41, 96, 111, 119, 337, 340, 346, 347, 350, 354, 355
resolution, 27, 290, 299, 362
response format, 348
responsibilities, 231, 369, 441
retirement, 347
returns, 84
revenue, 78
rewards, 68, 69, 71, 72, 119, 164, 165, 169, 209, 210, 386, 440
rhetoric, 37, 323, 326
rhythm, 206, 379
rice, 407

risk, 4, 26, 28, 30, 32, 33, 34, 35, 38, 39, 40, 41, 42, 77, 96, 127, 187, 211, 244, 292, 343, 362, 387, 390, 398, 402, 406
risk factors, 28
risk management, 40
risk perception, 28, 30, 35, 38, 39, 244, 343, 362
risks, 27, 28, 29, 30, 31, 32, 33, 34, 35, 41, 59, 96, 186, 215, 252, 363, 373, 378, 379, 390, 393
risk-taking, 387
risky driving, 206, 224
rivers, 167, 388
RMSEA, 53, 56, 136, 193, 197, 198, 214, 219, 238, 241, 257, 258, 259, 400, 401, 445
Rome, 43, 50, 51, 125, 139, 366, 382, 427
Rouleau, 342, 357
routines, 436
rule-breaking, 386
rural, 200, 318, 344, 345, 369, 372, 427
rural people, 369
Russia, 20

S

sadness, 251
safety, 292, 338, 343, 415, 417
salary, 189, 329
sales, 187, 387
salinity, 24
sample, 29, 64, 91, 98, 99, 103, 107, 116, 214, 237, 245, 255, 256, 280, 285, 290, 306, 308, 348, 352, 362, 366, 368, 369, 373, 375, 390, 398, 422, 425, 434, 442, 443, 444, 445, 446
sanctions, 13, 34, 169, 389, 390, 393, 396, 403, 408
SAS, 278, 279
satellite, 4
satisfaction, 31, 93, 99, 212, 244, 247, 250, 252, 253, 262, 322, 343, 346, 387, 413, 429, 437, 438, 439, 440, 441, 446, 448
saturation, 99
savings, 62, 63, 69, 70, 71, 72, 73, 145, 285
scandal, 405
scarcity, xi, 9, 16, 43, 55, 232, 298, 299, 362, 366, 367, 369, 370, 373, 378
Scheffe test, 353
schemas, 416
school, 58, 119, 130, 146, 152, 214, 228, 229, 232, 233, 234, 241, 242, 245, 293, 306, 308, 366, 421
schooling, 52, 186, 193, 214, 255
scientific community, 23
scientific progress, 357
scores, 95, 99, 130, 177, 178, 188, 232, 236, 243, 348, 394, 398, 422, 437
SCP, 79

SCT, 386, 387
SDT, 387, 402
sea ice, 24, 25
sea level, 24
search, 23, 45, 110, 111, 114, 116, 188, 323, 387, 440
search terms, 23
searching, 9, 130, 439
Seattle, 106
Secretary General, 20
secular, 115
security, 17, 90, 172, 177, 216, 318, 319, 322, 339, 379
selecting, 275
selectionist principles, 275
Self, 17, 51, 159, 171, 172, 173, 184, 223, 261, 262, 282, 283, 309, 387, 392, 402, 406, 447, 448
self help, 437
self worth, 435
self-concept, 116, 355
self-control, 208, 209, 210, 211, 223, 251, 387, 398, 399, 406
self-determination theory, 404
self-discipline, 172
self-efficacy, 246, 345
self-enhancement, 31, 66, 90, 172
self-esteem, 210, 345
self-image, 231
self-interest, 90, 102, 113, 114, 164, 165, 168, 172
self-presentation, 395
self-regulation, 315
self-report, 10, 14, 30, 44, 52, 53, 63, 74, 80, 126, 131, 132, 170, 186, 188, 192, 201, 206, 214, 221, 257, 260, 261, 272, 315, 353, 397, 399, 442, 446
self-reports, 63, 74, 80, 261
SEM, 52, 53, 132, 257
semantic, 370, 419, 420, 422
semantics, 430
semi-structured interviews, 50
senior citizens, 133
sensation, 210, 211, 222, 387
sensation seeking, 222
sensitivity, 145, 275, 392
sensory systems, 290
sentences, 390, 394
sentencing, 408
separation, 117, 229, 246
series, 13, 67, 87, 88, 125, 129, 130, 146, 171, 174, 209, 210, 232, 254, 344, 353, 365, 367, 369, 440
services, vi, 54, 62, 64, 68, 119, 189, 329, 338
SES, 9, 44, 52, 55, 193, 196, 199
settlements, 318, 319, 323, 325, 328
severity, 393, 394, 397, 399

sewage, 396, 399
sex, 247, 251, 388, 436, 448
sexism, 190, 198
sexual behavior, 270
sexual harassment, 189
sexual orientation, 128, 185
sexuality, 435
shame, 248, 252, 253
shape, 354, 364, 375, 376, 380
shaping, 91, 209, 231, 343, 354, 356
shares, 187, 211
sharing, 99, 188, 363, 374, 380, 439
sheep, 167
shelter, 319
shock, 345
shortage, 48, 369
shortages, 49, 373
short-term, 15, 31, 35, 168, 281, 362, 375, 379
signalling, 341
signals, 26, 32, 34
signal-to-noise ratio, 26
signs, 26
similarity, 290, 436
simulation, 308
simulations, 246, 306
Singapore, 24
singular, 330
sites, 50, 246, 343, 366, 373, 374, 375
skills, 3, 7, 8, 11, 50, 199, 225, 227, 228, 229, 230, 231, 232, 233, 234, 235, 236, 237, 238, 241, 242, 243, 246, 249, 260, 295, 296, 311, 322, 375, 433, 438
slavery, 189, 190
sleep, 418
sleep disorders, 418
Slovenia, 188
slums, 319
smiles, 437
smog, 135, 258
smoke, 210, 263, 405
smoking, 210, 222, 292
social acceptance, viii, 110, 337, 358
social behavior, 101, 162, 164, 165, 170, 171, 174, 210, 253, 301, 397, 398, 402, 403
social capital, 332
social change, 6, 85, 96, 326, 336
social class, 133
social cognition, 312
social cohesion, 184, 292
social comparison, 71, 449
social conflicts, 186, 363
social consensus, 391
social consequences, 169, 211

social construct, 321, 326, 334, 358, 407
social constructivism, 334
social context, 3, 13, 70, 122, 245, 289, 342, 354, 362, 363, 364, 365, 398, 431
social desirability, 281, 284, 301
social development, 85, 327
social dilemma, 30, 31, 32, 35, 39, 40, 42, 75, 78, 113, 114, 123, 167, 168, 182, 184, 222, 292, 304, 363
social distance, 29, 30, 32, 35
social environment, 8, 85, 137, 227, 300, 311, 334, 363, 393, 439
social evaluation, 92
social events, 364
social exchange, 364
social exclusion, 189
social factors, 169
social group, 45, 87, 94, 188, 212, 225, 228, 288, 370, 388
social identity, 45, 88, 101, 317, 324, 391, 392
social inequalities, 374
social influence, 35, 167, 182, 221, 391, 403, 407
social justice, 172, 291
social learning, 164
social movements, 79, 123, 183
social norms, 8, 11, 65, 67, 69, 70, 72, 76, 78, 165, 167, 169, 170, 183, 272, 275, 276, 278, 279, 280, 286, 292, 299, 364, 388, 389, 392, 397, 398, 401, 403, 404, 405, 407, 408
social order, 172, 388, 391
social organization, 317
social phenomena, 340, 347
social problems, xi, 162, 182, 185, 197, 325
social psychology, 18, 40, 75, 78, 123, 169, 174, 180, 182, 183, 223, 271, 289, 290, 293, 301, 345, 358
social relations, 48, 206, 290, 364
social resources, 3, 7, 191, 199, 332, 386
social responsibility, 167
social rewards, 164, 165
social roles, 231
social sciences, xi, 44, 45, 85, 273, 296, 311, 321, 341
social situations, 12, 15, 269, 275
social status, 192
social stress, 428
social support, 394
social welfare, 85
social work, 447
social workers, 447
socialisation, 358
socially responsible, 219, 251, 260
socioeconomic background, 298

socioeconomic status, 278
sociologists, 73, 342
sociology, 39, 85, 86, 250, 251, 264, 297, 339
software, 234, 278, 348
soil, 4, 367
soil erosion, 367
solar, 118, 338, 339
solar panels, 118
solid waste, 9, 139, 201, 246, 322, 448
solidarity, 77, 88, 101, 187, 207, 208, 213, 222, 362, 363
sounds, 13, 216, 411, 412, 413, 417, 418, 419, 420, 421, 422, 423, 424, 425, 426, 427, 429, 430
South Africa, 24, 31, 188
South America, 373
Southeast Asia, 4
Spain, 17, 58, 59, 83, 99, 104, 161, 164, 210, 229, 244, 313, 314, 375, 385, 394, 399, 406, 407, 429, 430
species, 3, 4, 6, 14, 15, 16, 46, 86, 87, 90, 93, 96, 104, 126, 127, 128, 133, 172, 176, 185, 190, 197, 226, 247, 251, 252, 256, 259, 272, 367, 388, 392, 396, 399, 414, 421, 438
specificity, 91, 170, 181, 368
spectrum, 287, 373, 374
speech, 20
speed, 211
speed limit, 211
spheres, 3, 186, 189, 318, 440
spills, 399
spiritual, 87, 172
spirituality, 414
springs, 436
stability, 89, 94, 210, 345, 364, 368, 378, 403
stages, 100, 223, 341, 347, 348, 353, 354, 415
standard deviation, 99, 150, 155, 157, 256, 280, 368, 442
standard of living, 52
standardization, 228
standards, 5, 91, 115, 119, 188, 330, 375, 392
statistical analysis, 256
statistics, 52, 53, 54, 59, 132, 133, 193, 194, 195, 215, 218, 235, 239, 256, 257, 258, 259, 320, 351, 371, 399, 442, 443, 444
STD, 155
stereotypes, 299, 301
stimulant, 129, 230, 231
stimulus, 118, 119, 416, 418
stock, 7, 232
storage, 338, 339, 343, 357, 358
storms, 26
strategic planning, 327
streams, 396

strength, 67, 289, 296, 302, 303, 304, 308, 315, 344, 351, 352, 354, 394
stress, 9, 11, 45, 110, 115, 118, 119, 135, 179, 186, 223, 245, 247, 354, 412, 414, 416, 418, 430, 431, 439
stress level, 418
stressors, 231, 264, 420, 428
structural changes, 102
structural equation model, 52, 98, 126, 193, 236, 237, 248, 257, 385, 399, 403, 434, 442
structural equation modeling, 193
Structural Equation Modeling, 58, 202, 222
structuring, 164, 326, 328, 364
students, 14, 74, 96, 232, 235, 241, 242, 245, 250, 278, 293, 306, 308, 344, 370, 399, 434, 441, 442, 446, 448
subjective, 13, 28, 30, 32, 143, 144, 145, 147, 151, 159, 171, 188, 206, 220, 270, 272, 275, 279, 284, 299, 322, 341, 342, 392, 402, 404, 419, 430, 434, 435, 436, 439, 441, 442, 447, 448, 449
subjective well-being, 13, 430
subjectivity, 342
Sub-Saharan Africa, 202, 441
subsidy, 397
subsistence, 117
substance abuse, 223
substance use, 222
substances, 399
suburban, 414, 418, 430
suffering, 164, 174, 314, 319
summer, 26, 80, 421
superiority, 87
supervision, 365, 427
supply, 25, 43, 51, 52, 53, 54, 366, 369, 373, 375, 380
surgery, 184, 431
surprise, 251
surveillance, 390
survival, 7, 15, 16, 88, 89, 97, 187, 197, 247, 251, 252, 253, 260, 261, 264, 319, 327, 381
surviving, 189, 388
suspects, 117
Sweden, 77, 89, 93, 104, 146, 188, 345, 395, 418, 441
switching, 63, 208, 213
Switzerland, 24, 159
symbolic, 48, 66, 76, 79, 340, 345, 346, 350, 353
symbolic meanings, 346, 353
sympathetic, 165
sympathy, 11, 163, 165, 211, 221
syndrome, 189, 222
synthesis, 58, 92, 121, 245, 246, 327

T

tactics, 275, 288, 341
Taiwan, 272
tangible, 127, 300, 311
Tanzania, 441
target behavior, 175
target population, 72
targets, 30, 147, 158, 179, 227, 338, 339, 351, 352
taxonomic, 279
taxonomy, 69, 288, 393, 407
teachers, 234, 243, 245, 333, 373
teaching, 232, 234, 243
technical assistance, 320
teenagers, 446
teens, 436, 442
teeth, 214
television, 328
temperature, 8, 21, 22, 24, 26, 142, 297
temporal, 9, 11, 15, 26, 27, 28, 29, 31, 32, 35, 40, 44, 49, 51, 52, 53, 55, 91, 97, 140, 168, 169, 205, 206, 207, 208, 213, 220, 223, 334, 345, 354, 362, 363, 368, 375, 378, 380
tension, 135, 172, 415, 418, 422
territory, 84, 361, 370, 372, 395
Terror Management Theory, 435, 450
terrorism, 5
terrorist, 5
terrorist acts, 5
textbooks, 169
textiles, 58, 201, 448
Theory of Planned Behavior, 65, 165, 171, 269, 270, 272, 283, 290, 292, 299, 386, 404
thinking, 25, 27, 34, 35, 85, 92, 219, 251, 305, 324, 347, 380, 408, 416, 435, 449
Third World, 374, 375
Thomson, 223
threat, 3, 13, 43, 114, 174, 337, 345, 346, 347, 349, 350, 353, 354, 358, 389, 393, 403
threatened, 5, 126, 127, 128, 345, 348, 352, 355, 438
threatening, 4, 28, 29, 30, 126, 174, 370, 402
threats, xi, 20, 87, 114, 127, 260, 345, 354, 358, 378, 379
three-way interaction, 288
thresholds, 26, 390
time frame, 23, 205, 206, 207, 208
timetable, 157
Tokyo, 153
tolerance, 130, 137
Tony Blair, 20
top-down, 34
total energy, 9, 61, 63, 72
tourism, 347, 351, 352

tourist, 347, 349, 350, 390
toxic, 5, 188, 246, 399
toxic substances, 399
toxicity, 139, 140
trade, 85, 278
trade-off, 278
tradition, 86, 87, 90, 110, 172, 174, 177, 273, 391
traffic, 23, 76, 79, 106, 146, 151, 418, 419, 420, 422, 425, 426
training, 226, 229, 230, 233, 242, 243, 318, 321, 322
traits, 109, 111, 115, 188, 210, 211, 231, 387, 402
trajectory, 339
trans, 141, 172, 322
transactions, 324, 325, 343
transcendence, 90, 172
transfer, 291
transformation, 321, 364, 375
transformations, 12, 317, 380, 383, 384
transgression, 389, 390, 394, 395, 396, 397, 404, 407
transition, 244, 378
transitions, 5
transmission, 338, 358, 382
transparency, 23
transport, 30, 64, 68, 73, 74, 75, 78, 79, 106, 146, 150, 151, 153, 154, 156, 157, 168, 169, 171, 274, 338, 339, 412
transportation, 16, 57, 62, 64, 76, 89, 114, 123, 146, 152, 153, 156, 157, 184, 209, 253, 254, 262, 297, 388, 412, 413
traps, 182
travel, 11, 65, 68, 72, 73, 75, 76, 121, 141, 145, 146, 147, 149, 150, 151, 152, 154, 158, 159, 171, 181, 315, 405
treaties, 37
trees, 22, 117, 256, 259, 428
triggers, 375
tropical forest, 127
tropical forests, 127
trust, 114, 328, 337, 350, 351, 352, 354, 368, 413
Turkey, 91, 93, 318, 335, 430
twins, 436, 439
Type I error, 281
typology, 207

U

UNCED, 318, 335
uncertain outcomes, 32
uncertainty, 28, 32, 34, 38, 40, 42, 44, 51, 52, 53, 54, 55, 158, 304, 312, 323, 363, 365, 375, 376, 379
undergraduate, 14, 276, 289
undergraduates, 201, 434, 441
underlying mechanisms, 220

UNDP, 319, 335
unemployment, 5
UNEP, 127, 140, 231, 246, 318, 334
UNESCO, 44, 45, 59, 229, 232, 241, 243, 246, 370
UNFCCC, 21, 22
unfolded, 279
UNFPA, 319, 320, 336
UN-Habitat, 319, 336
unhappiness, 197, 210, 211, 212, 441
uniform, 15
United Kingdom, 24, 61, 337, 411, 413, 434
United Nations, 16, 21, 22, 44, 45, 52, 55, 59, 102, 127, 138, 139, 140, 188, 200, 203, 231, 246, 318, 319, 334, 335, 336
United Nations Development Program, 319, 335
United Nations Environment Program, 22, 246, 318, 334
United States, 24, 38, 40, 95, 164, 189, 200, 404, 434
univariate, 53, 214, 215, 218, 234, 257, 442
Universal Declaration of Human Rights, 189
universe, 86, 370
universities, 434, 441
university students, 370
urban areas, 4, 94, 345, 430
urban population, 319, 371
urban settlement, 319
urbanization, 127
USDA, 356

V

vacuum, 269
Valdez, 209, 223
valence, 344
validation, 93, 208, 245, 391, 449
validity, 53, 75, 93, 95, 97, 132, 193, 201, 218, 234, 236, 242, 257, 260, 341, 400, 442, 444
variability, 22, 26, 91, 126, 127, 173, 237, 238, 274, 278, 286
variance, 12, 53, 91, 95, 99, 100, 111, 117, 118, 137, 150, 175, 177, 196, 199, 248, 254, 255, 260, 261, 269, 270, 272, 276, 280, 281, 284, 286, 287, 288, 290, 368, 369, 403, 418, 445, 446
variation, 26, 91, 125, 260, 417
vegetation, 415, 425
vehicles, 338, 357, 422
vein, 55, 95, 165, 416
Venezuela, 13, 317, 330, 331, 335
Vermont, 105
versatility, 6, 243
veterinarians, 327
victims, 29, 30, 389, 390
Victoria, 19, 38, 40, 50, 51, 366

vignette, 277, 278, 284
village, 345, 419
violence, xi, 3, 185, 186, 188, 197
violent, 221
visible, 425
vision, 6, 83, 97, 135, 175, 177, 179, 190, 321, 326, 361, 371, 376, 378, 379, 418
visual images, 419
visual perception, 139, 222, 245, 383
visual stimuli, 129, 140
vitamins, 270
vocabulary, 362
volatility, 13, 385, 399, 400, 402
voters, 20
vulnerability, 23, 38, 375, 376
vulnerable people, 25

W

Wales, 337, 347, 349, 353, 357
walking, 30, 135, 146, 147, 152, 195, 257, 258, 417, 418, 443, 444
war, 20, 185, 186, 189, 197
waste disposal, 297, 367
waste management, 36, 358
waste water, 11, 54, 59, 219, 368, 369, 370
wastes, 257, 369
water quality, 45, 51, 54, 365, 366, 367, 368, 369, 370, 373, 376
water recycling, 391, 403
water resources, 25, 44, 45, 50, 55, 361, 365, 367, 370, 374
waterways, 374
weakness, 394
wealth, 45, 55, 84, 85, 96, 101, 167, 172, 187, 320, 374, 413, 436, 437, 441
web, 23, 89, 278, 306, 308, 335, 343
web-based, 278, 306, 308

weight loss, 270
welfare, 27, 162, 164, 170, 172, 264, 322, 371, 412, 439
West Bank, 358
western countries, 65, 389
Western philosophy, 251
WHO, 431
wildlife, 351, 352, 413, 425
wind, 13, 24, 337, 338, 339, 340, 341, 342, 344, 347, 348, 349, 350, 352, 353, 356, 358
wind farm, 13, 337, 340, 341, 347, 348, 349, 350, 352, 353, 356, 358
wind turbines, 339, 340, 350
windows, 135, 396
winter, 26
wisdom, 172, 435
withdrawal, 379
witnesses, 373, 378
women, 4, 99, 131, 188, 189, 190, 194, 196, 199, 255, 318, 369, 439, 441, 444
wood, 263, 397, 405
woods, 397
workers, 286, 370, 397, 422
working groups, 23
workplace, 146, 147, 148, 151, 152
World Bank, 320, 334, 335
World Health Organization, 4, 18, 418, 431
worldview, 47, 55, 83, 86, 88, 91, 92, 94, 96, 97, 101, 102, 115, 174, 175, 435
worry, 216, 217
writing, 9, 15, 16, 171, 308, 337, 348, 353, 438, 446
wrongdoing, 402

Y

yield, 63, 344
young adults, 306, 308